THE DRYDEN PRESS

CHICAGO   NEW YORK   PHILADELPHIA
SAN FRANCISCO   MONTREAL   TORONTO
LONDON   SYDNEY   TOKYO   MEXICO CITY
RIO DE JANEIRO   MADRID

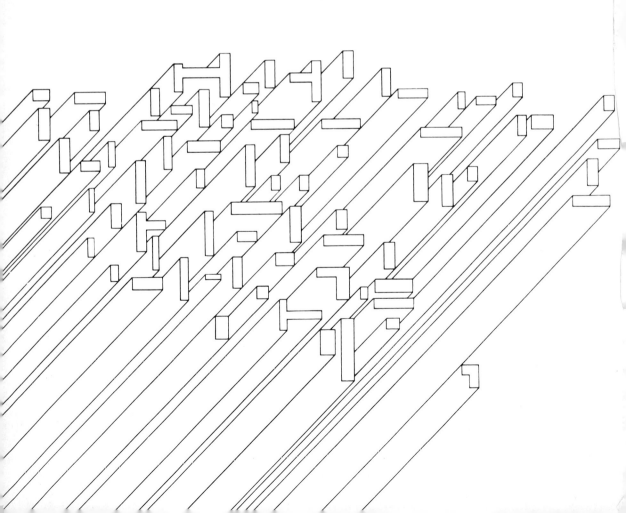

MACROECONOMICS

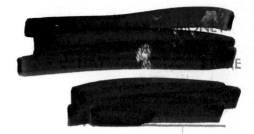

Contents

MACROECONOMICS
SECOND EDITION

J. C. POINDEXTER

NORTH CAROLINA
STATE UNIVERSITY

To Betsey

Acquisitions Editor: Glenn Turner
Developmental Editor: Nedah Abbott
Project Editors: Bernice Gordon, Brian Link Weber
Design Director: William Seabright
Production Manager: Peter Coveney

Cover design by William Seabright
Copy editing by Madelyn Roesch
Indexing by Ann Heinrichs

Address orders to: 383 Madison Avenue
                   New York, New York 10017

Address editorial correspondence to:
                   901 North Elm Street
                   Hinsdale, Illinois 60521

Library of Congress Catalog Card Number: 79–51107
ISBN: 0–03–050271–3
Printed in the United States of America
123–056–987654321

CBS COLLEGE PUBLISHING
The Dryden Press
Holt, Rinehart and Winston
Saunders College Publishing

Preface

The first edition of *Macroeconomics* was written to provide a comprehensive but compact presentation of macroeconomic theory, measurement, and policy making, suitable for students in upper level macroeconomics courses. The empirical nature of modern macroeconomics was accorded prominent, though not paramount, attention in that edition, and an effort was exerted to transmit the excitement generated by the controversies that provide progress in our efforts to understand and influence the macroeconomy.

The current edition retains the objectives and method of approach of the first edition. As before, students who study the text sequentially will first be exposed to a discussion of the basic concerns of macroeconomics and the methodology employed in macroeconomic model building and testing. The essential data for monitoring macroeconomic events (the national income and product accounts, price indexes, and measures of employment and unemployment) is then discussed. Readers are then involved in the modeling of macroeconomic processes. While policy concerns are confronted throughout the text, the degree of concentration on those concerns increases as the text proceeds and as the reader's understanding of the macroeconomy becomes more complete.

The major revisions in content and emphasis in the second edition reflect macroeconomic events since the early 1970s, when the first edition was written. The stubborn persistence of inflation in spite of economic slack has prompted the economics profession in recent years to devote far more attention to the role of expectations. This emphasis is reflected in the models employed in this text as they fully incorporate inflationary expectations that may perfectly anticipate inflation (in the long run) or fail to match actual inflation (in the short run). Discussion of the recent controversy over the relevance of adaptive versus rational expectations highlights the new emphasis on the role of expectations in the second edition.

Along with the persistence of inflation, other concerns, including an increased awareness of the threat of disruptions in the flow of energy resources and a marked decline in the rate of growth of labor productivity, have attracted additional attention to the role of supply in macroeconomic events. Current interest in the reasons for anemic growth in productive capacity and the possibilities for *supply-management* policies are carefully explored.

The overriding policy issues of the last decade have naturally diverted attention from the perhaps more abstract and doctrinal concerns of the profession in the earlier postwar era. The second edition reflects this shift in emphasis with reduced coverage of the *great debates* of the past. A series of *cases in point,* case studies of events and issues that have been prominent in recent years, have been introduced in the text to demonstrate the relevance of macroeconomics and to stimulate interest in macroeconomic controversies.

In addition to the extensive revision in emphasis in the second edition, there has been a thorough updating of the data series provided in the text and, where necessary (as in the discussions of price indexes and of the money stock), in the explanation of those data series. The results of recent empirical studies have also been integrated into the text, while discussion of the fundamental contributions in the post-Keynesian era is retained.

In preparation of the second edition I have benefitted from the comments and suggestions of a number of users of the first edition. I owe an even greater debt to my colleagues at North Carolina State University who have read and commented on sections of both editions of the text and to the following reviewers: Donald G. Heckerman, Univ. of Arizona; Michael Babcock, Kansas State University; F. Scott Wilson, Canisius College; Michael Salemi, University of North Carolina; John J. Klein, Georgia State University; Ziad Keilany, University of Tennessee at Chattanooga; Douglas B. Diamond, North Carolina State University; Doug W. Cho, Wichita State University; and Micha Gisser, University of New Mexico. Also I would like to thank the professional editorial staff provided by The Dryden Press. A special acknowledgement is due to Gwen Joyner, who has now managed to survive typing two text manuscripts.

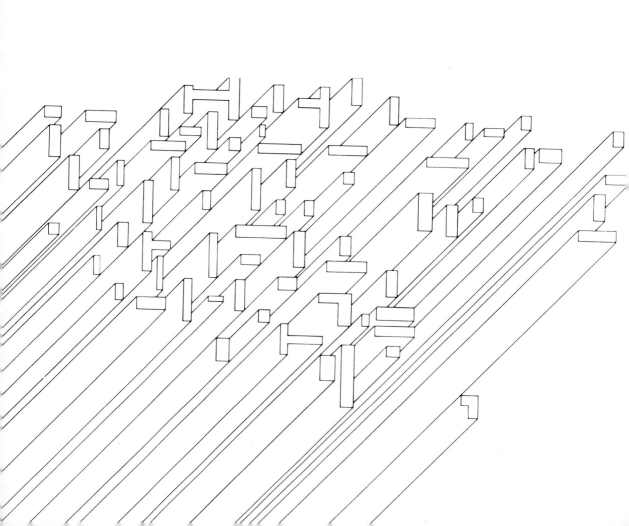

In the Beginning . . .

The history of market-oriented, capitalist-style economies shows a persistent progression of technical advances, an impressive growth in material productivity, and an enormous capacity to absorb labor and other resources. At the same time, that history reflects the fragility of prosperity as, over the centuries, economic commentators have described the "convulsions," "crises," "panics," and, in more modern times, "recessions," "depressions," and "inflationary spirals" that have afflicted such economies. It is an understanding of this ongoing experience that this text is intended to provide. Part I (Chapters 1–3) focuses on explaining the concerns of macroeconomics and on describing the most prominent measures of economic activity. Part II of the text (Chapters 4–10), titled "Building the Core Macro Model," then begins the analytical quest that offers the promise of an explanation of macroeconomic events. Throughout the text, an effort is made to tie description and analysis to real world events. Toward the end of Part II and continuing into Part III (Chapters 11 and 12), which deal with inflation, unemployment, and government policy, this effort becomes more rewarding as, by that time, a complete model of the domestic economy has been developed. This model can be applied in explaining current problems and is useful in exploring the possibilities of both beneficial and detrimental government intervention in the market place. Part IV of the text (Chapters 13 and 14) concentrates on the implementation of *monetary* and *fiscal* policy actions as the primary means by which policy makers attempt to influence economic activity.

Parts I through IV of the text provide coverage of the functioning of the domestic macroeconomy and of stabilization policy making for that system. Part V of the text (Chapters 15–17) extends and refines the macroeconomic model to deal in detail with international economic linkages, with economic growth, and with business fluctuations and forecasting.

Chapter 1

What Is and What Should Be

Macroeconomics is the study of *aggregate* economic activity. In contrast to *microeconomics,* which focuses on explaining the economic behavior of small units, such as individual households, individual firms, and individual markets or industries, macroeconomics is concerned with the performance of the economic system *as a whole.* As such, it represents an attempt to explain how the level of employment and output, the level of prices, the rate of growth of output, and the rate of price level change are determined for the entire economic system. Assuming that that capability exists, macroeconomic analysis can be used to provide government policy prescriptions which, successful or not, are intended to improve the economy's performance.

The problems that macroeconomics deals with are among the most prominent concerns of the nation's leaders and of average citizens alike. The breadth of concern over macroeconomic problems is clearly reflected in newspaper headlines that announce: ''Prices Rose at an 18 Percent Annual Rate in the First Quarter,'' ''Unemployment Rises for Third Consecutive Month,'' ''The Dollar Plunges Again on the Foreign Exchange Market,'' ''Output Grew by Only 1.6 Percent in Last 12 Months.'' Of course, those who lose their jobs during periods of rising unemployment, those who graduate from college and fail to find employment during periods of retarded

3

economic expansion, and those who suffer a reduction in economic well-being because of rising living costs hardly need a news account of the significance of recession, "anemic" expansion, or inflation.

Because of their importance, macroeconomic problems are frequently the basis for major public policy actions. Federal budgets are made "expansionary" or "restrictive" in response to economic conditions, and deliberate alterations in the volume of money in circulation are undertaken in an effort to stimulate or retard economic activity. Meanwhile, always looking for political opportunity, the opposition political party can be expected to provide a critical review of any major macroeconomic policy action the government undertakes. Indeed, while both major political parties in the United States accept the notion that the government is duty bound To use the weapons it has at its disposal to contribute to the economy's vitality, some of the most prominent issues that divide our political parties reflect differences of opinion on how that responsibility should be met. But met it must be, as every candidate for a high federal office is aware.

Recognizing the political opportunity afforded him by several years of sluggish economic expansion during the 1950s, John Kennedy, pledging that he would revitalize the economy, was elected president in 1960. Most economists agree that the government policies that were subsequently implemented under the guidance of Kennedy and, later, Lyndon Johnson, contributed substantially to a vigorous expansion of the U.S. economy that continued through nearly the entire decade following the 1960 election, the longest unbroken expansion the U.S. economy has ever experienced. Still, the government-engineered expansion of the 1960s must be rated as a qualified success. With the rapid escalation of U.S. involvement in Vietnam during the mid-1960s, inflationary forces were aroused that have persisted to the present. Richard Nixon, pledging to stop inflation without raising unemployment, won the presidential election in 1968. However, much to the detriment of the common good, the administrations of Richard Nixon and his successor, Gerald Ford, saw virulent inflation, excessive unemployment, international payments deficits, an energy crisis, and other economic woes as, in the 1973–74 period, the economy slumped into its deepest contraction since the Great Depression. In campaigning for the 1976 presidential election, Jimmy Carter pledged his efforts to restore economic order—to lower unemployment and reduce the inflation rate. While a significant decline in the unemployment rate occurred after his election, inflation accelerated into the double digit range during 1979 and remained the primary macroeconomic problem facing the United States economy and the newly elected Reagan administration at the beginning of the 1980s.

In spite of policies the macroeconomic ills of the last decade have elicited, and, many would argue, in part *because* of those policies, the economy's performance has remained unsatisfactory since the late 1960s. As a consequence of the duration and intensity of the macroeconomic difficulties endured, the government's response to the forces that have rocked the economy in the last decade has been the subject of considerable public scrutiny. Reflecting the general public's concerns, we might wish to ask: Why did the United States suffer its deepest recession since the 1930s in 1974 and 1975? Why have prices risen at such a rapid rate for over a decade? Why do we suffer from the twin evils of simultaneous inflation and slack economic conditions—a combination that is labeled inflationary recession or, inelegantly, stagflation? How can we account for the kinds of federal government intervention in the macroeconomy that we have witnessed in recent years? Why are some of its policies successful and some not? What policies should our leaders implement in the future? These are important questions that no informed citizen can ignore. Fortunately, they are questions that modern macroeconomic analysis can shed a great deal of light on.

Because of its concern with economic conditions that impinge directly on our lives, the study of macroeconomics has the appeal of relevance. Do not, however, expect macroeconomics to provide pat, cookbook solutions to all the problems that confront the macroeconomy. What macroeconomic analysis can provide is a framework for analyzing those problems and for pinpointing the considerations that are most relevant in dealing with them. Within this framework there will remain room for disagreement among competing analysts over the proper solutions to particular problems. While economists agree on a great many things, there are disagreements that distinguish "monetarists," "Keynesians," " new economists," and devotees of "rational expectations." The controversies that separate economists into such competing camps add excitement to the study of macroeconomics and reflect the fact that macroeconomics is a lively and evolving discipline.

This text will help you to untangle the complexities of modern macroeconomic analysis and provide an introduction to the most prominent disagreements that have characterized macroeconomic discussions in recent decades. As a background for these tasks the remainder of this chapter concentrates, first, on outlining the general nature of the analytical procedures employed in macroeconomics and, then, on reviewing the goals we might want to set for the economy.

The Methodology of Macroeconomics— Normative Versus Positive Economics

As modern macroeconomics has evolved, economists have tried to carefully separate their analysis of how the economic system functions to determine the volume of output, the general price level, the rate of growth of output, and so on from assertions about what values those variables *should* have. The first activity falls in the realm of *positive economics,* often described as the study of "what is." The second activity, dealing with questions of "what should be," falls in the realm of *normative economics.* As an application of positive economic analysis, using an understanding of the internal workings of the economy and the best data sources available, an economist might *predict* that unemployment in the United States will involve between

6 and 7 percent of the labor force next year. With positive analysis the economist might also predict how that unemployment rate could be changed through alternative government actions, but positive analysis cannot tell us whether society would be *better off* next year with some different unemployment rate. It is true, of course, that the economist who predicts a 6 to 7 percent unemployment rate might believe that society would be better off with a different rate, such as 4 percent or 9 percent. If so, that economist might advocate the government policies that positive analysis indicates would move the unemployment rate to the level he thinks *should* prevail for maximum social welfare (taking full account of any other effects these policies might have). However, his opinion of what the unemployment rate *should be* reflects his own preferences or value judgments on the link between unemployment and social welfare; that is, it rests on a normative judgment, rather than on objectively determined facts, because we have no way of objectively measuring human happiness.

The primary focus of this text, like the focus of most professional macroeconomists, is on positive analysis. Positive economic analysis has the responsibility of providing a set of generalizations or ''laws'' that can be used to make valid and useful predictions about the impact of various changes in circumstances. As is the case in all analytical endeavors, the generalizations positive economics provide take the form of ''if A, then B'' propositions. Such generalizations clearly imply *causality* because they tell us that, with the occurrence of a specified event or set of circumstances (A), another specific event (B) will occur. The performance of positive economic analysis is judged by the consistency of its generalizations and their implications with experience. As in all scientific disciplines, a set of macroeconomic laws that yields conclusions (predictions) which are more consistent with experience will displace one that yields less consistent conclusions.

The Interaction between Positive Analysis and Normative Judgments

While our primary interest is in positive economic analysis, we cannot ignore the unavoidable interaction between positive economics and value judgments. That interaction begins early in the analytical process because the very choice of the problems we decide to analyze rests on value judgments. Indeed, the concern over unemployment, inflation, and sluggish growth that was voiced earlier in this chapter reflects a set of normative judgments on the link between employment, price stability, and economic growth on the one hand, and social welfare on the other.

Perhaps more dramatically, but no more fundamentally, the normative concerns of macroeconomics are highlighted when macroeconomics is applied to the formal process of government policy making, for the major responsibility of normative economics is to select a set of government policy goals, the pursuit of which leads to an improvement in society's overall welfare (itself a normative policy goal). Of necessity, a great deal of art is involved in selecting a set of goals that adequately reflects the collective desires of society at large, and economic analysis has little to contribute to policy makers' understanding of what society values. Still, the rational selection of a set of goals must rest heavily on the conclusions of *positive* economics because, without an objective understanding of how the macroeconomy functions, policy makers cannot know what potential policy goals are attainable or the means through which chosen goals may be pursued. The useful application of macroeconomics clearly involves a blending of positive analysis with norms.

While modern macroeconomics involves a fundamental blending of positive analysis with social values, a student of economics should be able to distinguish normative from positive assertions, and should make a habit of doing so when evaluating economic statements, whether they appear in political speeches, in newspaper columns, or in the utterances of academic economists.

The Practice of Positive Economics

The practice of positive economic analysis begins with the confrontation of an economic phenomenon we want to explain (changes in meat prices, unemployment, the price level, and so on). Providing an explanation requires: (1) the formation of hypotheses (tentatively accepted assumptions) about the behavior patterns involved; (2) accounting for any interrelationships among the hypotheses specified in step one; and (3) deriving the implications or predictions logically deducible from the relationships constructed in steps one and two. On completion of step three, we have a *model* for explaining the economic phenomenon of interest. The fourth step consists of testing the predictions that model provides against observed reality.

Probably the most demanding task in the practice of positive analysis is step one, the selection of a set of tentatively accepted assumptions that permits us to *explain* complex reality. The assumptions employed must always provide a simplified caricature of reality—that is, an *abstraction* from reality—because the maze of information that confronts us when we observe a real world phenomenon we wish to explain obscures the fundamental causal relationships we seek. A good model will contain assumptions that capture the essential causal relations involved in producing the phenomenon we wish to explain, so that its predictions will be consistent with observed reality, while eliminating the maze of superfluous information with which reality confronts the observer.

As a simple, familiar, and compelling example of the skillful use of *simplifying* assumptions, recall the well-known Newtonian gravitational principle which states that, because of the force of gravity, a free body in space will fall with a constant rate of acceleration of some 32.2 feet per second. That law was developed for a body falling in a vacuum, attracted by just one other body. Still, the predictions it yields are impressively corroborated year after year by students dropping ball bearings in college physics labs. Clearly, the influence on acceleration of an atmosphere and of the gravitational pull of the sun, the moon, the stars, and other heavenly bodies that can attract our laboratory ball bearings, complicates and obscures the causal relationship we seek. The only viable method for obtaining an understanding of the behavior of falling bodies is that of constructing a model which abstracts from the many small forces that affect those bodies while concentrating on the major causal force(s).

Once the basic assumptions in our model have been specified and proper account has been taken of any relationships that link those assumptions, the model-building process must be completed by logical deduction of the conclusions that flow from those assumptions. This step requires careful application of the rules of logic because any logical errors made in this step can alter the conclusions our model provides. As a consequence, the resulting explanation of an observed phenomenon will be invalid no matter how skillfully the underlying assumptions were chosen. Presuming successful application of the techniques of logic, our model will provide us with a set of "if A, then B" predictions that can be compared to observed reality.

Familiar Economic Models. Now, if, by chance, the preceding discussion of the process of model building has left you wondering whether economic analysis is not something practiced by witch doctors or some other modern form of mystic, brief reference to a few standard examples of economic models should convince you that you have already worked through the model-building process in your basic economics courses. To begin with, recall the supply-demand market model used for determining prices in microeconomics. The construction of that model required the specification of two hypothesized behavioral relations: a supply function and a demand function. On the supply side of the market, the quantity of output offered for sale was assumed to be positively related to price, other things being held constant; while on the demand side of the market, the quantity of output purchased was assumed to be negatively related to price, other things being held constant (step one of the analytical process). The hypothesized supply and demand functions were linked (step two of the analytical process) by the market equilibrium condition that requires equality of supply and demand. Completing the market model you were able to deduce (step three) what market price and quantity would prevail with the market in equilibrium and, more importantly, that model provided a logical prediction of the impact on price and quantity of a change in circumstances. For example, a change in tastes that raised demand typically produced an increase both in price and in the quantity of output bought and sold.

Turning our attention from microeconomics to macroeconomics, it should be noted that macroeconomic models are distinctive only in that they concentrate on the behavior patterns of *aggregated groupings* of economic units. Consequently, this text spends a good deal of time separately analyzing the behavior of the household, business, foreign, and government *sectors* of the economy, and then in examining the interactions among these groupings or sectors to see how the values of important aggregate variables such as output, employment, and the price level are determined. From your introductory macroeconomics course, you may recall the construction of a simple income-determination model that performed this set of tasks.[1] The simplest macroeconomic model dealt with probably consisted of the hypothesis that aggregate consumption depends on the level of disposable income, the definition that total spending in a simple economy which has no government and no foreign trade is just the sum of consumption and investment spending, recognition that total spending and income in such an economy are identical, and the equilibrium condition that planned spending must be equal to output. That model allowed you to explain how the equilibrium levels of output and consumption are determined, to find their values, and to predict the impact on overall economic activity of any change in circumstances involving shifts in the consumption or investment functions.

Taxing your memory once more, you may recall that more complete macroeconomic models—those that took into account the economic role of government—not only allowed you to explain how the level of economic activity was determined but also illustrated the aggregate influence on the economy of government actions. That is an important accomplishment because most capitalistic systems in the world today have governments that are macroeconomic activists; governments that use their economic muscle in efforts to deliberately influence economic aggregates. That activism could not be rationalized if we did not have models that allow us to evaluate the effects of the government's policy actions on economic activity.

The fourth step of the analytical process involves the testing of our models. Among the social sciences, economics is distinctly fortunate in that the phenomena with which it deals are generally quantifiable, that is, they can be measured. As illustrations, we can and do collect *numerical* observations on the level of unemployment, the level of output, the level and rate of change of prices, the size and state of balance (or imbalance) of the government budget, the size of the money stock, and a wide array of other variables. Because economic analysis develops hypothesized relationships between concepts that are measurable, economists can employ the powerful techniques of modern statistics to *quantify* and *test* those hypothesized relationships. The combination of economic theory and statistical analysis, which allows the quantification and testing of economic models, is called *econometrics*.

In the four decades that have elapsed since macroeconomic analysis became a fashionable activity for economists, the theoretical models that macroeconomic analysts employ have been subjected to countless statistical

---

[1]If that basic macroeconomic model defies recall, you need not worry at this stage. It will be carefully reviewed in Chapter 4.

tests. An explanation of the econometric techniques that a skilled economic analyst might employ is outside the scope of this text. However, it is easy to illustrate what can be learned through the most commonly employed technique of econometric analysis.

For illustrative purposes, supppose a researcher sets out to ascertain what determines aggregate consumer spending. While recognizing that a number of other factors (perhaps the interest rate, wealth, family size, and so on) could have some effect on consumption, our researcher *hypothesizes* that aggregate consumption is positively related to the level of aggregate income with the magnitude of other influences on consumption small enough to be ignored. To test that hypothesis, suppose our researcher collects yearly data on aggregate income and aggregate consumption for, say, the

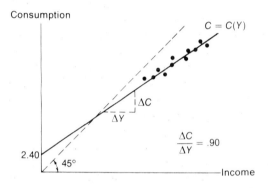

Figure 1—1 / An Econometrically Fitted Income-Consumption Relation

period 1970–1980 and plots his income-consumption observations on a graph like Figure 1—1.

The plotted points in Figure 1—1 seem to indicate clearly that the level of aggregate consumer spending rises as the level of aggregate income rises. Further, it appears that a simple straight line "fitted" to the plotted data does a good job of representing the fundamental relationship between income and consumption within the range of observations on those two variables.

It would seem that our econometrician has shown that his hypothesis is consistent with observed reality. In addition, he has *quantified* the relationship between aggregate income and consumption. The vertical intercept of the straight line fitted to the 1970–1980 data points, which serves only as a reference point to indicate the *position* of the consumption function in Figure 1—1, is assumed to have a value of 2.40. The assumed slope (rise over run) of that line is $\Delta C/\Delta Y = .90$, indicating that a $1 million increase in aggregate income would raise consumption by $900,000. Thus, the equation of the straight-line relationship between income and consumption is $C = 2.40 + .90Y$. From the "actual" observations available on income and consumption, our researcher's econometric analysis has provided us with a quantified relationship that can be used to predict the level of consumption that would accompany any observed income level. For example, if income in 1981 should turn out to be $2,500 billion, our income-consumption relation tells us consumption would be $2,252.4 billion.

Because our straight-line function does not fit all the plotted data points perfectly, we should not be surprised if actual consumption in 1981 is a bit different from the predicted value. The fact that observed values of consumption differ from, or, as an econometrician would say, *deviate* from, the values predicted by our straight line suggests that one or more other factors besides income have some influence on consumption. By specifying what those other factors are and building them into our econometric model we might be able to improve its predictions. However, based upon the straight-line relationship in Figure 1—1, $2,252.4 billion is our best prediction of 1981 consumption.

The line plotted through the data points in Figure 1—1 is called a *regression* line and the equation for that line is a regression equation. In conjunction with a regression equation our researcher is apt to report the value of the "coefficient of determination," designated R^2, for that equation. With limits of 0 percent and 100 percent, the R^2 value indicates the proportion of variation in the dependent variable accounted for (in the confines of the regression equation) by variation in the independent variable. A reported R^2 = .92 accompanying our example regression would indicate that 92 percent of the movements in consumption over the 1970–1980 period are explained by movements in income over that period.

If the hypothesized relationship between Y and C were invalid, we would expect the fitted regression equation to do a very poor job of explaining C, so the value of R^2 would be low, perhaps in the range of 0 to .30. However, one note of caution must be added here. The fact that a fitted regression line explains a large proportion of the variation in a variable in which we are interested does not always mean we have discovered a true causal relation between that variable and the independent variable in the regression. Instances of spurious, coincidental correlation are commonplace in economics. For example, it is frequently observed that movements in women's skirt lengths and in the Dow-Jones average of stock prices are closely correlated. It should not be concluded from that observation that changes in hem lengths *cause* changes in stock prices. Because of the risk of just such a coincidental correlation, no empirical test can absolutely confirm a hypothesis we want to employ for economic analysis. At best, all that can be claimed is that the statistical test results are consistent with the hypothesis being tested. Consequently, confidence in any hypothesis is achieved only by finding that hypothesis consistent with experience in numerous alternative sets of circumstances.

While our primary concern in this text is with the construction of theoretical models and their application in explaining macroeconomic events, in later chapters we will at times want to support the use of specific behavioral functions in our models by referring to regression equations that have been fitted for those functions. As already indicated, in addition to serving as tests of the behavioral patterns we will assume to exist, those regression equations can yield valuable quantification of the assumed responses our models incorporate. While our regression illustration involved only two variables, we should note that regression analysis can be easily extended to test for the importance of multiple explanatory variables. Regression analysis is the most powerful technique we have for performing the tests that permit economics to be an empirical science.[2]

Macroeconomic Goals

As our positive analysis of the macroeconomy progresses, we will discover why a free market economy may be afflicted by extended periods of underemployment, anemic expansion, and inflation. We will also review arguments on just how the federal government may influence the economy's performance. For now, with our brief summary of the methodology of macroeconomics completed, attention must be turned to the aggregate economic *goals* our government presumably pursues.

The now common view that government activities can exert an important influence on the economy, and that the government should try to improve the economy's performance, was explicitly recognized by Congress just after World War II in a landmark piece of economic legislation known as the Employment Act of 1946. That act declared that ". . . it is the continuing responsibility of the Federal government to use all practicable means. . .to promote maximum employment, production, and purchasing power." Policy makers have considered this act to be a *normative* mandate for active government efforts to maintain "full employment," "price stability," and "rapid economic growth." As we shall see, this list of goals is not exhaustive. Moreover, it is possible that the government may act in ways that are antithetical to these goals, or that the government may have no effective means by which it can pursue these goals. Each of these possibilities will be addressed in the chapters ahead.

Full Employment

Everyone has some notion of what the term *full employment* means. We will try to formalize those notions shortly. Meanwhile, the burdens of failing to maintain full employment during much of our history should be vividly apparent. In 1929, just prior to the Great Depression, a mere 3 percent of

---

[2]An intuitive explanation of the "ordinary least squares" technique that is most often employed in fitting regression equations is provided in Appendix 1—A. For complete treatments of regression analysis, including discussions of the shortcomings of the ordinary least squares technique and of the sophisticated techniques available for overcoming those shortcomings, consult a standard econometrics text such as Jan Kmenta, *Elements of Econometrics* (New York: Macmillan, 1971) or J. Johnston, *Econometric Methods,* 2nd ed. (New York: McGraw-Hill, 1972).

the U.S. labor force was unemployed. Four years later, in the depths of the depression, one of every four members of the labor force was unemployed, and unemployment rates remained above the 14 percent level throughout the 1930s. The families of the unemployed suffered a loss of income, and, in most cases, a massive reduction in the savings that had accumulated during their lifetimes. Even those workers who remained employed typically worked fewer hours and for lower wages than they would have under normal conditions so that their incomes, too, were reduced. Further, the psychological effects of the inability to find useful work that could provide support for one's family left permanent scars on many breadwinners.

While these unfortunate effects of unemployment are most obvious during severe depression, similar effects result from every deviation of employment below the full employment level. With unemployment rising above the 8 percent level in 1974–75, droves of current generation college students have selected technical fields—engineering, business, and even economics—in the hope that employment prospects will be brighter in the future in those fields. This phenomenon clearly reveals the discomfort that unemployment brings.

It is also noteworthy that swings in unemployment are not evenly distributed across the population. Notably, economic events that alter the overall level of unemployment have particularly harsh effects on low-skill, low-wage workers. As an illustration, unemployment rates among teenagers and blacks, groups that contain a large proportion of low-skill, low-wage workers, are particularly sensitive to recessions and expansions, as the charts in Figure 1—2 show. Respectively, those charts show the teenage unemployment rate and the black unemployment rate varying from lows of 12.24 percent and 6.4 percent in 1969 to 19.9 percent and 13.9 percent in 1975. According to the regression equations for the lines plotted in that figure, a one percentage point increase in the national unemployment rate was associated, on average, with a 1.49 percentage point increase in teenage unemployment and a 1.61 percentage point increase in black unemployment over the 1960–1978 period. Clearly, one group's mild recession may be another group's depression.

The Full Employment Unemployment Rate. If the maintenance of full employment is to be a policy goal, a working measure of the extent to which the economy is falling short of that goal is necessary. As a conceptual matter, it is often argued that full employment exists when employers are willing to employ every member of the labor force who wants to work at the prevailing wage rate. This does not mean that every member of the labor force who wants to work has a job. Ours is a dynamic economy in which changes in tastes and changes in production methods cause the disappearance of some jobs while others are created. It is an economy in which workers (voluntarily and involuntarily) exit from one job only to search or train for another, "more appropriate" job, and it is an economy in which new entrants into the labor force are seeking jobs.

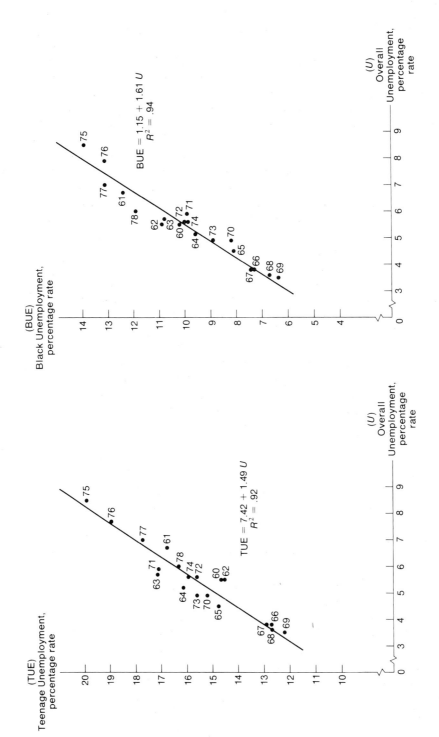

Figure 1—2 / The Association of Teenage and Black Unemployment with Overall Unemployment

Unlike the stock market and some agricultural commodity markets, the labor market is not a centralized auction market where offers to buy and offers to sell are readily matched. Because of imperfections in the market, notably the lack of readily available information on diverse job vacancies and heterogeneous unemployed workers, plus the lack of mobility on the part of labor, some unemploment must exist continuously if the labor market is to perform satisfactorily the socially desirable function of allocating labor to its most productive use. The important question for macroeconomics is how much measured unemployment must be tolerated at *full employment* due to those imperfections. En route to providing an answer to that question we will review the linkages between labor market imperfections and unemployment.

Search Unemployment and Structural Unemployment. No work seeker can know with certainty the wage offers that would be available to him from different employers. He can obtain information on job opportunities only by "searching" in the labor market, that is, by sampling job opportunities. Often an employed worker must quit the job he holds to search for more rewarding employment. In point of fact, a perusal of unemployment data typically shows that a large fraction of the pool of unemployed persons consists of individuals who have voluntarily quit their last job. Once a worker has terminated his previous employment and entered the unemployment pool, whether voluntarily or due to a layoff, his self-interest would compel him to sample job openings as long as the expected return from an additional sample is greater than the loss of current income from not accepting the best job offer already received. This is also true, of course, for a new entrant into the labor force seeking a suitable job slot. The job search procedure takes time and, during that time, the job seeker will be counted as unemployed, contributing to the maintenance of a revolving pool of unemployed job seekers.

The kind of temporary unemployment just described, which coexists with unfilled job vacancies, has traditionally been labeled *frictional unemployment*. With growing frequency in recent years, it has also been referred to as *search unemployment* in recognition of the basic justification for its existence. While search unemployment must always leave a significant fraction of the labor force unemployed, that unemployment cannot be considered an unmitigated evil either from an individual or a social perspective. The search process allows individuals to gravitate toward better employment opportunities—those in which they will be paid better because the *market value* of their production, reflecting society's evaluation of that production, is higher. Thus, the job search process provides higher wages to the work seeker and an enhanced value of production for society.

In addition to search unemployment, our summary measures of unemployment always reflect some *structural unemployment*. When shifts in product demand or changes in production techniques displace workers who then cannot find alternative employment because they lack suitable skills or geographic mobility, those workers are structurally unemployed. Teenagers, the aged, the handicapped, and perhaps those who live in decaying urban areas are the common victims of this form of unemployment.

Seeking a Numerical Value for the Full Employment Unemployment Rate. Because of the existence of structural and search unemployment, a positive level of measured unemployment must be accepted as full employment. However, determining the precise level of measured unemployment that must be tolerated as a reflection of the sum of structural and search unemployment is a difficult task. In the early 1960s, an "official" target unemployment rate of 4 percent was judged to be "reasonable and prudent" by the President's Council of Economic Advisers. It was thought that a 4 percent unemployment rate could be achieved *without producing significant upward pressure on prices.* In view of changes in the structure of the labor market in recent years and our recent experience with inflation, the target value for unemployment has gradually been revised upward until a number of government officials and economists have suggested that an unemployment rate for the United States as high as 5 percent or more is acceptable, and that any lower unemployment rate would create inflationary forces. As an operational matter, then, full employment exists when unemployment is at the lowest level that can be attained without an acceleration of inflation.

It is impossible to pin down a precise numerical value for the full employment level of the measured unemployment rate, but most economic analysts might currently agree to a target unemployment rate of somewhere between 4 1/2 and 5 1/2 percent of the labor force. With increasing frequency, this full employment unemployment rate is referred to as the *natural* rate of unemployment. (Chapters 3 and 9 will have more to say about the natural rate of unemployment.) The closer the economy presses to the lower limit of the natural unemployment rate range, the stronger we would expect upward pressures on the price level to become. Conversely, when the unemployment rate soars above the upper limit of that range, concern over the production society might have enjoyed with unemployment reduced is aroused.

From a brief look at the postwar record, it is apparent that the economy's actual employment performance has frequently fallen short of the full employment ideal. Between 1948 and 1979, unemployment averaged 5.1 percent of the labor force, and in the 1974–1979 period, unemployment averaged 6.8 percent. Of course, a primary concern of macroeconomic analysis is to explain why the actual unemployment rate is frequently above the level necessary to accommodate structural unemployment and an optimum volume of search unemployment. It is that additional unemployment that economy-stimulating government policies aim at eliminating.

Employment and Output. It should be clear that employment and aggregate output are closely related because by employing more labor, more output can be produced. By explicitly recognizing the interdependence of employment and output, crude aggregate measures of the economic costs of unemployment may be constructed. Unemployment of labor is accompanied by idleness of plants and manufacturing equipment (that is, of capital) and, with productive labor and capital idle, aggregate output is reduced. In Figure 1—3, the movements in U.S. unemployment and output from 1954 through 1979 are charted. In addition, part (A) of that figure provides a measure of *potential output,* the output level that could be achieved with full employment maintained.

As mentioned, in the early 1960s, the Council of Economic Advisers chose a *measured* unemployment rate of 4 percent as its full employment target. The potential output measure plotted in Figure 1—3 is then obtained through the following calculation:

$$\text{Potential output} = \text{96 percent of labor force} \times \begin{array}{c}\text{standard number}\\ \text{of work hours}\\ \text{per year}\end{array} \times \begin{array}{c}\text{average value of}\\ \text{output per}\\ \text{man-hour}\end{array} \qquad [1\text{—}1]$$

This equation indicates that the growth of potential output over time is determined by the growth of the labor force and the growth of labor's productivity. The labor force grows with increases in: (1) the population, (2) the proportion of the population in the working age range, and (3) the rate of participation in the work force. In turn, labor productivity, measured in terms of output per man-hour of labor, grows with the education and skill level of the population, and with increases in the quantity and quality of the machinery and equipment that labor has to work with. The plot of potential output in Figure 1—3 reflects the government's assumptions in projecting potential output until around 1976.

Figure 1—3 shows clearly the link between unemployment and output. The peak unemployment rates of 1953–54, 1957–58, 1960–61, 1969–70, and 1974–78 correspond to sizable gaps between actual and potential GNP. On the other hand, during the 1965–68 period, in which actual output was at or above potential, the unemployment rate was quite modest.

For the quarter of a century represented in Figure 1—3, the cumulative value of lost GNP due to excessive unemployment is nearly $700 billion in 1972 dollars. While representing a relatively small fraction of total output over this period, this is the current dollar equivalent of roughly a half of one year's output. Failure to maintain full employment is clearly costly. It's no wonder that maintaining full employment is a primary concern of macroeconomic policy.

Price Stability

Prices serve a resource allocation function of paramount importance in a capitalistic economic system. Rising prices in markets where demand exceeds supply call additional productive resources into those markets and reduce demand pressures. Falling prices in markets where supply exceeds demand serve as a signal for resources to leave such markets and for buyers

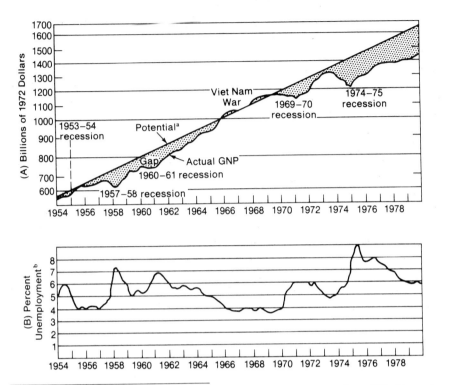

^aTrend line of 3 1/2 percent from 1954 to 1962:4th quarter; 3 3/4 percent from 1962:4th quarter to 1965:4th quarter; 4 percent from 1965:4th quarter to 1979:4th quarter.
^bUnemployment as a percent of civilian labor force; seasonally adjusted.

Figure 1—3 / Actual and Potential
Gross National Product and Unemployment Rates, 1954–1979

Sources: Department of Commerce, (Washington, D.C.: U.S. Government Printing Office, various years); *Business Conditions Digest*, Council of Economic Advisers, *Economic Report of the President* (Washington D.C.: U.S. Government Printing Office, various years).

to increase their purchases. It is clearly not the prevention of movements of individual prices, or of what we refer to as *relative* prices, that macroeconomic policy should attempt because prices could not serve their allocative function in that case. Yet, it is a goal of macroeconomic policy to restrict movement in the average or *absolute* price level. Relative prices may be left free to change (for example, the price of oil may be rising while that of electronic calculators is falling) so that the allocative role of prices is served while the average price level remains reasonably stable.

The justification of price stability as a policy goal is not as obvious as that of full employment. However, a sample of the problems inflation causes should be adequate for now to convince you that price stability is desirable. In periods of inflation, the prices society pays for goods and services increase. Sales revenues, ultimately divided up into wages, rent, interest, and profits, rise in step with prices because every transaction has two sides (expenditure and receipt). However, not everyone's income rises at the same rate in inflation periods. Hence, inflation may redistribute income, possibly in a pattern inconsistent with society's normative desires for a fair income distribution. Inflation may also be a burden to lenders as, after a price increase, the credit they extend is repaid with dollars that have reduced purchasing power.

Inflation also distorts the financial records of business firms (particularly their measures of depreciation and profit) and, hence, results in lower quality information for business decisions. If this results in poorer business decisions being made, society's material well-being will be damaged. A more detailed discussion of the burdens of inflation will be provided in Chapter 11. In the meantime, we will accept price stability as an important policy goal.

Figure 1—4 provides measures of the level of prices and their rates of change in the U.S. economy over the period 1952–1979. As the graphs show, from the end of the Korean War in 1954 until the middle of the 1960s, in spite of some notable peaks and ebbs, the U.S. price level crept upward at a moderate average rate of some 2 percent annually. That rate of *creeping inflation* evoked only mild concern. During the late 1960s, the annual rate of price rise had accelerated to the 5 percent per year range, evoking concern over price stability. The inflation rate then slowed again in the 1971–72 period but accelerated to rates not seen in the last five decades in the 1972–74 period and, after a subsequent decline, accelerated again beginning in 1978 and continued at a rapid rate as the 1980s began.

With the bursts of inflation into the "double digit" range in recent years, the goal of price stability has acquired a loftier status than it had enjoyed since prior to the Korean War. In fact, inflation has had the distinction of being identified by the president as public enemy number one. Judging from historical experience, then, it appears that society and its policy makers are willing to tolerate a creeping inflation rate (say, 1 to 2 percent annually) while deeming higher inflation rates, like those we have experienced since the late 1960s, unacceptable. You might note, finally, that until the later 1960s, periods of accelerating inflation were linked to periods of low unemployment, suggesting that a reduction in unemployment might be bought through an acceleration of inflation. The existence of that trade-off is brought into question, however, by the experience of recent years, as high inflation rates have been accompanied by high unemployment rates.

Rapid Economic Growth

Our third macroeconomic goal, rapid economic growth, has enjoyed an unquestioned position of importance for much of our history. With the rate of economic growth typically measured by the percentage rate of increase in output per capita, growth has been looked upon as synonymous with an improvement in society's well-being. It has been widely recognized that

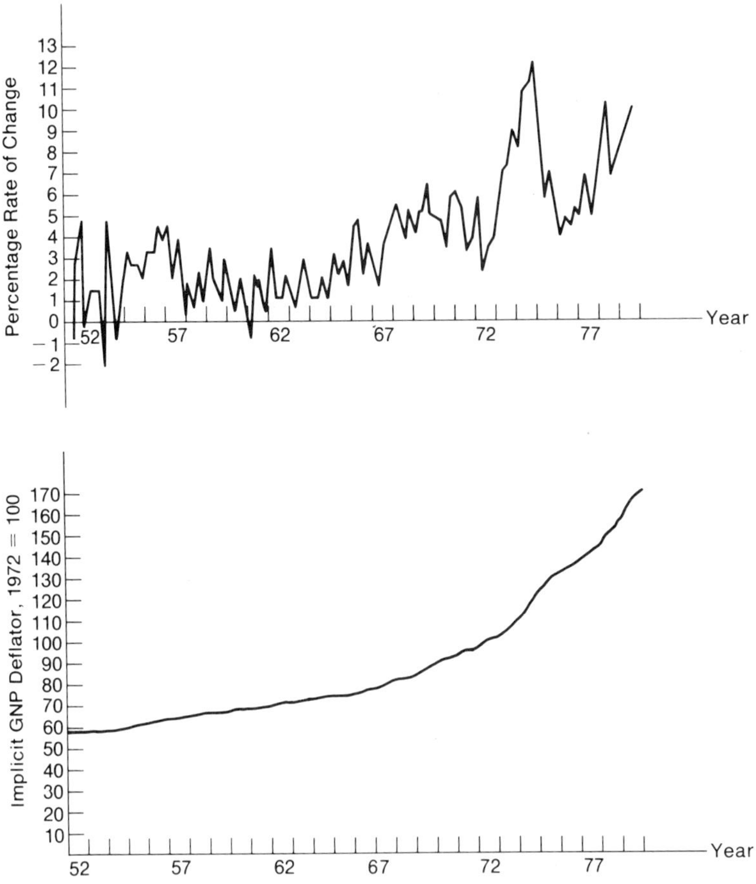

Figure 1—4 / The General Price Level and its Rate of Change 1952–79

rising levels of per capita income allow the achievement of higher levels of private consumption; the provision of a larger volume of such public goods as education, national defense, and parks; the enjoyment of an increasing amount of the important commodity leisure as increasing productive capacity permits a shortening of the workweek; and the provision of resources for offering aid to less developed countries. In addition, economic growth is closely tied to another of our goals, the maintenance of full employment. The labor force expands with the population, and labor-saving innovations tend to free labor from productive use. Maintaining full employment in the face of these forces has required the absorption of a volume of output that has grown briskly over time.

Still, in recent years the devotion to growth that we inherited from a simpler age has lost its near universal grip. It has become increasingly apparent that economic growth, as traditionally measured, imposes some painful burdens on society as well as benefits. Polluted air and water; unsightly scars on the land where forests have been cleared and where minerals and rocks have been gouged out; beaches littered with cans, bottles, and oil residue; congested and noisy streets—these have been the by-products of rapid growth. With recognition of these unpleasant, indeed, some even life-threatening, by-products of growth, it has become fashionable to argue that far too much attention has been devoted to the production of *things* and too little attention to the quality of life. More dramatically, citing the environmental damage and mineral resource depletion that rising output levels portend, numerous ecologists have called for no-growth policies to preserve resources (including the scarce endowments of clean air and water).

The issues raised by antigrowth forces are vital and cannot be ignored. Doubtless it is true that, for much of our history, we have failed to recognize fully the overall costs that the pursuit of ever higher levels of measured output has generated. Indeed, even now relatively little is known about the total environmental impact of most production processes. A rational growth policy, one aimed at maximizing society's overall welfare, cannot ignore the heavy costs of environmental protection. Maintaining the cleanliness and purity of our air, water, and land requires a diversion of resources away from producing other goods and services which, as revealed by their positive market prices, society values. Likewise, slowing production to save exhaustible mineral resources requires that society forgo valued current consumption. Rationality demands that we recognize these costs as well as the costs of environmental destruction. We cannot ignore the typical household's quest for a higher living standard, a quest that generally calls for the extra leisure time and additional manufactured goods that growth, as traditionally measured, provides.

There is, of course, no question but that we need to take account of the negative by-products of growth. Output growth can enhance society's welfare only if the value of that increased output more than covers the total cost to society of producing that output, including the value of the negative by-products generated or the cost of eliminating those by-products. Thus, if the ultimate concern of economic policy is social welfare, we should strive to permit output growth only in those lines of production that will provide a net benefit to society after provision for any unpleasant by-products of that growth. The value to society of increasing volumes of net output per capita still prevents us from relinquishing rapid growth as an important goal, but we now clearly recognize the need for new measures of output that adjust our production totals to allow for the destruction of our limited and exhaustible resources.

Other Policy Goals

There are, of course, additional socially desirable goals with which the informed citizen must concern himself. A partial list would include an equitable distribution of income, balance-of-payments equilibrium, and freedom of choice (both in economic and noneconomic matters). The goal of freedom of choice is not clearly macroeconomic in nature; so the requirements for assuring that freedom will not be treated at any length in this text. However, it should be recognized that economic woes can and have contributed to dramatic losses of freedom. The Bolshevik Revolution in Russia, the rise of Hitler in depression-torn Germany, and the communist takeover in Cuba stemmed in large part from seething dissatisfaction with economic conditions.

Like freedom of choice, the goal of maintaining an *equitable distribution of income* is hardly an exclusive concern of macroeconomics. However, government policies aimed at controlling the economy (particularly those that involve changes in taxes and government spending) do affect income distribution, and choices among alternative policies are influenced by the respective impacts on distribution. So, no macroeconomic analyst can ignore the goal of equity in the distribution of income, and we will have occasion in this text to see how distribution concerns have impinged on actual policies.

By allowing each country to specialize in the production of those commodities in which its relative efficiency is greatest, trade among countries allows total world production to increase. As a consequence, each trading country can enjoy a greater volume of real goods and services than would be possible without international trade. For a country to continue enjoying a desirable volume of international trade, *balance-of-payments equilibrium* must be maintained. Balance-of-payments concerns have, at times, influenced macroeconomic policies and consequently are an important macroeconomic concern, one that will be dealt with in Chapter 15.

While balance-of-payments, the distribution of income, economic freedom, and a number of other concerns cannot be ignored, macroeconomics is primarily concerned with the determinants of the growth in potential output, with deviations from the potential output path, and with changes in the general price level. Those are the concerns that will receive detailed examination in the core of this text.

Constraints and Conflicts in the Pursuit of Admirable Goals. Government efforts to achieve such macroeconomic goals as full employment, price stability, and an optimum growth trajectory fall under the label *stabilization policy*. The basic objective of stabilization policy in the past has been to keep the economy-wide demand for goods and services, referred to as *aggregate demand,* growing in step with the economy's productive capacity. This focus reflects the assumption that instability in aggregate demand is the root cause of macroeconomic problems.

In this light, a simple view of stabilization calls for government to stimulate aggregate demand when business activity is depressed (when there is excessive unemployment), and to reduce aggregate demand when prices rise too rapidly. The government can influence aggregate demand through the use of either fiscal or monetary policy. Fiscal policy involves changes in the government's budget. For example, to stimulate demand using fiscal policy, the government might cut taxes, leaving society with more income to dispose of, hence stimulating spending. Monetary policy involves changes in the stock of money in circulation. An increase in the money stock can result in a decline in the interest cost of borrowed funds and an increase in the availability of funds.

Unfortunately, although the government has tools available for influencing aggregate demand, this does not mean that a stabilization program that achieves the macroeconomic goals discussed earlier can be successfully administered. To begin with, this is so because there may be conflicts between policy goals. For example, it has frequently been argued that high employment and price stability are incompatible goals, that there is a trade-off between the two such that lower unemployment rates must correspond to higher inflation rates.

In Figure 1—5, observations on U.S. unemployment and inflation rates over the period 1960–1979 are provided. The solid schedule *(PC)* plotted for the 1960–1969 observations seems to support the view that there is an inflation/unemployment trade-off such that low unemployment can be achieved with a higher inflation rate, and inflation can be slowed by letting unemployment increase. The observations since 1969, a period in which we have experienced a sustained inflation, indicate that the unemployment/inflation trade-off is not stable. Indeed, changes in the rate of inflation that society *expects* play a crucial role in determining the link between inflation and unemployment, and changes in expectations shift the short-run trade-off schedule, providing the pattern shown by the broken line in Figure 1—5. In the long-run, we will discover, there does not appear to be much of a trade-off between unemployment and inflation as full employment is possible with an unlimited number of different inflation rates. Stabilization policy, however, must pay close attention to the short-run trade-off between inflation and employment, and to the effects of stabilization actions on expectations.

In addition to possible conflicts between policy goals, stabilization efforts are hampered by incomplete knowledge of the timing and strength of impact of different policies. A fiscal policy undertaken today with the objective of stimulating aggregate demand may not have that effect until several months in the future, by which time the demand stimulus may not be needed. In that case, the fiscal policy action would be destabilizing, boosting aggregate demand excessively.

Ponder for a moment, too, which stabilization actions are desirable when both the inflation rate and the unemployment rate are at excessive levels, as they have been for much of the past decade. This unpleasant combination of evils has attracted attention to the supply side of the economy and to proposals for policy actions that may influence the aggregate supply of goods and services as well as demand.

Within the economics profession, a great deal of controversy centers on the nature of the relationships between different policy goals, on the role that government should play in attempting to stabilize the economy, and on

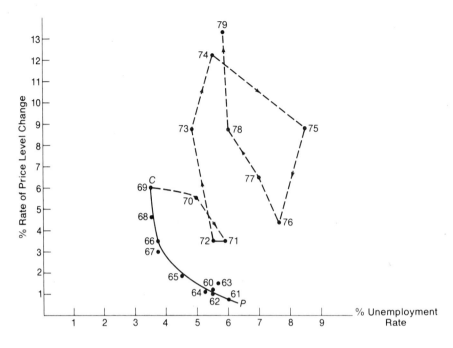

Figure 1—5 / Unemployment Versus Inflation, 1960–1979

the effectiveness of the tools that government has available for stabilization purposes. While almost everyone would agree that full employment, price stability, and sustained economic growth are admirable goals, we shall see that there are strong disagreements over the extent to which those goals may be achieved and over the best means for pursuing them.

Summary

As indicated in this introductory chapter, the remainder of this text will be concerned with explaining how public policy may contribute to the attainment of a number of important goals, including minimum unemployment (maximum output), price level stability, growth in per capita output, and so on. While such policy goals are sometimes complementary, as in the case of full employment and rapid growth, inconsistencies cannot be ruled out. As we saw, there is substantial evidence of a conflict between full employment and price stability, at least in the short-run. Moreover, to pursue any goal or set of goals, the government must know how its policy action will affect the economy. Uncertainty over the size and timing of the impact of public policies limits the government's ability to improve economic performance. Of course, the degree to which policy makers succeed in achieving the goals listed above is important to each of us because our individual, and collective, economic well-being depends heavily on the state of the economy as a whole.

It is worth reemphasizing the point that the methods through which government can pursue its chosen goals cannot be rationalized without understanding the functioning, at the macroeconomic level, of the economic system. To gain an understanding of how the system does work and, thus, of how government can affect the outcome of the economic process, we must build simplified models of the economy. The components of these models and the predictions the models provide must survive the scrutiny of careful statistical testing if we are to have confidence in our policy actions.

Taking a brief look ahead, in Chapter 2 a set of aggregate production and income measures that macroeconomists have employed intensively in constructing, testing, and refining their models are described. Chapter 3 provides a close look at available measures of unemployment, employment, and the price level. Chapter 4 then begins our direct involvement in the process of macroeconomic model building.

Questions

1. What is the distinction between macroeconomics and microeconomics?

2. What is positive economics?

3. Try to determine whether the following statements are positive or normative, and explain why.
   a. Smoking is bad for your health.
   b. According to the Brookings model of the U.S. economy, unemployment next year will be 6.2 percent.
   c. The government should reduce taxes next year to stimulate the economy.
   d. The government should set strict emission limitations on automobiles.
   Do any of the statements mix norms and positive analysis?

4. The proposition that consumption depends on income is common to all macroeconomic models. How might you test this hypothesis?

5. Suppose that regressing consumption on income provided the function:

$$C = 31.4 + .73Y \text{ with } R^2 = .974.$$

   Explain these results.

6. Whose preferences should government's macroeconomic goals reflect, society's or those of the Council of Economic Advisers?

7. Select two macroeconomic goals and account for their importance.

8. Would you prefer to buy drinks in no-deposit bottles and cans or in containers that require payment of a deposit that is refundable? Why? What difference would the kind of container used make in the overall level of U.S. output?

Suggested Readings

Asimov, Isaac. *Asimov's Guide to Science,* Chapter 1. New York: Basic Books, 1972.

Blaug, Mark. *Economic Theory in Retrospect,* Chapter 16. 3rd ed. New York: Cambridge University Press, 1978.

Bronfenbrenner, Martin. "A 'Middlebrow' Introduction to Economic Methodology." In *The Structure of Economic Science,* edited by S. R. Krup, pp. 5–24. Englewood Cliffs, N.J.: Prentice-Hall, 1966.

Council of Economic Advisers. *Economic Report of the President.* Washington, D.C.: U.S. Government Printing Office, annual.

"The Employment Act: Twenty Years of Policy Experience." In Council of Economic Advisers. *Economic Report of the President,* Chapter 7. Washington, D.C.: U.S. Government Printing Office, January 1966.

Friedman, Milton. *Essays in Positive Economics,* Chapter 1. Chicago: University of Chicago Press, 1953.

Huff, D. *How to Lie with Statistics.* New York: W. W. Norton & Co., 1954.

Popper, Carl. "On the Sources of Knowledge and Ignorance." In *Conjectures and Refutations: The Growth of Scientific Knowledge,* edited by Carl Popper, pp. 3–30. New York: Harper & Row, 1968.

Robinson, Joan. *Economic Philosophy,* Chapter 1. New York: Anchor Books, 1964.

White, William H. "Econometric Models: General Considerations." In *Dimensions of Macroeconomics,* edited by S. Mitra, pp. 38–54. New York: Random House, 1971.

Appendix to Chapter 1

An Intuitive Discussion of Ordinary Least Squares Regression

As stated in this chapter, regression analysis is the most frequently employed technique for testing and quantifying economic models. The linear "regression line" between income and consumption that was plotted in text Figure 1—1 to illustrate the role of regression analysis was selected "visually." That is, it looked to the author like the one straight line that *best* fitted the data points in that figure.

In actual econometric research, linear regression equations and any corresponding plot of these equations are obtained using a more objective statistical technique called the *ordinary least squares technique.* In ordinary least squares regression, a set of formulas is employed to derive linear regression equations which, in a particular way, best fit our statistical data. The way in which the derived regression equations best fit can be demonstrated readily with an abbreviated form of our income-consumption example. As we did before, consider the hypothesis that the value of consumption (C) is dependent only on the value of income (Y). With observations of Y and C we can look for a regression line (or equation) that reveals that relationship. Now, supposing that we have only three observations on income and consumption, as graphed in both (a) and (b) of Figure 1—A1, we must find the one straight line that best fits those data points. Of the unlimited number of different straight lines that could be fitted to them, two candidates are sketched in Figure 1—A1.

Looking at part (a) of the figure, we see that when income is at level Y_0, actual observed consumption (C_0) differs or deviates from the value predicted by the regression line $(\hat{C}_0)$ by amount c_0; when income is at level Y_1, observed consumption deviates from that predicted by our regression line by amount c_1; and so on. Because we want our models to predict as accurately as possible, we want to select a regression line (equation) using a criterion that, in some sense, minimizes errors of prediction. The ordinary least squares technique provides the one regression line that *minimizes the sum of the squares* (thus, "least squares") of the deviations of actual observed values of the dependent variable from predicted values. Should the regression line sketched in part (a) of Figure 1—A1 make the total area in the squares of deviations (the shaded squares) as small or smaller than the analogous area that would be associated with any other regression line, it would be the *linear ordinary least squares regression line* relating Y and C. The regression equation for that straight line would, of course, take the form $C_y = a + bY$ where, with actual data on Y and C, a and b would be numerical constants. The regression line in part (b) clearly cannot meet the least squares criterion since the sum of squared deviations associated with that line is more than twice as large as the analogous value for the regression line in part (a). To fully explain why the least squares criterion is used in fitting regression equations would carry us far afield, but we can, in passing, note that it is largely because of the desirable statistical properties of the estimates of the constants a and b provided by this procedure.

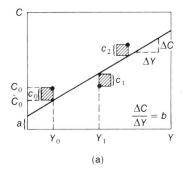

(a)

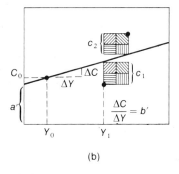

(b)

Figure 1—A1 / Effect on Sum of Squared Deviations of Altering the Values of the Slope and Intercept of the Regression Equation

If the hypothesis that the value of C is determined by the value of Y is correct, we would expect our regression equation to do a good (statistically significant) job in predicting or *explaining* the variations in the dependent variable C as the independent variable Y changes. As indicated in the text, the *proportion* of the variation in the dependent variable explained by movements in the independent variable is called the *coefficient of determination*. If all the observations of C and Y values should fall exactly on our regression line, the coefficient of determination, denoted symbolically as R^2, would be one; i.e., the regression would permit *all* the variation in the dependent variable C to be explained by movements in Y. For a regression that explains 90 percent of the variation in Y, $R^2 = .9$; for a regression that explains 80 percent of the variation in Y, $R^2 = .8$, and so on.

Deriving the Least Squares Formulas. The mathematically inclined student who is interested in statistical techniques should be able to derive the formulas for fitting least squares regression lines to observed data. Suppose we believe any two variables X and Y to be linearly related so a regression equation fitted to the available data on X and Y would appear as $Y_x = a + bX$. Actual values of Y will deviate from the predicted values (Y_x), the amount of deviation for any one observation being $(Y - Y_x)$. It is the sum, over our n observations, of the squared values of all such deviations, that is,

$$\left[\sum_n (Y - Y_x)^2 \right], \qquad\qquad [1\text{—}A1]$$

that we wish to minimize. Because $Y_x = a + bX$, we may claim we are minimizing $\sum_n (Y - a - bX)^2$. Our immediate objective is to derive the a and b values that minimize this term. To do that, we need to take the partial derivatives of $\sum_n (Y - a - bX)^2$ with respect to a and b and set them equal to zero. This yields,

$$\frac{\partial(\ )}{\partial a} = -2\sum_n (Y - a - bX) = 0$$
$$[1\text{—}A2]$$
$$\frac{\partial(\ )}{\partial b} = -2\sum_n X(Y - a - bX) = 0$$

Simplifying these equations yields the two equations (for n observations):

$$\sum_n Y = na + b \sum_n X$$

$$\sum_n XY = a\sum_n X + b\sum_n X^2$$

With data on X and Y inserted, these two equations can be solved simultaneously for the values of a and b that provide the best-fitting straight line through the available data points, that is, for the a and b values that provide the straight-line equation that minimizes the sum of squared deviations.

Solving symbolically for the values of a and b yields:

$$a = \frac{\sum_n X^2 \sum_n Y^2 - \sum_n X \sum_n XY}{n\sum_n X^2 - (\sum X)^2}$$

and

$$b = \frac{n\sum_n XY - \sum_n X \sum_n Y}{n\sum_n X^2 - (\sum X)^2} \qquad [1—A3]$$

For computational purposes, an exactly equivalent, but more convenient, set of expressions may be obtained with values of a and b expressed in terms of deviations of X and Y from their respective mean values. These expressions are:

$$b = \frac{\sum_n xy}{\sum_n x^2} \qquad [1—A4]$$

and $a = Y - bX$.

Chapter **2**

Measurement 1: The National Income and Product Accounts

The most important data for macroeconomic analysis and policy making are the national income and product accounts compiled by the Bureau of Economic Analysis of the Department of Commerce.[1] These national accounts are of quite modern origin, having been compiled and published on a regular basis only since World War II. While a number of other analysts contributed to the development of national income accounting, the U.S. accounts themselves were created under the guidance of Simon Kuznets.[2] In tribute to the importance of his creative efforts, Kuznets was awarded the Nobel prize in economics in 1971.

Like the accounting systems employed by private business firms, the national income and product accounts attempt to provide a summary description of economic performance—specifically, of the *production* performance of the aggregate economy. Consequently, the values of a number of

---

[1]National income and product statistics appear regularly in the *Survey of Current Business,* published monthly by the Department of Commerce. The July issue each year is a summary issue.

[2]Kuznets' pioneering work on national accounts for the United States is recorded in his two-volume tome, *National Income and Its Composition, 1919–1938* (New York: National Bureau of Economic Research, 1941).

31

variables in which we will be intensely interested, measures of national output, national income, consumption, investment, and so on, appear in those accounts. While the purpose of the national accounts is to measure and describe aggregate economic activity rather than to explain it, a skilled macroeconomic analyst can often gain valuable insights into sources of economic disturbances with a quick review of the data in those accounts. For example, with a brief reference to the national income accounts, we can often tentatively determine whether a decline in investment or a rise in private saving is responsible for a recession. In addition, when more refined analysis is required to explain macroeconomic events, as is usually the case, the national income and product accounts typically serve both as the prime source of descriptive evidence on the nature of those events, and as the source of data needed to test and quantify our theoretical explanations of those events. Needless to say, government policy makers keep a close watch on the national accounts as they evaluate the success of past policy actions and formulate policy for the future. Likewise, the heads of business enterprises use the national accounts in their efforts to predict changes in general economic conditions and, thus, in the markets for their products. The obvious importance of the national income and product accounts compels us to become familiar with them even though studying the accounts can be somewhat tedious.

Our primary objectives in working with the national accounts will be, first, to gain an understanding of the conceptual foundations of national income accounting and, second, to familiarize ourselves with the format and content of the actual U.S. national accounts. In working with the national accounts, we will find that a number of rather arbitrary decisions on the handling of specific items within those accounts must be made. Still, the assumptions employed in constructing the national income and product measures rest, for the most part, on sound analytical footing. If, while studying the national accounts, we can keep in mind the idea that their central objective is the measurement of the current *production* performance of the economy, some otherwise puzzling accounting decisions will make more sense.[3]

Developing a conceptual understanding of the national income and product accounts will serve an additional objective by clarifying the relationships that exist among output, income, and spending, three crucial macroeconomic variables. It will be shown that total, economy-wide spending on goods and services is identical to the value of output. Moreover, because the total spending that prompts current production is responsible ultimately for the income generated in the production process, it can be seen that there is a direct link between total spending and the level of income in an economy.

---

[3]Not infrequently, the measures of production provided in the national accounts are employed in roles for which they are ill suited. Most notably, production measures are often viewed as indicators of social welfare so that quantitative ''social welfare'' comparisons can be made between countries and across time.

The Components of Current Production

In organizing measures of the economy's aggregate production and income, an unlimited number of classification schemes could be used. Income and output could be measured and reported on a regional basis, subdivided, say, into income and output originating in the Southeast, Southwest, Northeast, and Northwest. Alternatively, production and income could be classified according to industrial sources, or according to whether they are generated during daylight hours or darkness. The classification scheme employed must be dictated by the phenomena we want to explain, and by our theoretical notions of how those phenomena occur.

The national income and product accounts were designed to provide data on those variables that macroeconomic theory tells us are important in explaining the overall level of economic activity, the course of price level changes, and the rate of economic expansion. The models most frequently employed in macroeconomic analysis subdivide the aggregate economy into four sectors: the household, business, foreign, and government sectors. The measures of total output in the national income and product accounts are correspondingly subdivided into consumption (by households), investment (by business firms), net exports (in the foreign sector), and government purchases. Each of these component parts of aggregate output (the sum of which is all of current output) is explained below. On the income side of the national income and product accounts, aggregate income is divided according to type of income. That subdivision is formally explained beginning on page 44.

Consumption

Consumption, as measured in the national income and product accounts, consists of the market value of purchases of those goods and services that directly yield human satisfaction. For example, the value of a pound of hamburger bought by a private household counts as personal consumption spending. The same pound of hamburger bought by the local spaghetti parlor is not counted as consumption until its value is reflected in the price of a spaghetti dinner, which yields satisfaction directly.

While the economy's output of consumer products is measured by summing the expenditures made by all households and nonprofit institutions, it must be recognized that consumer spending does not, in every case, measure the true "using up" of consumer goods. The reason is that the household sector devotes a sizable fraction of its total spending to the purchase of *durable* goods like cars, home appliances, furniture, and so on. Because those commodities have service lives greater than our one-year accounting period, households truly *use up* only a fraction of the consumer durables purchased during any selected accounting period. A household's purchase of an $8,000 automobile adds $8,000 to our measure of consumption when the purchase is made. However, if the car's life is eight years, the household actually enjoys a stream of transportation services over that eight-year period. On average, only one-eighth ($1,000) of the value of the car is used up providing transportation services each year.

A true measure of the yield of consumer services that provide satisfaction directly should obviously count only the annual *use value* of consumer durables and the full purchase value of those other *nondurable* consumer purchases that presumably are fully used up during the accounting period. Because of the insurmountable statistical difficulties that would be encountered in trying to measure the value of the services rendered each year by the massive accumulated stock of consumer durables, national income accountants treat durable purchases like other consumer expenditures, as though the durable goods acquired were fully consumed in one accounting period.

Investment

Investment is, essentially, the value of spending on newly produced, physical "capital goods" acquired for the purpose of providing a stream of productive services in the future. In the national income accounts, investment takes the form of spending on plants and equipment, inventories, and residential construction. Because the objective of the national accounts is the measurement of current production, only acquisitions of *newly produced* capital goods are counted as investment. The purchase by firm Z of an already existing plant, previously owned by firm X, reflects no current production. One firm's investment is matched by another firm's disinvestment. Similarly, purchases of stocks, bonds, and other interest-yielding financial assets, representing "financial investment," are excluded from the measure of investment recorded in the national income and product accounts because, again, such financial investment by a security buyer is offset by the equivalent disinvestment of the security seller (or issuer of new securities).[4]

The total expenditure on newly produced, physical capital goods in one period is called *gross investment*. A part of every period's gross investment is absorbed in the *replacement* of capital goods that wear out, become obsolete, or are accidentally destroyed during that period. The rest represents a net addition to the capital stock and is called *net investment*.

Net Exports

Net exports are the measure of the difference in value of exports and imports. U.S. exports consist of domestically produced goods and services that are sold abroad. Imports, on the other hand, consist of foreign-produced goods and services bought by economic units in this country. U.S. exports

---

[4]In the process of buying and selling existing assets, real or financial, some commissions and fees, representing payments for services currently rendered, are typically generated. The value of such "production" is included in the national accounts.

must be included in the measure of U.S. production, while imports should be excluded. Because our measured values of household consumption, business investment, and government purchases include expenditures on imported items, total imports must be subtracted from our summary measures of the components of *domestic* output if those measures are not to overstate the level of that output.

Government Purchases

Government purchases consist of purchases made by federal, state, and local government units. The government buys vast quantities of finished products including tanks and planes, bridges, schools, roads, and so on. In addition, it buys a substantial volume of factor inputs for use in its own "production" activities (think of the ink, paper, and manpower purchased by the Pentagon, your governor's office, and city hall). Unfortunately for the national income accountant, the "output" of most government operations is not exchanged in markets where a measure of its value (a market price) can be observed. The relatively small component of government production that does appear in markets, such as government-produced electric power, transit service, and postal service, is valued at market prices just as is private business production. For lack of a better approximation, the rest is assumed to equal the factor cost of providing governmental functions. Thus, the value of most of that portion of the nation's production that is absorbed in government use is set equal to the sum of government spending on factor inputs and finished products.

Gross National Product: Its Meaning and Measurement

To shift our focus from the components of aggregate production to summary measures of production, we will take a close look at the concept of *Gross National Product,* the most frequently cited summary measure of an economy's production. As the name implies, Gross National Product (often abbreviated as GNP) is the broadest measure of an economic system's aggregate production performance. By definition, GNP is the total *dollar* value of all *final* goods and services produced by the economy during a specified time period, typically one year.

While this definition of GNP is straightforward, some elements of that definition are deserving of elaboration. First, it is worth noting that GNP must be measured in dollars because of the impossibility of adding physical quantities of different commodities. It is not meaningful, for example, to compute the sum of 3 apples + 4 dozen eggs + 5 autos.[5] In addition, great

---

[5]The term "national" in Gross National Product indicates that our interest is in measuring the output of the residents (nationals) of a particular country. Thus, U.S. measures of output include the production (reflected by their earnings) of Americans that occurs abroad while excluding some income earned in the United States by foreign residents.

care is required to ensure that GNP figures measure just the value of *final products*, thereby avoiding the problem of double counting. A *final good* is one that is produced during the observed accounting period but not resold during that period. Items purchased for resale, whether destined for additional processing or not, are *intermediate goods*. For example, water bought for household use is a final good. Water bought by a manufacturing firm, the cost of which will be reflected in the sales price of the firm's product, is an intermediate good. If we counted in GNP both the value of the firm's water purchases and of its output (the price of which includes provision for the cost of water used in production), we would be overstating the value of GNP. In fact, we would have counted the value of water purchased by this firm twice. (Do the same claims hold for the household versus spaghetti parlor purchase of hamburger on page 33.

Finally, the items counted in GNP must actually be *produced* during the accounting period. If a wave of notalgia prompts me to purchase a 1950 Ford from you, that purchase entails no current production and must not be counted in GNP. In contrast, my purchase of a *new* Ford would reflect current production and must be counted in GNP.

Conceptual Techniques for Computing GNP

There are three important conceptual techniques that can be used to compute a value for GNP. They are commonly designated the *expenditure, income,* and *value added* techniques.

The Expenditure and Income Techniques. If GNP is the dollar value of all final goods and services currently produced, it should be possible to measure GNP by adding up all spending on final products during the accounting period. Doing so provides an *expenditure approach* measure of production. Alternatively, since for every dollar of spending on final products there must be a dollar *received,* we should also be able to obtain a value for GNP by adding up all *incomes* generated during the accounting period, that is, by using the *income approach.*

The *circular flow* diagram in Figure 2—1 illustrates the validity of the expenditure and income approaches to measuring the value of output and also shows the basic equivalence of those two measurement techniques. In the simple economic system represented by Figure 2—1, there are only two sectors. All production activity is assumed to take place in business firms, which are consolidated in the *business sector,* while all output is shown absorbed by the *household sector.* Business firms combine factor inputs, land, labor, capital, and entrepreneurial talent, to produce a flow of final goods and services. Looking at the upper loop of the flow diagram, it is clear that the dollar flow of household expenditures on final products must be identical to the dollar value of the flow of final goods and services that businesses produce and sell to households. Even if it is difficult to measure output directly, we can evaluate its flow indirectly simply by measuring total

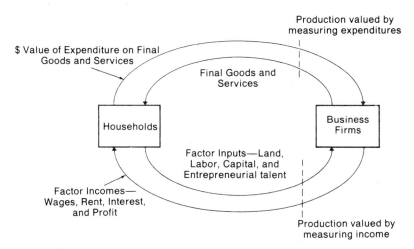

Production valued by measuring expenditures

$ Value of Expenditure on Final Goods and Services

Final Goods and Services

Households

Business Firms

Factor Inputs—Land, Labor, Capital, and Entrepreneurial talent

Factor Incomes— Wages, Rent, Interest, and Profit

Production valued by measuring income

Figure 2—1 / The Circular Flow in a Simple Economy

dollar spending on final products. But what becomes of those revenues that business firms receive from households? The lower loop of our flow diagram answers that question graphically. The factor inputs business firms use in the production process must be hired from households. In return for the factor services they provide, households receive a flow of income, wages for labor, rent for property, interest for money capital, and profit, as the reward of entrepreneurial talent. Those income payments completely exhaust the business sector's revenues because any business revenues left over after payment of wages, rent, and interest are, by definition, fully absorbed by profit which is income accruing to the households that own business firms. Once again, it is easy to see that, even though a direct measure of output is difficult, we can readily measure the value of output indirectly, in this case by measuring the value of income generated in the production process.

For the simple economy represented by the flow diagram in Figure 2—1, the expenditure and income techniques provide equally valid measures of aggregate economic activity. Indeed, for that simple economy measured output and income are numerically identical. That identity is invalidated by taking account of the real world complications (such as the existence of a government and a foreign sector) that are reflected in the actual U.S. national accounts. However, the expenditure and income approaches remain equally valid methods of measuring aggregate economic activity, and there remains a direct link between the level of spending and the level of income generated in the production process.

The Value Added Technique. As well as employing basic factor inputs (land, labor, and so on), business firms purchase *intermediate* commodity and service inputs from other firms. In creating their own products, firms *add value* to the intermediate inputs they receive from other firms. To measure one firm's contribution to current production, the value of the intermediate commodity and service inputs it purchases must be subtracted from the value of its own output, the difference being the firm's *value added*. As a simple example, a college bookstore that buys an economics text (an intermediate good) for sixteen dollars and resells it for twenty dollars has contributed four dollars worth of *value added* to the book.

Agriculture, mining, and similar basic industries provide high volumes of raw material inputs to the U.S. economy. These basic inputs move through successive layers of industry that process them into new forms until, ultimately, they emerge transformed into homes, automobiles, clothing, machine tools, office buildings, and other *final* products. In each stage of the production process, value is added to the material and service inputs from the preceding stage. By simply adding up the amounts of value added at each production stage where market transactions take place, we can derive a measure of the total dollar value of current (*final* goods and services) production.

Table 2—1 provides a simple numerical example of a national income measurement task. In addition to demonstrating the equivalence of the expenditure, income, and value added techniques of measuring production, that concrete numerical example should make the national income accounting concepts we have reviewed more meaningful.

The economic system represented in Table 2—1 is very simple, producing only two final products. One of the products is an investment or capital good, say, a bread-making machine, with an unlimited life. The other is the consumer product, bread. Table 2—1 lists the various market transactions that take place in producing these two final goods during the chosen accounting period. The first row shows the sale of twenty dollars worth of steel to a firm that manufactures bread-making machines. The second row shows this manufacturing firm selling bread-making machines to the bread company for fifty dollars. The third row shows a wheat grower selling his product to a flour-producing mill, with the remaining rows showing the successive market transactions that take place in the process of producing and selling bread.

Column 5 shows the *value added* to purchased inputs as they are processed by the listed firms. The first entry shows, assuming that the steel company buys nothing from other firms, that its value added is twenty dollars. The company that manufactures bread-making machines buys steel for twenty dollars and turns the steel into bread-making machinery which it sells for fifty dollars. The value added by the bread machine company then is thirty dollars. The value added by the wheat farmer, assuming he buys nothing from other firms, is the full five dollar sales price of his wheat. The flour mill is shown paying five dollars for the wheat which it turns into flour and resells for ten dollars. The mill's value added then is five dollars. Continuing down column 5 yields value-added figures of ten dollars for the firm that transforms the flour into bread, and five dollars for the retailers who display and sell bread to consumers, the *final* purchasers of the bread.

Table 2—1 / Determination of GNP by Expenditure, Income, and Value Added Techniques

Good (1)	Seller (2)	Buyer (3)	Value of Transaction (4)	Value Added (5)	Expenditure on Final Good (6)	Factor Earnings (Incomes) (7)
Steel	Steel company	Producer of bread-making machines	$ 20	$20	—	$20
Bread-making machine	Producer of bread-making machines	Bread-making company	50	30	$50	30
Wheat	Wheat-growing farmer	Flour-producing mill	5	5	—	5
Flour	Flour-producing mill	Bread-making company	10	5	—	5
Bread	Bread-making company	Retail groceries	20	10	—	10
Bread	Retail groceries	Consumers	25	5	25	5
Total dollar value of transactions			$130			
Gross National Product			—	$75	$75	$75

GNP, which is simply the sum of the value-added contributions of all our firms, is seventy-five dollars.

By looking at column 6, we see that the same GNP figure can be obtained by adding up all expenditures on *final* goods and services. There are only two items in our example that are final goods (goods produced during the accounting period but not resold), the bread-making machines and the bread sold to consumers. Adding the fifty dollar expenditure on bread-making machines to the twenty-five dollar consumer expenditure on bread yields a value of seventy-five dollars for GNP.

Finally, GNP can be computed by adding the factor earnings (incomes) that appear in column 7. Interestingly, the factor income figures in any one row are identical to the value added figures in that row. That is not sheer coincidence; a moment's reflection on the entries in any row will explain that equality (or identity). The total revenue the flour mill in row 4 received for sales of flour was ten dollars. However, five dollars of that went into payments for the intermediate input of wheat purchased from the farmer in row 3. Only five dollars was left for income payments to the factor inputs used by the mill. Out of that five dollars must come wages for labor, rent for use of property, and interest for use of borrowed funds. Any leftover revenue is, by definition, fully absorbed in profit, which is another factor income payment. Thus, all of the difference between total revenues and payments to other firms for intermediate inputs (that is, the full amount of value added) goes to factor earnings.

In the actual U.S. accounts, there are, as we will see, a few complications that must be taken into account in computing GNP using the techniques we have described. Nevertheless, GNP figures can be obtained using any of the three methods illustrated in our simple example. Before leaving that example, you should spend a few minutes looking at column 4 and thinking about the sources of double counting in the $130 total value of all transactions obtained by summing the entries in that column.

The Actual U.S. National Income and Product Accounts

We must now concentrate our attention on the actual computation of the output and income values in the national income and product accounts for the United States. We will concern ourselves only with calculating those values using the expenditure and income approaches. An actual sample account for the United States appears in Table 2—2.

GNP from the Expenditure (Product) Side

From the expenditure side of the accounts, we know that a value for GNP can be obtained by adding up all spending on final goods and services. Consistent with the classification scheme described earlier, our total expenditure measure of output can be broken up into consumption spending, investment spending, net exports, and government spending. Thus, for measured values of consumption *(C)*, *gross* investment (I_G), government spending *(G)*, and net exports (net exports = exports minus imports or $X - M$):

$$GNP = C + I_G + G + (X - M) \qquad [2—1]$$

Part A of Table 2—2 shows this breakdown of final spending with a further subdivision of each major component of spending. Total consumption spending, for example, is broken down into spending on durable goods (once again, cars, refrigerators, stoves, and so on), spending on nondurable goods (mainly food and clothing),[6] and spending on services (housing, medical and dental treatment, domestic help, and so on). While looking through the components of expenditure in Table 2—2 part A, it is worth noting that, in 1979, approximately 64 percent of GNP went into consumption, 16 percent into investment, and just over 20 percent was absorbed by government.

Other Measures of Output (Income)

As indicated before, GNP is our broadest measure of production. It is so comprehensive, in fact, that it fails to recognize the fact that some of the existing stock of capital is consumed in the production process. In any accounting period though, some capital is used up by being worn out, becoming obsolete, or by being accidentally destroyed. Subtracting the amount of ''capital consumption allowance'' from the GNP figure for our selected accounting period leaves the dollar value of *net* output available for society's use as a result of the productive efforts of all the factor inputs used in the production process. This measure of net output is labeled *net national product* (NNP).[7] Thus,

$$NNP = GNP - D,$$

---

[6]Commodities classified as consumer durables are those that generally last more than a year, while nondurables generally last less than a year.

[7]Conceptually, GNP is too broad a measure of true output because there is one source of double counting left unpurged in the GNP figure. The GNP figure includes all current spending on capital goods even though capital goods are used as inputs in the production of other goods and services. For example, the purchase in 1980 of a loom by a textile mill is included in GNP even though that loom will be used in 1980 in producing the final product cloth. As firms sell their final products, they include in their sales prices an allowance for the capital stock used up in the production process (that is, the price of final goods includes a charge for the capital embodied in those final goods). Thus, there is an element of double counting present in GNP figures, investment expenditures being counted twice. The deduction of depreciation charges eliminates this source of double counting, yielding that measure of net output that we call net national product. The GNP account includes this trouble-creating spending on investment goods purchase only in order to better represent the *timing* of changes in the level of *production.*

Table 2—2 / The National Income and Product Accounts   (1979)

			A. GNP from the Expenditure Side (in billions of dollars)
1. Personal consumption expenditures			1509.8
2. Durable goods		212.9	
3. Nondurable goods		597.0	
4. Services		699.9	
5. Gross private domestic investment			386.2
6. Fixed investment		367.8	
7. Nonresidential	253.9		
8. Structures	92.3		
9. Producers' durable equipment	161.6		
10. Residential structures	113.9		
11. Change in business inventories		18.4	
12. Net exports of goods and services			−3.5
13. Exports		257.4	
14. Imports		260.9	
15. Government purchases of goods and services			476.1
16. Federal		166.3	
17. National defense	108.3		
18. Other	58.0		
19. State and local		309.8	
20. Gross National Product			2368.6

where D stands for the capital consumption allowance (essentially depreciation). Recognizing that the deduction of depreciation from gross investment leaves net investment (I_n), we also know that the measured value of NNP is

$$NNP = C + I_N + G + (X - M). \qquad [2-2]$$

Because part of the capital stock is used up in the act of production, it is clear that not all of GNP represents income *earned* by the factor inputs involved in the production process. We might, however, think of our net (after depreciation) measure of output as representing income earned by factor inputs. This is not the case in the U.S. economy, however. The dollar value of NNP measured at market prices still is larger than earned income because of some *nonfactor* payments business firms must make. These nonfactor payments consist primarily of *indirect business taxes*. Included in this category of nonfactor payments are sales and excise taxes, property taxes, and franchise fees and fines collected by government agencies. A part of producers' sales revenues must be absorbed by these payments for which no specific productive service is rendered. Thus, market prices and the dollar value of NNP are larger, by the amount of indirect business taxes, than the value of income *earned* by the factors of production used in the production process. Deducting the value of indirect business taxes (T_i) from

Table 2—2 / The National Income and Product Accounts (1979) *(Continued)*

			B. GNP from the Income (Factor Earnings) Side (in billions of dollars)
21. Compensation of employees			1459.2
22. Wages and salaries		1227.3	
23. Supplements to wages and salaries		231.9	
24. Employer contributions for social insurance	109.2		
25. Other labor income	122.7		
26. Proprietors' income			130.0
27. Business and professional		97.9	
28. Farm		32.1	
29. Rental income of persons			26.9
30. Corporate profits, adjusted			178.4
31. Profits before tax		237.0	
32. Profits tax liability	92.7		
33. Profits after tax	144.4		
34. Dividends	52.7		
35. Undistributed profits	91.7		
36. Inventory valuation and capital consumption adjustments	−58.6		
37. Net interest			129.7
38. National income			1924.2
39. Indirect business tax liability and other minor adjustments			199.7
40. Net national product			2123.9
41. Capital consumption allowance			243.0
42. Gross National Product from factor earnings			2366.9
43. Statistical discrepancy			1.7
44. Gross National Product from expenditures			2368.6

Source: U.S. Department of Commerce, *Survey of Current Business* (Washington, D.C.: U.S. Government Printing Office).

earned income = Bus

NNP then does yield a value for *earned* income, which is labeled *national income* (NI). Algebraically,

$$NI = NNP - T_i$$

or   [2—3]

$$NI = GNP - D - T_i.$$

Going a step further, in the actual U.S. economy, income payments that are in fact *received* are typically smaller than the value of earned income. Why is not all of earned income paid out to the factor inputs involved in the production process? There are a number of reasons. First, a part of earned income typically takes the form of corporate profit against which the government levies a corporate income tax. That tax on profits reduces the dollar volume of profit income available for payment, in the form of dividends, to the owners (stockholders) of incorporated businesses. Further, firms typically pay out only part of their after-tax profits, keeping a portion (called *retained earnings*) for further internal expansion, enhancement of their liquid reserves, or acquisition of shares of other firms.

Another deduction from earned income is required to reflect the impact on received income of the social security system. Both employers and employees make (required) contributions to this *social insurance program*. The portion of earned income that is absorbed in the social security contribution is, consequently, not available for current income payments to our factors of production.

There is one final item that causes received income to differ from earned income. That item is the *transfer payment*, a payment for which no current productive service is rendered. Included in transfer payments are welfare payments, payouts on private and public (government) pension programs, including social security, and payments of interest on the national debt. Such payments make a positive contribution to received income, although they do not reflect current *earnings* from the provision of productive services.

To transform national income into a measure of received income, denoted *personal income,* we must subtract from national income the amount of corporate taxes (T_b), retained earnings (R_t), and Social Security contributions (SS), all components of income that is earned but not received; and we must add net transfer program payouts (T_r), representing income received but not earned, to that value. Algebraically,

$$PI = NI - (T_b + R_t + SS) + T_r, \qquad [2—4]$$

where PI is personal income, our measure of received income.

To summarize briefly the accounting relationships developed in this section, we obtained GNP from the expenditure side of the accounts by adding consumption, gross investment, govenment spending, and net exports. The resulting GNP figures differed from our measures of net output, called net national product (NNP), by the amount of capital consumption. In turn, NNP differed from personal income (PI), our measure of received income, because of indirect business taxes, the corporate profits tax, social security contributions, retained earnings, and transfer payments. Can you write the equation that allows GNP figures to be converted to PI figures?

GNP from the Income Side

We should now be able to go to the income side of the national accounts and sum the values of income earned by each of the four basic productive factors—land, labor, capital, and entrepreneurial talent—to obtain values for GNP and the other output and income measures that appear in the national accounts. The measures derived should be comparable to those obtained from the product (expenditures) side of the accounts. While our discussion up to this point has implied that we should find total income subdivided into wages, rent, interest, and profit, a look at the income side of the actual national accounts (Table 2—2 part B) reveals a somewhat different breakdown. Each of the entries in Table 2—2 part B is discussed below.

Labor's Reward. Most of the income *earned* by labor is reflected in the first line of Table 2—2 part B, compensation of employees. The largest component of employee compensation, wages and salaries, includes (along with ordinary wages and salaries) executives' compensation, commissions, tips, bonuses, and payments in kind which represent earned income to the recipients. Supplements to wages and salaries include such items as employer contributions for social insurance (social security, federal and state unemployment insurance, and so on); employer contributions for private pension, health, unemployment, and welfare funds; compensation for injuries; and pay for military reserve duty. Labor's take-home pay is substantially smaller than its total earned income because part of its earnings take the form of *fringe benefits* of the type outlined here, part is withheld to meet personal income tax liabilities, and part is absorbed by each employee's own contribution to social insurance.

Rent (and Royalties). Rental income of persons (line 29 of Table 2—2 part B) consists of the earnings of persons from the rental of property, *except* the earnings of persons engaged in the real estate business as a primary source of income (in that case earnings from rent are reflected in the business sector's earnings); the imputed net rental value to owner-occupants of nonfarm dwellings;[8] and the royalties received by persons from patents, copyrights, and rights to natural resources.

Net Interest. Net interest (line 37) is the excess of the business sector's interest payments over its interest receipts. Interest paid by consumers and by government enterprises is excluded on the assumption that it does not represent a factor cost of production. A consumer's current interest payments on a loan he obtained a year ago to buy an auto reflect no current production; it is merely a transfer payment. Similarly, most of government's interest payments are to service debt incurred during past war periods and, thus, cannot be interpreted as payments for current productive use of money capital. The outstanding debt of business is, however, assumed to reflect current productive use of borrowed capital. Thus, the interest payments for use of that capital are counted as a component of GNP.

---

[8]This imputation is necessary if we want to measure the actual value of housing services made available to society and do not want the value of those services to change every time a renter buys the house he has been renting.

Profit. Profit is a residual. It is what is left over after, out of available revenues, all other expense items have been taken into account. In the national account in Table 2—2 part B, total profit appears under two headings; profit of corporations and profit of unincorporated enterprises, that is, of single proprietorships and partnerships. The earnings of the owners of unincorporated enterprises, denoted *proprietors' income* (line 26), include farm earnings and professional income (the income of doctors, lawyers, consulting engineers, and so on).[9] The profit earned by corporations appears in line 30 and is labeled *corporate profits, adjusted*.

Both corporate profits and proprietors' income are modified by an *inventory valuation adjustment* and by a *capital consumption adjustment*. The inventory valuation adjustment is necessary to negate the impact on measured profit of changes in the level of prices. If prices rise during the accounting period, part of measured profit can represent simply a *markup* of the value of inventories that were bought at a lower price. If the inventory used in the production process was bought at prices lower than current replacement cost, firms' computed production costs (most frequently obtained using original purchase prices for inventory used) will be understated and their profits will be overstated. Conversely, during a period of price decline, production costs would be overstated and profits understated.[10] The inventory valuation adjustment is an attempt to offset the effect on profits (and on actual measured changes in inventories and GNP) of such changes in prices. Its value was quite large in 1979, reflecting the substantial increase in prices that year.

The capital consumption adjustment is necessary because the capital consumption allowances reported for income tax purposes under internal revenue service guidelines can seriously misrepresent the value of capital being used up during the accounting period. The capital consumption allowance is the difference between tax return-based depreciation allowances and allowances based on estimates of the actual economic service lives of capital assets, straight-line depreciation, and replacement costs.

---

[9]In practice, it is impossible to judge what portion of proprietors' income is truly profit income and what portion is the reward for the proprietor's own labor, money, capital, and property use. It is precisely because of the impossibility of disentangling the returns to the four basic factor inputs that the income side of our national accounts must be subdivided into the five earnings categories that appear in Table 2—2B.

[10]Correspondingly, the *product side* measure of inventory investment (a component of GNP), valued in money terms, will yield an overstatement of the actual physical change in inventories (thus in GNP) when prices are rising, and an understatement when prices are falling. The size of the inventory valuation adjustment depends on the extent to which businesses rely on the FIFO [First In—First Out] or LIFO [Last In—First Out] methods of charging inventory usage against current sales. A simple demonstration of the implications of using these alternative methods of measuring inventories and of the need for an inventory valuation adjustment can be found in Sam Rosen, *National Income and Other Social Accounts* (New York: Holt, Rinehart and Winston, 1972), pp. 49–52.

Investment, Productivity Growth, and the Distribution of Income. In recent years, the U.S. economy has experienced a low rate of growth in labor productivity and a lower level of investment than most other countries in terms of the proportion of GNP allocated to investment use. Many analysts directly relate these facts, arguing that low levels of investment are at least partly responsible for the anemic growth of productivity. In turn, it is argued that investment is decreased because of the low returns on investment. Our national income accounts provide a rough indication of these analysts' concerns over the returns to capital. Ignoring proprietors' income (which mixes profits, wages, etc.), corporate profits in 1979 were just over 9 percent of national income. In contrast, wages and salaries comprised nearly 64 percent of this income total. Apparently, the share of income accruing to capital has declined; in comparison, that share comprised roughly 14 percent of income in the mid-1960s.

Earned Income and Its Relation to Our Other Income and Production Measures. Combining the components of earned income that appear in Table 2—2B (compensation of employees, rental income of persons, net interest, and proprietors' income plus corporate profit) provides a summary measure of the income *earned* by the factor inputs used in the process of production. The resulting value of earned income, *national income,* appears in line 38 of Table 2—2 B.

You should recall that adding the value of nonfactor payments (basically the indirect business taxes shown in line 39) to national income yields a value for NNP, and adding the value of capital consumption to NNP yields a value for GNP. Making these adjustments to the value of national income derived from the income side of the accounts results in a value for GNP of $2,366.9 billion with the adjustments required shown in lines 39 to 42 of Table 2—2 B. As indicated by the entry in line 43 of that table, the value of GNP derived from income measures generally can be expected to differ by a relatively small magnitude from the GNP value obtained from summing expenditures on final goods and services. Such discrepancies are of a magnitude that can be attributed quite easily to statistical errors in independently compiling the data on earned income and expenditures.[11]

Moving in the other direction again, we showed above that national income can be altered to provide a measure of actual received income (PI). Again, to obtain personal income values, national income was modified by subtracting corporate income taxes, retained earnings, and social security contributions, and by the addition of transfer payments.

---

[11]The bulk of our income-side measures comes from income tax returns and employment tax records. Data for the product-side measures come from records on sales, inventories, and product shipments. Generated, as they are, from two different data sets, the income- and product-side estimates of GNP will never be precisely equal. Usually the income-side estimate is the lower of the two, suggesting that income reported for tax purposes is somewhat less than actual earnings.

The Disposition of Received Income. In the models macroeconomists construct, the manner in which the household sector of the economy disposes of its received income is crucial. A primary obligation that the recipients of money income must meet is the personal income tax liability.[12] The expendable income that is left after meeting this tax liability is labeled *disposable personal income*. It is income available to households to dispose of as they see fit. Thus,

$$Y_d = \text{PI} - T_p \qquad\qquad [2\text{—}5]$$

where Y_d is disposable personal income, PI is personal income, and T_p is the personal tax obligation, primarily income tax.

Households can divide their disposable income between consumption and saving as they choose. That part of disposable income that is not consumed is, by definition, saved. Thus,

$$Y_d = C + S$$

or $\qquad\qquad\qquad\qquad\qquad\qquad\qquad\qquad\qquad [2\text{—}6]$

$$S = Y_d - C$$

where C is consumption, S is personal saving, and Y_d, as before, is disposable income.

A Summary of National Income and Product Account Relationships. The accounting relationships we have developed can be summarized as shown in Table 2—3. Our ability to derive values for output or income from either the expenditures or the income side of the national income and product accounts should be apparent from a brief look at that table.

An understanding of the structure of the national income and product accounts will make the construction of models of the economic system much easier, and that chore awaits us. Before proceeding we should take note of a few of the special problems encountered in constructing the U.S. accounts, and of some of the limitations on those accounts.

The National Accounts—Some Notable Complications

While appropriate conceptual measures of a nation's economic activities may be readily formulated, the practical implementation of those conceptual measures is much more difficult. Compromises and approximations, some of which we have already touched upon, must frequently be tolerated. A number of the special difficulties involved in producing the U.S. national income and product accounts are reviewed below.

---

[12]In fact, most income recipients have a portion of their income withheld from their paychecks to meet personal income tax liabilities.

Table 2—3 / Relationships Employed in the National Income and Product Accounts

$$
\Sigma \text{ Final expenditures} =
\left\{
\begin{array}{l}
\text{Consumption} \\
+\text{Gross investment} \\
+\text{Government spending} \\
+\text{Net exports} \\ \hline
\text{Gross National Product}
\end{array}
\right.
$$

$$
\text{Gross National Product} =
\begin{array}{l}
\text{Gross National Product} \\
-\text{Capital consumption} \\ \hline
\text{Net National Product} \\
-\text{Indirect business taxes} \\ \hline
\text{National income} \\
-\text{Corporate profits tax} \\
-\text{Retained earnings} \\
-\text{Social Security} \\
+\text{Transfers} \\ \hline
\text{Personal income} \\
-\text{Personal income tax} \\ \hline
\text{Disposable income} \\
-\text{Consumption} \\ \hline
\text{Personal saving}
\end{array}
= \left.
\begin{array}{l}
\text{Compensation} \\
\text{of employees} \\
+\text{Rental income} \\
\text{of persons} \\
+\text{Net interest} \\
+\text{Proprietors' income*} \\
\&\text{ Corporate profits} \\ \hline
\text{National income}
\end{array}
\right\} = \Sigma \text{ Earned income}
$$

*Both items modified by the inventory valuation.

Depreciation

To know what is happening to the stock of capital and, correspondingly, to know the value of *net* output, we must know the rate at which the existing capital stock is being used up. Business firms' income statements provide a measure of depreciation, but there are reasons for questioning the usefulness of that measure. If the dollar value of measured depreciation is exactly equal to current gross investment, our accounting definitions tell us that the capital stock is unchanged. However, the newly produced capital goods will typically be technologically superior to the ones they replace, and an improvement in the quality of the capital stock is equivalent, in terms of its impact on productive capacity, to an increase in the stock of capital with no quality improvement. Clearly, our measures of net investment that, in turn, tell us what is happening to the accumulated stock of capital over time are somewhat misleading.

As implied by the discussion of adjustments to profit earnings, an additional problem exists because current depreciation charges as reported in tax returns typically are based on the original purchase prices of capital assets rather than on their replacement cost. Consequently, when prices are rising, the actual value of depreciation is understated. With depreciation understated, business profits are overstated, and so is NNP. During a period of falling prices, depreciation would be overstated, resulting in an understatement of profits and NNP.

Finally, business firms' depreciation charges are mere bookkeeping adjustments. The depreciation lifetimes that business firms *assign* to capital assets depend more heavily on the Internal Revenue Service's guidelines for "allowable lives" than on actual economic capital consumption. Hence, another possibility for error in our measurements of profit, net investment, and NNP arises.

Our measures of true capital consumption are clearly quite crude in spite of current efforts to correct for some of the more glaring deficiencies in those measures. In this regard, it is notable that many macroeconomic analysts prefer to work with GNP figures rather than NNP figures because of the potential inaccuracy in NNP introduced by shortcomings in available measures of depreciation.

Capital Gains and Losses

The occurrence of capital gains and losses, changes in the market value of assets, also causes problems for the national income accountant. If I hire a contractor and have him build an addition onto my home which increases its market value, the value (cost) of the addition is included in our measures of output. If, however, the market value of my house is increased by a favorable shift in demand (for example, due to the opening of a new factory within easy commuting distance) or by a generalized inflation, no entry in the national accounts would reflect the capital gain I enjoy. The familiar reason is that no current production is involved in the latter type of increase in market value.

Similarly, if the value of a tract of land increases because of the discovery of oil or uranium ore, no record of that increase in national wealth appears in the national income and product accounts. However, with the value of such discoveries omitted from our accounts, the depletion of natural resources must also be omitted; that depletion cannot be charged against current national output. Broadening our example, it must be recognized that no deterioration in the quantity or quality of natural endowments a nation is blessed with, including environmental quality, is directly reflected in the national income and product accounts. Our traditional measures of output and income clearly omit consideration of some economic activities that profoundly affect human well-being.

Nonmarket Production

The list of economic activities that are excluded from the national accounts can be extended with no difficulty. While GNP is defined as a measure of the dollar value of *total* production of final goods and services, there are a number of highly important productive activities that are not measured. The value of a housewife's performance of her duties as dietician, cook, housecleaner, chauffeur, baby-sitter, and so on are omitted from the national income and product accounts. When those same services are performed for pay, their value does appear in GNP. If a man marries his hired housekeeper, GNP is reduced by the amount of her previous pay even though actual output has not changed.[13] In recent years, the proliferation of home gardening, home canning, and even do-it-yourself construction of cabin homes has attracted widespread attention. The value of the production these activities involve is not measured. Similarly, the value of lawn maintenance, plumbing, auto repairs, and a host of other productive services performed by husband, wife, or child is omitted from GNP.

Home production is omitted from GNP measures only because of the practical difficulty of valuing such productive activity because, typically, home production does not go through market channels that would enable its value to be established. If two neighboring housewives should agree to do each other's housework, paying each $10,000 yearly for the services provided, GNP would rise by $20,000, though actual production remains unchanged. It is worth noting that the same practical difficulty of measurement is also characteristic of the production of externalities, i.e., costs that individual producing firms do not have to bear but which are a cost to society. For example, pollutants that enter the air or water are not "marketed" products. Thus, we are hard-pressed to value their *negative* contribution to output.

---

[13]The value of a "typical" housewife's services, as estimated in 1978 by Jefferson Standard Life Insurance Co., was around $18,000 a year.

Illegal Activities

Incomes earned in illegal activities are also, and for obvious reasons, concealed. Still, such activities do provide services and commodities that some members of society desire. Those who like moonshine whiskey, marijuana, and the services of male and female prostitutes would certainly argue that the providers of those items are involved in *productive* activity. Still, such production is ignored in the computation of GNP. As long as the relationship of illegal production to total production is stable, the omission of illegal production will not affect the usefulness of our output figures for measuring *changes* in production. The same, of course, can be said about the value of uncounted "housework." It is notable that, with rising tax burdens, the incentive to underreport productive activities (and the resulting income) is strengthened.

Imputations

Some components of unmarketed production are judged to be sufficiently important and sufficiently easily valued that an *imputed* value is estimated for them. Imputed values are assigned to these items by using observed prices on similar or identical items that do pass through the market.

An imputed value is assigned to farm production that is consumed on the farm. The imputed total value of retained output is counted as consumption on the expenditure side of the accounts and, on the income side of the accounts, an imputed net profit entry is made, with any difference between the value of retained production and net profit credited to the appropriate expense items. For payments in kind, consumption expenditures and wages are increased by an imputed amount.

As indicated earlier, an imputation is also made for the value of productive services flowing from owner-occupied homes. Conceptually, each household is treated as a business enterprise that owns a home as a business and rents it to the household as a consumer. This imputation makes up a sizable proportion of the net rental figure that appears on the income side of the national accounts under rental income of persons. The net rent entry from this source falls short of total imputed rent by the amount of depreciation of the owner-occupied homes and the amount of indirect business taxes resulting from home ownership.

Other imputations are made for certain financial enterprises (such as banks, investment funds, and insurance companies) which produce services that have no observed market price or that have a price which does not cover the cost of providing the service (as is the case, for example, with commercial bank checking account services). Certainly, any of the imputations employed in the national accounts may give biased estimates of the true value of production they represent. This would be the case if, for example, retained farm production differed in quality from marketed production. It would also be the case if the appearance on the market of retained goods and services would change the observed prices of those goods and services. However, even if the imputations are not precise, they would appear to adequately represent some important components of actual production which, without imputations, would have to be ignored.

While the list could be expanded substantially, our limited sample of the specific complications that national income accountants have to deal with is sufficient to provide a firm understanding of the nature of the practical difficulties confronted in constructing aggregate measures of economic activity. Because of the practical impossibility of obtaining precise measures of aggregate economic activity, there are strict limitations to the uses of national income accounting data. The next section of this chapter focuses attention on these limitations.

Recognizing Our Limitations

As indicated repeatedly in this chapter, the national accounts were designed to measure the economy's productive performance, and, presumably, it is the production of *real,* physical goods and services that we are interested in. However, our measures of output are in *nominal* (dollar) terms. If the general price level changes over time, our measures of output change even if real output stays constant. For example, if prices had risen by 10 percent during 1979 while real output was constant, the measures of output discussed in this chapter would have shown a 10 percent increase. Fortunately, we do have devices, called *price indexes,* that allow us to convert all our *nominal* measures into *real* measures. We will take a critical look at the construction and use of price indexes in Chapter 3, but, for the moment, we will assume that price adjustments can accurately deflate nominal output and income measures.

Even when our measures of output are deflated by an appropriate price index, they are still imperfect measures of production. As we have seen, a substantial portion of output is ignored (housework, illegal production). Furthermore, even when measured in terms of constant prices, output must still be valued in dollar terms because adding physical quantities of different goods and services is not meaningful. Thus, our measures of production provide little useful information in *absolute* terms (e.g., how much output is represented by the $2,368.6 billion worth measured for 1979?). It is only the *change* in output that can have meaning for us, and this only if we are willing to assume that omitted production is a stable proportion of total output.

Most analysts do have considerable confidence in the national accounts when they are used to provide measures of *change* in the level of economic activity over relatively short periods of time. When those accounts indicate that GNP is 3 percent smaller than last year's, or 9 percent larger than its value two years earlier, we accept those figures. However, as the time interval across which comparisons are made lengthens, faith in our measures of output change diminishes. Why? Because over time the fraction of production that is uncounted can change substantially and, also, because the very composition of output changes, tending to make output levels incomparable.

As an example of a *proportion* change in the composition of output, suppose we compare two market baskets of commodity production, one consisting of 100 turnips, 20 bicycles, and 500 ballpoint pens, and the other of 80 turnips, 24 bicycles, and 470 ballpoint pens. Which basket is larger? The answer is certainly not obvious. Just the change in the proportionate composition of the two baskets makes their volume incomparable. You can readily see that changing the *kinds* of commodities produced (introduce autos, electric lights, and so on where they previously did not exist) makes comparisons even more difficult, as do changes in the *quality* of existing products. Expressing output values in dollar terms (even constant dollars) provides little relief from this dilemma.[14] We merely have to accept the fact that measures of output changes are subject to more uncertainty as the time horizon we are working with lengthens. However, for purposes of monitoring those variables that are of fundamental concern in macroeconomic analysis, some of the limitations on available aggregate production measures are irrelevant. For the most part, the existence of nonmarket production (e.g., by households) and of omitted transactions has little to do with the functioning of the massive industrial complex that dominates modern economies. It is that complex which suffers from inflationary booms and employment-killing contractions, and, hence, it is that complex that requires monitoring. The problems of inflation and unemployment are not the result of improper measurement of housewives' productive services.

International Comparisons of Production

The use of national income data for comparisons of output levels between countries is even more difficult than its use for domestic comparisons across time. A major complication arises because the proportion of uncounted production varies from country to country. In more developed (industrialized) countries, uncounted home production is relatively less important. Also the proportion of production that is uncounted because of its legal status varies markedly. Gambling is perfectly legal in England while outlawed in the United States (with local exceptions), and the French explicitly include a value for black market activities in computing output values. Even the influence of political ideology affects the proportion of total production captured in a country's income accounts, as shown by the complete omission of any entry for the value of services in the accounts of Russia and its satellites; their national accounts show only the production of *commodities*, the provision of services being deemed *nonproductive*.

---

[14]The problem in generating an index of output is one of correctly assigning price *weights* that reflect society's subjective estimates of the relative values of different items. As demonstrated in Chapter 3, there is no completely satisfactory way to deal with this problem.

The problem of differences in the composition of output also affects international comparisons of output figures, compounding the mechanical difficulties of expressing different countries' output levels in terms of a common currency. Major data adjustments are clearly necessary for meaningful international comparisons of production levels, and even with adjustments any comparisons must be looked upon, at best, as crude approximations of the truth.

Aggregate Output as a Measure of Social Welfare

Despite the limitations of aggregate output data, even for measuring production, those data are often used in discussions of national welfare (i.e., some grand total of utility for society at large).[15] Rates of change of output are compared over two periods of time or between two countries, with conclusions derived on *progress* toward higher levels of social well-being. Levels of output are compared (again, both across time and between countries) to spot differences in standards of living. However, a moment's reflection will provide a healthy skepticism for conclusions drawn from such comparisons.

By forcing its labor force to work 25 percent longer each day, a country could substantially increase its per capita output. Would society be better off? (Would you recommend that policy for the United States?) Restricting our concern to a ''free'' society, even with accurate measurement, would all of the increase in U.S. per capita GNP between 1929 and 1979 represent an increase in economic welfare when more than $100 billion was spent on national defense in 1979? Once again, the composition of output is clearly important.

Even in a free society in which the composition of output is unchanged, higher levels of measured output may not correspond to higher levels of social welfare. With measures of production that fail to take account of the negative effects on society's welfare of the extra air and water pollution, the noise and congestion, the destroyed scenery, and other negative by-products that may accompany additional production, not every increase in measured output represents a positive contribution to society's welfare. Reintroduce the practical difficulties in measuring total physical production, and the use of output measures as welfare proxies becomes more suspect still.

Further, with any redistribution of income accompanying an increase in the level of output, even if it leaves just one individual worse off than before, we are left unable to conclusively argue that total social welfare is enhanced by the income increase. We would have to be able to measure and sum up individual utility values to provide proof for that supposition, a task that is not possible.

---

[15]In fact, most comparisons of output levels implicitly treat output measures as proxies for the economic welfare of society at large.

Finally, national income and product account measures are deficient for purposes of measuring welfare because they make no allowance for the value of leisure. Additional leisure time is one of the most sought after consequences of increasing productive capacity. With no change in actual production of physical goods and services, society would undoubtedly consider its welfare increased with any increase in leisure time. Yet no measure of the value of extra leisure appears in national income and product accounts.

While the national income and product accounts have been invaluable as measures of the economy's production performance, those accounts must be used with care. Even as production measures, the aggregate income and output totals require careful interpretation. When faced with the more demanding task of providing a summary measure of overall economic welfare, the national income totals are exceedingly crude.

Improved "Measures of Economic Welfare." In recent years, recognition of the shortcomings of national income accounts as measures of well-being has prompted considerable interest in altering those measures to compile welfare indexes. The most prominent effort in that direction has been provided by James Tobin and William Nordhaus of Yale University.[16] Arguing that the ultimate purpose of economic activity is consumption, not production, Tobin and Nordhaus modify the currently used national income accounts data to provide a new index called the *measure of economic welfare* (MEW).

In broad terms, to obtain MEW gross national product totals are adjusted by: (1) reclassification of GNP expenditures into consumption, investment, and intermediate production where only consumption contributes to current economic welfare; (2) imputations of the value of the services of consumer capital, the value of leisure, and the value of household work; and (3) a negative correction for some of the negative by-products of urbanization. While the list of specific modifications of GNP is quite long, prominent among the positive adjustments are the imputations for the value of leisure time and household production, while notable negative adjustments are made for air and water pollution and for other forms of ecological damage not reflected in the traditional measures of GNP. With large entries for the value of leisure and household production, estimates of MEW are considerably larger than the corresponding GNP measures. However, while both the absolute and per capita values of MEW have been rising, GNP measures, which ignore the negative by-products of production and growth, have grown more rapidly.

Tobin and Nordhaus themselves consider the measure of economic welfare a first, primitive attempt at providing an index of social welfare. They recognize the practical problems involved in obtaining a broadly defined

---

[16]William Nordhaus and James Tobin, "Is Growth Obsolete?" in *Economic Growth, Fiftieth Anniversary Colloquium V* (New York: National Bureau of Economic Research, 1972). Also see Robert Eisner, "Total Incomes in the United States, 1959 and 1969," *Review of Income and Wealth,* March 1978, pp. 24, 41–70.

measure of consumption, and, more fundamentally, they admit to an inability to correlate individual and collective happiness with consumption. Still, with creation of the MEW index the hard task of developing measures of the *quality of life* has been initiated. In the future, we can expect development of additional statistical indicators that will be used in conjunction with national income measures to provide *informed* judgements on the rate of economic progress.

Summary

Three conceptual techniques for obtaining a measure of the economy's output—which provided, in the process, measures of a number of other variables of interest to economic analysts (including disposable income, consumption, investment, and so on)—were reviewed in this chapter. The three techniques are: (1) adding up all spending on final goods and services, (2) adding up all earned income, and (3) summing the "value added" that results from the production efforts of all producers. In practice, these three techniques must yield values for national output that, except for small statistical discrepancies, are identical. It is worth reemphasizing that our conceptual discussion of national income accounting revealed that it is the value of production that determines the value of total income generated in the production process and available for disbursement as wages, rent, interest, and profits. In like fashion, total expenditures on final goods and services were found to be equal to the value of output.

Confirming the accounting relationships that will be prominent in the macroeconomic models developed later, this chapter dealt with the actual U.S. national income and product accounts. As is usually the case in series that attempt to measure economic activity, these accounts have shortcomings. They fail to measure some production; they measure production using an elastic yardstick (the dollar); and they do not provide an accurate measure of social welfare. We should not, however, be unduly critical of the national accounts. They were designed to measure production, not social welfare, and the Bureau of Economic Analysis which compiles those accounts presents them in just that light. For purposes of short-run analysis ("business cycle" analysis) and policy making, measured changes in output appear to be adequate if properly interpreted. Even more positively, data that appear in these accounts, despite their limitations, have helped macroeconomists bridge the gap between theory and policy practice. They have allowed the testing and refinement of economic theories and have provided quantification of the behavioral relationships used in modern models of the economic system.

Even when forced into uses for which they were not designed, such as measuring social welfare, measures in the national accounts have traditionally provided proxy measures superior to any alternatives available to us, and recent work suggests that GNP figures can be used as the basis for substantially improved (though not perfect) proxy measures of general economic welfare; we simply need to adequately add up the total flow of "goods" society has to enjoy and subtract the "bads." Despite its limitations, it would be hard to exaggerate the importance of the national income accounts to the progress of modern macroeconomics.

Questions

1. You are given the following scrambled data in billions of dollars:

Government and business transfers (T_r)	15
Indirect business taxes (T_i)	30
Gross National Product (GNP)	630
Social Security contributions (SS)	20
Personal taxes (T_p)	25
Capital consumption (D)	80
Residential construction (RC)	70
Retained earnings (R_t)	0
Personal consumption expenditures (C)	390
Direct business taxes (T_b)	40

   a. Work out in symbolic form (for example, $R_t - SS + T_b = ?$) and calculate the numerical value of net national product (NNP), national income (NI), personal income (PI), and disposable income (Y_d).
   b. Could you perform the same manipulations with data from the income side of the national accounts?

2. What is a transfer payment and why are such payments not included in our GNP measure?

3. Using the latest available issue of the *Survey of Current Business,* update the expenditures side of the national income and product measures that appear in Table 2—2 and compare the revised measures to those in the table. Have all the measures grown in step? How has the allocation of output to different end uses changed?

4. There have been complaints about the use of GNP values as an indicator of the nation's well-being. Outline those complaints.

5. In terms of measured output, what difference does it make whether I repair my own car or hire a mechanic to do it? Is the difference important?

6. Suppose an infestation of pine trees by a fast-spreading, tree-killing insect requires all pines west of the Mississippi to be cut and burned. Let the cost of this program be $2 billion and assume some resources (including labor) are used which otherwise would have been idle. What happens to GNP? Is the nation's welfare improved because of the insect infestation?

7. Distinguish between gross and net national product, and between gross and net investment. What linkage do the investment measures have with estimates of aggregate output made using the expenditures approach?

8. Describe some issues of fairness or equity that you think require attention in efforts to measure social welfare. (Hint: as an example, compare the interests in economic growth and job creation of high school dropouts and well-heeled, ecology-minded Hollywood performers).

Suggested Readings

Kendrick, John W. *Economic Accounts and Their Uses*. New York: McGraw-Hill, 1972.

Kuznets, Simon. *National Income and Its Composition, 1919–1938*, Chapter I. Vol. I. New York: National Bureau of Economic Research, 1941.

Kuznets, Simon. "National Income: A New Version." *The Review of Economics and Statistics*. 30 (1948): 151–179.

National Bureau of Economic Research. *A Critique of the United States Income and Wealth*. Vol. 22. Princeton, N.J.: Princeton University Press, 1958.

Nordhaus, William, and Tobin, James. "Is Growth Obsolete?" In *Economic Growth, Fiftieth Anniversary Colloquium V*. New York: National Bureau of Economic Research, 1972.

Rosen, Sam. *National Income and Other Social Accounts*, Chapters 1–6. New York: Holt, Rinehart and Winston, 1972.

Ruggles, Richard. "The U.S. National Accounts and Their Development." *American Economic Review*. 49 (March 1959): 85–95.

Stewart, Kenneth. "National Income Accounting and Economic Welfare: The Concepts of GNP and MEW." *Federal Reserve Bank of St. Louis Review*, April 1974, pp. 18–24.

U.S. Department of Commerce, Office of Business Economics. "National Income and Product Accounts of the United States, 1929–74." *Survey of Current Business*, Supplement, 1977, pp. vii–xi.

U.S. Department of Commerce, Office of Business Economics. "The Economic Accounts of the United States: Retrospect and Prospect." *Survey of Current Business, 50th Anniversary Issue*. 51 (July 1971): 230.

Chapter **3**	Measurement 2: Nominal and Real Values, Price Indexes, and Employment-Unemployment Statistics

This brief chapter completes our survey of the summary statistical series available for monitoring and analyzing the aggregate performance of the U.S. economy. Attention will be focused on two sets of statistical series. The first set consists of measures of the level and rate of change of prices, while the second consists of measures of the economy-wide levels of employment and unemployment. Because full employment is a primary goal of macroeconomic policy, the employment and unemployment measures described in this chapter have long been closely watched indicators of the economy's health. In the inflationary era that has persisted since the late 1960s, measures of the price level and its rate of change have also moved into the spotlight of national concern. The price level measures described in this chapter permit evaluation of the success (or failure) policy makers experience in the quest for reasonable price stability. Further, as suggested in Chapter 2, a properly measured index of price level change can be used to convert nominal measures of output into more meaningful *real* (price deflated) measures.

Nominal Versus Real Values
and the Need for Price Indexes

As indicated in Chapter 2, the important variables that appear in the national income and product accounts must be measured in dollar terms because of the impossibility of adding up the output of apples, oranges, autos, roller skates, haircuts, factory buildings, and the thousands of other products provided by a modern economy in anything other than money terms. With current output valued in money terms, the total value of one year's output of a particular product is just the price *(p)* of that product times the quantity *(q)* produced that year or $p \cdot q$. In an economy that produces n different final products, the value of total output (Y) is the summed market value of the output of each of the n final products. That is, the total value of output, measured in dollar terms, is

$$Y = p_0 q_0 + p_1 q_1 + p_2 q_2 + \ldots + p_n q_n \qquad [3-1]$$

where $p_i q_i$ is the value of the output of the ith product, say, bicycles. It is abundantly clear that the measured, *nominal* values of output and the other variables (consumption, investment, and so on) that appear in the national accounts are altered both by changes in the *real,* physical volume of measured economic activity (production, consumption, and so on), and by changes in the general price level. Of course, measures of the real, physical volume of output are required to evaluate the production performance of the economic system, and separate measures of price level change are interesting in their own right. Thus, the need for a technique that separates the nominal changes recorded in the national accounts into real changes and price level changes is clear-cut. To understand the meaning and usefulness of the devices, called *price indexes,* which provide that separation, we need to know how those indexes are constructed.

Price Index Construction

Suppose we are interested in measuring the extent of change in the general price level between 1970 and 1980. Now, because any economic system produces a very large number of different products, it is immediately apparent that any price index that purports to reflect changes in the general price level must combine, or *average,* the movements in a number of different prices of different products. The price of oranges in 1980 will differ from what it was in 1970, the price of new Cadillacs will have changed between 1970 and 1980, and so on. The simplest way of obtaining a summary index measure of the general price level in 1980 relative to its level in 1970 would be to calculate the ratios of 1980 to 1970 prices for each product our economy provides, then take the simple average of all those ratios. If the economy were extremely simple, that task would be easily accomplished. Suppose, for example, the economy produced only the two consumption goods, bread and wine. In that case we would have to find only two price ratios and average their values to find what had happened to the *general* price level. If the price of bread (p_b) had doubled between 1970 and 1980, while the price of wine (p_w) had remained unchanged, the two ratios we would have to average would be

$$\frac{p_b \text{ in } 1980}{p_b \text{ in } 1970} = 2 \quad \text{and} \quad \frac{p_w \text{ in } 1980}{p_w \text{ in } 1970} = 1 \qquad [3\text{--}2]$$

The simple average of those two ratios, our calculated price index, is just

$$(2 + 1)/2 = 3/2, \text{ or } 1.5. \qquad [3\text{--}3]$$

According to this index, the general price level in our simple economy rose by one half, or 50 percent, between 1970 and 1980.

While the simple technique just used to calculate a price index cannot be dismissed as completely invalid, we can easily improve on our computational methods to provide more accurate measures of price level change. In the price index calculation above, each product was implicitly assigned the same weight, or importance, in determining the extent of change in the general level of prices. However, in the simple and primitive two-good economy, it might be that wine is a very unimportant component of consumption, and that bread and free spring water provide the bulk of society's consumption needs. In that case, a sizable increase in the price of wine, while it would exert a strong upward push on our *calculated* price index, would have little effect on the *true* average price level society faces.

Because a simple average of price ratios assigns the same weight to every commodity, we have an obvious opportunity for development of improved measures of price level change. What is required, of course, is that we weight measured price changes in a way that more accurately accounts for the relative importance to society, or to an average consumer, of different products. In practice, individual product prices are often weighted by the number of units of the product actually purchased during a specified time period. Unfortunately, the specific mix of products society consumes changes over time so that there remains some question about precisely which time period's purchase quantities should be used as weights in price index calculations. The difficulties that arise from the lack of a universally valid set of quantity weights will be dealt with after a review of the standard methods that are employed in calculating actual price indexes.

The Laspeyres Index. Virtually all of the price indexes that are calculated on a regular basis are *Laspeyres indexes* in which earlier year (*base* year) quantities are used as weights. The formula for computing a Laspeyres price index can be written

$$I_{2,1} = \frac{\sum_i p_2 q_1}{\sum_i p_1 q_1}, \qquad i = 1, 2, 3, \ldots, n, \qquad [3\text{—}4]$$

where $I_{2,1}$ represents the value of the index in year 2 *based* upon year 1 prices, p_1 and p_2 represent prices of individual items bought in years 1 and 2 respectively, q_1 represents quantities of individual items bought in year 1, and $\sum_i$ indicates that we are to sum the products of price and quantity over the n commodities that were bought in the base year (that is, in year 1). This index is really the ratio of two expenditure measures, the denominator being the actual base period expenditure required in year 1 to buy the market basket of goods and services identified as "typical" in that year, while the numerator represents the amount of expenditure that would be required in year 2, at year 2 prices, to buy the same combination of items. With the combination of items bought held identical in both years (the quantity weights held constant), any change in the dollar volume of expenditure necessary to buy that market basket must be the result of a change in the price level.

The Paasche Index. An alternative form of price index is the *Paasche index.* The Paasche index uses latter period quantities (usually denoted *current* period) as weights. The formula for the Paasche index is

$$I_{2,1} = \frac{\sum_i p_2 q_2}{\sum_i p_1 q_2}, \qquad i = 1, 2, 3, \ldots, n. \qquad [3\text{—}5]$$

This index, too, is a ratio of two expenditures. The numerator in the Paasche index measures the actual, observed expenditure in year 2 (the current year) on a typical market basket of goods and services, while the denominator measures the amount of spending that would have been required in year 1, at year 1 prices, to buy the specific mix of items that composed the market basket in year 2.

Index Construction—A Simple Example. The mechanics involved in constructing both Laspeyres and Paasche indexes can be readily illustrated. Assuming that the world is only slightly more complicated than in our earlier example, suppose we have data on a "typical" household's actual expenditures, as recorded in Table 3—1.

Table 3—1 / Spending Data for 1970 and 1980 for a Typical Household

	1970		1980	
Item	Price	Quantity Bought	Price	Quantity Bought
Wine	$2.00	80	$1.00	120
Bread	4.00	30	8.00	20
Song	1.00	40	2.00	30

As indicated in the table, our typical household consumes only three items: wine, bread, and song (which could be interpreted more broadly as food, goods, other necessities, and luxuries).

It remains for us to determine what happened between 1970 and 1980 to the general level of prices our household was required to pay for the collection of items it purchased. The Laspeyres index tells us:

$$I_{1980,\ 1970} = \frac{\text{required spending in 1980 to get 1970 collection}}{\text{actual spending in 1970 on 1970 collection}} = \frac{\sum_i p_2 q_1}{\sum_i p_1 q_1}$$

$$= \frac{(1.00 \cdot 80) + (8.00 \cdot 30) + (2.00 \cdot 40)}{(2.00 \cdot 80) + (4.00 \cdot 30) + (1.00 \cdot 40)} = \frac{400}{320}$$

$$= 1.25 \text{ with a value of 1 assigned to the base year price level}$$

or

$$= 125\% \text{ with a value of } 100\% \text{ assigned to the base year price level.}$$

It appears that the price level our typical household faces increased by 25 percent between 1970 and 1980.

Computing the Paasche index reveals:

$$I_{1980,\ 1970} = \frac{\text{actual spending in 1980}}{\text{required spending in 1970 to get 1980 collection}} = \frac{\sum_i p_2 q_2}{\sum_i p_1 q_2}$$

$$= \frac{(1.00 \cdot 120) + (8.00 \cdot 20) + (2.00 \cdot 30)}{(2.00 \cdot 120) + (4.00 \cdot 20) + (1.00 \cdot 30)} = \frac{340}{350}$$

$$= .971 \text{ with a value of 1 assigned to the base year price level}$$

or

$$= 97.1\% \text{ with a value of } 100\% \text{ assigned to the base year price level.}$$

According to the Paasche index, the price level facing our household fell nearly 3 percent between 1970 and 1980.

We must wonder, what is the true index number? Unfortunately, there is no simple answer to that question. All we can say is that the true index value lies somewhere between the two values yielded by the computations above. As you may have noted already, what our simple price index example has just succeeded in doing is dramatically demonstrate what the lack of a universally correct set of quantity weights can do to measures of price level change. Quite simply, with standard weighting schemes (Laspeyres and Paasche), computed price indexes are biased. Perhaps, fortunately, these indexes are biased in opposite directions so that (ignoring any other difficulties in price level construction) their values can be expected to bracket the true index value.

For expository purposes, our example permitted a marked difference between the Laspeyres and Paasche price index values. Fortunately, the difference in index values computed from actual data would be that striking only under exceedingly rare conditions. The actual price indexes calculated for the United States, despite some inherent biases, do contain important, usable information. After describing the most prominent price level measures that are calculated in the United States, we will try to gain some perspective on the quality of our price indicators by taking a formal look at the most serious criticisms that are lodged against those measures.

Actual Price Indexes

Computing a Paasche index on a regular basis would require the gathering of a new set of data on both current period sales quantities (current period weights) and current prices for every update of the index. The first burden, which in practice is quite costly, is avoided in computing the Laspeyres index, because only *base year* quantity weights are required. Primarily because of the practical difficulty of obtaining the sales data necessary for an updating of quantity weights each period, virtually all the price indexes compiled on a regular basis are of the Laspeyres type. While a large number of different price indexes are regularly calculated and reported in the United States, the lion's share of attention is focused on three: the *consumer price index,* the *producer price index,* and the *implicit price deflator.* The first two are calculated on the Laspeyres basis, while the implicit price deflator, which is derived in an indirect manner, is a Paasche index.

The Consumer Price Index

Of all the price indexes compiled in the United States, perhaps the most prominent in terms of public recognition is the consumer price index (CPI). This index, which is issued monthly by the U.S. Department of Labor, is particularly closely watched by government officials, union leaders, and consumer advocates. As protection against an erosion of their living standards through inflation, well over 50 million U.S. residents, including, in 1980, some 9 million unionized workers, and some 34 million social security recipients, federal government pensioners, and food stamp recipients, have their incomes tied to movements in a consumer price index.

Until 1978, there was a single consumer price index value computed for a market basket of goods and services intended to represent the typical mix of purchases of *urban wage earners and clerical workers.* Because such consumers comprise less than half of the population, the Labor Department, as part of an effort begun in the early 1970s to improve price measures, broadened the focus of its survey of buying patterns to capture the mix of purchases of *all urban consumers* (some 80 percent of the population). It was intended that when the improved CPI was available, the old, more narrowly focused measure would be phased out. However, those whose incomes are tied to consumer price movements (particularly unionized labor), fearful that the new and more broadly focused index might not fully capture the price increases indicated by the older CPI, pressured the Labor Department to continue publishing the old CPI in conjunction with the new for the foreseeable future.

The items included in the market basket of goods and services used for calculating the CPI fall into one of six categories: food, housing, apparel, transportation, health and recreation, and miscellaneous services. The weights applied to different items now included in the market baskets used for consumer price index calculations were obtained from a survey of consumer purchases conducted in 1972–73. Price observations are obtained through visits to around 24,000 retail outlets in eighty-five urban areas across the country.

To end our brief description of the CPI, it is worth noting that, while computed values of the current CPI may measure very well changes in the general level of prices facing the average urban consumer, it is likely to perform that feat less well for Robert Redford, a U.S. senator, a surgeon, a southern tobacco farmer, a college professor, a college student, or a ghetto dweller. There is no universally correct set of weights that can represent the spending patterns of different individuals and, consequently, there is no universally applicable cost-of-living index. A brief look at price increases over the last decade in each of the product groups included in the CPI indicates that the biggest increases have occurred in home prices, food prices, medical care charges, and in the prices of fuel oil and coal. A recent college graduate facing home purchase and child-rearing expenses might well feel that the CPI has understated the degree of inflation since 1965, particularly if he or she is a heavy eater, heats with oil or coal, and drives a long distance to work.

The Producer Price Index

The "all commodities" producer price index (previously called the wholesale price index) covers some 2,800 commodities with their prices measured at the level of the first important commercial transaction in which they are involved. The commodities encompassed in the sample are chosen to represent movements in prices on all commodities produced in the manufacturing, agriculture, forestry, fishing, mining, gas and electric, and public utilities sectors of the economy. The base year weights currently employed in calculating this Laspeyres index were derived primarily from shipment values of commodities as recorded in 1972. Price data are gathered monthly through mail questionnaires to a sampling of representative producing companies.

Because of the many commodities covered in the producer price index, and because changes in prices at the wholesale level have traditionally appeared later in retail prices, many analysts have looked at this price index as a better measure of price movements than the consumer price index. However, the wholesale index completely omits the price level of services, and, at least in the last decade and a half, the increasing cost of services has been an important contributor to virtually everyone's cost of living. Moreover, in the 1973–1974 period, a persistent and dramatic divergence between the yearly price increases registered by the equivalent of today's producer price index and those indicated by other price indexes demonstrated that, under some conditions, the producer price index may provide highly misleading signals. In that period, price increases were not evenly distributed. The biggest increases were concentrated in products, such as wheat and petroleum, that have their first important commercial transaction at a very primitive stage of processing. Because it is difficult to avoid having products at all different stages of the production process reflected in the producer price index, price changes that occur at early stages of the production process can be double and triple counted. As William Nordhaus and John Shoven have recognized, petroleum illustrates this difficulty particularly clearly. According to Nordhaus and Shoven, "Petroleum shows up first as crude petroleum, then as refined petroleum products. The value of the petroleum products is then included again when they are sold as electric power, plastics and resins, and so on."[1] With the direct and indirect weights of crude products included repetitively, a producer price index can be seriously biased in an uneven inflation when price increases are originating in the earlier stages of production (as was the case in the 1973–1974 period.)

Table 3—2 / Percentage Changes in Producer Prices, 1973–1979

Year	All Commodities	Finished Goods
1973	15.2	11.7
1974	21.0	18.4
1975	4.2	6.6
1976	4.5	3.3
1977	6.0	6.5
1978	9.8	9.2
1979	14.7	12.6
Average	10.8	9.8

Source: Federal Reserve Bank of St. Louis, *National Economics Trends*, January 1980.

---

[1]William Nordhaus and John Shoven, "Inflation 1973: The Year of Infamy," *Challenge*, May–June, 1974, pp. 14–22.

Because of double-counting problems in the all-commodities producer price index, in 1979 the Bureau of Labor Statistics began preparing a "finished goods" index. This index measures prices at only one stage of the production process: prices on commodities that are to be sold to *final* demanders, consumers, and producers. Table 3—2 compares the percentage changes in the all-commodities and finished goods indexes for recent years. As expected, the all-commodities index indicates a higher inflation rate.

The Implicit GNP Deflator

In addition to consumer and producer price indexes, a host of other measures of changes in the prices of detailed subgroupings of commodities are computed. For example, individual measures of price level change are kept for textiles, fuels, metals, machinery and equipment, nonmetallic minerals, and so on; and, in addition to compiling values for the CPI, the Bureau of Labor Statistics compiles price index values for a detailed subgrouping of the goods and services consumers buy. In fact, for every one of a substantial number of subcomponents of GNP, a separate price index is maintained.

As previously suggested, price indexes permit the separation of changes in *dollar magnitudes* (i.e., the products of prices and physical quantities) into changes in *real,* physical units and pure price changes. With an understanding of the simple mechanics of making that separation, and thus of deflating nominal quantities to convert them to real quantities, we will be ready to explain how the third important summary price index, the *implicit GNP deflator,* is calculated.

Suppose that the total dollar expenditures on machinery and equipment in 1980 were $85 billion. To be able to compare the real volume of machinery and equipment acquired in 1980 to the volumes in other years, each year's purchase must be expressed in terms of constant purchasing power dollars deflated to eliminate the effects of price level change. Simply dividing the 1980 dollar expenditure on machinery and equipment by the price index for that category of production accomplishes the desired deflation for that year. If, for example, the index value for 1980 were 1.114 in terms of 1972 prices, the real value of 1980 machinery and equipment production would be $85 billion/1.114 = $78.30B valued at 1972 prices. This deflated value can be compared to any other year's output of machinery and equipment, also valued in 1972 prices, to see what has happened to real output.

To obtain the implicit price deflator, each of the components of GNP is deflated separately by its own price index. The resulting deflated measures are then combined to provide estimates of GNP and its four major expenditure components valued at *constant,* base year prices. For 1979, the resulting estimates valued in 1972 prices were:

Gross National Product	$1,431.1B
Personal consumption expenditures	924.5
Gross private domestic investment	214.8
Net exports of goods and services	17.7
Government purchases of goods and services	274.1

Λ quick reference to the sample national income accounts in Chapter 2 reveals that the 1979 GNP in *nominal* terms was $2,368.6B, markedly more than the deflated figure for 1979. Dividing the *inflated* nominal value of GNP by the constant price measure yields an implicit measure of the extent to which the price level has risen. The measure is the *implicit price deflator* for GNP. For our example, the ratio of 1979 GNP at current prices to GNP at constant prices is $2,368.6/$1,431.1 = 1.66, indicating that the price level rose by some 66 percent between 1972 and 1979. Derived indirectly from measures of GNP, our most aggregative measure of production, the implicit price deflator is the best measure we have of changes in the *general* price level. Postwar values for the implicit price deflator, along with values for the consumer and producer price indexes, are shown in Table 3—3. These price level measures move in a roughly parallel fashion. As noted earlier, however, this need not always be the case. For example, note the striking divergence in the 1973–74 period between price inceases measured using the producer price index and the other indexes.

Table 3—3 also provides measures of the nominal and real (deflated) values of GNP, illustrating the magnitude of adjustments needed to separate real output changes from price level changes. To confirm your understanding of the link between real output, nominal output, and the general price level, you should select a few observations from that table and calculate the value of one of these variables using the other two. For example, the value of real output in 1977 can be obtained by deflating nominal output by the implicit price deflator. Its value is:

$$1977 \text{ GNP in 1972 prices} = \$1,887.2/1.42 = \$1,332.7B. \qquad [3\text{—}6]$$

Price Index Limitations

Clearly, price indexes are highly useful, indeed essential, if we want an accurate indication of the rate of price level change, and if we want measures of the *real* performance of our economic system. It is no wonder so much attention is devoted to the regularly reported indexes. Of course, we expect our indexes to provide us with reliable price level measures. However, while most economists and statisticians think the government does an admirable job of compiling price index values, the inherent complexities of real world price index construction provide ample opportunities for the introduction of biases in price level measurement. We need to be aware of what the most prominent sources of bias are.

The Classic Index Number Problem. As our price index example demonstrated, in measuring price level changes, the quantity weights assigned to each product price must be held constant; in effect, this assumes that the quantities of each commodity consumed are the same in different periods. This requirement is the source of a systematic bias in all price index values, often referred to as the *index number problem*.

Table 3—3 / Price Indexes and GNP Values, 1947–1979

Year	Price Indexes (1972 = 100) Consumer	Producer finished goods	Implicit Price Deflator 1972 = 100	GNP in Current Dollars	GNP in Constant Dollars (1972)
1947	53.4	48.0	49.70	231.30	465.39
1948	57.5	52.3	53.13	257.60	484.85
1949	57.0	54.9	52.59	256.50	487.74
1950	57.5	56.2	53.69	284.80	530.45
1951	62.1	61.7	57.27	328.40	573.42
1952	63.5	62.7	58.00	345.50	595.69
1953	63.9	63.7	58.88	364.60	619.23
1954	64.3	64.6	59.69	364.80	611.16
1955	64.0	66.5	60.98	398.00	652.67
1956	65.0	71.4	62.90	419.20	666.45
1957	67.3	75.9	65.02	441.10	678.41
1958	69.1	77.7	66.06	447.30	677.11
1959	69.7	79.3	67.52	483.70	716.38
1960	70.8	79.4	68.67	503.70	733.51
1961	71.5	79.6	69.28	520.10	750.72
1962	72.3	79.9	70.55	560.30	794.19
1963	73.2	80.1	71.59	590.50	824.84
1964	74.1	80.9	72.71	632.40	869.76
1965	75.4	81.8	74.32	684.90	921.56
1966	77.6	83.9	76.76	749.90	976.94
1967	79.8	86.7	79.02	793.90	1004.70
1968	83.2	89.7	82.57	864.20	1046.63
1969	87.6	92.6	86.72	930.30	1072.76
1970	92.8	97.0	91.36	976.40	1068.74
1971	96.8	98.0	96.02	1050.40	1093.90
1972	100.0	100.0	100.00	1171.10	1171.10
1973	106.2	104.1	105.80	1306.60	1235.00
1974	117.9	120.7	116.02	1413.20	1218.00
1975	128.7	135.4	127.15	1516.30	1192.50
1976	136.1	143.4	133.76	1700.10	1271.00
1977	144.9	152.7	141.61	1887.20	1332.70
1978	155.9	163.7	152.09	2107.60	1385.70
1979	176.6	181.6	165.51	2368.60	1431.10

Source: U.S. Department of Labor, Bureau of Labor Statistics; U.S. Department of Commerce, Office of Business Economics.

Traditional demand analysis indicates that price and quantity demanded are inversely related. In the price index example on page 65, the price of bread and song increased from 1970 to 1980, while that of wine decreased. With the prices of bread and song increasing from 1970 to 1980, the quantities of those items demanded would be expected to fall (*ceteris paribus*) while, with the price of wine falling during that period, the quantity of wine demanded should have risen. Thus, wine would have become a more important part of the market basket of goods *actually bought* in 1980, the other two items becoming less important. To compute a Laspeyres price index, we used 1970 quantity weights, involving ourselves in a violation of the law of demand. Using base year weights to compute our price index caused us to weight too heavily the 1980 purchases of bread and song, the prices of which had risen, and caused us to weight too lightly the purchases of wine, the price of which had fallen. Generalizing, if tastes, incomes, and the other nonprice factors that affect demands for real goods and services should remain unchanged, any price index that uses base year weights (a Laspeyres index) gives too much weight to items that have experienced the greatest price increases (or smallest declines), and too little weight to those items that have experienced the smallest price increases (or greatest declines). Thus, these indexes would always be biased upward, overstating the true value of increases in the *general* price level or understating any fall in that level.

Conversely, price indexes computed with current year weights (Paasche indexes) would always attach too much weight to items that have experienced the smallest price increases (or greatest declines), and too little weight to items that have experienced the largest price increases (or smallest declines). Thus, Paasche indexes would always yield downward biased estimates of changes in the general price level. Consequently, we could expect to bracket the true change in the price level by computing both Laspeyres and Paasche indexes, because they are biased in opposite directions. Further, if the downward biased Paasche index indicated that the price level had risen, we could feel confident that, indeed, it *had* risen, while an indication from the upward biased Laspeyres index that the price level had fallen would be accepted with equal confidence. However, in reality we can expect tastes, incomes, and every other nonprice factor that affects demand to change over time so that we cannot be certain of the direction of price index bias that stems from the need of a fixed weighting scheme. For example, as a reflection of a change in tastes, we might see bicycle purchases multiplying. The increased demand for bicycles would likely cause an increase in bike prices with the *resulting* higher bike prices associated with a larger quantity of sales. With fixed-quantity weights, the importance of increased bike prices would be undervalued, introducing a downward bias in a fixed-weight index.

Quite clearly, if the composition of society's purchases changes over time, the necessity of using fixed-quantity weights introduces biases into our price indexes. The direction of bias, though, depends on whether changes in prices are the dominant source of changes in the composition of purchases or whether changes in the other factors that affect demand are the dominant influence on purchases. At any rate, whatever the direction of the bias, most analysts think the degree of bias is small, particularly if price comparisons are made over relatively limited periods of time so that drastic changes in the composition of purchases are unlikely.

Quality Changes. An additional bias may be introduced if there are qualitative changes in the products included in the collection of goods and services used for computing a price index. Clearly, product quality can change in two directions. A more fuel-efficient or longer-lasting auto engine with no increase in auto prices means more auto per dollar due to quality improvement. A reduction in the size of a "ten cent" candy bar is quality deterioration. Quality improvement (more car per dollar spent) is clearly equivalent to a unit price decline while quality deterioration (less candy bar per dime spent) is equivalent to a unit price increase.

Product improvement is easy to spot in normal times. Quicker-to-fix and more nutritious frozen foods, quicker and safer appendectomies and sterilizations, safer and faster air trips are all examples of quality improvements. If such quality improvements are not accounted for in price index construction, the computed indexes will be biased upward. While efforts are made to adjust our indexes for qualitative changes, many such changes are subtle ones and may not be adequately incorporated into the computed indexes. A related problem results from the introduction of wholly new products. While new products typically raise living standards, their introduction is usually not properly accounted for in price index calculations, reinforcing the upward bias in price indexes.[2]

Other Problems. A number of other limitations in price indexes should be briefly noted. First, actual sales prices may differ from list prices. Where actual prices are available, they are usually employed in price index calculations. Often, however, actual prices, frequently discounted from list, are unavailable. Measured changes in the price level would not be affected by this problem if deviations from list prices stayed constant over time, but that is not likely to be the case. Discounts become increasingly important during business contractions and decreasingly important in expansions. Consequently, the lack of information on actual sales prices can introduce an upward bias in price indexes during recessions. Price indexes that suffer such a bias understate the size of both price declines and increases as the level of business activity fluctuates.

In addition, many prices vary systematically as the season changes (for

---

[2]To highlight the role of qualitative changes in affecting our price measures, you might ponder the following question: With $1,000 to spend, would you prefer to order exclusively from a 1958 Sears catalogue or exclusively from a 1981 Sears catalogue?

instance, the prices of lettuce, fresh strawberries, and construction services), so that price indexes that are not adjusted for such seasonal variations provide misleading measures of price level change during the year. Happily, the widely watched consumer price index is seasonally adjusted.

A further limitation in price indexes arises because the price figures used for computing those indexes are obtained by survey and represent a small sample of actual transaction prices. Of course, the sample may be biased. Finally, it is worth reemphasizing that there is no truly general price index. As indicated before, the consumer price index measures the price level of a basket of products purchased by the "average" factory and clerical worker. Because my own purchasing patterns may differ substantially from those of factory and clerical workers, I would be likely to somewhat misrepresent changes in my real income if I deflated changes in my money income by the consumer price index.

An Overview. Everyone recognizes that available price indexes have limitations. They cannot be perfectly general and most of them are likely to be biased upward to some degree so that real income figures obtained by deflating money income figures for price changes are biased downward. Unfortunately, the extent of bias in our indexes cannot be satisfactorily measured in any objective way. In years past, some analysts argued that the "creeping" inflation recorded in the late 1950s and early 1960s was illusory; that it was simply a failure of our price indexes to adequately recognize product improvements and changes in the composition of purchases. Others have contended there is no significant bias in our price indexes. Wherever the truth lies, no one claims that the inflation measured since 1966 has been an illusion, and virtually everyone pays close heed to the latest recorded values of the price level measures the government compiles.

Over relatively brief periods of time, the composition of the market basket of products society purchases is rather stable, justifying the use of fixed weights in price index calculations. Moreover, product quality changes and the introduction of new products can normally be expected to occur quite gradually. Thus, the bias in available measures of price change over any short time period is likely to be small. The year-to-year changes in price measures and the reported year-to-year changes in real (price deflated) GNP, NNP, consumption, and so on are likely to be close to actual values under normal conditions. As periods that are further separated in time are compared, the accuracy of the price indexes employed and, thus, of the changes in real variables obtained with those indexes, is reduced. Still, even for comparisons over fairly extended time intervals, price-adjusted data are, in most cases, more meaningful than unadjusted data. For example, we can be sure that real GNP in the United States did not rise by 732 percent between 1950 and 1979, although that is what the undeflated-dollar figures in Table 3—3 indicate. We know that there was considerable inflation during that period, especially during the Korean War and the period since our Vietnam military involvement. The price-deflated GNP figures tell us that the rise in real output was a much more modest 170 percent. Though this measure is likely to be somewhat biased, its value is sure to be a better indicator of the true change in real output than the unadjusted figures yield.

U.S. Employment and Unemployment Statistics

We now need to shift our attention from price index values and their uses to the employment and unemployment measures compiled for the U.S. economy. These series, collected on a monthly basis for the Bureau of Labor Statistics by the Bureau of the Census, are based on a sample survey of about 56,000 households across the country. Like our other statistical series, these measures are essential but have their own shortcomings.

Employment

According to the Bureau of Census definition, an individual is employed if, during the survey week, he was at work for any amount of time as a paid employee, or was self-employed, or worked unpaid in a family enterprise (e.g., a family business or farm) for fifteen hours or more. He or she is also counted as employed, even if not working during the survey week, as long as he or she had a job but was temporarily absent due to illness, a labor dispute, vacation, bad weather, and so on.

This is clearly a crude measure of employment. An individual is counted as fully employed whether working for pay on an average of ten hours or forty to sixty hours weekly. Realistically, though, an individual who would like to work forty hours a week at the prevailing wage rate is three-fourths unemployed if only ten hours of weekly work are available. Because the average number of hours worked by employed individuals varies significantly with the level of overall economic activity, average workweeks are lengthened when economic activity is buoyant and are shortened when economic activity is depressed, the employment statistics compiled by the Bureau of Labor Statistics tend to hide an increased volume of *underemployment* when the economy is depressed and obscure the existence of *overtime* work during boom periods.

In a similar vein, if an unemployed Ph.D. in English takes a job as a short-order cook, he or she is not counted as unemployed. However, when an individual is forced, by the state of health of the economy, to work in a job that does not fully utilize his or her abilities, that individual is in part unemployed or underemployed. When economic activity is depressed, the number of individuals forced to accept such underemployment multiplies. Further, seasonal variations in the number of workers on vacation, and in the number temporarily out of work because of bad weather, are not adequately represented if we want our employment data to measure the productive use of labor. While the official measure of employment generally can be expected to move in a roughly parallel fashion with a more refined measure of actual productive labor input, substantial improvements in the measure the Bureau of Labor Statistics provides are undoubtedly attainable.

Measured Unemployment

An individual sixteen years old or older who was not employed during the survey week but who is currently available for work and has engaged in some specific job-seeking activity (interviewing with a prospective employer, answering an ad, and so on) during the preceding four weeks is counted as unemployed.[3] In addition, individuals waiting to be recalled to jobs from which they have been laid off, and individuals scheduled to report to new jobs within thirty days, are counted as unemployed. Table 3—4 provides a sample of the questions used in the actual survey conducted monthly to estimate the size of the labor force, the amount of employment, and the size of the pool of the unemployed, along with some other measures of labor market conditions.

The definitions of the labor force and of employment that are used in the measurement of unemployment exclude from unemployment those who would happily accept employment but who, after becoming convinced that no job is available, have simply quit making specific efforts to find employment. Of course, such "discouraged" job seekers are in every economically meaningful sense unemployed, and they would resume active participation in the labor market if only they became convinced that favorable opportunities for employment exist. Moreover, there is evidence that housewives, retired workers, and students become more active participants in the labor force when, in the course of an economic expansion, attractive opportunities for employment become available. However, like the discouraged worker, the *potential* worker receives no recognition in the U.S. unemployment statistics.

By counting workers whose skills are not fully utilized and by ignoring discouraged and potential workers, the official unemployment data hide or disguise a considerable volume of true unemployment.[4] In addition, that data series fails to fully reveal the employment and unemployment changes

---

[3]Being available for work does not require one to take any job offered. For example, a laid-off aerospace engineer is not *required* to take a job as a cook or a draftsman. He or she may refuse such jobs, remain unemployed, and still receive unemployment benefits for the normal duration of eligibility. However, if a job opening which is compatible with the individual's training and experience is refused, unemployment benefits may be terminated though he or she remains unemployed.

[4]See T. Dernburg and K. Strand, "Hidden Unemployment, 1953–1962: A Quantitative Analysis by Age and Sex," *The American Economic Review* 56 (1966): 71–95. According to this investigation, unemployment figures would be some 50 percent higher if discouraged workers were counted as part of the labor force. Of course, to the extent that discouraged workers are involved in nonmarket production, the economic loss from unemployment is less than the adjusted unemployment figures would suggest. See also J. Mincer, "Labor Force Participation and Unemployment: A Review of Recent Evidence," in *Prosperity and Unemployment,* ed. R. A. Gordon and M. S. Gordon (New York: John Wiley & Sons, 1966), pp. 73–112.

Table 3—4 / Excerpt from the Monthly Current Population Survey

brought about by cyclical swings in the overall level of economic activity. As the economy expands, the number of job opportunities increases. In response—discouraged workers and potential workers are enticed into becoming active participants in the labor force. With increased labor force participation, an increase in the number of job slots obviously cannot provide an equivalent reduction in unemployment, and the measured reduction in unemployment understates the true impact of economic expansion. By the same token, when job opportunities become less abundant during a business contraction, frustrated work seekers may abandon the job search that makes them an official part of the labor force. As a consequence, the measured increase in unemployment is an underestimate of the impact on true unemployment of a shrinkage in economic activity.

Another Overview. As just explained, it cannot be assumed that the size of the labor force is constant because labor force participation is itself a function of the level of unemployment. During a business expansion employment opportunities expand and participation in the labor force is encouraged. During contractions, opportunities for employment shrink and labor force participation is discouraged as measured unemployment rises. We have also noted that available employment and unemployment data are on a job versus no-job basis, so that whether a worker is working part-time or overtime, at his "best" occupation or in one that does not fully utilize his abilities, he is counted as employed. Typically, then, true unemployment (in, say, man-hours) is understated during recessions when part-time work becomes more commonplace and more labor is discouraged from participation in the labor force while, with overtime work common and labor force participation encouraged, the unemployment series might overstate the extent of unemployment in periods of exuberant economic activity.[5]

Postwar data on employment, unemployment, and the unemployment rate, i.e., the percentage of the civilian labor force that is unemployed, are presented in Table 3—5. Despite their shortcomings, these data series are our best sources of information on the productive use of labor. Consequently, every monthly variation in each of these series, and most particularly in the unemployment rate series, is carefully scrutinized. The last two columns of that table provide estimates, constructed by Michael Wachter and by Robert Gordon, of the natural rate of unemployment in a number of different years.[6] In any year, actual unemployment could be compared to a valid measure of the natural rate of unemployment to reveal the degree of pressure on prices. Later on, we will want to take a close look at the link between the inflation rate, on the one hand, and gaps between the actual and natural unemployment rates. In the meantime, it is notable that the estimated value of the natural unemployment rate has changed considerably in recent years, rising with the increase in female and teenage labor force participation rates and with the improvement of income support levels available to nonworkers through unemployment compensation, social security, welfare, and so on.

Okun's Law. A quick look down the fourth column in Table 3—5 reveals variations in the unemployment rate that may or may not strike you as

[5]In the slack year 1961, the official unemployment rate was around 6 percent. Adjusting for part-time work, the full-time equivalent unemployment rate was around 9 percent. For a discussion of this adjustment see Council of Economic Advisers, *Economic Report of the President* (Washington, D.C.: U.S. Government Printing Office, 1962) p. 43.

[6]See Michael L. Wachter, "The Changing Cyclical Responsiveness of Wage Inflation," *Brookings Papers on Economic Activity*, 7, no. 1 (1976): 115–159; and Robert J. Gordon, "Structural Unemployment and the Productivity of Women," in *Stabilization of Domestic and International Economy*, ed. K. Brunner and A. Meltzer, *Journal of Monetary Economics*, vol. 5, 1977, pp. 189–191. Also, Robert J. Gordon, *Macroeconomics* (Boston: Little Brown and Company, 1978), pp. 248–251 and Appendix B, Table B–1.

Table 3—5 / Employment and Unemployment, 1947–1979

Year	Employment	Unemployment	Unemployment Rate Percent of Civilian Labor Force	Wachter's Estimates	Gordon's Estimates
	Thousands of Persons Age 16 and Over			The Natural Rate of Unemployment	
1947	57,039	2,311	3.9%		
1948	58,344	2,276	3.8		
1949	57,649	3,637	5.9		
1950	59,920	3,288	5.3	4.3	4.1
1951	59,962	2,055	5.3		
1952	60,254	1,833	3.0		
1953	61,181	1,834	2.9		
1954	60,110	3,532	5.5		
1955	62,171	2,852	4.4	4.0	4.3
1956	63,802	2,750	4.1		
1957	64,071	2,859	4.3		
1958	63,036	4,602	6.8		
1959	64,630	3,740	5.5		
1960	65,778	3,852	5.5	4.2	4.4
1961	65,746	4,714	6.7		
1962	66,702	3,911	5.5		
1963	67,762	4,070	5.7		
1964	69,305	3,786	5.2		
1965	71,088	3,366	4.5	4.5	4.7
1966	72,895	2,875	3.8		
1967	74,372	2,975	3.8		
1968	75,920	2,817	3.6		
1969	77,902	2,832	3.5		
1970	78,627	4,088	4.9	5.0	5.1
1971	79,120	4,993	5.9		
1972	81,702	4,840	5.6		
1973	84,409	4,304	4.9		
1974	85,935	5,076	5.6		
1975	84,783	7,830	8.5	5.5	5.4
1976	87,485	7,288	7.7		
1977	90,546	6,855	7.0		
1978	94,373	6,047	6.0		
1979	96,945	5,963	5.8		

Source: U.S. Department of Labor, Bureau of Labor Statistics.

impressive. A moment's reflection will magnify their importance. The increase in the unemployment rate from 5.6 percent of the labor force in 1974 to 8.5 percent in 1975 means a 52 percent jump in measured unemployment, or, as the figures in column 3 of our table indicate, a measured increase of some 2.7 million workers unemployed. With what we already know about labor market responses to altered levels of economic activity, it should come as no surprise that a change in the measured unemployment rate can be associated with an even more striking change in output. That fact is illustrated clearly by a useful rule-of-thumb known as Okun's Law, named after its discoverer, Arthur Okun, who was chairman of the President's Council of Economic Advisors in the early 1960s.[7] In Chapter 1, a chart of the time path of potential output was provided in which potential output, which was viewed as a target for actual output, was assumed to grow at around a 4 percent annual rate. According to Okun's Law, it takes a rate of growth of 2½ percent annually over and above the growth rate of potential output (4 percent or otherwise) to reduce unemployment by 1 percentage point. This 2½ to 1 ratio, viewed from the other direction, implies that a 1 percentage point change in unemployment corresponds to a 2½ percent change in output. A rise in unemployment from 5 to 7 percent then translates into a quite impressive shrinkage in output.

How can this be? Because as the number of unemployed falls, the number employed rises even more as labor force participation rates increase. Also, expansion of the number of employed workers typically is accompanied by an increase in the average workweek. Finally, labor's output per hour usually rises during expansions because employed workers are more fully utilized. A two-pilot airline crew may, for example, carry more passengers per flight as well as make more flights when business conditions improve. Our unemployment statistics appear to seriously understate the economic cost (in terms of measured output) of a slack economy because a substantial fall in national output can be accompanied by an increase in unemployment of an apparently small magnitude.

Okun's Law also provides a handy rule-of-thumb in policy discussions dealing with the link between growth of real output and unemployment. Suppose, at the end of 1980, unemployment was 8 percent. To reduce that unemployment rate to 5 percent by the end of 1984 (one presidential term) would require a growth in output of $(3\% \times 2.5) = 7.5\%$ over and above the growth in potential output. That means just under a 6 percent annual growth rate of real output each year if potential output expands at roughly 4 percent annually.

Case in Point I

An Important Source of Policy Disagreement

The discussion above explained the crucial link between the size of the gap separating actual and potential output on the one hand, and the rate of desired expansion of the nation's output on the other. Clearly, major differences in the size of that gap would call for markedly different rates of expansion and, hence, for decidedly different government policies to pro-

---

[7]See Arthur Okun, "The Gap Between Actual and Potential Output," reprinted in *The Battle Against Unemployment*, ed. A. Okun (New York: W. W. Norton & Company, 1972), pp. 13–22. Also, Council of Economic Advisers, *Economic Report of the President* (Washington, D.C.: U.S. Government Printing Office, 1979), pp. 72–76.

mote expansion. Unfortunately for the purpose of policy making, erratic movements in labor productivity and a changing composition of the labor force in recent years have led to a good deal of uncertainty over the path of potential output and controversy over what the rate of expansion of the economy should be.

The chart below shows the actual and potential output series charted for the last decade in the *1979 Annual Report* of the President's Council of Economic Advisors. The line labeled 1976 potential corresponds to the potential output estimates charted in Chapter 1, assuming around a 4 percent annual growth in potential real output. The lines labeled 1977–78 potential and 1979 potential reflect successive downward revisions of the potential output target in response to a slowing of growth in labor productivity and a change in labor force composition that yields a higher full employment unemployment rate.

Table 3—6 / Actual and Potential Gross National Product

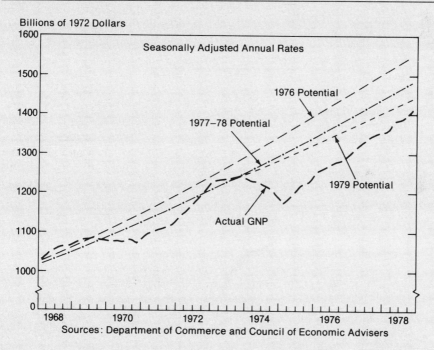

Sources: Department of Commerce and Council of Economic Advisers

Of course, with every revision of the potential output series, the size of the gap between actual and potential output is altered, possibly dramatically as the chart shows, and the appropriate degree of government initiated stimulus or restriction on the economy is changed. Unfortunately, the projected values of potential GNP are *estimates,* subject to a good bit of uncertainty. Indeed, different groups of economists can and do argue persuasively for different potential GNP targets (like the three plotted in the chart) and, as a consequence, must disagree over what policy actions are appropriate.

Summary

Among the goals of macroeconomic policy listed in Chapter 1, the maintenance of full employment and of reasonable stability in the general price level enjoyed lofty status. This chapter has reviewed the data series, price indexes and employment/unemployment statistics, that are used to monitor our success or failure in achieving those goals. While both the price measures and the employment/unemployment statistics compiled for the U.S. economy are subject to biases, they rank among the few most closely watched indicators of the macroeconomy's performance.

It is noteworthy that, even though our concerns up to now have been mainly descriptive, with a focus on quantitative measures of economic activity, we have already encountered controversy and potential disagreements among different economists. This will continue to be the case as our efforts become more analytical.

Questions

1. ───

Item	Prices		Quantities	
	1970	1980	1970	1980
Blue jeans	$ 8.00	$15.00	500	600
Drive-in movie tickets	2.25	3.00	400	450
Electronic calculators	150.00	35.00	40	120

   a. Calculate the Laspeyres index for 1980.
   b. Calculate the Paasche index for 1980.
   c. What biases would you expect in each of these index values?
   d. What practical advantages do you see in computing Laspeyres rather than Paasche price indexes?

2. Explain how price indexes can be used to deflate nominal values.

3. In a *Wall Street Journal* article a few years ago, a number of criticisms were lodged against the consumer price index. As an example the article said, ". . . if tomatoes skyrocket in price and consumers thus switch to apples, the index may exaggerate the jump in the cost-of-living since it gives the unused tomatoes the same weight as before."
   a. Elaborate on the "exaggeration" in the rate of inflation cited in the *Wall Street Journal* article.
   b. Suppose tomatoes skyrocket in price because of a change in tastes, thence in demand. What bias would be introduced into the CPI?
   c. Cite two other likely sources of bias in the CPI and explain how they produce that bias.

4. How is the U.S. unemployment rate computed?

5. In what ways is the measured unemployment rate a biased measure of true unemployment?

6. In Chapter 1, it was argued that full employment does not mean zero percent measured unemployment. Evaluate that assertion in light of the definition of unemployment you now have.

7. In a *Wall Street Journal* article that appeared in 1977, Paul McCracken (a former Council of Economic Advisers chairman) noted that while, during the preceding year, total U.S. spending on goods and services rose 11.6 percent, total purchases of U.S. produced goods and services rose only 10.4 percent. McCracken argued that this gap was responsible for nearly an extra one-half percentage point of unemployment. Provide an explanation of this claim.

Suggested Readings

Council of Economic Advisers. *Economic Report of the President*. Washington, D.C.: U.S. Government Printing Office, 1979.

Cullison, William E. "An Employment Pressure Index as an Alternative Measure of Labor Market Conditions." *The Review of Economics and Statistics* 42 (February 1975): 115–121.

President's Committee to Appraise Employment and Unemployment Statistics. *Measuring Employment and Unemployment*. Washington, D.C.: U.S. Government Printing Office, 1962.

Ruggles, Richard. "The Problems of Our Price Indexes." *Challenge*, November 1961. Reprinted in *The Battle Against Unemployment*, edited by Arthur Okun, pp. 77–82. 1st edition. New York: W. W. Norton & Co., 1965.

Wallace, William. *Measuring Price Changes*. Richmond, Va.: Federal Reserve Bank of Richmond, 1972.

Wonnacott, T. H. and Wonnacott, R. J. *Introductory Statistics for Business and Economics*, Chapter 23. New York: John Wiley & Sons, 1972.

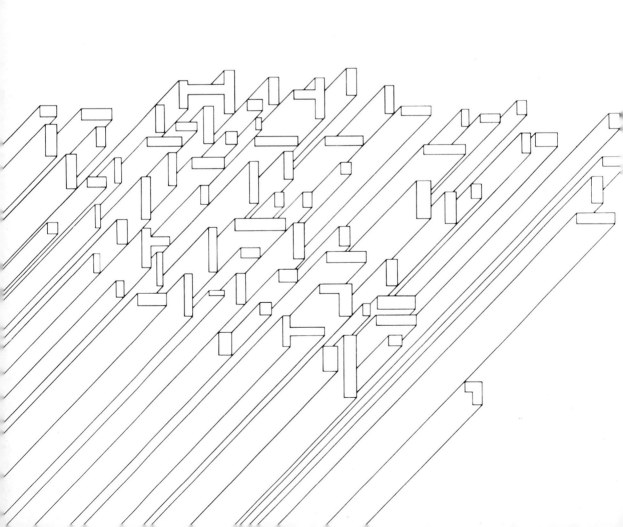

Part **II**

Building the Core Macroeconomic Model

The first three chapters, which you have now completed, are essentially descriptive, explaining both what the concerns of macroeconomics are and the methods commonly used in macroeconomics, then providing familiarity with the most important quantitative indicators of the economy's performance. In this second part of the text, our interests will be primarily analytical. The seven chapters (4–10) that comprise this section provide a detailed exposition of the form of macroeconomic model that the mainstream of the economics profession employs in analyzing events that may alter employment, output, and the general price level. The structure of the model considered also forms the basis for more detailed econometric models of the aggregate economy.

The model of the economy that we will construct emphasizes the role of disturbances in the economy-wide or aggregate levels of both demand and supply. It is disturbances that affect aggregate demand and/or aggregate supply which result in deviations in employment and output from their optimum values and in unwanted changes in the general price level.

Part (a) of Figure II—1 contains supply and demand schedules that *appear* to be typical of the supply and demand schedules you have worked with in microeconomics. Note, however, that rather than a single product and its price, the axes in Figure II—1 represent economy-wide output levels *(Y)* and the average or general price level *(P)*. Thus, the schedules in that figure are aggregate supply and aggregate demand schedules. The structure of the model underlying those schedules is sufficiently involved that it will not be fully explained until the end of Chapter 10. In the meantime, the simple supply/demand model may be used to anticipate some of our future concerns.

As will be shown in the chapters ahead, the equilibrium levels of output and the general price level are determined through the interaction of aggregate supply and aggregate demand. Generally, demand for output can be expected to be negatively related to the general price level, and output supplied positively associated with prices (though this may not always be the case). The response of the macroeconomy to the disturbances that confront it depends, of course, on the properties of the aggregate supply and demand schedules. Illustrating that point, parts (a) and (b) of Figure II—1 show the decidedly different responses to a shift in aggregate demand that a nearly horizontal or a steeply sloped supply schedule would require. In the first diagram, the demand shift results mostly in a change in real output *(Y)* with a weak response in the general price level. In contrast, the same demand shift in diagram (b) results primarily in a price level change with only a slight change in real output. Finally, diagram (c) illustrates the possibility that the responses to a significant shift in demand may vary with the level of economic activity. In that diagram, a shift in demand from D_0 to D_1, in a range where output is depressed (small relative to full employment output level Y_f), is associated with a weak price response and a strong output response. With the economy operating close to the full employment output level, diagram (c) shows a weak output and strong price response to a shift in demand.

The conditions under which the conflicting patterns of price and quantity adjustments pictured in Figure II—1 arise will be clarified in Chapters 9 and 10. In the meantime, for the next several chapters, aggregate demand will occupy

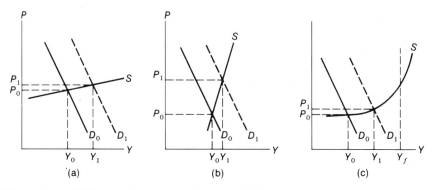

Figure II—1 / Differing Responses to Demand Shifts

center stage as the household, business firm, and government actions that influence demand for goods and services will be considered. Chapter 4 begins that task with a review of models of the demand for goods and services, in the process showing that consumption spending, business investment, and government purchases can exert powerful influences on the level of economic activity. Chapters 5 and 6 provide detailed examinations of the forces that determine consumption and investment demand, respectively, providing insight into sources of stability and instability in aggregate demand and, hence, in employment and production.

Chapter 7 introduces money and the financial market place into our analysis of economic events, allowing the interactions between money and the *real* market for goods and services to be examined. In Chapter 8, a formal model, the well-known IS–LM model, is developed for combining the financial market place with the market for goods and services.

Chapter 9 extends our analysis by adding a third market, the market for labor services. With this addition, the supply side of the economy can be formally represented and integrated into the macro model. With aggregate supply as an integral part of the *complete* macro model, economy-wide responses to a sample of disturbances when sufficient time is allowed to elapse for a "full information" adjustment of the economy to be completed are examined in Chapter 9. Chapter 10 extends the application of the complete macroeconomic model to examine the economy's *short-run* or *cyclical* responses to various disturbances. As our analysis will show, government actions may exert a rather potent influence on aggregate demand over somewhat limited time intervals while, over longer time intervals, its actions can significantly influence aggregate supply.

Chapter **4**	Models of Simple Economic Systems

To understand why the economy performs as it does and how its performance might be improved, we have to build models of that complex system. As indicated in Chapter 1 such models are always simplified abstractions of reality for, if our models did not vastly simplify the world, we could never hope to understand their workings (or, hence, the workings of the real world). The models constructed in this chapter are incomplete but crucial components of more complete *Keynesian-style* models. They owe their heritage to a revolutionary book, *The General Theory of Employment, Interest, and Money,*[1] written in 1936 by a British economist named John Maynard Keynes.

Prior to the 1930s, economists placed great faith in the ability of a market economy to generate and maintain full employment automatically. While they recognized that the economy was subject to periodic slumps, pre-Keynesian economists believed that natural forces within the economy could be depended on to restore full employment within an acceptable time period. However, the experience of the Great Depression, which began in 1929, required a reconsideration of the prevailing faith in an automatically adjusting economy. Unemployment hovered above 15 percent year after year with no evidence of any powerful forces working to restore full employment. Indeed, not until the mobilization for World War II was the economy freed from the lingering malaise that began a full decade earlier.

---

[1]John Maynard Keynes, *The General Theory of Employment, Interest, and Money* (New York: Harcourt Brace Jovanovich, 1936).

In marked contrast to the analysis of his predecessors, the model Keynes constructed in *The General Theory* argued that automatic forces within a market economy cannot be depended upon to maintain full employment or to restore full employment equilibrium once the economy has been rocked from that position. It follows that government intervention in the economy may, at times, be required to elicit a satisfactory performance from that system. In the postwar era, the majority of economists have adopted the Keynesian framework for macroeconomic analysis.

As a natural consequence of their birth during the Great Depression, Keynesian macroeconomic models have focused attention on the determinants of aggregate *demand* for real goods and services. During the depression a skilled labor force and a massive store of factories and sales outlets languished in the face of pressing unfulfilled consumer needs. Business firms were shut down simply because their output could not be profitably sold; aggregate demand for real goods and services was just too weak to sustain full employment production. With a major portion of the industrialized world's productive capacity idle, Keynes recognized the essentially passive role played in the depression by the supply side of the economy. His analysis emphasized the need for stimulating aggregate demand in order to return the economy to full employment.

The models constructed in this chapter reflect Keynes' depression era emphasis on the role of aggregate demand. As future chapters will show, these models would adequately represent only some very special economy; specifically, one in which there is a perfectly elastic supply of goods and services to match changes in aggregate demand with no change in the price level, and, what's more, one in which interest rates (and, hence, monetary policy actions by the central bank) have no influence on aggregate demand. Yet, the lessons learned about the role of aggregate demand and its determinants from the simple models in this chapter will be valid as a more complete and realistic model of the economy is developed, and we will carry the demand schedules developed in this chapter with us as our modeling of the economy continues.

Model I: Analyzing a Simple Economy

As neophytes at model construction, we will begin our own model-building activities as painlessly as possible, putting together a model of the most basic kind of economic system. No modern real-world economy could be adequately represented by this first model, but the analytical sequence required for constructing such a model will be directly applicable to the construction of more sophisticated and realistic models. If you thoroughly understand the development of this simple model, you will be able to work through the more complex models developed in this chapter very quickly. Indeed, reflecting your rapidly developing skill as a model builder, you may conclude that the analysis in this chapter is unduly repetitious.

The simplest sort of economic system is *closed* (that is, it is involved in no economic transactions with agents of any other country) and has no government. Moreover, it can be assumed that all production takes place in the "business" sector of the economy with all resulting profits accruing to firms' owners,[2] that all consumption takes place in the "household" sector, and that there are no transfer payments. Reflecting our concern with the *real* performance of the economic system, all the magnitudes dealt with throughout this chapter are measured in *real* terms, for, as indicated in the introduction to this chapter, no changes in the price level are considered among the factors affecting aggregate demand.

Measuring the Level of Production: National Accounts for a Simple Economy

As a first step toward analyzing this simple economic system, let us see whether a correspondingly simple system of descriptive national accounts, comparable to the U.S. national income and product accounts, can be constructed. The broadest measure of production will again be GNP, which can be calculated using either the expenditure or the income approach. From the expenditure side of the accounts, total GNP can be obtained by adding consumption spending by households and gross investment spending by business firms because, with no government and no foreign trade, government spending and net exports are nonexistent. From the income side, total received income will consist of the sum of wages, interest (paid by business to households), rent, and profit. This figure must be adjusted in the manner described below in order to provide a figure for GNP.

The *net* output generated in the production process still falls short of GNP by the amount of capital consumption, just as it did in the full accounts for the United States. Thus, net national product is still GNP minus capital consumption. Of course, it is also the sum of consumption and net investment spending.

At this point, our simple country's accounts begin to differ from those for the United States. With no government, there are no indirect business taxes. Thus, net national product is no different from national income (which represented *earned* income in the U.S. accounts). With no taxes on corporate profits, no social security system payments, no retained earnings by business, and no transfer payments, there is no difference between *earned* income and actual *received* income; that is, national income is the same as personal income for our simple economy. Finally, with no personal income taxes, all of received income is available to households as disposable income. We have clearly simplified the world. Households' disposable income is now identical to net national product. GNP figures can be obtained by adding up all consumption and investment spending or (from the income

---

[2]In the case of incorporated business, this assumption requires all profits to be paid out to stockholders. These payments are cash *dividends*.

side) by adding to actual received income the amount of capital consumption. The national accounts for this economy are summarized algebraically as follows using the same symbols used in Chapter 2.[3]

$$\text{Expenditure} \atop \text{Approach:} \left\{ \begin{array}{l} \Sigma \text{ (spending on final} \\ \qquad \text{goods and services)} \end{array} \right\} = C + I_G$$

$$= \text{GNP} - D = \text{NNP} = C + I_N.$$

$$\text{Income} \atop \text{Approach:} \left\{ \begin{array}{l} \Sigma \text{ (wages, interest,} \\ \qquad \text{rent, dividends)} \end{array} \right\} = \text{NNP}$$

$$= \text{NI} \quad \text{since there are no } T_i$$
$$= \text{PI} \quad \text{since there are no}$$
$$\qquad \qquad T_b, SS, R_t, T_r.$$
$$= Y_d \quad \text{since there are no } T_p.$$

The national account manipulations above demonstrate that, for *measured* values of the consumption, investment, and income terms,

$$Y = C + I_N, \qquad\qquad [4\text{—}1]$$

where Y is NNP, C is consumption, and I_N is net investment. Those manipulations also show that disposable income is identical to NNP. Because all of disposable income must be consumed or saved, and disposable income is the same as NNP, for *measured* values of the variables:

$$Y = C + S \qquad\qquad [4\text{—}2]$$

where S is personal saving by the household sector and the other variables retain their definitions. Combining the accounting identities in Equations 4—1 and 4—2 yields the identity:

$$S = I_N. \qquad\qquad [4\text{—}3]$$

Thus, the accounting identities for our simple world show that *measured* spending is always identical to the *measured* value of output (Eq. 4—1) and *measured* saving is always identical to *measured* investment (Eq. 4—3).

Why should measured saving always equal measured investment? A moment's reflection on one of our accounting identities (use Eq. 4—1) will make sense of this claim. Suppose the value of *net* output produced in the simple economy in 1980 were $1,000 billion. (The value of income generated in the production process must, of course, also be $1,000 billion because, in the simple economy, any commodity's "value" or "price" is exhausted

---

[3]Those symbols are: T_i = indirect business taxes, T_b = taxes on corporate profits, SS = social security contributions, R_t = retained earnings, T_r = transfer payments, NI = national income, PI = personal income, Y_d = disposable income, T_p = personal taxes, and so on.

by factor payments: the sum of wages, rent, interest, and any residual profit.) This $1,000 billion worth of output might have consisted of $200 billion worth of investment goods (goods produced to add *intentionally* to the existing stock of plants, equipment, and inventories held by the business sector), and $800 billion worth of output that business produced for consumption by the household sector. If, during 1980, the household sector chose to consume out of its $1,000 billion of received income only $700 billion worth of goods and services, there would be an *unplanned* addition of $100 billion worth of goods to business inventories. Because additions to inventory count as investment, whether intended or not, *actual* or *measured* investment in 1970 would have been $300 billion, matching 1980's personal saving figure. The total $1,000 billion worth of output would be absorbed by *measured* consumption and investment. Counting the unplanned, unintended change in inventories as investment ensures the identity of measured saving with measured investment, and of measured spending with output.[4]

While measured total spending must always be equal to the measured value of output (and income), the value of *planned* or *intended* total spending need not always be equal to output. In the example above, consumers *planned* to buy $700 billion worth of output, and business *planned* to buy $200 billion worth. Also, business "bought" an *unplanned* addition of $100 billion worth of inventories. Analogously, while *measured* saving and *measured* investment are always equal, *planned* investment may differ markedly from *planned* saving. (In our example, planned investment of $200 billion fell short of planned saving by $100 billion, resulting in an unintended increase in inventories of $100 billion.) This distinction between planned and measured equalities is essential to macroeconomic analysis. As we shall see, equality of planned saving and investment (or of planned total spending and output) is necessary for our simple economic system to be in *equilibrium*. In contrast, measured equalities in the national income accounting measures tell us nothing about equilibrium.

Before proceeding to the next section, you should be certain you understand the distinction between planned and measured values of consumption, saving, and investment. To be sure that you do, repeat the exercise above but do it assuming that households choose to consume $900 billion worth of goods and services out of their $1,000 billion of received income.

Equilibrium in the Simplest Model. With the descriptive national accounts for our simple economy completed, attention can be focused now on the requirements for equilibrium in that economy. An economic system is in *equilibrium*, at rest, when there are no forces tending to alter the prevailing

---

[4]It is also true that, for measured values, $Y_G = C + I_G$ and $Y_G = C + S_G$, where Y_G is GNP, C is consumption, I_G is gross investment, and S_G is "gross" saving, consisting of personal saving by households plus business saving in the form of depreciation funds. Therefore, $\cancel{C} + I_G = \cancel{C} + S_G$ so $I_G = S_G$. In the measured sense, gross spending $(C + I_G)$ must be equal to current gross output and gross investment must be equal to gross saving.

levels of output, spending, and so on. To determine the specific requirements for an economy to be in equilibrium, it is helpful to represent the
flows of aggregate income (and spending) in that economy in a simple schematic diagram. For our basic economy, Figure 4—1 provides such a schematic description using the $1,000 billion figure for the assumed level of net
output (*Y*).

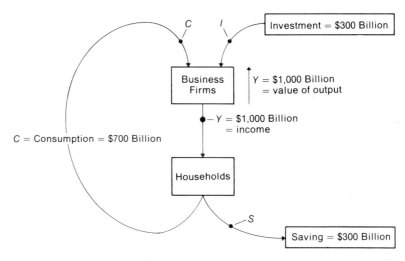

**Figure 4—1 / The Flow of Income
(Spending) in a Closed Economy with No Government**

Briefly relating what we already know to this flow diagram, we see again
that output and income are identical. As previously indicated, the value of
total output must be the same as total costs of production where those total
costs include payments for wages, rent, interest, and the residual item profit.
These payments for factor inputs by business are, of course, income to the
owners (households) of the employed factor inputs.

Figure 4—1 shows households in the simple economy collectively spending part of their received income and saving part (in this case amounts of
$700 billion and $300 billion, respectively), with consumption plus saving
equal to total received income. That diagram clearly reflects the point that
consumption spending absorbs part, but only part, of the output of businesses (in this case, $700 billion of the $1,000 billion worth of output).
However, if this economic system is to be in equilibrium, the remaining
$300 billion worth of output must be *willingly* absorbed by that other com-
ponent of spending, business investment in plants, equipment, and inventories (the necessary flow of planned investment spending is shown in the
diagram). Total *planned* spending on output is, of course, the sum of
planned consumption and *planned* investment spending (*C* + *I*). This total

of *planned spending* must be exactly equal to the value of output (income) for our simple economic system to be in equilibrium. (That is, *it is required that* $Y = C + I$ *in the planned sense for equilibrium to exist.*)[5]

Disequilibrium. What happens if, at the $1,000 billion level of output, total *planned* spending *(C + I)* is less than the value of output? For example, if this year output is $1,000 billion but planned $C + I$ is only $900 billion, what would we expect to happen?[6]

Clearly, $900 billion of spending cannot clear the market of $1,000 billion worth of output. Business inventories will be growing, and this expansion of inventories is *unintentional.* Businesses would surely not continue to produce $1,000 billion worth of output period after period if only $900 billion worth is willingly purchased for final use each period, requiring the unintended addition of $100 billion of output to inventory each period. Eventually, firms would cut back production (output), reducing income generated in the production process by an equivalent amount. Generalizing from this example, if the value of output (income) exceeds the value of total planned spending *(C + I)*, output will fall. *The economy cannot be in equilibrium if unintended increases in inventory are occurring.*

Similarly, if total planned spending, or *aggregate demand,* exceeds the value of output (for example, if planned $C + I = \$1,100$ billion while $Y = \$1,000$ billion), inventories will suffer an unplanned shrinkage. If firms observe such an unintended decrease in their inventories period after period, they are likely to respond by increasing their rate of production if they have any unused capacity to produce. Thus, if the value of total planned spending exceeds the value of output, output (income) will rise. *The economy cannot be in equilibrium if unintended decreases in inventory are occurring.*

The basic rule we have drawn from our discussion of disequilibrium will be valid for every model we construct, no matter how complicated. *The market for goods and services can be in equilibrium only if there are no unintended increases or decreases in inventory.*

An Alternative Statement of the Formal Equilibrium Condition. Again, the basic equilibrium requirement of no unintended change in inventory will be met if all of received income is spent (that is, if total planned spending is identical to the value of output, or $Y = C + I$). Referring to Figure 4—1 again, we can see that there is an alternative way of stating this rule. Total spending will remain equal to the value of output as long as any *leakage* from the circular flow of income (such as the $300 billion of saving) is exactly offset by an identical *injection* of spending into the income stream (such as

---

[5]Again, output and spending are always equal in value in the observed, measured, or "realized" sense.

[6]To illustrate this question graphically, you can redraw Figure 4—1, replacing the flow of $300 billion of measured investment with $200 billion of *planned* investment, making total *planned* spending equal to $900 billion (planned $C + I = \$700$ billion + $200 billion = $900 billion).

the $300 billion of investment). That is, total planned spending will equal the value of output $(Y = C + I)$ if leakages equal injections. For the simple economy we are analyzing, saving is the only leakage from the income stream, and investment is the only injection into that stream. Thus, equilibrium will prevail if planned saving is equal to planned investment, or $S = I$. Because our two fundamental equalities are fully equivalent statements of the same equilibrium condition, in addition to both holding true when the simple economic system is in equilibrium, they both must be violated when that system is in disequilibrium. Glancing back at Figure 4—1, it is easy to see that, when planned spending falls short of current output $(C + I < Y)$, planned saving must exceed planned investment $(S > I)$. In this case, inventories will experience an unplanned growth, and production will be reduced. When planned spending exceeds current output $(C + I > Y)$, planned saving will be less than planned investment; and, with inventories shrinking unexpectedly, business firms will step up the rate of production.

A Quantitative Estimate of Equilibrium Income

We now know what condition(s) must hold if an equilibrium income level is to prevail in the simple economic system, but we do not know what the value of equilibrium income will be. To find out we need to introduce some specific quantitative information about the spending behavior of the households and business firms in the simple economy. Specifically, estimates of planned consumption and planned investment are needed. Simple Keynesian models hypothesize that the volume of consumption spending society plans to undertake during any period is directly related to the volume of income it has to spend. Typically, consumption is taken to be a linear function of disposable income so that the *consumption function* in our model can be written algebraically as

$$C = a + bY$$

where Y is the value of aggregate income (net output), and the coefficients a and b are behavioral constants. The second coefficient, b, which measures the slope of the straight-line consumption function, is called the *marginal propensity to consume* (or MPC). It is a measure of the response of aggregate consumption per dollar of change in disposable income.[7] The first coefficient, a, is just the intercept of the straight-line consumption function.

---

[7]As we have already demonstrated, society must either consume or save all of its disposable income. If only a fractional portion of any $1 dollar increase in income is consumed, the remaining fraction must be saved. Thus, the response of saving per dollar of change in income, the so-called *marginal propensity to save*, is $(1 - b)$.

With data on aggregate consumption, C, and income, Y, over time, linear regression analysis can be used to ascertain the values of a and b in the consumption function (review Chapter 1, pp. 9–12 if this assertion is not clear). In the process of fitting the hypothesized consumption function, we would be testing the validity of the simple hypothesis that consumption is linearly related to income. If the linear consumption function appears to adequately capture the linkage between income and consumption, the fitted function could be used as a predictor of the level of consumption society would *plan* to undertake at any selected level of income.

function could be used as a predictor of the level of consumption society would *plan* to undertake at any selected level of income.

We can now turn our attention to accounting for planned investment spending. Unfortunately, explaining what determines planned investment is relatively complex. To keep our model-building efforts as simple and straightforward as possible, we will avoid that complexity for now by assuming that the volume of planned investment in the time period with which we are concerned is a constant, the value of which is *given* (say, through a survey of businessmen's investment plans). In the jargon of economic analysis, we are assuming that the value of planned investment is *exogenous* to our model; that is, its level does not depend on the value of any variable in the model we are building but is determined by forces outside the scope of that model. In contrast, the values of income and of consumption (which depends on income) are to be determined within our model. Thus, these variables are *endogenous*.

We are now ready to solve for the quantitative value of equilibrium output. Restating our two equivalent formulations of the equilibrium condition, plugging in our "behavioral hypotheses" for consumption and investment, and solving algebraically for the equilibrium level of output (income), yields the following results:

Form 1:

$$\text{Aggregate demand} = \text{value of output (income)},$$

or

$$Y = C + I.$$

With $C = a + bY$ and $I = \bar{I}$ (the bar indicating exogenous), the equilibrium condition becomes

$$Y = a + bY + \bar{I},$$

so the equilibrium level of income ($Y_{eq.}$) is

$$Y_{eq.} = \frac{1}{1-b}(a + \bar{I}).$$

$\longrightarrow Y - by = a + \bar{I}$

$Y(1-b) = a + \bar{I}$

$Y = \dfrac{a + \bar{I}}{1 - b}$ [4–4]

Form 2:

Leakages (saving) = injections (investment),

or

$$S = I.$$

With

$$S = Y - C$$

$$= Y - a - bY$$

$$= -a + (1 - b)\, Y,$$

[handwritten: $= Y - (a + bY)$]

[handwritten: $= +a + (Y - bY)$]

the equilibrium condition becomes

$$-a + (1 - b)\, Y = \bar{I}$$

so the equilibrium level of income is

$$Y_{eq.} = \frac{1}{1 - b}(a + \bar{I}). \qquad [4\text{—}5]$$

[handwritten: $(1-b)Y = \bar{I} + a$]

[handwritten: $Y = \dfrac{\bar{I} + a}{1 - b}$]

Because the two forms of the equilibrium condition are equivalent, the level of income that satisfies either statement of the equilibrium condition must be the same ($Y_{eq.} = (1/(1 - b))\,(a + \bar{I})$ for this model).

Graphical Solutions. We can also solve this simple algebraic system graphically. Plotting our assumed consumption and investment functions would yield schedules C and $\bar{I}$ in part (a) of Figure 4—2. Total demand (planned spending) in this model is, again, just $C + I$. Graphically summing the C and $\bar{I}$ schedules vertically yields the aggregate demand schedule $C + \bar{I}$. Because this schedule lies above the consumption schedule by amount $\bar{I}$ at every income level, it has the same slope as the consumption schedule.

The 45° line in part a of Figure 4—2 is purely a reference line. With the same dollar scale on the horizontal and vertical axes of our diagram, this reference line simply serves to identify points at which spending is equal to the value of income (output). For example, when income is Y_1, consumption (C_1) is exactly equal to income, as the intersection of the consumption schedule with the 45° reference line demonstrates. Because income and spending must be equal for equilibrium, this reference line is at the locus of all potential equilibrium positions in our market for goods and services.

The reference line in part (a) of Figure 4—2 identifies the *one level* of income at which spending equals income as $Y_{eq.}$. As we can also readily see

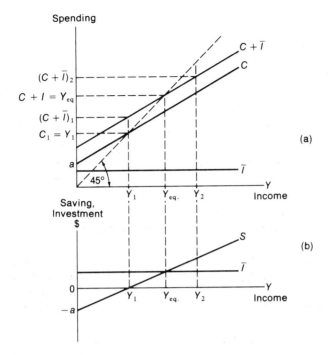

Figure 4—2 / Equilibrium Income

from that diagram, if the business sector incorrectly anticipates the strength of aggregate demand, there will be unplanned inventory investment prompting an adjustment in output (income). For example, if the business sector produces a volume of output smaller than the equilibrium quantity (such as Y_1), planned spending $(C + \bar{I})$ will exceed the value of output by $(C + \bar{I})_1$ minus Y_1, resulting in an unplanned depletion of inventories. As inventories suffer an unintended decline, business firms may step up production, raising the level of output toward Y_{eq}.

On the other hand, if the business sector overestimates the strength of aggregate demand and produces a volume of output larger than Y_{eq} (say, Y_2), not all of current output will be willingly purchased. There will be unintended inventory investment which will prompt business firms to cut back on production. Only at output level Y_{eq} is there neither unintended inventory accumulation nor depletion.

We can also produce a graphical solution for this system by plotting leakages (saving) and injections (investment) against income. These schedules are, respectively, S and $\bar{I}$ in part (b) of Figure 4—2. In part a of that figure, as a mathematical proposition, consumption was amount a when income was zero, so that all consumption at that unlikely income level would be provided by *dissaving*. That is, saving at $Y = 0$ is $S = Y - C = 0 - a$ $- (b \cdot 0)$ or $S = -a$. When income was Y_1, consumption was equal to income (saving was zero) as reflected by point Y_1 in Figure 4—2. By knowing any two points on the linear saving schedule we can, of course, plot the entire schedule as we have in part (b) of the figure. The investment schedule plotted in that figure is the same one employed in part a of the figure.

The relationship that must hold between leakages and injections for there to be equilibrium is that leakages and injections must be equal *(S = I)*. This equality holds only for $Y_{eq.}$ ($Y_{eq.}$ must, of course, be the same in both parts (a) and (b) of the figure). With output below $Y_{eq.}$, the investment injection into the income stream exceeds the saving leakage from that stream, so aggregate demand must exceed the volume of output. Consequently, inventories would suffer an unplanned depletion, prompting an increase in production. With output above $Y_{eq.}$, the saving leakage is larger than the investment injection, indicating that output exceeds planned spending. Thus, there would be an unplanned swelling of inventories prompting a production cutback.

With statistical estimates of the behavioral constants *(a and b)* in the consumption function and with an estimate of planned investment $(\bar{I})$, we could solve for the specific numerical value of equilibrium income. If, for example, statistical analysis showed $a = \$100$ billion, $b = .60$, and $\bar{I} = \$300$ billion, the equilibrium level of income would be $\$1,000$ billion. *Prove this result both algebraically and graphically.*

The exercise you have just been through is a clear-cut application of the methodology of macroeconomic analysis. For several decades, economists have involved themselves in similar exercises, building models and, then, using statistical analysis to test and quantify their models. Quite probably you are thinking: "Is that all there is to macroeconomic analysis? This model must be too simple for practical application." Your concern is well founded; the model *is* too simplistic. However, introducing real-world complexities into the analytical framework we have just constructed is straightforward and easily understood if you have a firm grasp of the basic model. The rest of this chapter is devoted to constructing more complex models of the market for real goods and services (what is often labeled the *commodity market*), and to demonstrating the use of those models for predicting not only the level of output, but also the changes in output that would result from various shocks to the economic system.

Model II: A Closed Economy with a Government Sector

Perhaps the single most important modification we could use to make our product market model more realistic is the introduction of a government that has the power to collect taxes and spend. Through its expenditures and tax levies, the government plays an important role in determining the overall level of aggregate demand. Indeed, through changing its levels of spending or tax collections the government can and does exert considerable influence on the economy, and model II can illustrate the meaning of expansionary or restrictive government "budgets" of the sort referred to in Chapter 1.

The impact on our original income flow diagram (Figure 4—1) of the introduction of a government that taxes and spends is reflected in Figure 4—3. When there is a government that collects taxes, the value of income available to be disposed of as households see fit (disposable income) is no longer the same as received income Y. Instead, disposable income is received income less taxes $(Y_d = Y - T)$, and it is this reduced level of income that households have available to consume or save as they choose, as indicated schematically in Figure 4—3. To accommodate government spending, it must be recognized that such spending comprises an additional source of demand for the output of the business sector, as also shown in that diagram.

For equilibrium in this more complicated economic system, the same *basic* condition must hold as for the economy without a government: *there must be no unintended changes in inventories.* Total planned spending *(C + I + G)* must be just sufficient to clear the market of the current level of output *(Y)* or, in algebraic terms, we must have $Y = C + I + G$ for equilibrium in this closed (no foreign sector) model with a government that taxes and spends.

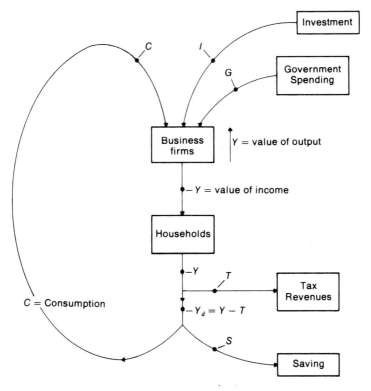

Figure 4—3 / The Flow of Income (Spending) for a Closed Economy

As was the case with our simpler model, for aggregate demand to be just equal to the value of output, any leakage from the circular flow of income must be precisely offset by an equal injection into the income stream. However, in this model there are two sources of leakage, private saving (S) and tax collections (T), and two sources of injections into the spending stream, investment (I) and government spending (G). For equilibrium, then, it is also necessary that $S + T = I + G$.

A Quantitative Estimate of Equilibrium Income

With the equilibrium condition(s) for this model in hand, we can now solve for a quantitative estimate of the equilibrium level of income if we have the necessary quantitative information on *planned* consumption, investment, taxes, and government spending. Suppose our information on the consumption function indicates that the simple straight-line form of the consumption function we have already employed can be retained. In this case, the only modification needed in the treatment of consumption in order to accommodate the role of government is the explicit recognition that consumption depends on *disposable income* (Y_d), rather than on received income Y. We will also retain the same value for investment assuming, again, that this variable is exogenously determined. Finally, we will assume that the levels of government spending (G) and tax collections (T) are exogenously determined (they are government policy decisions). In summary, our model of income determination has become:

$$\left. \begin{array}{l} Y = C + I + G \\ S + T = I + G \end{array} \right\} \text{ the equilibrium condition(s),}$$
or

$$C = a + bY_d \text{ where } Y_d \equiv Y - T \text{ by definition,}$$

$$\left. \begin{array}{l} I = \bar{I} \\ G = \bar{G} \\ T = \bar{T} \end{array} \right\} \text{ bar indicates values determined exogenously.}$$

In equation form, the above equilibrium condition(s), behavioral functions, and exogenous variables constitute the *structure* of our model of the commodity market. Once again, we can solve our model algebraically for the equilibrium level of income beginning with either of our two equivalent statements of the equilibrium condition. Doing so yields:

Form 1:

$$\text{Aggregate demand} = \text{value of output}$$

or

$$Y = C + I + G.$$

Substituting for C, I, and G,

$$Y = a + bY_d + \bar{I} + \bar{G}$$
$$= a + b(Y - \bar{T}) + \bar{I} + \bar{G}$$
$$\therefore Y_{eq.} = \frac{1}{1-b}(a + \bar{I} + \bar{G} - b\bar{T}) \qquad [4\text{--}6]$$

(handwritten annotations in right margin:)
$$Y = a + bY - b\bar{T} + \bar{I} + \bar{G}$$
$$Y - bY = a + \bar{I} + \bar{G} - b\bar{T}$$
$$(1-b)Y = a + \bar{I} + \bar{G} - b\bar{T}$$

Form 2:

$$\text{Leakages} = \text{injections}$$

or

$$S + T = I + G.$$

Substituting for S, T, I, and G yields

$$(Y_d - C) + \bar{T} = \bar{I} + \bar{G},$$

so

$$Y - \bar{T} - a - bY + b\bar{T} + \bar{T} = \bar{I} + \bar{G}$$

or

$$Y(1 - b) = a + \bar{I} + \bar{G} - b\bar{T}.$$

$$\therefore Y_{eq.} = \frac{1}{1-b}(a + \bar{I} + \bar{G} - b\bar{T}). \qquad [4\text{--}7]$$

In both cases, of course, the equilibrium values of income are the same and show the relationship between the values of the exogenous variables in our system $(\bar{I}, \bar{G}, \bar{T})$ and the endogenous variable, income $(Y_{eq.})$. The derived equations that show these linkages may be referred to as *reduced form* equations derived from the complete structural model of an economy. The reduced form equations for model II indicate that, with $a = \$100$ billion, $b = .60$, and $\bar{I} = \$300$ billion as before, and $\bar{G} = \$100$ billion, and $\bar{T} = \$83.3$ billion (the government budget $\$16.7$ billion in *deficit*), the equilibrium level of income is $\$1,125$ billion.

Graphical Solutions. A solution for the equilibrium level of income can also be obtained graphically, as illustrated in Figure 4—4. In part (a) of that diagram, the aggregate demand schedule is obtained by vertically summing the consumption, investment, and government spending schedules. The equilibrium output level, where aggregate demand and output are equal, is

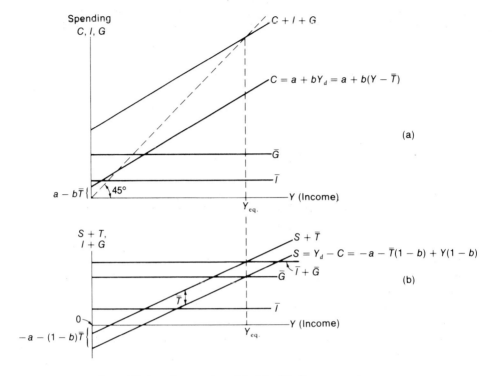

Figure 4—4 / Equilibrium Income in a Model with Government

$Y_{eq.}$ The government's tax levies can be seen influencing aggregate demand (hence equilibrium output) by reducing consumption spending out of net national product by amount $b\bar{T}$, the volume of tax collections times the fraction of those tax revenues that would be spent if left in the hands of consumers.

In part (b) of Figure 4—4 total injections into the spending stream are obtained by summing the exogenous investment and government spending schedules, $\bar{I}$ and $\bar{G}$. Total leakages are the sum of saving out of *after-tax* income and exogenous tax levies $\bar{T}$. Equilibrium prevails, at output level $Y_{eq.}$, where total leakages and total injections are equal. While graphical solutions to the equation systems we have constructed to represent simple economies remain possible, it should be clear that the graphical technique becomes intractable quite rapidly as our models become more complicated.

Model III: A Closed Economy with Government, Endogenous Investment and Tax Revenues

Our model of the economy can be made still more realistic by introducing some simple but compellingly sensible modifications in the investment and tax revenue schedules employed. Dealing first with the investment function, it should be noted that the extent of utilization of existing plants and equipment is positively related to the level of income. Furthermore, businessmen's expectations of future business conditions are likely to be more optimistic when the economy is healthy. With these notions in mind, many macroeconomic analysts allege that business investment in new productive facilities is a positive function of income. A simple investment function that allows investment to change with income, but still accounts for the existence of an *autonomous* component of investment spending *not influenced by the level of economic activity,* is the straight-line function $I = \bar{I} + cY$, where $\bar{I}$ is the autonomous component of investment (representing, for example, investment that results from innovations); c, which could be called a "marginal propensity to invest," represents the *induced* response of investment to changes in the level of income; and Y is aggregate income as usual.

Turning now to the tax function, in practice government tax policy typically specifies not the total volume of tax receipts to be collected, but instead, the structure of tax *rates* with the revenues generated by the tax system changing as the level of income changes. A simple tax function that accounts for this behavior of tax receipts is the linear relationship $T = \bar{T} + tY$, where T is total tax revenues, $\bar{T}$ is the autonomous component of taxes, t is the marginal tax rate representing the response of tax collections to a change in income, and Y is total received income.

Altering the form of our tax and investment functions has little impact on the analytical framework we have employed for finding the equilibrium value of income. The schematic income flow diagram for our new model is the same as it was for the preceding model (Figure 4—3) because no new sources of leakages or injections have been introduced into that model. Thus, the basic conditions that must hold for equilibrium are the same (that is, $Y = C + I + G$, or equivalently, $S + T = I + G$).

Retaining the same behavioral assumptions for our other schedules but employing the modified investment and tax schedules, our model can be algebraically summarized as:

$$\left.\begin{array}{l} Y = C + I + G \\[4pt] S + T = I + G \end{array}\right\} \text{the equilibrium condition(s)}$$

$$\left.\begin{array}{l} C = a + bY_d \\ I = \bar{I} + cY \\ G = \bar{G} \\ T = \bar{T} + tY \end{array}\right\} \text{spending and tax functions.}$$

Plugging into the first form of the equilibrium condition for this model, a solution for the equilibrium level of income can be obtained as follows:

$$Y = C + I + G \text{ for equilibrium}$$

so

$$Y = a + bY_d + \bar{I} + cY + \overline{G}$$
$$= a + b(Y - T) + \bar{I} + cY + \overline{G}$$

or

$$Y = a + b(Y - \overline{T} - tY) + \bar{I} + cY + \overline{G}$$

where

$$Y_d = Y - T \text{ and } T = \overline{T} + tY.$$

Collecting the Y terms and moving them to the left side of our equality yields

$$Y(1 - b - c + bt) = a + \bar{I} + \overline{G} - b\overline{T},$$

and solving for Y alone yields the reduced form equilibrium equation

$$Y_{\text{eq.}} = \frac{1}{1 - b - c + bt}(a + \bar{I} + \overline{G} - b\overline{T}) \qquad [4\text{--}8]$$

or

$$Y_{\text{eq.}} = \frac{1}{1 - b(1 - t) - c}(a + \bar{I} + \overline{G} - b\overline{T}).$$

With numerical values for a, b, c, $\bar{I}$, $\overline{G}$, t, and $\overline{T}$, we could solve for the numerical value of equilibrium income. You should be able to prove that the same value for the equilibrium level of income can be derived from the alternative form of the equilibrium condition $(S + T = I + G)$.

There are many additional modifications that could be introduced into our income determination models. For example, as a next logical step the economy could be *opened* to permit international trade, the export of do-mestically produced goods and services and the import of their foreign pro-duced counterparts (indeed, a foreign sector will be built into the macro model in Chapter 15). However, the prime objective of the first half of this chapter has been to provide familiarity with the model-building process as applied in the construction of simple Keynesian income-determination models, and no further complexities need be entertained to acquire that familiarity. As our exercises have already demonstrated, the introduction of additional complexities in no way alters what we have determined to be the basic requirement for equilibrium in the market for goods and services. For equilibrium, there must be no unintended inventory changes (requiring equality of planned spending with output, and of planned injections with planned leakages). With unplanned additions to inventories, business firms will reduce output; and with the unplanned shrinkage of inventories, they will endeavor to raise production. With no more than a comprehension of the basic requirement for commodity market equilibrium and an ability to visualize income and spending flows, as we have done schematically in this chapter, you can construct models of surprising complexity which, with information on planned spending totals, can be used to predict income. Of course, every swing in production and income means accompanying swings in employment and unemployment.

Multiplier Analysis

We have now seen that we can build simple, mathematical models of the product market and solve for the equilibrium level of income with those models. This leads us to a question of direct importance to policy makers: What happens to the level of income if equilibrium is disturbed by a change in some parameter in the system (for example, a shift in the consumption, investment, government spending, or tax schedule)? The macroeconomist's construction for ascertaining the impact on equilibrium income of such shocks to the system is called the *multiplier*.

The Multiplier for Model I: A Closed Economy without Government

To develop the multiplier concept, let us return to our simplest model of the product market. In that model, there was no government and no foreign sector, consumption was a function of received income $(C = a + bY)$ because there were no taxes, and investment was exogenous $(I = \bar{I})$. Using Equation 4—4 or 4—5, the equilibrium level of income in that model was:

$$Y_{eq.} = \frac{1}{1 - b}(a + \bar{I})$$

or, in specific "numerical" terms,

$$Y_1 = \frac{1}{1 - b}(a_1 + \bar{I}_1)$$

for the particular *numerical* values of a and I, of $a = a_1$, and $\bar{I} = \bar{I}_1$. That equilibrium level of income appears in Figure 4—5, corresponding to the solid aggregate demand schedule $C_1 + \bar{I}_1$.

Suppose now that this equilibrium is disturbed by the shock of an increase in planned investment spending, reflected in the upward shift of the investment demand schedule from $\bar{I}_1$ to $\bar{I}_2$ in Figure 4—5. What happens to the equilibrium level of income as a result of this shift in the investment schedule?

An upward shift in the investment schedule requires an equivalent upward shift in the aggregate demand schedule (to $C_1 + I_2$ in Figure 4—5) because aggregate demand is the sum of C and I. With the aggregate demand schedule at $C_1 + \bar{I}_2$, the equilibrium level of income becomes Y_2. Thus, the

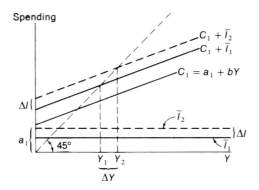

Figure 4—5 / Impact on Income of a Change in Investment

increase in investment in amount ΔI results in an increase in the equilibrium level of income of ΔY. The ratio of ΔY to ΔI (the *change* in income that results from a specified *change* in investment) gives the value of the *investment multiplier* (K_I). If the schedules in our graph were accurately constructed, by measurement of ΔY and ΔI we could obtain a numerical estimate of this multiplier's value.

Equivalently, and with less effort, the value of this investment multiplier can be obtained algebraically. Solving our equilibrium income condition using specific values of the consumption function intercept and investment $(a = a_1$ and $I = \bar{I}_1)$ gave us the specific value of equilibrium income:

$$Y_1 = \frac{1}{1-b}(a_1 + \bar{I}_1)$$

If we now let investment rise from $\bar{I}_1$ to $\bar{I}_2$, the equilibrium level of income becomes

$$Y_2 = \frac{1}{1-b}(a_1 + \bar{I}_2)$$

The *change* in income is

$$Y_2 - Y_1 = \frac{1}{1-b}(a_1 + \bar{I}_2) - \frac{1}{1-b}(a_1 + \bar{I}_1)$$

Collecting terms provides the measure of income change

$$\Delta Y = \frac{1}{1-b}(\cancel{a_1} + \bar{I}_2 - \cancel{a_1} - \bar{I}_1)$$

$$= \frac{1}{1-b}(\bar{I}_2 - \bar{I}_1)$$

or,

$$\Delta Y = \frac{1}{1 - b} \Delta I$$

Because the investment multiplier is simply $K_I = \Delta Y/\Delta I$, this expression for ΔY can be rearranged to yield[8]

$$K_I = \frac{\Delta Y}{\Delta I} = \frac{1}{1 - b} \qquad [4\!-\!9]$$

If the value of b were .75, the investment multiplier would have a value of 4, indicating that a $10 billion increase in investment would increase the equilibrium level of income by $40 billion (a *multiple* of the original shift in the investment schedule). The justification for the name "multiplier" for this concept should be clear. But why should a $10 billion increase in investment result in an even larger increase in total spending? A step by step answer to this question is provided just ahead, but basically it is because the $10 billion of extra investment spending is also extra income, inducing a further increase in consumption spending. Before proceeding, think about the impact of a $10 billion reduction in investment spending and be sure you know the value of the accompanying shrinkage in equilibrium income.

An Autonomous Shift in the Consumption Function. With planned investment unchanged, suppose our original equilibrium were disturbed by a parallel shift in the consumption function (a change in the autonomous component of consumption as a result, for example, of a change in consumer preferences). The impact of an upward shift in the consumption function by amount Δa is shown in Figure 4—6. A parallel upward shift in the consumption function shifts the aggregate demand schedule $(C + \bar{I})$ upward by the same vertical distance. As a result, the equilibrium level of income increases from Y_1 to Y_2 (by ΔY).

We can easily solve algebraically for the impact on income of the shift in the consumption function. Following a familiar sequence, we know

$$Y_1 = \frac{1}{1 - b} (a_1 + \bar{I}_1) \text{ for } a = a_1$$

and,

$$Y_2 = \frac{1}{1 - b} (a_2 + \bar{I}_1) \text{ for } a = a_2$$

---

[8]Students who have had differential calculus should recognize that attempting to find the *change* in the value of income that results from a *change* in investment simply requires the differentiation of the expression for equilibrium income with respect to investment. Thus, if $Y_{eq.} = [1/(1 - b)] (a + \bar{I})$, then $K_I = dY/d\bar{I} = 1/(1 - b)$.

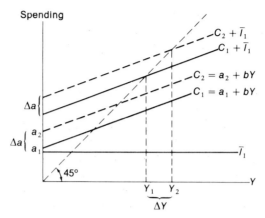

Figure 4—6 / Impact on Income of a Shift in the Consumption Function

Hence,

$$\Delta Y = Y_2 - Y_1 = \frac{1}{1-b}(a_2 + \bar{I}_1) - \frac{1}{1-b}(a_1 + \bar{I}_1)$$

$$= \frac{1}{1-b}(a_2 + \bar{I}_1 - a_1 - \bar{I}_1)$$

$$\text{or } \Delta Y = \frac{1}{1-b}\Delta a$$

Dividing this expression for ΔY by Δa to obtain the consumption multiplier yields

$$K_a = \frac{\Delta Y}{\Delta a} = \frac{1}{1-b}, \qquad\qquad [4\text{—}10]$$

the same value obtained above for the investment multiplier.[9] Indeed, <u>it does not matter whether the original autonomous change in spending is in consumption or investment; the impact on income is the same.</u>

The Logic of the Multiplier

So far, we have established the existence of the multiplier in a mechanical manner without attempting to explain the economic logic of the process by which an autonomous change in some spending schedule generates a multiple expansion of income. To illuminate that process, suppose we again

---

[9]Differentiating the equilibrium condition with respect to a, with $Y_{eq} = [1/(1-b)](a + \bar{I})$, the consumption multiplier is $K_a = dY/da = 1/(1-b)$.

disturb equilibrium in our model by letting investment increase, then trace the individual rounds of income expansion that ensue. Let businessmen increase their spending on plants, equipment, and inventories (that is, on investment goods) by some specified amount, say one dollar. A dollar increase in investment spending means one dollar of extra income to the recipients of that spending. As shown in "Round 2" of Table 4—1, the typical recipient of this new one dollar flow of income will spend part of the dollar and save part, passing on a reduced increment of new income ($1 × MPC) to the recipients of spending in this second round of the expansion process. The recipients of this new income (in amount $1 × MPC) will spend part (fraction MPC) and save part (fraction 1 − MPC), and so the process goes *ad infinitum*.

The remaining rows in Table 4—1 trace the overall expansion of spending (income) and saving. The numerical values in each round are generated assuming an MPC of .75. As shown there, summing the changes in spending and saving that take place in each round of adjustment yields an overall increase of four dollars in total spending and one dollar in saving in response to the original increment of one dollar in investment spending. These mathematical results are perfectly consistent with the requirement for macroeconomic equilibrium. With a marginal propensity to save of .25, income must rise by four dollars to *induce* a sufficient increase in the saving leakage ($4 × .25) to offset the original one dollar increase in investment.[10] Keeping in mind this spending expansion process that is responsible for the multiplier effect, we can proceed to develop multiplier formulas for more complicated models of the economic system. In the meantime, it should be recognized that the multiplier just developed for the simplest sort of economic system sheds light on some important policy issues. For example, with the economy in equilibrium at an output level that is $40 billion below full employment, the multiplier can reveal the amount by which planned investment by business firms or planned consumption by households would have to increase to restore full employment.

---

[10]Values for the total change in spending and saving can be derived algebraically quite easily by summing, over all rounds of adjustment, the increments in spending and saving respectively. For spending, the total change is (for $\Delta I = \$1$):

$$\text{Total } \Delta Y = \$1(1 + MPC + MPC^2 + MPC^3 + \cdots + MPC^n + \cdots).$$

From a well-known algebraic formula, the value of the sum of a geometric series of the form in parentheses is $1/(1 - MPC)$ for $MPC < 1$. Thus, $\Delta Y = \$1[1/(1 - MPC)]$, implying that the multiplier ($\Delta Y/\Delta I = \Delta Y/\$1$ in this case) is $1/(1 - b)$, as we have shown previously.

$$\Delta S = \$1 \cdot (1 - MPC)(1 + MPC + MPC^2 + MPC^3 + \cdots + MPC^n + \cdots).$$

Again, the value of the sum of the geometric series in parentheses is $1/(1 - b)$. Thus,

$$\begin{aligned}\Delta S &= \$1 \cdot (1 - MPC)[1/(1 - MPC)]\\ &= \$1(1)\\ &= \$1\end{aligned}$$

Table 4—1   Expansion of Income Through the Multiplier

Round	Overall Level of Investment	Change in Total Spending (Income)	Change in Saving
0	$\bar{I}$	0	0
1	$\bar{I} + \Delta I = \bar{I} + \$1$	$\$1$ (the original increase in investment)	
2	$\bar{I} + \Delta I = \bar{I} + \$1$	$\$1 \times MPC = .75$	$\$1 \times MPS = \$1(1 - MPC) = .25$
3	.	$\$1 \times MPC^2 = .56$	$\$1 \times MPC \times MPS = \$1 \times MPC(1 - MPC) = .19$
4	.	$\$1 \times MPC^3 = .42$	$\$1 \times MPC^2 \times MPS = \$1 \times MPC^2(1 - MPC) = .14$
5	.	$\$1 \times MPC^4 = .32$	$\$1 \times MPC^3 \times MPS = \$1 \times MPC^3(1 - MPC) = .10$
.	.	.	.
.	.	.	.
∞	.	.	.
Totals		$\$1 \times \dfrac{1}{1 - MPC} = \$4.00$	$\$1 \times \dfrac{(1 - MPC)}{(1 - MPC)} = \$1.00$

Multipliers for Model II: A Closed Economy with a Government Sector

Our second model of income determination was built for a closed economic system, but one that had a government with the power to collect taxes and spend. The addition of government spending and taxes makes this second model far more interesting than the simple model for, as indicated earlier, the government influences the economy through alterations in the levels of its spending and tax revenues. With investment, government spending, and total tax revenues determined exogenously, the equilibrium level of income for this model was

$$Y_{eq.} = \frac{1}{1 - b}(a + \bar{I} + \bar{G} - b\bar{T}) \qquad [4\text{--}11]$$

as indicated earlier in Equations 4—6 and 4—7.

The Spending Multiplier

For the specific values of the autonomous terms $a = a_1, \bar{I} = \bar{I}_1, \bar{G} = \bar{G}_1$, and $T = T_1$, equilibrium income in this second model is

$$Y_1 = \frac{1}{1 - b}(a_1 + \bar{I}_1 + \bar{G}_1 - b\bar{T}_1).$$

If investment should rise from $\bar{I}_1$ to $\bar{I}_2$, income would be

$$Y_2 = \frac{1}{1 - b}(a_1 + \bar{I}_2 + \bar{G}_1 - b\bar{T}_1).$$

Subtracting Y_1 from Y_2 yields

$$\Delta Y = Y_2 - Y_1$$
$$= \frac{1}{1 - b}(a_1 + \bar{I}_2 + \bar{G}_1 - b\bar{T}_1) - \frac{1}{1 - b}(a_1 + \bar{I}_1 + \bar{G}_1 - b\bar{T}_1)$$

or

$$\Delta Y = \frac{1}{1 - b}\Delta I$$

Thus, the investment multiplier must be

$$K_I = \frac{\Delta Y}{\Delta I} = \frac{1}{1 - b} \qquad [4\text{--}12]$$

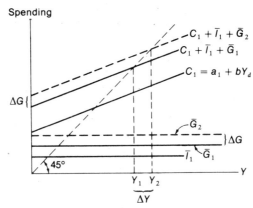

Figure 4—7 / Impact on Income of a Change in Government Spending

the same value that was obtained for the simple model (model I) without government. This is a sensible conclusion for, just as in model I, the only spending response that is induced by an income change in this model is a change in consumption. Repeating this derivation for a change in the autonomous component of consumption spending *or for a change in government spending* would yield the same result; like the investment multiplier, the consumption multiplier and the government spending multiplier for model II have a value of $1/(1 - b)$. It makes no difference whether the original change in spending is in the form of a change in investment, consumption, or government spending; the impact on income is the same.[11] Any first-round change in spending, no matter what its source, generates the same series of induced increments in spending. Thus, there is only one value for a particular model's *spending* multiplier, and there is no necessity to distinguish between consumption, investment, and government spending multipliers.

The impact of a change in one spending schedule, a change of amount ΔG in the government spending schedule, is illustrated graphically in Figure 4—7. As shown, an increase in government spending of ΔG leads to an increase in the equilibrium level of income of ΔY. As we already know, the value of the ratio $\Delta Y/\Delta G$, the spending multiplier for this model, is $1/(1 - b)$. With that knowledge, the change in government spending required to produce any selected change in the equilibrium level of output can be determined easily as $\Delta G = \Delta Y(1 - b)$ or $\Delta G = \Delta Y/K_{\text{spending}}$.

---

[11]With differential calculus we can quickly show this. If

$$Y_{\text{eq.}} = \frac{1}{1 - b}(a + \bar{I} + \overline{G} - b\overline{T})$$

then

$$K_a = \frac{dY}{da} = K_{\bar{I}} = \frac{dY}{d\bar{I}} = K_{\overline{G}} = \frac{dY}{d\overline{G}} = \frac{1}{1 - b}$$

The Tax Multiplier

In addition to wielding control over its expenditures, the government in our second model has the power to change the "lump sum" amount of tax revenues it collects. If it does so, the equilibrium level of income changes. Beginning with the economic system in equilibrium at income level Y_1, as shown in Figure 4—8, what will be the impact of an increase in taxes from $\overline{T}_1$ to $\overline{T}_2$ dollars?

An increase in taxes reduces disposable income by the amount of the increase in taxes (recall that $Y_d = Y - T$). Since consumption is a function of disposable income (Y_d), an increase in taxes that reduces disposable income would reduce consumption at every level of received income (Y). Graphically, this means a downward shift in our plotted consumption function.

By how much would the consumption function shift? By $\$\Delta T \cdot$ MPC at every level of income; that is, by the change in disposable income resulting from the tax change times the fraction of that income that would have been spent had it been left in the hands of consumers. The new consumption function (C_2) is shown in Figure 4—8. The parallel downward shift in the consumption function requires an equivalent downward shift in the aggregate demand schedule, establishing a new equilibrium level of income at Y_2 in Figure 4—8. Thus, an increase in tax receipts by amount ΔT leads to a *decrease* in income of ΔY. The ratio $\Delta Y/\Delta T$ can be called the tax multiplier, K_T.

Clearly, the tax multiplier ($K_T = \Delta Y/\Delta T$) is negative in value. We can readily demonstrate this fact and simultaneously derive a formula for finding the size of the tax multiplier by employing the same algebraic procedure used to evaluate spending multipliers.

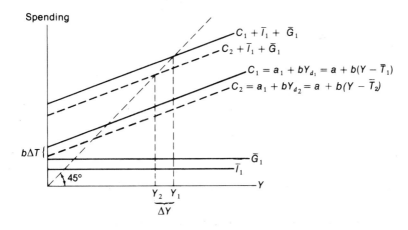

Figure 4—8 / Impact on Income of a Change in Taxes

For $a = a_1$, $I = \bar{I}_1$, $G = \bar{G}_1$, and $T = \bar{T}_1$, equilibrium income is

$$Y_1 = \frac{1}{1-b}(a_1 + \bar{I}_1 + \bar{G}_1 - b\bar{T}_1)$$

Similarly,

$$Y_2 = \frac{1}{1-b}(a_1 + \bar{I}_1 + \bar{G}_1 - b\bar{T}_2)$$

for $a = a_1$, $I = \bar{I}_1$, $G = \bar{G}_1$, and $T = \bar{T}_2$, which is greater than $\bar{T}_1$ by amount ΔT. Subtracting Y_1 from Y_2,

$$\Delta Y = Y_2 - Y_1 = \frac{1}{1-b}(a_1 + \bar{I}_1 + \bar{G}_1 - b\bar{T}_2) - \frac{1}{1-b}(a_1 + \bar{I}_1 + \bar{G}_1 - b\bar{T}_1)$$

or

$$\Delta Y = \frac{-b}{1-b}\Delta T$$

Dividing through by ΔT to obtain the tax multiplier yields

$$K_T = \frac{\Delta Y}{\Delta T} = -\frac{b}{1-b} \qquad [4\text{---}13]$$

or

$$K_T = -b\left(\frac{1}{1-b}\right) \qquad [4\text{---}14]$$

The tax multiplier is indeed negative and its value is smaller than that of the spending multiplier. For an MPC of .75, the tax multiplier has a value of -3.

In fact, in absolute size it is only b times as large as the spending multiplier. The reason for the smaller size of the tax multiplier can be readily seen by recalling our discussion of the logic of the multiplier. Unlike a shift in a spending schedule, which means an equivalent change in first-round spending in the multiplier adjustment process, a change in taxes alters first-round spending by only the MPC times the change in taxes. With the impact on first-round spending of a change in taxes only b times as large as the impact of an equal change in investment, consumption, or government spending, the overall change in income will be reduced to a value b times as great as the spending multiplier.[12]

Government Transfers. At this point, we can easily expand our comprehension of the government budget's impact on economic activity by recognizing that, in essence, government transfer payments are negative taxes. Like taxes, transfer payments do not directly affect aggregate demand but, instead, alter the volume of disposable income. A $100 increase in transfer payments generates first-round spending of $100 · MPC, which is then subject to the normal multiplier expansion process. Hence, the algebraic expression for a "transfer" multiplier $\left[K_{TR} = b/(1 - b) \right]$ shows that it is equal in magnitude but opposite in sign to the tax multiplier.[13]

In the interest of simplicity of exposition, we will consolidate our positive and negative tax collections as one variable, which, if you like, can be thought of as *net* tax collections (total tax revenues minus transfers). The value of this variable will always be positive (taxes always exceed transfers) but will change in response to either tax revenue or transfer payment changes. We will continue to use the letter T to represent (net) tax revenues.[14] What would be the impact on equilibrium income of an equal increase in both tax revenues and transfer payments?

---

[12]Using differential calculus to simplify our efforts, with

$$Y_{eq.} = \frac{1}{1 - b}(a + \bar{I} + \overline{G} - b\overline{T}), \; K_T = \left[\frac{1}{1-b} \right] \times \left[-b\left(\frac{d\overline{T}}{aT}\right) \right] = \frac{-b}{1-b}$$

[13]To the extent that the recipients of transfer payments have different MPCs from those of taxpayers, the aggregate impact of a one dollar change in taxes may differ from the impact of an equivalent change in transfers. It is, in fact, commonly alleged that recipients of transfer payments (social security payments, welfare payments, unemployment compensation, and so on), occupying the lower range of the income distribution, consume most or all of any change in income (that is, their MPC $\simeq$ 1). As a consequence, the numerical magnitude of the transfer multiplier would be closer to that of the government spending multiplier than to the tax multiplier. At this juncture, however, there is no need for us to distinguish between taxpayers and transfer recipients in our models.

[14]We are defining net taxes as tax revenues minus transfers. That is,

$$T = R - tr$$

where T is net taxes, R is tax revenues, and tr is transfers. The introduction of transfer payments has made the value of disposable income in our model equal to earned income minus taxes plus transfers, or

$$Y_d = Y - R + tr$$

which is simply

$$Y_d = Y - T$$

Thus, we have done nothing to alter the form of any of the models developed in this chapter. To make the models relevant for analysis of a system that has transfer payments, we simply need to think of our tax variable as a measure of *net* taxes, affected both by tax collections and transfers.

The Balanced Budget Multiplier

Having considered the independent effects of both government spending and tax alterations, we can now ask: What would be the impact on the equilibrium level of income of an equal change in government spending and tax revenues? Given that the spending multiplier has a value of $K = 1/(1 - b)$, a change in government spending changes income by $\Delta Y = 1/(1 - b) \cdot \Delta G$. Also, because the tax multiplier is $K_T = \Delta Y/\Delta T = -b/(1 - b)$, a change in tax revenues changes income by $\Delta Y = -b/(1 - b) \cdot \Delta T$. The total impact on income of a simultaneous change in both government spending and taxes is simply the sum of the two separate effects, or

$$\Delta Y = \frac{1}{1 - b} \cdot \Delta G - \frac{b}{1 - b} \cdot \Delta T$$

Because a "balanced budget" change in taxes and government spending requires an equal change in taxes and government spending ($\Delta G = \Delta T = \Delta B$ where ΔB is the "balanced" change in the size of the budget), we can substitute the common term (ΔB) for ΔG and ΔT. Doing so yields

$$\Delta Y = \frac{1}{1 - b} \cdot \Delta B - \frac{b}{1 - b} \cdot \Delta B$$
$$= \Delta B \cdot \frac{1 - b}{1 - b}$$

or

$$\Delta Y = \Delta B$$

The balanced budget multiplier must have a value of 1 no matter what the value of the marginal propensity to consume! That is

$$K_B = \frac{\Delta Y}{\Delta B} = 1 \qquad\qquad [4\text{—}15]$$

Quite logically, because the tax multiplier has a value that is 1 less in absolute value than the government spending multiplier, equal changes in government spending and tax revenues will change equilibrium income by precisely the same dollar amount no matter what the size of the MPC and no matter what the initial state of balance or imbalance in the budget. Tax collections reduce society's purchasing power, but if tax revenues are "respent," the purchasing power in the hands of consumers is exactly restored and the sequence of consumer spending is unaltered. Thus, total production is increased by the volume of additional goods and services government purchases when it enlarges its budget in a balanced fashion.[15] This same conclusion holds even in models that include an induced increase in taxes as income rises (as our model III does) so long as the increase in government spending is matched by the total increase in tax revenues when equilibrium has been restored.[16]

While real-world complications, including possible differences in the MPCs of taxpayers and government spending recipients, along with aggregate supply responses more complex than those permitted in this chapter, weaken the conclusion that the balanced budget multiplier has a value of precisely 1, the conclusion that equal changes in government spending and tax revenues exert a strong influence on the equilibrium level of output has played an important role in economic policy making. A notable illustration of the application of the balanced budget multiplier concept occurred in 1964. Early that year Congress enacted an $11 billion tax cut to stimulate the economy. Prior to its passage, opponents of the tax cut said they would favor the bill if government spending were cut by an equal amount. In response, the Council of Economic Advisors argued that cutting taxes and government spending by the same amount would not only fail to stimulate the economy but would result in a sharp contraction.

Multipliers for Model III: Investment and Tax Revenues Endogenous

We attempted to make our third model of income determination more realistic by allowing investment and tax revenues to respond positively to changes in the level of income. The functional relationships employed in that model were

$$C = a + bY_d$$

$$I = \bar{I} + cY$$

$$G = \bar{G}$$

$$T = \bar{T} + tY$$

---

[15]An equal change in government spending and tax revenues generates the following series of income changes in the model we are working with:

(1) ΔY from an increase in $G = \Delta G + \Delta G \cdot \text{MPC} + \Delta G \cdot \text{MPC}^2 + \cdots + \Delta G \cdot \text{MPC}^n + \cdots$

(2) ΔY from an increase in $T = -[0 + \Delta T \cdot \text{MPC} + \Delta T \cdot \text{MPC}^2 + \cdots + \Delta T \cdot \text{MPC}^n + \cdots]$

If $\Delta G = \Delta T$, all the terms on the right-hand side of the two series are the same except the term ΔG. Combining the two series for $\Delta G = \Delta T$ shows that overall $\Delta Y = \Delta G = \Delta T$.

[16]When taxes are a function of income, the *total* change in tax revenues when the size of the government's budget is altered consists in part of an autonomous change in taxes and in part of a change in tax revenue that occurs as income changes. A mathematical proof that the balanced budget multiplier has a value of 1 in this case can be found in T. F. Dernburg and Judith D. Dernburg, *Macroeconomic Analysis* (Reading, Mass.: Addison-Wesley, 1969), pp. 17–20.

with the variables defined as before. As it originally appeared in Equation 4—8, the equilibrium level of income for this model was

$$Y_{eq.} = \frac{1}{1 - b - c + bt}(a + \bar{I} + \bar{G} - b\bar{T}) \qquad [4\text{—}16]$$

The value of the spending multiplier for this model is

$$K_{spending} = K_a = K_I = K_G = \frac{1}{1 - b - c + bt} \qquad [4\text{—}17]$$

or

$$K_{spending} = \frac{1}{1 - b(1 - t) - c} \qquad [4\text{—}18]$$

a result you should be able to prove.[17] The multiplier for a change in taxes through a change in the autonomous component $(\bar{T})$ of tax collection is

$$K_T = -\frac{b}{1 - b - c + bt} = -b\left(\frac{1}{1 - b - c + bt}\right) \qquad [4\text{—}19]$$

or

$$K_{\bar{T}} = \frac{-b}{1 - b(1 - t) - c} \qquad [4\text{—}20]$$

Again, the impact of a change in taxes is weaker than, and opposite in direction to, the impact of an equivalent autonomous change in spending.[18]

---

[17]The calculus proof is simple:

$$K_{spending} = \frac{dY}{da} = \frac{dY}{d\bar{I}} = \frac{dY}{d\bar{G}} = \frac{1}{1 - b - c + bt}$$

[18]We might also be interested in the impact on equilibrium income of a change in the *marginal* tax rate (t). Of course, raising the marginal tax rate increases the total volume of taxes collected at any specified income level, inducing a contraction in equilibrium income, while reducing the tax rate lowers total tax collections stimulating income. Moreover, the first-round change in spending produced by a tax rate change depends on the initial level of income, so that the total multiplier effect of a tax rate change varies positively with the level of income. Differentiating the expression for equilibrium income with respect to t yields

$$\frac{dY}{dt} = -\frac{b(a + \bar{I} + \bar{G} - b\bar{T})}{(1 - b - c + bt)^2}$$

or $\dfrac{dY}{dt} = -\dfrac{b}{1 - b - c + bt} \cdot Y_{eq.}$ since $Y_{eq.} = \dfrac{a + \bar{I} + \bar{G} - b\bar{T}}{1 - b - c + bt}$

The size of the impact on Y of a change in t clearly depends on the level of income at which the economy is initially operating.

It is important to note, as some unfamiliar terms appear in the denominators of our multiplier expressions, that the sizes of both the spending and the tax multipliers for this model are different from the sizes of those respective multipliers derived for models I and II. We can readily account for the differences. If investment is a positive function of the level of income, an autonomous shift in any spending schedule will induce a spending response from investment as well as from consumption, as income changes. With both consumption and investment responding to movements in income, it is not surprising that the total change in spending brought about by an autonomous increase in spending is larger than it would be if only consumption responds to such movements. That the multiplier is larger with this positive investment response to income changes is apparent from the presence of the c term in the denominator of the multiplier formula (the c term makes the denominator smaller, thus the value of the multiplier larger).

In probing the logic of the multiplier process, we noted that, when equilibrium was disturbed, income would always have to adjust by enough to generate a change in leakages from the spending stream sufficient to offset the increment in injections into the spending stream. If tax receipts respond positively to changes in income, a *smaller* change in income is sufficient to generate the leakages (saving plus taxes) necessary to offset any increment in spending injections. That the multiplier is indeed weaker with taxes responding to income changes is apparent from the presence of the positive term bt (which appears only because taxes are assumed to respond to income changes) in the denominator of the multipliers derived in this section. In economic analysis, factors that decrease the size of the multiplier are frequently called *automatic stabilizers*. Such factors stabilize the economy in the sense that, for any shock to the system (any shift in a spending schedule), whether expansionary or contractionary, the size of the resulting *change* in aggregate output is reduced by their presence. The tax structure in this model would be such a stabilizer.

Equilibrium Income, the Multiplier, and Employment

As our last major task in this chapter, we can relate the changes in income that our multiplier analysis has dealt with to changes in employment by introducing the concept of an *aggregate production function*. The aggregate production function is simply the relationship between aggregate output and the inputs necessary to produce that output. Letting N be hours of labor and A the volume of nonlabor inputs (capital, land), the production function in algebraic terms is $Y = Y(N,A)$ with output (Y) positively related to both the number of hours of labor and the volume of nonlabor resources employed. In the short-run, the total stock of nonlabor inputs can be assumed to be constant and technological change can be ignored. Thus, the only way to change the volume of output is through changes in the volume of labor employed. For the short-run, then, the production function can be rewritten as $Y = Y(N)$. If the economy is operating with substantial excess capacity (that is, with underemployment of both labor and nonlabor inputs), a given percentage change in output could be associated with an approximately equal percentage change in *properly measured* employment. That is, we might expect essentially constant returns to *fully utilized* labor and capital inputs as larger volumes of those inputs are put to work because idle labor could be put to work with existing, but idle, nonlabor inputs. Of course, to the extent that business firms hoard partially idle labor during periods of depressed economic activity, an expansion of employment as measured in the United States can yield an even greater percentage increase in output. In fact, as indicated in Chapter 3, output per hour of measured employment typically does rise during economic expansions as employed workers are more fully utilized, and, as a consequence, total output expands by a larger percentage than employment does. As the level of economic activity expands toward full utilization of the nonlabor factors of production, larger increments in labor utilization become necessary for attaining specified additions to output. (We are in the region of diminishing returns.) To know precisely the impact on employment of any particular change in the level of output, we would need empirical knowledge of the exact form of the production function. At the moment, however, it is sufficient to note that for our multiplier analysis to indicate that output is increasing, it must also be indicating an increase in employment.[19] The analysis in this chapter indicates that, if the government wants to alter the level of employment (or unemployment), it can do so by changing government spending, taxes, or both. Remember, though, that this chapter deals with models that are too simplified to represent an actual economy except under some quite special circumstances.

The Size of the Multiplier

By estimating the size of the behavior parameters in our multiplier models (the MPC, the marginal tax rate, and so on), we can obtain numerical values for our multipliers. Keynes himself believed the spending multiplier for the United States had a value between 2.5 and 3.[20] Other investigators have typically found multiplier values for periods of normal economic activity to lie between 2 and 3 1/2. Paul Davidson's estimate of the spending multiplier yields a value of 2.11.[21] Arthur Okun, one-time member of the President's

---

[19]It is also worth recalling from the discussion in Chapter 3 that every increase in measured employment need not decrease measured unemployment. It would if the labor force were constant, but it is not. Instead, the size of the measured labor force itself depends on the rate of unemployment. If additional employment opportunities become available, tending to lower unemployment, labor force participation tends to increase; that is, housewives, teenagers, and other categories of "discouraged workers" will actively enter the labor force as employment opportunities improve. See T. Dernburg and K. Strand, "Hidden Unemployment, 1953–1962; A Quantitative Analysis by Age and Sex," *The American Economic Review* 56, (1966): 71–95.

[20]See Keynes, *The General Theory of Employment*, pp. 127–128.

[21]Paul Davidson, "Income and Employment Multipliers, and the Price Level," *The American Economic Review* 52 (1962): 738–752.

Council of Economic Advisors, has estimated the spending multiplier to have a value of 3.[22] With a model that allows the time path of output's response to spending changes to be tracked, the Bureau of Economic Analysis (BEA) has projected the response of real output to changes in government purchases of goods and services. Based on historical experience in the 1955–1974 period, the peak response of output to changes in government purchases of privately produced goods and services has averaged 3.4 times the increase in spending according to BEA estimates.[23] The value of the tax multiplier is, of course, one less than the value of the spending multiplier in simple commodity market models constructed in this chapter.

Complicating matters, the multiplier's value is likely to change over the business cycle as businesses' *investment* responses to change in aggregate demand vary with the stage of the cycle and because changes in demand elicit changes in real output and prices in proportions that vary with business conditions. As an illustration, the Bureau of Economic Analysis model projects a peak real output response of 3.8 times the change in government purchases in an economy with "high" (8 percent) unemployment, but a peak response of 2.5 (and, ultimately, a negative response) times the change in government purchases when unemployment is low (4 1/2 percent).

If the government budget is to be used deliberately to alter the level of economic activity, good estimates of multiplier values are a necessity. If, for example, aggregate output is $25 billion below the full employment level and we want to know how much to change government spending or tax collections to achieve full employment, we need to know the values of the government spending and tax multipliers. With those values, the required dose of budget adjustment can be prescribed. If the spending multiplier were 2.5, a $10 billion increase in government spending would increase output to the full employment level (remember, $K_G = \Delta Y/\Delta G$ or $\Delta Y = K_G \cdot \Delta G$). What change in taxes would provide full employment?

With the correct set of fixed numerical values for the tax and spending multipliers, the policy maker's task of prescribing government spending and tax programs for altering aggregate output and employment would be a straightforward arithmetic exercise. Unfortunately, not enough is known about the size or timing of the impact of budget changes to make fiscal control measures simple.[24] That is so even though a great deal of research effort with models of varying degrees of complexity has focused on the economy's response to changes in spending and tax levies. This note of humility should serve to reinforce our earlier suggestion that the models constructed in this chapter are simplistic. Even the most complex model in

[22]U.S. Congress, Joint Economic Committee, *State of the Economy and Policies for Full Employment*, 87th Congress, 2nd Session, 1962, p. 199.

[23]See Albert A. Hirsch, ''Policy Multiplier in the BEA Quarterly Econometric Model,'' *Survey of Current Business*, June 1977, pp. 60–72.

[24]The Hirsch article cited above contains a simple exposition on the time path of output's response to changes in spending, taxes, and so on.

this chapter treated the supply of real goods and services as passive, ignored international trade, and took no account of the economic impact of changes in the supply of money. Multipliers that are to be used for real-world policy making must take account of these complications. Further, for policy purposes we must know more than the impact on equilibrium income of a specific government expenditure or tax policy action, because it takes time for the economy to adjust from one equilibrium to another. We need to know the timing of the income response to policy actions as well as the size of that response.

The Price Level

So far we have also failed to discuss any price level response to changes in the level of output. That omission has been possible only because it has been tacitly assumed that the economic systems we are analyzing are operating with substantial excess capacity. In that case, any increase in aggregate demand might be satisfied by an increase in real output with little or no change in the price level. However, as the economy approaches full employment it becomes increasingly difficult to meet growing demand with an increase in output. Clearly, if the economy were operating at full capacity so that output could not expand, any increase in aggregate demand would have to result in an increased price level. There is much more that we need to say about the behavior of the price level. We will, however, delay any involved discussion of that topic until Chapter 9.

Case in Point II

The Multiplier in the Depression Era

While a complete explanation of macroeconomic events in the decade following 1929 would be quite involved, the fundamental macroeconomic forces that were at work during that depression era can be vividly clarified through application of the multiplier concept. In 1929, GNP was $103.1 billion and investment was $16.2 billion, or about 16 percent of GNP. Ignoring price changes to keep our illustration simple, four years later, with a collapse of business confidence, investment had declined to just $1.4 billion and GNP to $55.6 billion. Changes in autonomous consumption and in the government budget were rather minor during this period, so the direct cause of the $47.5 billion contraction in GNP that had idled 25 percent of the labor force by 1933 was, by and large, the $14.8 billion decline in investment. The spending multiplier appears to have had a value of around 3 in this period

$$(k = \frac{\Delta Y}{\Delta I} = \frac{47.5}{14.8} = 3.2).$$

With the multiplier concept in mind, Keynes urged the Roosevelt government to increase government spending to stimulate the economy, and it is often assumed that the government became actively involved in fiscal stimulus during that period. A glance at government budget data, however, suggests otherwise. From 1932 to 1938 (the end of Roosevelt's second term), government spending rose by $2.4 billion. With a multiplier of 3, this would raise GNP by just over $7 billion, not nearly enough to restore full employment. Moreover, at the same time the government increased its tax collections by $5 billion, negating the stimulus from added spending, in an effort to maintain a *balanced* government budget.

Finally, in the 1940s, a test of the potency of large changes in the government budget during a deep depression situation occurred. From 1940 to 1944 government spending swelled from $9.6 billion to $94.0 billion, and the budget deficit widened from $2.7 billion to $46.1 billion as taxes were not raised in step. During that period, GNP rose from $100 billion to $210.5 billion and full employment was restored. Of course, this was not the result of a sudden acceptance of Keynesian doctrine by policy makers but the side effect of America's involvement in World War II. The experience, however, vividly demonstrated the potency of fiscal actions in a depression period when the simple models developed in this chapter come closest to adequately representing reality.

Summary

In this chapter, attention has been focused on one market: the commodity market. We have built models of the commodity market for economic systems of varying complexity to find: (1) how the equilibrium level of income is determined and what its value is; and (2) how the equilibrium level of income changes in response to autonomous changes in consumption, investment, government spending, and tax collections. Equilibrium in these models could exist only when total planned spending was exactly equal to the value of output (i.e., when any leakages out of the spending stream were offset by equal injections). The equilibrium level of income was increased by an increase in consumption, investment, or government spending, or by a decrease in taxes. Conversely, income was reduced by a reduction in C, I, or G, or by an increase in taxes. The size of the multipliers depended on the values of the MPC, the marginal propensity to invest (MPI), and the marginal tax rate *(t)*, with their size enlarged by a bigger MPC and MPI but reduced by a larger *t*. We also showed that, with estimates of these parameters, we could solve for values of the spending multiplier and the tax multiplier, constructs that have important implications for government policy.

While the mechanics of model construction presented in this chapter are essential to the construction of macroeconomic models suitable for policy application, we cannot claim to have constructed such models at this time. Most importantly, the models we have constructed relegate the entire supply side of the economy to a minor and passive role. In addition, these models have not taken account of the role of international trade, and they have completely ignored the role of the nation's money supply. Further, our behavioral assumptions have not been quantified using observed values of income, consumption, investment, and so on. Quantification would suggest that the multiplier processes we have reviewed take a substantial amount of calendar time and might convince you that the level of aggregation has been pushed too far. Whatever the shortcomings of the models we have constructed, they clearly demonstrate the paramount importance of planned spending in determining the level of economic activity. In deference to this role, a substantial portion of this text is devoted to explaining the behavioral relations that generate final spending on consumption, investment, government purchases, and net exports.

Taking a quick look ahead, in Chapter 5 the determinants of personal consumption in a complex modern economy are examined. While a number of potential determinants of consumption, including wealth, interest rates, and the distribution of income, are considered, disposable personal income remains the key consumption determining variable, as it was in this chapter.

The determinants of business investment in plant and equipment are dealt with in Chapter 6. The arguments will indicate that we must, in any serious attempt at modeling a modern economy, rely on an investment-demand relationship that is considerably more complicated than the one employed in this chapter.

Chapter 7 allows the introduction of the role of money into our analysis by focusing on the role the interest rate plays in determining the level of economic activity. The following two chapters, which rely on information from Chapters 4–7, build fairly sophisticated income determination models. As was the case with the simple models in this chapter, the more sophisticated models constructed in Chapters 8 and 9 will be "Keynesian" or "post-Keynesian" models.

Over the years, Keynesian analysis has had, and continues to have, its critics, many of them prominent economists. And modern macroeconomics has been influenced to a substantial degree by *non-Keynesians,* as we shall see in future chapters. Yet, mainstream macroeconomic analysis has been dominated by the analytical framework developed by Keynes in *The General Theory.* As though he could predict the influence his analysis would have even long after his death, in his own "modest" appraisal of *The General Theory,* Keynes asserted:

I believe myself to be writing a book on economic theory that will largely revolutionize—not, I suppose, at once but in the course of the next ten years —the way the world thinks about economic problems.[25]

---

[25]Letter from J. M. Keynes to George Bernard Shaw, New Year's Day, 1935. Quoted in John K. Galbraith, "How Keynes Came to America," in *Readings in Economics,* ed. Paul Samuelson, 7th ed. (New York: McGraw-Hill, 1973) pp. 91–96. This article is an excellent description of the process by which Keynesian analysis came to be embraced in America.

Questions

1. At one point in this chapter, we claimed that measured saving and investment are always equal while at other times we argued that the equality of saving and investment is necessary for the economy to be in equilibrium. Explain this apparent inconsistency.

2. A change in inventory investment is the adjustment mechanism that ensured equality of realized saving and investment in our simple model. Explain.

3. In the table below, there is data on planned consumption and investment for a closed economy with no government.

Income	Consumption	Investment
in billions	in billions	in billions
$ 0	$ 50	$25
100	125	25
200	200	25
300	275	25

   a. Find the equilibrium value of income for this model both algebraically and graphically.
   b. Derive the spending multiplier formula and calculate its value.
   c. Determine the equilibrium values of consumption, saving, and investment.
   d. Explain the adjustment that would occur should current income be less than equilibrium income.

4. The last problem you had to solve ignored the existence of government. Suppose we introduce a government sector into the model in Question 3, letting the government spend $50 billion and collect $50 billion in taxes.
   a. Using whatever parameter values you need from your solution to Question 3, find the new equilibrium value of output.
   b. Derive the formulas for the government spending and tax multipliers and calculate their values.
   c. Find the equilibrium values for C, S, and I.

5. Assume the government spending multiplier has a value of 3 and the tax multiplier a value of -2.
   a. Find the impact on equilibrium income of a $20 billion increase in government spending; of a $20 billion reduction in tax collections.
   b. If equilibrium output is $30 billion below the target (full employment) level, what change in government spending could eliminate the gap? What change in tax collections would have the same effect?
   c. How would a $15 billion reduction in both tax revenues and government spending affect output? How do you know?

6. See whether you can sketch the flow diagrams and identify the equilibrium conditions for:

   a. A closed economy with a government that taxes but does not spend.
   b. A closed economy with a government that spends but does not tax.
   c. An open economy (one with exports and imports) with no government.

7. What difference does it make if investment depends on the level of output or does not? Explain.

8. What difference does it make if net tax revenues depend on the level of aggregate income or do not? Explain.

9. How would a step-up in military spending affect economic activity? A cutback in military spending? What tax policies could be used to offset those government spending changes?

10. Because, in reality, tax revenues vary with the level of income, an autonomous shift in any spending schedule results in a change in tax revenues. For example, a fall in investment lowers income through the multiplier, in turn reducing tax revenue. Analyze the implications of requiring the government to maintain a balanced budget (tax revenue and spending equal) in the face of shifts in non-governmental spending schedules. Is that requirement likely to enhance or reduce economic stability?

Suggested Readings

Friedman, Milton. "Weak Links in the Multiplier Chain." In *Capitalism and Freedom*. Chicago: University of Chicago Press, 1962. Reprinted in *The Battle Against Unemployment*, edited by Arthur Okun. Revised edition. New York: W.W. Norton & Co., 1972.

Goodwin, Richard M. "The Multiplier." In *The New Economics*, edited by Seymour E. Harris, pp. 482–499. New York: Alfred A. Knopf, 1947.

Heller, Walter W. *New Dimensions in Political Economy*, Chapter 2. New York: W. W. Norton & Co., 1967.

Hirsch, Albert A. "Policy Multipliers in the BEA Quarterly Econometric Model." *Survey of Current Business*, June 1977, pp. 60–72.

Machlup, Fritz. "Period Analysis and Multiplier Theory." *Quarterly Journal of Economics* 54 (1939): 1–27. Reprinted in *Readings in Business Cycle Theory*, pp. 203–234. Philadelphia: Blakiston Co., 1944.

Musgrave, Richard. *The Theory of Public Finance*, Chapter 18. New York: McGraw-Hill, 1959.

President's Council of Economic Advisers. "The Workings of the Multiplier." In *The Battle Against Unemployment*, edited by Arthur Okun. Revised edition. New York: W.W. Norton & Co., 1972.

Samuelson, Paul A. "The Simple Mathematics of Income Determination." In *Income, Employment, and Public Policy, Essays in Honor of Alvin H. Hansen*. This selection is reprinted in *Readings in Macroeconomics*, edited by M. G. Mueller, pp. 24–36. 2nd edition. New York: Holt, Rinehart and Winston, 1971.

Chapter 5

The Consumption Function

The models of income determination developed in the last chapter demonstrated that planned consumption plays an integral role in the determination of aggregate demand, and thus of income. That role is retained in all Keynesian income-determination models, including the most sophisticated variants. It goes without saying that, to construct Keynesian macroeconomic models which can be relied on to predict economic developments and to tailor policy prescriptions to the economy's needs, a clear understanding of the consumption function is needed; we must know what the determinants of consumption are and how consumption responds to changes in its determinants. Paralleling these concerns, we need to know whether consumption spending is subject to abrupt, hard-to-predict changes so that it is a source of economic instability, or whether consumption exerts a steadying influence on economic activity. These are the primary concerns of this chapter. By explaining the behavior of consumption, we will be simultaneously explaining the behavior of saving, because any income that is not consumed is, by definition, saved. Thus, we can discuss the consumption function and the saving function simultaneously and interchangeably.

Income-Consumption and Income-Saving Functions

The models constructed in Chapter 4 employed a simple, linear consumption function. Although some repetition of effort is involved, the analysis in this chapter will begin by looking a bit more intensively at that simple function.

While we have ignored the point up to now, there are obviously factors other than income that can affect consumption demand. Thus, the simple linear relationship we assumed to hold between income and consumption in Chapter 4 must be qualified. The formal hypothesis we implicitly employed was that *ceteris paribus* (other things held constant), *real* consumption spending[1] is a linear function of *real* disposable income as reflected in the equation

$$C = a + bY_d$$

Because saving is income less consumption, it follows that saving is also a linear function of real disposable income. Algebraically, saving must be

$$S = Y_d - C$$
$$= Y_d - (a + bY_d)$$

or

$$S = -a + (1 - b)Y_d \qquad\qquad [5\text{--}1]$$

As shown in Chapter 4, with a positive value for the intercept *(a)*, and with a value of the slope *(b)* that is positive but less than 1, the consumption and saving functions would plot like those in Figure 5—1. The slope of the consumption function, called the *marginal propensity to consume* (MPC), measures the response of real consumption spending to a change in real income. Symbolically, that response is

$$\text{MPC} = \frac{\Delta C}{\Delta Y_d} = b$$

The slope of the saving function, the *marginal propensity to save* (MPS), measures the response of saving to changes in income. Symbolically, the

---

[1] For some purposes a different concept of consumption would be more appropriate. If our objective were to measure the actual using-up (consumption) of final products, we would be better off to break down aggregate expenditure into spending on nondurables (eggs, bacon, balloons, and so on) and spending on durables (autos, refrigerators, washing machines, and so on). Because only a part of a durable good is used up in a typical accounting period (one-fifth of an auto if the accounting period is one year and the auto's life is five years), actual consumption (using-up of products) is the sum of expenditure on nondurables and depreciation (using-up) of durables, not total expenditure on final products.

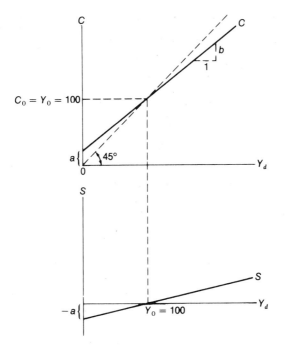

Figure 5—1 / Consumption and Saving Functions

MPS is MPS $=\Delta S/\Delta Y_d = (1-b)$.[2] Further, because every one dollar change in income must either be consumed or saved, the MPC and the MPS must sum to one. That is, because

$$\Delta Y_d = \Delta C + \Delta S$$

dividing through by ΔY_d yields

$$1 = \frac{\Delta C}{\Delta Y_d} + \frac{\Delta S}{\Delta Y_d}$$

or

$$1 = \text{MPC} + \text{MPS} \qquad\qquad [5-2]$$

It should be clear that accurate measures of the marginal propensities to consume and save would be of great value in macroeconomics forecasting and policy planning. As an illustration for the simplest macro models built in Chapter 4, the multiplier value would be $1/(1-b) = 1/(1-.75) = 4$ if the MPC is .75 and twice as large $\left[1/(1-b) = 1/(1-.88) = 8 \right]$ if the MPC is .88.

---

[2]Students with a background in calculus will recognize that the marginal propensities to consume and save are the first derivatives of the consumption and saving functions, respectively, with respect to disposable income. For $C = a + bY_d$, MPC $= dC/dY_d = b$ and for $S = -a + (1-b)Y_d$, MPS $= dS/dY_d = (1-b)$.

We also need to define *average* propensities to consume and save. The *average propensity to consume* (APC) is simply the portion of the average dollar of income that is consumed, symbolically represented as

$$APC = \frac{C}{Y_d}$$

The *average propensity to save* (APS) is the fraction of the average dollar of income that is saved. Thus,

$$APS = \frac{S}{Y_d} = \frac{Y_d - C}{Y_d} \text{ since } S = Y_d - C.$$

Making the division indicated in this expression for the APS yields,

$$APS = 1 - \frac{C}{Y_d}$$

or

$$APS = 1 - APC \qquad [5\text{—}3]$$

reflecting the fact that the portion of the average income dollar that is not spent must be saved.

With values for the parameters a and b, we can formally graph the consumption and saving functions, trace those schedules in tabular form, or leave them in algebraic form. For example, with $a = 20$ and $b = .8$, consumption is $C = 20 + .8Y_d$ and saving is $S = -20 + .2Y_d$. These are the specific functions that were used to plot the schedules in Figure 5—1. In addition, these schedules were used to provide the values for consumption, saving, and the propensities to consume and save entered in Table 5—1. Quite apparently, what is known about consumption and saving behavior can be conveyed in a number of different formats with no loss of information. You might also note that, for the particular consumption and saving functions represented in Table 5—1, the MPC and MPS are constant while, with an increase in income, the APC falls and the APS rises.

Table 5—1 / Propensities to Consume and Save for a Specific Consumption (Saving) Function

Y_d	$C =$ $(20 + .80Y_d)$	$S =$ $(-20 + .20Y_d)$	APC $= \left(\frac{C}{Y_d}\right)$	APS $= \left(\frac{S}{Y_d}\right)$	MPC $= \left(\frac{\Delta C}{\Delta Y_d}\right)$	MPS $= \left(\frac{\Delta S}{\Delta Y_d}\right)$
0	20	−20	−	−		
50	60	−10	1.2	−.2	.8	.2
100	100	0	1.0	0	.8	.2
150	140	10	.93	.07	.8	.2
200	180	20	.90	.10	.8	.2

Other Forms of Consumption and Saving Functions

While the consumption function we have employed up to this point served us well in the simple models of Chapter 4, it should be recognized that other forms are possible, perhaps even more realistic. Two alternative, but still simple, consumption functions are plotted in Figures 5—2 and 5—3. The function in Figure 5—2 is a variant of the linear function that has a zero vertical intercept. For such a function the APC and MPC are equal to each other and are constant as income changes. This would be referred to as a *proportional consumption function* because the same proportion of income is consumed at every income level along the function. In contrast, a straight-line consumption function that has a positive intercept (i.e., the consumption function we have employed to this point) is *nonproportional*. We could also have a nonlinear function like the one plotted in Figure 5—3, reflecting the tendency of both the MPC and APC to fall as disposable income rises. The possibility that this shape is the appropriate one for the aggregate consumption function is ominous, for as income grows over time a larger fraction of income is saved.[3] To avoid *stagnation* in economic activity due to slack aggregate demand, this growing proportional difference

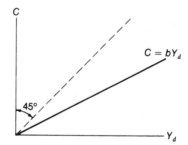

Figure 5—2 / A Linear
Consumption Function with Zero Intercept

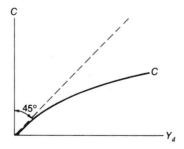

Figure 5—3 / A Nonlinear
Consumption Function with Zero Intercept

[3]It is also true for the function graphed in Figure 5—1 that the fraction of income saved rises as the level of income rises. However, for the function graphed in Figure 5—3, the gap between income and consumption widens at an increasing rate as income rises.

between income and consumption would have to be made up by some other form of spending (for example, private investment or government spending). The higher income becomes, the greater the burden imposed on nonconsumption spending. In the immediate post-depression period of the 1930s a number of prominent economists were concerned that the U.S. propensity to save would outrun the inducement to invest, resulting in a chronic depression of economic activity.[4] Happily, the dour predictions of the "stagnationists" have not been fulfilled.

It is apparent that different forms of the consumption function are possible, and that these differences in form can give rise to important differences in implications for government policy. The rest of this chapter reviews what economists have learned about the precise form of the aggregate consumption function beginning with Keynes' own description of that function.

The Appropriate Form of the Consumption Function

Keynes' absolute income theory of the consumption function is described quite succinctly in *The General Theory*. According to Keynes:

The fundamental psychological law, upon which we are entitled to depend with great confidence both *a priori* from our knowledge of human nature and from the detailed facts of experience, is that men are disposed, as a rule and on the average, to increase their consumption as their income increases, but not by as much as the increase in their income. . . .

Apart from short-period *changes* in the level of income, it is also obvious that a higher absolute income will tend, as a rule, to widen the gap between income and consumption. For the satisfaction of the immediate primary needs of man and his family is usually a stronger motive than the motives toward accumulation, which only acquire effective sway when a margin of comfort has been attained. These reasons will lead, as a rule, to a greater *proportion* of income being saved as real income increases.[5]

Thus, for Keynes, $C = f(Y_d)$ such that $0 < \text{MPC} < 1$. The APC was expected to fall as income rose. With which of the specific forms of the consumption function discussed above is this hypothesis consistent?

This was a firmly stated if not very restrictive hypothesis that, with data on disposable income and consumption, could be statistically tested. Unfortunately, adequate observations on the levels of aggregate income and consumption that the economy had enjoyed over time were not available in the 1930s. Without appropriate time series data, empirically oriented economists in the late 1930s and early 1940s had to rely heavily on cross-section

---

[4]This stagnation thesis is most often associated with Alvin H. Hansen. See A. H. Hansen, "Economic Progress and Declining Population Growth," *The American Economic Review* 29 (1939): 1–15, reprinted in *Readings in Macroeconomics,* ed. M. G. Mueller, 2nd ed. (New York: Holt, Rinehart and Winston, 1971), pp. 265–276.

[5]John Maynard Keynes, *The General Theory of Employment, Interest, and Money* (New York: Harcourt Brace Jovanovich, 1936), pp. 96–97.

data for testing and quantifying consumption function hypotheses. Specifically, from cross-sectional family budget surveys of the population conducted in 1935–1936, and again in 1941–1942, observations on the level of disposable income and the associated level of consumption spending were obtained for individual families. Until the World War II era, economists employed those cross-section surveys in empirical studies of the consumption function. If the families surveyed in the budget studies are divided into groups by income level (for example, those with incomes between $3,000 and $3,500 per year could constitute one group), a plot of average family consumption spending versus average disposable income for the selected ranges of disposable income yields an income-versus-family consumption curve of the form shown in Figure 5—4. While this function is consistent with Keynes' requirements, we should have little faith in this evidence from cross-section data as corroboration of a Keynesian consumption function. The consumption-income relationship we need is one that tells us how *aggregate* consumption (by all families) depends on *aggregate* disposable income (received by all families). The function plotted in Figure 5—4 tells us how *different families* at different levels of income divide their income between consumption and saving.[6]

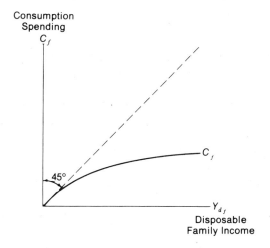

**Figure 5—4 / Average Family
(Budget Study) Consumption Function**

[6]To conclude that the results from budget study data provide strong support for the Keynesian consumption function we would have to be willing to accept some rather strong assumptions. Most notably, we would have to assume that families are quite homogeneous in terms of spending desires across broad ranges of income levels, and we would have to assume that *relative income* (a concept to be developed later in this chapter) is unimportant as a determinant of consumer behavior.

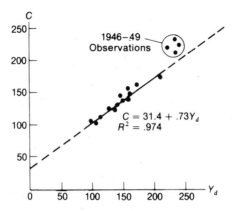

**Figure 5—5 / The Consumption Function
from Time Series Data, 1929–1941 (Data in Billions)**

By the early 1940s, enough annual measures of aggregate income and consumption had become available (such figures were compiled beginning in 1929) to provide a much needed time series test of the Keynesian consumption function hypothesis. As shown in Figure 5—5, the time series data available through 1941 provided support for a simple, linear consumption function consistent with Keynesian assumptions. Consumption was shown to rise as income rose, but the consumption rise was less than the income rise, and the proportion of income consumed appeared to decline with income growth.

Seemingly supported by both time series and cross-sectional data, the simple, linear consumption function, exhibiting a gap between income and consumption that widened with income growth, was widely employed in macroeconomic forecasts made during the middle 1940s. However, faith in that function was short-lived. With a postwar cutback in government spending anticipated, many economists predicted a severe economic slump at war's end. In fact, there was a postwar boom fueled by a volume of consumption spending substantially larger than the level predicted by extrapolating the consumption function in Figure 5—5 forward to higher income levels. (The levels of actual consumption and disposable income for 1946–1949 are plotted in Figure 5—5 for comparison.)

Extrapolating the aggregate consumption functions that had been fitted to *interwar* data backward also provided highly suspicious predictions for consumption spending. In fact, with the consumption function in Figure 5—5, at any income level below $116 billion consumption exceeds current output, a possibility only if society consumes its accumulated wealth; and it is hard to imagine society doing that on an extended basis. Moreover, during World War II Simon Kuznets generated additional annual observations on disposable income and saving (consumption) backward in time to 1869, and that data indicated there had been no long-run change in the proportion of income consumed even though income had quadrupled between 1869 and 1929.[7]

We can readily update the conclusions from time series data that the crude empirical investigations conducted through the early 1940s provided. When regression analysis is employed to fit a consumption function to aggregate data over a long time span (including the span from 1869 to the present) a straight-line function that emanates from a point near the origin results (just like the hypothetical consumption function in Figure 5—2). As you already know, the marginal and average propensities to consume are equal and constant for such a function, as are the marginal and average propensities to save.

Clearly, the long-run or *secular* consumption function is inconsistent with Keynes' belief that a larger proportion of income would be saved as the level of aggregate income rose. However, we can also fit consumption functions to shorter time periods (like the interwar and postwar periods). Doing so yields flatter consumption functions (functions with positive intercepts), each of which by itself is consistent with the Keynesian specification of the income-consumption relationship.

A graph of consumption functions fitted to an extended time period (denoted by C_s for secular consumption function) and to shorter time periods (denoted by C_c for cyclical consumption function) would appear as shown in Figure 5—6A. It appears that the short-run (cyclical) consumption function, marked with a c subscript, is flatter than the long-run relationship, with the short-run function somehow shifting upward over time to yield the observed long-run function. The differences in the properties of secular and short-run consumption functions are exaggerated for expository purposes in Figure 5—6A. In Figure 5—6B, the short-run consumption function from Figure 5—5 is replotted along with another cyclical function fitted to data from 1946–1978. Comparing the postwar function to the extension of the prewar schedule makes it apparent that the short-run function has shifted substantially. Modern research on consumption functions has focused on reconciling the apparent conflict between short- and long-run evidence and on providing a theoretically more complete consumption behavior model than that implied by the simple Keynesian hypothesis. A satisfactory model of consumption behavior must meet a quite restrictive set of requirements, not only reconciling nonproportional short-run and proportional long-run consumption schedules, but also permitting cross-sectional income-consumption patterns that are consistent with budget study data, and accounting for the higher than predicted postwar consumption level. Our basic concern in the rest of this chapter is in developing an understanding of

---

[7]See Simon Kuznets, *Uses of National Income in Peace and War* (New York: National Bureau of Economic Research, 1942). Similar results were later obtained by Raymond Goldsmith for consumption and *personal* income. According to Goldsmith, a "main enduring characteristic [of saving behavior is] long-term stability of aggregate personal saving at approximately one-eighth of income." See Goldsmith, *A Study of Saving in the United States,* vol. 1 (Princeton, N.J.: Princeton University Press for the National Bureau of Economic Research, 1955), p. 22.

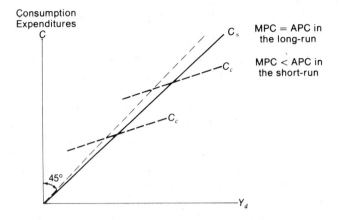

Figure 5—6A / The Long-Run and Short-Run (Secular and Cyclical) Consumption Functions

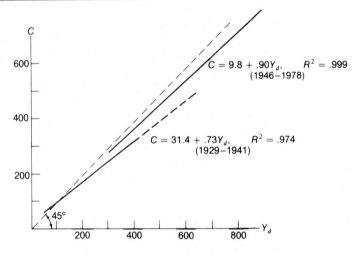

Figure 5—6B / Actual Cyclical Consumption Functions for 1929–1941 and 1946–1978 (measured in billions of 1958 dollars)

modern consumption theories and examining their explanations of differences in short- and long-run consumption functions.

Modern Consumption Function Hypotheses

Economists have traveled a number of different paths in their efforts to improve our understanding of consumption behavior and, hence, to account for the conflicting evidence provided by short- and long-run investigations of the consumption function. Some studies have tacitly assumed that the basic income-consumption linkage is nonproportional, as suggested by short-run data. Emphasizing the *ceteris paribus* nature of the income-consumption relationship, these investigations rely on changes in one or more factors other than income to shift the consumption function upward over time so that consumption remains a constant proportion of income in the long-run. Other studies have assumed that the income-consumption relationship is proportional, with short-run data simply showing cyclical deviations from the basic relationship. While many of the early efforts to improve our understanding of the behavior of consumption casually added non-income variables to consumption function regressions, more recent efforts have concentrated on the construction and testing of formal and sophisticated models of consumer behavior. It is these models that are our main concern as they have played a dominant role in the construction of macroeconomic models of the economy in the last two and one half decades.

Past and Relative Income

One of the first models to offer a systematic resolution of the conflict between long- and short-run consumption functions was developed by James Duesenberry shortly after World War II.[8] Duesenberry's consumption model involves a skillful combination of two hypotheses about human consumer behavior: the *relative income hypothesis* and the *past income hypothesis*. Rejecting a basic tenet of standard consumption theory, the assumption that individual household consumption is independent of the actions of other households, the relative income hypothesis treats man as a social animal. As such, his behavior, including the economic behavior of consuming, is assumed to depend very heavily on the actions of members of his peer group (his neighbors, business associates, and so on). If consumers are concerned with social status, and if income or, more precisely, consumption expenditure as a demonstration of income, is an accepted guide to social position, the proportion of income a consumer unit spends will depend heavily on its relative income position.

Suppose we are observing the behavior of individual consumer units in a peer group with average income Y_m. For a unit with income below the average ($Y < Y_m$), we could expect to find an APC above the average as the lower-income family tries to "keep up with the Joneses." On the other hand, those with above-average incomes can consume a smaller fraction of their incomes and still maintain their social status. Hence, we should expect to find a nonproportional cross-sectional consumption function for our sample of families, just as family budget study data revealed. Formally stated, the relative income hypothesis indicates that, for the ith individual consumer

---

[8]James S. Duesenberry, *Income, Saving, and the Theory of Consumer Behavior* (Cambridge, Mass: Harvard University Press, 1949).

unit, the APC is

$$\text{APC}_i = \frac{C_i}{Y_i} = f\left(\frac{Y_i}{Y_m}\right)$$

[5—4]

where

C_i = real consumption by the ith consumer unit,
Y_i = real income for the ith consumer unit,
Y_m = average income of the relevant peer group.

Applied to the economy as a whole, this hypothesis contends that families with below-average incomes will have larger APCs than those that enjoy above-average incomes.

The APC for a consumer unit will change only if his percentile position in the income distribution changes. For example, if a consumer unit's income rises more slowly than average income over time, its APC would be expected to rise, while, if its income rises faster than Y_m, its APC would be expected to decline. If everyone's income is rising over time, and at the same rate, relative income positions would be unchanged and there would be no reason for any consumer unit's APC (or, therefore, for the aggregate APC) to change. The aggregate APC (total consumption/total income) would change only as a result of a significant change in the overall distribution of income. If the distribution of income is stable over time, the aggregate APC should be stable over time. Thus, the long-run (trend) constancy of the APC can be rationalized if the hypothesis that a consumer unit's APC depends only on his percentile position in the relevant peer group is accepted.

As we know, though, there are cyclical movements in aggregate income and consumption, and cyclical (short-run) deviations of the APC from its trend value that must be explained. To do that, Duesenberry employs the past income hypothesis. According to the past income hypothesis, when there are cyclical movements in income, consumption expenditures depend not only on the current level of income but also on the highest level of income attained in the past. According to Duesenberry:

> The fundamental psychological postulate underlying our argument is that it is harder for a family to reduce its expenditures from a high level than for a family to refrain from making high expenditures in the first place.[9]

A family with a high income, given time for adjustment, will become accustomed to an accordingly elevated standard of living. If income moves cyclically, in response to a fall in income such a family would attempt to maintain its standard of living at the expense of saving. Thus, "past income" is an important determinant of consumption expenditures as well as current income. The precise past income figure which Duesenberry thinks important is the previous peak income. "The peak year's consumption sets the stan-

---

[9]Duesenberry, *Income, Saving, and the Theory of Consumer Behavior*, pp. 84–85.

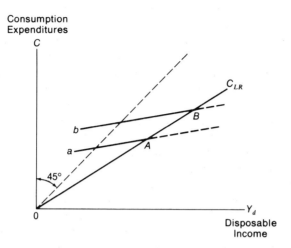

**Figure 5—7 / Duesenberry's
Secular and Cyclical Consumption Functions**

dard from which cuts are made (provided the peak did not represent a mere spurt in income)."[10] Duesenberry relied on both the relative and the past income hypotheses to attempt to reconcile the long- and short-run consumption/income relations.

According to Duesenberry, if income increases along a steady trend path, the aggregate APC would be affected only by changes in income distribution (the relative income hypothesis rules). If the income distribution stays the same over time, then we should expect to obtain the long-run consumption function, OC_{LR} in Figure 5—7, along which consumption is proportional to income.

If, however, income varies cyclically (as well as increasing secularly), Duesenberry would expect deviations from the secular path OC_{LR}. With cyclical movements, the past income hypothesis comes into play and consumption at any point in time would be expected to depend not only on current income but also on the highest level of income previously attained.

Suppose we are at point A in Figure 5—7. If consumption depends only on current income, a decline in income would result in a movement back along OC_{LR} (the APC constant). If the past income hypothesis holds, however, such a cyclical fall in income would be met first with a sacrifice in saving, a movement back along the flatter short-run consumption schedule aA. Along this schedule, the APC rises as income falls and declines as income grows.

As the economy passes through the trough of the income cycle and income rises, consumers would first restore the desired level of saving until point A (corresponding to previous peak income) was reached. As income

---

[10]Duesenberry concedes that a weighted average of past income levels might be better but claims that too few observations are available to statistically estimate the weights, op. cit. p. 89.

continues to increase, a more "normal" saving ratio can be restored because previous peak income has lost its sway. Consequently, the economy would move along the proportional schedule OC_{LR} until the next cyclical downturn, at which point we would again see a movement along a flatter consumption function such as bB. A nonproportional, short-run (cyclical) consumption function is perfectly consistent with a proportional long-run consumption function.[11]

Duesenberry's consumption model has enjoyed prominence in the development of macroeconomic analysis as one of the first of the systematic reconciliations of observed long- and short-run income/consumption relations. However, because Duesenberry's model is not derived through the direct application of traditional consumer behavior theory—indeed, it rejects some of the basic tenets of that traditional theory—it has never been fully accepted by the economics profession as a general explanation of aggregate consumption behavior. Economists have responded with considerably more favor to consumption function hypotheses that are derived assuming utility maximization by rational households that are not imprisoned by habitual consumption patterns or social pressures. Such households save to make the time pattern of their consumption more gratifying, with both current and future consumption contributing to utility. Milton Friedman's *permanent income hypothesis* fits this mold.[12]

The Permanent Income Hypothesis

Duesenberry's attempt to explain consumption behavior implicitly assumes that the national income and product accounts definitions of income and consumption are the appropriate ones for explaining consumer behavior. In Friedman's treatment of the permanent income hypothesis that assumption is rejected. As with most simple consumption functions fitted to national income and product accounts data, those described earlier in this chapter assume that consumption in each year depends on income in that same year. Friedman would contend that there is nothing special about a one-year-long accounting period or any other fixed time period. Certainly we would not want to argue that this week's consumption depends only on this week's income, or that today's consumption depends on today's income alone.

---

[11]Duesenberry fitted a simple linear relation of the form $S_t/Y_t = a(Y_t/Y_0) + b$ to aggregate data for the years 1923–1940, obtaining

$$S_t/Y_t = .166(Y_t/Y_0) - .066 \qquad (R^2 = .9)$$

This relationship can account for both secular and cyclical behavior in saving.

(a) Secular: looking at the trend of income, Y_t/Y_0 can be, say, 1.03 (reflecting a 3 percent annual growth in income) because Y_0 is the previous year's income in any year t only if a smooth upward trend of income levels is relevant. In this case, $S_t/Y_t = .166$ (1.03) − .066 = .105 = 10.5% = APS or APC = 1 − APS = 89.5%, a value consistent with Kuznets' data on the secular value of the APC.

(b) Cyclical: as income falls the ratio (Y_t/Y_0) falls so that S_t/Y_t falls (APS ↓ , APC ↑), as cyclical data typically demonstrate.

[12]Milton Friedman, *A Theory of the Consumption Function* (Princeton, N.J.: Princeton University Press for the National Bureau of Economic Research, 1957).

Instead, consumption in any such period depends heavily on the income we expect to be receiving in the future. Indeed, for any particular short accounting period, consumption may be practically independent of that period's income, as consumption decisions are made based on some average expected value of future income receipts. Friedman calls the value of spendable income that an individual counts on as being available for consumption use, based on expected future income, *permanent income.*

Of course, measures of this longer time horizon income are not available in the national income and product accounts, so it is necessary to determine the link between Friedman's conceptually appropriate measure of income (i.e., permanent income) and observed income.

According to Friedman, observed income can be divided into two components, a "permanent" component and a "transitory" component. That is,

$$Y = Y_p + Y_t$$

where

$$Y = \text{observed income}$$
$$Y_p = \text{permanent income}$$
$$Y_t = \text{transitory income.}$$

In similar fashion, observed consumption may be divided into permanent and transitory components so

$$C = C_p + C_t$$

where

$$C = \text{observed consumption}$$
$$C_p = \text{permanent consumption}$$
$$C_t = \text{transitory consumption.} \qquad [5\text{—}5]$$

According to Friedman, "The permanent component (of income) is to be interpreted as reflecting the effect of those factors that the unit regards as determining its capital value or wealth."[13] Thus, Y_p is a measure of expected expendable income available over the consumer's life.[14] Envision a consumer unit who, this period, intends to sell the rights to its future earnings from working for an immediate lump-sum payment. Add to the market value of its future labor earnings the current value of its accumulated property wealth, providing a sum that the consumer unit can contract to lend at interest. The yearly interest income that the consumer unit could spend

---

[13]Friedman, *A Theory of the Consumption Function,* p. 21.

[14]Realistically, Friedman's empirical work implies that the consumer's time horizon is more limited in duration, close to three years.

each year without reducing its capital (wealth), is permanent income. Permanent consumption (C_p) is that consumption which the consumer unit systematically chooses to enjoy based upon its permanent income.

Y_t and C_t are unexpected, "chance" movements in income and consumption, respectively. Microeconomic examples would include income loss due to an unexpected illness, gains due to an unexpected inheritance, losses due to a crop failure for Y_t, and such items as unexpectedly good opportunities to make purchases, or spending due to an unexpected illness for C_t. The possibility of transitory disturbances at the aggregate level, and their role in aggregate consumption behavior, is explored in the next section.

The Formal Hypothesis. Friedman's formal hypothesis states that the systematic relationship between consumption and income is the relationship between the permanent components, C_p and Y_p. He hypothesizes that the true relationship is proportional, and that the proportion (the APC designated k) is affected by several factors other than income. That is

$$C_p = k\ (i,w,u) \cdot Y_p \qquad\qquad [5-6]$$

The factors affecting the size of k are i, the rate of interest (or a set of rates); w, a proxy variable that measures the relative importance of property and nonproperty income; and u, a catchall variable included to capture the impact on k of such factors as tastes, the size and age of consumer units, and so on.[15] With no significant secular tendency for the interest rate to change, and with no demonstrated empirically significant role for w and u in altering the value of k at the aggregate level, the secular income-consumption relationship for the economy should exhibit a fairly constant APC.

To make the hypothesis testable (subject to refutation), Friedman assumes that "the transitory components of income and consumption are uncorrelated with one another and with the corresponding permanent components."[16] *The substantive implication of the formal hypothesis is that a change in observed income would systematically affect consumption (if at all) only to the extent that it affects the value of permanent income.*[17] If a consumer has a long time horizon, a change in the level of income currently received could have little impact on his "permanent" income level and, thus, could have little effect on his consumption behavior.

At the aggregate level then, transitory (cyclical) swings in current, mea-

---

[15]Because it is easier to borrow against nonhuman wealth than human wealth, the higher the value of w (the higher the ratio of "property" to "nonproperty" wealth), the weaker the motivation to accumulate (save) and the larger the value of k. How would k be related to i and u?

[16]Friedman, *A Theory of the Consumption Function*, p. 26. The assumption in rigorous terms is $\rho_{Y_tY_p} = \rho_{C_tC_p} = \rho_{Y_tC_t} = 0$, where ρ is the partial correlation coefficient between the variables indicated by subscripts.

[17]That is, if $C_p = f(Y_p)$, then MPC $= dC_p/dY$, $= \partial C_p/\partial Y_p \cdot (dY_p/dY)$, with the size of dY_p/dY declining as the consumer's time horizon lengthens.

sured income would have little effect on aggregate consumption. Faced with a decline in current income to a subnormal level during recessions, consumers would reduce their saving rate without significantly reducing consumption, which is based on permanent income. Hence, in recessions an increased fraction of current measured income would be consumed. On the other hand, in boom periods measured income rises more rapidly than historical experience tells us is normal. Households, continuing to base their consumption on what they perceive as normal or permanent income, save an unusually large fraction of the transitory increase in earnings. As long as income varies cyclically, in addition to growing steadily over the long-run, we should expect flat (nonproportional) short-run consumption functions to coexist with a proportional long-run income-consumption relationship. The corresponding macroeconomic policy implications are striking for, according to the permanent income hypothesis, a change in received income stemming from a government policy action (for example, a change in tax collections) that is temporary would have a negligible impact on consumption spending. Thus the explicitly temporary increase in tax collections imposed under Lyndon Johnson in 1968 (in the form of a 10 percent income tax surcharge), having little impact on permanent income, could not have been expected to depress consumption very substantially. Appearing to support that view, aggregate demand remained at an inflationary level through 1968 and 1969. Of course, statistical series cannot unequivocally reveal what would have happened without the tax surcharge.[18] In the same vein, advocates of the permanent income hypothesis would argue that the one-time 10 percent rebate on personal income tax liabilities, which Congress provided in 1975 as part of a stimulative fiscal program, would generate relatively little additional consumption.

Though Friedman's application of the permanent income theory to numerous empirical situations has demonstrated its consistency with real-world observations in a broad array of circumstances, there are studies that have failed to support the hypothesis. An investigation by Bodkin[19] found that the MPC out of unexpected (transitory) income from National Life

---

[18]For an explanation of the "weak" effects of the 1968 surcharge, see Robert Eisner, "Fiscal and Monetary Policy Reconsidered," *The American Economic Review* 59 (1969): 897–905. Other economists have argued that the tax surcharge was effective in reducing consumer spending. See Arthur Okun, "The Personal Tax Surcharge and Consumer Demand, 1968," *Brookings Papers on Economic Activity* 1 (1971): 167–200.

[19]Ronald Bodkin, "Windfall Income and Consumption," *The American Economic Review* 49 (1959): 602–614.

[20]If the appropriate time horizon for consumers is three years, as Friedman's estimates have indicated, the MPC out of windfalls should be approximately one-third. A shorter horizon is obtained in an investigation by R. Holbrook, "The Three-Year Horizon: An Analysis of the Evidence," *Journal of Political Economy* 75 (1967): 750–754. Negative results have also been produced by Hendrick Houthakker, "The Permanent Income Hypothesis," *The American Economic Review* 48 (1958): 396–404; and by Robert C. Jones, "Transitory Income and Expenditures on Consumption Categories," *American Economic Association Proceedings* 50 (1960): 584–592.

Insurance dividends in 1950 fell between 0.72 and 0.97, values considerably larger than allowable in Friedman's model.[20] Studies of the impact of the 1968 tax surcharge, a temporary tax on taxes, and the one-shot 1975 tax rebate indicate that temporary tax changes are 50 to 90 percent as effective as permanent tax changes in altering consumption spending.[21] Friedman's own empirical work with time series data for the years 1905 through 1951 has yielded a function of the form $C = 0.88Y_p$. For this function the APC is clearly a constant proportion of permanent income (thus both the average and marginal propensities to consume out of permanent income are 88 percent). Because there is no direct way to observe permanent income, as a proxy Friedman used a weighted average of current and past values of observed income.[22] The assumption is that individuals base their expectations of future income on past and current experience. However, expectations of future income levels certainly can incorporate information that is not included in current and past income observations. Thus, reliance on a weighted average of observed income values to predict permanent income and consumption builds a degree of momentum into those predictions that can result in sizable errors when turning points in consumption occur. In spite of difficulties like this one, which must be tolerated in the empirical application of the permanent income hypothesis, that hypothesis plays a dominant role in modern discussions of aggregate consumption behavior. The fundamental conclusion that income changes which are viewed as temporary (transitory) have a significantly weaker effect on consumption than those that are perceived as permanent is aired commonly now, even in newspaper discussions of proposed tax policy changes. More controversial is the notion emphasized by Friedman and his most ardent supporters that the multiplier is an undependable tool for policy making and forecasting because households have to translate observed income changes into permanent and transitory components. In an effort to control the economy, the government can alter taxes and its spending levels, in both cases altering disposable income. According to Friedman, however, policy makers cannot know how much of the income change a fiscal policy action produces will be considered permanent and how much transitory. Hence, they cannot know the MPC (or the multiplier) and they cannot reliably predict the impact of fiscal actions.

[21]See Walter Dolde, "Temporary Taxes as Macro-Economic Stabilizers, *The American Economic Review* 69(1979): 81–85, and F. Modigliani and C. Steindel, "Is a Tax Rebate an Effective Tool for Stabilization Policy?" *Brookings Papers on Economic Activity* 1(1977): 175–209.

[22]Friedman uses a weighted average of incomes for the previous seventeen years with weights declining rapidly as the observation becomes more distant in time (current year's income has a weight of .33, the previous year's income a weight of .22, and so on). With this weighting scheme, a one hundred dollar change in current income changes Y by thirty-three dollars. The MPC out of current income is $dC/dY = \partial C/\partial Y_p \cdot dY_p/dY = .88(.33) = .29$. Clearly, with an MPC of .29, this short-run aggregate consumption function is flatter (nonproportional) than the long-run function. Approximately one-third of a measured change in current income is currently consumed. Hence, it is argued that, on the average, increments to income appear to be spread out over an approximate three-year planning horizon.

The Life Cycle Hypothesis

A hypothesis similar in implications to Friedman's permanent income hypothesis is Modigliani's so-called *life cycle hypothesis.* The central theme of this hypothesis is that men are "forward-looking animals."[23] Accordingly, "there need not be any close and simple relation between consumption in a given short period and income in that same period. The rate of consumption in any given period is a facet of a plan which extends *over the balance of the individual's life,* while the income accruing within the same period is but one element which contributes to the shaping of such a plan."[24]

For the typical individual, income is low during the early years of life, rises toward a peak in the late years of full-time employment, then returns to a low level in the late years of life. With current income only a relatively minor determinant of current consumption, the life cycle hypothesis suggests that an individual will spread out his consumption in a pattern that is much smoother than that of his income stream. The predicted form of behavior is shown in Figure 5—8, with our individual saving during his peak earning years and dissaving in his low-income years.[25]

In summary terms, the life cycle hypothesis indicates that an individual's consumption in any period depends on the total resources he has to spend over his remaining life (once again on his total wealth, consisting of the value of the property he owns plus the market or discounted value of the

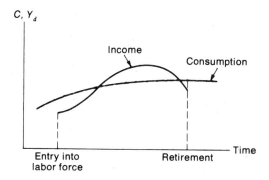

Figure 5—8 / Life Cycle Income and Consumption

---

[23]See Franco Modigliani and Richard Brumberg, Utility Analysis and the Consumption Function: An Interpretation of Cross-Section Data" in *Post-Keynesian Economics,* ed. K. Kurihara (New Brunswick, N.J.: Rutgers University Press, 1954). Also, Albert Ando and Franco Modigliani, "The 'Life-Cycle' Hypothesis of Saving," *The American Economic Review* 53 (1963): 55–84.

[24]Modigliani and Brumberg, op. cit., pp. 391–392.

[25]This pattern of behavior corresponds to lifetime utility maximization. If the marginal utility from consumption diminishes with an increase in consumption, overall utility is increased by cutting back on consumption in "peak" consumption years and adding to consumption in other years.

future stream of income he expects to earn by working)[26] and the number of years he expects to live. The greater an individual's wealth or the shorter his expected life, the larger his yearly consumption will be, according to the life cycle model.

In formal terms, this hypothesis suggests that, in a simple setting, a consumer would spend the same proportion of what he perceives to be his total wealth each year, no matter what the level of received income is in that one year. That is, for an individual consumer consumption is[27]

$$C_t = \frac{1}{L_t} V_t$$

where

C_t = consumption in year t
L_t = the consumer's expected remaining life in year t (in years)
V_t = the consumer's total wealth in year t.

With an individual's total wealth in year t dependent on the value of his property wealth at the beginning of year t, the income he earns from his labor efforts in year t, and his expected stream of labor income receipts over the remaining years until retirement, the individual's consumption function can be rewritten as

$$C_t = C(Y_t, Y_t^e, a_t) \qquad\qquad [5\text{—}7]$$

where

Y_t = labor income in year t
Y_t^e = income expected from working in the consumer's remaining earning years $(Y_{t + 1}, Y_{t + 2}, \ldots)$
a_t = net value of assets owned by the consumer at the beginning of year t.

An increase in current income above the expected level increases the individual's net worth. According to the life cycle hypothesis, if the increase in that one year's income is not perceived as permanent, the resulting *small* increase in net worth, spread evenly over the consumer's remaining life with equal additions to consumption in each period, would have a *small* impact on current consumption. For the typical individual then, the marginal propensity to consume out of current income would be small relative to the average propensity to consume. However, the larger the impact of an unanticipated increase in current income on the level of income *expected* in

---

[26]The process, called discounting, allows us to convert a stream of expected future income receipts into an equivalent value of wealth held currently as a stock. The mechanics of discounting are covered in Chapter 6.

[27]The model was first developed, in the form used here, assuming a zero interest rate, then extended to a world with a positive interest rate.

the future (and thus on the consumer's net worth) the larger is the response in consumption and, of course, the larger the MPC. The implications of the hypothesis for an individual's consumption behavior are clearly quite similar to those of the permanent income hypothesis. Once again, an explicitly temporary change in current income, for example, because of a temporary income tax change, would be expected to have little impact on consumption.[28] On the other hand, a change in current income that is viewed as reflecting a shift in the entire time stream of future income receipts (for example, a *permanent* change in tax rates) would have a far larger impact on consumption.

To employ the life cycle hypothesis in explaining aggregate consumption behavior, we need to recognize that the proportion of aggregate income society would consume in any period would change with the age distribution, rising as the proportion of the population in the early or late stages of life increases. However, the life cycle hypothesis does not rely on changes in the population's age distribution to reconcile the behavior patterns observed in short-run and long-run studies of the consumption function.

Holding the age composition of the population constant, the life cycle hypothesis implies that aggregate consumption depends on society's current income, its expected future labor earnings, and the value of its assets. In linear form then, aggregate consumption in period t is expected to be

$$C_t' = b_1 Y_t' + b_2 Y_t^{e'} + b_3 a_t'$$

where the superscript (') indicates the variables are *aggregate* measures (of consumption, current labor income, expected labor income, and assets).

Unfortunately for purposes of testing this model, future expected income cannot be measured. However, if expected income depends on current income (let expected income be $Y_t^{e'} = Z Y_t'$), our consumption function can be rewritten as

$$C_t' = b_4 Y_t' + b_3 a_t' \text{ with } (b_4 = b_1 + b_2 Z) \tag{5—8}$$

This function allows predictions of changes in consumption based just on changes in the observable variables: current labor income (Y_t') and asset

---

[28]If N is the number of remaining working years for our consumer, Y^e is the average yearly value of labor income expected in the future, the other variables are defined as before, and the interest rate is zero, then

$$C = C(Y, Y^e, a, t) = 1/L_t(Y) + N/L_t (Y^e) + 1/L_t(a)$$

so $\partial C/\partial Y = 1/L_t + N/L_t (dY^e/dY)$.

If an unexpected change in received income has no impact on income expected in the future, then the second term disappears leaving $\partial C/\partial Y = 1/L_t$, which typically would be extremely small in value. If, as is more reasonable, an unexpected change in income causes expected future income to change in the same direction ($dY^e/dY > 0$), then the MPC will be larger. How much larger it would be depends on the size of dY^e/dY.

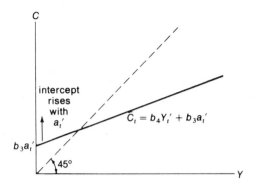

Figure 5—9 / The Life Cycle Consumption Function

holdings (a_t'). Moreover, this equation can be readily employed to reconcile short- and long-run patterns of consumption behavior. In the short-run, the value of assets remains virtually unchanged so that the short-run income-consumption relationship is nonproportional, its intercept $(b_3 a_t')$ dictated by the value of assets, as shown in Figure 5—9. With a steady growth of property wealth in the long-run, the value of the intercept of the short-run function is steadily increased, shifting the consumption function upward in the manner necessary for generating a proportional long-run consumption function.[29] Wealth, which we identified early in this chapter as a candidate for explaining observed consumption patterns, plays a crucial role in the life cycle hypothesis.

---

[29] Ando and Modigliani fitted a number of empirical forms of this hypothesis to time series data for the United States. A representative result is the equation

$$C_t' = 0.7\,Y_t' + .06\,a_t'$$

where Y_t' is labor income, a_t' is the value of property wealth, and C_t' is consumption. This equation says, of course, that the MPC out of current income is .7 and the MPC out of assets is .06. For short-run, or cyclical, movements in income a_t' is near constant. Thus, the short-run consumption function is nonproportional with a virtually fixed intercept (an intercept value of $.06 a_t'$). As the time period lengthens, saving will result in growth of the value of accumulated assets. As property wealth increases, the short-run consumption function will shift upward because its intercept is simply $.06 a_t'$ and the value of a_t' is growing.

Dividing the fitted consumption function by total disposable income (Y_d') to provide a measure of the APC yields

$$\text{APC} = \frac{C_t'}{Y_d'} = .7\frac{Y_t'}{Y_d'} + .06\frac{a_t'}{Y_d'}.$$

Clearly, the APC can remain constant over time if labor's share of total income (Y_t'/Y_d') stays constant *and* if wealth grows at the same trend rate as income (keeping a_t'/Y_d' unchanged). Both those conditions have approximately held in the United States.

Summary

The discussion in this chapter began with Keynes' rough "psychological law" that consumption is a positive function of the absolute level of current disposable income with a marginal propensity to consume that is smaller than the average propensity to consume and also less than one. As demonstrated, this crude hypothesis is not supported unequivocally by available data on income and consumption, is incapable of reconciling the conflict between short-run and secular time series data, and is open to criticism on theoretical grounds.

Three formal hypotheses that have been developed to try to overcome the shortcomings of the Keynesian *absolute income hypothesis* are the Duesenberry *relative (and past) income hypothesis,* the Friedman *permanent income hypothesis,* and the Modigliani *life cycle hypothesis.* Each of these appears to be more general and, thus, more satisfying theoretically than the Keynesian function. Each is capable of reconciling the conflict between long-run and short-run consumption functions. Making a choice among these hypotheses on purely *a priori* grounds is impossible, though the fact that Duesenberry's consumption model is not firmly grounded in standard consumer behavior theory has prevented its general acceptance by economists. It is also difficult to make a clear-cut choice on empirical grounds because all three hypotheses yield consumption functions that fit the data quite well (that is, all three functions yield high R^2 terms when fitted to data on income and consumption).[30]

It is frustrating that available test methods are unable to identify the one best model among the several logical constructions that are capable of reconciling the conflict between short- and long-run evidence on the consumption function. For our purposes it is sufficient to note that all of the empirical investigations we have reviewed agree on the basic form of the income-consumption relationship. Both the proportional long-run function and the nonproportional short-run function have important applications in macroeconomic analysis. For short-run analysis, which is the primary concern of this text, a nonproportional function of just the form employed in Chapter 4 *(C = a + bY_d)* is appropriate. On the other hand, for analyzing

---

[30]The very high measured correlations between income and consumption, in fact, do not provide compelling evidence that income changes *cause* consumption changes. While the income level no doubt does influence consumption, in turn consumption spending is by far the largest component of aggregate spending (income). Whether consumption is high because income is high or whether income is high because consumption is high cannot be ascertained from the statistical tests reported in this text. The statistical difficulties that result from correlating one variable *(C),* with another variable *(Y),* of which the first is a component part, are beyond the scope of this text. However, it should be recognized that a "spuriously" high correlation results. Daniel B. Suits has suggested that with consumption comprising near 90 percent of income, the correlation between income and consumption should be expected to be around .9 even if income changes do not cause consumption changes. See D. B. Suits, "The Determinants of Consumer Expenditure: A Review of Present Knowledge," *Impacts of Monetary Policy,* Commission on Money and Credit (Englewood Cliffs, N.J.: Prentice-Hall, 1963), pp. 1–57.

the long-run growth of the economy, as we will do in Chapter 16, a proportional consumption function is appropriate. Moreover, there is basic agreement between the two consumption function hypotheses that are most intensively employed in current research (the life cycle hypothesis and the permanent income hypothesis) on the impact of government budget changes. Most notably on this score, both hypotheses agree that changes in government outlays or tax collections that are perceived as temporary will have a significantly smaller impact on current consumption, and hence on overall demand, than those that are perceived as permanent. As a consequence, great care is required in attempting to devise fiscal policy actions that will have the desired effect on aggregate spending. It is also widely agreed that, according to these hypotheses, consumption is based on a measure that is decidedly more stable than current income, and, hence, that consumption follows a relatively stable expansion path. Consumption demand, then, is viewed as a stabilizing influence on the economy according to these models, rather than as a source of fluctuations.[31]

In comparing the permanent income and life cycle hypotheses, it is notable that the permanent income hypothesis pays more attention to the formation of expectations regarding future income than does the basic life cycle model, while the life cycle model provides a rationale for including wealth along with income in the consumption function. Happily, the best attributes of both models can be combined as richer expectation formation models may be employed in life cycle style consumption functions. The major econometric forecasting models of the U.S. economy in fact do just that.

In light of the indicated weakness of explicitly temporary income tax changes, a few economists have recently suggested that the government could more effectively control the level of consumption spending by applying (or relaxing) a temporary sales tax on consumption goods. Such a temporary tax would alter the relative cost of current as opposed to future consumption. You should be well equipped now to provide a theoretical evaluation of the impact on aggregate consumption of such a tax levy and to compare its effects to those that would stem from a permanent change in the sales tax rate. (Be careful, this is trickier than it sounds!)

Finally, it is worth noting that the government still looks upon income tax changes as a basic tool for controlling consumption spending. In the spring of 1975, Congress instituted a personal income tax cut to spur anemic consumption demand in the midst of a steep contraction in economic activity. Combining a 10 percent rebate on 1974 income tax liabilities with a one-year cut in tax obligations, that tax-cut package was designed to materially increase disposable income in 1975. How should consumption have been expected to respond?

---

[31]John F.O. Bilson has constructed a model which shows that, depending on the manner in which expectations of future income are formed, consumer expenditures might respond abruptly to events that alter the income path. In that case, consumption demand may act as a destabilizing force. See Bilson, "The Rational Expectations Approach to the Consumption Function—A Multi-Country Study" (Paper presented at the International Seminar on Macroeconomics, Paris, 1979).

Case in Point III

The Stagnation Thesis and the Saving Ratio

Recall that the text referred to the "Stagnation Thesis" which was popular in the 1930s. This thesis held that, with income rising over time, a greater proportion of income would be saved and a smaller proportion consumed. This argument was based largely on Keynes' description of the consumption function and on cross-section data on family income and consumption.

Of course, as the models of Chapter 4 reveal, if a larger fraction of income is saved, the fraction of output absorbed by investment and/or government spending must be increased. With a fear that investment opportunities would not be adequate to fill the gap between high employment output and consumption, stagnationists argued that a very large increase in government spending (without an offsetting increase in taxes) would be required to maintain high levels of employment.

The chart below shows the actual saving ratio (personal saving as a fraction of disposable personal income) from just before 1900 through 1978. As

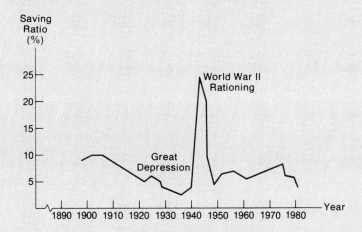

the chart shows, the saving ratio was quite low, as all of the modern consumption function hypotheses predict, when income was extraordinarily low during the Great Depression. On the other hand, the very high saving ratios experienced during World War II were the result of a special restriction, the nonavailability of many consumer goods. With virtually no consumer durables to spend their earned income on and restricted quantities of other consumer goods, households saved extraordinarily large fractions of their incomes during the war.

Outside of the Great Depression/World War II era, the saving ratio has remained relatively stable over time. This is particularly true from 1910 to the present, though real income has more than tripled during that interval. In sharp contrast to the fear of the stagnationists, the saving ratio, if anything, now seems lower than it was at the turn of the century. Rather than excessive saving threatening us, we are now more frequently concerned with an inadequate rate of saving to free the resources needed for investment to modernize and expand our capital stock. As you know, all of the modern consumption function hypotheses are consistent with a secular stability in the fractions of income that are saved and consumed. The life cycle and permanent income theories also provide a ready rationalization of lower-than-normal saving ratios in the immediate post-World War II period, as the massive saving taking place during the war provided a substantial increase in wealth during that period which households were eager to spend on consumer goods as industry converted from war materials production to peacetime production.

Questions

1. Suppose you have the observations presented in the table below generated by a consumption function of the form: $C = a + bY + cA$.

Year	C	Y	A
1	670	800	800
2	750	900	900
3	770	900	1000
4	850	1000	1100
5	910	1100	1100

   From the data, find the constant a and the marginal propensities to consume out of Y and A. What is consumption when Y (income) is zero? When Y is zero and A is 1000?

2. From the data in the *Survey of Current Business* plot the real consumption and real disposable income figures for 1965 through last year. Using a straightedge, draw the straight line that, by eye, seems to fit best through your plotted observations.
   a. Is your plotted line a usable short-run consumption function?
   b. From your consumption line, find the approximate value of the marginal propensity to consume.
   c. What does your MPC make the value of the multiplier in models I and II of Chapter 4?

3. Suppose you are given the hypothetical consumption function $C = a + bY + cW + di + eA$ in which C is real consumption spending, Y is real disposable income, W is real wealth, i is the interest rate, and A is a measure of the age distribution of the population. Explain how C would respond to changes in each of these variables and why.

4. By extrapolating short-run, or cyclical, consumption functions (like $C = 31.4 + .73Y_d$ in Figure 5—6B) fitted to prewar data, economists predicted a growing

gap between consumption spending and full employment output after World War II. With government spending expected to decline at the war's end, predictions of massive recession were commonplace. In fact, consumers went on a buying spree after the war and inflation was more of a problem than stagnation. Account for the major error in forecasting consumption that gave us misleading forecasts of postwar economic performance.

5. In recent years, the government has increased social security payments to the aged and has provided that group with medical care. With these programs financed through general tax revenues and increased social security contributions, what impact should we expect these programs to have on aggregate consumption spending?

6. In the biblical story about the seven good years and seven bad years, a community stored up grain during seven years of extraordinarily good harvests and was thereby able to live "normally" during seven subsequent years of crop failure. Identify a consumption function hypothesis that accommodates the behavior described above and briefly explain the logical foundation of that function.

7. In her last album, *Pearl,* recorded by Columbia Records, the late Janis Joplin sang:

    "Lord, won't you buy me a Mercedes Benz?
    My friends all have Porsches, I must make amends."*

    Identify the consumption function hypothesis that reflects the sentiment expressed in the song and explain how economists have used that hypothesis to account for observed consumer behavior.

8. What do the permanent and life cycle consumption function hypotheses have to say about: (1) the effect on consumption of a temporary income surtax? (2) The size and predictability of the multiplier?

Suggested Readings

Ando, Albert, and Modigliani, Franco. "The 'Life-Cycle' Hypothesis of Saving: Aggregate Implications and Tests." *The American Economic Review* 53 (1963): 55–84.

deLeeuw, Frank, and Gramlich, Edward. "The Federal Reserve—MIT Econometric Model." *Federal Reserve Bulletin* 54 (1968): 11–13 and 21–25.

Duesenberry, James S. *Income, Saving, and the Theory of Consumer Behavior.* Cambridge, Mass.: Harvard University Press, 1949.

Farrell, M. J. "The New Theories of the Consumption Function." *Economic Journal* 69 (1959): 678–695. Reprinted in *Readings in Macroeconomics,* edited by M. G. Mueller, pp. 77–92. 2nd ed. New York: Holt, Rinehart and Winston.

Ferber, Robert. "Research on Household Behavior." *The American Economic Review* 52 (1962): 19–63.

Ferber, Robert. "Consumer Economics, a Survey." *Journal of Economic Literature*. 11 (1973): 1303–1342.

Mayer, Thomas. *Permanent Income, Wealth, and Consumption: A Critique of the Permanent Income Theory, the Life-Cycle Hypothesis, and Related Theories.* Berkeley: University of California Press, 1972.

Suits, Daniel B. "The Determinants of Consumer Expenditure: A Review of Present Knowledge." In *Impacts of Monetary Policy.* Commission on Money and Credit. Englewood Cliffs, N.J.: Prentice-Hall, 1963.

Tobin, James. "Relative Income, Absolute Income and Saving." In *Money, Trade and Economic Growth: Essays in Honor of J.H. Williams,* pp. 135–156. New York: Macmillan, 1951.

Chapter 6   Investment

The permanent income and life cycle hypotheses of Chapter 5 suggest that consumption, the largest component of aggregate demand, is to some extent insulated from short-run changes in income. Consequently, consumption may generally exert a stabilizing influence on the economy. (What does a "small" MPC imply for the value of the multiplier?)

The other major component of private (nongovernment) demand is investment which, for purposes of simplicity, we assumed was exogenous in all but one of the income determination models developed in Chapter 4. We now need to assess the role of investment as a source of changes in aggregate demand and identify the forces that influence investment spending. In so doing, we will discover a linkage between the market for goods and services and money, and we will see that tax policy actions may influence investment.

While investment is a far smaller component of aggregate demand than is consumption (net investment rarely exceeds 12 percent of aggregate output), analysis of its determinants and attempts to predict its level have received a disproportionate share of economists' attention. This is so, first, because of its volatility. Because aggregate demand is the sum of investment and some other components of spending, variations in investment can produce, through the multiplier, magnified changes in aggregate demand and, hence, in the levels of output and employment. Indicative of the volatility of investment and its link to economic activity, Figure 6—1 shows the relationship between net investment as a percentage of output and unemployment (along an inverted scale) over the period 1946–1979. Clearly, there

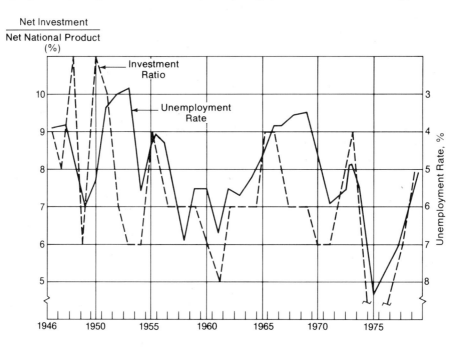

**Figure 6—1 / The Investment Ratio
and the Unemployment Rate, 1946–1979**

Source: Council of Economic Advisers, *Economic Report of the President* (Washington, D.C.: U.S. Government Printing Office, various years).

are sizable variations in the investment measure plotted in the figure; and there is little doubt but that they are strongly related to fluctuations in output and employment, with unemployment rising in the face of declining investment and shrinking with increased investment. This evidence of sizable and continuing variations in a component of aggregate demand comprises a strong invitation for government efforts to stabilize aggregate demand. Of course, it does not tell us whether the government's efforts to do so, say by altering taxes, can succeed, or whether government intervention may further destabilize the economy.

As we know, the government does attempt to stabilize economic activity; and, as a second reason for the attention investment has received, we will see that some of the important weapons the government employs in this effort work through altering the level of planned investment. Of course, accurate predictions of the size and timing of investment responses to policy actions are essential for the design of those actions.

Before embarking on an analysis of what determines aggregate investment, we need to recall (from our treatment of the national income and
product accounts) that the term *investment* applies only to the purchase of
new, physical assets, not to the purchase of existing physical assets nor to
the purchase of financial assets (stocks, bonds, and so on). The acquisition
of an existing physical asset represents investment to the purchaser but, in
the aggregate, is offset by an equal amount of disinvestment by the previous
owner. The same can be said for exchanges of financial assets. In neither
case do the exchanges reflect current production (except for the services of
the broker in the exchange process).

We should also recall that total investment spending (so-called *gross investment*) is composed of two components: *replacement investment,* that
part of gross investment required to replace the capital consumed during
the production process, and *net investment,* the net addition to the existing
stock of capital.

The Business Investment Decision

As explained in our discussion of national income and product accounts,
investment consists of: (1) businesses' expenditures on structures and equipment, (2) spending on residential structures, and (3) inventory investment.
As the figures for 1979 listed below indicate, business *fixed* investment (on
structures and equipment) is the largest component of investment, and our
immediate concern is to analyze the business investment decision.

1979 Gross Private Domestic Investment — $386.2 Billion

Nonresidential structures and equipment	$253.9 B
Residential structures	113.9 B
Inventory change	18.4 B
Total	$386.2 Billion

As we all know, firms invest in new, productive assets (new machinery, a
new store, a new office building, and so on) only because they expect that
investment to be profitable. More specifically, a firm will buy a new capital
asset because it expects that asset to yield a future stream of receipts sufficient to cover all direct costs involved in production utilizing that asset
(labor costs, energy costs, and so on), and still leave revenues sufficient to
amortize (pay the depreciation costs on) the asset and provide a residual
representing the *return on capital investment.*

We can clarify these ideas and set the stage for further development of
the investment decision-making process by looking at a simple example.
Suppose I am considering investing in a peanut stand for this year's county
fair. Before I can rationally decide whether this investment is worth-while

(that is, if it will be profitable), I need to develop estimates of the revenues I can expect to receive and of the costs that will be involved in establishing, maintaining, and operating the peanut stand. Such estimates may range from rough, crude, intuitive "guesstimates" to precise, sophisticated estimates supported by data generated and analyzed by engineers, accountants, and business forecasting specialists. The quality of such estimates will typically vary with the size of the company, the sophistication of its managers, the size of the investment project being considered, and so on.

Regardless of the technique of estimation I employ, suppose I judge the set of values in Table 6—1 to be my best estimates of revenue and costs.

Table 6—1 / Data for Investment Decision on a Capital Asset with a One-Year Life

Original cost of equipment (peanut stand)		$1,000
Expected life of equipment	1 year	
Total revenue expected from operation of stand (total revenue = number of bags of peanuts sold x price per bag)		1,500
Operating expenses (expenses other than depreciation and interest)		400
Labor $300		
Franchise fee 50		
Raw materials 50		
Expected gross revenue from investment before depreciation and interest charges (total revenue minus operating expenses)		$1,100
Depreciation cost		1,000
Net revenue before deduction of interest cost		$ 100

Deducting the $400 of operating expenses from the $1,500 of expected revenues leaves receipts of $1,100 to amortize my investment and provide a residual return on investment. With an expected life of one year and no salvage value on my peanut stand, the depreciation charge is the full $1,000 of original cost, leaving $100 as the net return on investment. You should note that no interest charges have been entered in Table 6—1. Typically, investment decision analysts compare the net return on a proposed investment (ignoring interest costs) to the interest cost of that investment in order to decide whether the project will be profitable. In our example, if I had to borrow $1,000 for one year to finance the peanut stand investment, the interest cost of the investment would be $1,000 times the rate of interest I had to pay on the loan. With a market interest rate of 9 percent, interest charges would be $90. With net revenue of $100 before interest charges, $10 would be left after paying interest costs. I would be $10 better off making the investment than I would be if I did not make it. If the interest rate I had to pay were 10 percent, interest costs would have completely exhausted pre-interest net revenue. If the interest rate should exceed 10 percent, I would clearly be worse off making the investment than I would be if I did not invest. An investment in the peanut stand should be made only if the expected revenues from using the peanut stand would cover all direct costs involved in peanut sales and still leave sufficient revenue to cover the depreciation cost of "using up" the stand plus a residual, representing the return on capital, which must exceed the interest cost of the investment.

Generalizing from this example, the investment decision is made by comparing the net return on investment before interest charges to those interest charges. Typically, both figures are expressed in percentage terms rather than in absolute figures. In our example, the percentage rate of return on investment before interest charges is 10 percent (net revenue ÷ original investment = $100 ÷ $1,000 = .10 or 10%). If the cost of capital (the market rate of interest) is less than 10 percent, the project should be undertaken. If the interest rate is greater than 10 percent, it should not.

Our conclusions are unchanged if the investment is to be financed out of our own funds instead of by borrowing, for firms can lend as well as borrow at the market interest rate. Unless the expected rate of return on our physical investment project exceeds the interest rate at which we can lend (or borrow), we will not invest in that project.

While the mechanics of investment decision-making for the peanut stand example are clear-cut, to handle more complicated projects some of the concepts introduced only by implication in that example must be explored. However, the decision rule developed for the peanut stand investment has general validity. If the rate of return on investment exceeds the going interest rate (the cost of capital to the firm considering the investment project), the investment should be undertaken. If the rate of return on investment is less than the interest rate, the project should not be undertaken.

The Return on Capital

The pre-interest cost rate of return on the asset considered in our example is what investment analysts often call the *internal rate of return on investment*. It is ". . . that rate of discount which would make the present value of . . . [net receipts] expected from the capital-asset during its life just equal to its supply price."[1] We can readily develop an understanding of this definition of the internal rate of return through the example above in which $1,000 invested in a one-year project yielded pre-interest cost revenues of $1,100. That is, $1,000 invested for one year grew in value to $1,100. The internal rate of return on that investment is 10 percent. Clearly, with investment opportunities that yield a 10 percent rate of return available to the business firm, $1,000 in the present is precisely equivalent to the receipt of $1,100 one year from now.

So far, all we have done is illustrate that there is a *time value* of money.

---

[1]John Maynard Keynes, *The General Theory of Employment, Interest, and Money* (New York: Harcourt Brace Jovanovich, 1936), p. 135.

$1,000 in the present is worth more than $1,000 to be received one year from now simply because the $1,000 now can be invested at a positive rate of return. Finding the equivalent value *now*, the so-called *present value*, of expected future income receipts, is called the *discounting* of those future receipts. In investment analysis the percentage *rate of discount* that makes the cost of an investment project just equal to the present or discounted value of the future receipts expected to result from that project is its internal rate of return. Because, in our example, a $1,000 investment grew to $1,100 at the end of one year, the rate of discount that made the present value of the expected earnings equal to the $1,000 cost of the asset was 10 percent.

In algebraic terms, the equation $1,000 (1 + .10) = $1,100 demonstrates the equivalence of $1,000 in the present with $1,100 a year hence, when investments yielding 10 percent annually are available. Generalizing from our example, the equivalence of C invested in the present with revenues of R one year later, when investments yielding rate of return r are available, is illustrated by the equation $C (1 + r) = R$. Of course, this equation can be rearranged, for example, to appear as $C = R/(1 + r)$. Clearly, there is some percentage rate of return, some discount rate, that will make these equalities hold. In our example, with $C = $1,000 and $R = $1,100, the solution value for r is 10 percent.

Investment Projects with Lives of More Than One Year. When the investment project being considered has a life greater than one year, the necessity of allowing for compound interest makes the computation of the internal rate of return on investment slightly more complicated. Suppose a project is being considered that costs C dollars, has a life of two years, and is expected to return revenues in the amount of R_2 in one lump payment at the end of its two-year life. The stream of relevant money flows can be schematically represented as in Figure 6—2. What is the rate of return on this project, or, asking the same question in a different form, at what rate must C grow to become amount R_2 in two years? Invested at rate of return r, C would be worth $C (1 + r)$ after one year and, with compound interest, would be worth $[C (1 + r) \cdot (1 + r)]$ or $C (1 + r)^2$ after two years. If $C (1 + r)^2$ must grow to value R_2 $[$ that is, $C (1 + r)^2 = R_2]$ and we have estimates of C and R_2, we can solve for r, the internal rate of return. Again, it is the rate that allows C to grow to value R_2 in two years, or it is the rate that

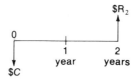

Figure 6—2 / Cash Flows for a Project with a Two-Year Life

can make the present discounted value of $\$R_2$, received two years hence, equal to $\$C$ now:

$$C = \frac{R_2}{(1 + r)^2}$$

The relevant cash flows for an asset that has a life of three years, costs $\$C$, and promises to pay a lump sum of revenue of $\$R_3$ at the end of its three-year life can be schematically represented as in Figure 6—3. For such a project, the internal rate of return can be obtained by solving the equation $C = R_3/(1 + r)^3$ for r. In this case, the lump revenue payment must, of course, be discounted back three periods. What relationship would you use to find the internal rate of return on a project with a life of four years? Six years? Ten years? It should be clear that for any investment of $\$C$ which, after a period of n years, promises to pay $\$R_n$, the equation $C(1 + r)^n = R_n$ $\left[\text{or } C = R_n/(1 + r)^n\right]$ portrays the link between the cost of the asset, its payoff, and its internal rate of return. With information on any two variables in the equation, the solution value for the remaining variable may be found.

Figure 6—3 / Cash Flows for a Project with a Three-Year Life

Rate of Return in the General Investment Problem. Typically, an investment project may be expected to yield a stream of receipts throughout its life rather than one lump sum of receipts at a single point in time. A cash flow schematic for this more typical investment project, with a life of n years, would appear as shown in Figure 6—4, with each year's receipts assumed

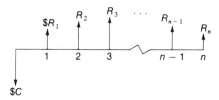

Figure 6—4 / Cash Flows for a Project with an n-Year Life

to accrue at the end of the respective year. For this project, how do we find the internal rate of return, the rate of discount that will make the discounted (present) value of the future stream of receipts equal to $\$C$, the current acquisition cost of the capital asset? As shown earlier, the present value of

R_1 can be found by discounting R_1 back one year; the present value of R_2 can be found by discounting R_2 back two years; and so on. For the project in Figure 6—4, the rate of return can be found from the equality

$$C = \frac{R_1}{(1+r)} + \frac{R_2}{(1+r)^2} + \frac{R_3}{(1+r)^3} + \cdots + \frac{R_n}{(1+r)^n} \qquad [6\text{—}1]$$

With estimates for the cost of the asset (C) and for expected receipts $(R_1, R_2, \ldots, R_n)$ there is only one unknown, r, which can be found by trial and error.[2]

No matter what the specific time pattern of revenue flows, with estimates of those flows and of the cost of the asset that provides them, a value for the rate of return on that asset can be computed. This computed rate of return can be compared to the cost of funds to the firm in order to determine whether the project should be undertaken. If the internal rate of return exceeds the market rate of interest, the project should be undertaken. If the internal rate of return is less than the interest rate, the project should not be undertaken. Of course, the larger the expected future receipts, or the smaller the cost, the higher will be the rate of return on an investment project. On the other hand, with smaller expected revenues, or with a higher acquisition cost, the rate of return on a capital asset is reduced. A moment's reflection may also suggest that the *timing* of the stream of receipts a capital asset provides has an important influence on its rate of return, a point that will be investigated later in this chapter.

---

[2]If our investment project yields a *uniform* stream of annual receipts, that is, $R_1 = R_2 = R_3 = \ldots = R_n = R$, Equation 6—1 can be rewritten as

(a) $C = \dfrac{R}{1+r} + \dfrac{R}{(1+r)^2} + \ldots + \dfrac{R}{(1+r)^n} = R\left[(1+r)^{-1} + (1+r)^{-2} + \ldots + (1+r)^{-n}\right].$

Multiplying both sides of this expression by $(1+r)^{-1}$ yields

(b) $C(1+r)^{-1} = R\left[(1+r)^{-2} + (1+r)^{-3} + \ldots + (1+r)^{-(n+1)}\right].$

Subtracting (b) from (a) yields

$C\left[1 - (1+r)^{-1}\right] = R\left[(1+r)^{-1} - (1+r)^{-(n+1)}\right]$

which, multiplied by $(1+r)$, yields

(c) $C = \dfrac{R}{r}\left[1 - (1+r)^{-n}\right].$

With values for R and C this single equation can be solved for the rate of return (r), which equates the discounted value of future receipts generated by a capital asset with its acquisition cost.

Should the stream of uniform payments from an asset continue forever, equation (c) reduces (as $n \to \infty$) to

(d) $C = \dfrac{R}{r}.$

Once again, with R and C known, the rate of return can be found.

An Alternative Approach. The method of investment decision-making just reviewed is called the *internal rate of return technique.* An alternative approach is provided by what is known as the *present value technique.* We saw above that we can solve for the internal rate of return: the discount rate that makes the discounted value of anticipated revenues from an investment project equal to its acquisition cost. If, alternatively, expected receipts are discounted using the *market rate of interest* as the discount factor, the present value obtained reflects the *current market value* of the expected stream of receipts.

The purchase of a capital asset gives the purchaser the right to the stream of receipts expected from its use. Going back to the peanut stand example, our investment provided revenues of $1,100 at the end of one year. With a market interest rate of 10 percent available, the present value of that expected revenue is $1,000. A firm would be willing to pay up to $1,000 for the peanut stand because, at any acquisition price lower than that amount, the rate of return earned would exceed the market interest rate. At a purchase price of exactly $1,000, the firm should be indifferent with regard to buying the peanut stand or lending at the 10 percent market interest rate. In either case, $1,000 in the present grows to $1,100 in one year. The firm would, of course, be reducing its profits by paying more than $1,000 for the peanut stand.

In general terms, the present value of an asset with a life of n years, that is expected to yield receipts $R_1, R_2, \ldots, R_n$ in years one through n, is

$$V = \frac{R_1}{1+i} + \frac{R_2}{(1+i)^2} + \ldots + \frac{R_{n-1}}{(1+i)^{n-1}} + \frac{R_n}{(1+i)^n} \qquad [6\text{--}2]$$

where V is present value, i is the market rate of interest, and R_j would be the expected net revenue in year j.[3]

What general investment rule should a profit-maximizing firm, using present value calculations, follow in its investment decision process? The present value calculation tells the firm what the *right* to the expected stream of earnings from an asset is worth *now* (that is, the present value of the earnings expected from use of the asset). The firm also knows, or has an estimate of, the price it must pay for the asset now. If the present value of the expected receipts made available to the firm by buying an asset exceeds that asset's purchase price, the firm should invest. Conversely, if the purchase price of the right to those receipts (the asset) exceeds the present value of the receipts, the firm should not undertake the investment project.

For our purposes, it can be assumed that the decisions made on potential investment projects using the present value technique are always the same

---

[3] For an asset with an infinite life that is expected to yield net receipts of the same size each period throughout its life, the present value is $V = R/i$.

as those obtained using an internal rate of return calculation.[4] To see the basic equivalence of the two techniques, compare Equations (6—1) and (6—2), assuming, initially, that the market rate of interest is the same as the internal rate of return $(i = r)$ for the investment project under consideration. With $i = r$, the present value of the project is equal to the original cost of the asset being considered. With the market rate of interest higher $(i > r)$, the internal rate of return decision rule would tell us not to undertake the project. Looking at Equation (6—2) tells us that as i increases, making $i > r$, the present value of the asset under consideration falls, making $V < C$, which also tells us not to undertake the project. With $i < r$, so that an investment project appears profitable on the basis of the internal rate of return decision rule, we will find $V > C$, making that project appear favorable on the basis of the present value-cost comparison.

To summarize, the decision rules for these two alternative techniques of investment analysis are shown in Table 6—2. The interest rate (i), prices of capital assets (C), and the expected size and time pattern of net receipts (the Rs) are important determinants of business firms' investment decisions. A change in any of these factors will affect the level of investment by individual firms and, thus, aggregate investment spending.

Table 6—2 / Investment Decision Rules

Decision Technique Employed			
Internal rate of return versus interest rate comparison	$i < r$	$i > r$	$i = r$
Present value versus cost comparison	$V > C$	$V < C$	$V = C$
Fate of project	should be undertaken	should *not* be undertaken	indifferent

Our primary concern in the next section of this chapter will be with the relationship between the market rate of interest and the aggregate level of investment. Before progressing to that topic, a brief discussion of the precision with which individual firms' investment decision calculations can be made is in order. Investors' estimates of the original cost of a prospective investment project are frequently quite precise (though this is not always the case). Their estimates of future net receipts are, however, subject to considerable uncertainty because they typically accrue over an extended time horizon. Future net receipts may differ from estimates because of changes in demand (thus in product price and quantity sold) or because of changes on the supply side (changes in current operating costs due to

---

[4]In a number of special cases, the internal rate of return rule breaks down. Among the reasons for failure are the assumption of an interest rate that remains constant over time and the mathematical possibility of multiple rates of return for the same capital asset. For a discussion of the conditions under which the internal rate of return criterion fails, see Jack Hirshleifer, *Interest, Investment, and Capital* (Englewood Cliffs, N.J.: Prentice-Hall, 1970), especially pp. 74–81.

changes in wage rates, materials costs, and so on). Costs may also change unexpectedly because of government edicts that require additional outlays, say, for pollution abatement equipment, and sales may change because of restrictions imposed on products. (An example is the requirement that new cars use lead-free gasoline.)

Forecasts of future movements in demand and costs (and thus in net receipts from, and the rate of return on, a new capital asset) are often crude and quite subjective.[5] The subjective element in those forecasts can lead to substantial volatility in businessmen's estimates of the profitability of new investment projects and, hence, in investment expenditures. Business confidence is frequently assumed to be so sensitive as to cause a revision of profitability estimates in response even to political developments (for example, the switch from a conservative to a liberal government). Keynes emphasized the delicate nature of profit expectations in the following passage:

If the fear of a Labour Government or a New Deal depresses enterprise, this need not be the result either of a reasonable calculation or of a plot with political intent;—it is the mere consequence of upsetting the balance of spontaneous optimism. In estimating the prospects of investment, we must have regard, therefore, to the nerves and hysteria and even the digestions and reactions to the weather of those upon whose spontaneous activity it largely depends.[6]

Investment decision-making, appearing as a precise art in an example in which future net receipts are known with certainty, is fraught with uncertainty and subjectivity in practice.

The Rate of Interest and Aggregate Investment Behavior

Assuming that business firms attempt to maximize profits, and that to do so they employ investment decision techniques like those discussed above, Keynes alleged that there was an aggregate investment demand schedule that slopes downward from left to right, as shown in Figure 6—5. The

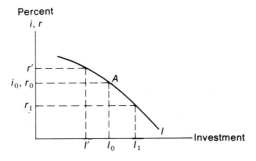

Figure 6—5 / Investment Demand

[5]Such estimates can be quite misleading. Where did the Edsel go?

[6]Keynes, *The General Theory*, p. 162.

schedule in that figure shows the percentage rate of return that could be expected on *new* investment during a specified time period for any level of investment expenditure. It indicates, for example, that if investment in this period were taking place at rate I_0, at the margin the rate of return on investment would be r_0.

In what sense is schedule I in Figure 6—5 a demand curve? A *demand curve* relates the cost of an item to the quantity of that item demanded, and schedule I does just that. The price of capital goods, the "cost of capital," is the market rate of interest at which the firm can borrow and lend. Thus, the schedule in Figure 6—5, which shows what volume of real investment (the rate of purchase of capital goods) will take place at every possible market interest rate we might observe, serves as a demand curve for investment. If the interest rate *(i)* were just equal to internal rate of return r_0, businesses would choose collectively to invest amount I_0. With any smaller volume of investment, the rate of return on investment at the margin would be higher, hence, greater than the cost of capital. For example, at investment level I', the rate of return on investment would be r'. Total profits of any firm are, of course, always increased by investing, even if the firm must borrow to finance that investment, as long as the return on investment exceeds the market interest rate. Thus, there would be an incentive for investment to be increased as long as r exceeds i. Only when investment has increased sufficiently to drive the rate of return on investment down to equality with the rate of interest (as at point A in Figure 6—5 for an interest rate equal to i_0) does the inducement to increase investment disappear.

Analogously, if the market rate of interest remained equal to i_0, but investment exceeded I_0 (for example, increased to I_1), the rate of return on investment (r_1 if $I = I_1$) would be less than the cost of capital. Firms would be reducing the size of their total profits by this overinvestment, and would be induced to contract investment expenditures sufficiently to allow the rate of return on investment to return to equality with the market interest rate ($i = r_0$). It should be clear that, for any rate of interest, the investment demand schedule can tell us the equilibrium (profit-maximizing) rate of real investment expenditure.

The Demand for Capital. So far, we have merely asserted that there is an inverse relation between the flow rate of investment and the rate of return on investment. We have not provided a convincing theoretical explanation of why such a demand for investment schedule should exist. In fact, standard explanations of the functioning of business firms account for the demand for a stock of capital, not a flow of investment, and we must first understand what determines the amount of capital demanded before we can explain the flow demand for investment.

The capital stock is the existing physical accumulation of productive facilities in the form of factories, machinery, office buildings, sales outlets, and so on. As the simple example developed early in this chapter suggested, the rate of return on capital goods depends upon the value of sales revenues

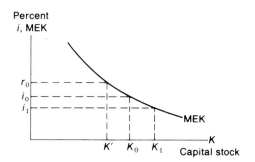

Figure 6—6 / The Demand for Capital

that can be generated through their use, and on the operating costs associated with their use. Further, as the concept of *diminishing returns* suggests, for any other factor of production, an increase in the capital stock, with the size and quality of the existing labor force, the technique of production, and the stock of natural resources and land given, should lead to a lower return at the margin. Thus, the schedule, which we shall call the *marginal efficiency of capital* (MEK), slopes downward from left to right, as in Figure 6—6, reflecting, due to diminishing returns, a fall in the expected return to capital assets as the stock of capital increases. That is, with diminishing returns, adding successive units of capital to the existing stock adds successively smaller increments to output, and hence to the sales revenues generated through the use of that capital. For a given acquisition cost of capital, then, the yield on extra units of capital falls as the size of the total stock grows.

Given the marginal efficiency of capital stock schedule and the market rate of interest, there will be one unique *equilibrium stock* of capital. For example, if the interest rate is i_0, the equilibrium capital stock in Figure 6—6 is K_0. A smaller capital stock, like K', could not be an equilibrium stock because the return on additions to the capital stock (r_0) would exceed the interest cost of capital (i_0). Thus, additional investment would take place, increasing the capital stock until the return to capital is driven down to equality with the market rate of interest. Similarly, a capital stock larger than K_0 could not be an equilibrium stock with a market rate of interest equal to i_0 because the return on capital would be less than the return available for lending. Net disinvestment in capital assets would occur until the capital stock had shrunk to size K_0.

Once investment has equalized the actual stock of capital with the desired (profit-maximizing) stock, as long as no shocks are allowed to disturb equilibrium (nothing happens to change the position of the MEK curve and the interest rate stays constant), the capital stock will remain unchanged. *Net investment will be zero because no change in the size of the capital stock is desired.* Gross investment must, however, be positive with a magnitude equal to the value of capital consumption allowances for the optimum capital stock to be maintained.[7]

The Interest Rate and the Equilibrium Capital Stock. If the market interest rate changes, the equilibrium value of the capital stock changes. The capital stock demand (MEK) schedule shows the impact of a change in the market rate of interest on the equilibrium capital stock. The MEK schedule in Figure 6—6 shows a fall in the rate of interest from i_0 to i_1 increasing the desired or equilibrium capital stock by amount ΔK. It indicates nothing, however, about how rapidly the desired adjustment in the size of the capital stock will take place. That is, it tells us nothing about the flow rate of *net investment* we can expect to observe during the adjustment process initiated by the change in the market rate of interest.

Shifts in the MEK Schedule and the Equilibrium Capital Stock. The optimum value of the capital stock will also change if the MEK schedule shifts. Because, for any existing stock of capital (i.e., at any point on the MEK schedule), the rate of return on capital depends upon the sales revenues that that firm's managers can expect to generate through the use of capital assets in the future, and on the future costs they can expect to incur, there is a long list of factors that can shift the MEK schedule. Among the most important are:

1. A change in the demand for firms' products. As an illustration, an increased demand would result in higher sales, higher prices, or both, with gross and net revenues (the big Rs in our investment analysis) pulled upward. The yield rate on capital would be increased at any level of capital stock so the MEK schedule is shifted upward.
2. Innovation (the introduction of new products, new and more efficient production facilities, or advanced production techniques). By stimulating sales (of new products) and raising revenues, or by producing at lower cost (with improved facilities or techniques), firms can enjoy increases in net revenues from the use of capital. Again, this shifts the MEK schedule upward. In like fashion, innovations that lower the acquisition costs of capital assets would raise their expected yields, shifting the MEK schedule outward.
3. Changes in factor costs. Particularly changes in the labor, materials, and energy costs that firms face through the use of capital assets alter the yield on capital. Militant and successful wage bargaining that firms expect to raise future labor costs, anticipated jumps in energy prices due to OPEC actions, and rising materials prices for whatever reason would lower the expected yield on capital, shifting the MEK curve downward.
4. Government actions. For example, tax policy changes or changes in

---

[7]As indicated in Chapter 2, capital consumption encompasses the depreciation, obsolescence, and accidental destruction of capital assets.

safety and environmental protection regulations can exert a potent influence on the demand for capital. Of course, it is the after-tax yield that business is concerned with, so tax changes shift the MEK schedule by altering after-tax profits. Specify for yourself some possible results of safety and/or environmental protection regulations.

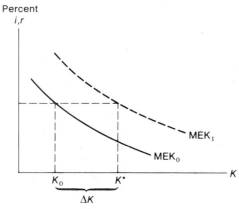

Figure 6—7 / A Shift in the MEK Schedule

Figure 6—7 illustrates the effect of an event (say, a change in the tax treatment of business profits) that raises the expected yield on capital assets. The demand for capital schedule shifts to MEK_1 and the desired stock of capital becomes K^*. With the existing stock of capital unchanged at K_0, firms must undertake ΔK of net investment (over and above replacement investment) in order to restore capital stock equilibrium.

Similar shifts would result from changes in any factor that, like those described above, affects the yields on capital, whether it does so through changing expected Rs or asset purchase costs. When such shifts create capital stock disequilibrium (a gap between the actual and desired stocks of capital), net investment takes place because it is through net investment that the actual capital stock can change to match the desired stock.

The Adjustment Process. It is now clear that either changes in the interest cost of capital, which prompt movements along a given MEK schedule, or shifts in the MEK schedule itself, produce gaps between the actual and desired stocks of capital, prompting a flow of net investment to close those gaps. What is not clear is the rate at which the adjustment of the actual capital stock to its new desired value will take place. If there were no *adjustment costs,* costs that are a function of the rate at which the capital stock is changed, there could be a *full adjustment* of the capital stock in just one period after the change in the desired capital stock. In this case, the return on capital and on increments in the flow of investment would decline only as the size of the capital stock grew (because of diminishing returns).

There are, however, good reasons to believe that there are significant adjustment costs that, by raising the effective cost of adding to the capital stock, depress the yield on investment independently of diminishing returns. Moreover, these costs are apt to increase with the flow rate of investment so that the yield on investment falls as the rate of investment increases. As a consequence, only a *partial adjustment* of the capital stock toward its new desired value will occur in any single accounting period following the emergence of capital stock disequilibrium. A full adjustment could not occur for, if it did, the reduction of the yield on capital from diminishing returns combined with the reduction in yield due to adjustment costs would push the yield on capital and investment additions to the capital stock well below the interest cost of capital, decidedly not an optimum situation.

Figure 6—8 illustrates the nature of the adjustment process when capital stock equilibrium is disturbed by a fall in interest. With a lowering of interest from i_0 to i_1, the desired capital stock becomes K^*. As net investment is undertaken, adjustment costs depress the yield on investment along schedule MEI_0 (note that we are measuring both the stock of capital and the flow of investment along the horizontal axis of Figure 6—8). With those costs rising as the rate of investment increases, the MEI (marginal efficiency of investment) schedule slopes downward from left to right showing a decline in the yield rate on investment as its flow rate increases.

It, of course, adds to firms' profits if they undertake any investment that offers a yield in excess of the interest cost of funds. Hence, the optimum investment rate in the period following the emergence of capital stock disequilibrium is $I_1 = \Delta K_1$, equating the return on investment with the interest cost of funds. Of course, the net investment undertaken in period 1 after equilibrium is disturbed increases the capital stock, in this case to level K', and because of diminishing returns the rate of return on any flow rate of investment will be lower in the next period. This is reflected in a marginal

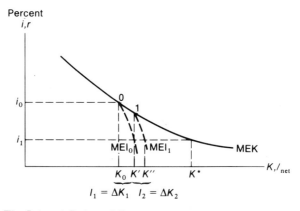

Figure 6—8 / The Interest Rate and Investment

efficiency of investment schedule (MEI$_1$) and that schedule calls for net investment in the reduced amount $I_2 = \Delta K_2$ in the second adjustment period. Of course, this partial adjustment process would continue until the actual capital stock is increased to volume K^*. Where would the MEI schedule be with the capital stock adjustment completed?

Adjustment Costs. There may be capital stock adjustment costs that are internal to business firms and those that arise apart from the capital-acquiring firms. As an illustration of the former, undertaking plant and equipment purchases and integrating the new assets into a firm's operations diverts management efforts away from the firm's ongoing activities. This is sure to raise costs as operating inefficiencies emerge. The faster investment additions to capital are undertaken, the greater is the diversion and the higher are the costs of acquiring and integrating the capital into existing operations.

Like any other industries, those that produce capital assets face rising marginal costs as their outputs expand. Consequently, higher prices are required to induce them to produce at a faster rate. For firms that are buying capital assets to invest in them at a faster rate, capital goods-producing industries must step up their output, which they will do only at higher prices. Thus, the higher the level of investment, the higher the purchase price of capital goods, and the lower the return on investment. It is because of adjustment costs of the sort cited that the marginal efficiency of investment schedule is decidedly more steeply sloped than the MEK schedule.

The Investment Model in Summary

Our analysis has shown that no net investment takes place unless there is a gap between the desired stock of capital and the existing stock. Hence, the factors that determine the position of the MEK schedule, factors affecting future Rs and acquisition costs, belong in an investment model. Given the MEK schedule, the existing stock of capital dictates the position of the MEI schedule, with a larger existing stock reducing the returns to investment. Finally, interest rate changes result in movements along existing MEK and MEI schedules, prompting a change in investment. Part (a) of Figure 6—9 shows the change in the desired stock of capital (from K_0 to K^*) and the first period response in net investment (I_1) that a decline in the interest rate generates. Part (b) of that diagram shows the impact on the desired stock of capital (from K_0 to K^*) and the first period investment response (I_1) to an event that raises the expected yield on capital (by raising the Rs or reducing the price of capital goods). Part (c) of that figure simply shows, after several adjustment periods following a shock like either of those represented in (a) and (b), the position of the MEI schedule and the rate of investment as the actual stock of capital has expanded most of the way toward K^*. It is apparent from (c) that as the actual capital stock gets closer to its desired level, the incentive to invest is reduced.

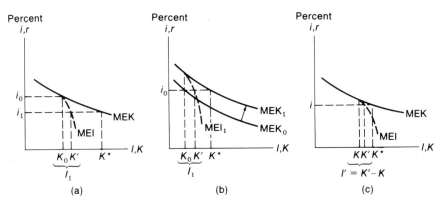

Figure 6—9 / A Summary of Factors Affecting Investment

An algebraic statement of the link revealed above between net investments and its determinants might take the form

$$I_{net} = I(i,R,C,K) \ \text{ with } \ \frac{\Delta I}{\Delta i} < 0$$

$$\frac{\Delta I}{\Delta R} > 0$$

$$\frac{\Delta I}{\Delta C} < 0 \qquad \qquad [6\text{—}3]$$

$$\frac{\Delta I}{\Delta K} < 0$$

In this equation, net investment (I_{net}) is negatively related to the interest cost funds, positively related to the expected revenues after deduction of operating costs (R), negatively related to the prevailing level of capital goods prices (C), and negatively related to the existing stock of capital.

Over relatively short periods of time, changes in the stock of capital can be ignored for practical purposes because they are likely to be very small relative to the existing stock. In addition, the structure of capital goods prices may be taken as given in the short-run.[8] Hence, the investment function reduces to

$$I = I(i,R). \qquad\qquad [6\text{—}4]$$

Because "expected net revenues" are not observable in the real world, for empirically testing investment functions some proxy variable that is thought

---

[8]The change in the price of capital goods *induced* by a change in the level of investment is fully captured; indeed, it is one of the adjustment costs that is responsible for the relatively steep slope of the MEI schedule. If there are autonomous changes in capital goods prices, the investment demand schedule shifts. An autonomous increase (decrease) in capital goods prices would shift the MEK and MEI schedules downward (upward).

to be closely related to expected net revenues must be relied on. A variable that has frequently been assumed to exhibit the necessary close association with expected revenues is the current level of sales (output). If current output is a reasonable proxy for expected revenues, then we can employ as our investment model the function

$$I = I(i, Y), \qquad\qquad [6\text{—}5]$$

where i is the market interest rate and Y is the output level.

This simple investment function has been supported by a number of empirical tests, and as a reasonable, basic model of investment behavior this function is commonly employed in simple models of the economic system such as the ones that will be constructed in this text beginning in Chapter 8.

Unfortunately, recent empirical research on investment demand involves complexities that prevent us from being able to look directly at fitted regression equations for the response of investment to changes in output and the interest rate. However, a simple summary may be helpful. There is widespread agreement in recently conducted studies that investment demand is positively related to the level of output and negatively related to the interest rate. In a survey of results generated from data on manufacturing industries, Evans has concluded that: (1) "A change of 1 percent in output will produce an average change of 1 1/2 to 2 percent in investment over a two-year period," and (2) "A change of one point in the long-term interest rate, say from 4 to 5 percent, will change investment from 5 to 10 percent over a two-year period."[9] Little of this impact is generated until over a year has elapsed, according to Evans, because an interest rate change does not affect projects that are already under way.

The Flexible Accelerator

Virtually all modern explanations of aggregate investment agree that it is the gap between the actual and desired stocks of capital that prompts investment, and that only a portion of the gap that exists at any point in time is apt to be closed by investment in the next period. A particularly simple model that formalizes this proposition, and that can be used to provide a stronger basis for the inclusion of income in empirical investment functions, is called the flexible accelerator.

The flexible accelerator model simply assumes that a constant fraction λ of the gap between the desired and actual capital stocks is filled by net investment each period. As a result, firms' investment is increased in proportion to the size of that gap. In algebraic terms, net investment according to the flexible accelerator model is

$$I_{net_t} = \lambda(K_t^* - K_{t-1}) \qquad 0 < \lambda < 1 \qquad [6\text{—}6]$$

---

[9]Michael Evans, *Macroeconomic Activity: Theory, Forecasting, and Control* (New York: Harper & Row, 1969), p. 138. Chapters 4 and 5 provide an extensive review of the modern empirical literature on investment demand.

That is, net investment in period t is fraction λ of the gap between the desired stock of capital in that period (K_t^*) and the existing stock inherited from the preceding period (K_{t-1}). Of course, the larger the *partial adjustment coefficient* λ, the faster gap $K_t^* - K_{t-1}$ would be closed. From our earlier discussion of the factors that affect the demand for capital *(i, R,* and *C)* it is clear that the flexible accelerator provides an explicit investment function of the form

$$I_{net_t} = \lambda[K(i,R,C) - K_{t-1}] \qquad [6\text{—}7]$$

Again, the roles of the interest rate *(i)*, expected net revenues *(R)*, capital goods prices *(C)*, and the existing stock of capital *(K_{t-1})* are clear-cut; and because future *Rs* are not observable, some proxy for the combination of *R* and *C* must be chosen. Let us look at an alternative explanation of the choice of output *(Y)* as the appropriate proxy.

Output and Capital. Microeconomic reasoning indicates that, for a given set of relative factor costs (on land, labor, and capital), there is one optimum stock of capital for every output level. Thus, for a given set of factor costs, for output level Y_0 there is one desired capital stock K_0^* given by the equation

$$K_0^* = A Y \qquad [6\text{—}8]$$

In this equation, the proportionality constant $A = \dfrac{K_0^*}{Y_0}$ is the preferred capital to output ratio. For output to increase, more of some or all factor inputs in production must be employed. With constant returns to scale and unchanged relative factor costs, firms would alter the volume of all factor inputs employed, including capital, in proportion to the increase in output. So, at output Y_1, the desired capital stock would be given by[10]

$$K_1^* = A Y_1 \qquad [6\text{—}9]$$

---

[10]See Richard S. Eckaus, "The Acceleration Principle Reconsidered," *Quarterly Journal of Economics* 67 (1953): 209—230. A more rigid "accelerator" model has been prominent in the economics literature for many decades. That model assumed a capital to output ratio that was absolutely fixed by technical or engineering requirements; e.g., it takes exactly ten shoemaking machines, each capable of producing 8,000 pairs of shoes annually, to produce 80,000 pairs annually. With output of Y_0 in period 0 and Y_1 in period 1, the *required* stocks of capital would be $K_0 = A Y_0$ and $K_1 = A Y_1$, respectively. Net investment, the change in capital required by a change in sales of ΔY, is, thus,

$$I_{net} = \Delta K_0 = K_1 - K_0 = A Y_1 - A Y_0 = A\Delta Y.$$

This rigid model, which is excessively restrictive in that it requires a *full adjustment* of the capital stock each period to maintain the required capital to output ratio, makes net investment a function of the *rate of change* of output (ΔY) rather than its level. This contrasts with the less restrictive *flexible* accelerator model.

with A the same proportionality constant as before. Thus, ignoring changes in relative factor costs and employing the flexible accelerator model, net investment in period t is

$$I_{net_t} = \lambda(K_t^* - K_{t-1}) \qquad\qquad [6\text{—}10]$$
$$= \lambda(A Y_t - K_{t-1})$$

Here, net investment is proportional to the gap $K_t^* - K_{t-1}$ and the desired stock of capital is proportional to output. Investment then is a positive function of output as the economy's production function links the output level to the profit-maximizing stock of capital required to produce that output. Of course, the flexible accelerator model allows for any specification of the value of K^*, so we may take account of changing relative factor costs (e.g., by including a measure of interest rates) and relax the requirement of constant returns to scale (hence, the *proportional* link between Y and K) and still retain the strong justification for inclusion of output as an argument in the investment function. Quite simply, we have appealed to the economy's production function to justify using Y as a shifter of the MEK and, hence, MEI schedules. In this context, a change in sales, to the extent that it is judged permanent, alters the profit-maximizing stock of capital.[11]

Disinvestment and Replacement Investment

Our discussion of investment responses up to this point has focused on events that increase the desired stock of capital and induce a positive flow of net investment. Generally, reversing those events reduces the desired stock of capital (shifting the MEK schedule leftward) so the existing capital stock is larger than the desired stock. In this case, net disinvestment takes place. It is reasonable to expect the resulting flow of disinvestment to be a stable fraction of the existing capital stock, as the capital stock shrinks through the abandonment of assets as they become obsolete or "worn out."

Our discussion of investment may also be extended to allow for replacement investment. We know that the sum of replacement investment (I_r) and net investment (I_n) is gross investment (I_g). With the reasonable assumption that a constant proportion (d) of the existing capital stock (K) is worn away and replaced each year, aggregate gross investment is

$$I_g = I_n + I_r \qquad\qquad I_r = dK_{t-1} \qquad\qquad [6\text{—}11]$$

which, plugging in Equation (6—10) for net investment is

$$I_g = \lambda(A Y_t - K_{t-1}) + dK_{t-1}$$

or $\qquad\qquad\qquad\qquad\qquad\qquad\qquad\qquad\qquad\qquad\qquad\qquad [6\text{—}12]$

$$I_g = \lambda A Y_t + (d - \lambda)K_{t-1}$$

---

[11]For an attempt to develop an accelerator model in which investment responds only to permanent changes in output, see Robert Eisner, "Investment: Fact and Fancy," *The American Economic Review* 53 (1963): 237–246.

According to this equation, gross investment rises with output and may either rise or fall with an increase in the capital stock depending upon the relative size of λ (the partial adjustment coefficient that influences the net investment response to gap $(K^* - K_{t-1})$ and d (the replacement requirement fraction).

The Tax Treatment of Business Income and Investment

While in developing the core of business investment analysis we have noted that the tax requirements businesses face may influence their investment, there are some specific tax policy actions that deserve examination. In that regard remember that when businessmen are making an investment decision, they are concerned with the after-tax profitability of that investment; that is, the stream of expected net receipts upon which they base their investment calculations is the after-tax stream. An increase in the tax rate on business income will lower expected after-tax receipts, shifting the MEK and MEI schedules downward and thus depressing investment.[12] Conversely, a reduction of business income tax rates would shift the MEK and MEI schedules outward and stimulate investment.

In addition, while with existing Internal Revenue Service rules depreciation costs are deductible as current expenses, a change in depreciation rules will alter a firm's current expenses and, thus, its total profit. Moreover, because it is a firm's profit that determines its direct tax liability, after-tax profits will be altered by changes in depreciation rules.

When depreciation rules are altered to allow a firm to depreciate a capital asset more rapidly, the current measured expenses of using that asset are raised in the early years of its life, lowering taxable profits in those years. That is, *accelerated depreciation* can lower a firm's tax liability in the early years of the asset's life by raising the costs the firm reports for tax purposes. In the later years of the asset's life, taxable income and the firm's tax liability will be increased equivalently (the asset will be fully depreciated before its economically useful life is ended). Thus, the overall effect of accelerated depreciation rules is to allow an alteration of the *time pattern* of the firm's tax liabilities, permitting the firm to pay lower taxes in the early years of a capital asset's life and higher taxes in the later years. This, of course, alters the time pattern of the after-tax stream of revenues expected from use of a capital asset, raising the values of the after-tax *Rs* expected from that asset during the depreciation period, and lowering the values expected in the later years of the asset's life. Changing the time pattern of expected revenues in this manner raises the present value of the asset (or, *ipso facto*, raises the internal rate of return on that asset) because, taking account of

---

[12]The greater the ability of producing firms to pass the tax increase on to the public in the form of higher prices, the smaller will be the shift. Even if tax increases are ultimately completely passed on to the public, the required price adjustments take time and expected after-tax receipts will be depressed during that interval.

the time value of money, a dollar of revenue in the near future is worth more now than a dollar of revenue in the more distant future. Thus, a shift to accelerated depreciation rules should stimulate investment while a shift to a less liberal set of depreciation rules should reduce investment.[13] Accelerated depreciation was adopted in 1954 and liberalized in 1962. More recently, a further shortening of allowable depreciation lives on equipment was provided at the beginning of 1971.

In 1962, a special form of tax reduction was introduced in the United States in an effort to stimulate investment. The provision, usually called the *investment tax credit,* allowed business firms to deduct, as a credit against their tax liabilities, 7 percent of the amount of their new investment spending during the accounting period. In effect, this provision lowered the purchase price of any prospective capital asset by the amount of tax-saving that asset purchase entailed, and thus raised the after-tax rate of return projected for that asset. Hence, introducing a tax credit or raising the effective rate stimulates investment while removal of such a credit or reducing the rate reduces investment.[14] The 7 percent tax credit was suspended in 1966 in an effort to slow economic expansion, reinstated in 1967, and suspended again in 1968. More recently, the tax credit was reinstated with minor modification in August of 1971, and in the spring of 1975 was boosted to 10 percent in an effort to stimulate investment.

Other Factors Affecting Investment

There are a number of other, for our purposes "minor," potential determinants of investment spending. A brief discussion of a small sample of such factors follows.

Credit Rationing or Availability. It is sometimes argued that investment depends not only on the interest rate firms have to pay on borrowed funds but also on the availability of credit. The central argument is that "nonprice" rationing of loan funds may prevent some investment projects from being undertaken. For nonprice rationing of credit to be important, the interest

---

[13]Tilting the time pattern of expected after-tax revenues does not alter the total undiscounted dollar value of those revenues. If the rate of interest were zero, changing the time pattern of the after-tax *Rs* would not affect the present value of a capital asset and, thus, would not affect investment.

[14]For a test of the impact on investment of tax policy changes, see Dale W. Jorgenson and Robert E. Hall, "Tax Policy and Investment Behavior," *The American Economic Review* 57 (1967): 391–414. According to Jorgenson and Hall, both the liberalization of depreciation guidelines and the introduction of a tax credit substantially stimulate investment, net investment enjoying a temporary increase and gross investment permanently increasing due to an enlargement of the optimum capital stock. To a sizable extent, however, the Jorgenson and Hall results are built into their investment model. Alternative and more modest appraisals of the impact of tax policies on the level and timing of investment appear in *Tax Incentives and Capital Spending,* ed. G. Fromm (Washington, D.C.: Brookings Institution, 1971).

rate must, for some reason, be prevented from rising to a market clearing level.

The one component of investment that is likely to be most affected by credit rationing is residential construction. Legal ceilings on mortgage interest rates and limits on the rates that can be paid to depositors by those financial institutions that specialize in mortgage loans can result in a flight of lendable funds away from the mortgage market and toward higher-yielding alternatives during periods when market interest rates rise abruptly. In such circumstances borrowable funds for residential construction may simply not be available, and investment in such assets will be diminished.

Proxies for Expected Profitability of Investment. The current level of output is not the only variable that can be chosen as a proxy for expected revenue or expected profitability from investment spending. To cite one alternative, some analysts have suggested that current profit is a better predictor of investment than output is. While the two variables are closely correlated (when output rises profits typically rise), empirical tests seem to favor an income variable as a superior indicator of changes in investment.

Cash Flows. By ignoring the issue, our theoretical analysis suggests that, in making an investment decision, it is immaterial whether the funds to be invested are borrowed or whether they come from the savings (retained earnings and depreciation funds) of the firm. The interest cost (explicit or "opportunity" cost) is the same and, thus, the same investment decision should be made. However, there is some empirical evidence that investment spending is positively related to the flow of internally generated funds. Such a relationship suggests that firms do not consider the true cost of internally generated funds to be as high as that of funds generated by borrowing (which raise a firm's fixed obligations) or funds generated by stock issue (which dilute management's control).[15]

Summary

As the material in this chapter suggests, determination of the aggregate level of investment is quite complex. However, with a thorough grasp of the methods by which individual firms make their investment decisions we were able to build a fairly sophisticated model for explaining investment spending, a model that was capable of telling us the direction of investment response to changes in the interest rate, the size of the capital stock, the confidence of businessmen, tax policy, and so on. Of course, all the specific factors that can alter investment in the short-run do so by affecting the expected profitability (the stream of future Rs or acquisition costs) of capital or its

---

[15]See W. H. Locke Anderson, "Business Fixed Investment: A Marriage of Fact and Fancy" in *The Determinants of Investment Behavior,* ed. Robert Ferber (New York: National Bureau of Economic Research, Columbia University Press, 1967), pp. 413—425.

interest cost. Hence, we were able to summarize our investment model in the simple algebraic form

$$I_{net_t} = I(Y,i)$$

with current output *(Y)* providing a proxy measure for expected business conditions and *i* the market interest rate. While we will employ this some-what simplified investment function in the income determination models constructed in later chapters, the role of the several specific determinants of investment discussed in this chapter cannot be forgotten. Perhaps most importantly, we must remain mindful of the impact on investment of changes in the tax treatment of business income; the government, which possesses discretionary control over tax regulations, can use tax changes to stimulate or retard planned investment.

It may be noted that the highly aggregative treatment of investment developed in this chapter was based on an analysis of business firms' decisions on investment in *plant and equipment*. No special theory of inventory investment or investment in residential housing has been provided. Fortunately, that is only a minor limitation on your understanding of the determinants of investment, which can be quickly eliminated by a brief look at the special nature of those two components of investment. Because inventories are held to meet anticipated sales requirements, the desired stock of inventories may be expected to vary roughly in proportion to the level of expected sales. While differences in the rate of inventory turnover, distance from suppliers, storage bulk, and so on may result in variations among firms in the desired inventory-sales ratio, in the aggregate the desired inventory-sales ratio can be expected to be relatively stable. Hence, an accelerator model can be employed to link net inventory investment with the appropriate sales (output) variable. With current sales employed as a measure of expected sales, empirical evidence indicates that over a year's time, actual inventory investment largely reflects desired changes in inventories, i.e., there is a *full adjustment* to the change in output. Hence, with annual data the accelerator with a λ value of 1 provides a suitable explanation of inventory investment, mirroring the considerable volatility of that component of aggregate investment. For shorter time periods, a partial adjustment form of the accelerator is clearly superior. In no case is there any compelling evidence that inventory investment is influenced significantly by changes in the interest cost of maintaining inventories.[16]

One category of investment, investment in residential housing, is highly sensitive to credit market conditions. By and large, residential housing purchases are mortgage loan financed. Because houses are durable, their purchase can be postponed easily if the interest cost of mortgage loans rises (that tendency should be particularly pronounced if interest rates on mortgages are expected to go down in the future). Moreover, as indicated earlier,

---

[16]See Evans, *Macroeconomic Activity*, Chapter 8.

there are reasons for expecting the availability of mortgage funds to change dramatically as market interest rates vary. At the same time, the income variable that influences households as they consider the long-term commitment to buy a house is surely permanent income. The influence of current income on home purchases is sufficiently small that residential investment typically varies countercyclically, increasing during contractions (when interest rates decline and the availability of mortgage funds increases) and shrinking during expansions.[17] As they do with the other components of investment, empirical investigations of residential investment rely heavily on partial adjustment forms of the accelerator with close attention paid to permanent income, population, and credit market conditions as determinants of the desired stock of housing at any point in time.

In closing our formal discussion of investment it should be recalled that we began our discussion by showing the volatile cyclical pattern of investment in the past. This volatility is readily understood now that we have shown how dependent investment is on expected future events. Expectations, of course, may change quite abruptly, prompting changes in investment that tend to destabilize the economy.

Questions

1. Suppose, as a personal investment, you have the opportunity to purchase a suburban lot for $10,000. You estimate that in five years you will be able to sell the lot for double its purchase price. You now own $10,000 worth of corporate bonds that are yielding a 10 percent annual rate of return. Should you sell the bonds and buy the lot?

2. Suppose the Fizzmore Cola Company has the opportunity to invest in a new cola plant that costs $272,500 and has a life of three years. The company expects the plant to generate annual net revenues of $100,000, $50,000, and $150,000 at the end of the first, second, and third years, respectively. The market interest rate is 5 percent.
   a. Find the present value of this project and determine whether it should be undertaken.
   b. Use the internal rate of return calculation to make that decision.
   c. Make the same calculations you made in (a) and (b) but assume the expected net revenue stream is reversed. What difference does this change in the *timing* of net revenues make? What does this have to do with the tax treatment of business profits?

3. How would the outbreak of all out-war between Japan and China affect the marginal efficiency of investment in the United States?

---

[17]See Jack M. Guttentag, "The Short Cycle in Residential Construction," *The American Economic Review* 51 (1961): 275–298; and William E. Gibson, "Protecting Home-Building from Restrictive Credit Conditions," *Brookings Papers on Economic Activity* 3 (1973): 647–699.

4. Our investment theory provides an inverse relationship between the market interest rate and the level of investment. In reality, we typically find that the level of investment is high when the interest rate is high, and low when the interest rate is low. Can our investment theory be correct? Explain.

5. Suppose, in a new empirical study of investment, you find investment explained by the regression equation:

$$I_t = .25\,(K_t^* - K_{t-1})$$

with

$$K_t^* = a + b_1 Y_t + b_2 i_t$$

where K_t^* is the desired capital stock in period t, K_{t-1} the actual capital stock in the preceding period, Y_t the real income in period t, and i_t the interest rate in period t. Explain the investment theory represented.

6. Explain how the investment tax credit and changes in the depreciation rules business firms are allowed to employ can be used to alter investment.

7. Use the accelerator model with a λ value close to 1 to explain changes in the demand for college teachers. What is wrong with that model?

8. It is frequently observed that during periods of generally exuberant economic activity, with interest rates at relatively high levels, residential construction is depressed while other components of gross investment remain strong. Account for the special behavior of residential construction.

9. Opponents of activist government intervention in the economy often contend that stable budgetary and related policies would eliminate most of the economy's fluctuations. Evaluate this proposition in light of what you know about investment expenditures.

10. There is no concrete upper limit on the level of investment spending. However, because gross investment cannot be negative, the lower limit on negative net investment is dictated by the rate at which the capital stock depreciates. Speculate on how this asymmetry might affect the economy's ability to recover from depression.

Suggested Readings

Anderson, W. H. Locke "Business Fixed Investment: A Marriage of Fact and Fancy." In *The Determinants of Investment Behavior,* pp. 413–425. New York: National Bureau of Economic Research, Columbia University Press.

Eckaus, Richard S. "The Acceleration Principle Reconsidered." *Quarterly Journal of Economics* 67 (1973): 209–230.

Eisner, Robert. "Investment: Fact and Fancy." *The American Economic Review* 53 (1963): 237–246.

Eisner, Robert, and Strotz, R. H. "Determinants of Business Investment." In *Impacts of Monetary Policy,* Commission on Money and Credit, pp. 60–333. Englewood Cliffs, N.J.: Prentice-Hall, 1963.

Evans, Michael. *Macroeconomic Activity: Theory, Forecasting, and Control,* Chapters 4 and 5. New York: Harper & Row, 1969.

Hirshleifer, Jack. *Investment, Interest, and Capital.* Englewood Cliffs, N.J.: Prentice-Hall, 1970.

Johnson, Harry G. *Macroeconomics and Monetary Theory,* Chapter 5. Chicago: Aldine Publishing Co., 1972.

Jorgenson, Dale W. "Anticipations and Investment Behavior." In *The Brookings Quarterly Model of the United States,* edited by James Dusenberry, et al., pp. 35–92. Chicago: Rand McNally and Co., 1965.

Jorgenson, Dale W. "Capital Theory and Investment Behavior." *The American Economic Review* 53 (1963): 247–259.

Jorgenson, Dale W. "Investment Behavior and the Production Function." *The Bell Journal of Economics and Management Science* 3 (1972): 220–251.

Jorgenson, Dale W., and Hall, Robert E. "Tax Policy and Investment Behavior." *The American Economic Review* 57 (1967): 391–414.

Jorgenson, Dale W., and Siebert, C. D. "A Comparison of Alternative Theories of Corporate Investment Behavior." *The American Economic Review* 58 (1968): 681–712.

Keynes, John M. *The General Theory of Employment, Interest, and Money,* Chapters 11 and 12. New York: Harcourt Brace Jovanovich, 1936.

Witte, James G. "The Micro-Foundations of the Social Investment Function." *Journal of Political Economy* 71 (1963): 441–456.

Chapter 7

Money and Interest

The simple income determination models in Chapter 4 showed that investment is an important determinant of the level of economic activity. Through the multiplier, it was shown that an increase (decrease) in the level of planned investment results in an even larger expansion (contraction) in the equilibrium level of output. In turn, the analysis in Chapter 6 indicated that the interest rate is one of the important determinants of the level of planned investment. The relationship between investment and the interest rate was shown to be an inverse one with low rates of interest stimulating investment (*ceteris paribus*) and high interest rates retarding investment. Clearly, interest rate changes can have an impact on the overall level of economic activity that cannot be ignored in a comprehensive model of the macroeconomy. Logically, it would appear that we now must turn our attention to discovering what forces determine the value of the interest rate and, hence, cause the interest rate to change. With that objective in mind, this chapter introduces the *financial sector* of the economy.

In the financial sector, until recently, it has been convenient to distinguish between *income-earning financial assets* and those that provide no income yield, with the latter serving as *money* (providing the convenience yield of being readily spendable). Monetary assets were prevented by law from paying interest. Innovations in the financial market are now threatening to blur the distinction between nonmonetary financial assets, which yield an interest return, and monetary assets, as some assets that are readily spendable now pay interest. Still, those assets that qualify as money cannot be expected to pay an explicit interest reward as high as the yield on nonmonetary assets (which do not offer the convenience yield of being readily spendable).

In our discussion of the financial market place, we will refer to all income-earning, nonmonetary financial assets as *bonds*. Following this distinction between money and bonds, our exploration of the financial sector of the economy will look at both the money and bond markets with emphasis on the former. As it does in the market for goods and services, we will see that the government has the ability to influence events in the financial market place. In conjunction with consideration of the factors that affect interest rates, we will focus close attention on the manner in which the government can do this. In turn, we can begin to assess the reliability with which the government's actions may be translated into predictable responses in the market for goods and services.

The Rate of Interest

As always, to understand complex reality we must construct simple representations of that reality. The *rate of interest* is just such a simple, abstract, representation. There is no such item in the real world, as a glance at the financial pages of any of the country's major newspapers will verify. Indeed, in every actual economic system one observes not one rate of interest but many. At one point in time there is one rate of interest on each of the alternative forms of time deposits at your local bank, another set of rates on U.S. government bonds, a different rate on the credit extended by the local furniture store, and so on. There is not one of these observed rates that can obviously be singled out as the rate of interest.

Observed interest rates should be thought of as *gross* interest rates, which include charges for risk, administrative costs, and the *pure* rate of interest.[1] It is this last component of observed interest rates that we can take as our measure of the interest rate.

The pure rate of interest is the rate that would be observed on a perfectly riskless asset, in a purely competitive market, if administrative costs were zero. Because that interest rate is the opportunity cost of holding noninterest-yielding money, it must be the reward to wealth holders that is just sufficient to entice them to sacrifice the convenience yielded by money balances and hold their wealth in the form of bonds. Although this pure rate of interest is not observable, it is present (and equal in value) in every gross interest rate. In a competitive financial market, differences in observed in-

---

[1] In addition, where capital markets are not perfectly competitive, there will be an additional charge representing pure profit or monopoly rent earned by lenders in the market.

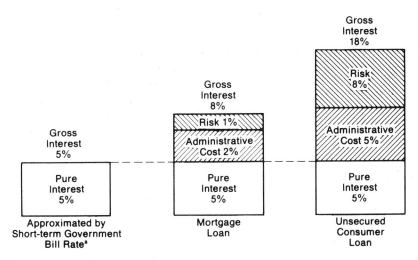

**Figure 7—1 / Components of Observed
Interest Rates on Different Types of Loans**

[a]Short-term U.S. government bonds are virtually riskless because of the government's effective tax-levying power. Also, because government bonds are sold in large "lots," the per unit administrative cost is very low. Thus, the observed interest rate on short-term U.S. debt provides a close approximation of the pure rate of interest.

terest rates are the result of differences in administrative costs or risk allowances, as shown in Figure 7—1. Because the pure rate of interest is a component of every gross rate, a change in the pure rate of interest will change every observed interest rate. That is, an increase in the pure rate of interest, our measure of the interest rate, raises the entire structure of interest rates, and a decrease in the pure rate lowers the entire structure of interest rates. The models developed in this chapter demonstrate how this pure interest rate is determined and how changes in that rate, and, thus, in the entire structure of interest rates, can occur. In these terms, all *bonds* in the following discussion may be viewed as homogeneous.[2]

Interest Rate Determination

In the well-developed financial markets in the United States, a household, business firm, or government unit can easily borrow money to enhance its current purchasing power. Interest is the price paid for the borrowed funds.

---

[2]As a practical matter, with securities that are not homogeneous but that differ in time to maturity, risk of default, etc., a weighted average of the array of observed interest rates can be used as a measure of the interest rate; or, if all market interest rates move together, any one of them can be used as an index of overall interest rate movements. Macroeconomic analysts most often look at movements in long-term bond rates and in the "prime rate" at which banks lend to their best commercial customers for indexes of interest rate movements.

At the same time, interest payments constitute the reward that lenders receive for abstaining from current commodity purchases and lending. For the financial sector to be in equilibrium, the prevailing interest rate must equate borrowers' demands for credit with lenders' supplies. Apparently, the determinants of the equilibrium interest rate can be analyzed in a model consisting of credit supply and demand schedules. The interest rate also serves as an index of the opportunity cost of holding money (which, while it offers a convenience yield, offers no interest or, at most, an interest yield that is less than the yield on bonds). Consequently, the interest rate that provides financial sector equilibrium must also equate society's *demand for money balances with the available money stock.* Hence, analysis of the determinants of the interest rate can also be conducted, concentrating on the supply of and demand for money. The *liquidity preference theory* of interest rate determination, developed by Keynes in *The General Theory,* employs this second approach.[3]

Money Supply

To identify those forces that alter money supply or demand, and hence influence the interest rate, we certainly need to know exactly what "things" should be counted as money. According to a frequently accepted definition, money is anything that is generally accepted as a medium of exchange. While in different times and places gold, silver, jewelry, cigarettes, stones, and other items have served as money, in the United States today only currency (paper and coins) and deposits on which drafts (checks) for payments to third parties can be drawn are generally accepted as a means of payment. The bulk of deposits on which drafts can be drawn continue to be demand deposits in commercial banks. In addition, however, drafts can be drawn against some deposits that pay interest, including NOW (Negotiable Orders for Withdrawal) account balances, automatic transfer from savings (ATS) balances, and credit union share draft balances. As the usage of such deposits grows in the future, a larger proportion of the money stock will be in interest-bearing form.

In addition to serving as a medium of exchange, money also functions as a store of value and as a standard or measure of value. Of course, both of these functions are performed as well by a number of other financial assets. Passbook time deposits, for example, serve as a store of purchasing power and a measure of value just as efficiently as do currency and demand deposits. However, such time deposits are not generally accepted as a medium of exchange. Short-term government securities also serve as an excellent store of purchasing power even though their value is not strictly fixed in dollar terms at every point in time. Yet, government securities are certainly not generally accepted as a medium of exchange.

---

[3]John Maynard Keynes, *The General Theory of Employment, Interest, and Money* (New York: Harcourt Brace Jovanovich, 1936), Chapter 13. The tight link between the money market and the market for credit (bonds) is developed more fully later in this chapter.

Clearly, different financial assets possess different degrees of "moneyness" or "liquidity." Passbook savings deposits are slightly less liquid than currency and demand deposits; short-term government securities are less liquid than time deposits; and other financial assets (long-term government bonds, corporate bonds, and so on) are less liquid than short-term government securities. Because there is a continuum of financial assets that offer differing degrees of liquidity, the selection of a dividing point in the liquidity spectrum for determining which assets are money and which are not involves some element of arbitrariness. For consistency with the mainstream of macroeconomic analysis, which emphasizes the role of money as a medium of exchange, the division must be made so as to exclude from the money stock all assets except currency and checking-type deposits, the two assets that are readily accepted as mediums of exchange. That definition (or any other) is satisfactory if it permits the derivation and statistical estimation of stable money demand and supply functions that can be relied on for predicting interest rate changes. As we proceed, we will see that this requirement: (1) prompts different analysts to favor different definitions of money; and (2) can call for changes in the generally accepted definition of money as the financial system evolves.

Restricted to encompassing currency and checking type deposits, we are focusing on money narrowly defined. Beginning in 1980, the narrowest measure of the money supply reported by the U.S. central bank, the Federal Reserve System, was composed of currency and demand deposits in commercial banks. This money supply measure is labeled M–1a. Adding interest-bearing "checkable" deposits at all depository institutions (including savings and loan associations, mutual savings banks, and credit unions, as well as commercial banks) provides a slightly broader money supply measure labeled M–1b. For purposes of this chapter, the Federal Reserve System can be viewed as controlling the number of dollars of money held by the public (under either definition) so that once the central bank has selected a desired level for the nominal money supply, it can hit and maintain that target stock with considerable precision.[4] As a result, the nominal money stock is fixed by a policy decision of the central bank and is exogenous to the money market models constructed in this chapter.

To correspond to our treatment of the commodity market in which the real demand for goods and services was of major concern, we will focus on the *real* (purchasing power) value of money supplied and demanded in the money market. This is not only more convenient for model-building purposes but also reflects an absence of "money illusion" on the part of the money-using public. That is, in an economy in which all money wages and prices suddenly were doubled, but nothing else changes, twice as many dollars (a doubled value of *nominal* money balances) would be required to

---

[4]Chapter 13 looks at the mechanics of money supply control more closely to explain the assertion that the central bank can and does control the money supply.

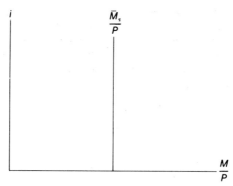

Figure 7—2 / The Real Money Supply

purchase an unchanged volume of goods. A public that recognizes this simple fact, doubling its demand for *nominal* money balances to leave its *real* stock of money balances unchanged, is free of money illusion.

The real value of the existing money stock is nothing more than the nominal money stock deflated by an appropriate index of the general price level. With the central bank setting the nominal money stock at $M_s = \bar{M}_s$, and with a prevailing price level P, the real stock of money can be represented by the vertical schedule $\bar{M}_s/P$ shown in Figure 7—2. By increasing (decreasing) the nominal money stock, with prices held constant, the central bank can shift the money supply schedule to the right (left).

Money Demand

Because the interest rate reflects the opportunity cost of holding money, it seems reasonable to expect the demand for money to rise as its interest cost falls. Recalling that the public demands money because of its purchasing power, Figure 7—3 shows a demand for real money balances M_D/P that agrees with our intuition. That money demand schedule is combined with

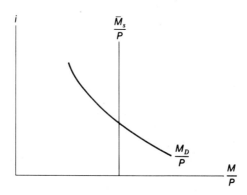

Figure 7—3 / Money Supply and Demand Combined

the money supply schedule from Figure 7—2 to provide an intuitively appealing representation of the money market where forces may be viewed as acting to influence the interest rate. Unfortunately, a great deal of explanation and empirical verification of the demand for money schedule is necessary for us to fully understand the functioning of the money market and appreciate the disagreements among economists over the role that money plays in the economy. That is the task to which we now turn.

The Classical Transactions Demand for Money—If Only it Were So. While it involves some intellectual exertion in reviewing old and outmoded theories, current disagreements over the role of money are clarified by looking at alternative explanations of money demand and at a related concept, the velocity of money. Our departure point is the classical, or what we may think of as pre-Keynesian, *quantity theory of money*. The framework for analysis in the quantity theory is a simple identity called the *equation of exchange*. This equation (identity) can be written as

$$MV = PY$$

where M is the nominal money supply, V is velocity (the number of times each period the average dollar of money is used to buy final goods and services), P is the price level, and Y is real output.

The product MV in the equation of exchange, the number of dollars in circulation times the average frequency with which dollars are used to finance final purchases, is total spending on final goods and services. The product PY, the price level times the volume of real output, represents total receipts from the sale of final goods and services. The identity says simply that total spending equals total receipts. Of course, this identity can be expressed in other forms. For example, it can be rewritten as $V = PY/M$ to define velocity. This expression shows that the velocity of money[5] is the ratio of the value of output purchased to the stock of money available for use in paying for final purchases. With a value of output (GNP) of $2,369 billion in 1979 and a money stock of $382 billion, each dollar of the money stock, on average, was used 6.2 times to buy final goods and services. That is, velocity in 1979 was 6.2.

Rearranging the equation of exchange to isolate the volume of money society possesses yields

$$M = \frac{1}{V} \cdot PY \qquad\qquad [7\text{—}1]$$

or, in terms of real purchasing power,

$$\frac{M}{P} = \frac{1}{V} \cdot Y \qquad\qquad [7\text{—}2]$$

---

[5]Technically, this has been referred to historically as the *income* velocity of money.

In these equations, <u>1/V is the fraction of output (nominal in the first case, real in the second) that society holds command over in money form.</u>

At this point, we have looked just at definitional equalities that, by themselves, are devoid of theoretical content. With one simple step though, the equation of exchange becomes a theory with a prominent history, capable, according to its supporters, of explaining the role of money in the economy. That step involves explaining what determines the velocity (V) with which society willingly uses its money stock, or its inverse $(1/V)$ which is the fraction of output that society willingly holds (i.e., demands) command over in money form.

<u>The basic reason for demanding money recognized by classical theory is the lack of synchronization between income receipts and expenditures.</u> Consider, in this regard, a household that receives its income, say $900 of wages, at the end of each month. Generally, we would not expect that household to immediately spend the full $900, but to face spending needs that gradually use up the $900 income payment during the following month. Figure 7—4 illustrates a simple case in which the household that receives a $900 income payment uses all that income at a steady rate during the following month, spending $30 per day. With a money payment of $900, this household has a full $900 of money balances at the start of the first day of the month, has $870 at the start of the second day, $840 at the start of the third day, and an amount on each subsequent day that is reduced by $30 daily. The average cash balance during the month would be $450. If the household's income

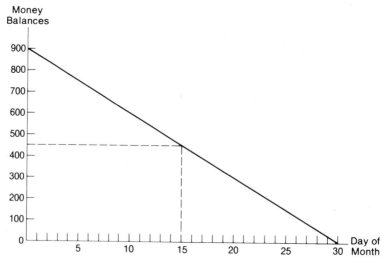

**Figure 7—4 / Transactions Money
Holdings with a Uniform Spending Path**

receipts were instantly spent, i.e., its income receipts and disbursements exactly synchronized, the value of money balances held to finance transactions would be zero. Without that perfect synchronization there is a positive transactions demand for money (at an average of $450 for the household in the example). In like fashion, business firms have expenditures that are not synchronized with their income receipts, and so they demand money for transactions purposes.

According to classical analysis, velocity *(V)* and its inverse *(1/V)*, the fraction of income that society demands to hold command over in money form, are both determined by existing conventions and "institutions." The transactions need for money would be reduced, for example, by an increase in the use of credit, as that results in a better synchronization of income receipts and money payments. Imagine the impact of the creation and popularization of credit cards.

Because, according to the "classicists," institutions and traditions change slowly over time, if at all, over limited time periods *V* and its inverse *(1/V)* can be treated as constants for an economy in equilibrium. The role of money in such a world is easily explained. For an economy producing output Y_0 at price level P_0, a specific fraction $(1/V)$ of income is demanded in money form. That is, money demand is $M_D = (1/V)\,(P_0 \cdot Y_0)$ in nominal form or $M_D/P_0 = (1/V)Y_0$ in real terms. If the existing money stock matches money demand, equilibrium prevails with velocity at the *desired* level. In this case, an increase in the money supply would leave society with larger money balances than it demands. (Remember, it demands fraction $1/V$ of output.) The excess money balances would be spent, raising spending *(P Y)* until the new, larger money stock is the desired fraction $(1/V)$ of the enlarged level of spending on output. Pre-Keynesian classical analysis assumed, further, that prices were sufficiently flexible that the bulk of adjustments in the value of output *(P Y)* would take the form of price changes rather than quantity (real output) changes.

Keynesian Money Demand. As we have seen, understanding the role of money would be wonderfully simple with velocity stable. However, examining the historical record raises doubts about the usefulness of assuming that velocity is stable. Figure 7—5 shows velocity values for three countries over the period 1900–1975. Clearly, there are significant changes in velocity, even over quite brief time intervals. With emphasis placed on the variability of velocity, Keynes had to alter the classical treatment of money demand in order to explain that variability.

Like his classical predecessors, Keynes recognized a transactions demand for money. In addition, however, Keynes recognized an *asset* demand for money; not a demand for money to spend but a demand for money to hold (or, in Keynes' more colorful terms, to *hoard*) as a financial asset. It is from this recognition of an asset demand for money that the modern-day

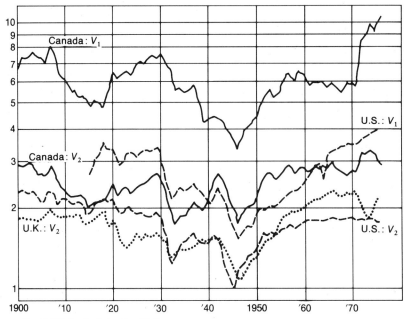

**Figure 7—5 / Velocity[a] in the U.S.,
Canada, and the United Kingdom, 1900—1975**

---

[a]Velocity V_1 is the velocity of money defined narrowly as currency plus demand deposits. Velocity V_2 adds savings deposits.

portfolio-balance money demand models which explain systematic changes in velocity evolved.[6]

As did classical analysis, Keynes' transactions demand for money reflected the need for money balances to bridge the gap between the receipt and disbursement of income. For individuals and firms alike, a larger volume of output purchases would require that more command over goods and services be held in money form. That is, the transactions demand for real money balances (M_t/P) is positively related to real output (Y) both for individual economic units and in the aggregate as shown in Equation (7—3).

$$\frac{M_t}{P} = M(Y) \qquad s.t. \quad \frac{\Delta(M_t/P)}{\Delta Y} > 0. \qquad\qquad [7—3]$$

Because interest is an opportunity cost of holding money for any purpose, assuming that money demand is a negative function of interest rates is compatible with Keynes' specification of the transactions demand for money.

---

[6]It is undeniably true that some classical economists provide more sophisticated explanations of velocity than the standard Keynesian critique of their arguments indicates. For an example of the most sophisticated of classical analyses see Irving Fisher, *The Purchasing Power of Money* (New York: Macmillan, 1911).

However, Keynes himself emphasized the interest sensitivity of speculative, rather than transactions, money demand.

Grouping all income-earning financial assets together and calling them *bonds,* Keynes described the speculative demand for money as a demand for money as an asset in place of bonds *in order to avoid capital losses.* Bonds are merely contractual agreements that obligate a borrower (the bond issuer) to pay fixed sums of money, interest and principal, at stated time intervals. Typically, over the life of a bond the issuer is obligated for semi-annual or annual interest payments while, upon maturity, the *face* or maturity value of the bond must be paid. As an example, an 8 percent coupon yield bond due in twenty years would pay $40 semiannually (or $80 annually) for twenty years plus $1000 at the end of twenty years. What would the present value of such a bond be at prevailing interest yields? Of course, money does not offer the interest earnings that bonds do, so the only time an individual would want his speculative wealth held in money form is when he or she expects bond prices to fall, i.e., when capital losses are expected on bonds.

Because bonds represent contracts for specific money payments, a decline in bond prices corresponds to an increase in interest yields. The expectation of a decline in bond prices, then, is an expectation of increases in interest rates.[7] In Keynes' analysis, while there is a great diversity of opinion, it was contended that all participants in the financial market have some notion of what the normal level of interest is. Those who think interest rates are above normal would expect a decline in yields (a rise in bond prices) and would choose to hold their speculative wealth in bonds. Those who think interest yields are below normal would expect a rise in yields (a decline in bond prices) and, to avoid capital losses, would want their spec-

---

[7]Less common than bonds with specified maturity dates, some bonds are designed never to mature but to provide a perpetual stream of equal semiannual or annual interest payments. Such *perpetual* bonds are particularly easy to work with computationally. If an individual with $100 of savings can choose between holding that savings in money and a $100 perpetual bond currently paying a 10 percent annual coupon yield ($10 per year in interest payments), his choice depends on what he *expects* to happen to the market rate of interest in the future. If he expects the market interest rate to rise, say, to 12 percent in the next year, he will keep his savings in money form rather than buy the bond, for with an increase in the market interest rate from 10 to 12 percent, the market price of a perpetual bond paying $10 yearly would fall from $100 to $83.33. At a price of $83.33, our saver's perpetual bond would be yielding a 12 percent rate of return like all other securities in the bond market. Of course, this equilibrium market price is just the present value of the bond, obtained using the 12 percent market interest rate as the discount rate applied to future income receipts generated by that bond. From the section on present value calculations in Chapter 6, you may recall that the present value of an asset that yields a perpetual stream of uniform payments (as the perpetual bond does) is $PV = R/i$, where R is the yearly payment and i is the market interest rate. The loss in capital (market) value of $16.67 on the bond more than offsets the $10 coupon payment our saver would receive in one year as a bond-holder, so he clearly would be worse off holding the bond than if he kept his $100 savings in idle, money form.

ulative wealth in money form.[8]

Given the state of expectations regarding interest rates, a decline in actual yields would convince more financial market participants that interest rates are below normal and will rise in the future, adding their asset demands for money to existing speculative demand. In real terms, then, the speculative demand for money (M_{sp}/P) is a negative function of the interest rate (i) as Equation (7—4) shows.

$$\frac{M_{sp}}{P} = 1(i) \qquad s.t. \; \frac{\Delta(M_{sp}/P)}{\Delta i} < 0 \qquad [7\text{—}4]$$

Overall demand for real money balances (M_D/P) is the sum of transactions demand $\left[M_t/P = M(Y)\right]$ and speculative demand $\left[M_{sp}/P = 1(i)\right]$. Thus total money demand is positively related to output (transactions demand expanding with output) and negatively related to the interest rate as indicated in Equation (7—5).

$$\frac{M_D}{P} = \frac{M_t}{P} + \frac{M_{sp}}{P}$$

$$= M(Y) + 1(i) \qquad [7\text{—}5]$$

$$= M(Y,i) \qquad s.t. \; \frac{\Delta M_D/P}{\Delta Y} > 0$$

$$\frac{\Delta M_D/P}{\Delta i} < 0$$

In Figure 7—6, a money demand function with the properties described above is drawn for output level Y_0. As that schedule shows, interest rate changes call forth movements along the prevailing money demand schedule (as from point (a) to point (b) for a drop in the interest rate from i_0 to i_1). In contrast, a change in real output shifts the money demand schedule, for example, to the position of (M_D^*/P) for an increase in output to level Y_1. Finally, from Equation (7—5), note that as long as Y and i stay unchanged, the demand for *real* money balances is not altered by a change in the price level so the *nominal* demand for money changes in step with prices. That is, for a price level that is multiple λ of the original price level, P^0, the real demand for money is

$$\frac{M_D}{P} = \frac{\lambda M_D^0}{\lambda P^0} = M(Y,i) \qquad [7\text{—}6]$$

so nominal demand λM_D^0 has increased in step with prices.

---

[8]To be more specific, the total yield from bond holdings consists of the interest yield plus any capital gain (loss) from a change in bond prices. The percentage yield is:

$$\% \text{ yield} = i + \frac{1}{B}\frac{\Delta B}{\Delta t}$$

where i is the interest yield at the price the buyer purchases the bond and B is the bond price, making $1/B(\Delta B/\Delta t)$ the percentage rate of capital gain yield. As long as wealth-holders expect the overall yield to be positive $\left[i > -1/B(\Delta B/\Delta t)\right]$, they prefer to hold bonds rather than money, according to the Keynesian analysis. If bond prices are expected to fall (interest rates rise) at a rate that exceeds the interest yield on bonds, wealth-holders would be better off holding their savings in money form.

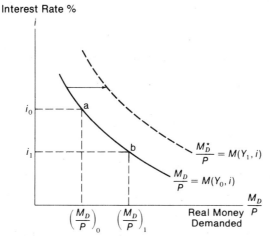

Figure 7—6 / Money Demand

Velocity Again. In light of some weaknesses in Keynes' original explanation, we will have a bit more to say about the transactions and speculative demands for money. To complete Keynes' critical response to the classical treatment of money demand, recall that for money market equilibrium (with real money balances equal to the demand for them), the equation of exchange indicates that money demand is fraction $1/V$ of real output, or

$$\frac{M_D}{P} = \frac{1}{V} \cdot Y \qquad [7-7]$$

Keynes' analysis indicates that real money demand (M_D/P) is a function of real output and the interest rate so it follows that

$$M(Y,i) = \frac{1}{V} \cdot Y \qquad [7-8]$$

Velocity then is given by the equation

$$V = \frac{Y}{M(Y,i)} \qquad [7-9]$$

Clearly, velocity cannot be considered constant but varies with output and the interest rate. Notably, an interest rate increase lowers the real demand for money and raises velocity; society squeezes more work out of its money balances, economizing on the quantity held as interest rates rise to allow an existing money stock to finance more purchases. Conversely, a decline in the interest cost of holding money raises money demand and lowers the average frequency of use of each unit of the money stock. Velocity is no longer constant but may change abruptly in the face of changes in financial market conditions.

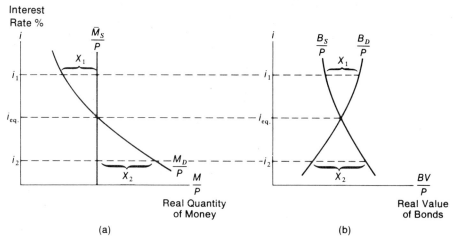

Figure 7—7 / The Equilibrium Interest Rate

The Equilibrium Interest Rate

Combining the money supply schedule from Figure 7—2 with the money demand schedule from Figure 7—6 provides the money market diagram in part (a) of Figure 7—7. In this diagram, the equilibrium interest rate occurs (like any other competitively determined price) at the intersection of the market supply and demand schedules. Hence, $i_{eq.}$ is the equilibrium interest rate.

Moreover, because, in the simple Keynesian model, savers have only two financial assets in which they can hold their accumulated savings, money and bonds, the interest rate that makes wealth-holders just satisfied to hold the existing stock of real money in their portfolios must also make them just satisfied to hold the existing real stock of bonds. Illustrating that point, the market for bonds is depicted in part (b) of Figure 7—7, with bond supply and bond demand equated at interest rate $i_{eq.}$.

Briefly focusing attention directly on the bond market representation in part (b) of Figure 7—7, you should notice that our bond supply and demand schedules have an unusual appearance; the bond supply schedule (B_s/P) slopes *downward* from left to right and the bond demand schedule (B_D/P) slopes *upward*. The apparent reversal of the normal slopes of those schedules is the result of plotting bond supply and demand against the interest rate instead of against bond prices (remember, bond prices are inversely related to the interest rate). Also, for consistency with part (a) of Figure 7—7, the horizontal axis of the bond market diagram shows the real value of bonds supplied and demanded. With the bonds in our analysis assumed to be perpetuities, the market value of every bond is $V = R/i$ and, if there are B bonds in existence, the total real value of the existing stock (supply) of bonds is $B \cdot V/P = B \cdot R/iP$. With an increase in the interest rate, the value of every bond, hence of the entire existing supply of bonds, falls as reflected in the bond supply schedule B_s/P. On the other hand, because an interest rate increase convinces more wealth-holders that their savings should be held in bonds rather than in money, the bond demand schedule slopes upward.[9]

With the aid of the bond market, we can now corroborate the claim that $i_{eq.}$ is the equilibrium interest rate and, furthermore, we can demonstrate that it is a stable market-clearing rate. Suppose that the actual market interest rate should somehow rise to a level i_1. With more wealth-holders wanting to hold their accumulated savings in bonds and fewer wanting their savings in money form at this elevated interest rate, there would be an excess supply of money and an excess demand for bonds. Further, because our wealth-holders are confined to placing their wealth either in money or bonds, the excess supply of money must be equal in real value to the excess demand for bonds (value X_1 in both the money and bond markets). However, despite the efforts of those individuals who hold larger real money balances than desired to reduce those money hoards through the purchase of bonds, the total stock of money balances that society must hold remains unchanged. What will change is the interest rate, for the excess demand for bonds, which must accompany an excess supply of money, will drive bond prices upward. As bond prices rise (the interest rate falls), the quantity of money demanded increases, closing the gap between money demand and the constant supply of money. Likewise, the fall in the interest rate (increase in bond prices) closes the gap between bond supply and bond demand. Clearly any excess supply of money (excess demand for bonds) will set in motion forces that depress the interest rate toward the equilibrium rate, a rate that makes society willing to hold the existing stock of money.

Should the interest rate somehow fall below the equilibrium level, say, to level i_2 in Figure 7—7, there will be an excess demand for money and, correspondingly, an excess supply of bonds. The resulting effort by society to build up its money balances by selling the alternative asset, bonds, will not change the total money stock but will raise the rate of interest (lower the price of bonds) sufficiently to make society satisfied with the available supply of money balances.

Changes in the Interest Rate. The equilibrium interest rate can change only as a result of a shift in either money (bond) supply or money (bond) demand. Suppose the central bank chooses to increase the money stock, say, from $\overline{M}_S/P$ to $\overline{M}_S'/P$ as shown in Figure 7—8a. One way the central bank can do this is by purchasing bonds, in effect swapping money for bonds. Without going into detail regarding the central bank's action (again, money supply control is covered in Chapter 13), the addition of the central bank's demand for bonds shifts the bond demand schedule from BV/iP to BV'/iP in Figure 7—8b.

---

[9]Because our analysis is basically short-run, we can ignore the flow change in bond supply, which will be negligible compared to the existing physical stock of bonds.

Interest Rate %

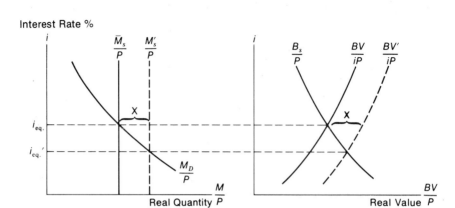

(a)   (b)

**Figure 7—8 / The Interest Rate
Response to an Increase in Money Supply**

The shift in the money supply schedule creates an excess supply of money balances (an excess demand for bonds) in amount X. As before, though, the effort to swap money for bonds will not alter the total money stock, but it will drive the interest rate down (bond prices up) to a level that makes the public just willing to hold the existing stock of money balances. That is, the interest rate must fall from $i_{eq.}$ to $i_{eq.}'$ in response to this money supply increase as we can see either from the money market model or its mirror image, the bond market.

With the bond market model carrying the same information as the money market model, we may simplify our graph by dropping one; and, by convention, it is the bond market that is supressed. Following this convention, Figure 7—9 uses the money market model to show the effect of a money supply reduction. Reducing the money supply creates an excess demand for money (an excess supply of bonds), pushing down bond prices and raising the interest rate until, at $i_{eq.}'$, society is just willing to hold the reduced real volume of money balances that the central bank has provided.

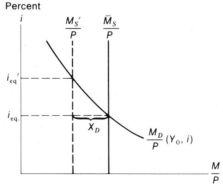

Figure 7—9 / A Money Supply Reduction

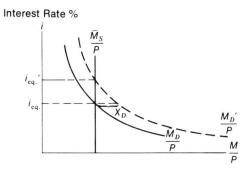

Interest Rate %

Figure 7—10 / An Increase in Money Demand

Shifting our focus to the demand side of the money market, suppose, with the money supply fixed, something happens to increase money demand from M_D/P to M_D'/P as shown in Figure 7—10. The resulting excess demand for money balances (excess supply of bonds) would drive the interest rate up to $i_{eq.}'$. Conversely, a decrease in the demand for money would result in a fall in the interest rate. In this regard, it must be emphasized that any one money demand schedule is valid only for one real income level. A change in the level of real income shifts the money demand schedule, to the right for an income increase and to the left for an income decline. What else would cause the demand for money to change?

Note that, with an income increase, if the money stock is unchanged, velocity must have increased; and it is the increase in the interest cost of holding money that makes society willing to "economize" on money balances, using the existing money stock to finance a larger volume of purchases. Rather than being an institutionally determined constant, velocity changes systematically in response to shocks that alter output and the interest rate.

Extending What We Know

For events that occur in the financial arena, such as a change in the money stock, to have a predictable influence on the economy, the relationship between the demand for money and the factors that affect it must be stable. Table 7—1 provides a summary of some prominent empirical studies of the factors that affect money demand. This table need not be studied in detail; indeed, we will review a more recent and detailed study of money demand a bit later. However, a brief scan of the table sheds needed light on the reasonableness of the Keynesian form of the money demand function.

The studies cited in Table 7—1 were for different time periods, used different measures of the interest rate (for example, some used a long-term "bond" rate and some a short-term "bill" rate for the interest variable), and fitted functions that differ in precise algebraic formulation. While the resulting measures of response in money demand to changes in income and

Table 7—1 / Empirical Studies of the Money Demand Function

(1) Authors	(2) General Form of Demand Function[a]	(3) Elasticities[b] Interest	(3) Elasticities[b] Income	(4) Period of Study	(5) R^2
Bronfenbrenner-Mayer	$M = M(Y,i,NW)$ NW = Net Worth or "Wealth"	−.33	1.23	1919–1956	.91
Latané	$M = M(Y,i)$	−.89	1.00	1909–1958	n.a.
Christ	$M = M(Y,i)$	−.58	1.00	1892–1959	.76
Teigen	$M = M(Y,i)$	−.05	.51	1946–1959	.99
Heller	$M = M(Y,i)$	−.104	1.076	1957–1958	.92
Lee	$M = M(Y,i)$	−.75	1.076	1951–1965	.94

[a]The equations are found in Martin Bronfenbrenner and Thomas Mayer, "Liquidity Functions in the American Economy," *Econometrica* 27(1960): 810–834; Henry Latané, "Income Velocity and Interest Rates: A Pragmatic Approach," *Review of Economics and Statistics* 42(1960): 445–449; Carl Christ, "Interest Rates and 'Portfolio Selection' Among Liquid Assets in the U.S.," in *Measurement in Economics,* ed. Carl Christ, et al. (Stanford, Cal.: Stanford University Press, 1963), pp. 201–218; Ronald Teigen, "The Demand for and Supply of Money," in *Readings in Money, National Income and Stabilization Policy,* ed. Ronald Teigen and Warren Smith (Homewood, Ill.: Richard D. Irwin, 1965), pp. 44–76; H. R. Heller, "The Demand for Money: The Evidence from the Short-Run Data," *Quarterly Journal of Economics,* 1965, pp. 291–303; Tong Hun Lee, "Alternative Interest Rates and the Demand for Money: The Empirical Evidence," *The American Economic Review* 57(1967): 1168–1181.

Other important contributions to the literature on empirical tests of money demand functions include Karl Brunner and Alan Meltzer, "Some Further Evidence on Supply and Demand Functions for Money," *Journal of Finance* 19(1964): 240–283; Milton Friedman, "The Demand for Money—Some Theoretical and Empirical Results," *Journal of Political Economy* 67(1959): 327–351; David Laidler, "The Rate of Interest and the Demand for Money—Some Empirical Evidence," *Journal of Political Economy* 74(1966): 545–555; and Stephen Goldfield, "The Demand for Money Revisited," *Brookings Papers on Economic Activity* 3(1973): 577–646; Edgar Feige and Douglas Pearce, "The Substitutability of Money and Near Monies: A Survey of the Time-Series Evidence," *The Journal of Economic Literature* 15(1977): 439–469.

[b]To refresh your memory, price elasticity is the percentage of change in quantity divided by the percentage of change in price, and income elasticity is the percentage of change in quantity divided by the percentage of change in income. The interest rate is the price of holding money. You might also note that the Christ and Latané studies employed regression models that constrained the income elasticity of money demand to be unitary.

the interest rate differ in size, all agree that there is a statistically significant positive relationship between income and money demand, and a significant inverse relationship between money demand and the interest rate. Certainly, the evidence appears to suggest that money demand is a stable (hence predictable) function of income and the interest rate. Moreover, it definitely indicates that the Keynesian form of the money demand function $[M_D/P = M(Y,i)]$ is consistent with experience.

Uncertainty and Money Demand

Despite its consistency with empirical evidence, there are shortcomings in the Keynesian liquidity preference explanation of the money demand function that have necessitated the development of alternative explanations. One of these focuses on the speculative motive for holding money. Keynes' speculative demand for money provided an aggregate money demand schedule that was negatively related to the interest rate. However, in Keynes' explanation, a smooth, continuous, functional relationship between the interest rate and money demand is possible only if there is a diversity of opinion about the value of the "normal" rate of interest among the millions of individual demanders of money. That is, there is no comparable smooth, continuous interest response in individual money demand functions because, in Keynes' analysis, every individual would want to hold *all* of his speculative wealth either in money (expecting bond prices to fall) or in bonds (expecting bond prices to rise), never part in each. This kind of behavior is reasonable if individuals feel certain they know the future path of movement of the interest rate (bond prices). However, the real world rarely allows individuals to hold expectations about the future with certainty. The existence of uncertainty or risk is likely to prompt an individual to hold wealth in both money and securities, that is, to diversify his portfolio. The arguments below, developed by James Tobin, show that, in a world characterized by uncertainty or risk, an individual's speculative money demand can be a continuous inverse function of the interest rate.[10] As a consequence, a smooth aggregate relationship between the interest rate and money demand is possible without appeal to a diversity of opinion that would gradually erode as the interest rate rests at a near-constant level for substantial time periods. We know that individuals hold diversified portfolios (for example, one individual might be observed holding money, stocks, bonds, and savings deposits simultaneously). This would not be the case if there were certainty with respect to yields on various assets. Instead, individuals would hold only one asset, the one that offers the highest yield.

In a Keynesian world where there are only two liquid assets, money and long-term bonds, an individual can increase the expected yield on his portfolio of wealth holdings only by increasing the proportion of his portfolio held in the form of interest-yielding bonds. However, if interest rates (thus bond prices) are subject to unexpected movements, raising the proportion of the portfolio held in bonds increases the risk of capital loss the individual wealth-holder faces. With all bonds assumed to be identical, we can graphically describe the risk-yield trade-off available to an individual, as in Figure 7—11. In that figure, the expected percentage yield on the individual's total portfolio of liquid assets is measured on the vertical axis while the total portfolio risk he is exposed to is measured on the horizontal axis. As indicated by the straight-line trade-off schedule, with identical bonds both expected yield and risk increase in direct proportion to the allocation of speculative wealth to bond holdings. If an individual's entire portfolio is held in money form (point A in Figure 7—11), there is zero yield and zero risk of loss from interest rate changes (for simplicity, it is assumed that there is *no* interest paid on money, but all that is necessary is that the yield on money

---

[10]See James Tobin, "Liquidity Preference as Behavior Toward Risk," *Review of Economic Studies*, 25(1958): 65–68.

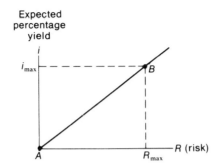

Figure 7—11 / Risk-Yield Trade-off Available to a Wealth Holder

be less than it is on bonds). In contrast, with a specific total stock of liquid wealth in the portfolio, both expected yield and risk attain their maximum values of i_{max} and R_{max} respectively when the entire portfolio is held in the form of bonds (point B in Figure 7—11).

If the typical wealth holder finds risk unpleasant (is risk-averse[11]), he will be willing to hold a higher-risk portfolio of assets only if compensated by a higher expected yield on that portfolio. We can represent an individual's willingness to trade yield for risk by a set of indifference curves, as shown in Figure 7—12. By definition, an individual is indifferent to alternative positions on any one indifference curve. For example, an individual would feel equally well off at position A or A' on indifference curve II. However, a movement to a higher indifference curve provides an unequivocal improvement in the individual's well-being (in our diagram, a movement to a higher indifference curve provides a higher expected yield with no increase in risk or equal yield with lowered risk).

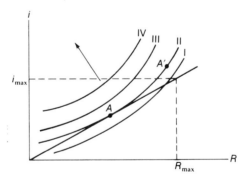

Figure 7—12 / Utility-Maximizing Portfolio Equilibrium

---

[11]Individuals who are risk-averse would prefer to receive $100 with certainty to having a 50 percent probability of receiving $0 and a 50 percent probability of $200, the *expected value* of which is $100.

As indicated earlier, a risk-averse individual will accept a riskier portfolio only if compensated for the accompanying disutility by a higher expected rate of return. Further, it is usually assumed that the higher the level of risk the portfolio is subject to, the larger must be the compensatory addition to the expected yield on the portfolio. It is this set of assumptions that dictates the shape of the indifference curves in Figure 7—12. Our utility-maximizing individual would choose to hold the one determinate mix of money and bonds that would place him on the highest attainable indifference curve (point A on curve II), given the initial endowment of wealth that constrains the size of his portfolio, the interest rate, and the degree of uncertainty with respect to future interest rates (bond prices).

Now, suppose the market interest rate (the expected percentage rate of return on bond holdings) rises with no change in the perceived riskiness of bonds. This change in the expected percentage yield on bonds would rotate the available risk-yield trade-off schedule counterclockwise, as shown in Figure 7—13. As a consequence, our utility-maximizing individual would change the composition of his portfolio to move from point A to point B. The new portfolio (point B) could be subject to more risk (R_1 instead of R_0) only if the proportion of the portfolio held in bonds were to increase and, therefore, if the proportion held in money were to decrease. Thus, for the individual represented by Figure 7—13, we have shown that an increase in the interest rate can reduce the speculative demand for money. Direct aggregation of such individual speculative demand schedules would generate a market speculative money demand function exhibiting the same property of inverse interest sensitivity without relying on a diversity of opinion about a normal interest rate in the process.

Tobin's analysis is surely a clever generalization of the Keynesian speculative demand for money. Because it shares a serious weakness with the Keynesian analysis, however, it cannot stand by itself as the explanation of interest elasticity in money demand. The common weakness stems from the

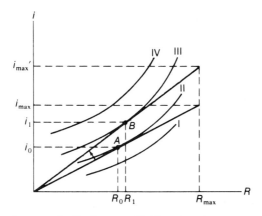

Figure 7—13 / An Increase in the Interest Yield on Bonds

fact that both Keynes and Tobin develop their arguments in an artificial world that has only two assets: money which is constant in nominal value, and bonds, the market value of which varies with changes in the interest rate.

In the real world, wealth can also be held in stocks, short-term bonds, savings bonds, savings accounts, and so on. The existence of a significant speculative demand for money in such a world has been seriously questioned because individuals who fear bond price declines can still hold their wealth in an interest-bearing form other than money with little or no fear of capital losses from interest rate changes; for example, in a savings account, in a certificate of deposit, or in ninety-day treasury "bills," all of these assets being essentially free of the risk of loss from interest rate changes and virtually instantly convertible into money or other assets. Hence, the effort to avoid risk by holding a diversified portfolio can account for the demand for "safe" assets, such as savings deposits, but that motivation alone cannot explain the interest sensitivity of the demand for money defined narrowly.

Interest-Sensitive Transactions Demand for Money

If speculative demand cannot account for money demand's interest sensitivity, the interest responsiveness of transactions money demand must. That a significant interest sensitivity in transactions demand should be expected has been demonstrated by both William Baumol and James Tobin.[12]

Baumol's analysis suggests that transactions money holding should be treated as an inventory from which gradual drains occur. There are costs involved in maintaining this inventory (as is the case with every inventory), and it is in the interest of any individual or business firm to minimize the costs of maintaining an inventory of money that allows transactions needs to be met.

Let us look at an individual's inventory control task assuming, for simplicity, that his or her purchase transactions are perfectly foreseen and occur in a steady stream. If, at the beginning of each time period, money balances in amount w are acquired and steadily expended through the period until exhausted at the end of the period, average transactions balances held will be $w/2$. This familiar flow pattern is graphed, basically as before, in Figure 7—14.

There are two components of the total cost of maintaining the inventory of money balances from which the individual draws. First, if i is the available market interest rate (or, with a positive interest yield on money, the gap between the yield on nonmonetary assets and the interest yield on monetary assets), then the value of one cost component each period, the foregone

---

[12]William Baumol, "The Transactions Demand for Cash: An Inventory Theoretic Approach," *Quarterly Journal of Economics* 46(1952): 545–546, and James Tobin, "The Interest-Elasticity of Transactions Demand for Cash," *Review of Economics and Statistics* 38(1956): 241–247.

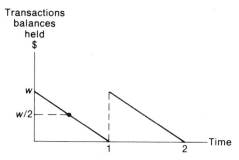

Figure 7—14 / The Time Path of Transactions Balances

interest income on an average volume of money inventory of $w/2$, is simply $i\,w/2$. In addition, each time a cash acquisition occurs there are noninterest transactions costs, such as brokerage fees for converting securities into cash, postage, bookkeeping expenses, and transportation costs to a bank or broker. If T is the value of transactions that must be financed in our selected time period, and w is the size of withdrawals, then T/w is the number of cash acquisitions (withdrawals) required. If the dollar transactions cost of making one cash acquisition or withdrawal is n, then the noninterest cost of money inventory management in our selected period is $N = n\,T/w$.

Thus, the total cost of money inventory management is

$$tc = i \cdot w/2 + n \cdot T/w, \qquad [7\text{—}10]$$

the interest cost plus transactions (withdrawal) cost. If an individual holds large cash balances, there will be few withdrawals and $n \cdot T/w$ will be small. Foregone interest costs will be large, however. Conversely, small average cash balances will result in relatively high transactions costs and low interest costs. Only one size of withdrawal (thus of average cash balances) will minimize the total cost of maintaining adequate cash inventory.

Figure 7—15 shows how the interest and transactions costs of maintaining an inventory of transactions balances vary with the size of withdrawal.

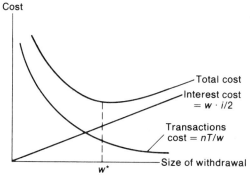

**Figure 7—15 / The Costs of a Cash Inventory
for a Specified Volume of Transactions per Period**

Vertically summing these two components of inventory cost yields the total cost schedule plotted in that figure. The size of withdrawals that minimizes the total cost of maintaining an inventory of cash balances sufficient to finance our T dollars of transactions per period is w^*. In this example then, average money balances would be $w^*/2$.

An increase in the interest yield on nonmonetary assets would rotate the interest-cost schedule counterclockwise, shifting the total cost curve upward and leftward. The leftward shift of the total cost schedule would reduce the cost-minimizing size of cash withdrawals and, thus, reduce the average volume of desired transactions balances. Quite simply, the increase in the interest cost of holding an inventory of transactions balances induces a reduction in the quantity of dollars demanded for that purpose.

An increase in the volume of transactions to be financed during our observation period would shift the transactions cost schedule upward because more withdrawals of any selected size would be required to meet transactions needs. As a result, the total cost schedule would be shifted to the right, increasing the optimum size of withdrawal and average size of transactions balances.[13]

The inventory model argues, then, that transactions demand for money is positively related to the volume of transactions and inversely related to the interest rate. These conclusions have general applicability because our model was developed to analyze either individual or business firm behavior. That is not to say, however, that we should expect to see the average individual investing a fraction of his monthly salary in interest-yielding securities which he expects to exchange for money during the following month in order to meet his transactions needs. For most individuals, the fixed cost of converting cash into securities and, later, back into cash exceeds the incremental interest income that could be earned during the period between income receipts. On the other hand, a large business firm that must accumulate sizable cash balances to pay annual employee bonuses or to meet

---

[13]The *formula* for the optimum size of withdrawal is $w = \sqrt{2nT/i}$. This formula makes it clear that the optimum size withdrawal and corresponding average cash inventory ($w/2$) varies inversely with the interest rate. It also suggests that transactions demand for money is proportional to the *square root* of the volume of transactions, implying that there are some *scale economies* in cash holding.

The derivation of the optimum withdrawal formula is a straightforward application of the classical calculus maximization process. If the total cost of maintaining the cash inventory is

$$tc = \frac{i}{2} \; w + n \; \frac{T}{w}$$

the rate of change (first derivative) of total cost with respect to withdrawal size is

$$\frac{d(tc)}{dw} = \frac{i}{2} - n\frac{T}{w^2}.$$

Setting the rate of change equal to zero (an extreme value of the total cost function) and solving for the withdrawal size yields the formula above. The second derivative of the total cost function is positive, indicating that the extreme value for total cost is a minimum value.

quarterly tax liabilities may well profit from investing those funds temporarily in interest-earning securities.

It should be apparent that the inventory model provides an aggregate money demand function that is qualitatively equivalent to the Keynesian money demand model. According to either model, aggregate money demand is a positive function of the income level and an inverse function of the interest rate. Significantly though, the inventory model can explain the empirically observed interest sensitivity of money demand without resorting to a speculative demand for money.

Goldfeld's Tests. The most comprehensive effort to expose the modern view of money demand to empirical testing was conducted in 1973 by Stephen Goldfeld.[14] Goldfeld's tests were designed to measure both: (1) the size of the response in money demand to interest rates and real income; and (2) the timing of that response. As with other important macroeconomic variables (notably consumption and investment), the response of money demand to the factors that influence it involves a time lag with the response accumulating gradually to its full, long-run value.

Goldfeld uses two interest rates as measures of the opportunity cost of holding money. The first, reflecting the fact that time deposits can be substituted for household demand deposit balances, is the yield rate on time deposits (i_{TD}). The second is the rate on *commercial paper* (i_{CP}), which is a short-term debt instrument issued by corporations. In practice, commercial paper is highly liquid and, as a consequence, is often purchased by businesses that have surplus funds for short time intervals and wish to earn some return on those funds. For that reason, the commercial paper rate is chosen as the index of the opportunity cost to business firms of holding money balances.

Table 7—2 shows, for one, four, and eight quarters, and in the long-run (∞), the real income and interest elasticities of the demand for money. According to that table, a one percentage point increase (as from 5 percent to 6 percent, a 20 percent increase) in interest rates in general, which would include like rises in i_{TD} and i_{CP}, would eventually reduce the demand for money by a bit over 4½ percent $\left[(-.160 - .067) \cdot 20\% = 4.54\%\right]$. This full response takes time, however, with about 73 percent $\left[\dfrac{.117}{.160} = \dfrac{.049}{.067} = .73\right]$ of the response occurring in the first year after interest rates rise. The elasticity entries in the real income column show that a rise in real income raises the demand for money. This response, however, is not fully felt immediately but accumulates gradually. Moreover, even in the long-run, the demand for money does not rise in the same proportion as real income, but only by 68 percent of income's increase. It appears that there may be "economies of scale" in the use of money, a result that is implied by the inventory approach to money demand (see footnote 13).

---

[14]Stephen Goldfeld, "The Demand for Money Revisited," *Brookings Papers on Economic Activity* (1973:3) 577–646.

Table 7—2 / Elasticities of Narrowly Defined
Money Demand to Real Income and Interest Rates

Quarters after Change in:	Income (Y)	Time Deposit Yields (i_{TD})	Commercial Paper Yields (i_{CP})
1	0.19	−0.045	−0.019
2	0.33	−0.077	−0.033
3	0.43	−0.100	−0.042
4	0.50	−0.117	−0.099
8	0.63	−0.148	−0.062
Long-run (∞)	0.68	−0.160	−0.067

Source: Stephen Goldfeld, "The Demand for Money Revisited," *Brookings Papers on Economic Activity* (1973:3).

Goldfeld's study also involves statistical tests of the stability of the response of money demand to changes in income and interest rates. In this regard, what he found ". . . most interesting is the apparent sturdiness of a quite conventional formulation of the money demand function." He concludes that ". . . the conventional equation exhibits no marked instabilities."[15] Thus, the "conventional" money demand function, with money demand dependent on income and interest rates, has been widely supported theoretically and empirically, both in terms of its form and its reliability (stability). Still, recent experience indicates that there are limits remaining on our ability to predict money demand responses.

Case In Point IV

The Case of the Missing Money

While a great deal of effort has been expended in trying to construct and statistically test money demand functions, since 1974 demand has not changed in the manner predicted by money demand regression equations fitted to data prior to that time. There has been an unpredicted shift in the money demand function as society's demand for money began expanding much more slowly, beginning at the start of 1974, than predicted by available money demand equations.[16]

Table 7—3 illustrates the magnitude of prediction errors based on Goldfeld's money demand equation.

---

[15]Goldfeld, "The Demand for Money," p. 632.

[16]See Stephen Goldfeld, "The Case of the Missing Money," *Brookings Papers on Economic Activity* (1976:3): 683–730.

Table 7—3 / Actual Values, Forecast Values, and Errors in Money Demand, Quarterly from 1974:1 to 1976:2

	Billions of 1972 dollars		
	M_1 money demand		
Year and Quarter	Actual	Forecast	Error
	244.4		
1974: 1	241.2	245.6	−1.2
2	236.7	244.1	−3.0
3	232.3	242.5	−5.8
4	226.9	241.8	−9.5
1975: 1	228.9	241.6	−14.7
2	228.6	242.6	−14.0
3	228.7	243.8	−15.2
4	226.1	245.9	−19.4
1976: 1	225.9	248.2	−22.3
2	227.9	250.3	−22.3

For the ten-quarter period actual money demand averaged $13 billion less than predicted and the error for 1976:2 is nearly 10 percent. Of course, this underprediction of money demand is matched by an equal percentage underprediction of velocity. With a velocity value of 6, which is a bit less than its actual value at the end of 1979, and a money stock of $390 billion (its value at the end of 1979) a 10 percent underprediction of velocity corresponds to a $234 billion underprediction of spending. You might expect a monetary policy that aims at providing a particular money stock based on a money demand function this much in error to be more than a little bit destabilizing.

Institutional innovations, such as the emergence of telephone transfers of funds from saving to checking accounts, the appearance in the Northeast of Negotiable Orders for Withdrawal (NOW) accounts, automatic transfers from savings to checking accounts, and overnight loans from large depositors to their banks have been cited as explanations of the apparent shrinkage in money demand. Economic factors such as: (1) the acceleration of inflation in recent years, and (2) rising tax burdens that divert money, in currency form, into unrecorded transactions in the "underground economy" may be causing an apparent shift in the money demand function. The case of the missing money has not, however, been fully solved in a convincing manner at this time.

With the apparent shift of the money demand function after 1973, a great deal more research has been devoted to testing for the stability of money demand functions. A number of the studies conducted in recent years conclude that the demand for money, narrowly defined (currency plus demand deposits), does not meet the statistical requirements for stability, although some broader definition of money may provide stable regression results.

The issue of the degree of stability of the money demand function at this point is unresolved and it is crucial to the conduct of stabilization policy.[17]

Changing Prices and Interest Rates

In our money (bond) market discussion of the factors that affect interest rates, we took account of once and for all changes in the general price level. However, we have not entertained the possibility of a continuing, nonzero rate of price change. Hence, we have been able to tacitly assume that the general price level is expected to remain unchanged in the future. That assumption is clearly untenable in a period like the mid-1960s to the present when the general price level has risen rapidly.

When no change in the general price level is anticipated, the *nominal* interest rate that is observed in the money (bond) market measures the expected *real* interest yield on bonds. When the general price level is expected to change, the real (price adjusted) yield on bonds can differ substantially from the observed interest rate, requiring us to distinguish between the nominal and real rates of interest.

Without attempting at the moment to explain how those expectations are generated, suppose that borrowers and lenders have come to expect an increase in the price level. With prices rising over time, the purchasing power of money shrinks. Hence, lenders (bond holders), whose financial claims for interest and principal payments are fixed in dollar terms, would suffer capital losses while borrowers (bond issuers) would enjoy equivalent capital gains. Of course, instead of lending, savers could exchange their savings for real property (land and commodities), the dollar value of which rises with the general price level. With this option available, savers who anticipate inflation would be willing to lend their savings (buy bonds) only if the nominal interest yield is sufficient to both compensate for the loss of purchasing power of the dollar repayments they receive and provide the real interest reward they require to forego the current use of funds. By the same token, borrowers who anticipate inflation would be willing to pay a higher nominal interest rate because they expect their future interest and principal payments to be made in depreciated dollars.

If lenders and borrowers share a common expected rate of change in the general price level, the nominal interest rate will differ from the real rate by

---

[17] A recent study that provides evidence that the demand for money function is not stable was conducted by G. S. Laumas, "Liquidity Functions for the United States Manufacturing Corporations," *The Southern Economic Journal,* October 1977, pp. 271–276; idem, "The Stability of the Demand for Money by the Household Sector—A Note," *The Southern Economic Journal,* October 1979, pp. 603–608. Further tests showing that the issue of stability of the money demand function is unresolved are discussed in Thomas F. Cargill and Robert A. Meyer, "Stability of the Demand Function for Money: An Unresolved Issue," *The American Economic Review,* May 1979, pp. 318–323. A contrasting view on the stability of money demand is provided in R. W. Hafer and Scott E. Hein, "Evidence on the Temporal Stability of the Demand for Money Relationship in the United States," *Federal Reserve Bank of St. Louis Review,* December 1979, pp. 3–14.

that expected rate of price change. In algebraic terms, with prices expected to change at the rate $\Delta P^e/P$ each period, the nominal interest rate would be

$$i = \rho + \frac{\Delta P^e}{P}$$

where ρ is the real rate of interest, i.e., the percentage interest rate that would prevail if no change in the price level were expected.[18] If, with no price level change expected, the equilibrium interest rate (nominal and real) were 4 percent, with prices expected to rise by 4 percent per period, the nominal interest rate that we observe would be 8 percent; if prices were expected to rise 6 percent per period, the market interest rate would be 10 percent; and so on. If the substantial inflation the United States began experiencing in the mid-1960s produced the expectation of continuing inflation, the record high interest rates witnessed in the United States in recent years may have largely reflected the price expectations term in the equation above rather than a rise in the real rate of interest. However, what portion of observed interest yields does, in fact, represent an inflation premium must remain to some extent a matter of conjecture because we can observe neither the real interest rate nor the value of expected price changes.[18]

To complete our discussion of the role of expected changes in the price level, we must determine whether it is the nominal or the real rate of interest that our previous analytical efforts have identified as an important determinant of both money demand and planned investment spending. First, for the holders of money balances, the nominal interest rate is relevant because it is the nominal interest rate that must be sacrificed when one holds money instead of bonds. In contrast, it is the real interest rate that firms expect to prevail which determines the level of investment spending. To justify that claim, consider an inflationary period, a period in which the prices business firms would receive for the goods and services they produce would be rising. At the same time, during a generalized inflation the production costs firms

---

[18]To be mathematically complete, our expression for the nominal interest rate should be written as

$$i = \rho + \frac{\Delta P^e}{P} + \rho\frac{\Delta P^e}{P}$$

where the last term $[\rho(\Delta P^e/P)]$ measures the expected change in the real value of interest payments. Because this term is quantitatively negligible, it is normally ignored in attempts to explain movements in the nominal interest rate.

[19]For the most part, investigations of the formation of price expectations conclude that expectations are modified slowly in response to experienced price level movements. For example, see Thomas J. Sargent, "Commodity Price Expectations and the Interest Rate," *Quarterly Journal of Economics* 83 (1969): 127–140; and William E. Gibson, "Price Expectations Effects on Interest Rates," *The Journal of Finance,* 25 (1970): 19–34; idem, "Interest Rates and Inflationary Expectations: New Evidence," *The American Economic Review,* December 1972, pp. 854–865. A shorter adjustment period is found in William P. Yohe and Dennis S. Karnosky, "Interest Rates and Price Level Changes," *Federal Reserve Bank of St. Louis Review,* December 1969, pp. 19–36.

face would be rising in the same proportion as their prices. Hence, the net revenues firms would expect to flow from any investment they undertake would be increased by just the expected rate of inflation. Because the nominal interest cost of investment would also be increased by just the expected inflation rate, the same investment decisions would be made no matter what the size of the inflation premium built into the nominal interest rate. That is, the level of investment must depend on the real interest rate, and nominal yield rates do not serve as good guides to the financial market's influence on investment.

Summary

The first important task of this chapter was to provide a model for explaining movements in interest rates. With the classical (pre-Keynesian) quantity theory of demand for money as a background, we followed the Keynesian tradition by identifying forces that determine interest rates within the confines of the money (bond) market. Within the money market, the nominal stock of money was taken to be exogenously determined (by the central bank) so that, with an existing price level, the real money stock is fixed. The demand for real money balances, on the other hand, was treated as a positive function of real output and negatively related to interest rates. This specification remained valid even as we identified shortcomings in the original Keynesian explanation of money demand and probed more modern versions of money demand models.

Through 1973, empirical studies of the demand for money appeared to confirm that the conventional specification of the money demand function was appropriate and that money demand responded in a stable (hence, predictable) manner to changes in output and interest rates. After 1973, however, episodic evidence and statistical investigation have given rise to serious questions with regard to the stability of money demand. Accurate forecasts of money demand, which a stable money demand function would permit, are crucial in the conduct of monetary policy. This is especially true for monetarist (non-Keynesian) policy prescriptions as we shall see a bit later.

To complete our discussion of money and the interest rate, we introduced the expectation of a nonzero rate of change in the general price level, concluding that observed interest rates would differ from the real rate by the expected rate of price level change. Of course, as long as no change in the general price level is expected, the nominal and real rates of interest are identical. Because it is convenient to develop models of the aggregate economy without having to distinguish between those measures, the analysis in the next chapter assumes that no change in the general price level is expected. With the groundwork provided in this chapter, we will be able to assess easily the role of nonzero inflation (deflation) expectations in the model developed in that and the following chapter.

Questions

1. It is often alleged that the central bank can control either the money supply or the interest rate but not both simultaneously. Explain.

2. You are considering buying a bond that has a maturity value of $1,000, a life of five years, and provides an annual (coupon) payment of $40. With the market interest rate 5 percent, what will the price of this bond be? Explain the intrinsic link between bond price changes and interest rate changes.

3. Consider a bond with ten years to run until maturity and a $5,000 face value, which pays an annual coupon rate of 6 percent. Find the price of this bond when the market interest rate is 4 percent. Is this bond selling at a discount or a premium?

4. From the *Wall Street Journal* or *The New York Times,* select a government bond that has fifteen or more years until maturity, and use the yield rate on that bond as your measure of the market interest rate.
   a. Use the observed market interest rate to determine the market value of a bond like the one in Question 2.
   b. Make your one best prediction of what the market interest rate will be one year from now and use that predicted interest rate to determine the market value of the bond.
   c. Would you be better off holding the bond or money, given your prediction of the interest rate a year from now?

5. Suppose the president, by executive order, decreed that all workers should be paid monthly instead of weekly or semiweekly. What would you expect to happen to the interest rate?

6. Suppose the election of a liberal government, by reducing confidence in future economic stability, increases liquidity preference (money demand). What would happen to the interest rate?

7. Suppose the market interest rate should remain in a narrow range between 7 and 7 1/2 percent for several years. What would be the impact of this experience on the diversity of opinion assumed in the liquidity preference theory, and what is the implication for the shape of the aggregate money demand function?

8. For a risky world, build a model that shows an individual increasing his speculative demand for money as the interest rate rises. Is this possible?

9. To finance $400 worth of transactions per month, find the cost-minimizing volume of transactions balances with the cost of converting securities to money equal to $2 per conversion and an interest yield on securities of .01 (1 percent) per month.

10. Explain the link between instability in money demand and instability in velocity.

11. Use the classical quantity theory of money framework to assess the implications for economic stability of unpredictable shifts in money demand.

12. You are given the following information:

$$
\text{Money Market}
\begin{cases}
\text{Money Supply} \quad \dfrac{\overline{M}}{P} = \$250 \\[2em]
\text{Money Demand} \quad \dfrac{M_D}{P} = 1/3\,Y + \dfrac{2}{i}
\end{cases}
$$

$$
\begin{matrix}
\text{Goods and} \\
\text{Service Market}
\end{matrix}
\begin{cases}
\text{Consumption} \quad C = 20 + 4/5\,Y_d \\[1em]
\text{Investment} \quad I = 20 + \dfrac{.8}{i} \\[1em]
\begin{matrix}\text{Government} \\ \text{Spending}\end{matrix} \quad \overline{G} = 60 \\[1em]
\text{Tax Revenue} \quad \overline{T} = 0
\end{cases}
$$

You should inspect these simplified equations to make sure they represent (roughly) the behavioral patterns we would expect to observe for the aggregate economy.

To anticipate one of the tasks we will face in the next chapter, see whether you can solve this algebraic (simultaneous equation) representation of the economy for the equilibrium values of income, the interest rate, consumption, investment, and saving.

13. On a $100 loan for a five-year period, with both principal and interest to be paid in a lump sum at the end of the five years, the lump payment would be $R = \$100\,(1 + .04)^5 = \$121.70$.

Now, suppose that the lender who is satisfied with a 4 percent real annual return comes to expect a 5 percent annual inflation rate. Calculate the dollar payment at the end of five years that would make him willing to lend the $100; then calculate the nominal interest rate he would have to charge to compensate for the anticipated inflation.

Suggested Reading

Baumol, William. "The Transactions Demand for Cash: An Inventory Theoretic Approach." *Quarterly Journal of Economics* 46(1952): 545–556.

deLeeuw, Frank, and Gramlich, Edward. "The Federal Reserve—MIT Econometric Model." *Federal Reserve Bulletin,* January 1968, pp. 11–40.

Gibson, William E. "Price Expectations Effects on Interest Rates." *Journal of Finance* 25(1970): 19–34.

Goldfeld, Stephen M. "The Demand for Money Revisited." *Brookings Papers on Economic Activity* (1973:3): 576–646.

Goldfeld, Stephen M. "The Case of the Missing Money." *Brookings Papers on Economic Activity* (1976:3): 683–730.

Hafer, R. W. and Hein, Scott E. "Evidence on the Temporal Stability of the Demand for Money Relationship in the United States." *Federal Reserve Bank of St. Louis Review,* December 1979, pp. 3–14.

Keynes, John Maynard. *The General Theory of Employment, Interest, and Money,* Chapter 13. New York: Harcourt Brace Jovanovich, 1936.

Laidler, David E. W. *The Demand for Money: Theories and Evidence.* 2nd ed. New York: Dun-Donnelley, 1977.

Simpson, Thomas D. "The Redefined Monetary Aggregates." *Federal Reserve Bulletin,* February 1980, pp. 97–114.

Teigen, Ronald. "The Demand for and Supply of Money." In *Readings in Money, National Income, and Stabilization Policy,* edited by W. L. Smith and R. L. Teigen, pp. 68–103. 3rd ed. Homewood, Ill.: Richard D. Irwin, 1974.

Tobin, James. "Liquidity Preference as Behavior Toward Risk." *Review of Economic Studies* 25(1958): 65–86.

Yohe, William P., and Karnosky, Dennis S. "Interest Rates and Price Level Changes." *Federal Reserve Bank of St. Louis Review,* December 1969, pp. 19–36.

Chapter **8**

Money in a Keynesian System: The Constant Price *IS-LM* Model

In Chapter 4, we built several Keynesian models of macroeconomic systems that could be solved for equilibrium values of income. Though these models differed in complexity and sophistication, they shared one important trait; they all dealt exclusively with the behavior of the commodity market (the market for goods and services), completely ignoring the existence of the money market and, for all practical purposes, the labor market, as though the behavior of those markets would have no effect on the equilibrium level of income. Chapters 5 and 6 looked in considerable detail at the determinants of consumption and investment, the major private sector (as opposed to government) components of demand for real goods and services. Because it was demonstrated that the interest rate is an important determinant of investment spending, Chapter 7 was devoted to introducing the financial sector of the economy. The forces that influence the interest rate were analyzed, concentrating on the money market.

Putting it all Together

In this chapter, the commodity and money markets are formally combined. With money integrated into our Keynesian model, the fundamental interactions between the commodity and money markets can be explicitly and systematically included in our analysis of the macroeconomy. Because the resulting models will have two markets, when we speak of our system being in equilibrium we will mean that both of those markets are in equilibrium. As we proceed, we will try to take full advantage of what was learned about consumption and investment demand in Chapters 5 and 6. However, detail will be added gradually as we proceed from the construction of very simple models to models that are fairly complex. The first model constructed will be for a closed economy with no government expenditures or taxes. In developing this model it is assumed that the price level is constant. That convenient, but unrealistic, assumption will be retained until the last section of this chapter.

With the money and commodity markets combined in this chapter, we can begin to provide a realistic appraisal of the patterns of adjustment the economy experiences when it is subject to a wide array of shocks. In addition, we will gain some insights into the conditions that favor the use of *monetary policy* on the one hand or *fiscal policy* on the other, as policy makers try to stabilize economic activity.

A Graphical Summary of What We Know

Figure 8—1 graphically summarizes the component parts of the model of the macroeconomy which has now been developed (again, ignoring government spending and tax collections). In part (a) of that figure, interest rate i_0 is shown equating money supply and demand. In turn, given the investment demand schedule plotted in part (b) of that figure, the equilibrium level of investment at interest rate i_0 is I_0. Finally, in part (c) of Figure 8—1 investment demand of I_0 is combined with a nonproportional consumption function to yield the equilibrium level of income labeled Y_0. If the money demand and investment demand schedules plotted in Figure 8—1 are the schedules that correspond to income level Y_0, Figure 8—1 provides a completely satisfactory graphical representation of our model of the economy *in equilibrium*. (We are about to discover the magnitude of that "if.") However, that graphical summary of the component parts of the macroeconomy is of little use in assessing the full response of the economic system to any of the shocks it must endure. To illustrate that claim, suppose equilibrium (at i_0, I_0, Y_0) is disturbed by an increase in the stock of money. Were the real money stock to expand to level $\overline{M}'/P$, the interest rate would have to fall to level i_1 for money market equilibrium to be maintained. At that lower interest rate, the equilibrium volume of investment would be increased to I_1 and, through the multiplier, that increase in planned investment would raise equilibrium income to level Y_1. However, with income increased, the demand for money would be increased, raising the equilibrium interest rate at least part of the way back toward its initial level.[1] In turn, with the interest

---

[1]The investment demand schedule would also be shifted to the right if investment is a positive function of the output level. However, to avoid an excessive number of complications, investment's response to income changes can be ignored for the time being without altering our conclusions.

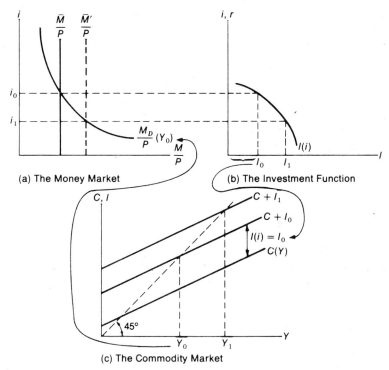

(a) The Money Market

(b) The Investment Function

(c) The Commodity Market

**Figure 8—1 / A Graphical Summary
of a Two-Market Macroeconomic Model**

rate raised, investment would be reduced leading, through the multiplier, to a lower equilibrium level of income, hence a reduced demand for money, a lowered interest rate, and so it goes *ad infinitum*. With developments in the commodity market causing adjustments in the money market, and money market adjustments, in turn, having feedback effects on the commodity market, the task of searching out the new equilibrium values of income and the interest rate could be quite tedious if we had to rely on the graphical summary in Figure 8—1. Thanks to the efforts of a British economist named John Hicks, what we already know about the macroeconomy can be presented in a far more convenient format.[2] To construct that alternative format for a simple economic system we will focus formal attention first on the commodity market, then on the money market.

Commodity Market Equilibrium—The *IS* Curve

For a closed economy with no government spending or taxes, expenditures on goods and services can only exist in the form of household expenditures

---

[2] See John R. Hicks, "Mr. Keynes and the 'Classics': A Suggested Interpretation," *Econometrica* 5(1937):147–159.

on consumer goods and business expenditures on investment goods. The analysis in this chapter continues to assume that real consumption spending is a positive function of real income with a marginal propensity to consume between 0 and 1. That is, real consumption is given by

$$C = C(Y)$$

such that

$$0 < \frac{\Delta C}{\Delta Y} < 1 \qquad [8\text{—}1]$$

In Chapter 6 on the determinants of investment, it was argued that aggregate investment is a positive function of the level of income and an inverse function of the interest rate. For the analysis in this chapter a simplified form of the investment function will be used, one that reflects the interest sensitivity of investment but ignores any link between investment and the level of income. Consequently, the investment function takes the form

$$I = I(i)$$

such that

$$\frac{\Delta I}{\Delta i} < 0 \qquad [8\text{—}2]$$

In Keynesian models of the economy it is primarily through this interest rate-investment linkage that developments in the money market have their influence on the commodity market.

   In an economy without a government, we know that for commodity market equilibrium, total planned spending (planned $C + I$) must equal the real value of output (Y) or, *ipso facto,* planned saving must equal planned investment (thus the designation $I = S$ or IS curve for the commodity market equilibrium relationship we are developing). Substituting the behavioral relationships for consumption (saving) and investment into either of the two equivalent forms of the commodity market equilibrium condition,

$$Y = C + I \qquad [8\text{—}3]$$

or

$$S = I \qquad [8\text{—}4]$$

yields respectively

$$Y - C(Y) = I(i) \qquad [8\text{—}5]$$

or

$$S(Y) = I(i) \qquad\qquad [8\text{—}6]$$

These equilibrium conditions are the fundamental ingredient in the arguments that follow.

If any one value for the interest rate is arbitrarily selected, the investment schedule $[I(i)]$ defines the accompanying equilibrium value of investment. Because saving is a function of income, there is some income level that will generate a saving flow that is precisely equal to the flow of investment, permitting commodity market equilibrium to be restored. Suppose, for the particular investment and saving (consumption) functions prevailing in our simple economy, such a saving-investment equality holds for $i = i_0$ and $Y = Y_0$, as shown in Figure 8—2. This is one *equilibrium* combination of i and Y. Suppose now that the interest rate falls, say, to i_1. Because the investment function indicates that a fall in the interest rate increases investment, for our equilibrium conditions to continue to hold after the interest rate declines, saving $[S(Y)$ or $Y - C(Y)]$ must rise. To induce a rise in saving, Y must increase. Thus, *any* fall in the interest rate, which increases aggregate planned spending through its stimulative effect on investment, would have to be accompanied by an increase in income (say to level Y_1 for a drop in i to i_1) if commodity market equilibrium is to be maintained. For our specified saving and investment schedules, a curve showing all the possible combinations of i and Y that yield equilibrium in the commodity market

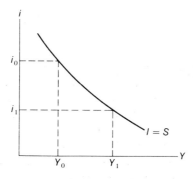

Figure 8—2 / Commodity Market Equilibrium: The *IS* Curve

(the $I = S$ or IS curve) slopes downward from left to right, as Figure 8—2 shows.[3]

Shifts in the *IS* Schedule

Maintenance of commodity market equilibrium requires the entire IS curve to shift if there are shifts in the investment or consumption (saving) schedules. An autonomous increase in investment (a rightward shift in the investment demand schedule) means a higher level of investment spending at *any* interest rate, such as i_0 in Figure 8—3. For equilibrium, the higher level of investment must be matched by an increase in saving. Because saving increases only if income increases, to maintain equilibrium the autonomous increase in investment must be associated with an increase in income, an increase large enough to generate extra saving in an amount equal to the increase in investment. An autonomous increase in investment then implies a rightward shift in the IS schedule, as shown in Figure 8—3. Conversely,

---

[3]The IS curve is frequently derived graphically with a four-part diagram such as the one shown below. Employing simple linear functions, part (a) of the diagram below is a plot of the investment function (the MEI); part (c) plots the saving function; part (b) is simply a 45° identity line; and part (d) plots the commodity market equilibrium, or IS curve.

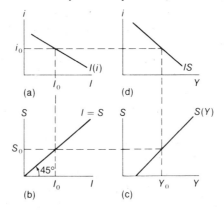

Picking an initial interest rate level (say, i_0) fixes the level of investment (at I_0) and, thus, the volume of saving (S_0) necessary for equilibrium. Given the volume of saving required, the saving function defines the level of income (Y_0) necessary for equilibrium. This establishes one point on the IS-LM schedule. Altering the initial interest rate selected by any amount and tracing through the diagram counterclockwise yields another point on the IS curve. The resulting IS curve will slope downward from left to right as shown.

The downward slope of the IS curve can also be quite easily demonstrated mathematically. For equilibrium, $Y - C(Y) = I(i)$. Differentiating with respect to Y yields

$$1 - \frac{\partial C}{\partial Y} = \frac{\partial I}{\partial i}\frac{di}{dY}$$

Thus

$$\frac{di}{dy} = \frac{1 - \partial C/\partial Y}{\partial I/\partial i}$$

Because $0 < \partial C/\partial Y < 1$, the numerator of this expression, is positive and, by assumption, the denominator is negative, di/dY, the slope of IS curve must be negative.

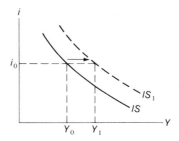

Figure 8—3 / Shifts in the *IS* Schedule

an autonomous reduction in investment implies a leftward shift in the *IS* schedule.[4]

Shifts in the consumption function have similar effects. An autonomous upward shift of the consumption function (an increase in the value of the intercept) is the same as an autonomous downward shift of the saving function; the volume of saving at any level of income is reduced. To maintain sufficient saving to offset the investment that takes place at any selected interest rate, the level of income would have to rise. Because commodity market equilibrium at any selected interest rate could be maintained only with income increased, this shift in the consumption (saving) function implies a rightward shift of the *IS* schedule. Conversely, an autonomous decrease in consumption (increase in saving) implies a leftward shift of the *IS* schedule. You should prove that the shift is a parallel one with a magnitude equal to the shift in the consumption function times the spending multiplier. You may do this with the four-part diagram in footnote 3 or mathematically. Alternatively, you may shift the consumption function employed in any specific algebraic representation of the commodity market (such as the one in Question 12 in Chapter 7) and algebraically or graphically trace its impact on the *IS* schedule.

In brief, the *IS* curve is a schedule showing every possible combination of the interest rate and income level that can yield commodity market equilibrium. Its position and slope depend on the positions and slopes of the investment and consumption (saving) functions that underlie it. By itself,

---

[4]These shifts in the *IS* curve will be parallel shifts, the magnitude of which is equal to the autonomous change in investment times the investment multiplier. This result is easily proved. For equilibrium, $Y = C(Y) + I(i)$. Taking the total differential of this expression yields

$$dY = \frac{\partial C}{\partial Y} dY + \frac{\partial I}{\partial i} di + dI$$

where dI is an *autonomous* change in investment. Holding the interest rate constant ($di = 0$) and recognizing that $\partial C/\partial Y$ is the MPC, we have

$$dY(1 - \text{MPC}) = dI \text{ or } dY|_{i = const.} = \frac{1}{1 - \text{MPC}} \cdot dI$$

This expression tells us the required change in income, holding the interest rate constant at *any* level, to restore equilibrium after an autonomous increase in investment. In this expression we can readily recognize $1/(1 - \text{MPC})$ as the simple spending multiplier for a closed economy in which investment and tax revenues are independent of the level of income.

the *IS* schedule cannot reveal which combination of *i* and *Y* will prevail as the overall equilibrium combination in both the money and commodity markets.

Money Market Equilibrium—The *LM* Curve

For economy-wide or general equilibrium it is necessary that we also have equilibrium in the money market. This will occur, of course, when money supply and money demand are equal. Continuing to assume that the nominal money supply is exogenously determined, the real money supply is also an exogenously given constant as long as the price level is constant. Based on the analysis in Chapter 7, it is assumed that the real demand for money is an inverse function of the interest rate and a positive function of real income. Thus, in algebraic form our real money supply function is

$$\frac{M_s}{P} = \frac{\overline{M}}{P} \qquad [8\text{—}7]$$

and our real money demand function is

$$\frac{M_D}{P} = M(i, Y) \qquad [8\text{—}8]$$

with $\Delta M/\Delta i < 0$ and $\Delta M/\Delta Y > 0$. For equilibrium, money supply must equal money demand or

$$\frac{\overline{M}}{P} = M(i, Y) \qquad [8\text{—}9]$$

Now, let us suppose we know one combination of *i* and *Y* (i_0 and Y_0 in Figure 8—4) that will produce equilibrium in the money market. Then, letting the interest rate rise by any selected amount, say, to i_1, we must ascertain how *Y* has to change if money market equilibrium is to be maintained. An increase in the interest rate reduces money demand tending to

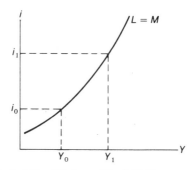

Figure 8—4 / Money Market Equilibrium: The *LM* Curve

create an excess supply of money. The public would willingly hold these excess funds (and thus be willing to hold the given real money stock $\overline{M}/P$) only at a higher level of income (say, Y_1). Thus, a rise in the interest rate must be accompanied by a rise in the level of real income if money market equilibrium is to be maintained. Clearly the money market equilibrium curve (the $L = M$ or LM curve where L represents money demand and M money supply) must slope upward from left to right. That schedule shows all the combinations of i and Y that produce equilibrium (equality of supply and demand) in the money market.[5]

---

[5]Making use of Keynes' original distinction between transactions and speculative money demands, the LM schedule is frequently derived graphically using the four-part diagram, below. The schedule in part (b) of the diagram represents transactions demand for money, assuming demand to be proportional (with proportionality constant k) to Y. The schedule in (d) represents speculative demand for money. The schedule in (c) is simply an identity line that mechanically divides the total money supply into transactions and speculative components. That part of total money balances $(\overline{M}/P)$ not held in one form must be held in the other. The schedule in (a) is the LM curve.

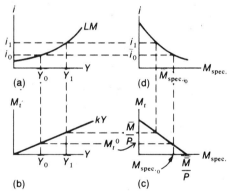

Beginning in (d), with a known interest rate (assume it is i_0), the volume of speculative demand is defined $[M_{(spec._0)}]$. Given the total money supply $(\overline{M}/P)$, that portion not held as speculative balances must be held in transaction balances $[M^0_t]$ as shown in (c). The schedule in (b) shows what level of real income (Y_0) must prevail in order to get the public to willingly absorb the money available for transactions balances in that form. Thus, as we see in (a), for interest rate i_0 the only possible money market equilibrium value for income is Y_0. Should the interest rate rise to i_1, the only possible equilibrium level of income would be Y_1 as we can see by again starting in (d) and proceeding clockwise through our diagram. Thus, the LM curve slopes upward from left to right.

This proposition can be quickly proved mathematically. For money market equilibrium the real money supply must equal real money demand, $\overline{M}/P = M(i, Y)$. With a fixed real money supply, total differentiation of this equilibrium condition yields

$$0 = \frac{\partial M}{\partial i} di + \frac{\partial M}{\partial Y} dY$$

so that

$$\frac{di}{dY} = -\frac{\partial M/\partial Y}{\partial M/\partial i}$$

The numerator of this expression is positive while the denominator is negative. Thus, di/dY, the slope of the LM schedule, is positive.

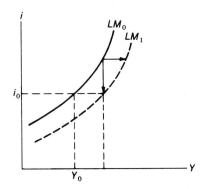

Figure 8—5 / Shifts in the *LM* Schedule

Shifts in the *LM* Schedule

The *LM* schedule will shift in response to shifts in the underlying money supply or money demand functions. Beginning in equilibrium, an increase in the supply of money would create an excess supply of money requiring either an increase in Y (thus in money demand) or a decrease in i (thus a rise in money demand) for the additional real money balances to be willingly absorbed. This means, of course, a rightward shift of the *LM* curve, as shown in Figure 8—5. Conversely, a reduction in money supply requires a leftward shift of the *LM* function.[6]

An autonomous increase in the demand for money would create an excess demand for money that could be eliminated only by a rise in the interest rate or a fall in income. Thus, an increase in the demand for real money balances means a leftward shift of the *LM* schedule. Conversely, a decrease in money demand would mean a rightward shift of the *LM* schedule. As suggested in Chapter 7, money demand will shift with a change in the degree of integration of industry, a change in the frequency of income payments, a change in expectations, and so on.

Clearly, the shape and position of the *LM* schedule depends on the shapes and positions of the underlying money supply and demand schedules, a shift in either of those schedules shifting the *LM* curve. As was the case with the *IS* curve, although the *LM* curve shows all the combinations of i and Y that can yield an equilibrium in the money market, it cannot tell us which combination will prevail as the equilibrium combination when there is system-wide or general equilibrium.

---

[6]The shifts will be parallel shifts with a magnitude (measured horizontally) equal to the change in real money supply times the "velocity of circulation," where the velocity of circulation measures the number of times per accounting period each dollar of transactions balances is, on average, used for an income payment. This makes intuitive sense; for all of the change in money supply to be absorbed in transactions balances, at a given interest rate spending on final goods and services (which is the same as income) must have changed by the increment in money supply multiplied by the number of times each new dollar is, on average, spent on final goods and services. Can you prove this proposition mathematically? Hint: If you assume $M_{t+p} = kY$, then $1/k = Y/M_{t+p}$ is the velocity of circulation of transactions balances.

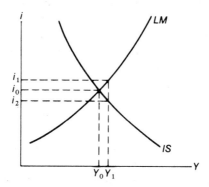

Figure 8—6 / General Equilibrium: *IS* and *LM* Combined

Simultaneous Equilibrium

By combining the commodity and money market equilibrium schedules (the *IS* and *LM* curves) as in Figure 8—6, we can see that only one combination of i and Y (the combination i_0 and Y_0) can simultaneously clear both the money and commodity markets.[7] That is, given the money supply and demand schedules that underly the *LM* curve, and the consumption and investment schedules that underlie the *IS* curve, the only possible equilibrium values of i and Y are the combination at the *IS-LM* intersection. At any other combination of an interest rate and an income level the commodity market or the money market, or both markets, will be in disequilibrium. If, for example, the level of income should rise (say to Y_1), the rate of interest determined in the money market (i_1) would exceed the interest rate that is necessary (i_2) to stimulate sufficient investment to make Y_1 the equilibrium level of income in the commodity market. With excess supply in the commodity market, income would be forced downward. If income should ever fall below Y_0, the money market interest rate would fall below the level that would restrict investment to a volume small enough to produce equilibrium in the commodity market. That is, planned investment would exceed

---

[7]The *IS* schedule and *LM* schedule are just graphical representations of single equations in the two unknowns i and Y. With the two equations in i and Y we can solve simultaneously for the values of i and Y that satisfy both of these equations. This is, of course, what we are doing graphically in Figure 8—6.

The equilibrium conditions represented in Figure 8—6 $\left[\overline{M}/P = M(i, Y) \text{ and } S(Y) = I(i) \right]$ could be written in simple linear form as $m = kY + ni$ and $a + sY = I + vi$ where $m = \overline{M}/P$ and k, n, s, and v are the coefficients measuring the responses of transactions demand for money, speculative demand for money (if that is the only source of interest sensitivity), saving, and investment, respectively, to changes in income, the interest rate, income, and the interest rate. Solving these two equations simultaneously for the two unknowns i and Y yields:

$$Y = \frac{1}{s + vk/n}(-a + \overline{I} + vm/n) \text{ and } i = -\frac{1}{s + vk/n} \cdot \frac{k}{n}(a + \overline{I} - ms/k)$$

which are specific values for i and Y.

planned saving and income would rise. A formal mathematical proof that stability of equilibrium is always ensured by the forces that are aroused whenever the existing i and Y combination differs from the equilibrium combination is beyond the scope of this text.[8] However, there is little question but that stability of equilibrium is provided by those forces.

Using the Model

We now have a simple macroeconomic model that can be used to trace the impact of various economic disturbances on an array of important economic variables. Specifically, we can introduce shocks into the system (changes in money supply or demand, changes in consumption, or changes in investment) and trace the impact of those shocks on income (output), the interest rate, consumption (saving), investment, and, if we wish to make the distinction, on transactions and speculative demand for money.

To illustrate the use of our simple *IS-LM* model, suppose equilibrium is disturbed by an autonomous increase in the money supply. According to our analysis, an increase in money supply, which immediately creates an excess supply of money (excess demand for bonds), reduces the interest rate and stimulates investment spending. In Figure 8—7, the increase in money supply is represented by a rightward shift of the *LM* schedule (from *LM* to *LM'*), providing the new equilibrium at reduced interest rate (i_1) and higher income level (Y_1). Because consumption and saving are positive functions of income, the values of both of these variables will be greater in the new equilibrium. Demand for money will also have increased due to the increase in income. The lower interest rate results in a higher level of investment spending and a further increase in the demand for money. What would be the impact of a reduction in money supply?

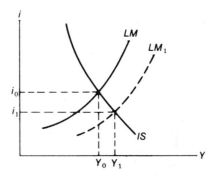

**Figure 8—7 / A Change in General
Equilibrium due to a Shift in the *LM* Curve**

[8]The dynamic issue of stability is dealt with in Thomas F. Dernburg and Judith D. Dernburg, *Macroeconomic Analysis* (Reading, Mass.: Addison-Wesley, 1969), pp. 7–8 and Chapter 12.

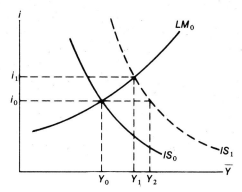

**Figure 8—8 / A Change in General
Equilibrium due to a Shift in the *IS* Curve**

Shifting attention to the demand side of the money market, an increase in the frequency of income payments or an increase in the fraction of transactions that are credit financed could reduce the transactions demand for money, resulting in an excess supply of money (excess demand for bonds). In that case, the unchanged stock of money would be willingly held only at a lower interest rate or higher income level. Thus, these *institutional changes* would shift the *LM* curve rightward and the interest rate would fall, stimulating investment and, hence, raising the equilibrium level of income.[9]

Equilibrium is also disturbed by shifts in the *IS* schedule. Suppose the initial equilibrium in Figure 8—8 (i_0 and Y_0) is disturbed by an autonomous increase in investment. This shock would shift the *IS* curve rightward to a position like that of IS_1, showing that the increase in investment provides higher equilibrium values of both the interest rate and income (i_1 and Y_1).

Why does the equilibrium level of income not increase by the full amount of the horizontally measured shift in the *IS* curve (that is, by $Y_0 - Y_2$) which is the amount of change in income that the simple multipliers in Chapter 4 would predict in response to our hypothetical increase in investment? The reason is that the interest rate rises as income rises, tending to reduce the amount of investment spending. The initial increase in investment spending starts the multiplier process working. However, as income rises, the demand for money rises, creating excess demand in the money market (excess supply in the bond market). This results in a rise in the interest rate that squeezes out some investment, tending to reduce the size of the multiplier effect on income. This feedback phenomenon, which appears because the monetary sector of the economy has been combined with the commodity

---

[9]To be precise, these institutional changes would rotate the *LM* schedule in the clockwise direction because, for example, a halving of the volume of transactions balances that must be held to finance each dollar's worth of transactions would double the volume of transactions that any given volume of money balances could support.

market, is often referred to as a "crowding out effect." It acts to reduce the size of any spending (or tax) multiplier, and, as such, it serves as an automatic stabilizer originating in the monetary sector of the economy. Of course, any increase in spending must be financed, and, with no increase in the money stock, existing money balances must be spent with a higher average frequency. That is, velocity $[V = PY/M]$ must have increased to permit any rise in Y. The interest rate increase that depresses investment also prompts a rise in velocity by inducing society to economize on its money demand.

What has happened to the other variables in our model? With income up, consumption and saving will have risen. There was an initial increase in investment, then a negative investment response to the rising interest rate. However, the overall level of investment must end up higher than it was before the autonomous shift in the investment schedule. Otherwise, there would be no reason for income, the interest rate, and so on to end up with any values other than their initial values. What would be the impact of an autonomous decrease in investment? Of an autonomous shift in the consumption (saving) function? These are questions that you can answer easily with the *IS-LM* model. You may have noted from the exercise above that the interactions which take place between the money and commodity markets are no longer a major source of confusion as we search for new equilibrium values of i and Y.

Government in the *IS-LM* Model

As always, the basic objective of the effort we have expended in constructing the *IS-LM* model of the economy was that of providing a simplified representation of reality, permitting us to make conditional (if a, then b) predictions about real world events. As demonstrated above, our *IS-LM* model predicted that *if* investment should experience a once-and-for-all increase, *then* the equilibrium values of income, consumption, and saving would increase. In like fashion, the basic *IS-LM* model permits analysis of the impact of all the other shocks that could shift either the *IS* schedule or the *LM* schedule: an autonomous shift in the consumption function, an autonomous change in money demand, or a change in the size of the money supply. Among the forces that affect the macroeconomy, those that emanate from the government's economic activities are probably the most important, and the model we have constructed in this chapter has certainly not provided an adequate role for government. To be able to assess the aggregate impact of government's economic activities, we must formally recognize the existence of government and build the relevant activities of government into the *IS-LM* model.

We will continue to assume that the central bank, which you now may recognize as an agent of the government, has complete control over the stock of nominal money balances so that, with this control and a constant price level, it can make the stock of real money balances $(\overline{M}/P)$ what it wants it to be. Consequently, no changes in the behavioral relationships in the monetary sector of our model are necessitated by the introduction of a government. The demand for real money balances is still a function of real income and the interest rate, and, for equilibrium, real money supply must equal demand. *The LM curve is unaffected by the introduction of a government.*

The introduction of a government in the commodity market is more involved but follows a familiar path. In Chapter 4 a government was introduced into models of the commodity market and that government was allowed to spend and to collect taxes. In terms of the behavioral functions in the commodity market, as we did in Chapter 4, we must recognize government as a source of spending on final goods and services, and we must recognize the dependence of household consumption on the level of real *disposable income,* which differs from total (received) income by the amount of taxes collected.

Equilibrium in the commodity market with government included in the *IS-LM* model requires equality of planned spending with output, or, alternatively stated, equality of total leakages from the spending stream (saving plus taxes) with total injections into the spending stream (investment plus government spending). That is, the commodity market equilibrium conditions with government are

$$Y = C(Y) + I(i) + G \qquad [8\text{—}10]$$

or

$$S(Y) + T = I(i) + G \qquad [8\text{—}11]$$

The general properties of the *IS* curve are unchanged. It still slopes downward from left to right because a fall in the interest rate still stimulates investment, requiring a higher level of income to generate sufficient leakages (now saving plus taxes) from the income stream to offset the volume of injections (now investment plus government spending) into that flow. Further, the *IS* curve is still shifted rightward by an autonomous increase in consumption or investment and leftward by a fall in either of those functions. In addition, however, with government included in our model, the *IS* schedule will be shifted by any change in government spending or tax collections. Starting at any point on the *IS* schedule, an increase in government spending would create an excess demand for commodities, requiring a higher interest rate or an enlarged volume of output (income) to maintain equilibrium. Thus, an increase in government spending has the same effect on the *IS* curve as an increase in consumption or investment; they all shift the *IS* curve rightward. Conversely, a decrease in government spending, resulting in an excess supply of commodities, shifts the *IS* leftward just as a fall in consumption or investment does.[10]

An increase in taxes, because it reduces disposable income and thus consumption spending, shifts the *IS* curve leftward. Conversely, a reduction in taxes, by raising disposable income and consumption, shifts the *IS* curve rightward. A given dollar volume change in tax collections shifts the *IS* curve less than an equivalent dollar change in government spending does, because first-round spending in the tax change case is altered only by the change in tax collections times the marginal propensity to consume, not by the full amount of the tax change.[11]

A Brief Glance at Monetary and Fiscal Policy

It should be apparent by now that government, by altering its spending, its tax receipts, or the money supply, can affect the equilibrium position of the economy. What, specifically, are the changes it can bring about?

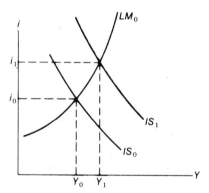

Figure 8—9 / The Effect on Equilibrium of an Increase in Government Spending

---

[10]The shifts due to changes in government spending are parallel and have a magnitude equal to the change in government spending times the spending multiplier, as you can demonstrate using the method illustrated in footnote 4 of this chapter.

[11]That is, the magnitude of the shift in the *IS* curve resulting from a change in tax collections is the *tax multiplier* times the change in taxes. Explicitly introducing tax revenues into the consumption function, equilibrium income is $Y = C(Y - T) + I(i) + G$. Taking the total differential of this expression yields

$$dY = \frac{\partial C}{\partial(Y - T)}(dY - dT) + \frac{\partial I}{\partial i}\,di + dG$$

Holding the interest rate and government spending constant ($di = dG = 0$), and recognizing that $\partial C / \partial(Y - T) = \text{MPC}$, we have $dY\,(1 - \text{MPC}) = -\text{MPC} \cdot dT$ or

$$\frac{dY}{dT} = \frac{-\text{MPC}}{1 - \text{MPC}}$$

the simple tax multiplier for a closed economy in which investment and tax revenues are independent of the level of income.

Beginning with our model in general equilibrium (position i_0, Y_0 in Figure 8—9), let the government increase its spending. The increase in government spending shifts the *IS* curve rightward (say, to IS_1), raising the equilibrium level of income to Y_1 and of the interest rate to i_1.[12] The increase in income will result in a rise in consumption and saving, and will raise the demand for money while the rise in the interest rate will result in the crowding out of some investment and will tend to reduce money demand. Overall, the demand for money must end up equal to the unchanged money supply so velocity must have increased. You can trace the effects of a decrease in government spending on your own.

An increase in tax collections, which reduces disposable income and hence consumption, would shift the *IS* curve leftward lowering income, the interest rate, consumption, and savings. The drop in the interest rate would stimulate investment. With an unchanged money stock and output reduced, velocity is reduced. These results are reversed for a reduction in tax receipts.

This model indicates that, if government wishes to change the level of income by the use of *fiscal policy,* that is, through discretionary changes in government spending and/or tax collections, it can do so. In addition, the government can use monetary policy, alterations in the quantity of money

---

[12]To prove this mathematically, assume that both government spending and tax collections are autonomous so that the money and commodity market equilibrium conditions are

$$\frac{\overline{M}}{P} = M(Y,i) \text{ and } S(Y) + \overline{T} = I(i) + \overline{G}$$

Differentiating both equilibrium conditions with respect to G yields

$$\frac{\partial M}{\partial Y}\left(\frac{dY}{dG}\right) + \frac{\partial M}{\partial i}\left(\frac{di}{dG}\right) = 0$$

and

$$\frac{\partial S}{\partial Y}\left(\frac{dY}{dG}\right) - \frac{\partial I}{\partial i}\left(\frac{di}{dG}\right) = 1$$

Solving simultaneously for dY/dG and di/dG yields:

$$\frac{dY}{dG} = \frac{\dfrac{\partial M}{\partial i}}{\dfrac{\partial S}{\partial Y}\dfrac{\partial M}{\partial i} + \dfrac{\partial M}{\partial Y}\dfrac{\partial I}{\partial i}}$$

and

$$\frac{di}{dG} = \frac{-\dfrac{\partial M}{\partial Y}}{\dfrac{\partial S}{\partial Y}\dfrac{\partial M}{\partial i} + \dfrac{\partial M}{\partial Y}\dfrac{\partial I}{\partial i}}$$

Both the numerator and denominator of dY/dG are negative, making dY/dG positive, while di/dG is positive because a negative sign prefixes the negative ratio expression (positive numerator and negative denominator) for di/dG. Thus, both income and the interest rate respond positively to changes in government spending.

held by the public, to alter the economy's equilibrium position. The effects of money supply changes are those spelled out beginning on page 230, an increase in the money stock raising income and reducing the interest rate. It goes without saying that monetary and fiscal policies can also be used together to pursue the government's policy goal(s). For a particular income target, the equilibrium level of our other variables, the interest rate, consumption, investment, and so on, will differ with the particular mix of monetary and fiscal policy actions employed.

The Policy Mix and Investment. Figure 8—10 shows two alternative sets of IS and LM schedules, with each set yielding the same equilibrium level of income (Y_0). Schedule LM_1 represents a more expansive (larger money stock) monetary policy than schedule LM_0 does. To maintain equilibrium at output level Y_0 with the more expansive monetary policy represented by schedule LM_1, fiscal policy must provide the commodity market equilibrium schedule IS_1. As compared to schedule IS_0, schedule IS_1 involves a more restrictive fiscal policy requiring smaller government outlays, higher taxes, or both.

Now, while the output level is the same in both cases, the interest rate is lower in the expansive monetary/restrictive fiscal policy case and the allocation of resources differs.

$$Y = C(Y - T) + \overset{\uparrow}{\underset{\downarrow}{I(i)}} + G \qquad [8\text{—}12]$$

Focusing attention on the commodity market equilibrium expression given by Equation (8—12), it is clear that to maintain output level Y_0, the higher investment level that expansive monetary policy provides requires an offsetting reduction in government demand for output (a cut in government spending), in consumption demand (through a tax increase), or both.

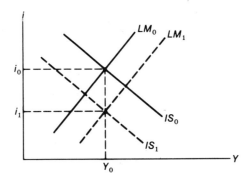

Figure 8—10 / Equilibrium with Alternative Policy Mixes

In recent years, the share of GNP allocated to business investment has declined and the rate of growth of productivity, the output per hour of labor services that the economy provides, has declined. A society that values continuing gains in material goods consumption levels might favor a policy mix that encourages investment at the cost of, say, government resource usage, i.e., a policy like the expansive monetary/restrictive fiscal policy mix reviewed above. As an alternative, determine for yourself what policy mix would be favored by a society that values *current* consumption and consider the resource usage trade-offs that could be exploited.

The Relative Strength of Monetary and Fiscal Policies

With the *IS-LM* framework, we have shown that output responds to monetary and fiscal policy actions, but we have not determined how large the output responses are or what the size of responses depends on. Of course, we already know that the size of output responses is partly dependent on the size of the commodity market multiplier (in the case of a fiscal policy action) or the velocity of money balances usage (in the case of a monetary policy action). However, the response also varies with the interest elasticities of the *IS* and *LM* schedules. Figure 8—11 shows output's response to monetary and fiscal shocks, given differing interest elasticities of the *IS* and *LM* schedules.

The *LM* Schedule and Output Changes

Part (a) of Figure 8—11 shows how output's response to a *fiscal* policy action differs with the slope of the *LM* curve. Part (b) of that figure shows how output's response to a *monetary* policy action differs with the slope of the *LM* curve. In each case, the flatter *LM* schedules (*B* subscripts) exhibit a much larger interest elasticity, reflecting a larger interest elasticity of money demand.

From part (a) of the figure it is clear that a more interest-elastic *LM* schedule raises the potency of fiscal policy. In fact, if, in the limit, money demand and, correspondingly, the *LM* schedule should approach an infinite interest elasticity, fiscal policy would have the full strength predicted by the simple commodity market multiplier of Chapter 4 because there would be no significant interest rate change as output changes, and no crowding out of investment. Keynes himself suggested that this extreme case might be relevant in a deep depression situation in which interest rates have fallen so low that everyone expects them to rise in the future. In this case, the demand for money could be flat at the prevailing low interest rate because no-one would willingly exchange money for bonds. Instead, expecting interest rates to rise (bond prices to fall), they would hoard additions to their money balances. With surplus, hoarded money balances available, a substantial rise in output could be financed without the appearance of a sizable excess demand for money and an attendant increase in interest rates.

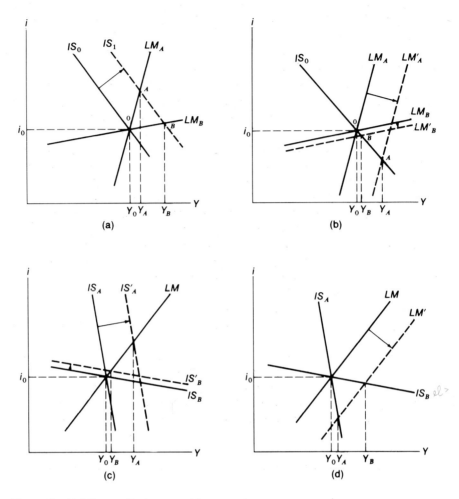

**Figure 8—11 / Output Responses with
Different Elasticities of the IS and LM Schedules**

In contrast, should money demand exhibit very little interest elasticity, fiscal policy would be quite weak. In this case, the rise of interest rates with output exerts a potent damping effect on investment. In the extreme case of virtually no interest elasticity of money demand (a vertical *LM* schedule), there would be complete crowding out and fiscal policy would be impotent.

Part (b) of Figure 8—11 shows that the more interest elastic is money demand and, hence, the *LM* schedule, the weaker is monetary policy. For the same size *parallel* rightward shift of the *LM* schedule (i.e., the same size monetary policy action) output rises only to level Y_B with the highly interest-elastic schedule LM_B but expands to level Y_A with schedule LM_A. In the extreme case with money demand and the *LM* schedule approaching an infinite interest elasticity, monetary policy would become powerless. This is Keynes' "liquidity trap" in which additions to the money stock are hoarded with no additional money balances exchanged for bonds (which are expected to decline in value) and, hence, no downward pressure on interest rates to stimulate investment.

Doubtless, the *LM* schedule is never either perfectly horizontal or vertical, but differences in opinion over just how interest elastic that schedule is can clearly lead to disagreements over the relative strength of monetary and fiscal policies and, hence, to disagreements over the administration of stabilization policy.

The *IS* Schedule and Output Changes

Part (c) of Figure 8—11 shows how the interest elasticity of the *IS* schedule affects the strength of fiscal policy. The more interest *inelastic* the *IS* schedule, the more potent is fiscal policy. In turn, the more interest elastic is investment spending and the smaller is the marginal propensity to save, the greater is the interest elasticity of the *IS* schedule.

In contrast, part (d) of the figure shows that the more interest inelastic the *IS* schedule, the weaker is monetary policy. If, however, investment and/or some other component of spending is highly interest elastic, a monetary policy action has a potent effect on the commodity market, raising equilibrium output substantially. Once more, there are clear opportunities for disagreements over the interest elasticity of the *IS* curve and, consequently, over the proper conduct of stabilization policy.

Additional Policy Complications: Market Instabilities and Optimum Policy Strategies

In Chapters 5–7, we examined the behavior of consumption, investment, and money demand. In the process we discovered that there is substantial volatility in at least one component of commodity demand, investment demand, and not all of the variations in investment can be explained by available investment models. In related fashion, our investigation in Chapter 7 indicated that there may be unpredictable shifts in money demand. In the framework of this chapter, unpredictable shifts in the investment schedule result in instability in the *IS* curve, while unpredictable shifts in money demand constitute instability in the *LM* schedule. The issue of which schedule, the *IS* or *LM*, is more unstable is an important one for stabilization policy because the proper target of monetary control depends to a crucial extent on which schedule is "stable."

As the analysis of money demand in Chapter 7 indicated, the central bank can choose to control the money stock (in which case money demand dictates the interest rate) or to control the interest rate (providing the amount of money demanded at the target interest rate). It cannot control both. Which strategy should it employ? Figures 8—12 and 8—13 illustrate the

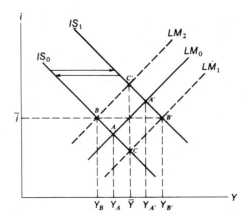

Figure 8—12 / Monetary Strategies when the _IS_ Curve Is Unstable

manner in which the stability (instability) of the _IS_ and _LM_ schedules influence the answer to that question.

Instability in the _IS_ Schedule

In Figure 8—12, money demand and the _LM_ schedule are treated as stable while it is assumed that there is instability in the _IS_ curve. The _IS_ curve may be viewed as shifting randomly between IS_0 and IS_1. The _LM_ schedule, on the other hand, shifts only when there is a central bank-engineered change in the money supply.

Suppose, in a world that matches our assumptions, the central bank chooses to control the money supply, holding the money stock constant so the _LM_ schedule is fixed at LM_0. In this case, output will vary between Y_A and Y_A' as the _IS_ curve shifts and equilibrium moves between A and A'.

Alternatively, the central bank can control the interest rate, keeping it at a constant level like $\bar{i}$. In this case, when the _IS_ curve shifts to position IS_1, the central bank must pump sufficient money into the economy to hold the interest rate at $\bar{i}$ (shifting the _LM_ schedule to LM_1). When the _IS_ schedule shifts leftward to IS_0, maintaining the interest rate requires a reduction in the money stock (shifting the _LM_ schedule to LM_2). With this strategy, output varies over the wider range from Y_B to Y_B' as equilibrium shifts between points B and B'.

Clearly, a constant money stock strategy is superior to a constant interest rate strategy when the _IS_ schedule is subject to erratic shifts. However, if the central bank is not required to adhere to naive rules but is permitted to pursue an activist countercyclical policy, output may be far more effectively stabilized _if_ the central bank has adequate information on developments in the commodity market and their dependence on monetary policy actions. As illustrated in Figure 8—12, if the central bank can identify an upward shift in commodity demand that corresponds to schedule IS_1, it could reduce the money stock to provide money market equilibrium schedule LM_2. Equilibrium would occur at point C'. If the central bank can identify a contraction in commodity demand that shifts the *IS* curve downward to position IS_0, it could stimulate the economy by raising the money stock to provide money market equilibrium schedule LM_1. Equilibrium would occur at point C. The activist policy, then, could stabilize output fully if the central bank has the information necessary to properly alter the money stock. Much larger variations in interest rates would be required, however, than would be necessary in other stabilization programs.

Instability in the *LM* Schedule. In Figure 8—13, commodity demand and the *IS* curve are treated as stable while it is assumed that there is instability in money demand and, hence, in the *LM* schedule. The *LM* schedule is viewed as shifting randomly between LM_0 and LM_1.

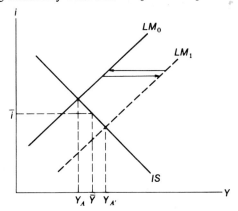

Figure 8—13 / Monetary Strategies when the *LM* Curve Is Unstable

In the face of a shifting demand for money, following a rule of holding the money supply constant would allow income to fluctuate between output levels Y_A and Y_A'. In contrast, if the central bank chooses the strategy of holding the interest rate constant (say at $\bar{i}$), providing the money required to satisfy money demand at that interest rate, output would be stabilized at $\bar{Y}$.

As Chapters 5–7 indicated, both commodity demand (hence the *IS* curve) and money demand (hence the *LM* curve) are subject to some instability. Which is more unstable is not a settled issue. Here, then, is a clear-cut reason for differing viewpoints on how monetary policy should be conducted. A belief that money demand is more stable than commodity demand tends to favor stabilizing the money stock in order to improve the economy's functioning. Of course, it is better still to pursue a countercyclical policy if adequate information is available to the central bank. A belief that money demand is less stable than commodity demand leads to favoring the strategy of stabilizing the interest rate.

The Monetary Effects of Fiscal Operations

As a final complication in the *IS-LM* framework we need to account for the monetary effects of fiscal actions. The *IS-LM* model with government has allowed us to easily evaluate the effects of monetary and fiscal policy actions. Money supply changes produced shifts in the *LM* curve with no impact on the *IS* curve, while fiscal actions (a change in government spending or in tax collections) shifted the *IS* curve with no impact on the money supply and thus no effect on the *LM* curve.

To avoid the confusion that has led to some pointless debate in recent years, we should take care to label the policy actions we have analyzed in this chapter *pure* monetary and fiscal policies. A pure monetary policy alters the money supply without directly affecting the current flow of income, while a pure fiscal operation, which does directly affect the income stream via a change in government spending or tax collections, leaves the money supply unchanged.

While the standard operational methods of money supply control that are available to the central bank[13] provide pure monetary policy actions, fiscal operations can and often do have an accompanying effect on the money supply. The potential for having a monetary effect accompany a fiscal operation is easy to see. Suppose the Treasury makes a $1,000 payment to a presidential aide. Mechanically, the Treasury would make that payment with a check drawn on its account with the central bank, a check that the presidential aide would take to his own bank for deposit or for conversion to currency. In either case, the publicly held stock of money would be increased by this $1,000 *fiscal* operation unless the monetary effect were offset by a compensatory reduction in the publicly held money stock. Whether it is offset or not depends on the method employed to finance the $1,000 expenditure.

When the government collects tax revenues, in addition to reducing disposable income, it also reduces the publicly held money stock by the amount of tax collections. Consequently, the monetary effect of a $1,000 government expenditure would be offset if the expenditure were tax financed. A tax-financed fiscal operation is a pure fiscal operation.

Similarly, if the government finances an expenditure program by selling government bonds to the public, the fiscal operation is pure. In this case, the public exchanges money for government bonds but also has its money stock restored by the bond-financed government expenditure. Whenever we are discussing fiscal policy in this text, it is to be understood that any government deficit is financed by borrowing from the public (that is, the public sale of newly issued government bonds) and that any surplus (which would otherwise reduce the money stock) is used to retire publicly held government bonds.

The Treasury can finance a deficit by borrowing from (selling bonds to) the central bank. In this case, there is no offset to the monetary effect of

---

[13]Those methods are described in Chapter 13.

the expenditure. Thus, an increase in the level of government expenditure financed by bond sales to the central bank would constitute a combined monetary-fiscal operation. In fact, the resulting one-shot rightward shift in the *IS* curve would be accompanied by a continuing rightward shift in the *LM* curve if, in every subsequent period, the deficit is central bank financed and, hence, increases the money stock.

The Price Level and Equilibrium Output

In developing and using the *IS-LM* model we have held the price level constant. This, by implication, means that we have been treating the supply of output as completely passive, expanding and contracting with aggregate demand with no attendant change in the general price level. That is, for any event that shifted the *IS* or *LM* schedule rightward (an autonomous increase in consumption, investment, government spending, or money supply, or an autonomous decline in taxes or money demand), equilibrium output was allowed to rise with no change in prices, as illustrated by the movement from Y_0 to Y_1 in Figure 8—14 along the implied supply curve *S*. Clearly, the *IS-LM* analysis focuses on changes in aggregate demand and neglects the supply side of the economy. We will rectify that situation in Chapter 9, but, to complete our efforts to exploit the *IS-LM* model, we need now to probe the relationship between the general price level and the equilibrium level of output demanded.

Figure 8—15 shows an economy at rest at output level Y_0. Note, from the labeling of the *LM* schedule, that the real money stock that provides the initial *LM* schedule and equilibrium output position corresponds to the specific general price level P_0. Given the nominal money stock, a different price level would provide a different *LM* curve and a different equilibrium output level. For example, a fall in the price level to P_1 would raise the real money stock, shifting the *LM* schedule rightward $\left[\text{to } LM(P_1)\right]$ to represent the

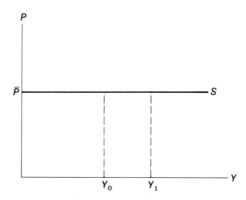

Figure 8—14 / Passive Supply at Price Level $\bar{P}$

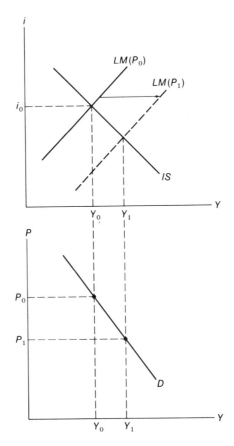

**Figure 8—15 / Changes in the
General Price Level and Aggregate Demand**

interest rate decline and output demand stimulus that this price reduction
generates. Any further decline in the price level would further stimulate the
demand for output, moving the economy along the downward sloping aggregate demand schedule *(D)* in the bottom half of Figure 8—15. On the
other hand, a rise in the price level, which reduces the real money stock
and drives up interest rates would reduce the demand for goods and services.

All the disturbances that, with the price level constant, were treated as
causing output to adjust can also be represented as shifts in the aggregate
demand schedule in Figure 8—15. Illustratively, an increase in government
spending that shifts the *IS* curve rightward results in a higher level of equilibrium output at *any* price level. That is, the aggregate demand for output
schedule is shifted rightward by this increase in government spending (or
by an autonomous increase in consumption, investment, or money supply,
or by an autonomous decline in taxes or money demand). In the next chapter, we will combine aggregate demand with a more realistic aggregate sup-

ply schedule, providing the framework for furthering our understanding of the economy's functioning.

Summary

In this chapter a simple model that takes account of the interactions between the money market and the market for goods and services has been constructed. That model enabled us to assess the impact of a number of common economic disturbances on a broad array of important macroeconomic variables. Among the disturbances considered, those that result from the *fiscal* and *monetary* policy actions of government were of particular interest. Our analysis indicated a standard route through which monetary policy actions are viewed as affecting the economy. Specifically, in the *IS-LM* model described, monetary policy actions are transmitted to aggregate demand through interest rate changes that alter investment demand.

Now, it must be recognized that other channels for the transmission of monetary policy have been emphasized by some analysts. For example, classical economists viewed an expansionary monetary policy as increasing the real value of wealth, held in the form of money balances. A part of this increase in wealth was assumed to be used for consumer purchases of goods, directly increasing aggregate demand. More recently, tests with some prominent statistical models of the U.S. economy have indicated that increases in money supply can prompt a rise in stock prices, which raises the wealth society perceives itself as having and adds to aggregate demand.

Different analysts have emphasized different links between money supply changes and aggregate demand, with some paying heed to more than one asset when the money supply changes, and viewing yield changes as affecting more than one component of aggregate demand. Concisely summarizing the major routes through which money supply changes influence the economy, Warren Smith has said:

Monetary policy induces portfolio adjustments which . . . affect income and employment. A purchase of, say, Treasury bills by the Federal Reserve will directly lower the yield on bills and, by a process of arbitrage involving a chain of portfolio substitutions will exert downward pressure on interest rates on financial assets generally. . . .

With the expected yield on a unit of real capital initially unchanged, the decline in the yields on financial assets, and the more favorable terms on which new debt can be issued, the balance sheets of households and businesses will be thrown out of equilibrium. The adjustment toward a new equilibrium will take the form of a sale of existing financial assets and the issuance of new debt to acquire real capital and claims thereto. . . . This stock adjustment approach is readily applicable, with some variations to suit the circumstances, to the demands for a wide variety of both business and consumer capital—including plant and equipment, inventories, residential construction, and consumer durable goods.[14]

---

[14]Warren L. Smith, "A Neo-Keynesian View of Monetary Policy," in *Controlling Monetary Aggregates* (Boston: Federal Reserve Bank of Boston, 1969), pp. 106–107.

The *IS-LM* model lacks the rich detail that a more elaborate representation of macroeconomic responses to policy actions provides. However, it incorporates the linkage between portfolio adjustments and real asset purchases that is common to most macroeconomic analyses, even the most sophisticated. By incorporating the rudiments of macroeconomic responses to policy actions, it has provided substantial insights into the factors that enhance the relative strength of monetary or fiscal policies, namely a set of interest and income elasticities; and it has allowed us to show how instabilities in the commodity or money market affect the optimum choice of stabilization tools.

With the *IS-LM* model, we probed the monetary implications of the requirement that the government finance its outlays. It does this through a combination of taxes and bond issue. It was demonstrated that expenditures that are financed by taxes or bond sales to the public represent pure fiscal actions (no shift in the *LM* curve), while expenditures financed by bond sales to the central bank increase the money supply (shift the *LM* curve as well as the *IS* curve).

A serious limitation on the use of the basic *IS-LM* model in analyzing economic events is the requirement of a constant price level which, we discovered, reflects our failure to deal explicitly and convincingly with the production or supply side of the economy. Indeed, with the price level allowed to change, we showed that the *IS-LM* model provides an aggregate demand schedule for the economy. The task of constructing an equivalent representation of the supply side of the economy is the primary concern of the next chapter.

Questions

1. In much of this chapter the *IS-LM* model assumes a constant price level. Discuss the reasonableness of that assumption.

2. Use the *IS-LM* model to analyze the impact on income, the interest rate, consumption, saving, investment, and velocity of the disturbances listed below:
    a. a change (+ or −) in government spending,
    b. a change (+ or −) in tax revenues,
    c. an increase in society's "thriftiness,"
    d. an autonomous increase in liquidity preference,
    e. a central bank-engineered reduction in the money supply,
    f. an autonomous reduction in the price level,
    g. a simultaneous increase in the money supply and reduction in government spending.

3. Explain the impact that consideration of the role of the money market had on the multiplier analysis developed in Chapter 4.

4. How would the model developed in this chapter be altered if:
    a. investment spending were unaffected by changes in the interest rate?

    b. the demand for money were insensitive to interest rate changes?
How would the strength of monetary and fiscal policy actions be affected?

5. If you have sufficient mathematical background, derive for the *IS-LM* model
with government:
    a. the slopes of the *IS* and *LM* schedules;
    b. the size of the shift in the *IS* schedule that stems from an autonomous change
in spending, and the size of shift resulting from an autonomous change in tax
collections;
    c. the size of the shift in the *LM* schedule stemming from a change in the real
money supply;
    d. the system-wide impact of an autonomous change in any spending schedule,
the tax schedule, or the money supply.

6. Suppose that the central bank acts to hold the interest rate constant as the
government increases its expenditures. What are the implications for the money
supply and for the size of change in output?

7. With instability in commodity market schedules, discuss the optimum choice of
stabilization instrument and the information requirements involved in that
choice.

Suggested Readings

Hicks, John R. "Mr. Keynes and the 'Classics': A Suggested Interpretation." *Econometrica* 5 (1937): 147–159.

Keynes, John Maynard. *The General Theory of Employment, Interest, and Money,*
Chapter 18. New York: Harcourt Brace Jovanovich, 1936.

Poole, William, "Optimal Choice of Monetary Policy Instruments in a Simple Stochastic Macro Model." *Quarterly Journal of Economics* 84 (1970): 197–216.

Ritter, Lawrence S. "The Role of Money in Keynesian Theory." In *Banking and
Monetary Studies,* edited by Deane Carson, pp. 134–150. Homewood, Ill.: Richard D. Irwin, 1963. Reprinted in M. G. Mueller, *Readings in Macroeconomics,*
pp. 161–172. 2nd ed. New York: Holt, Rinehart and Winston, 1971.

Chapter 9

Aggregate Supply and Economy-Wide Equilibrium

As indicated in Chapter 8, our analysis to this point has focused on the determinants of aggregate demand and neglected the supply side of the economy. The primary objective of this chapter is to construct a representation of the supply side and, then, to combine aggregate supply and demand, permitting a more realistic and complete assessment of the economy's responses to various shocks. With the addition of our aggregate supply model, the link between economic activity and employment (unemployment) will be clarified, and the general price level will be freed, permitting an explanation of price level changes.

Intuition suggests that, as in the case of individual firms, the relationship between price and quantity of output supplied should be positive, output rising with price. Through our efforts in this and the following chapter, we will see that such is the case in the short-run, a period that may involve a considerable interval of calendar time. In the long-run, however, there is reason to believe that the aggregate supply curve is vertical, with output left unchanged by movements in the general price level.

The Aggregate Production Function and Labor Demand

Our first task in modeling the supply side of the economy involves constructing a model of the market for labor services and exploring the link
between employment and output. In reality, a country's labor force includes
cooks, steeplejacks, welders, doctors, secretaries, bulldozer operators, and
a host of other categories of skilled and unskilled workers. Likewise, the
job slots that employers offer differ in skill requirements, working conditions, levels of pay, forms of pay, and so on. As always though, concern
for explaining the broad forces that influence the *aggregate* economy requires us to forego detailed examination of the many submarkets in which
labor is employed. Our attention must be focused on those common, per-
vasive forces that affect the supply of and demand for *labor in general* and,
hence, influence the *general wage level* and the *aggregate employment
level*. To that end, our development of the labor market can be thought of,
for now, as dealing with labor that sells homogeneous services at a common
wage economy-wide.

The Production Function

By first focusing attention on the technical link between employment and
output, we will be able to provide a straightforward explanation of the aggregate demand for labor. In general, we can expect a country's aggregate
output to be positively related to the quantity of capital and labor employed
(given the quality of the labor force and the state of technology). At a given

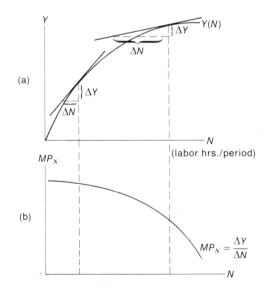

**Figure 9—1 / The Aggregate Production
Function and the Marginal Product of Labor**

point in time then, a country's *aggregate production function* would take the form $Y = Y(K,N)$, where K is the stock of capital and N is the number of hours of labor services employed. For short-run analysis, the stock of capital is constant, so output can change only if there is a change in the quantity of labor services firms utilize. As firms employ more labor, the volume of real output is increased as shown in part (a) of Figure 9—1. Thus, in the short-run, output is a positive function of labor employment or $Y = Y(N)$ with $\Delta Y/\Delta N > 0$. The downward concavity of the short-run aggregate production function reflects the presence of *diminishing returns*. While output rises as employment rises, it is assumed that the output growth takes place at a decreasing rate as the existing capital stock is spread out over more and more hours of labor input. Eventually output would attain a maximum value and then begin to fall if enough labor is crowded into employment with the stock of plants and equipment fixed.

The *marginal product of labor,* the extra output provided by a unit addition of labor input, is simply the slope of the aggregate production function $\left[\Delta Y/\Delta N, \text{ in part (b) in Figure 9—1}\right]$. By inspecting the production function in Figure 9—1, we can see that the assumption of diminishing returns requires the marginal product of labor to fall as employment increases.

Labor Demand

We can now explain what determines the quantity of labor input individual firms employ and use that information to explain the aggregate demand for labor. For simplicity, that explanation will be developed for firms that operate in competitive markets. As a firm increases the quantity of labor employed, it increases output by $(\Delta Y/\Delta N)\Delta N$, the marginal product of labor times the increase in employment. Because competitive firms face a given product price level, the dollar revenue increase from extra labor input is $\Delta R = (P \cdot \Delta Y/\Delta N)\Delta N$, the *value* of labor's marginal product times the increase in employment. Of course, with more labor employed, a firm's total costs are increased. The extra dollar costs faced by a firm employing ΔN additional units of labor is $\Delta C = W \cdot \Delta N$, the market-determined money wage rate times the increase in employment. A profit-maximizing firm will always increase its labor input as long as the increase adds more to revenue than to cost. Thus, for equilibrium, employment must be increased until the extra revenue generated by the last increment of labor employment just covers the cost to the firm of employing that last increment, that is, until $\Delta R = \Delta C$. If, in equilibrium, *marginal revenue* (ΔR) must equal *marginal cost* (ΔC), then

$$P \cdot \frac{\Delta Y}{\Delta N} \cdot \Delta N = W \cdot \Delta N \qquad [9—1]$$

or, canceling the common ΔN terms,

$$P \cdot \frac{\Delta Y}{\Delta N} = W \qquad\qquad [9\text{--}2]$$

where, once again, $P \cdot \Delta Y/\Delta N$ is the value of labor's marginal product and W is the money wage. Rearranging this equality in a form that is more useful for our purposes, we obtain

$$\frac{\Delta Y}{\Delta N} = \frac{W}{P} \qquad\qquad [9\text{--}3]$$

In this expression, $\Delta Y/\Delta N$ is the marginal product of labor and W/P is the real wage of labor. The real wage is determined for any specific prevailing values of the money wage and price level, and any one competitive firm will strive to employ the volume of labor that equates the marginal product of labor with the real wage. Should the real wage fall, through either a fall in money wages·or a rise in the price level, firms will find it profitable to increase the volume of labor employed. For the collection of all firms, this implies the aggregate labor demand function in the lower half of Figure 9—2, which is nothing more than the aggregate marginal product of labor schedule from Figure 9—1. According to this schedule, at real wage $(W/P)_0$ the business sector will employ N_0 units of labor and produce output at level Y_0. Should the real wage be reduced to $(W/P)_1$, the business sector

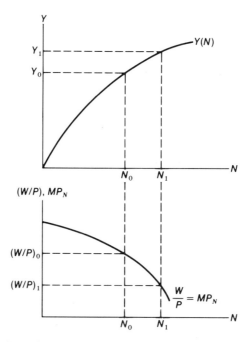

Figure 9—2 ⊦ The Real Wage Employment, and Output

would find it profitable to increase employment for, at real wage rate $(W/P)_1$, the marginal product of labor would exceed the real wage of labor for every level of employment less then N_1. Thus, business firms' profits would be increased by adding to employment until employment level N_1, the new equilibrium level that equates the marginal product of labor and the real wage, is established, with the corresponding increased level of production Y_1.

While changes in the real wage induce moves along the labor demand schedule, as firms equate the real wage with labor's marginal product, changes in any other factor that influences labor's productivity will shift the labor demand schedule (and, quite probably, the production function). As examples, changes in technology or changes in the quantity of other factors (capital, land, or energy inputs) used with labor would shift the labor demand schedule. After considering disturbances that, in a complete model of the economy, prompt movements along a fixed labor demand schedule, we will want to consider disturbances that shift the labor demand schedule.

Labor Supply

To complete our model of the labor market, we need to know what determines the number of hours of labor that will be supplied to the business sector. In deciding how to divide their time between labor and leisure, between working for pay and engaging in other time uses, workers consider the wage reward they receive for working. Of course, it is the command over goods and services which their money wages represent that workers are really concerned with, so it is the *real* wage workers expect to receive that influences their labor-leisure choice. A doubling of money wages and prices, leaving the real wage unchanged, would not alter the number of hours of labor time that a rational worker supplies to the labor market.

Two complications in labor's efforts to determine what volume of labor services to offer should be noted. First, because workers are paid a money wage, they must deflate their wage offers with what they judge to be an appropriate index of the prices of goods and services they purchase to determine their real wage reward for working. That is a complex task because most individuals are purchasers of many dozens of different goods and services. Second, because workers often contract to work for an extended time horizon (one, two, or three years) at a specific wage or on a specific wage schedule, it is the price level that workers expect to prevail during the work period that is relevant to their labor-leisure decision. Needless to say, workers may at times hold mistaken expectations regarding the general price level.

Now no mention was made of these complexities in our discussion of labor demand. The simple reason is that firms, which are labor demanders, have a relatively simple task in our labor market model. As producers of one or at most a few products, individual firms can keep up rather easily with (or even control) prices on their product(s), and they can easily keep up with (or even control) the money wage costs they face for labor. That is, firms are assumed to have at all times the information necessary for determining what the real wage cost of their labor is, while workers, with a much more complex information-gathering task, may at times be mistaken about the expected real value of wage offers they receive.[1]

Whether their expectations of prices and, hence, of their real wages are correct or not, workers can be expected to respond to an increase in expected real wages by offering more hours of labor services, with part of the increase stemming from increased labor force participation (say by women and teenagers), and part from an increase in the hours per week offered by existing members of the labor force.[2] Figure 9—3 shows labor being supplied as a positive function of the expected real wage, with quantity of labor services N_0 offered at expected real wage (W/P_0^e) and N_1 offered at (W/P_1^e).

Actual Versus Expected Prices and Labor Supply

Having recognized that the price level that labor expects can differ from the actual price level, let us consider two possible responses to a change in money wages and prices. With the prevailing money wage at five dollars per hour and a price index value of 1.0, let both the money wage and the actual price level rise by 20 percent to six dollars per hour and 1.2 respectively.

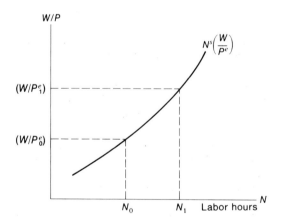

Figure 9—3 / Aggregate Labor Supply

---

[1]There are other sets of assumptions that provide supply schedule properties comparable to those that stem from this assumed asymmetry in the information-gathering tasks of firms and workers. Other schemes, however, involve more complexity.

[2]A rigorous derivation of the labor supply schedule, assuming utility-maximizing behavior on the part of laborers, can be found in W. H. Branson, *Macroeconomic Theory and Policy*, 2nd ed. (New York: Harper and Row, 1979), pp. 104–105.

Case 1: # Correct Expectations

Because both money wages and prices are increased by 20 percent, real wages are unchanged at $W/P = 5/1.0 = 6/1.2 = 5$. With the expected price level matching the actual price level ($P^e = P$), labor would offer an unchanged volume of services. This would be true for proportional money wage and price changes starting at any real wage, as long as expectations are correct. With full information, then, the labor supply schedule remains stable as in the figure below as money wages and prices change.

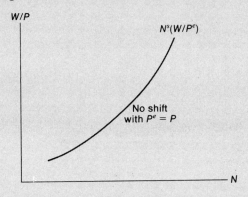

Case 2: # Partial or Zero Price Expectation Changes

While actual real wages are unchanged, suppose labor fails to adjust its price expectations as the money wage and actual prices rise by 20 percent. In this case, the real wage that labor expects to receive is $W/P^e = 6/1.0 = 6$. That is, with labor valuing the new money wage at the old (and now obsolete) price level, it expects a 20 percent increase in real wages. Acting on what it expects its real wage to be, labor would offer more hours of services at every *actual* real wage as reflected in the rightward shift in the labor supply schedule below.

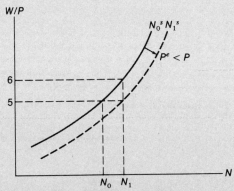

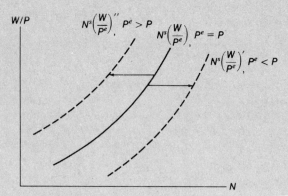

Figure 9—4 / Price Expectations and Labor Supply

The rightward shift of the labor supply schedule in Case 2 is the result of labor's failure to alter its price expectations so that actual and expected prices coincide. In this situation labor is offering more hours of services at every real wage than it would if it had full information on the price level that will prevail during its anticipated work period. Should workers expect a price level higher than actually prevails, valuing their money wages at the overestimated price level provides an underestimate of expected real wages and could lead labor to provide fewer hours of services at every actual real wage than it would if it had full information.

Figure 9—4 summarizes our discussion of the role of expectations in the labor supply schedule. With full information on the price level ($P^e = P$) labor services are provided along the solid schedule. The expectation of a price level lower than actually prevails ($P^e < P$) shifts the labor supply schedule rightward to a position like that of $N^s(P^e < P)$, and, if the expected price level is greater than actually prevails, the labor supply schedule is shifted leftward.

Aggregate Supply with Full Information. Figure 9—5 shows the labor market cleared at the full employment level of employment N_0 at a real wage W_0/P_0. Remember, full employment corresponds to some 5 percent measured unemployment, as a portion of the work force is always voluntarily unemployed and involved in job search activities. Without reproducing the economy's production function in Figure 9—5, we know that corresponding to employment level N_0 there is a level of output Y_0, as labeled in the top portion of our figure. Often, the market-clearing employment level represented in this figure is referred to as the *natural employment rate* with the corresponding output level labeled the *natural output level*. Of course, this full employment output level is the *potential output level* discussed in the first section of the text.

Now, beginning with the price level at P_0, consider the effects of an increase in prices to level P_1 if labor has full information on the price change, adjusting its expected price estimate accordingly. A rise in prices reduces the real wage to a level like W_0/P_1; and, with $P^e = P = P_1$, labor would offer only N' hours of services at this reduced real wage, while firms would demand N'' hours. The resulting excess demand for labor would force money wage offers upward as firms compete for the scarce labor supply. Of course, with full information (hence, no shift in the labor supply schedule), an excess demand for labor would persist until the real wage is restored to level W_0/P_0. That is, with prices up to level $P_1 = \gamma P_0$, money wages would have to rise by the same proportion to restore equilibrium with $W_1/P_1 = \gamma W_0/\gamma P_0 = W_0/P_0$. With full information then ($P^e = P$), a rise in the price level prompts an equal proportional increase in money wages, leaving the real wage, employment, and the level of real output unaffected.

In similar fashion, a fully anticipated reduction in the price level requires a compensatory fall in money wages as the price decline raises the real wage, creating an excess supply of labor. The resulting downward pressure on money wages would have to restore the original real wage (money wages reduced in proportion to the price decline) for equilibrium to be restored. Hence, with full information ($P^e = P$), a decline in the price level, as to P_2 in Figure 9—5, prompts a corresponding reduction in money wages with

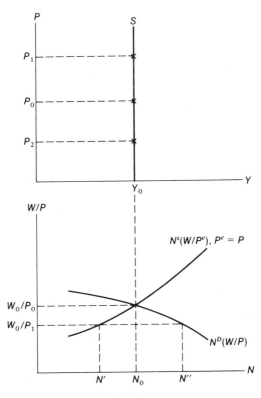

Figure 9—5 / The Supply Response to Price Changes: $P^e = P$

real wages unaffected and with employment and output unchanged at the natural employment rate and natural output level, respectively.

Because our conclusions would be the same for any size of increase or cut in the general price level, the economy's aggregate supply schedule is represented by the solid vertical line in Figure 9—5 when price expectations change in step with the actual price level. That is, *with full information on the price level, the economy's aggregate supply schedule is simply a vertical line at the full (natural) employment level of output.*

Aggregate Supply with an Incomplete Adjustment in Price Expectations. Our next task is to see how the aggregate supply schedule may differ if labor does not have full information on changes in the general price level so that a change in prices fails to induce an equal proportional change in the general price level that labor *expects* to prevail. Figure 9—6 illustrates this case.

Suppose that the labor market is initially cleared (at W_0/P_0, N_0) and that output is at level Y_0 with the general price level P_0. Then, as before, increase the general price level to P_1, reducing the actual real wage and causing an excess demand for labor to appear. Firms would bid up money wages as

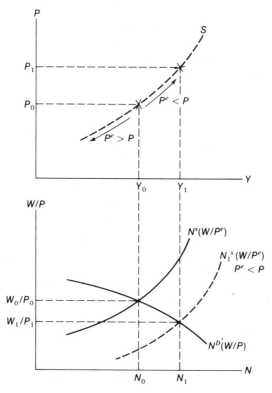

Figure 9—6 / The Supply Response to Price Changes: $P^e \neq P$

they compete for scarce labor, but, with labor not altering price expectations in step with actual prices, any money wage increase would be interpreted as a real wage increase. Consequently, the labor supply schedule is shifted rightward as to position $N_1^s(W/P^e)$. Equilibrium would then occur at the higher employment level N_1 and the correspondingly higher output level Y_1. The actual real wage is reduced at this point, but labor, valuing its higher money wage (W_1) at an expected price level that is less than actual prices, thinks its real wage has increased and offers more labor services. In effect, the unanticipated price increase has fooled workers into reducing search unemployment, raising employment and output above their natural levels.

Similar reasoning indicates that a cut in prices would lower output and employment. In this case, labor would be receiving reduced money wage offers and, evaluating them at an expected price level above the actual price level, would conclude that real wages had dropped. In turn, labor would withdraw labor services, accepting additional search unemployment as long as the *expected* real wage is viewed as being below the market-clearing level.

With costly-to-obtain and, hence, imperfect information, aggregate output is clearly positively related to the price level. That is, *with unanticipated changes in the general price level, the economy's aggregate supply schedule slopes upward from left to right,* as represented by the broken line in Figure 9—6.

Which form of the aggregate supply schedule should we view as more appropriate for analyzing the macroeconomy's responses to the shocks that confront it? You should be aware that the answer to that question can differ markedly depending on what particular school of thought the authority you are questioning adheres to. Most economists, however, would say: (1) that both forms of the aggregate supply schedule are useful in explaining the economy's functioning; and (2) that the *time horizon* of your analysis of the economy's reactions to shocks is fundamentally important in determining what the supply responses to those shocks will be. We will explore the role of time in the economy's dynamic functioning as our discussion proceeds. In the meantime, exploring the economy-wide reactions to disturbances with contrasting restrictions on the adjustment of price expectations is instructive, and that is our next task.

Economy-Wide Adjustments with Full Information

To complete this chapter, we will look at a sample of disturbances that affect an economy in which it is assumed that labor has full information on the general price level. As we now know, this assumption permits expected prices to always match actual prices and leaves the labor supply curve unaltered in the face of a price level change.

An Increase in Government Spending

Figure 9—7 shows an economy initially in equilibrium at output level Y_0 and price level P_0. Along with the aggregate supply and demand schedules, the *IS-LM* model is drawn to represent the demand side of the economy, and the labor market is presented as representing the supply side of the economy with employment level N_0 corresponding to output level Y_0. With full information always available on the general price level ($P^e = P$), employment is at the natural rate with output corresponding.

In the *IS-LM* model, an increase in government spending shifts the *IS* schedule rightward (as to *IS'*), raising the equilibrium level of aggregate demand to level Y'. In the aggregate supply and demand model, the increase in government demand corresponds to a rightward shift in the aggregate demand schedule to position *D'*. Note that the "constant price" increase in demand in the *IS-LM* model matches the "constant price" (at P_0) increase in demand in the aggregate demand and supply model.

With aggregate demand exceeding supply ($Y' > Y_0$), prices must increase to level P_1 before supply and demand will again coincide. As prices rise, there are reactions on both the demand and supply sides of the economy that we need to keep track of. In the labor market (i.e., on the supply side), a price increase tends to reduce the real wage; and, with labor fully recognizing the real wage decline, this creates an excess demand for labor. Competing for the scarce labor force, firms will bid up the money wage. The upward pressure on money wages will persist as long as the real wage is below the market-clearing level, pushing the real wage back to that level. With the economy's reaction to the government spending increase completed, money wages will have risen in the same proportion as prices so the real wage and employment will remain unchanged.

On the demand side of the economy, the price rise reduces the real value of the money supply, shifting the *LM* schedule leftward. With the shrinkage in real money balances, the interest rate rises and the increased interest cost of investment reduces investment demand. It is this mechanism that provides the shrinkage in aggregate demand. The price increase must continue until the *LM* schedule is shifted to position *LM'* because aggregate demand must shrink back to equality with the unchanged level of potential or natural output.

Overall, the increase in government spending has raised prices and the interest rate but has left employment and output unchanged. What has changed is the allocation of resources. Recall that aggregate real output is $Y = C + I + G$. With real output (income) unchanged, real consumption will also be unchanged. Hence, the increase in government spending must be matched by an equivalent decline in investment spending. That is, the additional government spending has *crowded out* an equal volume of private purchases, leaving aggregate demand and output unchanged. This set of conclusions matches those yielded by classical analysis in assessing the effects of fiscal actions.

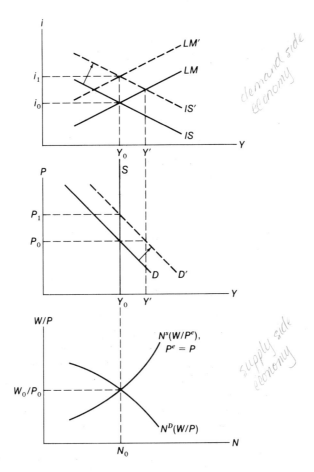

Figure 9—7 / Increased Government Spending with Full Information

As alternatives to a government spending increase, aggregate demand would also be increased (and the *IS* schedule shifted rightward) by an autonomous increase in consumption or investment, or by a cut in taxes. As in the government spending example, these shocks would raise prices and the interest rate but leave employment and output unaltered. Of course, the composition of output would differ depending on which schedule(s) are shifted, as you can determine for yourself. In contrast, with a cut in government spending, consumption, or investment, or with a tax increase, prices and the interest rate would fall while employment and output again remain unchanged with only the composition of output altered.

Money Supply Changes

Beginning once again with an economy at rest (at Y_0, P_0, i_0, N_0, W_0/P_0), Figure 9—8 illustrates the economy's reaction to an increase in the nominal

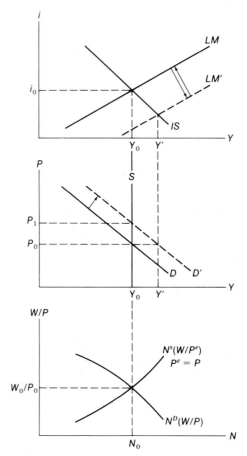

Figure 9—8 / A Money Supply Increase

money supply to a level $M_1 = \gamma M_0$. In the *IS-LM* model, an increase in the nominal money stock shifts the *LM* curve rightward to a position like *LM'*. This shift illustrates money's role in stimulating spending; the money supply increase drives interest rates down, stimulating investment and, hence, aggregate demand to level Y' in the diagram. Of course, this constant price increase in aggregate demand is matched in the aggregate supply and demand model by the shift in the aggregate demand schedule to position D'.

The increase in aggregate demand forces prices upward, eventually to level P_1. In the labor market, as prices rise money wages will be bid up as well, as firms compete for workers. With the price adjustment complete, money wages will have risen in the same proportion as prices, leaving the real wage, employment, and, hence, output unchanged.

In the meantime, the rise in prices, by reducing the real value of the money stock, would be shifting the *LM* schedule leftward, with the interest rate rising and aggregate demand shrinking back toward their original levels.

With output (supply) unchanged, prices would have to continue rising until the LM schedule is at its original position with aggregate demand back to level Y_0. What size price increase does this require? Recall that money market equilibrium requires equality of the real money supply $(\overline{M}_S/P)$ with real money demand, which is a function of income and the interest rate $[M(Y,i)]$. That is, money market equilibrium prevails when

$$\frac{\overline{M}_S}{P} = M(Y,i) \qquad\qquad [9\text{—}4]$$

Of course, with the economy's adjustment complete, output and the interest rate are at their original levels (Y_0 and i_0), so the real demand for money will be unchanged. The only way money market equilibrium could prevail, then, is if the real money supply is unchanged, which it will be if, and only if, the price level has increased in the same proportion as the money supply. That is, the real money supply will be $\gamma M_0/\gamma P_0 = M_0/P_0$ as the increase in the money supply elicits an equal proportional increase in prices.

In like fashion, a reduction in the nominal money stock would reduce the general price level and the nominal value of wages in proportion to the money stock decline. Again, the value of the *real* variables in the system, real output and its component parts, the real wage, employment, and the interest rate, would be unaltered by a money supply shrinkage.

Once again, we have generated classical conclusions with our full information model. As the classicists claimed, money in this model is *neutral*, i.e., changes in the money stock alter prices and nominal values but leave the values of real variables unchanged. Moreover, the link between money and prices is fully illustrated by the equation of exchange, $MV = PY$. With velocity unchanged in our alternative positions of static equilibrium and output stationary at the full employment level, the nominal money stock and prices are proportional: $(\gamma M)V = (\gamma P)Y$ is the same as $MV = PY$.

Our model's reactions to a money supply change reflect a *classical dichotomy,* a conceptual division in the economy between real forces that determine real variables (employment, the real wage, real output and its division into its component parts, and the real interest rate) and monetary forces that have the very limited role of altering only prices and nominal values. These classical conclusions hold even though our model contains a money demand function consistent with modern portfolio views of financial asset demand rather than the mechanistic money demand function often associated (not necessarily correctly) with classical analysis. The essence of classical analysis, then, appears to be the assumption that economic agents (firms, consumers, and, particularly, workers) have full information with which to make rational economic decisions.

Of course, the longer the time interval over which the economy is allowed to respond to any disturbance, the more complete will be the information on economic events, notably on changes in the prevailing price level. In recognition of this fact, some analysts define the long-run as a period of time adequate for acquiring the full information needed to make rational economic decisions. Consequently, the economy would function according to classical rules *in the long-run*. In actuality, classical analysis focused by and large on long-run concerns and, in the long-run, it appears that classical reasoning is basically valid. What happens in the economy over shorter time intervals, which may be quite lengthy in calendar time, will be examined in the next chapter. With a look at a supply side disturbance, we can complete this chapter's review of the full information (classical) economy's reactions to an instructive sample of shocks.

A Supply Side Shock

To illustrate the full information model's reaction to a supply side disturbance, consider a significant reduction in the supply of energy inputs into the production process. With less energy to work with, labor will be less productive. That is, this shock alters the economy's short-run production function, as shown in the top part of Figure 9—9. The fall in labor's productivity rotates the production function clockwise from $Y(N,E_0)$ for energy input E_0 to $Y(N,E_1)$ for energy input E_1, as any level of employment would provide less output than before. In addition, because the slope of the pro-

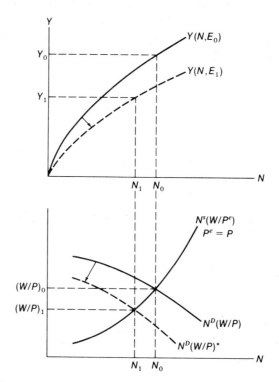

Figure 9—9 / The Impact of a Production Function Shift

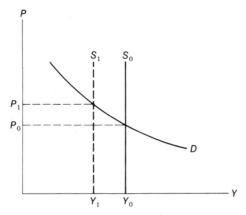

Figure 9—10 / An Aggregate Supply Shift in the Full Information Model

duction function is the marginal product of labor, the shift in the production function shifts the labor demand schedule leftward from $N^D(W/P)$ to $N^D(W/P)^*$.

It is notable that, as a consequence of the loss of energy inputs, the market-clearing level of output supplied declines from Y_0 to Y_1 as both the level of employment and labor's productivity are reduced. Moreover, with labor's productivity reduced, the real wage that equates labor supply and demand is reduced.

Figure 9—10 uses the aggregate supply and demand model to illustrate the economy-wide impact of our energy loss shock. With an initial equilibrium at output level Y_0 and price level P_0, the reduction in aggregate supply that the loss of energy inputs portends, shifts the aggregate supply schedule leftward from S_0 to S_1. At the initial price level P_0, there would be excess demand ($Y_0 - Y_1$) driving prices upward toward level P_1. As in our earlier examples, the rise in prices reduces the real money stock, raising interest rates, and reducing investment (hence, total) demand until demand is down to the reduced level of equilibrium supply S_1.

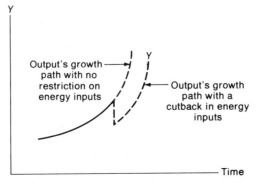

Figure 9—11 / Output's Expansion Path with an Energy Input Cutback

Clearly, the loss of energy inputs has caused a once-and-for-all decline in the economy's production (hence, consumption) standard. Of course, over time, with continued improvements in technology and in labor force skills, and with increases in the quantities of labor and capital employed, output will expand. As Figure 9—11 illustrates, however, as long as the restriction in energy inputs, or correspondingly in any other major factor of production, persists, the expansion path of output over time will lie below that which would prevail without the cutback in a major input in the production process.

With the Organization of Petroleum Exporting Countries (OPEC) cartel raising the price of oil by a sizable multiple since 1973, oil-importing countries like the U.S. have endeavored to economize on oil (and related energy) inputs. Our illustration shows clearly the long-run (full information) impact of a reduction, *ceteris paribus*, in energy usage.

Case In Point V   # OPEC and U.S. Output

In the Fall of 1973, OPEC embargoed oil shipments to the United States. Several weeks later, oil shipments were resumed but at a price that, in 1974, was nearly four times the pre-embargo price. Since 1974, OPEC has maintained the upward pressure on oil prices.

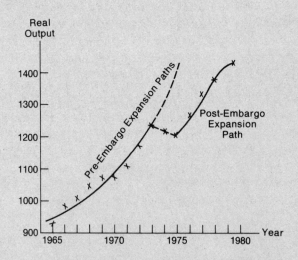

The U.S. Economy's Pre- and Post-Embargo Expansion Paths

The United States is a heavy petroleum user, relying on imports for roughly half of its oil flows. It is notable, too, that with the OPEC cartel jacking up the cost of oil, the increased demand for energy substitutes (coal, natural gas, etc.) has raised their prices markedly. We might expect the output expansion paths of economies that have voracious energy appetites to be shifted downward in the post-embargo period as they economize on the usage of markedly more costly energy inputs.

While data from a handful of years does not offer convincing evidence of a significant shift in long-term trends, the data on output in the U.S. economy from 1965–1979 is strongly suggestive that a downward shift in our output expansion path has occurred, coinciding with the abrupt change in energy costs in the 1970s.

Time and Economic Adjustments

We have now used the full information form of our macro model to analyze the economy's response to both demand and supply shocks. We have seen that in this model there is an asymmetry in that demand disturbances produce only price adjustments in aggregate variables, leaving quantities (output and employment) unaltered, while a supply side disturbance, our example being a cutback in energy usage, was necessary to call forth quantity changes.

These "classical" results can only be viewed as valid if we are talking about a response period long enough in time to permit the full adjustment of expected prices necessary to restore equality between actual and expected prices. This may involve a substantial period of calendar time, and for that reason we must question the usefulness of the classical analysis in predicting economic events of interest to policy makers. Indeed, it is painfully clear that in the real world shifts in aggregate demand cause sizable changes in quantities—both output and employment. In the post-World War II era, unemployment in the United States has fluctuated between approximately 3 and 8½ percent of the labor force, and in the Great Depression of the 1930s unemployment rose from predepression levels of far under 5 percent to a full 25 percent. To understand fully how quantity adjustments can occur, we need to investigate the functioning of an economy in which there is not full information on price changes. That restriction implies that we are focusing on a time interval too short for labor to fully recognize and come to anticipate price changes. Such a short-run time horizon, however, may extend for a period of calendar time that is many months or even years in duration. At the beginning of this chapter, we developed an aggregate supply schedule that, because of labor market responses based on imperfect information, sloped upward from left to right. Chapter 10 will employ that supply schedule to assess the economy's short-run response to demand shocks, then our short- and long-run arguments will be combined.

Summary

The major task of this chapter was to develop a representation of the supply side of the economy and integrate it into our macroeconomic model. That task necessitated focusing on the economy's production function and on the market for labor services. In dealing with the labor market, it was shown that price changes lead to different effects on employment and, hence, the aggregate supply of output, depending on whether the price changes are anticipated or not. An increase (decrease) in prices not matched by a proportional increase (decrease) in expected prices shifted the labor supply schedule rightward (leftward), permitting output and employment to change with prices. In contrast, with full information so that the expected price level matches the actual price level, price changes due to demand shifts leave employment unaltered and output constant along a vertical aggregate supply schedule.

Using the full information model, we explored the economy's responses to a sample of disturbances and showed that the economy displayed *classical* properties even though our model includes modern day views of the determinants of spending and, in particular, money demand. It appears, then, that the essence of classical analysis is the focus on adjustment periods long enough to permit full information on prices to be acquired. Of course, the classical form of analysis can be quite useful; notably, we employed it to analyze the long-term effects of a cutback in energy usage. However, the classical form of our model fails to provide an acceptable explanation of the quantity adjustments that, under the label business fluctuations, have been a dominant concern of macroeconomic analysis.

Questions

1. Explain the slope of the labor supply curve and account for shifts in that schedule that stem from changes in price expectations.

2. What do you expect the price level to be one year from now? Two years from now? Upon what are your estimates based?

3. Use the full information model to analyze the effects of:
   a. an increase in "thrift," i.e., an increase in saving at every income level,
   b. an increase in investment,
   c. a technological innovation that enhances labor's productivity,
   d. an increase in female labor force participation.

4. In what sense do the conclusions drawn from the macroeconomic model depend on time?

Suggested Readings

Alchian, Armen A. "Information Costs, Pricing, and Resource Unemployment." *Western Economic Journal* 7(1969), pp. 109–128.

Keynes, John Maynard. *The General Theory of Employment, Interest, and Money,* Chapters 18 and 20. New York: Harcourt Brace Jovanovich, 1936.

Appendix to Chapter 9 # A Simple Classical Model

In this chapter, we generated classical conclusions but with a model that, for the interested student, may not clearly illuminate the basis of classical reasoning. For those who are interested, this appendix attempts to provide that illumination.

Say's Law

The essence of the simple classical model of income determination is captured in a proposition known as *Say's Law*. Briefly summarized, Say's Law claims that "supply creates its own demand," i.e., that the very act of production increases demand by an amount equal to the increase in output so that a condition of overproduction, inducing a persistent contraction of output and employment, could not occur.

The logic of Say's Law seems clear for a barter economy. An individual increases his output of some product only in order to trade the extra output (over and above his own demand) for products produced by others. An increase in output carries with it an identical increase in demand in real terms.

An elegantly simple, formal, mathematical statement of Say's Law can be readily provided. While there is no money, that is, no one item that is generally used as a medium of exchange, in a barter economy, for simplicity suppose that there are "accounting prices" for every product. These prices reflect the rate at which any commodity will exchange for another; for example, the rate at which shoes exchange for cloth. Because any individual might produce one or more commodities, in general the *value* of any individual's production of n different commodities (measured at accounting prices) is

$$p_1 s_1 + p_2 s_2 + \ldots + p_n s_n \qquad [9\text{—A1}]$$

An individual produces so that he or she can demand commodities for personal use. The total *value* of the commodities demanded is

$$p_1 d_1 + p_2 d_2 + \ldots + p_n d_n \qquad [9\text{—A2}]$$

If an individual produces only for his or her own use or for exchange with other producers, then it must be the case that

$$p_1 s_1 + p_2 s_2 + \ldots + p_n s_n = p_1 d_1 + p_2 d_2 + \ldots + p_n d_n \qquad [9\text{—}A3]$$

The value of an individual's production (of one commodity or n commodities) is identical to the value of his or her total demand for goods and services. With this identity holding for any and every individual then *the value of aggregate supply must be identical to the value of total demand,* or

$$\sum_{i=1}^{n} p_i S_i \equiv \sum_{i=1}^{n} p_i D_i \qquad [9\text{—}A4]$$

where S_i is the *aggregate* output of commodity i from all individuals and D_i is the *aggregate* quantity of commodity i demanded by all individuals. Equation (9—A4) allows one or more commodities to be in excess supply at existing accounting prices, while, for some one or more other commodities, there is excess demand. However, Equation (9—A4) requires the total value of excess supplies to be matched by the total value of excess demands. Output *in general* cannot differ in value from the level of demand because the act of supplying commodities is, at the same time, the act of demanding commodities.

A Money Economy

What about the case of a money economy in which exchanges are made using money, and individuals can *save* a portion of their money income? In this case, because part (or all) of any increase in income may be saved in money form, an increase in income (output) may not imply an increase in spending sufficient to clear the market of the increased level of output. How would Keynes' classical predecessors respond to this point?

They would claim that the introduction of money makes no difference. Total spending would always be sufficient to clear the market of any specified level of output (income). In a monetary economy, however, the mechanism that ensures equality of income and spending is a flexible interest rate, a rate that can equate aggregate demand and supply (or *ipso facto,* investment and saving) at any level of income.

The Commodity Market. In our classical model, investment is an inverse function of the interest rate because classical economists assumed that the return on investment fell as the level of investment rose. The level of saving out of any specified level of income was a positive function of the interest rate. Further, it was assumed to be irrational for anyone to hold savings as idle money balances if there were any positive yield available from lending. Thus, any saving was promptly loaned. An interest return (that allows net worth to grow, permitting increased future consumption) was the reward for abstinence, that is, for not consuming. The higher the reward, the larger the fraction of income saved. With both investment and saving quite sensitive to the interest rate, it was believed that interest rate adjustments would always allow saving and investment to be equal at any level of income. Thus, for any selected level of income, the classical saving and investment functions are

$$I = I(i) \quad \text{such that} \quad \frac{\Delta I}{\Delta i} < 0 \qquad \text{[9—A5]}$$

and

$$S = S(i) \quad \text{such that} \quad \frac{\Delta S}{\Delta i} > 0$$

with

$$S = I \text{ always.}$$

These schedules are plotted in Figure 9—A1.

An increase in thriftiness (a shift of the saving function to the right such as shown in Figure 9—A1) with the interest rate at level i_0 would leave an excess supply of saving, with some savers frustrated in their attempt to earn a reward (i_0) for abstaining from consumption. If any of these savers offer to lend their savings at a reduced rate, the interest rate must fall (competitive market). Thus, the interest rate is flexible and adjusts to maintain the equality of S and I. Clearly, any level of income can be an equilibrium level. The level of income must be determined elsewhere. Only the interest rate, the proportion of income consumed (and saved), and the level of investment are determined here in the commodity market. Note that the interest rate is a *real* variable determined in the commodity market, with its value dependent on the "productivity of capital" (our marginal efficiency of investment) and "thrift" (the saving schedule).

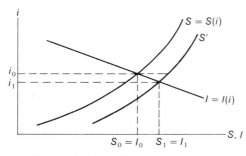

Figure 9—A1 / Commodity Market Equilibrium

Similarly, a shift in the investment function would require a change in the equilibrium interest rate, with an increase in investment (a rightward shift of the investment function) raising the interest rate, and a decrease in investment lowering it. Once again, the level of income does not need to change to maintain the equality of investment and saving needed for commodity market equilibrium. The flexible interest rate mechanism ensures that equality.

The Labor Market. Say's Law, even extended to a money economy, allows *any* level of income to be an equilibrium level. It says nothing about what level of income will actually be established. In our simple classical model the level of output is established in the labor market by the demand for and supply of labor.

The classical economists assumed that the quantity of labor supplied and the quantity demanded depended on the real wage. Labor supply was a positive function of the real wage. The higher the reward for foregoing leisure, the larger the quantity of labor services offered. In addition, the real wage was known with certainty.

Demand for labor was a derived demand as indicated by standard marginal productivity theory. Additional labor would be hired by a firm (and thus by the economy as a whole) as long as the marginal product of labor exceeded the real wage of labor. Given the stock of land, the capital stock, the state of technology, and the quality of the labor force, with diminishing returns to the quantity of labor employed, the demand schedule for labor sloped downward from left to right. Thus,

$$N^s = N\left(\frac{W}{P}\right) \qquad \frac{\Delta N^s}{\Delta\left(\dfrac{W}{P}\right)} > 0 \qquad\qquad [9\text{---}A6]$$

$$N^D = N\left(\frac{W}{P}\right) \qquad \frac{\Delta N^D}{\Delta\left(\dfrac{W}{P}\right)} < 0$$

and $N^S = N^D$ in equilibrium.

The classical supply and demand schedules appear in Figure 9—A2.

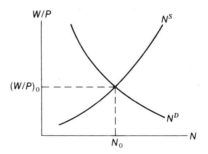

Figure 9—A2 / Labor Market Equilibrium

The figure shows that unemployment can exist only if the real wage is above $(W/P)_0$. If labor actively competes for employment, the classicists argued, unemployment could not persist. By bidding down the money wage, labor could bid down its real wage (prices are determined elsewhere!), reducing the quantity of labor supplied and increasing the amount demanded until any excess supply is eliminated.

Clearly, competitive forces are sufficient to ensure full employment equilibrium! Any change in the labor supply or demand schedules can only temporarily disturb full employment equilibrium. Thus, the equilibrium level of employment is established at the full employment level. Further, given the production function, which describes the relationship between employment and output, equilibrium output is determined. That is,

$$Y = Y(N) \qquad\qquad [9\text{—}A7]$$

so that for

$$N = N_0, \; Y = Y(N_0) = Y_0$$

Prolonged unemployment could exist only if for some reason, such as the existence of powerful labor unions or minimum wage laws, labor is unable to reduce its real wage by bidding down the money wage.

Thus, all real variables (W/P, N, Y, r, C, S, and I) are determined in the *real* sectors of the economy, that is, in the commodity market and in the labor market. The only role left for the money market is the determination of nominal values.

The Money Market. The role of money was analyzed through the well-known *equation of exchange* which states that:

$$MV = PY \qquad\qquad [9\text{—}A8]$$

where:

M = money supply;

V = velocity, the number of times each dollar is, on average, used to buy final goods and services during any given time period;

P = the average price of goods and services sold;

Y = the quantity of output or the level of output in real terms.

The equation of exchange is an identity which recognized that:

Total spending (MV) = receipts or value of goods purchased (PY).

The equation of exchange becomes a theory with causal content, *the quantity theory of money,* when a theory of velocity is introduced.[1] A common classical assumption was that velocity was determined by institutional factors such as the frequency of income payments maintained by tradition, contract, and so on along with the degree of integration of business firms. Hence, it was assumed that velocity was constant (at least in the short-run because institutional arrangements change only gradually over time, if at all).

With velocity constant and the level of real output established at the full employment level by the labor market, money supply and the price level (and thus the nominal value of income and output) are directly related. An increase in M must lead to a proportional increase in P, but can have no permanent impact on any *real* variable. Thus, the quantity of money determines the price level and nominal values of Y, C, S, I, and W, but the real values of these variables are determined in the labor and commodity markets. The economy is dichotomized!

The only way for equilibrium income to change in this classical model is for a shift to occur in the labor supply or demand curve. For example, an autonomous increase in labor supply would lower the real wage, raise employment and output, and thus raise consumption, saving, and investment. In contrast, an autonomous fall in consumption (rise in saving) results, in the classical model, in a fall in the interest rate that stimulates additional investment to maintain equilibrium in the commodity market. Income and employment would remain unaffected.

---

[1]As indicated earlier, a theory of velocity is the equivalent of a theory of the demand for money. Assume that the volume of nominal money demanded for transactions purposes is proportional to the level of money income with proportionality a constant k. That is,

$$M_D = kPY$$

For money market equilibrium, money demand must, of course, equal money supply. From the equation of exchange in the text,

$$MV = PY$$

we see that $M = (1/V)PY$. Thus, $1/V$ and k (or *ipso facto,* $1/k$ and V) are identical. A theory that explains the value of V also explains the value of k.

Chapter 10

Quantity and Price Changes

This chapter, which picks up where Chapter 9 left off, has two basic objectives. The first is to determine how the economy may react to disturbances when actual prices differ from expected prices, that is, over time intervals that are inadequate to permit full information on prices to be acquired. The second objective is to integrate these "short-run" predictions with the long-run analysis of Chapter 9 so as to provide a comprehensive view of the economy's response to events that push it out of equilibrium.

Adjustments in the Short Run

Recall, from the construction of the labor supply schedule in Chapter 9, that when the actual price level differs from the expected level the labor supply schedule is shifted. When actual prices exceed expected prices, the labor supply schedule is shifted rightward as labor, valuing higher money wage offers at too low a price level, expects a real wage higher than what actually will prevail. With more labor supplied, employment and output are increased by a price rise as the economy moves upward along a nonvertical aggregate supply schedule. Of course, for labor to be fooled in the manner assumed, we are confined to a time horizon too short to permit full information on prices to be acquired; we are looking at the economy's short-run responses to events that create disequilibrium.

A Contraction in Demand

As the first exercise in this chapter, suppose that the changes in world energy supplies that have taken place in recent years cause a once-and-for-all change for the worse in businessmen's expectations of future profits from the use of capital assets. This wave of pessimism would reduce planned investment expenditures and, thus, cut aggregate demand for goods and services in general.

Figure 10—1 shows an economy originally in equilibrium at i_0, Y_0, P_0, N_0, W_0/P_0, with the actual and expected price levels equal. A <u>cutback in</u>

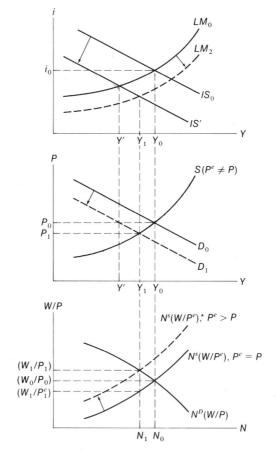

Figure 10—1 / A Decline in Investment with $P^e \neq P$

planned investment would manifest itself in the $IS=LM$ component of our model as a leftward shift in the IS schedule to, say, IS' as aggregate demand is reduced to level Y'. This corresponds to the downward shift in the aggregate demand schedule from D_0 to D_1.

With excess supply ($Y_0 - Y'$ is an index indicator of the actual gap between aggregate supply and demand at the original price level), prices would decline, ultimately to level P_1, and this price decline prompts responses on both the demand and supply sides of the economy. On the demand ($IS=LM$) side, the price decline increases the real value of the money stock, shifting the LM schedule rightward (as to LM_1) to show the resulting stimulus to aggregate demand.

On the supply (labor market) side of the economy, the price reduction would tend to raise the real wage, creating an excess supply of labor and, hence, forcing the money wage downward. Should the money wage fall as fast as prices, the real wage and employment could remain unchanged. With labor failing to adjust its expectation of future prices in step with the actual price decline (thus valuing reduced money wage offers with too high a price level), it withdraws labor services, shifting the labor supply schedule leftward, as to position $N^s(W/P^e)$.*

As long as labor remains fooled with regard to the general price level, expecting real wages to be lower than those that actually prevail, the labor supply schedule will remain to the left of its original position. In this case, the economy would rest at the depressed employment and output levels N_0, Y_0. With output (income) reduced, consumption and saving would be reduced. In addition, the demand for money will have fallen with output, lowering the interest rate and stimulating investment. With both real output and the price level reduced, velocity ($= PY/M$) is reduced. In the labor market, with employment reduced, labor's productivity and actual real wage (W_1/P_1) are increased while labor *expects* the real wage to be lower (W_1/P_1^e). As Keynes emphasized in *The General Theory,* and as casual observation of reality indicates, a contraction in aggregate demand has prompted quantity adjustments (a contraction in the economy's employment and output levels) and not just price changes as emphasized in the classical model of the economy.

Table 10—1 / Responses to Demand Shocks when $P^e \neq P$

Source of Disturbance	Impact on: ($-$ means decrease, $+$ increase)								
An autonomous:	Y	C	S	i	I	P	V	W/P	N
Decrease in investment	$-$	$-$	$-$	$-$	$-$	$-$	$-$	$+$	$-$
Decrease in government spending	$-$	$-$	$-$	$-$	$+$	$-$	$-$	$+$	$-$
Decrease in consumption	$-$	$-$	$+$	$-$	$+$	$-$	$-$	$+$	$-$
Increase in taxes	$-$	$-$	$-$	$-$	$+$	$-$	$-$	$+$	$-$

As with the investment example, an autonomous reduction in any other component of aggregate demand—consumption, government spending, or, for an open economy, net exports—would result in a decline in employment and output as long as labor fails to fully recognize and fully adjust its price expectations to the resulting fall in prices. Table 10—1 summarizes the directions of change in the array of important variables in our model (with $P^e \neq P$) that would be brought about by: a decline in investment, a decline in government spending, a decline in consumption, or an increase in taxes. You should be sure that you can use the model in Figure 10—1 to generate these predictions before going on to the next section.

From Short Run to Long Run

It was explicit recognition of the quantity adjustments described above that prompted Keynes, in the midst of the Great Depression, to reject classical reasoning and argue in favor of an activist role for government in economic activity, that is, for fiscal and/or monetary policy actions aimed at *stabilizing* the economy. The classicists, in contrast, had believed that competitive forces within the market economy were strong enough to restore full employment equilibrium in short order after any disturbance created a disequilibrium.

The Self-Adjusting Economy

Figure 10—2 reproduces the labor market and the aggregate supply and demand model shown in Figure 10—1. In both Figures 10—1 and 10—2, a contraction in demand and a resulting decline in prices that is not fully anticipated is responsible for the short-run contraction in employment and output to levels N_1 and Y_1, respectively. This contraction is actually not inconsistent with classical theory predictions; but, if money wages and prices are free to vary, the contraction is temporary, lasting only as long as labor remains unaware of the price level decline that has occurred. As labor becomes informed that prices have dropped and alters its expected price level estimate in light of that information, the labor supply schedule will shift back to the right, increasing the hours of labor services offered and pressing the real wage downward. As a consequence, employment and output supplied increase, prompting a further price decline that enlarges the real money stock and raises the demand for output (along schedule D'). With adequate time for full information on price adjustments to be generated and acted on, the labor supply schedule will have returned to its original full information position $N^s(W/P^e)$ and employment and output will be at their original levels $(N_0$ and $Y_0)$. That is, the shrinkage in demand will have prompted a *short-run* quantity adjustment from point 0 to point 1 in the aggregate supply and demand model above, but in the long run real quantities will be at their original levels with only prices and nominal values changed. In our example, the price level ultimately must fall from P_0 to P_2 for equilibrium at the natural employment rate to be restored, and, given sufficient time for adjustment, our model represents a self-adjusting economy.

Expectations Formation and the Adjustment Period. Classical economists contended that the economy was self-adjusting and needed no stabilization intervention by the government because they thought the time interval required for a full long-run adjustment of the economy of the sort described above was brief. Keynes, on the other hand, concluded that the automatic adjustment process could not be counted on to quickly cure a recession caused by a decline in aggregate demand. An important reason for this difference in conclusions is a difference in beliefs on the manner in which price expectations are formed and, hence, on the speed with which full information on price changes is reflected in economic actions. Of course, Keynesian support for the active use of stabilization policy reflects a longer assumed adjustment period than does the classical conclusion that the economy is self-regulating.

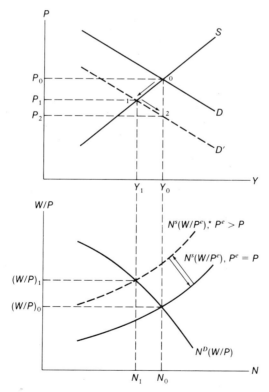

Figure 10—2 / Short- and Long-Run Adjustments

Marked differences of opinion on the rapidity with which the economy reacts to new information persist today, reflecting the existence of two readily distinguishable schools of thought on the manner in which expectations are formed. The labels "adaptive expectations" and "rational expectations" are generally used to identify these alternative views.

According to the first view, the price level that society expects to prevail is *adapted* to experienced prices in the market place. That is, the price level that is expected to prevail this period is based on the actual price level last period. It is typically assumed that when society changes its view of the expected price level (as from P^e_{t-1} in the last period to P^e_t in this period), the amount of change is in proportion to the gap between the price level expected to prevail last period and the price level (P_{t-1}) that actually prevailed. With proportionality factor γ, this period's change in the expected price level is

$$P^e_t - P^e_{t-1} = \gamma(P_{t-1} - P^e_{t-1}) \qquad [10\text{--}1]$$

as information on the error in predicting last period's price level is used to predict this period's price level.

If the proportionality constant (γ) in the adjustment equation is 1, expected prices are fully adjusted in the current period to changes in the price level in the immediately preceding period (indeed, the equation reduces to $P^e_t = P_{t-1}$). Factor γ need not have a value of one, however, but might in general be expected to be a fraction, reflecting a partial adjustment of expected to actual changes in the price level. For example, if $\gamma = \frac{1}{2}$, with a one-time increase in actual prices from level 1.0 to level 2.0, the expected price level would adapt in the manner illustrated by the dashed line in Figure 10—3. The solid line shows the actual price level jumping from 1.0 to 2.0 at the beginning of time period zero. During time period zero, the expected price level is raised by one-half of the gap between actual and expected

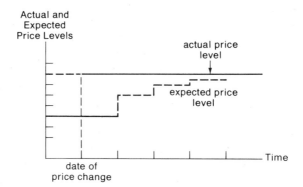

Figure 10—3 / The Adaptive Adjustment of Expected to Actual Prices

prices in period 0, that is, by ½ (2.0 − 1.0) = .5 to level 1.5. In period 2, the gap between actual and expected prices in period one (2.0 − 1.5) is partially closed, and so the adjustment process continues with expected prices gradually approaching the actual price level. It is notable that, the smaller is γ, the slower is the adjustment of expected to actual price changes. In terms of our description of the economy's short- and long-run responses to a contraction in demand, the smaller (larger) is γ, the longer (shorter) the time interval over which the economy would remain in a depressed state until informed price expectations permit restoration of full employment equilibrium.

In contrast, the rational expectations view assumes that society is far more sophisticated in its understanding of the economy's functioning. In our demand contraction example, the rational expectations model views society as understanding that a decline in investment demand will ultimately lower prices in proportion to the cut in aggregate spending. This information, then, is reflected in price expectations with no substantial lag. Needless to say, rational expectations arguments provide a basis for the conclusions of classical analysis on the self-regulating nature of the economy.

Slow Adjustments and Stabilization Policy. If expected prices are slow to adjust, fiscal and/or monetary actions undertaken by the government may improve the economy's performance. As Figure 10—4 shows, if a decline in aggregate demand, say from level D to D', prompts a contraction toward output level Y_1, the aggregate demand schedule could be returned to its original position, with equilibrium restored at output level Y_0, by the appropriate expansionary fiscal and/or monetary policy action. With this policy-induced shift in aggregate demand, the contraction would be reversed and an expansion back to full employment equilibrium initiated.

Of course, aggregate demand can be increased by an increase in government spending, a cut in taxes, institution of an investment tax credit or some other incentive program, an increase in transfer payments, or by an

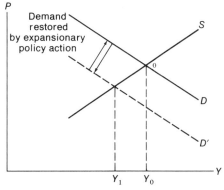

Figure 10—4 / Restoring Full Employment Demand

increase in the nominal money supply. All but the last action fall in the realm of fiscal policy actions and, ultimately, are administered by Congress. The last action is a monetary policy action that would be undertaken by the central bank.

To function in the manner illustrated in Figure 10—4, just restoring full employment equilibrium without having to wait for the economy's automatic adjustment process to work itself out, it is necessary that:

1. Stabilization authorities, fiscal and monetary, be able to recognize when a need for altering aggregate demand exists;
2. The means exist for calculating the appropriate size of policy action;
3. The time interval required for stabilization actions to be undertaken and have their influence on aggregate demand must be shorter than the automatic adjustment period.

Better yet, if it were only possible to predict ahead of time when aggregate demand would suffer an autonomous contraction and how large that demand shift would be, anticipatory policy actions could be undertaken to try to avoid any contraction in employment and output. For example, an anticipated $15 billion decline in planned investment could be offset with a $15 billion increase in government spending, or with a somewhat larger tax cut, leaving aggregate demand unchanged.

Strengthening the Case for Activism. By focusing attention on the role of labor's price level expectations, we have shown that fiscal and/or monetary policy actions may improve the economy's performance when expectations adjust slowly in the face of actual changes in the price level. This conclusion may be reinforced by recognition of some real world, "institutional" constraints on wage movements. Notably, wage contracts often extend for as long as three years, and they, along with minimum wage laws and the alternative support levels available under unemployment or welfare programs, may place an effective floor on money wages for extended time intervals. Formulated in money wage terms, these institutional factors may cause the money wage to be rigid in the downward direction in the short run.

Figure 10—5 repeats our demand contraction experiment with the money wage assumed to be completely rigid in the downward direction, as signified by the bar over the money wage term. As before, a cut in demand produces an excess supply $(Y_0 - Y')$ in the commodity market which prompts a fall in prices. As prices fall, increasing the real money stock and pushing interest rates downward, demand would recover in part as before (e.g., to level Y_1). In the meantime, the fall in prices raises the real wage, creating an excess supply of labor. In this case, however, money wages cannot fall to permit the labor market to return to a cleared position. Instead, employment would contract to a level, N_1, corresponding to the reduced output level Y_1.

Recognition of the institutional bars to money wage adjustments in the face of a contraction of demand is important because:

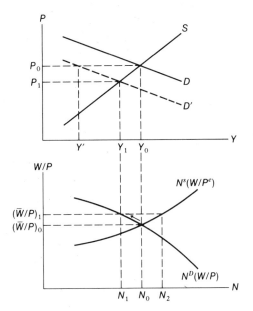

Figure 10—5 / A Contraction with a Rigid Money Wage

1. Those institutional factors reinforce the role of slow-adjusting expectations in generating *quantity* adjustments in the economy when demand changes.
2. This relieves "poorly informed" labor of bearing full responsibility for those quantity adjustments as labor's wage requirements, set by contract, may remain fixed as though labor were poorly informed when it actually is not.
3. This clearly demonstrates that a contraction in demand can create *involuntary* unemployment as, in Figure 10—5, N_2 units of labor would willingly work at real wage $(\overline{W}/P)_1$, while only N_1 units will be employed.

As before, in time money wages would decline, pushing the economy in the direction of full employment. However, Keynesian analysis indicates that the adjustment period would be unacceptably long and, what is more, unnecessary because stabilization weapons are readily available and can be used to raise aggregate demand enough to restore full employment.

As a matter primarily of historical interest, in Keynes' own attack on classical analysis he argued further that, even if money wages and prices were free to fall in the face of a demand contraction, the economy could fail to automatically return to full employment following a contraction in demand. One reason, he argued, was that in a depressed economy the interest rate might fall to a level so low that everyone expects interest yields to rise (bond prices to fall) in the future. In this case, no one would willingly exchange money for bonds. Hence, a price decline, which increases the real money stock, would not result in an interest rate reduction (bond price rise) to stimulate investment and, hence, aggregate demand. The additional real money balances would just be hoarded in this "liquidity trap," as Keynes labeled it, so aggregate demand would remain at a depressed level no matter how long prices are permitted to fall.

In turn, even if a price decline lowers the interest rate, Keynes argued that there was no guarantee that aggregate demand would rise. Why? In a depressed economy, firms are already operating with substantial volumes of idle plant capacity, so investment may not be stimulated significantly by an interest rate decline. These extreme conditions of a liquidity trap or an interest-inelastic investment demand schedule correspond, respectively, to a horizontal *LM* schedule and a vertical *IS* schedule. You may include such schedules in the macroeconomic model employed in this and the last chapter to prove that an automatic price decline in response to a drop in aggregate demand may not restore aggregate demand to its full employment level. Because empirical evidence offers little support for *IS* and *LM* schedules with these extreme properties, modern discussions of the desirability of stabilization policy pay little heed to the liquidity trap and interest-insensitive investment arguments.

Supply Shocks

Our macro model may also be applied to evaluating the economy's short- and long-run responses to disturbances that impinge upon or stem from the supply side of the economy. As an example of this application of the model, we will consider an increase in the labor force.

Now, the prospect of increases in the supply of labor has always been a prominent concern of the existing work force. Basically, the concern has been over the question: Can an increased supply of labor be employed without displacing already employed workers, or must chronic unemployment result as it would if there were only a fixed number of jobs available in our economic system? Particularly in debates over immigration laws this question has had a long and prominent history. Through the 1800s and into the present century, strict limits on immigration have been favored by countless organizations, including the American Federation of Labor, the American Legion, and the National Grange. A common concern, voiced most insistently by organized labor, has been that "The immigrant, with his low rate of wages, drives out of his trade men formerly employed therein. . . ."[1]

[1]John Mitchell, *Organized Labor: Its Problems, Purposes and Ideals* (Philadelphia: American Book and Bible House, 1903), p. 103. Mitchell was president of the United Mine Workers of America. The notion that there is "only so much work to be done" has also been responsible for organized labor's efforts to prevent the employment of women and children and for the widespread fear that adoption of machine production techniques would *displace* labor. A fascinating discussion of these venerable "workingman's" explanations of unemployment can be found in W. B. Catlin, *The Labor Problem* (New York: Harper & Row, 1926), Chapter 3.

More recently, marked increases in women's labor force participation rates have prompted outcries that "women are taking jobs away from male heads of households," implying that men are left jobless when more of a fixed array of jobs go to women. There are even proposals to shorten the workweek to thirty-five hours in order to "spread the available work" over an enlarged labor force. Our aggregate model can shed some light on whether or not there is just some fixed amount of work to go around, and on how the economy may respond to an increase in the work force. In applying that model to analyze a supply side shock, we will follow the same sequence used in dealing with demand shocks. That requires, first, determining how the equilibrium values of aggregate demand or supply are altered with prices constant, then permitting prices and, with a lag, expected prices to change, prompting further adjustments in the economy.

Figure 10—6 illustrates the short- and long-run responses to an increase in the labor force. Initially, the model in that figure represents an economy in long-run full employment equilibrium at $(W/P)_0$, N_0, Y_0, P_0. Note that the aggregate demand schedule that corresponds to this initial equilibrium is schedule D_0, along which demand is equal to supply Y_0 at price P_0. With an increase in the labor force, the *full information* labor supply schedule is shifted rightward to position $N_1^s(W/P^e)$. This is the new full information labor supply schedule. In a flexible wage and price system, the resulting excess supply of labor would depress the real wage toward the market-clearing level $(W/P)_1$. This real wage would provide the higher employment level N_1, corresponding to the higher output level Y_1.

Because we have not yet permitted actual and expected prices to change, however, the economy cannot have returned to equilibrium at N_1, Y_1 as there is now an excess supply $(Y_1 - Y_0)$ of goods and services. This excess supply would drive the price level downward, and, if labor does not revise its expected price level estimate at the same rate, the economy would be operating along the short-run supply schedule S'. This schedule permits a short-run adjustment to output level Y' as the price level declines to P'. Of course, with a reduced price level and no change in the expected price level, labor's supply schedule is shifted leftward to a position like that of $N_2^s(W/P^e)$, as labor is valuing its money wage offers at too high a price level $(P^e > P)$.

Until sufficient time has elapsed to permit labor to obtain full information on the price change and integrate that into the expectations on which it acts, employment and, hence, output must remain below their full information, market-clearing levels N_1 and Y_1. As information on the price level decline is obtained and acted on, the labor supply schedule will shift rightward toward the position of $N_1^s (W/P^e)$, increasing output and forcing prices further downward. In the long run, when the full information adjustment is completed, the economy will be at rest with employment (unemployment) at the new, full information natural rate (N_1), with output at the corresponding full employment or potential output level (Y_1), and with the general price level at P_1.

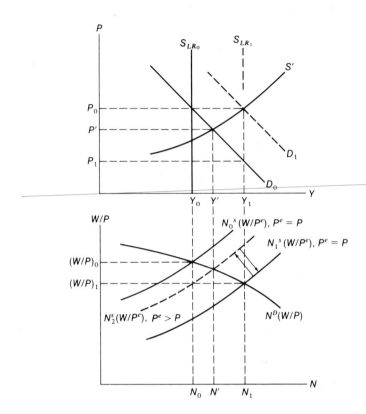

Figure 10—6 / An Increase in Labor Supply

Clearly, in the long run there is no limited number of jobs; an increase in the labor force does not require a permanent increase in the fraction of the labor force that is jobless. At the same time, there is an adjustment interval required to permit the additional labor to be absorbed in job slots, and that interval may be quite lengthy in calendar time. If the adjustment period is lengthy, either because of slow adjustments in price expectations or because of institutional rigidities, stabilization weapons may again be used to stimulate aggregate demand. Aggregate demand could be boosted to a level (D_1) that matches the new supply schedule at the new full employment output level Y_0. No change in actual or expected commodity prices would be required in this case, so the wage adjustment required to move to employment level N_1 might occur in a relatively brief time interval unless institutional rigidities prevented any money wage decline. In that case, a larger policy stimulus could, by raising prices, provide the needed decline in real wages.

Supply Shocks in General

With an increase in the labor force, our analysis has shown that the economy's productive capacity has increased, that its long-run supply schedule is shifted outward. Figure 10—7 illustrates this shift with schedules S_{LR_0} and S_{LR_1} representing the original and new long-run supply schedules for the economy. As we have shown, the long-run, full information adjustment to this shift in aggregate supply would automatically raise output to level Y_1 and drop the price level to P_1, given adequate time for the full adjustment to take place. However, lags in wage and/or price changes, from slow adjustments in expectations, institutional rigidities, or both, make the adjustment take place gradually with the economy, in effect, adjusting along the demand schedule from point 0 to point 1 as time elapses.

In like fashion, any other event that increases the economy's productive potential, i.e., that shifts the long-run supply curve rightward, would involve a similar sequence, with output, prices, and the other variables of interest to macroeconomists gradually adjusting toward their full information, full employment levels. As examples, represented in summary form by Figure 10—7, you might use the full model to illustrate the economy's short- and long-run responses to:

1. An advance in technology that enhances labor's productivity,
2. The discovery of sizable new energy sources or other important resource inputs in the production process,
3. The implementation of new incentive programs that motivate labor to work harder.

In contrast, examples of supply side shocks, which may reduce potential output, prompting a gradual contraction in output and an increase in prices, include:

1. Cartelization of world energy supplies (remember, we analyzed the *long-run* consequences of that event in Chapter 9);
2. A reduction in labor force participation rates;
3. The imposition of safety and health rules (OSHA regulations) if they lower worker productivity;
4. The imposition of environmental protection regulations that require abandonment of some production facilities, require partial cutbacks in the productive usage of some facilities, and direct capital investment from

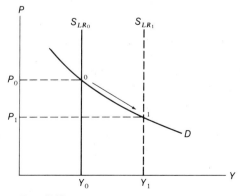

Figure 10—7 / Supply Side Shifts

productive usage of some facilities, and direct capital investment from assets that produce marketable commodities to assets that reduce plants' contributions to pollution problems.

Controlling Aggregate Supply

Conventional monetary and fiscal actions have traditionally been viewed as 'means for controlling the level of aggregate demand. With recognition of the fact that aggregate supply is also subject to systematic changes, however, it is reasonable to consider whether there are policies that might improve the economy's performance that impinge directly on the supply side of the economy. Actually, the government has long been engaged in stabilization policy actions that affect aggregate supply; but they generally have also altered aggregate demand, and economic conditions have favored emphasizing that role. As notable examples, investment tax credits and reductions of allowable guidelines for depreciating capital assets have been employed as fiscal tools, with most emphasis placed on their ability to stimulate investment and, thus, overall demand. By providing incentives for additions to the capital stock, these devices would lead, over time, to the accumulation of a larger stock of capital for labor to work with, shifting the aggregate supply schedule rightward as labor's productivity is enhanced. Since the mid-1960s, the rate of growth in labor's productivity has slowed dramatically in the U.S. economy, and many attribute a major portion of that slowdown to a failure of the capital stock to grow as fast as the work force. In light of this development, there has been a shift in focus to the supply side effects of stabilization actions and a renewed interest in fiscal and monetary policies that would stimulate "saving and investment."

Easy passage, in 1978, of a corporate tax cut has been credited to recognition of the (supply side) need for capital formation incentives (of course, demand was stimulated too), and proposals to offer labor tax relief in exchange for a reduction in money wage demands also reflect supply side considerations.

To illustrate the application of "supply control" actions, suppose that labor, on the basis of past experience, *expects* prices to rise by 8 percent this year and, so, demands an 8 percent increase in money wages to continue providing the same level of services. This increase in wage costs would force prices that firms must charge to cover their production costs upward at every employment and output level; i.e., it would shift the short-run aggregate supply schedule upward as illustrated by the shift from S_0 to S_1 in Figure 10—8. This shift in aggregate supply would raise prices, to P_1 in the short run and P_2 in the long run.

By exchanging compensatory tax relief on labor's earnings for the money wage boost, the government might succeed in holding the supply schedule at S_0, avoiding the price increase that an upward shift in aggregate supply would entail. Of course, the tax reduction would raise disposable income, so to hold aggregate demand constant (as at D_0) would require a compensatory stabilization action, say, in the form of a cut in government expen-

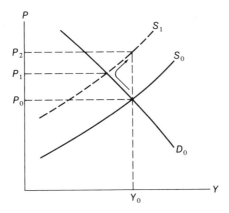

Figure 10—8 / Supply Management

ditures or a shrinkage in the money stock. As this example illustrates, the current focus on *supply management* highlights the significance of our earlier recognition (Chapter 8) that alternative mixes of fiscal and monetary policies can permit the pursuit of multiple goals, including full employment, price stability, and growth in productive capacity, because the composition of full employment output may differ substantially as the government alters incentives for saving and investing.

Demand Expansion at Full Employment

To complete our examination of the macro model's responses to the shocks that might befall it, we need to return to the demand side of the economy, combining our conclusions about the short- and long-run responses to expansion in aggregate demand *beginning with equilibrium at the natural (full information market-clearing) position*. This activity will set the stage for our consideration of inflation beginning in Chapter 11.

In Figure 10—9, Y_0 is the full employment (with full information) output level and P_0 is assumed to be the initial equilibrium price level. S_{SR_0} is the short-run aggregate supply schedule that is valid as long as actual and expected prices remain at P_0, and D_0 is the initial aggregate demand schedule.

Consider, now, an increase in aggregate demand to level D_1. With the resulting excess demand for goods and services, prices will rise; and, as we have shown before, as long as labor does not alter expected prices in proportion to the rise in actual prices, employment and output will rise along schedule S_{SR_0} toward the short-run equilibrium position Y_1, P_1. The expansion of real output and, correspondingly, employment, is possible only because labor is fooled (or functions as though it is), offering more services at a higher money wage but lower real wage. With labor fooled by the unanticipated increase in aggregate demand and prices, employment can be temporarily pushed above the natural or full employment level with output

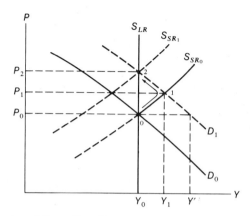

Figure 10—9 / Short- and Long-Run Responses to a Demand Expansion

correspondingly increased to a level above full employment *potential* output. Of course, this boost in employment and production is temporary for, as labor obtains information on the overall price level increase, adjusting its price expectations and acting on these expectations, it will reduce the volume of labor services offered, returning to the natural employment level with real wages at their original level.

As money wages and, hence, production costs rise, the prices firms must charge to cover costs rise; the short-run aggregate supply schedule is shifted upward, eventually to position S_{SR_1}. As the full adjustment to the demand increase takes place, the economy follows a looped path, as the arrow in Figure 10—9 shows, from point 0 toward point 1 and, finally, to rest at point 2 when the full information adjustment is completed. At the final equilibrium position (P_2, Y_0), output has returned to its original full employment level, and the long-run supply curve is vertical as discussed earlier. In the long run, then, a stimulative demand policy leaves the levels of output and employment unchanged but permanently raises prices.

If an expansion in demand at full employment is the result of a money supply increase, in the long run prices and *nominal* quantities increase in proportion to the monetary expansion; but all real variables, income, employment, the real wage, interest, etc., are left unchanged. Money is, again, neutral. This is not true in the short run, however, as our analysis has shown a demand expansion, whatever its source, will raise employment and output until full information on the resulting adjustment in prices is obtained and acted on.

If the expansion in demand is the result of a fiscal policy action, employment and output will return to their full information equilibrium values in the long run so the level of output is not permanently altered by the expansionary fiscal policy. However, the composition of output may be as we explained in Chapter 9. For example, an increase in government spending would, in the long run, raise interest rates until investment spending declines by the amount of increase in government outlay.

Case in Point VI

The Interest Rate: A Monetary or a Real Phenomenon

As an application of the reasoning employed in this chapter, we will consider an issue that has both historical and current significance. That issue involves the determinants of the interest rate and, consequently, the extent of control that the central bank has over interest rates. According to Keynes' classical predecessors, the interest rate was a *real* phenomenon, the value of which was determined by "productivity" (the yield on investment) and "thrift" (the saving schedule). In contrast, Keynes and his followers emphasized the notion that the interest rate is a *monetary* phenomenon determined by the supply of and demand for money and, hence, subject to control by the central bank.

Figure 10—10 combines the aggregate supply and demand model with the *IS-LM* model of demand determination to permit us to investigate whether the interest rate is under the control of the central bank or is determined in some other manner. The economy represented in that figure is initially in long-run equilibrium at full employment output level Y_0, price level P_0, and interest rate i_0. Suppose, however, that the central bank believes this is too high an interest rate level and would prefer an interest rate reduction to level i_1. By increasing the money supply, shifting the *LM* schedule rightward, the central bank can lower interest rates. For example, with a large enough money stock expansion the interest rate might momentarily be pushed to level i' corresponding to *LM* schedule *LM'*. With this *expansionary* monetary policy action, aggregate demand would be raised (schedule D_1) and, at the prevailing price level (P_0), would exceed supply, prompting a price level increase. In the short run, with labor unaware of the increase in the price level, the price level increase would prompt an expansion of output along the short-run supply schedule S_{SR} while demand is contracting along demand schedule D_1. The contraction of demand, of course, reflects the shrinkage in the money stock as the price level rises (shifting the *LM* schedule leftward to LM_1). With the price level increased to P_1, output demand and supply would match at Y_1 and equilibrium would prevail. Moreover, the central bank has reduced interest rates to the target level (i_1). So, it appears that the interest rate is a monetary phenomenon subject to central bank control. Remember, though, that this is in the short run, a time period inadequate for full information adjustments to take place.

In the long run, as labor, adjusting its wage requirements in light of new price level information, withdraws services until the natural employment rate is restored, the economy will move to the long-run price level P_2 that equates demand with full information, full employment output Y_0. The further price rise reduces the real money stock until the *LM* schedule is returned to its original position (LM_0). At this point, the interest rate is returned to level i_0. Given the investment demand and saving (consumption) schedules that dictate the position of the *IS* curve, there is only one per-

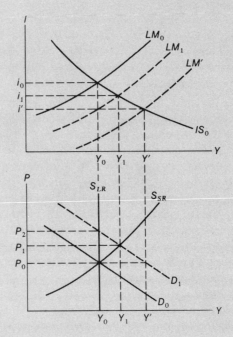

Figure 10—10 / Macroeconomic Adjustments and the Interest Rate

centage yield rate that provides commodity market (*IS* schedule) equilibrium at full information, full employment, and that is interest rate i_0. In the long run the interest rate is, indeed, dictated by productivity and thrift. So, both Keynes and the classicists might be considered to be right (and wrong) in their emphasis on monetary and real factors, respectively, as the determinants of interest yields. In the short run, interest is a monetary phenomenon when expectations do not adjust fully to actual price changes while, in the long run, with a full adjustment of price expectations, interest is a real phenomenon. As an additional matter of concern, provide yourself with an explanation of how interest rates vary in response to a money supply rise if expectations are "rational," so that society knows how a money supply increase translates into a price level rise.

Summary

In this chapter we have looked at the combined short- and long-run adjustments that the economy experiences as a consequence of events that alter either aggregate demand or supply. In the short run, the economy experiences *quantity* adjustments, significant changes in employment and output, as well as price adjustments in the face of shifts in either demand or supply; and the short run may persist for extended periods of calendar time. Short-run equilibrium cannot persist indefinitely, however, as it is based on incomplete information and, thus, incorrect expectations of the price level. With information generated over time, the economy's full information adjustment to demand shifts involves only price changes while supply shifts, e.g., a change in energy availability, produce lasting quantity changes even in the long run when actual and expected prices are equal.

Because many of the events that altered demand or supply in this chapter caused an increase in the general price level, it is likely that you have been thinking about inflation as an economic problem as you worked through the discussion. The next chapter permits you to concentrate directly on that problem. However, before going on to that chapter, you should note that, with every disturbance considered at this point, any resulting price adjustment (up or down) was a *one-time* adjustment. That is, prices did not go on changing forever but experienced a once-and-for-all adjustment to a new and stable level. In fact, the price changes we considered were *self-terminating* in that those price changes brought about the supply and demand expansions and/or contractions that reestablished equality between aggregate supply and demand.

Questions

1. Contrast the economy's short- and long-run adjustments to:
   a. an increase in society's "thriftiness,"
   b. a contraction in the money supply,
   c. an increase in government spending financed by bond sales to the public.

2. Why does the economy's short-run supply curve slope upward from left to right?

3. The central bank can control the nominal money stock. Can it control the real money stock? (Be sure to take account of both short- and long-run adjustments in your answer.)

4. Are the economy's short-run or long-run properties of more relevance for policy formulation? How would your answer vary depending on the length of time that constitutes the "short-run"?

Suggested Readings

Gordon, Donald F. "A Neo-Classical Theory of Keynesian Unemployment." *Economic Inquiry* 12 (1974): pp. 431–459.

Grossman, Herschel. "Aggregate Demand, Job Search, and Employment." *Journal of Political Economy* 81 (1973): pp. 1353–1369.

Modigliani, Franco. "The Monetarist Controversy, or Should We Forsake Stabilization Policies?" *The American Economic Review* 67 (1977): pp. 1–19.

Tobin, James. "How Dead Is Keynes?" *Economic Inquiry* 15 (1977): pp. 459–468.

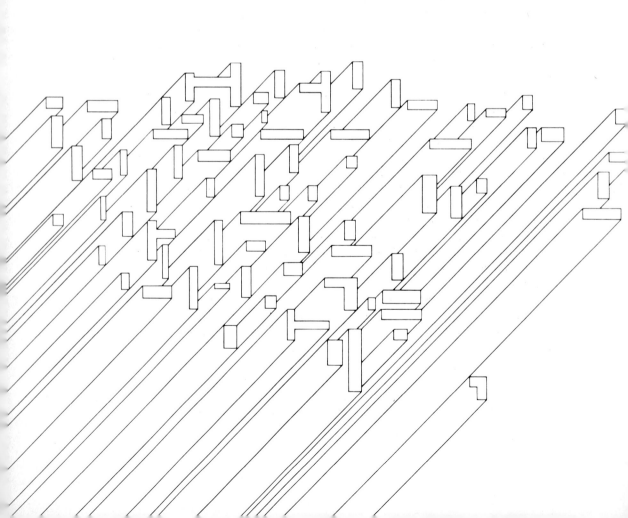

Inflation, Unemployment, and Government Policy

This section of the text focuses attention directly on the twin evils of inflation and unemployment, the links between them, and the policy options that are available for dealing with those problems. Chapter 11 reviews the dominant explanations of inflation and provides an integrated description of the inflation process in which both aggregate demand and supply play important roles. This explanation of inflation provides an interpretation of the Phillips Curve, the apparent empirical relationship between inflation rates and unemployment rates, and illuminates the conflicting positions of competing camps on the durability of the Phillips relationship.

Chapter 12 evaluates the policy options that are available in a world of stagflation, i.e., combined inflation and excessive unemployment, including traditional demand control tools, wage-price controls, proposals to deal with *structural* problems in the economy, and proposals to improve employment prospects while slowing inflation by altering aggregate supply. Evidence reviewed in this chapter is used to argue persuasively that, when traditional demand restraint is employed to combat inflation, employment, and output fall much more quickly than inflation abates.

Chapter **11**   Inflation

The term *inflation* is surely a familiar one to every member of contemporary society. It refers to a problem that has plagued the U.S. and most other countries with particular vengeance in the last fifteen years. In 1974, when the U.S. inflation rate crossed the threshold from a single to a double-digit (10 percent or greater) rate, inflation was conceded the distinction of being "Public Enemy Number One" by then President Gerald Ford. After receding a bit, the rate of price increase rose again in 1979, and we entered the 1980s with double digit inflation again.

In spite of our familiarity with inflation, it remains a source of a great deal of confusion. This chapter will attempt to remove some of that confusion by addressing such questions as: What is inflation? Who are the villains responsible for it? Is the central bank always to be blamed for our inflationary problems? What relationship is there between inflation and unemployment? To what extent is society burdened by inflation, if at all, and who bears the resulting burden? What can be done to eliminate inflation, and why has it not been done?

What Is Inflation?

Inflation is commonly defined as a significant and sustained increase in the general price level. It is not *high* prices, but *rising* prices that constitute inflation. We are concerned, then, with an explicitly dynamic process. While virtually all economists would accept these propositions, there remains a troublesome vagueness in just what price increases are significant and sustained.

Figure 11—1 shows the pattern of actual yearly changes in the Consumer Price Index, a widely monitored gauge of inflation, over the period 1950 through 1979. Over that time, price changes have ranged from ½ a percentage point decline in 1954 to a more than 13 percent increase in 1979. Over the first fifteen-year interval covered in the chart, prices rose some 32 percent, i.e., at an annual rate of just under 2 percent. Over the last fifteen years, the increase has been a whopping 144 percent and averaged about 6 percent yearly.

For obvious reasons, the period since 1965 is generally viewed as an inflationary era. By comparison, the preceding fifteen years are viewed as a period of relative price stability. Yet, with prices rising by more than 10 percent over the two-year span of 1950–1951, there were widespread concerns over inflation and those concerns were rekindled in the 1956–1958 period. By today's standards, the price increases in these periods were small. Thus, it appears that we cannot pin down quantitative measures that distinguish significant and sustained price level increases from others. We can, however, draw a clear distinction between events that result in one-shot price increases that will end automatically, and processes that, without "outside intervention," would permit an indefinite continuation of price increases.

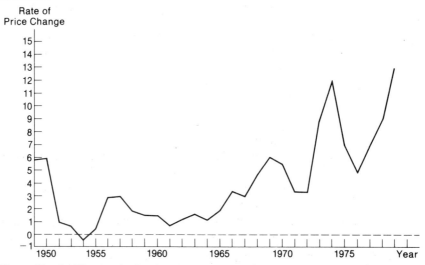

Figure 11—1 / Changes in the Consumer Price Index: December to December, 1950–1979

Demand-Pull and Cost-Push Explanations of Inflation

"Demand-pull" and "cost-push" theories have provided the traditional explanations of inflation. We can use the model in Chapters 9 and 10 to illustrate the mechanics of the inflation processes that correspond to these theories. That exercise will demonstrate the importance of the distinction between one-shot price increases and *sustained* inflations. In addition, it suggests that both demand and cost (supply) theories provide incomplete explanations of sustained inflations.

Demand-Pull

Demand-pull, or *excess demand,* inflation is a rising price level that results from disturbances which increase aggregate demand to a level exceeding the volume of output. It has frequently been described as the result of "too many dollars chasing too few goods."

With our aggregate model of the economy we have already shown that an increase in aggregate demand raises the general price level. Repeating the demonstration of that fact, with an increase in aggregate demand from D_0 to D_1 in Figure 11—2, the price level would rise to P' in the short run and P_1 in the long run. This would be the result no matter what is responsible for the increase in aggregate demand. So a money supply increase, a government spending increase or tax cut, a rise in consumption or investment, $= AD$ or an increase in net exports would prompt an upward adjustment in prices. Of course, the rise in prices takes time, and, as prices are rising over that time interval, the label inflation is apt to be attached to the price adjustment (again, what qualifies as a *significant* and *persistent* price increase is hard to determine). Of utmost importance from our viewpoint, however, is the fact that the price increase is self-terminating, ending automatically when demand and supply are reequated at the new long-run equilibrium price level P_1. Of course, at this point labor will have fully adjusted its price expectations so that the short-run supply schedule will have shifted to S_{SR_1}.

For the demand-pull increase in prices to continue after reaching level P_1, demand would have to shift upward again, as to level D_2, prompting a further adjustment of prices, ultimately to level P_2. For the price rise to continue indefinitely, the demand curve would have to continue shifting outward indefinitely, from position D_0 to D_1, to D_2, to D_3, and so on.

How could an inflation process continue in this manner? Aggregate demand may be increased and a price rise initiated by any number of events, including an increase in society's propensity to consume, a burst of business enthusiasm that increases investment, a foreign crop failure that boosts exports, or a rise in government spending. There are good reasons for believing that none of these sources of demand shifts can generate a long-lasting inflation. To begin with, it is unreasonable to expect any component of aggregate demand to spontaneously continue increasing period after period. This is true even of government purchases. At the worst logical ex-

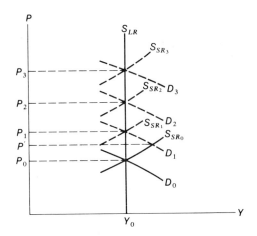

Figure 11—2 / One-Shot Versus Continuing Price Increase

treme, a government might continue raising its expenditures to enlarge its share of national output until all output goes to public use. At that point, there would be no incentive for further inflationary increases in government expenditures. In reality, government spending has been a rather stable fraction of output for many years and, so, could not generate a pattern of demand growth like that illustrated in Figure 11—2.

An additional impediment to a sustained inflation stemming from any of the sources listed above is limits on velocity. If the money stock is held constant as prices and the nominal value of output rise, the velocity with which money is used to purchase output must rise in step, i.e., society must increasingly *economize* on money holdings. However, barring abandonment of the national currency, society cannot be expected to raise money's velocity (lower the demand for money) without limit; the purchasing power (dollars to chase goods) will simply not be provided to sustain an inflation indefinitely with the money supply fixed.

Only with a continued *increase in the money supply* can demand continue growing in the manner necessary for inflation to persist. A continuing increase in the money supply generated by the central bank can raise aggregate demand and drive prices upward indefinitely.

In recognition of money's vital role, Nobel prize-winning economist Milton Friedman has argued that *inflation is always and everywhere a monetary phenomenon.*[1] So, in every persistent inflationary experience, the central bank's compliant participation is necessary. This does not mean, however, that the central bank should be singled out as the ultimate and sole *cause* of every inflation. In fact, most of our significant inflationary periods have

---

[1]See Milton Friedman, "Inflation: Causes and Consequences," in idem, *Dollars and Deficits* (Englewood Cliffs, N.J.: Prentice-Hall, 1968), pp. 21–71.

been associated with war periods when there were large increases in government spending, i.e., when there was strong fiscal stimulus. All that the Federal Reserve would have to do to permit inflation to occur under such circumstances is attempt to keep interest rates from rising dramatically. In addition, as we are about to discover, there are a number of supply or "cost" shocks that could prompt a price increase and induce the central bank to raise the money stock.

Cost-Push

While economic analysis has traditionally emphasized the role of demand pressure on the price level, in the post-World War II period there has been widespread interest in theories that focus on the role of aggregate supply in the inflation process. The simultaneous appearance of both inflation and excessive unemployment in the post-war period suggests, as we shall see, that inflation can stem from a *leftward* shift in the aggregate supply schedule.

Traditionally, either unionized labor or businesses that have some degree of market (monopoly) power have been identified as the groups responsible for supply side or "cost-push" inflation. Unionized labor has been blamed for causing inflation by bargaining successfully for higher wages (using the threat of strikes as the bargaining weapon), whereas firms have been accused of causing inflation simply by raising prices to expand their profit margins.

Labor is often accused of using its bargaining power to acquire *inflationary* boosts in wages. In evaluating such a claim, we must first recognize that not all wage boosts cause price increases. For example, should labor bargain successfully for a 4 percent money wage boost next year, and should labor productivity also rise by 4 percent next year, the wage boost cannot be viewed as inflationary. In that case, firms' labor costs per unit of output would be unaffected; the same number of workers could be employed and paid 4 percent more, but those workers would be producing a 4 percent larger volume of output, leaving unit labor costs unchanged. Hence a constant volume of employment could be maintained with a money wage increase that just matches the growth in labor productivity, yet the higher wage would require no boost in the price level. In contrast a money wage boost that exceeds the proportionate rise in labor productivity does raise the labor cost of producing at every employment and output level. Thus, if wages increase at a rate that exceeds the rate of growth of labor productivity, the aggregate supply curve is shifted upward.

A *profit-push* inflation is alleged to be the result of business firms' using any monopoly power they enjoy in product markets to directly raise product prices. With firms charging higher prices on any volume of output in order to enjoy greater profit margins, the aggregate supply curve is shifted upward.

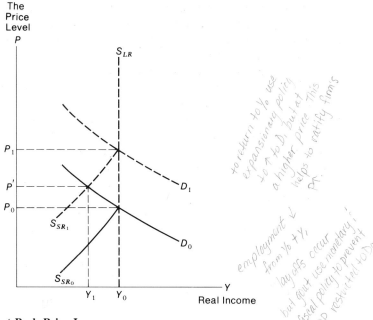

Figure 11—3 / Cost-Push Price Increases

Figure 11—3 illustrates cost-push inflation. Beginning with output at its full employment (natural) level, Y_0, and with prices at level P_0, the appearance of cost-push pressures shifts the aggregate supply curve upward as to position S_{SR_1}. With no change in aggregate demand, the upward shift in aggregate supply would raise the price level to P' but would reduce output to level Y_1. With the reduction in output, employment declines; i.e., because prices (at P') have risen by a smaller proportion than money wages, real wages are increased, prompting firms to lay off their least productive workers.

At this point, the government may prevent a continuation of price increases by employing fiscal and monetary policies that restrict demand to level D_0. However, if the government is concerned about unemployment, it may restore full employment by pursuing expansionary demand policies to shift aggregate demand to a level like D_1. In this case, equilibrium would be restored at output level Y_0, but at the higher price level P_1. Moreover, this may not be the end of the story for, with a full information adjustment to the new equilibrium position, real wages and the real income rewards of labor and capital will be at their original levels. In this case, those responsible for the initial cost-push pressures might be expected to push again for higher (wage or profit) rewards, which would continue the inflationary process. Thus, by using its policy weapons to raise aggregate demand as needed to maintain full employment in the face of a cost-push inflation, government would be ratifying or validating the uses of market power that were responsible for the inflation rather than permitting the price rise to end of itself.

Evaluating the Cost-Push Thesis. Is the cost-push thesis valid? Because the continuation of inflation appears to require accompanying shifts in aggregate demand, most economists would agree that the distinction between demand-pull and cost-push inflation is artificial. However, the question of whether an inflation can originate through the exercise of market power is the subject of disagreement. All would agree that firms with monopoly power will charge higher prices than competitive firms and that organized labor might succeed in winning a higher wage than unorganized labor would. However, *higher* prices and wages are not the same thing as *rising* prices and wages, and it is the latter that is the essence of inflation. Other things being constant, a firm with monopoly power that continues increasing its product prices will eventually reduce its profits as sales fall. In the same vein, a union that continues raising its workers' wages will, at the same time, be reducing the quantity of workers demanded, so that excessive wage increases will leave the workers worse off than before. Hence, according to standard economic theory, cost-push inflation requires irrational behavior and is unlikely to be a problem in reality. The supporters of cost-push theories argue that the "other things" that are assumed constant in standard economic analysis are, in fact, influenced by wage and price increases, so that the possessors of monopoly power can benefit from a push for a bigger share of the economy's output. As an illustration, we have already seen that the government may respond endogenously to a cost-push shift in the aggregate supply schedule, raising demand as needed to maintain full employment.

It is also possible that those responsible for cost-push pressures may be relatively insulated from its quantity (employment and output) effects. When layoffs occur, it is generally the younger, newer additions to the work force ("last hired, first fired") who lose their jobs. It is not the majority of older workers with union-protected seniority, and it is not the union leaders who face the unemployment penalty.

The validity of wage- and profit-push explanations of inflation remains a source of some disagreement among economists, though most feel that an inflation stemming from such sources cannot persist. However, the experience of recent years, in which both the unemployment rate and the inflation rate have been high and at times have risen together, argues forcefully that shifts in the aggregate supply schedule can play an important role in the inflationary process. Indeed, to fully understand the events of recent years, we must explore some nontraditional views of the forces that can shift the aggregate supply schedule, resulting in an active and pernicious role for aggregate supply in real world inflation processes.

Contemporary Supply Shocks and Price Increases

In Chapters 9 and 10 we identified factors that, by shifting the aggregate supply schedule, could cause a price increase. Included in our list were reductions in labor force participation rates, the imposition of safety and health (OSHA) regulations that lower productivity, environmental protection regulations and, perhaps most significantly in today's world, cartelization of world energy supplies. All of these factors have the potential of shifting aggregate supply upward, and, if the government attempts to maintain full employment in the face of those shifts, a sustained rise in prices might occur.

Using the world oil market for illustrative purposes, consider an attempt by OPEC to raise its members' share of world income by instituting a price increase. As before, this causes the U.S. economy's aggregate supply schedule to shift upward and to the left, as from S_0 to S_1 in Figure 11—4. With no government policy action, the price level would rise to level P' in the short run. However, the government is apt to respond to the accompanying contraction in employment and output by raising aggregate demand, as to level D_1, prompting a further price increase to level P_2 as government tries to maintain full employment.

Of course, with the rise in prices, dollars have lost purchasing power. Dollars are used as an international medium of exchange, a so-called "key" currency, and if OPEC members are paid for oil in dollars, the boost in oil prices does not bring in a correspondingly increased flow of purchasing power. OPEC members might then claim that the failure of the United States to control its own price level merited a further oil price boost. In turn, any further oil price increase would shift the aggregate supply curve further

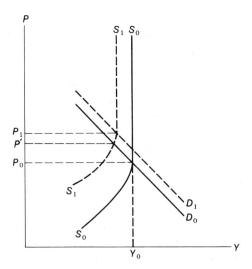

Figure 11—4 / OPEC and Inflation

upward, maintaining the cost-push pressure on domestic prices. Naturally, for the inflation to continue, demand would have to be boosted in step with supply.

Toward a Full Explanation of an Inflation Process

As a by-product of our discussion of factors that can raise prices by shifting either aggregate demand or aggregate supply, it should be clear that demand-pull and cost-push theories offer incomplete explanations of inflation. With an increase in aggregate demand prices rise and, as price expectations adjust, aggregate supply shifts, too. With an upward shift in aggregate supply, demand is apt to shift as government pursues the goal of full employment. To understand a full-fledged, sustained inflation process, we need to take account of the systematic interactions between aggregate demand and aggregate supply rather than treating them as independent of one another. To accomplish that task we need merely to modify our earlier treatment of labor's price expectations, permitting labor to deal with the dynamic concept of a rate of price change.

Inflationary Expectations

So far in our discussion of factors that might lead to inflation we have employed models in which the price level is a matter of foremost concern; it appears on the vertical axis of our aggregate supply and demand model and serves as a focus of labor's attention in making labor-leisure choices. However, in a sustained inflation it is the *rate* of inflation, the rate of change in, rather than the level of, prices, that is the matter of foremost concern. We will not abandon our interest in the price level or the models that include it, but we do need to take account of *inflationary expectations,* i.e., of projections of the rate of price increase; and we need to consider models that probe the links between the inflation rate and other macroeconomic variables, notably employment.

To anticipate the results of this effort, compatible with the results illustrated in our static models, we will conclude that: 1) the continuation of inflation requires a continuous growth in aggregate demand, ultimately via permissive monetary policy; 2) labor may be fooled by an acceleration of inflation into offering more services at a lower real wage in the short run, permitting a reduction in unemployment; 3) in the long run when labor has come to correctly anticipate the inflation rate, employment will return to the *natural* employment rate, with money wages and prices marching upward in step; 4) efforts to slow inflation once it has become anticipated require an employment and output reduction until labor has adjusted its inflationary expectations downward.

Inflationary Expectations and Labor Supply. Let $\dot{P}$ represent the change per period in the general price level, $\dot{P}^e$ the *expected* change per period, and P

the existing price level. With these definitions, the actual percentage inflation rate is $\dot{P}/P$ and the expected inflation rate in percentage terms is $\dot{P}^e/P$. Figure 11—5 shows a labor supply curve (N^s) which is assumed to prevail when the inflation rate that labor expects to prevail matches the actual inflation rate ($\dot{P}/P = \dot{P}^e/P$). There is nothing special about any particular inflation rate in that diagram, so for purposes of argument assume that prices are rising at a steady 2 percent annual rate. With that inflation rate fully anticipated, labor would require a 2 percent annual increase in money wages (ignoring productivity changes) to maintain its real wages. With a demand for labor N^D, the labor market would be cleared, in long-run equilibrium at the natural employment rate, with real wage $(W/P)_0$ and employment level N_0.

Now, consider the effects of an acceleration in the inflation rate due, say, to an increase in the rate of growth of the money supply. As before, we will assume that business firms require only a relatively short time interval to acquire full information on price developments, at least relative to labor, so it is again labor that may be fooled by an increase in the inflation rate.

With business firms quickly recognizing the more rapid inflation rate, say it has risen to 6 percent annually, but no demand by labor for a more rapid rise in money wages, firms will try to add to their work forces in light of reduced real wages. In competing for labor, firms will then bid money wages upward at an accelerated rate but, as long as wages are not increased in proportion with prices, real wages remain depressed and labor demand increased.

Labor, on the other hand, values the new money wage offers it receives, which have grown faster than anticipated, at the old and now outmoded price trajectory, concluding incorrectly that its real wages have risen. As a consequence, labor shortens its employment search periods, offering more

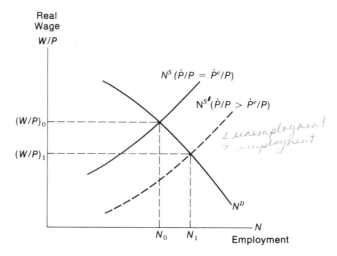

Figure 11—5 / **Unanticipated Inflation and Labor Supply**

labor services and reducing unemployment. The labor supply schedule is then shifted rightward, as to position $N^{s'}$, by the unanticipated acceleration of inflation. As long as labor's expected inflation rate lies below the actual inflation rate $(\dot{P}/P > \dot{P}^e/P)$, the labor supply schedule will remain to the right of its full information position permitting a higher employment level like N_1 at a lower real wage like $(W/P)_1$. Of course, over time, as labor acquires better information on the actual inflation rate, the labor supply schedule will shift back toward its original level until, with full information $(\dot{P}/P = \dot{P}^e/P = 6\%)$, the original labor supply schedule will be restored with employment at the full information, full employment level N_0. Real wages, then, would have returned to their original level, with money wages now increasing at the higher, steady state inflation rate of 6 percent.

In summary, then, any event (such as an acceleration in money supply growth) that raises the rate of growth of aggregate demand will accelerate the inflation rate, and *an unanticipated acceleration in the inflation rate will temporarily reduce unemployment. Employment and unemployment will return to their natural rates, however, when inflation expectations are fully adjusted to the new, higher inflation rate.* For a steady state inflation at any rate to persist indefinitely, an accommodating expansion in the money supply is required.

REREAD

Now, with inflation underway at a fully anticipated 6 percent annual rate, suppose the government slows the growth of aggregate demand, say through a restrictive monetary policy, in an attempt to slow inflation. Slack demand will slow the rate of rise in prices and optimizing business firms would respond with reduced money wage offers. However, with labor expecting price and money wage increases at the old rate, the reduced rise in money wage offers would be viewed (again, incorrectly) as a real wage reduction. In this case, labor would withdraw services; the labor supply schedule is shifted leftward with $\dot{P}/P < \dot{P}^e/P$, lowering employment and raising unemployment. As before, better information on the actual inflation rate would be generated over time, shifting the labor supply back to the right toward the full information position and raising employment (reducing unemployment). The return to full information, full employment then must await the generation of full information on the actual inflation rate.

The Inflation-Unemployment Trade-off

Our discussion of inflation expectations and the labor market reaction to altered inflation rates focused attention on the existence of an apparent trade-off, at least in the short run, between inflation and unemployment. By accelerating the inflation rate, unemployment was reduced below the natural rate (output raised above the full employment potential level) as work seekers were fooled into quickly accepting seemingly attractive job offers. Once labor acquired full information on the rise in the inflation rate and built that information into its wage bargains, unemployment returned to its original, "natural rate" level.

The extent and duration of the trade-off between inflation and unemployment has, for the last decade, been a focal point of research in macroeconomics. It is also at the center of heated policy debates over what goal of stabilization policy should receive priority. A close look at this trade-off relationship is clearly merited.

Figure 11—6 provides a schedule reflecting the behavior patterns described above. Beginning with a steady state inflation rate of 2 percent and with unemployment at its natural rate, U_0, an unanticipated acceleration in the inflation rate to 6 percent lowers the unemployment rate to U'. Again, this reflects the high cost to labor of information as the higher money wage offers labor receives at the new, higher price trajectory are valued on the basis of old, and now outmoded, price expectations. If the higher inflation rate is maintained, however, labor's expectations are apt to adjust to correspond to experience; and, with inflationary expectations matching actual inflation, unemployment is returned to its original, natural rate level (point 2 in the diagram). The sloped schedule (from point 0 to 1) in the diagram represents the short-run trade-off between inflation and unemployment, but Figure 11—6 shows no long-run trade-off between inflation and unemployment.

With unemployment returned to its original, natural rate, if the government should decide to try to squeeze unemployment back down to U', inflation would accelerate again as, once more, an unanticipated rise in the inflation rate is necessary to raise both labor demand and (with labor fooled) supply. Reducing unemployment to U' once a 6 percent inflation rate has come to be fully anticipated, then, requires a movement along a wholly new

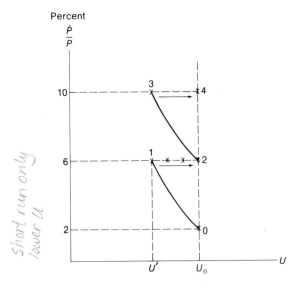

Figure 11—6 / Generating an Inflation-Unemployment Trade-off

trade-off schedule (2 to 3 in the diagram), and, as before, unemployment can be held below the natural rate only as long as labor has imperfect information. With the new inflation rate, 10 percent in our example, fully anticipated, equilibrium would be restored at the natural unemployment rate (point 4), with money wages rising each period to compensate for the fully anticipated 10 percent inflation.

In such a steady-state inflation, with all providers of factors of production building a 10 percent annual increase into their factor prices, the aggregate supply schedule would be shifting upward by 10 percent each year. For expectations to match experience, enabling the steady-state inflation to persist, demand would have to rise 10 percent in nominal terms each year, providing economy-wide equilibrium at price level P_0 in year 0, $1.10 \times P_0$ in year 1, $(1.10)^2 \times P_0$ in year 2, etc., as shown in Figure 11—7, but with output remaining at the full employment potential level.

Slowing Inflation

At this point, suppose the government decides that there are significant burdens associated with inflation and that it stops or reduces the growth in aggregate demand in order to slow inflation. Once more, the economy faces a short-run trade-off between inflation and unemployment, but in this case we are moving *down* along the prevailing trade-off schedule to higher unemployment rates. Figure 11—8 includes the trade-off schedules from Figure 11—6 and extends them to show the short-run employment cost of reducing the inflation rate.

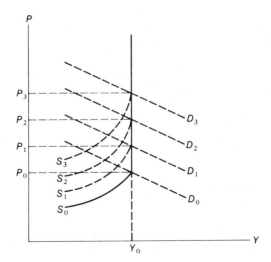

**Figure 11—7 / Aggregate Supply
and Demand with Steady-State Inflation**

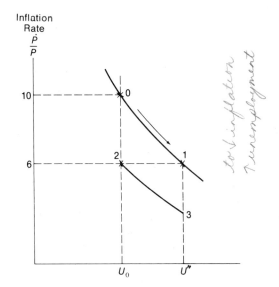

Figure 11—8 / Slowing Inflation by Contracting Demand

By cutting demand (or its rate of growth), a restrictive monetary or fiscal policy can slow the inflation rate. However, as Figure 11—8 illustrates, with labor anticipating a continuing 10 percent inflation, a reduction in the inflation rate to 6 percent will raise unemployment as to level U''. Again, this is a reflection of imperfect information flows to the suppliers of labor, as labor values the money wage offers it is getting, which are now rising at a reduced rate, with the old and now outmoded level of price expectations. Deflating its wage offers with prices that are "too high," labor undervalues its real wage. As a consequence, labor withdraws services and lengthens the duration of job search, raising unemployment to level U'' in the short run.

With the passage of time, labor will gradually learn that the actual inflation rate has slowed (to 6 percent in our example). With a full information adjustment of inflationary expectations, i.e., the expected inflation rate matching the actual 6 percent rate, unemployment would return to its natural rate (point 2). So for a slowing of inflation, too, there is a short-run inflation/unemployment trade-off, but no long-run trade-off as the economy loops from point 0 to point 1 to point 2 as the short- and long-run adjustments to restrictive stabilization policy are completed. With the economy at point 2, any further effort to slow inflation by restricting aggregate demand would involve a short-run adjustment along the new trade-off schedule (2–3).

The Role of Aggregate Supply

Clearly, in the inflation process described above, the supply side of the economy was an active participant. In addition, in any effort on government's part to stop an entrenched and fully anticipated inflation by means

of restrictive monetary and fiscal actions, aggregate supply plays a pernicious role; it is the supply side of the economy that guarantees that the
adjustment to price stability is slow and painful.

As our discussion of the trade-off between inflation and unemployment
reflected, to stop an ongoing inflation the government must slow the rate of
growth of aggregate demand and thereby create an excess supply of goods
and services (lowering prices or slowing their rate of increase). However,
with imperfect (and, after a cutback in demand, outmoded) information,
workers continue pushing up money wage demands at a rate based on expected inflation. In Figure 11—9, an economy's aggregate supply schedule
is shown to shift upward (from S_0 to S_1) even while aggregate demand is
held constant at D_0. The result, as the figure shows, is a rise in prices
(although it is smaller than what would occur if aggregate demand were
allowed to rise in step with supply), which is accompanied by declines in
output and, correspondingly, in employment. Thus unemployment is seen
to increase even while inflation persists, albeit at a reduced rate. As long as
labor pushes for further wage increases to compensate for expected inflation, the aggregate supply schedule will continue to shift upward, raising
prices. As long as aggregate demand is so restricted as to be inadequate to
clear the commodity market of full employment output, there will be a
slowing of the inflation rate, as well. Experience eventually provides society
with better information (in particular with information that the inflation rate
is slowing, so that smaller inflation-motivated adjustments in wages are acceptable), and then the rise in the aggregate supply schedule can slow down,
further reducing the inflation rate. If aggregate demand is restricted long
enough, according to the model we have been working with, inflation can
be halted completely, with the anticipated inflation rate reduced to zero.

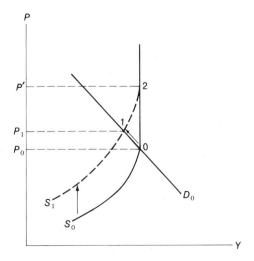

Figure 11—9 / Restricting Demand with Rising Supply

However, because inflationary expectations are adjusted downward only slowly by information-generating experience, the elimination of inflation is a painful process, involving a protracted period of inflation combined with depressed levels of employment and output. "Stagflation," referring to a combination of economic stagnation or depression with inflation, is a term that has frequently been employed to describe economic conditions in the United States in the last decade as inflation has persisted in spite of a slowed expansion of economic activity. Well-entrenched inflationary expectations must bear a large part of the blame for the economy's below par performance during this period as, in the manner described above, they have maintained upward pressure on wages and prices in spite of economic slack.

The Natural Rate View Versus the Long-Run Trade-off View. Economists label the view that changes in the inflation rate prompt changes in employment (unemployment) and output in the short-run, while leaving those variables at their full employment (natural) levels in the long run, the *natural rate hypothesis*. Advanced by Edmund Phelps, Milton Friedman,[2] and others, this thesis implies that the government has a very limited ability to alter employment and output; it can do so only in the short run as market forces return those variables to the natural employment rate levels in the long run.

The natural rate hypothesis, by focusing attention on the role of expectations in the inflation process, has attracted increasing numbers of adherents in recent years. Still, it is possible that over a limited range of unemployment rates there remains some long-run trade-off between inflation and unemployment as some continue to argue.[3] Within the confines of the model we have employed, it is possible that labor might never fully adjust its wage requirements to increased inflation rates, leaving the unemployment rate permanently reduced. Figure 11—10 illustrates this possibility. Beginning with a noninflationary equilibrium at point 0, an acceleration in inflation to, say, a 5 percent rate would move the economy along the trade-off schedule T_0 in the short run to unemployment rate U'. As labor recognizes that the inflation rate has accelerated and acts on that information, the trade-off schedule is shifted upward. If labor's wage requirements are adjusted by any proportion of the price path change less than one, the trade-off schedule is shifted upward less than in proportion to the acceleration of inflation (shifted in proportion to the change in the inflation rate, the trade-off schedule would go through point 3 in the diagram). In this case, by maintaining the 5 percent inflation rate, government could keep unemployment at level U_1, below what we had viewed as the "natural" unemployment rate and,

[2]See Edmund Phelps, *Inflation Policy and Unemployment Theory: The Cost-Benefit Approach to Monetary Planning* (New York: Norton, 1972), and Milton Friedman, "The Role of Monetary Policy," *The American Economic Review,* March 1968, pp. 1–17.
[3]See James Tobin, "Inflation and Unemployment," *The American Economic Review,* March 1972, pp. 1–18; and Robert Solow, "Down the Phillips Curve With Gun and Camera," *Inflation, Trade and Taxes,* Ohio State University, Columbus, O.: ed. D. A. Belsey, et al.

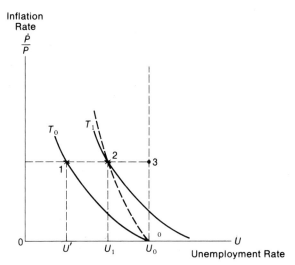

**Figure 11—10 / The Long-Run Trade-off
with a Partial Adjustment to Inflation Rate Changes**

hence, negating the existence of a single full employment/unemployment rate.

As an alternative possibility, an inflation-induced "temporary" increase in employment (which can occur only with imperfect information) would give some labor job experience that it otherwise would not have. If on-the-job training makes that labor more valuable (hence better paid), or if it encourages the development of a greater willingness to maintain employment at any wage, employment becomes more attractive relative to search unemployment, and the natural rate of unemployment is reduced. Illustrating this possibility, Figure 11—11 shows a short-run adjustment along schedule T_0 in response to an acceleration of inflation from 0 to 5 percent. With U_0 the original value of the natural unemployment rate, U_1 is the reduced natural unemployment rate that is provided by on-the-job training. The long-run adjustment to the accelerated inflation rate then involves a movement from point 0 to point 2, as even with a full information adjustment to the higher inflation rate, unemployment remains permanently below its original rate.

In both cases described above, there remains a long-run trade-off between inflation and unemployment, represented by the sloped broken lines that pass through U_0 and point 2 in Figures 11—10 and 11—11. It is noteworthy that, even if a trade-off persists in the long-run, it is a decidedly less favorable trade-off than the one that exists in the short-run when there has been inadequate time for major alterations in expectations.

Rational Expectations Again. As a final possibility, consider the extention of the natural rate hypothesis to accommodate rational expectations. Once again, with rational expectations society knows what forces influence the

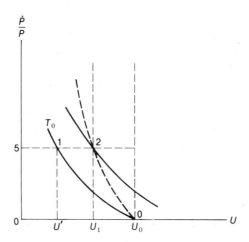

**Figure 11—11 / The Long-Run Trade-off with a Job
Experience Induced Reduction in the Natural Unemployment Rate**

economy; in this case, what determines the inflation rate. If the rate of
monetary expansion is the ultimate determinant of the inflation rate and
society knows it, with an acceleration in money supply growth, a corresponding acceleration in the inflation rate will be anticipated and built into
wage and other factor costs. Thus, the inflation rate would adjust simultaneously to changes in the rate of money supply growth, and there would be
no *real, quantity* (employment and output) adjustments in response to
changes in the inflation rate. It is only when there are errors in projected
inflation rates, e.g., when workers' price projections lag behind actual inflation rates, that employment and output adjustments occur.

Empirical Evidence: The Phillips Curve

In 1958, A.W. Phillips published the results of an empirical probe of the link
between inflation rates and unemployment rates in Britain.[4] Following
Phillips' lead, economists in other countries were soon generating a large
body of evidence on the empirical link between unemployment rates and
inflation rates. Reflecting this tradition, Figure 11—12 provides a schedule,

---

[4]A. W. Phillips, "The Relationship between Unemployment and the Rate of Change of Money
Wage Rates in the United Kingdom, 1861–1957," *Economica* n.s. 25 (1958): 283–299. As
indicated in the title, Phillips' original investigation was concerned with the link between
unemployment and the rate of wage inflation, not with unemployment versus the rate of change
of prices in general. However, the shift to the latter concern is simple and straightforward,
and the label *Phillips curve* is generally applied to both relationships. A follow-up study that
emphasized the link between unemployment and price change on the basis of U.S. data was
provided in Paul Samuelson and Robert Solow, "Analytical Aspects of Anti-Inflation Policy,"
The American Economic Review, May 1960, pp. 177–194.

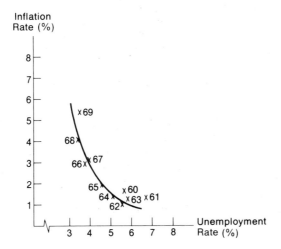

Figure 11—12 / The Phillips Curve: U.S. Data 1960–69

called a *Phillips curve,* relating U.S. unemployment rates and inflation rates for the period 1960 through 1969. The observations in that diagram fit the plotted Phillips curve quite well, and that schedule seems to imply that there is a long-run trade-off between inflation and unemployment. According to that schedule, to have limited inflation to 1 or 1½ percent annually in the 1960s, it appears that an unemployment rate between 5½ and 6 percent would have to have been accepted. To achieve the full employment goal of 4 percent unemployment, which was sought in the 1960s, the Phillips curve plot suggests that an inflation rate of some 3 percent annually would have been required. In the early 1960s, the Phillips curve was often viewed, in this vein, as representing a "menu of policy choices." With proper attention to the social costs of both unemployment and inflation, policy makers were to choose from the unemployment-inflation combinations that the Phillips curve showed were available, the one combination that would maximize social welfare.

Should the plot in Figure 11—12 be viewed as representing a stable trade-off between inflation and unemployment? Our arguments in this chapter have suggested not; the trade-off represented by that particular Phillips curve would persist only as long as inflationary expectations remain unchanged. According to this view, the apparent trade-off represented by Figure 11—12 is a reflection of the low rates of inflation that characterized the latter part of the 1950s and the early 1960s. With society anticipating no substantial rate of price rise, increases in aggregate demand that moderately accelerated the actual inflation rate could have been expected to lower unemployment. From 1965 until the end of the decade, though, inflation was maintained at a relatively high level and, with that persistent inflationary experience, we should expect inflationary expectations to be modified, shifting the Phillips curve.

Case in Point VII

The Clockwise Looped Path of Unemployment and Inflation Rates[5]

In fact, a closer look at the data for the United States over the extended period 1956 to 1979 seems to support the notion of a constantly shifting trade-off. As Figure 11—13 shows, instead of a stable Phillips Curve, there appear to have been four clockwise loops. Each loop includes: (1) a period of *declining* unemployment and *rising* inflation; (2) a period of *rising* unemployment and *rising* inflation; (3) a period of *falling* inflation and *rising* unemployment; and finally (4) a period of *falling* inflation and unemployment. This looping motion became very pronounced during the 1970s.

Why are loops formed by movement along and between shifting Phillips trade-offs? A plausible explanation requires extending our model of the shifting trade-off to recognize that workers not only attempt to anticipate inflation, but also to (1) "catch up" when unanticipated inflation has occurred, or (2) to reduce wage demands if there is excess unemployment. If

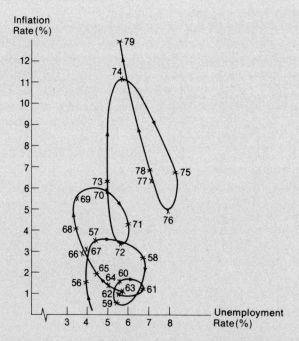

Figure 11—13 / Inflation and Unemployment Rates: 1956–79

---

[5]The case was provided by Douglas Diamond of North Carolina State University.

we assume that expectations of inflation are based on recent inflation rates, then we shall find the accelerated inflation accompanying the "catch-up" increase in wages leads to expectations of future inflation rates that are too high. This means that the economy will overshoot its return towards the natural rate of unemployment, and a period of excessive unemployment will be necessary before reductions in expectations of inflation and wage increases permit a return towards U_0.

This cyclical aspect of the expectations theory is illustrated in Figure 11—14. In our illustration, we are assuming that the rate of expansion in aggregate demand has increased; we are not assuming that the government can "fine tune" demand to maintain a more rapid but constant inflation rate. A permanent increase in the rate of expansion in aggregate demand leads initially to movement along trade-off T_1 to a higher inflation rate $(\dot{P}/P)_1$ and a lower unemployment rate of U_1. The decline in unemployment occurs because workers are slow to recognize the erosion of the real purchasing power of their incomes. Over time, they learn to expect continued inflation (say at $(\dot{P}/P)_1$). In adition, they recognize that their real wages were lowered by the unanticipated inflation. At this point, their demands for wage increases will be higher than their expectations of price increases to enable them to catch up with past price increases. Then a new trade-off curve (T_2) based on their inflation expectation is centered on $(\dot{P}/P)_1$ and U_0, but the actual inflation rate will be higher than $(\dot{P}/P)_1$ and unemployment will continue to be less than U_0. Unemployment may increase from U_1, though this is not necessary at this point.

Workers continue to fall behind inflation if they do not incorporate the effects of their own attempts to catch up with prices into their expectations of future price increases. The process of accelerating inflation will come to

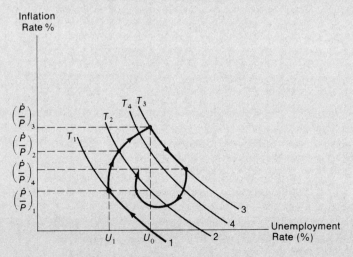

Figure 11—14 / A Clockwise Loop Adjustment Path

an end when increases in nominal aggregate demand cannot support the increase in prices and real demand declines. At some point, workers' wages will have caught up with prices and unemployment will be back at U_0.

However, a legacy of the delayed catch up in wages has been a rate of inflation higher than that supportable by the expansion in nominal aggregate demand. This higher rate of inflation is now built into the expectations of workers. They expect inflation of $(\dot{P}/P)_3$, but only something less, say $(\dot{P}/P)_4$, will occur. Workers are now overpricing their services and unemployment will rise. As this occurs, workers will start to reduce the rate of increase in their wage demands. This will further moderate inflation. Unfortunately, just as was the case on the upside of the loop, workers will lag behind in reducing their wage expectations, and only after an extended time interval will unemployment begin to fall. In fact, it is likely that unemployment will return to U_0 with workers having too low an estimate of the underlying rate of inflation, and the cycle will repeat itself on a smaller scale.

The looping of the economy has also been influenced by accelerations and decelerations in the rate of growth in aggregate demand. Higher loops were begun in the election years of 1964, 1972, and 1976, perhaps as incumbent presidents attempted to move the economy along the current Phillips trade-off. Each of these expansions was followed by periods of accelerating inflation and increasing unemployment. At about this time the rate of growth in aggregate demand was just as sharply reduced. These actions reinforced the inevitable downward part of the loop and, in the mid-1970s, brought the economy to much higher levels of unemployment. However, the downward portion of the most recent loop was suddenly brought to a halt in 1976, and the economy moved up again towards higher inflation rates and a (temporarily) lower unemployment rate.

To conclude our discussion on the linkage between unemployment and inflation, we should take special note of the following points:

1. The apparently attractive Phillips curve trade-off between inflation rates and unemployment rates that was observed in the United States in the 1950s and early 1960s was, in all likelihood, due to the stability of inflationary expectations.
2. With a change in inflationary expectations, the short-run Phillips curve is shifted so that the long-run trade-off between inflation and unemployment is far less attractive than the short-run trade-off (i.e., the long-run trade-off schedule is much steeper than the short-run schedule), if it exists at all.
3. It appears, then, that inflating the economy is a poor means of reducing unemployment if there are any significant social costs that stem from inflation.
4. In a well-entrenched inflation in which continued inflation is anticipated,

attempts to slow inflation by reducing aggregate demand can require protracted periods of depressed employment and output.

The Costs of Inflation

Virtually everyone agrees that extended periods of depressed employment and output are a heavy price to pay to slow inflation. Inflation is also generally viewed as burdensome, but the reasons for this view are generally less clear. To justify the pursuit of stability in the general price level as an important policy goal, our next task is to identify the costs that inflation imposes on society.

The vocal public response to inflation leaves the impression that rising prices reduce living standards across the board by reducing the purchasing power of received income. As a general proposition, however, this cannot be true because, economy-wide, money income is equal to real output times the average output sales price. If inflation does not cause real output to fall, then the price level and *aggregate* money income can only rise together. It seems, though, that individuals are often unwilling to attribute their increases in nominal income to generalized inflationary forces. They appear to feel that their money income increases are *earned,* while the increasing prices they have to pay for goods and services stem from the avaricious actions of some other individuals or groups.

Inflation and the Distribution of Income and Wealth

Even if aggregate money income rises with prices, inflation can benefit some groups at the expense of others; it can redistribute income and wealth. As we all know, anyone whose money income rises more rapidly than prices during periods of inflation enjoys an increasing real income level, and anyone whose money income rises more slowly than the general price level suffers a reduction in real income. What individuals or groups does inflation affect in these ways? While conclusive evidence is hard to come by, it has long been asserted that profit earners gain and wage earners lose from inflation because wage costs of production typically lag behind increases in selling prices. Indeed, at least in the unionized sector of the economy where wages are set by contract, there appears to be some lag between price level increases and money wage adjustments. However, while adjustments in wages do appear to lag behind movements in the price level during the early stages of an inflation, wages tend to catch up in later periods as inflation premiums are built into new wage agreements. Thus, any inflation-induced redistribution of income from labor to profit earners is likely to be transitory.[6]

---

[6]Evidence that real wages and employment tend to peak together during inflationary expansions appears in Ronald G. Bodkin, "Real Wages and Cyclical Variations in Employment," *Canadian Journal of Economics* 2 (1969): 353–374; see also George L. Bach and James B. Stephenson, "Inflation and the Redistribution of Wealth," *The Review of Economics and Statistics* 56 (1974): 1–13.

Tradition also holds that the salaries of white-collar workers adjust to price level changes with a long lag, permitting inflation to reduce the real income those workers enjoy. For some salaried workers, notably state and local government employees (including teachers), the reduction in real income from inflation is commonly alleged to be long lasting because their salaries are notoriously slow to adjust to changes in prices. Of course, as long as government salary adjustments lag behind increases in the cost of living, income is redistributed from government workers to taxpayers.

For some individuals, inflation results in a permanent reduction in real purchasing power. Anyone who is dependent on an income that is not just slow to adjust to price level changes but is absolutely fixed in nominal terms will suffer a permanent purchasing power reduction when prices rise. Because bond coupon and principal payments are fixed in dollar amount, bondholders suffer a reduction in real purchasing power as prices rise. Similarly, the beneficiaries of fixed value annuities from pension and life insurance programs have their real purchasing power reduced by inflation. Unlike a wage earner, a retired individual living off such fixed payments cannot bargain for catch-up increases in his income receipts. As a result, past savings that were thought to be ample to meet future needs (say, for retirement) can end up being woefully inadequate because of inflation. To partially alleviate the impact of inflation on the living standards of the retired, Congress in recent years has provided a number of boosts in Social Security benefits. Moreover, since 1972 Social Security benefits have been tied to the price level by an escalator formula that automatically increases those benefits when the Consumer Price Index increases.[7]

Inflation can also alter the distribution of wealth between creditors and debtors. While debtors are benefited by inflation because their debts are fixed in dollar terms, the real value of which is diminished by the price level increase, creditors are damaged. An individual (debtor) who buys a $50,000 house with a $40,000 (80 percent) mortgage might welcome inflation. If prices should rise by 50 percent, the market value of his house would be $75,000, while his mortgage remains at $40,000. While inflation has increased the buyer's equity in the house more than threefold (from $10,000 to $35,000), the lender has suffered a one-third reduction in the real value of the mortgage debt due to him. Should all mortgage holders favor inflation? Not necessarily. Most individuals are both creditors and debtors. Most have some savings which typically are loaned out (to a bank in a savings account, to government through bond purchases, and so on). The real value of the wealth they hold in the form of dollar claims is eroded as prices rise. To benefit from inflation, one must be a debtor on a net basis. With a large volume of outstanding debt, the wealth redistribution from creditors to debt-

---

[7]While Congress in recent years has provided boosts in Social Security benefits to offset the effects of inflation, the real value of payments on bonds, insurance, and other fixed-dollar assets retirees often rely on has fallen substantially. With the potential for loss of real income on fixed nominal-value annuities highlighted by recent experience, a number of variable payment retirement programs have been made available in recent years.

ors that inflation causes can be quite substantial. While unequivocally identifying debtor and creditor groups is difficult, older people are more frequently net creditors and younger people net debtors.

What broad conclusions on the equity of the redistributive effects of
inflation have we outlined? No hard and fast generalization on the general
nature of redistribution, on whether there is redistribution from poor to rich
or vice versa as a result of inflation, is justified.[8] It is clear though that some
persons, such as retired individuals living on pensions and other annuities,
have suffered real income cuts through inflation, as have the employees of
state and local governmental units and of educational and religious institutions. In addition, it is clear that inflation can produce large wealth redistributions *within* groups when there are both net creditors and net debtors
in these groups. Any redistributive effects of inflation, no matter what their
breadth of incidence, are highly arbitrary and would be consistent with
socially determined norms for income and wealth redistribution only by
coincidence.

Learning to Live with Inflation

It is important to note that the potential redistributive burdens we have
discussed arise as a result of *unanticipated* inflation. If the rate of inflation
is correctly anticipated by the general public, the redistributions of income
and wealth we have outlined above need not occur. With inflation anticipated, workers will demand contracts that include money wage or salary
adjustments to offset the anticipated price increases, and retirement plan
purchasers will demand retirement benefits that are tied to the price level.
In addition, nominal interest rates on bonds will rise to compensate lenders
for the erosion of purchasing power that inflation imposes on fixed money
payments. As we argued in Chapter 7, if an individual who would normally
lend at a 4 percent annual interest rate expects prices to rise at a 5 percent
annual rate over the life of the loan, he will demand a 5 percent inflation
premium in the nominal interest rate he requires for lending; that is, he
would lend only if he could receive a 9 percent or higher nominal interest
rate. A borrower who expects prices to rise by 5 percent annually would be
willing to pay the 5 percent inflation premium because he knows he will
repay the loan in dollars that have lost purchasing power at a 5 percent
annual rate. No wonder interest rates in the United States were in the 15
percent range in 1979 when the Consumer Price Index rose by 13 percent.

---

[8]Again, see Bach and Stephenson, ''Inflation and the Redistribution.'' For a discussion of the
problems involved in evaluating the redistributive effects of inflation, see George L. Bach and
Albert Ando, ''The Redistributional Effects of Inflation,'' *Review of Economics and Statistics*
39 (1957): 1–13; and Oswald Brownlee and Alfred Conrad, ''Effects upon the Distribution of
Income of a Tight Money Policy,'' in *Stabilization Policies,* Research Studies of the Commission on Money and Credit (Englewood Cliffs, N.J.: Prentice-Hall, 1963), ed. E. Cary Brown,
et al. pp. 499–558. For recent evidence on inflation's redistributive effects see Joseph J. Min-
arik, ''Who Wins, Who Loses from Inflation?'' *Challenge,* January/February 1979: pp. 26–31.

Of course, it is unreasonable to expect all of society to properly anticipate episodes of inflation, and with the extraordinarily rapid inflation of the 1970s there emerged a great deal of interest in institutional changes that could limit the uneven and arbitrary redistributive effect that an unanticipated inflation engenders. Attracting the most attention were proposals for universal *indexation*, i.e., the attachment of inflation escalator clauses to all forms of contractual arrangements involving money transfers. Already, escalator clauses that employ the Consumer Price Index as a measure of changes in the purchasing power of the dollar protect the real wages of some 5 million union workers, the real food-purchasing power of some 18 million food stamp recipients, and the real value of the pensions of more than 30 million Social Security recipients. With a comparable indexation of all loans, insurance premiums and benefits, long-term purchase agreements, rents, taxes, and so on, we might "learn to live with inflation," blunting its harshest redistributive effects.

On the other hand, it can be contended that learning to live with inflation through indexation is a sure-fire way of perpetuating and even accelerating inflation. With broad, if not universal, protection from inflation, the public and political support necessary for the sometimes harsh policies necessary to control inflation might well evaporate. Moreover, universal indexation would build momentum into any episode of inflation that an unavoidable, random disturbance might initiate as automatically escalated wages and prices chase each other upward. Because of such concerns universal indexation is supported by relatively few economists.

Indexing Income Taxes. While universal indexation is not widely favored, economists in general are united in their support of the indexation of the federal income tax system. At present, without automatic adjustments in the nominal values of exemptions, standard deductions, and tax brackets to match inflation, the progressive income tax system imposes a forced transfer of purchasing power from the private sector to the government as prices rise. As an illustration, consider a taxpayer with earnings of $20,000. If married and filing a joint return, this taxpaying unit's federal income tax obligation in 1979 would have been $3,225 or 16.125 percent of income. If, because of inflation, prices and money incomes were 10 percent higher a year later, the tax obligation at 1979 rates on $22,000 of money income would be $3,777 or 17.169 percent of income. The fraction of an unchanged level of real income going to government use is increased by inflation because the tax system does not distinguish between "real" and "nominal" increases in income. In 1980 dollars, our hypothetical taxpayer would have suffered a $229.50 "inflation tax" reduction in purchasing power from the 10 percent increase in nominal income.

In recent years, there have been a number of proposals presented to Congress to index the tax system. None has been adopted. In opposition to those bills it has been argued that: (1) the existing system provides an automatic brake on inflation as aggregate demand is dampened when the real tax burden rises; or (2) treating one aspect of inflation's unwanted effects would weaken the government's resolve to slow inflation.

There are other possible explanations of government's reluctance to index taxes that Congress might not be expected to focus attention on. Notably, the automatic increase in spending power available for government use may be viewed as desirable as it enables Congressmen to enlarge their favorite programs: national defense, welfare, education, or what have you. In addition, if the extra bite on private spending power is judged too harsh, Congressmen can receive credit for tax relief by voting to lower tax rates. In the inflationary era we have been involved in since the mid-1960s, tax reductions have been instituted several times. Still, the overall share of income going to government use has risen over that period with taxes absorbing just over 12 percent of earnings in 1964 but nearly 18 percent in 1979. Figure 11—15 shows how the fraction of the average worker's earnings going to federal income taxes has changed over that period.

The Inflation Tax on Money Balances. It should also be noted that, while correct inflationary expectations or widespread indexing can largely prevent the redistributive impact of inflation, there is one social cost of inflation that cannot be circumvented as long as interest (which rises to compensate lenders for expected inflation losses) is not paid on money holdings. Even with correct inflation expectations or widely dispersed escalator agreements, inflation still reduces the real value of any individual's cash balances. Recognizing the increased cost of holding money that inflation creates, the public will try to reduce its money holdings below the desired level that would prevail if no inflation were anticipated. Economizing on the use of money balances does reduce the "inflation tax" on money holdings, but at the

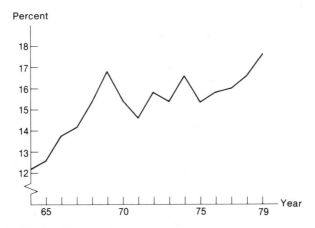

Figure 11—15 / Ratio of Personal Federal Income Tax Liabilities to Income: 1969–79

same time it entails a sacrifice of the convenience yield of the additional money balances. Specifically, households might squeeze their money balances by keeping more funds in savings accounts, necessitating the inconvenience of extra trips to the bank to transfer funds from savings to checking accounts. This sort of burden is often referred to as the "shoe leather" cost of the inflation tax on money. Of course, business firms, too, would devote scarcer resources to managing cash balances when the inflation tax on those balances is higher.

Effects on Production and Growth. With prices rising as rapidly as they have in recent years, inflation may affect the size of the real GNP as well as its distribution. To a large extent, any detrimental effects of inflation on current output stem from its effects on the quality of information available to guide economic decision making. For the business firms that do the producing in a developed economy, the major information distortions are in two elements of costs: depreciation on long-term assets and inventory costs. As suggested earlier, accounting measures of depreciation, generally based on historical costs, undervalue depreciation costs during inflation. With this element of costs undervalued, profits are overestimated. In addition, the nominal value of inventories rises with prices in general, and, unless cost measures are based on the *replacement* value of inventories, costs will be understated and profits overstated.

To avoid mistaken decisions based on erroneous information, firms may react to the information problems that inflation creates by employing additional economic analysts and accountants, and by purchasing more consultant's services. Such actions represent a diversion of resources from the production of "ordinary" goods and services and thus result in an inflation-induced decline in real GNP. Individuals, too, may direct substantial effort away from ordinary production activities and into speculative activities when inflation is anticipated, as they seek assets that can protect their accumulated wealth from erosion due to price increases.

Inflation may also depress future production levels. It is commonly assumed that the expectation of inflation, nurtured by experienced inflation, causes a reduction in the propensity to save (that is, an upward shift in the consumption function), as individuals, expecting prices to rise, buy now to beat the price increases. As an illustration, with the 13.3 percent rise in the Consumer Price Index in 1979, the fraction of disposable income saved, which has averaged about 6¼ percent annually in the United States since World War II, fell to 4.6 percent. With the rapid inflation rate that has persisted since 1974, the saving ratio has been well below its post-war average throughout the second half of the 1970s. From 1976 through 1979, the saving to disposable income ratio averaged 5.2 percent. Because it is only by saving (not consuming) that resources can be freed for the investment that enlarges the capital stock and, thus, future production capacity, any reduction in the propensity to save limits output growth. The link between inflation and the depressed level of capital formation the U.S. economy has experienced in the 1970s (accompanied by restricted improvements in labor productivity) should be apparent.

Of the threats to economic well-being posed by inflation, by far the worst stems from the possibility of a runaway inflation, a so-called *hyperinflation,* in which prices rise so rapidly that society loses faith in money. In that case, the diversion of resources from ordinary production to speculative activities can be substantial, and if money is abandoned in favor of barter exchange, production standards of the sort we are accustomed to cannot be maintained.

The best-known case of hyperinflation occurred after World War I in Germany. From 1913 to November of 1923, the index of wholesale prices in Germany rose from a level of 100 to 73 trillion, with most of the increases occurring in 1922 and 1923. The economic hardship that followed is commonly listed as a major contributing factor in the rise of fervent nationalism and, finally, Nazism. Hungary, Poland, Austria, and Russia also suffered from hyperinflation after World War I, but not on the scale that Germany did.[9]

Our list of the by-products of inflation is not exhaustive, but it is representative of the lines of reasoning followed in modern discussions of the costs of inflation. It is clearly sufficient to rationalize the common acceptance of general price stability as a national policy goal, and it sets the stage for consideration of the means by which price stability can be pursued. Chapter 12 will deal with anti-inflation policy. In the meantime, this chapter concludes with an explanation of the incorporation of inflationary expectations in the *IS-LM* model that has been a fundamental component of our analytical apparatus.

Incorporating Inflationary Expectations in the *IS-LM* Model

As first indicated in Chapter 7, when no inflation is anticipated, no distinction need be drawn between the nominal rate of interest, which is observed in the financial market place, and its *real* counterpart. However, with inflation anticipated, lenders will part with their loanable funds only if they receive their usual percentage of interest return plus an interest allowance sufficient to offset the impact of the expected inflation on the purchasing power of the dollars they are repaid. Hence, the nominal interest rate lenders require will be the sum of the real rate of interest (required when no inflation is anticipated) and the expected rate of inflation. Borrowers, if they share the inflationary expectations of lenders, will agree to pay the higher nominal interest rate. They expect to repay their loans with dollars that have lost real purchasing power at the expected rate of inflation. Hence, the

---

[9]A classic study of this hyperinflation was provided by Phillip Cagan, ''The Monetary Dynamics of Hyperinflation'' in Friedman (ed.), *Studies in the Quantity Theory of Money* (Chicago: University of Chicago Press, 1956), pp. 25–117.

nominal rate of interest can be represented algebraically (as in Chapter 7) as,

$$i = \rho + \frac{\Delta P^e}{P} \qquad\qquad [11-1]$$

with i the nominal (observed market) interest rate, ρ the real interest rate, and $\Delta P^e/P$ the expected rate of inflation.

In Figure 11—16 a standard and familiar set of commodity and money market equilibrium schedules are sketched (IS_0 and LM_0), providing an equilibrium level of aggregate demand at output level Y_f with market interest rate i_0. For convenience, it is asumed that Y_f is the full employment, full information level of output. If IS_0 and LM_0 represent the commodity and money market equilibrium schedules when there is a zero rate of expected inflation (as they have up to now), the equilibrium interest rate (i_0) is identical to the real interest rate (ρ).

As a first step in accommodating the appearance of nonzero inflation expectations, we must recognize that the nominal and real interest rates will diverge with the emergence of inflationary expectations (both measured along the vertical axis in Figure 11—16), and we must shift the IS curve upward. Investment is a function of the real interest rate. While the emergence of inflationary expectations raises the nominal interest cost of investment, the nominal expected returns from investment are increased by an identical percentage amount, and no revision of investment plans is called for. With the volume of investment associated with any real interest rate unaltered by changes in the expected rate of inflation, the IS curve would be shifted upward by (measured vertically) the expected rate of inflation. Hence, for expected inflation rate $\Delta P^e/P$ the IS schedule would become schedule IS_1 in Figure 11—16. Along that new IS schedule, an unchanged

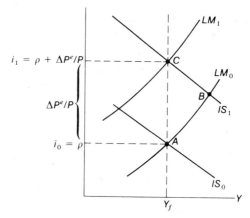

Figure 11—16 / Inflationary Expectations in the *IS-LM* Model

level of investment, hence aggregate demand, would accompany the unchanged real interest rate, ρ, and the higher nominal interest rate, i_1. Of
course, every increase in the expected rate of inflation would shift the *IS*
curve further upward, and every decrease would produce a decline in the
IS schedule. In contrast, the position of the *LM* curve is unaltered by
changes in the expected rate of inflation. It is the nominal interest rate that
is a measure of the (opportunity) cost of holding money balances. Thus, any
change in the nominal interest rate can be expected to change the demand
for money, and that response is already reflected in the standard *LM* schedule. With the nominal stock of money fixed, a change in the nominal interest
rate necessitates a changed level of spending (a movement along an existing
LM curve) for money market equilibrium to be maintained.

Beginning with the economy in equilibrium with no inflation anticipated
(at Y_f, i_0 in Figure 11—16), let us trace the complete adjustment in the *IS-
LM* model to a generalized expectation that prices are going to rise at rate
$\Delta P^e/P$ henceforth. As indicated above, with the emergence of the expectation of inflation at rate $\Delta P^e/P$, the *IS* curve is shifted upward (to position
IS_1), while the position of the *LM* curve is unaffected. At the new intersection of the commodity and money market equilibrium schedules (point *B*),
the nominal interest rate is above the original value of the real (and nominal)
rate, but not by the full amount of expected inflation. Hence, the real rate
of interest (the nominal rate minus the expected rate of inflation) is below
value ρ. Quite simply, with prices expected to rise, society's demand for
money, which loses purchasing power with inflation, has declined and the
resulting excess supply of money has produced a decline in the real interest
rate (even though nominal rates are increased).

With the real interest rate temporarily depressed, investment is stimulated, and aggregate demand at point *B* exceeds the full employment level
of output. Prices will then rise as a direct consequence of the adoption of
inflationary expectations. As prices rise the real stock of money shrinks,
shifting the *LM* curve leftward until aggregate demand is reduced to equality
with output. With expectations unchanged, that requires a shift of the *LM*
curve to position LM_1 in Figure 11—16, providing the new "equilibrium"
interest rate i_1.

While the mere existence of inflationary expectations results in a one-
shot price increase and a rise in the nominal interest rate equal to the expected inflation rate (a movement to position *C* in Figure 11—16), neither
the inflation nor the elevated interest rate can persist unless government
validates society's expectations. Specifically, only if the government increases the money stock and, correspondingly, the nominal demand for
output at the rate of expected inflation, can point *C* in Figure 11—16 remain
the equilibrium point in our *IS-LM* model. While an increasing money supply with stable prices would shift the *LM* curve rightward, with prices rising
at the same rate as the nominal money stock, the real supply of money
would be unchanged. The *LM* schedule would remain at position LM_1, and

the *IS-LM* model would reflect an equilibrium at point *C* with a steady-state inflation at the expected rate.[10]

If the government refuses to validate the public's inflationary expectations, holding the rate of money supply growth below the expected inflation rate, the inflation rate would decline (a continuation of inflation at the expected rate would shift the *LM* curve leftward, resulting in an excess supply of real goods and services). As inflation slows, society's inflationary expectations would be revised downward shifting the *IS* curve downward. If the expectation of a zero inflation rate is restored, equilibrium would be restored at i_0, Y_f in Figure 11—16, with no difference between the nominal and real interest rates.

Summary

In this chapter we have reviewed the two dominant explanations of price increases, the demand-pull and cost-push theories. Demand-pull price increases, the result of excess demand for aggregate output, were shown to be self-limiting unless the government pursues fiscal and, ultimately, monetary policies that cause aggregate demand to grow excessively. Preventing demand-pull price increases requires that aggregate demand be allowed to grow only as rapidly as aggregate supply grows.

Cost-push, or seller's, "inflation" resulted when the domestic possessors of monopoly power used that power in a way that would shift the aggregate supply curve upward or when some external shock shifted the supply curve upward. The upward shift in the supply curve raised the price level and reduced employment and output. Our model suggested that cost-push price increases would also lead to their own end, raising the unemployment rate and reducing total sales, unless the government validates cost-push efforts through an expansionary monetary and fiscal policy aimed at maintaining full employment.

While we agreed that prices are higher in markets that are monopolized, we sympathetically reviewed arguments that question the thesis that monopoly power (cost-push pressure) can be held responsible for sustained increases in prices such as the United States has experienced in recent years. Available empirical evidence does not indicate that there has been a sustained growth in monopoly power in the U.S. economy, a condition which the critics of the thesis claim is necessary to validate the cost-push explanation of inflation.

The inflationary role of the supply side of the economy is in maintaining an ongoing inflation after the elimination of excess demand. Stopping an inflation when that inflation is expected to continue was shown to be costly,

---

[10]It would seem to be worth recalling at this point our earlier suggestion that, with continued inflation in the late 1960s and through the 1970s, the "high" observed interest rates could have been expected to contain a substantial inflation premium.

necessitating an increased unemployment rate during the typically pro-tracted adjustment period. Given the importance of the link between the inflation rate and the unemployment rate, we focused a good bit of our attention on the nature of that link—the subject of a large and growing body of literature on the *Phillips curve*. We looked at both the short- and long-run properties of the Phillips curve, reviewing the conflict between sup-porters of the "natural rate" hypothesis and those who believe there is some long-run trade-off between unemployment and inflation. It was clear that the long-run Phillips curve is substantially more steeply sloped than the short-run schedule, strictly limiting the government's ability to lower un-employment permanently by accelerating inflation. On the other hand, ef-forts to slow a well-established inflation by reducing the growth rate of demand for output were shown to have a heavy cost in unemployment, suggesting that anti-inflation policies should be enacted only if inflation in-volves significant social costs. That there are important costs, actual and potential, which stem from inflation was explained in the last major section of this chapter.

Finally, we completed our analysis of the role of inflationary expectations by integrating such expectations into the *IS-LM* model. In so doing we verified, in a general equilibrium framework, our earlier partial equilibrium (bond and money market) argument that the existence of inflationary ex-pectations would result in an equilibrium value of the nominal interest rate that exceeds the real rate by the expected rate of inflation.

Questions

1. Explain the demand-pull and cost-push theories of inflation. For policy purposes, does it matter whether an unwanted inflation is of the cost-push or demand-pull variety?

2. Explain the link between the rate of increase in money wages, the rate of growth in productivity, and inflation.

3. Can inflation continue indefinitely without an increase in the nominal money supply? Explain.

4. Can a demand-pull inflation persist without the involvement of aggregate supply and labor supply? Explain why you would argue that demand-pull and cost-push models represent incomplete explanations of inflation.

5. It is often argued that moderate inflation (say, 3 to 4 percent annually) is a small price to pay for a buoyant level of economic activity when a substantial increase in unemployment would be necessary to maintain price stability. Evaluate that argument in light of what you know about the Phillips curve.

6. Many people appear to believe that inflation is a universal evil, reducing every-one's real well-being. Briefly dispel that notion and then give some legitimate reasons for the widespread concern over inflation.

7. What do inflationary expectations have to do with your answer to Question 6? Is a perfectly anticipated inflation of 50 percent per year more or less harmful than an unanticipated inflation of 10 percent per year?

Suggested Readings

Beals, Ralph E. "Concentrated Industries, Administered Prices and Inflation: A Survey of Recent Empirical Research." Report prepared for the Council on Wage and Price Stability, Washington, D.C., June 1975.

Bronfenbrenner, Martin, and Holzman, F. D. "Survey of Inflation Theory." *American Economic Review,* October 1963, pp. 593–661.

Eisner, Robert. "Factors Affecting the Level of Interest Rates." Reprinted in *Monetary Economics, Readings on Current Issues,* edited by William E. Gibson and George G. Kaufman, pp. 303–310. New York: McGraw-Hill, 1971.

Fisher, Irving. "A Statistical Relation Between Unemployment and Price Changes." Reprinted in the *Journal of Political Economy* 81 (1973): pp. 496–502.

Friedman, Milton. "The Role of Monetary Policy." *American Economic Review,* March 1968, pp. 1–17.

Frisch, Helmut. "Inflation Theory 1963–1975: A 'Second Generation' Survey."*Journal of Economic Literature* 15 (1977): 1289–1317.

Gibson, William E. "Interest Rates and Monetary Policy." *Journal of Political Economy* 78 (1970): pp. 431–455.

Humphrey, Thomas M. *Essays on Inflation,* Federal Reserve Bank of Richmond.

Johnson, Harry G. "A Survey of Theories of Inflation." In *Essays in Monetary Economics.* Cambridge, Mass.: Harvard University Press, 1969.

Laidler, David and Parkin, Michael. "Inflation: A Survey." *Economic Journal* 85 (1975): pp. 741–809.

Lucas, Robert E. and Rapping, Leonard A. "Price Expectations and the Phillips Curve." *American Economic Review,* June 1969, pp. 342–350.

Chapter 12   Policy Options and Stagflation

Why has the United States economy been plagued with such a persistent inflation? What can be done to stop it? Because inflation is burdensome, why have the steps necessary to stop inflation not been taken? Most of you have probably had questions similar to these drift through your mind. This chapter may reinforce your conclusions, and may suggest some additional possibilities to you as it focuses on the options that are available to macroeconomic policy makers.

Restricting Demand

For an inflation to persist unabated, the nominal value of aggregate demand must be permitted to rise at a rate consistent with anticipated inflation. Ultimately, this is possible only with a corresponding expansion in the money stock. It would seem, then, that to slow an inflation all that is necessary is a simple reduction in the rate of growth of aggregate demand. Unfortunately, slowing the growth of aggregate demand also reduces economic activity, and for an extended time period employment and output may be reduced far more dramatically than the inflation rate, as restrictive policy actions are taken.

In the 1970s, there were two periods when the economy could be viewed as reacting to restrictive stabilization policy, one in 1970–1972 and the other in 1974–1977. Figure 12–1 shows, on a semiannual basis, the resulting changes in employment and the inflation rate. The plots in that figure are consistent with our claims that restrictive policies, which raise unemployment, serve to reduce the inflation rate. Because the imposition of wage and price controls in the fall of 1971 may have distorted the adjustment path represented in part (a) of our figure, the plot in part (b) is a better indication of the inflation/unemployment response pattern when demand is restricted. In either case, it is clear that the adjustment period for reducing the inflation rate is quite long. In part (b) of Figure 12—1 inflation remained in the 5 percent range even after three and one-half years of unemployment in excess of 5½ percent of the labor force (each dot along the plotted schedule shows a semiannual observation). As our discussion of Okun's Law in Chapter 3 pointed out, each percentage point increase in the unemployment rate translates into an approximately 2½ percentage point decline in output. The *extent* of labor and product market slack and the *duration* of reduced economic activity that must be endured to slow inflation is clearly oppressive. With excessive inflation a top priority concern in 1980, the Congressional Joint Economic Committee sponsored a study by Data Resources (a well-known econometric modeling concern) which indicated that restrictive demand policies would have to hold the unemployment rate at 7.5 percent for five years in order to reduce the "core" rate of inflation (estimated to be 9 percent at that time) by one percentage point. Other investigations, with theoretical foundations that reflect Keynesian, monetarist, and other persuasions, have generated differing estimates of the employment and output

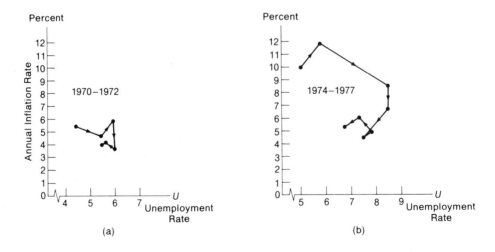

Figure 12—1 / Unemployment and Inflation in Two Contraction Periods

losses that would be necessitated by inflation-slowing restrictions in aggregate demand. Even the most optimistic studies indicate, though, that disinflation is a slow and costly process.[1]

Of course, the long time interval required for slowing inflation is a reflection of the slowness with which inflationary expectations are revised downward (the slowness with which the short-run Phillips curve shifts downward as demand restriction induces a clockwise loop adjustment toward a new equilibrium with unemployment at the natural rate and inflation slowed). Frequent policy statements alluding to the need to "bite the bullet," to "tighten our belts," and so on, in order to succeed in the battle against inflation, are reflections of the sizable and persistent burdens that combating inflation through demand-restricting actions involves.

Wage-Price Controls

Probably no other action so clearly reveals the frustration policy makers have suffered from the inability of the economy to enjoy simultaneously both high employment and price stability as their well-intentioned efforts to improve economic conditions by intervening directly in the market processes that determine wages and prices. Most recently, in August 1971, the United States adopted a wage-price freeze which was followed by multiple "phases" of *controlled* adjustments in wages and prices. Those controls, which were allowed to lapse in 1973, were imposed to help end the persistent inflation that began in the mid-1960s.

The rationale for wage-price controls differs with the explanation of inflation. Many of the advocates of wage-price controls believe that, in large part, inflation is the result of labor unions and large corporations using the monopoly power they possess to push up wages and prices; that is, in recent years we have been suffering from cost-push inflation. They contend that, if wage and price controls are employed to prevent the further use of that market power, cost-push pressures on the price level can be relieved.

In the last chapter, we briefly reviewed the theoretical arguments that are frequently employed to reject the cost-push explanation of inflation. Of course, there is no way we can *prove* whether the cost-push thesis is invalid or not. Even if the arguments of the critics of the cost-push thesis are correct, it may not be necessary to reject wage-price controls, "properly applied," as an aid in controlling inflation. We have seen that once a demand-pull-initiated inflation is under way, if labor and employers adapt their expectations to that experience (shifting the aggregate supply curve upward in anticipation of further price increases), inflation can continue unabated

---

[1]For a survey of recent studies of the short-run costs of reducing the inflation rate see Laurence H. Meyer and Robert H. Rasche, "On the Costs and Benefits of Anti-Inflation Policies," *Federal Reserve Bank of St. Louis Review,* February 1980, pp. 3–14. See also Phillip Cagan, *Persistent Inflation: Historical and Policy Essays* (New York: Columbia University Press, 1979), pp. 242–247.

long after the economy has been purged of excess demand. Further, with well-established inflationary expectations slow to adjust, we have seen that a restrictive aggregate demand policy can slow the inflation rate only with a lengthy adjustment period during which unemployment is substantially increased. If, somehow, expectations could be altered more rapidly, the adjustment period during which the economy suffers the twin evils of inflation and excessive unemployment could be shortened. In support of wage-price controls, it can be argued that if, in conjunction with a restrictive demand policy, the government should announce in the most convincing possible way that inflation was going to be stopped, backing up that claim by the application of strict wage-price controls, expectations might adjust far more rapidly than they would if sole reliance were placed on restrictive monetary and fiscal policy. Where expectations of inflation have become embedded in long-lived contracts, the inflationary wage and price increases those contracts provide can be circumvented, at least in part, with the application of wage-price controls.

To the extent that wage-price controls, by modifying inflation expectations, shorten the adjustment period required for lowering the inflation rate to the target level, they might be a valuable supplement to tools for controlling aggregate demand. However, most economists would agree there are a number of reasons that such controls should never be looked upon as a substitute for proper control of aggregate demand. If applied during a period when aggregate demand is excessive, those controls can only *repress* the officially measured symptoms (price increases) of excess demand. More important in that case are the well-known side effects of holding prices below market-clearing levels.

Figure 12—2 shows one market in which controls hold the official product price (P_c) below the market-clearing level $(P_{eq}.)$. In this market, price cannot serve its normal rationing function because, at the legal ceiling price, the quantity supplied (Q_c) falls far short of the quantity demanded (Q_d).

If wage-price controls are imposed when there is generalized excess demand, many individual product markets (like the one in Figure 12—2) will

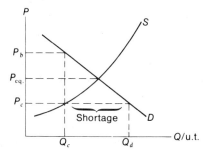

Figure 12—2 / A Market with Price Control

suffer shortages. With shortages at the legal price level, waiting lines and waiting lists will form to ration the short supplies. Black markets will develop as enterprising middlemen attempt to profit from those shortages. Looking again at Figure 12—2, with supply restricted to output level Q_c by the price ceiling (in effect the supply schedule becomes vertical above P_c at output level Q_c), society would be willing to pay a black market price of up to P_c and still take the full quantity producers are willing to supply. This price ceiling would reward lawbreakers while providing society with a reduced quantity of the price-controlled product.

Product quality is also likely to deteriorate as producers seek to escape the lid on prices. By reducing quality (fewer nuts in the candy bar, thinner chrome plating on auto parts, lower quality paper in books, and so on), producers can permit the increase in effective prices that market forces call for. Because a host of techniques are available for circumventing official price ceilings, effective prices cannot be strictly constrained for an extended time period, at least not without an army-sized network of enforcement agents that would be intolerably costly. (Even with public cooperation spurred by patriotism, the price control program instituted during World War II required a staff of 60,000!)

Wage controls are equally difficult to enforce. With excess demand in the labor market at the legal wage rate, nonwage benefits to labor (a company car, more stock options, longer paid vacations, and so on) will rise to attract the volume of labor services firms want to hire. These alternative forms of labor compensation contribute to employers' costs (thus required prices) just as wages do.

Experience in a number of countries has shown that eventually people always find ways to circumvent price constraints that attempt to hold prices below market-clearing levels for long time periods. It is frequently concluded on this basis that controls simply do not work; at best, they simply postpone inflation. Most economists, rather than being disturbed by that experience, find it pleasing! Why? A government cannot impose controls on the *general* price (or wage) level, but must apply controls on individual prices. If those controls were effective over an extended period, then the price signals that a market economy depends on to shift resources in concert with changes in society's wants would not be operative; i.e., with individual prices controlled, *relative* prices cannot change to induce changes in the composition of production. The social loss from price-control induced resource misallocation is minimized if techniques for maintaining relative flexibility in *effective* prices (techniques for circumventing controls) can be devised.

With circumvention the likely result of an extended application of wage-price controls, and with a costly distortion of resource usage likely in the long run if circumvention does not occur, controls must have their beneficial effect on expectations in a relatively short time interval (six months, one year?). Whether that is possible or not is an issue that cannot be settled unequivocally on the basis of our experience with controls.

In the meantime, there is some evidence available on the success of the controls instituted in the United States in August 1971. Survey data compiled by Dun & Bradstreet and by the University of Michigan Survey Research Center indicated that there were "modest" declines in the inflation rate *anticipated* by business purchasing agents and by households as controls were applied.[2] There are also a number of econometric studies that found inflation rates lower (with controls) than would have been predicted by price regressions in the absence of controls.[3] On the other hand, there is evidence that the controls only temporarily suppressed inflation and that catch-up wage and price increases occurred after removal of the controls, leaving the long-run inflation rate unaffected. For example, a study by Gordon estimated that controls lowered the actual inflation rate by about 3½ percent between mid-1971 and the third quarter of 1973, but that prices increased by about 3½ percent more than they would have in the absence of controls in the two years following removal of controls.[4] Moreover, there was growing dissatisfaction with the 1971–72 controls program, suggesting that it was maintained too long; that the distortions of normal economic processes engendered by those controls outweighed any continuing beneficial influence they had on the momentum of inflationary forces.

With a sharp acceleration in the inflation rate after the removal of controls, their credibility, and thus their potential for affecting expectations, had to suffer. With the passage of time, though, the unimpressive performances of the control programs used in the past tend to fade in the social memory, setting the stage for more insistent calls for wage and price restraints during subsequent inflations. Of course, there are always supporters (including prominent political figures) of what appear to be obvious and simple means of maintaining wage and price stability.

Reconciling High Employment with Price Stability. The evidence reviewed in Chapter 11 on the relationship between unemployment and price stability indicated that the United States must tolerate a relatively high level of measured unemployment, probably in excess of 5 percent of the labor force, if approximate price stability is to be maintained. Because of the high "natural rate" of unemployment, some economic commentators favor the untenable combination of a stimulative monetary and fiscal policy stance with wage and price controls. A more promising alternative, however, recognizes that the natural rate of unemployment is not the proverbial immovable object but, in fact, may be reduced (the long-run Phillips curve, whatever its slope, shifted leftward) by specific policy actions.

[2]See Phillip Cagan, "Controls and Monetary Policy, 1969–1973," in *A New Look at Inflation*, ed. Phillip Cagan, et al. (Washington, D.C.: American Enterprise Institute, 1973), p. 13.

[3]See Council of Economic Advisers, *Economic Report of the President* (Washington, D.C.: U.S. Government Printing Office, 1973), pp. 56–64.

[4]Robert J. Gordon, "The Impact of Aggregate Demand on Prices," *Brookings Papers on Economic Activity* 6 (1975): Table 5; p. 641.

Remember that the residue of measured unemployment which remains when aggregate demand begins exerting strong upward pressure on the price level is not the same animal that Keynes was concerned with in *The General Theory* (it is not the involuntary unemployment that, in our aggregate model, left labor off its supply curve with the real wage above the market-clearing level). Rather than reflecting a chronic aggregate shortage of jobs, this residual unemployment is a reflection of the difficulty of matching workers with available job openings and keeping them happily employed. This residual unemployment could be reduced by: (1) shortening the search time required for a job seeker (whether a job changer or a new entrant into the labor force) to find acceptable employment; and (2) reducing job instability, the frequency of job changes.[5]

Any program that improves the flow of information required for matching job openings and workers would reduce the time labor spends in job search and thus reduce search unemployment. Advocates of plans for regional "job banks" that keep computerized listings of job openings and applicants have such an objective in mind. To the extent that geographical barriers prevent the filling of job vacancies with qualified unemployed workers, the government could provide relocation aid in the form of loans or grants.[6]

An improved flow of job information could be of particular benefit to unskilled young workers whose average job search period is longer than the period for older adults. However, even with improved job information many economists feel that the search period for young workers would remain relatively high because of the effect of minimum wage laws. Young workers, particularly new entrants into the labor force, are low-skill workers. If the value of a young worker's contribution to a firm's production (his value marginal product) is less than the wage a minimum wage law requires the firm to pay for his services, he will not be hired. Thus, minimum wage laws that hold young workers' *reservation wages* above the market value of their output in some job slots limit the number of jobs available to those workers. Relaxing the minimum wage requirement for young workers would open up those job slots.

Job instability (frequency of job changes) is a reflection of job dissatisfaction. It is a characteristic common to low-skill jobs (clerk, deliveryman, manual laborer) that offer little hope of improved status in the future and, in many cases, scant economic advantage over the support available from public assistance programs. That unskilled workers change jobs frequently and often deliberately *choose* unemployment (or intermittent employment to take advantage of unemployment compensation) should come as no great surprise; self-interest is a potent force in rich and poor alike. In recent years,

---

[5]For a far more complete treatment of proposals to lower the U.S. unemployment rate, see Martin Feldstein, "The Economics of the New Unemployment," *The Public Interest,* Fall 1973, pp. 3–42.

[6]Even now, federal income tax deductions are allowed for relocation expenses involved in a move of more than fifty miles.

the United States has experimented with manpower training programs in the hope that, with higher skill levels, previously low-skilled labor would find more rewarding, hence more stable employment.[7] As a complementary policy, some analysts have advocated raising the costs of unemployment by reducing support levels in the public assistance programs relative to the rewards from continued employment. It is also worth noting that an improved flow of information in the labor market could reduce the frequency of job changes by allowing workers to better select the jobs they accept.

Special unemployment problems exist because some workers suffer from mental or physical disabilities. Many individuals with serious disabilities that limit their productive capacity rarely find employment even in the tightest labor market. Policies that can improve employment prospects for the disabled include vocational rehabilitation programs and direct government subsidization of employment of the handicapped. The subsidy could take the form of payments to employers in private industry who use handicapped labor or could be paid directly to handicapped workers who are employed by government.

Our list of specific explanations for the extensive measured unemployment we observe in the United States, even in inflation periods, could be extended easily, for example, by pointing out that the seasonal nature of some employment (notably in construction) contributes to measured unemployment. We could also list many more policy proposals for reducing unemployment. This brief review is sufficient, however, to demonstrate that there are programs that can improve the unemployment/inflation trade-off. The relevant question for government policy makers is whether the social benefits to be derived from implementing any selected program for reducing unemployment exceed the social costs of that program. Only if they do would society be better off with the program implemented. It is clear, for example, that vocational rehabilitation raises the skill levels of the disabled, but vocational rehabilitation is costly. In many cases, the productivity gain from rehabilitative efforts cannot cover the cost of those efforts. Society at large might be better off providing direct support to the disabled in those cases rather than depending on vocational rehabilitation to raise incomes to an acceptable level.[8]

Productivity Problems and Prospects

Productivity increases reflect the relationship between output and one or more of the factor inputs used to produce that output. The most frequently cited productivity measure is *labor productivity,* the ratio of output to labor

---

[7]A pessimistic view of the effectiveness of manpower training programs appears in Robert Hall, "Prospects for Shifting the Phillips Curve Through Manpower Policy," *Brookings Papers on Economic Activity* 3 (1971): 659–701.

[8]If the psychological well-being of disabled workers is enhanced by self-sufficiency, social welfare could be enhanced by providing vocational rehabilitation even in cases where the market value of productivity gains falls short of the cost of rehabilitation.

input. At a number of points we have called attention to the role of changes in labor productivity in economy-wide adjustments. For example, we have pointed out the link between labor productivity on the one hand, and labor's real wage reward for working and the aggregate supply of output on the other. Productivity improvements, we noted, lead to increases in real wages and an increased aggregate supply of goods and services.

Of even more immediate interest, we have noted the link between changes in money wages, changes in labor productivity, and changes in prices; money wage increases in excess of productivity growth were deemed "inflationary" as firms have to increase prices to maintain their profits under such circumstances. With labor costs making up the bulk (about three-fourths) of total factor costs, and with other factor charges a relatively stable fraction of total costs, the rate of increase in prices $(\dot{P}/P)$ is equal to the difference between the rate of increase in money wages $(\dot{W}/W)$ and the rate of growth in labor productivity (λ). That is, the inflation rate is

$$\frac{\dot{P}}{P} = \frac{\dot{W}}{W} - \lambda \qquad\qquad [12\text{--}1]$$

According to this equation, a money wage increase of 8 percent annually with a 3 percent growth in labor productivity translates into a 5 percent price increase. In contrast, with a 2 percent rise in labor productivity, the associated rate of price increase would be 6 percent.

The equation above indicates, then, that for any *given* rate of wage increases (as set, say, by prior contractual agreement or by expectations) the inflation rate is raised by one percentage point for every one percentage point decline in the rate of labor productivity growth. In like fashion, an increased rate of productivity growth would correspond to a lowered inflation rate corresponding to any ongoing rate of wage increase.

Productivity Growth in the Past

Figure 12—3 provides a plot of labor productivity in the private business sector over the interval 1947–1979. The long-run rate of productivity increases followed the trend line, based on a 3.2 percent annual rate of growth, rather closely until 1967. Since then the rate of productivity growth has slowed decisively. The annual rate of labor productivity growth in private businesses slowed to 2.2 percent in the 1967–1972 period, to 1.2 percent in the 1972–1978 period, was negative in 1978, and remained so in 1979. With rapid increases in money wages in recent years, many view the slowdown in labor productivity growth as a significant contributor to our sustained rapid inflation.

Possible Causes of the Decline in Productivity. The sources of improvements in labor productivity are: (1) an enlargement in the quantity of capital that

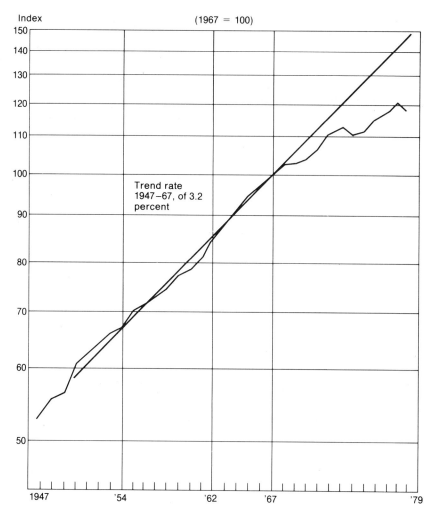

**Figure 12—3 / Output per Hour in Private
Business Sector 1947–79 Actual Levels and 1947–67 Trend**

Source: Bureau of Labor Statistics

each unit of labor has available to work with, or an improvement in its quality; (2) an improvement in the quality of labor itself; or (3) increased efficiency in combining labor and capital (often referred to as "organizational" improvements). Specific reasons for the recent decline in labor's rate of productivity growth must fall within these categories and a number of possibilities have been investigated.

The Cyclical View. Productivity growth usually slows (or even becomes negative) during high employment periods near the end of business expansion and as the economy sinks into recession periods. During recoveries, though, productivity growth accelerates to maintain the trend rate of increase in productivity. An important reason for the cyclical pattern, first confronted in Chapter 3, is the business practice of "hoarding" labor. Because of the search and training costs involved in replenishing their labor force when business expands, firms are reluctant to lay off workers (particularly skilled workers) during business contractions. Hence, with labor less intensively used, labor productivity declines during a contraction. On the other hand, sizable output increases are possible with little increase in *measured* labor usage in the early stages of recovery from a recession as hoarded labor is utilized more and more intensively. The large gains in labor productivity end, of course, as labor becomes fully utilized so productivity gains decline as the expansion continues. It is also notable that a sizable portion of labor employment is of the "overhead" variety (such as management), and there is little change in this form of employment as output varies over the "business cycle." The productivity of this labor declines, then, as output falls, and rises as output expands.

Table 12—1 shows the behavior of productivity in previous contractions and expansions from World War II until 1979. In that table, expansions and contractions are treated separately and are divided to show the annual growth rates of labor productivity in the first and second half of each period.

Table 12—1 / Average Annual Rates of Change in Labor Productivity (Output Per Hour) During Business Cycle Expansions and Contractions, Private Business Sector

Expansions			Contractions		
Period	Annual Rates of Change (Percent)		Period	Annual Rates of Change (Percent)	
(Year: Quarter)	First Half	Second Half	(Year: Quarter)	First Half	Second Half
1945:4–1948:4	—	3.0	1948:4–1949:4	−1.4	5.1
1949:4–1953:3	5.8	2.7	1953:3–1954:2	−1.2	1.2
1954:2–1957:3	3.5	2.2	1957:3–1958:2	2.0	2.4
1958:2–1960:2	4.4	1.3	1960:2–1961:1	−1.4	2.4
1961:1–1969:4	4.3	2.0	1969:4–1970:4	0.4	2.5
1970:4–1973:4	3.8	1.1	1973:4–1975:1	−4.0	−0.9
1974:4–1979:1	4.0	0.6	—	—	—

The figures in the table indicate that, in all cases, productivity rose much faster in the first half of expansions than in the second, with productivity rising much more slowly in the second half. During the first half of contractions, productivity rose very slowly or fell. In the second half of all but the last recession productivity began to rise rapidly. The 1973–1975 recession and subsequent recovery are distinctive (1) in the extent of the productivity decline, and (2) in the continuation of the decline in productivity in the second half of the recession. Productivity growth in the second half of the subsequent inflation was also notably weak. The evidence in this table and in Figure 12—3 suggests strongly that, rather than cyclical weakness in productivity growth, we have experienced a structural shift in the growth path of productivity with the new expansion path well below the one that existed through 1967. Because of the close association between business cycle developments and labor productivity, for a time it was easy to argue that the depressed post-1967 pattern of labor productivity growth was the result of depressed economic activity. However, with the data in labor productivity changes in the post-1975 expansion now in, that view is no longer tenable.

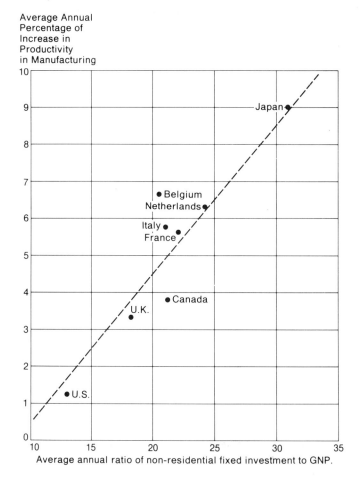

**Figure 12—4 / Investment and Productivity
in the United States and Other Nations, 1960–1976**

Source: Productivity Perspectives, American Productivity Center, Inc. Reprinted in Federal Reserve Bank of Kansas City *Economic Review*. November 1979, Washington, D.C.: U.S. Government.

Capital Formation's Role. Investment can raise labor productivity in two ways. First, if investment adds to the capital stock faster than the labor force expands, each unit of labor (on average) has more capital to work with and, consequently, enjoys a higher average and marginal productivity. In addition, it is through investment that new and technologically superior capital is put in place, again raising labor productivity. With capital formation capable of providing labor with both more and better production facilities, labor productivity can be expected to rise with the capital to labor ratio. The capital stock to labor force ratio peaked in the United States in 1974 and has declined since that time,[9] leading to widespread concern over the "weakness" of investment flows.

Figure 12—4 compares U.S. investment and productivity patterns over the period 1960–1976 to the comparable values for seven other countries. While charts cannot establish causality, the lesson that this commonly employed chart conveys on the link between the portion of a country's output allocated to investment and its rate of productivity growth is clear-cut. With a decidedly smaller share of GNP going into capital formation in the United States than in the other countries represented in that chart, productivity's growth rate has been correspondingly lower. In the interest of spurring investment and productivity growth, Congress has been confronted with a number of proposals including liberalization of the investment tax credit, revisions of depreciation schedules, and tax exemption of a limited volume of interest income on savings as an incentive to savers to provide more funds for business investment use.[10]

Research and Development. In modern economies, technological improvements in plant and equipment, in processes, and in business organization are often the result of research and development programs. Increased funding of such programs might be expected to bring about more rapid productivity gains. On the other hand, with a lowered level of outlays on research and development, productivity gains from that source might falter. Figure 12—5 shows that, compared to the expansion trajectory in the preceding decade and a half, outlays on research and development have slackened substantially since the late 1960s.

Environmental and Safety Regulations. The use of resources for pollution abatement, for improving safety and health conditions in the work place, and for attending to the administrative requirements of government regulations diverts businesses and the labor they employ from the production of *measured* output (cars, houses, etc.) to unmeasured production (cleaner air

---

[9]See U.S. Congress, *Joint Economic Committee Report, 1979,* Report No. 96–44, Washington, D.C.: U.S. Government, pp. 59–60.

[10]A critical evaluation of capital formation's potential to enhance productivity is provided in Edward F. Denison, "The Contributions of Capital to Economic Growth," *The American Economic Review,* May 1980, pp. 220–224.

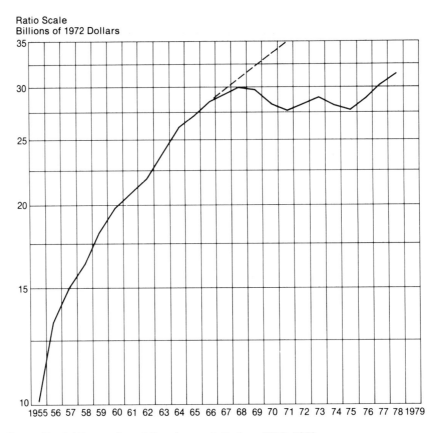

Ratio Scale
Billions of 1972 Dollars

Figure 12—5 / Research and Development Outlays 1955–1978

Source: U.S. National Science Foundation

and water, enhanced worker safety and health, etc.). It is frequently claimed that regulations in these areas have slowed the growth of labor productivity, and there is some empirical support for these claims. By way of example, Denison has estimated that pollution abatement regulations have reduced the annual growth rate of labor productivity by .15 percentage points, and health and safety requirements by .07 percentage points.[11] These costs lend credence to consideration of proposals to postpone achievement of certain pollution abatement and work safety goals.

Labor Force Developments. In recent years we have witnessed a now well-known increase in the proportions of the labor force comprised of women and young workers. To the extent that this compositional change in the work force lowers experience levels, productivity is apt to suffer. Figure 12—6 shows the magnitude of these phenomena.

[11]Edward F. Denison, "Effects of Selected Changes in the Institutional and Human Environment Upon Output Per Unit of Input," *Survey of Current Business,* January 1978, pp. 21–44.

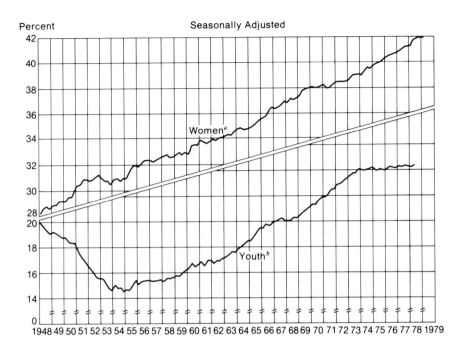

Percent   Seasonally Adjusted

Figure 12—6 / Women and Youth as a Percentage of the Labor Force

[a]Ratio of women in the civilian labor force to total civilian labor force.
[b]Ratio of the civilian labor force age 16–24 to total civilian labor force.
 Latest data plotted: 2nd quarter
Source: U.S. Department of Labor

The portion of women and young workers in the labor force is naturally limited; indeed, since 1973 the fraction of the labor force comprised of young workers has been quite stable, so productivity cannot decline indefinitely as a consequence of these compositional changes in the labor force. In fact, as younger workers mature and as the labor force participation rate of women levels off, the resulting older and more experienced work force should enjoy enhanced productivity.

Energy's Role. An embargo on U.S. oil purchases from OPEC would reduce the volume of oil available for use with labor and other production factors. A substantial rise in oil prices (relative to other factor costs) could result, too, in a cutback in the volume of oil used with other resources as firms economize on the use of inputs that become relatively more expensive. In either case, if labor has less energy to work with, labor's productivity is reduced. The extent to which OPEC's actions have depressed labor productivity is a matter of controversy. Studies by William Fellner and Edward Denison, covering several years in the mid-1970s, indicate that energy problems only slightly reduced labor productivity's annual growth rate (by .3

and .2 of a percentage point, respectively), while studies by Rasche and Tatom, by Peter Clark, and others have found much larger effects (for example a 1.3 percent per year decline in labor productivity's growth over 1973–1978, according to Rasche and Tatom).[12]

Summary

If the policy choices available for dealing with the inflation and unemployment ills of the 1970s did not face serious shortcomings, progress toward curing those problems would surely have been apparent by the end of the decade. Of course, the impediments are substantial. Most notable in the case of the policy tools employed in the past, restrictive demand policies impose harsh employment and production costs on the economy over an extended time interval, and wage-price controls can cause serious distortions in market processes. In turn, with restrictions on aggregate demand the slowdown in inflation is apt to come after the output and employment response (unfortunately, for an administration that is combatting inflation), and bursts of repressed inflation after the removal of wage-price controls can offset any apparent reduction in inflation while controls were in effect.

There are also some nontraditional, supply-oriented possibilities for dealing with our inflation and unemployment problems. Included are schemes to improve information flows and to make some specific groups more employable, say, through manpower training programs. In addition, there are possibilities for stimulating aggregate supply to slow price increases by spurring productivity growth. In this regard, there are current efforts to spur saving and investment through tax relief on interest income, through alterations in the investment tax credit, and through changes in business depreciation charges. Unfortunately, "supply control" policies are apt to require a very extended time interval to exert a sizable effect on employment and the inflation rate, and the costs associated with some proposed supply side policy actions may exceed the value of their benefits.

Not unexpectedly, the frustrations stemming from a persistent period of excessive inflation and excessive unemployment combined has evoked an explosion of specific policy proposals. This chapter has attempted to view

---

[12]For discussions of the results cited see William Fellner, "The Declining Growth of American Productivity: An Introductory Note, "in *Contemporary Economic Problems 1979*, p. 8; Edward F. Denison, "Where Has Productivity Gone?" in *U.S. Productive Capacity: Estimating the Utilization Gap.* (Washington University: Center for the Study of American Business, 1977), p. 76; idem, "The Puzzling Drop in Productivity," op. cit., p. 62, and idem, "Explanations of Declining Productivity Growth," op. cit., p. 15–18; Robert Rasche and John Tatom, "The Effects of the New Energy Regime on Economic Capacity, Production, and Prices" and "Energy Resources and Potential GNP" in *U.S. Productive Capacity;* and Peter Clark, "A New Measure of Potential Output," U.S. Congress, Joint Economic Committee, *Hearings on the Economic Report of the President,* 95th Congress, 1st session, 1977. Also see John Tatom, "The Productivity Problem," *Federal Reserve Bank of St. Louis Review,* September 1979, pp. 10–15.

in some detail the most important choices that are available to policy makers. A more comprehensive shopping list of policy proposals would have to be expanded to include but not be limited to: (1) restrictions on the market power of business and labor to induce more (competitive) price responsiveness to changes in demand; (2) removal of legislative impediments (such as minimum wage laws) to wage and price adjustments; (3) removal of barriers to the importation of cheaper foreign products; (4) steps to limit our dependence on a cartelized foreign oil market; (5) instead of controls, wage-price *guidelines* which businesses and labor could be urged to follow; and (6) alternative forms of business organization in which labor participates in the decision-making process with management.

What specific set of policy choices an economic analyst favors differs primarily with his or her view about the source of sustained inflation, that is, whether demand or supply (cost) is viewed as the villain in the inflation process. No matter what specific proposals economists support, they are generally pessimistic with regard to the near-term prospects for the economy. A typical view is that of Robert Solow who has argued that "Our inflation has been building for 15 years. There is no mechanical symmetry in such matters, but it would be reasonable to hope to eliminate it in about the same length of time."[13] Perhaps by the time you are reading this text prospects will be more pleasant.

Questions

1. Discuss the costs and benefits of restricting aggregate demand in order to slow inflation.

2. Taking account of the timing of the responses in inflation and unemployment (employment) to changes in aggregate demand, explain what might be meant by the term "political business cycle."

3. Discuss the costs and benefits of wage-price controls.

4. What does the rate of productivity growth have to do with inflation?

5. List and explain three reasons why the growth rate of labor's productivity may have been depressed in recent years.

6. List and explain three proposals you might favor for stimulating productivity growth.

---

[13]Robert M. Solow as quoted in David Mermelstein, "The Threatening Economy," *The New York Times Magazine*, 30 December 1979, p. 14.

Suggested Readings

Denison, Edward F. "Explanations of Declining Productivity Growth." *Survey of Current Business,* August 1979, pp. 1–24.

Denison, Edward F. *Accounting for Slower Economic Growth: The United States in the 1970s.* Washington, D.C.: The Brookings Institution, 1979.

Feldstein, Martin. "The Economics of the New Unemployment." *The Public Interest,* Fall 1973, pp. 3–42.

Fellner, William. *Contemporary Economic Problems 1979.* Washington, D.C.: American Enterprise Institute for Public Policy Research, 1979.

Gordon, Robert T. "The Impact of Aggregate Demand on Prices." *Brookings Papers on Economic Activity* 3 (1975): pp. 616–662.

Meyer, Laurence H., and Rasche, Robert H. "On the Costs and Benefits of Anti-Inflation Policies." *Federal Reserve Bank of St. Louis Review,* February 1980, pp. 3–14.

Perry, George. "Potential Output and Productivity." *Brookings Papers on Economic Activity* 1 (1977): pp. 11–47.

Tatom, John A. "The Productivity Problem." *Federal Reserve Bank of St. Louis Review,* September 1979, pp. 3–16.

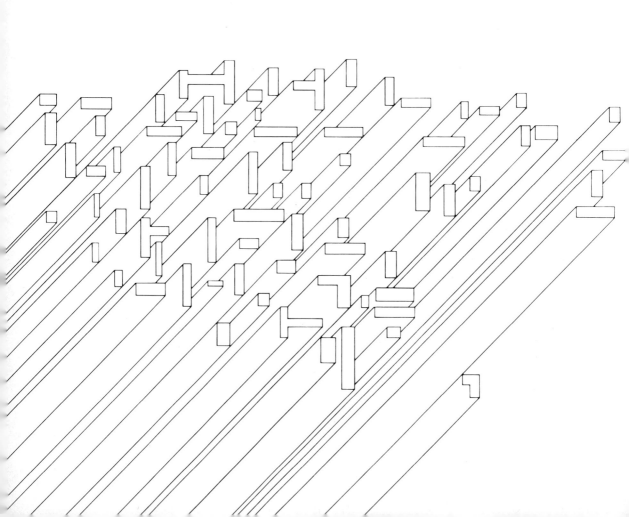

Part IV   **Aggregate Demand Control**

We have already seen that there are serious impediments to controlling the economy through control of aggregate demand. In the last two chapters it has been clearly demonstrated that, when the growth of demand is restrained in an effort to combat inflation, employment and output fall much more quickly than inflation abates. Earlier chapters showed that there are a number of factors other than government policies that influence aggregate demand so that precise control over the level of aggregate demand can be hard to achieve. As illustrations, changes in society's expectations of future ("permanent") income can shift consumption demand; changes in businesses' profit expectations alter investment demand; and shifts in the demand for money (that shift the *LM* schedule) result in altered levels of demand for final goods and services.

In spite of these and some other difficulties, traditional demand control, pursued through monetary (money supply control) and fiscal (budgetary control) policy actions, comprises the primary means by which the government strives to stabilize economic activity. The following two chapters examine the implementation of monetary and fiscal policy actions and consider some additional difficulties that those control tools involve.

Chapter 13   Implementing Monetary Policy

Up to this point, it has simply been asserted that the money supply is under the control of the central bank. In this chapter, that control over the money supply will be explained and the difficulties that monetary policy actions involve will be probed. It will be shown that, while actions of the public and of banks and related financial institutions can influence that money supply, the central bank has the ability to alter and, hence, control the money stock.

The American Banking System

As explained in Chapter 7, the money supply, narrowly defined, consists of currency and the deposits upon which checks can be drawn for the payment of debts to third parties. Commercial banks provide demand deposit accounts upon which checks may be drawn but on which no interest is paid. They also offer automatic transfer from savings (ATS) accounts and negotiable orders for withdrawal (NOW) accounts. Checks may be drawn on both of these and both may pay interest. Noninterest-bearing demand deposits and interest-bearing accounts on which checks may be drawn are also provided by mutual savings banks, savings and loan associations, and credit unions in the form of ATS accounts, NOW accounts, and share draft accounts. At present the bulk of "checkable" deposits in the United States is composed of noninterest-bearing demand deposits in commercial banks. The fractions that are interest-bearing and that are provided by nonbank financial institutions are growing, however.

The agency that monitors and attempts to control the amount of money in circulation—that is, the central bank—is called the Federal Reserve System in the United States. This agency is commonly referred to as "the Fed." At present, the Fed actually keeps track of two narrow measures of the money supply. As explained in Chapter 7, these are M1-A, which measures the consistency of currency in the possession of the nonbank public plus checkable deposits in commercial banks, and M1-B, which adds the volume of checkable deposits at nonbank financial institutions to M1-A.

To understand how the amount of money in circulation is determined, it is useful to think of the institutions that offer checkable deposits as existing primarily to hold deposits for the public (with the associated function of clearing checks drawn against those deposits) and to extend credit to the public. Remember that, while by drawing a check on a checkable deposit individuals can meet their debts, all other varieties of deposits (for example, passbook savings deposits) must first be converted into money (currency or checkable deposits) before debts can be paid.

Because checkable deposits are money (making up about 70 percent of the total money supply), the financial institutions that provide these deposits play a crucial role in determining the volume of money balances in existence. The supply of money is altered whenever those institutions create or destroy checkable deposits. This is a daily occurence. For example, when a bank extends a loan, it typically does so by merely crediting an approved loan applicant's checking account (a simple bookkeeping entry) with the amount of the loan extended. Since checking account deposits are money, the bank creates money with the stroke of a pen or with an electronic imprint on a computer tape whenever it extends loans. In like fashion, banks and other institutions that provide checkable deposits permit the money supply to shrink whenever they accept repayment of outstanding loans (eliminating checkable deposit liabilities from their books) without extending an equivalent volume of new loans. It is this intrinsic involvement in the money creation (and destruction) process, in conjunction with the important influence of money supply changes on the demand for goods and services, that makes our system of banks and related depository institutions uniquely important in macroeconomics.

The Need for a Central Bank

In the nineteenth and early twentieth centuries, money was provided by a banking system composed of thousands of independent, private banks, each operating in pursuit of profit with financial market forces providing the only central guidance on bank credit extension policy. Throughout that period the U.S. economy suffered from frequent and, on occasion, sizable expansions and contractions. From boom to bust, the profit-maximizing efforts of commercial banks produced large swings in the volume of bank loans, tending to amplify the economy's instability. During expansions, when demand for loans was strong, banks extended large volumes of new loans. This action increased the money supply, contributing to the strength of the expansion and any accompanying inflation. During contractions bank loan officers became more pessimistic about future business conditions and thus about the prudence of extending credit to loan applicants. They allowed their volume of outstanding loans to shrink, which reduced the money supply and amplified the contraction of economic activity.

Further, in the more severe contractions bank failures were commonplace. Such failures contributed to the financial ruin of countless depositors and, by adversely affecting expectations, accentuated the ongoing contraction. "Runs" on banks were frequent, with depositors lining up to convert their deposits into "safe" currency. Unable to honor all deposit liabilities at once, additional banks folded, eroding confidence in the banking system and, thus, in the economy in general.

Aside from cyclical crises in the financial market, it is also worth noting that, over the course of a normal year, there are systematic "seasonal" changes in the demand for money. For example, during the Christmas season the volume of business activity and, thus, of money demand, increases sharply. In the post-Christmas period business activity slumps and money demand falls accordingly. To avoid seasonal periods of money scarcity and surplus, which result in volatile movements in the interest rate, an "elastic" money supply is needed. The unregulated private banking system did not provide the needed elasticity in money supply.

The Federal Reserve System. In 1907, a financial panic in the United States precipitated the failure of an alarming number of commercial banks. Public and congressional disgust with the apparent inadequacy of unrestricted private banking led to the creation in 1913 of the Federal Reserve System. Among its other duties, the Fed was designed to provide an elastic currency and, more importantly, to prevent bank failures, first by setting limits on the amount of credit member banks could extend, and second by serving as a *lender of last resort* to provide funds to banks that faced extraordinarily large withdrawals.

Under the Federal Reserve System, the country was divided into twelve Federal Reserve Districts, each with its own Federal Reserve Bank.[1] This geographically dispersed central bank system is administered from Washington by the presidentially appointed, seven-member Board of Governors of the Federal Reserve System. Direct guidance in administering monetary policy is provided by a twelve-person Federal Open Market Committee, consisting of the Board of Governors and five of the district bank presidents, always including the president of the New York district bank.

---

[1]The twelve Federal Reserve District Banks are located in Boston, New York, Philadelphia, Cleveland, Richmond, Atlanta, Chicago, St. Louis, Minneapolis, Kansas City, Dallas, and San Francisco. In addition to the main district bank, there are a number of branch district banks in other cities.

The Federal Reserve currently performs a variety of services for member commercial banks, nonbank depository institutions, the U.S. government, and the public. The Fed provides currency for the use of financial institutions and the general public, clears and collects checks for depository institutions, provides loans to qualifying depository institutions, and, finally, holds deposits (called reserves) for depository institutions.[2] As a fiscal agent for government, the Fed carries the principal checking accounts of the U.S. Treasury and aids the Treasury in issuing and redeeming government securities. Also, the Federal Reserve Bank of New York acts as the agent of the U.S. Treasury in gold and foreign exchange transactions.

The above list of functions is representative, not exhaustive. In fact, that list fails to spotlight the one most important function of the Federal Reserve System. That function is the regulation of the nation's money supply. We have already used our income determination models to analyze the impact of changes in the nation's money supply. We are now ready to account for the ability of the Fed to deliberately alter the money stock.

A Brief Review of Simple Banking Transactions

Introductory economics courses usually review the mechanics of money creation in a simple setting. Typically, attention is focused on demand deposit money (currency holdings were ignored or assumed to be fixed). As noted above, the Fed holds reserve deposits for member banks and, in actuality, member banks are *required* to maintain reserves against their deposit obligations in a ratio set by the Fed. In simple money supply models, all banks are assumed to be members of the Fed, facing the same required reserve ratio on deposits. Finally, all banks are assumed to put any excess reserves over and above Fed requirements to work earning interest. A simple model based on these assumptions provides valuable insight into the money supply process and sets the stage for more sophisticated views of monetary control.

One Bank's Response to a Deposit Inflow

Within the confines of a simple banking system of the sort outlined above, suppose you deposit one hundred dollars in your checking account at the local bank. Because that bank is an *intermediary* that generates its revenues by lending deposits, by transferring funds from primary lenders to borrowers, it will seek to profitably lend as much of your deposit as it can. If the required reserve ration on banks' demand deposit liabilities is 20 percent,

---

[2]While Federal Reserve System membership entitles the member to all Fed services, there are other means by which such services may be acquired. Notably, nonmembers may obtain currency shipments, check-clearing, and other Fed services through "correspondent" relations with members.

your bank can legally lend up to eighty dollars of your deposit but must hold twenty dollars in reserves.

Table 13—1 / Simplified Balance Sheets for a Member Bank

Balance Sheet before Deposit		Balance Sheet after a $100 Deposit	
Assets	Liabilities	Assets	Liabilities
Reserves $ 200	Demand deposits $1,000	Reserves $ 300	Demand deposits $1,100
Loans and Investments 800		Loans and Investments 800	
$1,000		$1,100	

In Table 13—1, there is a set of simplified balance sheets for your bank, one for the period preceding your $100 deposit and one after. Before your deposit, it is assumed that the bank has $1,000 of demand deposit liabilities. With a 20 percent reserve ratio, the bank must hold $200 in reserves, leaving $800 free for the bank to lend and invest. Because there is an interest (opportunity) cost of holding idle deposits, for your bank to be in equilibrium we have assumed that it will hold no reserves in excess of its legal requirement. Thus, the bank is in equilibrium with a full $800 loaned and invested.

With your deposit of $100, the bank's demand deposit liabilities are increased to $1,000 and its reserves to $300. With deposit liabilities up by $100, *required* reserves are increased, but only by $20, leaving your bank with $80 of *excess* reserves which it can put to work (lend or invest).

Extending a Loan. With eighty dollars of excess reserves, your bank can now lend eighty dollars to any loan applicant it chooses. When the bank extends a loan, it does so by *creating* demand deposits for the loan recipient. The creation of those demand deposits requires nothing more than a set of entries in the bank's balance sheet.

Table 13—2 shows the changes in your bank's balance sheet when it extends an eighty dollar loan. This bank need not worry about holding reserves against the newly created demand deposits because the loan recipient will soon draw a check on those deposits to finance his or her spending. (Why else would he or she pay interest to borrow?) The recipient of the loan applicant's spending will deposit that check in his or her own bank.

Table 13—2 / Changes in a Bank's Balance Sheet When It Extends an $80 Loan

Assets	Liabilities
Loans + $80	Demand + $80 deposits

An Increase in Reserves. Backtrack a moment now and look in more detail at your original one hundred dollar deposit. Suppose that the one hundred dollars represented the payment you received when you sold a government bond to the Federal Reserve System (the Fed, as you may know, regularly buys and sells government bonds). In exchange for the bond, the Fed would have given you a check, drawn on itself, for one hundred dollars. It was when you deposited that one hundred dollar check that your bank's demand deposit liabilities were increased by one hundred dollars. By sending that check back to the Fed, your bank would have its reserve account with the Fed credited for one hundred dollars of added reserves.

By purchasing a bond from you, the Fed has increased the volume of reserves available to your bank and to the entire commercial banking system by one hundred dollars. With a 20 percent reserve ratio, the volume of demand deposit money can increase by a multiple of the increase in reserves, five times the increase in reserves, before all available reserves will be tied up as required reserves.

As we have already seen, with one hundred dollars of new demand deposit liabilities, one hundred dollars of new reserves, and a 20 percent reserve ratio, your bank has eighty dollars of excess reserves that it can lend, creating eighty dollars more of new demand deposits in the process, but that is not the end of the money expansion process. When our eighty dollar loan recipient spends his loan proceeds, the recipient of that spending will deposit the eighty dollar check in his or her own bank. As a consequence, that bank's demand deposit liabilities and its reserves are increased by eighty dollars. With a 20 percent reserve ratio, this second bank has sixty-four dollars of excess reserves that it can lend. On making a sixty-four dollar loan, it creates sixty-four dollars of new demand deposit money that, when spent, will be transferred to a third bank which, in turn, will have some fifty-one dollars of excess reserves, and so it goes. The total increase in money supply due to the Fed purchase of a one hundred dollar bond would be:

$$\Delta M = \$100 + \$80 + \$64 + \$51.20 + \$40.96 + \cdots$$

or

$$\Delta M = \$100 \left[1 + .8 + (.8)^2 + (.8)^3 + (.8)^4 + \cdots \right].$$

The geometric series in the brackets can be readily summed to give

$$\Delta M = \$100 \left(\frac{1}{1 - .8} \right) = \$100 \left(\frac{1}{.2} \right) = \$500.$$

(This geometric series, you will note, has the same form as the simple income multiplier expansion process in Chapter 4.)

With the reserve ratio value of .2, a $100 increase in reserves ("high-powered" money) resulted in a $500 increase in the money stock. With excess reserves available to the banking system, commercial banks literally create money with the stroke of a pen as they extend loans. Clearly, if the central bank controls the required reserve ratio (try a reserve ratio of .1 or .3) and the volume of reserves available to the banking system, it can exert control over the money stock in the simple world represented by this rudimentary model. A more realistic model would have to take account of the public's currency holdings, of its possession of a mix of interest-bearing and non-interest-bearing checking accounts, of the existence of nonbank depository institutions that offer checkable accounts, and of the possibility that financial institutions may choose to hold some excess reserves.

A More Realistic Money Supply Model

In reality society now holds its money partly in currency form, partly in noninterest-bearing demand deposits, and partly in interest-bearing accounts on which checks may be drawn. Currency holdings make up about 30 percent of the total money supply and checkable deposits, the remainder. With an increase in the money supply, both currency and checkable deposits can be expected to rise.

It is also worth noting, in the interest of realism, that reserves can be held either in the form of currency (called vault cash) or as reserve deposits in accounts at or monitored by the Fed.[3] Either form of reserves can support (meet the legal reserve requirement on) a multiple volume of checkable deposit money. As in our earlier exercise, with a 20 percent reserve ratio, every dollar of reserves, either vault cash or reserve deposits, can support five dollars of deposits. No wonder reserve money, including currency, is frequently referred to as "high-powered" money or "base" money.

With the institutional information in hand, we can proceed to construct a formal money supply model. In building that model, we will make use of the following definitions:

M = total money supply, narrowly defined (our measure will match the Fed's M1-B definition)
C = total currency held by the public
D = total noninterest-bearing demand deposits held by the public in banks and other depository institutions
N = total interest-bearing demand deposits held by the public in banks and other depository institutions
$M = C + D + N$

---

[3]Technically, reserves may be maintained in balances at the Federal Reserve Bank of which the depository institution is a member or at which it maintains an account. Reserves of nonmember depository institutions may be held at a correspondent depository institution holding required reserves at a Federal Reserve Bank, a Federal Home Loan Bank, or the National Credit Union Administration Central Liquidity Facility.

r = required reserve ratio on checkable deposits, whether they pay interest or not

R = total reserves or base money available to the financial system

R' = total required reserves

c = the ratio of the public's currency holdings to its holdings of noninterest-bearing demand deposits (D)

n = the ratio of the public's holdings of interest-bearing checkable deposits to its holdings of noninterest-bearing demand deposits

RA = total reserve money absorbed by required reserves and public currency holdings

For simplicity, our analysis continues to ignore the existence of time deposits against which checks cannot be drawn and, as indicated above, assumes that all depository institutions face the same reserve requirement on checkable deposits.

An Equilibrium Requirement

There are two absorbers of reserve, or base, money in this money supply model, required reserves and public currency holdings. Therefore, total absorbed reserves are

$$RA = R' + C \qquad\qquad [13\text{--}1]$$

Required reserves, R', are the sum of reserves required on both interest-bearing and noninterest-bearing checkable deposits. That is, $R' = r[D + N]$ and with $N = nD$, required reserves are $R' = rD[1 + n]$. The currency held by the public is $C = cD$. Substituting these expressions for R' and C into Equation (13—1) yields

$$RA = rD[1 + n] + cD \qquad\qquad [13\text{--}2]$$

or

$$RA = D[r(1 + n) + c] \qquad\qquad [13\text{--}3]$$

The Fed provides reserves to the financial system (the ways the Fed can do this are described below) and we have labeled the amount provided R. Should the volume of absorbed reserves *(RA)* fall short of the volume of reserves provided by the Fed *(R)*, there will be excess reserves that can be legally loaned to credit applicants.

The cost to lending institutions of holding excess reserves is the foregone interest income that could be earned by lending those reserves. We will initially assume that, as profit-maximizers, depository institutions always put any excess reserves to work by lending them, thus eliminating the excess. Remember, however, that these lenders are legally required to at least meet the legal reserve ratio even if they must borrow reserves or call in loans to do so. Thus, a desired goal of zero excess reserves may be employed as an equilibrium condition in this money supply model. In formal terms, then, for equilibrium absorbed reserves *(RA)* must equal the volume of reserves *(R)* the central bank makes available, or

$$R = D\big[r(1 + n) + c)\big].$$ [13—4]

The equilibrium volume of noninterest-bearing demand deposits, then, is

$$D = \frac{1}{r(1 + n) + c} \cdot R.$$ [13—5]

The Equilibrium Money Stock. Recalling that currency holdings are $C = cD$ and holdings of interest-bearing checkable deposits are $N = nD$, the money supply *(M = C + D + N)* is

$$M = cD + D + nD$$ [13—6]

or

$$M = D\big[1 + c + n\big]$$ [13—7]

From equations 13—5 and 13—7, the equilibrium money stock is

$$M = \frac{1 + c + n}{r(1 + n) + c} \cdot R.$$ [13—8]

With a 15 percent reserve ratio and assuming that the public's holdings of currency *(C)* and interest-bearing checking deposits *(N)* are, respectively, 30 and 5 percent of noninterest-bearing demand deposits (these are approximately the 1980 values), the equilibrium money supply is

$$M = 2.95R.$$ [13—9]

That is, each dollar of reserves provided by the Fed permits $2.95 of total money holdings by the public. As a simple mathematical proposition, inspection of Equations (13—8) and (13—9) shows clearly that *if the Fed can change the volume of reserves at will, it can change the money stock at will.* Specifically, the change in nominal money supply that can be provided by a change in reserves is

$$\Delta M = \left[\frac{1 + c + n}{r(1 + n) + c)}\right] \cdot \Delta R \quad \text{\textit{credit expansion or money multiplier}}$$ [13—10]

which, with our sample values for c, and r yields

$$\Delta M = 2.95\Delta R.$$ [13—11]

The term in brackets in Equation (13—10) can be called a *credit expansion,* or money supply multiplier $[\Delta M / \Delta R = 1/(c + r(1 + n))]$. It measures the impact on the nominal money stock of a change in the volume of reserves, assuming that, in equilibrium, the banking system holds no excess reserves.

Looking back at Equation (13—8), we also see that, with the volume of reserves fixed, the equilibrium stock of money will change with every change in the required reserve ratio *(r).* A reduction in the reserve ratio would make the denominator of Equation (13—8) smaller, increasing the size of the equilibrium money stock while, conversely, an increase in *r* would reduce the size of the equilibrium money stock. Because the Fed sets the value of the required reserve ratio, it should be able to use that ratio to control the nominal money stock. It is noteworthy, too, that by changing the mix of currency, interest-bearing checking deposits, and noninterest-bearing checking deposits (hence, the value of *c* and *n*), the public can alter the money stock that corresponds to any given volume of reserves.

Monetary Policy: The Tools of Money Supply Control

The Federal Reserve System has three important general instruments for controlling the money supply. They are the *reserve requirement,* the *discount rate,* and *open market operations.* With the money supply model we have just constructed, it is easy to see how these instruments affect the money supply.

The Reserve Requirement

The model developed above provides an accurate representation of the role of the reserve requirement. Still, we will enhance our understanding by carefully outlining the money supply adjustment to a change in the required reserve ratio. Let the financial system be in equilibrium (every lending institution has zero excess reserves) when the required reserve ratio is reduced (say, from 15 percent to 10 percent). Immediately after reduction in the reserve ratio, all lending institutions still possess the same volume of actual reserve holdings while required reserves have been reduced (cut in half!) Each lending institution will have excess reserves, which it can put to work by extending new credit.

As in our simpler, all-bank financial world, when a depository institution extends a loan, it typically does so by merely crediting an approved loan applicant's checkable account with the amount of the granted loan. As indicated before, since such deposits are money, a lender creates money with such bookkeeping entries. After a reserve ratio reduction, system-wide money creation of precisely this nature will continue as long as there are excess reserves in the system. According to Equation (13—8), after the financial system has adjusted to a required reserve ratio reduction from 15 to 10 percent, each dollar of reserves will support $3.33 of money holdings, a substantial increase from the initial $2.95 volume.

Conversely, should the required reserve ratio be increased while the financial system is in equilibrium, every lending institution will be faced with an unallowable reserve deficiency. They can respond by refusing to renew some loan commitments as loans come due, by calling in existing loans, and, temporarily, by borrowing reserves to meet the legal reserve requirement. As loans are repaid, our lender's checkable deposit liabilities are reduced, shrinking the money supply. To complete the system-wide adjustment to an increased reserve ratio, total deposit liabilities would have to fall sufficiently to allow the available volume of reserves to meet the system's increased percentage reserve requirement.

The reserve requirement is indeed under the control of the Board of Governors of the Federal Reserve System. Thus, the reserve requirement could serve as a powerful tool for controlling the money supply, with a reduction in the reserve ratio increasing the money supply and an increase in the reserve ratio reducing that supply.

The Discount Rate

The discount rate is the interest rate at which member banks and some other depository institutions can borrow reserves from the Fed. When an institution borrows at the Fed's "discount window," the Fed extends the approved loan by crediting the borrower's reserve account at the Fed with the amount of the loan. As we have seen, a change in reserves available to the financial system will result in a multiple change in the public's money holdings.

To encourage an increase in the money supply, the Fed can set the discount rate substantially below the short-term interest rate at which lending institutions can, in turn, lend. This strategy can normally be expected to prompt aggressive lenders to borrow reserves at the Fed in order to extend new loans to the public. Conversely, the Fed can induce the repayment of existing reserve loans (reducing reserves in the system and thus the money supply) by setting the discount rate above the rate on short-term credit.

Open Market Operations

Open market operations are the purchase and sale of securities in the open market. In practice, the Fed conducts open market operations by having the New York branch of the Federal Reserve System buy and sell government securities through a small number of firms that specialize in the government securities trade. A purchase of securities by the Fed increases the volume of reserves available to lending institutions and thereby increases lending (creation of checkable deposits). A sale of securities by the Fed drains reserves, inducing a contraction of the money stock.

The Fed may, through the securities specialists with which it deals, exchange securities with lending institutions and with the general public. When the Fed buys government bonds from lending institutions that maintain reserves in the Federal Reserve System, payment is made, in effect, by crediting those institutions' reserve accounts with the Fed for the amount of the Fed's bond purchases. With the financial system in equilibrium prior to the open market purchase, the additional (excess) reserves resulting from that open market purchase will prompt an expansion in the money supply as lending institutions attempt to put their excess reserves to work by extending interest-earning loans.

When the Fed sells securities to lending institutions that maintain reserves with the Fed, the purchasing institutions meet their debt by drawing checks on themselves made out to the Fed. When the Fed receives those checks, it debits the reserve accounts of the institutions on which the checks are drawn for the amount of the bond sale. Beginning in equilibrium, the deficiency of reserves resulting from the Fed's open market sale would prompt a reduction in the volume of outstanding loans (and thus, in the volume of "created" checking account money).

The money supply model we have built indicates that, when open market operations result in security exchanges between the Fed and depository institutions, the total money supply will change by the volume of open market purchases (or sales) times the money supply multiplier. Identical results are forthcoming when the Fed's security exchanges are with the general public.

The Fed would pay for a bond purchase from the general public with a check drawn upon itself. The recipient would deposit that check in his or her own checking account, directly increasing the volume of checking deposits (money) by the amount of the bond purchase and creating *excess reserves* equal to the bond purchase minus the reserve requirement on the bond seller's new deposit. The financial system could then expand its deposit liabilities until the excess reserves are absorbed. Because the open market purchase increases total available reserves by the full amount of the bond purchase, the total money supply can expand by the amount of the bond purchase times the money supply multiplier. You should be able to trace the impact on the money supply of a Fed sale of securities to the public.

Use of the Tools of Monetary Control

In practice, changes in the required reserve ratio are infrequently used in an effort to affect the money supply. The Fed has traditionally claimed that reserve ratio changes are too blunt and crude a tool for active monetary policy use. It is argued that even a small change in the reserve ratio results in undesirably large and abrupt changes in the money supply. In addition, the Fed claims that, because reserve ratio changes "announce" to the public the policy intention of the central bank, they may cause unwanted, potentially destabilizing reactions from the public. Whatever the justification for a policy of disuse, the reserve ratio is altered relatively infrequently.

In contrast, the discount rate is changed fairly often. It should not be assumed, though, that this is evidence of the active use of the discount rate as a money supply control weapon. In fact, the discount rate is generally changed only in response to changes that have already occurred in the market rate of interest. A restrictive monetary stance by the Fed, implemented, say, through open market operations, would cause market interest rates to rise. If the discount rate remains unchanged in the face of such a rise in market rates, depository institutions have an incentive to borrow reserves from the Fed to support an increased volume of loans—loans that, by increasing the money supply, reduce the upward pressure on the interest rate. To avoid such a slippage in its restrictive policy, the Fed must raise the discount rate as the market interest rate rises. In fact, historical observation shows that the discount rate systematically follows movements in market interest rates, reflecting the *passive* role of discount rate changes. In contrast to this typical behavior of the discount rate, in 1978, 1979, and 1980 the Fed found occasion to increase the discount rate dramatically, a full percentage point! Apparently, these were attempts to "announce" that the Fed was serious in its intentions to slow inflation by pursuing a restrictive monetary policy.

The general tool that is actively employed for the day-to-day implementation of monetary policy is open market operations. Because the Fed is continuously *both* buying and selling bonds in the open market, it is easy for the Fed to temporarily mask its policy objectives, preventing the announcement effects on economic behavior that it has traditionally feared.[4] Further, the Fed feels that open market operations are a precision tool, that both large and small desired adjustments in the money stock can be obtained quite precisely through open market purchases and sales. Also, the thrust of policy can be easily reversed with this flexible tool. Finally, it is argued that the initiative for a money supply change lies in the hands of the Fed with open market operations.[5] Thus, the Fed favors the active use of open market operations for monetary policy rather than variations in the reserve ratio or in the discount rate.

---

[4]Many economists believe that the stabilization efforts of the central bank would be enhanced by clear public statements of planned monetary policy actions.

[5]It is claimed that this site of rest for the initiative in money supply changes contrasts with discount rate changes. A change in the discount rate would result in a money supply change only if it *induced* commercial banks to change their volume of borrowing from the Fed. "You can take a horse to water. . . ." Of course, the Fed must also encourage purchases or sales of government securities; and, once it has altered reserves by doing that, the commercial banks can, as we are about to discover, limit the impact of open market operations by changing the volume of excess reserves they hold.

Excess Reserves and the Interest Elasticity of the Money Supply

To simplify matters, we constructed our money supply model assuming that depository institutions try to stay fully loaned, holding zero excess reserves. However, in practice, they typically hold a cushion of excess reserves. To explain that practice, we need to recognize that a depository institution's managers cannot know with certainty what the future holds. Without excess reserves, a period of unexpectedly heavy withdrawals or unexpectedly light deposit inflows can leave a reserve deficiency. While such a deficiency can be covered by borrowing reserves from the Fed or from other institutions, the cost (primarily interest) of borrowing reserves can exceed the rate of return the lender earns at the margin on its investments. Weighing the returns from squeezing excess reserves to acquire earning assets against the costs of borrowing reserves, depository institutions generally hold some excess reserves.

The Optimum Volume of Excess Reserves

Given that, when faced with an increased risk of a reserve deficiency from economizing on excess reserves, depository institutions determine the volume of excess reserves they want to hold by comparing the rate of return on earning assets to the discount rate, the total volume of excess reserves held by our system of depository institutions will change as financial market conditions change. For example, with "tight" credit conditions, if interest rates on loans rise relative to the cost of borrowing reserves from the Fed, excess reserves would be squeezed, since greater use is made of available reserves to extend credit. Indeed, aggressive lenders will happily expose themselves to a greater risk of having to borrow reserves from the central bank if the discrepancy between the discount rate and the rate of return on earning assets is large enough. Algebraically, the system-wide demand for excess reserves would be expressed as $X = X(i - i_d)$, where i is the market interest rate at which depository institutions lend and i_d is the discount rate at which reserves can be borrowed. This demand function assumes that the volume of excess reserves the depository lenders collectively choose to hold is a function of the gap between the borrowing and lending rate, with excess reserves reduced (credit extended more aggressively) as the gap widens.

The Revised Money Supply Model

Recognition that excess reserves may be voluntarily held requires only a slight modification of our formal money supply model. The central bank still controls the volume of reserves (R) available to the system, but with lenders holding excess reserves (X), only a portion of the provided reserves $[R - X(i - i_d)]$ will be used to support depository institutions' checking account liabilities. Thus, Equation (13—8) must be modified to read

$$M = \frac{1 + c + n}{r(1 + n) + c} \left[R - X(i - i_d) \right]. \qquad [13\text{--}12]$$

Our previous estimates of the volume of money that a given stock of reserves would support must now be taken as upper limit estimates—estimates that are valid only when our depository institutions choose to hold no excess reserves so that

$$M = \frac{1 + c + n}{r(1 + n) + c} \left[R - X\overset{0}{(i - i_d)} \right] = \frac{1 + c + n}{r(1 + n) + c} \cdot R$$

Equation (13—12) shows that, other things being equal, the central bank can change the money supply by changing reserves, just as it could in the simpler model. We must now recognize, however, that, by altering the volume of excess reserves they choose to hold, lending institutions can influence the response of the money supply to changes in reserves. For example, during a period of depressed economic activity with depository institution managers leery of loan extensions, a large portion of a central bank-engineered increase in reserves *could* be absorbed in excess reserves. In that case, to attain the expansionary effect it desires, the Fed would have to expand reserves much more than it would if all excess reserves were used for credit extension.

Equation (13—12) also shows that, in striking contrast to an assumption employed in all our models of the money market up to this point, we should expect the quantity of money supplied to be positively related to the market rate of interest. Other things being constant, as the market rate of interest rises, the gap between the rate of return on loans and the interest cost of borrowing reserves widens, enticing depository institutions to draw down their excess reserves as they take advantage of profitable opportunities to lend. With increased lending, the stock of money is expanded.[6] This tendency for lender behavior to result in an increase in the money supply as the interest rate rises may be reinforced by the general public's reaction to an increased interest rate. Because currency provides no interest yield, as the interest rate rises, raising the relative attractiveness of interest-paying savings deposits and of demand deposits on which some form of return may be paid (for example, gifts for opening new accounts, preferential loan treatment for larger depositors, explicit interest payments on NOW-type accounts, and so on), the public may economize on its currency holdings, exchanging them for demand and savings deposits. Because currency is *reserve* money, as the general public deposits some of its currency holdings in depository institutions, additional loans will be extended, raising the

---

[6]Because a reduction in the discount rate (i_d) with the market interest rate unchanged would also widen the gap between the borrowing and lending rate, it is clear that the money supply also depends on the discount rate.

money supply. Thus, if an increase in the interest rate entices these institutions to "dishoard" excess reserves and the general public to dishoard currency, the aggregate supply of nominal money balances would look like the schedule in Figure 13—1, with the money supply positively related to the market interest rate.

No longer can we take the nominal supply of money to be an exogenous variable that is controlled solely by the Federal Reserve. Indeed, its value is jointly determined by the actions of the commercial banking system, the other depository institutions that offer checkable deposits, the general public, and the Federal Reserve System.

An Interest-Elastic Money Supply. Several investigators have used regression analysis to test for the responsiveness of the money stock to interest rate changes. Their regressions have provided estimates of the elasticity of the money supply to changes in the market interest rate that range from .12 to .19.[7] These are important results, for the interest responsiveness of the money supply affects the slope of the LM curve in our aggregate model, and some modern arguments over the relative effectiveness of monetary and fiscal policy depend crucially on the shape of that LM curve. In figure 13—2, two *real* money supply schedules are sketched (holding the price level constant), one that assumes the nominal money supply is positively related to the interest rate (M_S'/P) and one that takes the nominal money stock to be exogenous, independent of the interest rate $(\overline{M}_S/P)$. If, at real output level Y_0, the demand schedule for real money balances is $(M_D/P)_{Y_0}$, the equilibrium interest rate is i_0. Because the interest rate/output combination (i_0, Y_0) is a money market equilibrium combination, it can be plotted

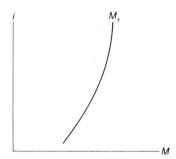

Figure 13—1 / The Interest Rate and the Nominal Money Supply

[7]If the money supply's elasticity with respect to the interest rate is .15, a 10 percent increase in the market interest rate, say, from a rate of 8 percent to 8.8 percent, would increase the money supply by 1.5 percent. Empirical evidence on the money stock's response to interest rate changes appears in Robert L. Teigen, "The Demand for and Supply of Money," in *Readings in Money, National Income, and Stabilization Policy*, ed. W. L. Smith and R. L. Teigen (Homewood, Ill.: Richard D. Irwin, 1974), pp. 65–103, and in Patrick H. Hendershott and Frank DeLeeuw, "Free Reserves, Interest Rates, and Deposits: A Synthesis," *Journal of Finance* 25 (1970): 599–613.

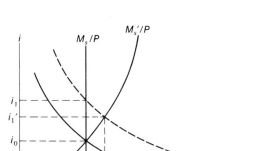

**Figure 13—2 / Money Market
Adjustments with an Interest-Sensitive Money Supply**

as one point on the money market equilibrium *(LM)* schedule, as in Figure 13—3.

With an increase in the level of real output, the money demand function is shifted rightward. For the higher output level Y_1, let us suppose the money demand schedule shifts to $(M_D/P)_{Y_1}$ in Figure 13—2. With the money supply fixed at $(\overline{M}_S/P)$, the money market equilibrium interest rate would rise to i_1, implying an *LM* schedule like LM_0 in Figure 13—3. With the money supply sensitive to the interest rate increase, the equilibrium interest rate rises only to i_1'. With the money *supply* expanded by an increase in the interest rate, even with the volume of reserves provided by the Fed, the required reserve ratio, and the discount rate held constant, a small interest rate increase can restore money market equilibrium after an increase in the level of output (thus money demand). Hence, the *LM* curve is more *interest elastic,* like LM_1 in Figure 13—3, the more interest elastic is the money supply schedule.

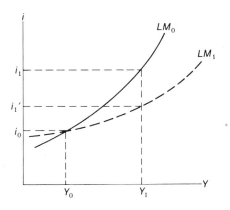

Figure 13—3 / The *LM* Schedule with Interest-Sensitive Money Supply

The Relative Strength of Monetary and Fiscal Policy

In Chapter 8 we showed that, with the stock of money given, the less sensitive the demand for money is to the interest rate, the steeper is the *LM* schedule. In turn, the steeper the *LM* schedule is, the weaker fiscal policy is. Indeed, in the extreme case in which the *LM* schedule is vertical, requiring both money supply and money demand to be interest inelastic, an expansionary fiscal policy causes the interest rate in the *IS-LM* model to rise until, by reducing investment expenditure, aggregate demand is restored to its original level. All an expansionary fiscal policy does in that case is raise the interest rate and reallocate an unchanged level of real output. A change in the money supply is necessary for the level of output to be altered. Thus, the classical conclusion that fiscal policy is powerless and monetary policy effective in altering the output level requires the assumption that the nominal supply of money is exogenous. If the money supply responds positively to the interest rate, providing an additional source of interest elasticity in the *LM* schedule, these classical conclusions are invalid in the *IS-LM* model, even if the demand for money is insensitive to the interest rate. Unless both money supply and demand are insensitive to the interest rate, both monetary and fiscal policy can alter aggregate demand in the simple *IS-LM* model.

A Brief Summary. Our first task in this chapter was to construct a money supply model that could be used to illustrate the techniques the Federal Reserve System possesses for controlling the money supply. With the help of the model we constructed, it was shown that the Fed, which provides reserves, or base money, to the financial system, can control the nominal money supply. It can do so utilizing three general control instruments: open market operations, the discount rate, and the required reserve ratio. By recognizing that lending institutions hold excess reserves and that the public can alter the credit expansion multiplier by changing its currency holdings, we paid homage to the practical difficulties the Fed must deal with if it chooses a target value for the money supply and tries to hit that target. (No one said a policy maker's life is easy.) The Fed must live with, and compensate for, the actions of banks, other depository institutions, and the nonbank public, still relying on its general control instruments for pursuing its monetary policy objectives. In spite of these complications, the Federal Reserve System's bond purchases and sales, discount rate changes, and reserve ratio alterations still change the money supply. Accurately predicting the size of money stock change resulting from application of these policy instruments is a difficult and challenging task because depository institutions and the general public are jointly responsible (with the Fed) for determining the size of the money stock.

Our last concern was to integrate our new understanding of the determinants of the money supply into the aggregate income determination model. With the nominal money supply endogenous, i.e., positively related to the market interest rate, the money market equilibrium *(LM)* schedule is more interest elastic than it is with the nominal money stock fixed. This revelation is important because the strength of fiscal policy is increased and the strength of monetary policy reduced by an enlarged interest elasticity of the *LM* schedule.

Case in Point VIII   ## Fed Pursuit of Monetary Targets

In monthly meetings, the Federal Open Market Committee (FOMC), composed of the seven-member Board of Governors of the Fed and five district bank presidents, decides on the operating targets of monetary policy. Its policy decisions are communicated to the manager of the Federal Open Market Account at the New York Federal Reserve Bank, usually in the form of directives that specify ranges of acceptable growth rates of money and reserve aggregates, as well as what it views as compatible tolerance limits on movements in the interest yield on federal funds. Originally, federal funds were exclusively excess reserves which banks with an excess loaned, often on an overnight basis, to banks that were short of reserves. In recent years the market has expanded to include other participants. Still, the market deals in very short-term obligations (often available in one day) and the interest rate prevailing in this market is widely viewed as a gauge of the cost of short-term funds. Federal reserve actions that add to (reduce) the financial system's reserve base can be expected to lower (raise) the interest cost of short-term funds.

The chart, on the next page, compares, for the period 1977–1979, actual changes in the narrowly defined money supply and in the federal funds rate with the tolerance ranges set by FOMC directives. On a month-to-month basis, it is evident that actual money supply changes can fall outside the tolerance ranges set by the FOMC, actual growth rates sometimes exceeding and sometimes falling short of the prescribed tolerance limits. The Fed recognizes that, with a number of factors other than its own policy actions altering the monetary base and the money multiplier, precise control over the rate of monetary expansion over intervals as short as a few months is unattainable. But, with the ability to apply compensatory adjustments in its security purchases and sales, the Fed can successfully maintain a desired rate of monetary expansion over periods of several months.

A perusal of the lower half of the chart through mid-year 1978 reveals that the Fed has little difficulty maintaining a federal funds rate within relatively narrow tolerance limits. Of course, information on the federal funds rate is available with little delay while the Fed cannot know until after the fact the extent to which its activities, in conjunction with the other events that influence the money stock, have combined to modify the money supply.

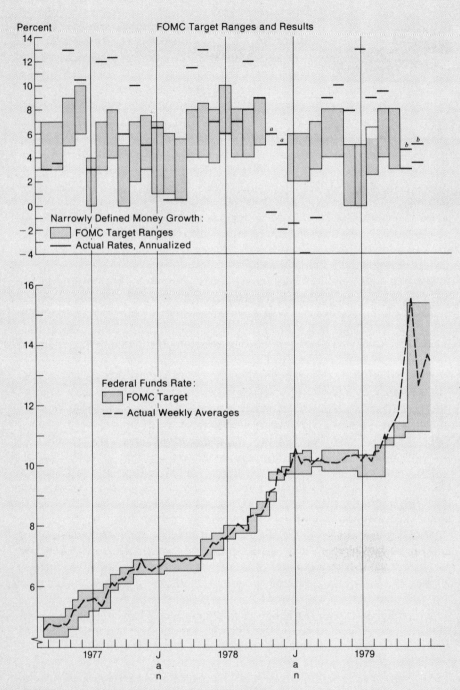

Figure 13—4 / FOMC Target Ranges and Results

aOnly a maximum growth rate specified.
bOnly a target growth rate specified.
cFOMC directed the open market account manager to pursue a target of "10 percent or slightly higher."
Source: Adapted from charts compiled by the Economic Analysis Department of Morgan Guaranty Trust Company

It is also possible, as is frequently claimed, that the Fed has enjoyed greater success in meeting the federal funds rate directive than it has in meeting the directive for monetary expansion. This results, some argue, because the Fed has focused its attention primarily on interest rates as an indicator of monetary stimulus or restriction; that is, that it has actually let monetary aggregates change as necessary to meet its desires for interest rate levels.

The much wider tolerance range for the federal funds rate that appears in the chart at the end of 1979 reflects a significant shift in emphasis in the day-to-day procedures used to conduct monetary policy. Among other announcements that it issued on October 6, 1979, the Fed indicated that it had shifted its emphasis from targeting on the federal funds rate to targeting on depository reserves. In the words of the Fed announcement: "This action involves placing greater emphasis on day-to-day operations on the supply of bank reserves and less emphasis on confining short-term fluctuations in the federal funds rate."[8] Whether the new reserve targeting emphasis will provide the Fed with tighter control over the money supply over short time intervals is a question that will receive close attention in the early 1980s.

Lags and the Effectiveness of Monetary Policy

We have already confronted a sample of problems that can impede the successful application of monetary policy to stabilize the economy. In the remainder of this chapter some additional difficulties in the application of monetary policy will be examined, beginning with consideration of the *timing* of monetary policy's influence on aggregate demand.

Figure 13—5 shows an idealized business cycle (the solid line) in which output peaks at time t_0, declines, then begins to rise once more. If an expansionary monetary policy could begin to stimulate aggregate demand immediately after the contraction in output begins (at t_0), the severity of the contraction could be sharply reduced with the time path of output looking more like the broken line in Figure 13—5. Unfortunately, there is a substantial lag between the point in time at which the need for an expansionary (or contractionary) monetary policy arises and the time at which that policy can alter aggregate demand.

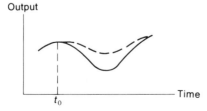

Figure 13—5 / Smoothing the Business Cycle

[8]"Announcements: Monetary Policy Actions," *Federal Reserve Bulletin*, (October 1979), p. 830.

Recognition, Administrative, and Operational Lags

Our idealized business cycle is reproduced in Figure 13—6. From that plot, it is clear that the need for an expansionary monetary policy arises at time t_0. However, the monetary authorities may not immediately recognize that need. Data on output, employment, and so on are available only at discrete time intervals. For example, figures on Gross National Product, a basic yardstick of the economy's vigor, are available only at quarterly intervals. To be sure, there are other important data series, including price indexes and unemployment rates, that are available at more frequent intervals. However, one or two monthly observations do not provide the clear-cut evidence of a major change in economic developments that the Fed needs to revise its policy stance. Thus, a *recognition lag* that may last several months must be endured before the monetary authorities become convinced that a need for policy action has arisen. That lag is represented by the time lapse between t_0 and t_1 in Figure 13—6.

The solution for the delay in recognizing the need for policy action is better forecasting, and a great deal of effort has been expended toward that end. As an aid in forecasting economic developments, several data series are available, including new orders for machinery and equipment, hiring rates, and even stock market prices, which appear to be leading indicators of economic activity. Over the business cycle, these data series tend to hit both peaks and troughs earlier than overall economic activity does. Data series on consumer buying intentions and business investment plans are also an aid to forecasters, and, increasingly, econometric models of the economy are being relied on for predicting the future. Experience shows, though, that in spite of our best efforts, forecasting is an uncertain affair. In 1929, a prominent group of economic forecasters predicted economic recovery within a year! As an aftermath to World War II, many economists predicted a major postwar recession. In fact, economic activity turned out to be excessively buoyant after the war.

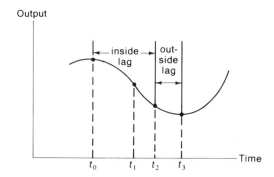

Figure 13—6 / The Lags in Monetary Policy

A second lag, the *administrative lag,* is the interval between recognition of a need for action and the implementation of policy action. Having recognized the need for an expansionary (or contractionary) monetary policy, the Fed must determine how to administer its policy action, and the size of policy action that is needed. Because policy decisions are made by a small group (the Federal Open Market Committee) that meets at frequent intervals, the administrative lag for monetary policy is usually brief. That lag is represented by the time interval between t_1 and t_2 in Figure 13—6. The recognition and administrative lags combined are frequently referred to as the *inside lag* (t_0 to t_2), the time interval between the emergence of a need for action and the administration of that action.

Even after the monetary authority has initiated a policy action, there is a sizable *operational lag,* or *outside lag,* before that policy has its effect on aggregate demand. For example, to stimulate economic activity the Fed can use open market operations to pump reserves into the banking system. The commercial banking system must then transform the injection of reserves, through the credit-expansion process, into an increase in the supply of money. It takes time for a general increase in available credit and the full decline in the interest rate to materialize. As that is accomplished, spending plans will be adjusted, but again time delays are involved. Decisions to undertake a factory expansion, construct an apartment complex, or even to contract for a new home are not made overnight. Once investment decisions are made, contracts must be formalized (typically requiring an evaluation period by the capital goods suppliers and, often, the submission of competing bids) before those decisions begin to affect production.

The operational lag is represented by the time interval between t_2 and t_3 in Figure 13—6, with the expansionary monetary policy's major impact on output distributed over an interval of time after t_3. While this operational, or outside, lag is generally conceded to be far more important than the inside lag in delaying the effective application of monetary policy, there is no clear evidence on the length of time comprising the outside lag. Milton Friedman argues, though, that this lag is both *long* and *variable.*[9] Empirical studies have suggested a diverse assortment of time values for the outside lag, ranging from one to two months to three years before a monetary policy action begins to exert a significant effect on the economy.

The implications for monetary policy of a long and variable lag between emergence of a need for policy and the impact of policy are clear-cut; monetary policy actions may frequently be destabilizing rather than stabilizing. Figure 13—6 illustrates that possibility. Our expansionary policy, aimed at

---

[9]For a sample of views on the length of the lag in monetary policy's effect, see Milton Friedman, "The Lag in Effect of Monetary Policy," *Journal of Political Economy* 48 (1960): 617–621; Robert H. Rasche and Harold T. Shapiro, "The F.R.B.-M.I.T. Econometric Model: Its Special Features," *The American Economic Review* 58 (1968): 123–149; Franco Modigliani and Albert Ando, "Impacts of Fiscal Actions on Aggregate Income and the Monetarist Controversy: Theory and Evidence," in *Monetarism,* ed. Jerome L. Stein (Amsterdam: North Holland, 1976), pp. 17–42.

combating the contraction that began at time t_0, does not begin to exert its expansionary effect on aggregate demand until t_3, when the contraction has ended and output is already expanding. Monetary stimulation at that point could produce an excessively strong and prolonged expansion, favoring the development of a needless inflation. Analogously, if the Fed sharply reduces the rate of growth of the money supply to stifle an expansion that it judges to be excessive, by the time that restrictive policy has its impact on aggregate demand, output may have already peaked with contraction underway. Monetary restriction at that time would reinforce the contraction.

Rules versus Discretion

For many years, economists have debated whether the central bank should have a free hand in determining the growth rate of the money supply, as it now does, or whether the rate of monetary expansion should be dictated by a simple rule. The majority of economists favor continuation of the discretionary implementation of monetary policy, but a vocal minority, led by Milton Friedman, favor establishment of a requirement that the Fed engineer a *steady* growth of the money supply at an annual rate approximating the long-run growth rate of real productive capacity, something between 4 and 5 percent annually.[10] That expansion rate, it is claimed, would provide the growing money stock needed to keep step with the financial requirements of an expanding economy.

Part of the rules versus discretion debate stems directly from differences in empirical judgment on the ability of the Fed, with its staff of professional economists, to predict the impact of monetary policy actions. Proponents of simple rules for monetary expansion argue, like Friedman, that the lags in monetary policy's impact are long and variable (thus hard to predict). As we have just seen, with the combination of a limited ability to forecast movements in economic activity and a long (not to mention variable) lag in monetary policy's impact, policy actions may be frequently destabilizing. Looking at the historical record on movements in the *money supply* and movements in *nominal output,* supporters of simple monetary rules find enough episodes of closely related, sometimes violent movements in those two variables to convince themselves that discretionary monetary policy has, on balance, been destabilizing and is likely to continue to be destabilizing in the future. This conclusion assumes, of course, a dominant role for money as an exogenous determinant of the level of economic activity, i.e., as the cause of the observed movements in output.

Advocates of discretion emphasize the endogenous nature of the money supply, pointing out that closely related movements in nominal income and

[10]See, for example, Milton Friedman, *A Program for Monetary Stability* (New York: Fordham University Press, 1959), p. 91. For a set of arguments that supports a much lower rate of monetary expansion, see Friedman's *The Optimum Quantity of Money and Other Essays* (Chicago: Aldine, 1969), pp. 1–50.

money, violent or otherwise, would be observed if the money supply re-sponds passively to money income changes (thus interest rate changes) gen-erated by real forces. They contend that constraining the growth rate of the money supply would often be destabilizing because the monetary authority could not respond to an excessive expansion or contraction originating in the real sectors of the economy or stemming from an autonomous change in money demand. As a simple illustration of their concern, if a bond-fi-nanced increase in government spending, say, for a military engagement, overstimulates the economy, adherence to a simple rule would prevent the monetary authorities from imposing a policy restrictive enough to prevent inflation. Implicit in that concern is the belief that the monetary authority can administer discretionary policy wisely; that the impact of monetary policy can be predicted accurately enough that the Fed can contribute to economic stability.

While our discussion has flirted with the issue, we should explicitly rec-ognize that a second difference in judgment also plays a prominent role in the rules versus discretion debate. Advocates of a monetary rule typically take the classical position that the economy is *inherently stable*. They at-tribute a large part of the responsibility for observed fluctuations in nominal output to monetary mismanagement (which would be eliminated with a mon-etary rule). With an inherently stable economy, little (stability) is gained and much can be lost through the well-intentioned but inadvertently mis-guided use of discretionary monetary policy.

Supporters of discretion typically believe, like Keynes, that sizable ex-pansions and contractions can be generated by nonmonetary forces and that the self-equilibrating forces in the economy are often unacceptably slow. Thus, they contend that discretionary monetary policy, properly applied, can significantly improve the economy's performance. While conceding that actual monetary policy has at times been destabilizing, proponents of dis-cretion argue that our understanding of macroeconomic forces and our fore-casting ability have improved dramatically in recent years so that policy errors now occur less frequently. They attribute the rather favorable per-formance of the U.S. economy from World War II to 1970 to the generally skillful use of discretionary stabilization policy and anticipate, with growing knowledge, an even better performance from stabilization policy in the fu-ture.

While in the 1960s and 1970s there was widespread support for the use of countercyclical policies to attempt to "fine tune" the economy's expan-sion path, enthusiasm for those efforts waned with the experiences of the 1970s. Reflecting the spreading loss of faith in the ability of stabilization policy to effectively combat short-run (cyclical) problems, the Congres-sional Joint Economic Committee concluded in its mid-year 1980 report that policy makers should focus their efforts on long-term solutions to economic problems. Citing the difficulties of anticipating or even identifying cycle turning points, along with timing problems from delays in implementing policy actions and having their effects transmitted to the economy, the committee argued that government efforts to shorten the duration or reduce the intensity of cyclical swings in economic activity are apt to be ineffective.

To close our discussion of the rules versus discretion issue, it is worth noting that supporters of monetary rules frequently have been politically conservative (classical or nineteenth-century liberals). They judge governmental intervention in human affairs to be at best inefficient and at worst freedom threatening. As a consequence, where government functions must be tolerated as necessary evils, they believe government should be strictly constrained. The advocates of discretion are much more frequently modern liberals. They typically have more faith in the ability of government agencies to skillfully and fairly administer their assigned tasks and generally do not feel threatened by active government involvement in economic affairs. The failure of government policy actions in recent years has surely played an important role in the much publicized recent drift toward conservatism in the United States.

Additional Limitations on Monetary Policy

In addition to timing problems, monetary policy makers face a number of other difficulties in using monetary policy for stabilizing output, employment, and prices. If the international monetary system depends on exchange rates that are not fully determined by free market forces (at present the Fed intervenes in foreign exchange markets to "manage" short-run changes in exchange rates between the dollar and other currencies), balance-of-payments concerns can limit the central bank's freedom to pursue domestic goals. Indeed, monetary policy was clearly constrained in the early 1960s (when exchange rates were *fixed* by international agreement) by balance-of-payments considerations. With the economy suffering from excessive unemployment and anemic growth in the early years of the Kennedy administration, expansionary monetary policy to stimulate investment was considered but rejected. The same interest rate reduction that would have stimulated domestic investment would have lowered the yield on U.S. securities relative to those in other countries. With short-run (money) capital highly sensitive to relative returns, lowering the U.S. interest rate would have prompted a sizable capital outflow, enlarging the already worrisome balance-of-payments deficit, which, by the decade's end, had led to the collapse of the dollar's international exchange value.

The Uneven Incidence of Monetary Policy

In addition to international considerations that can restrict the Fed's freedom to control the money supply and interest rates, there are a number of internal limits that arise because the interest rate changes that monetary policy actions produce can have a quite uneven impact on different groups within society. Perhaps most notably, a monetary policy that raises market interest rates can reduce the flow of funds into the home mortgage market to a trickle, dealing crushing blows to the home construction industry.

Historically, the extreme interest sensitivity of the construction industry has stemmed to a large extent from a set of institutional restraints imposed on interest rates. These included federal government-imposed ceilings on the interest rates that can be charged on Veterans Administration guaranteed and Federal Housing Administration insured mortgage loans as well as state-imposed *usury* laws that limit the interest charge that can be levied on mortgage loans. Finally, a large portion of all mortgage lending is done by savings and loan associations, specialized financial intermediaries that channel the bulk of their deposit inflows into mortgages, and the interest rates those associations can pay on a large portion of their obligations has been legally limited. As market interest rates rise above the level that savings and loan associations can legally offer, depositors shift their funds out of the savings and loan associations and directly into the securities market (a process called *disintermediation*), reducing the availability of mortgage funds. In addition, when market interest rates exceed federal or state government-imposed ceilings on mortgage rates, additional funds are shifted out of the mortgage market. The volatile response of the home construction industry is easy to see. As Table 13—3 reveals, in the four most recent periods of elevated interest rates (1966, 1969, 1974–1975, and 1979–1980) housing starts plummeted. From the levels of a year earlier, housing starts dropped by more than 20 percent in 1966, by some 3 percent in 1969 in spite

Table 13—3 / New Housing Starts

Year	Housing Starts (in thousands of units)
1965	1,473
1966	1,165
1967	1,292
1968	1,508
1969	1,467
1970	1,434
1971	2,052
1972	2,357
1973	2,045
1974	1,338
1975	1,160
1976	1,538
1977	1,987
1978	2,020
1979	1,743
1980	1,154*

*Annual rate over first six months
Source: *Federal Reserve Bulletin,* various issues

of sizable government support of the mortgage market, by nearly 35 percent in 1974 with a continuing decline in 1975, and by 14 percent in 1979 with the contraction deepening in 1980. These figures are a vivid reflection of the frustrations of: (1) potential new home purchasers who cannot find mortgage funds; and (2) home builders, many of whom are driven into bankruptcy because they are unable to sell the new dwellings they produce.

Of course, rising interest rates, as a signal of the pressure on scarce productive resources, must be allowed to reduce production if they are to ration scarce resources and contribute to a stable economic environment. However, the response in the housing construction industry illustrated in Table 13—3 does not reflect just a price-rationed reduction in the demand for housing (a movement up a demand curve). Instead, it reflects the perverse impact of restrictions on interest rates that have affected the housing industry. At allowable interest rates, the volume of funds potential home buyers would like is simply not *available* when market interest rates are at elevated levels.

In sweeping legislation aimed at reducing regulation in the financial sector of the economy, Congress scheduled in 1980 a gradual phaseout of interest ceilings to begin in 1981. With the removal of regulatory restrictions on interest rates and with innovative new loans issued to permit more frequent adjustments in mortgage interest charges as market interest rates vary, the institutions that lend to the construction market may feel the impact of monetary restraint less sharply in the future.

While the housing industry is the one sector of the economy that is most strongly affected by changed credit conditions, it is not the only sector so affected. State and local governments are often subject to legislative and administrative regulations that impose ceilings on the interest rates those governmental units can pay on bond debt. As a consequence, when interest rates are high, bond financing of the construction of roads, schools, parks, and so on may become impossible, even if the citizenry would be willing to pay the prevailing interest rate for the funds required to finance such projects. The impact of high interest rates is vividly apparent in survey data on the cutback in long-term state and local borrowing in the high interest rate years 1966 and 1969–1970.[11] In 1966 long-term borrowing by state and local governments was reduced by approximately 20 percent of planned levels. In fiscal 1970 (July 1969 to June 1970) the cutback was about 28 percent.

It is also frequently argued that *small* businesses are particularly sensitive to altered credit conditions. Large businesses, it is claimed, have ready access to national credit markets and can borrow funds either from banks or by direct sale of their own security issues. Under restrictive credit conditions banks may feel it is necessary to meet the needs of their large business customers first, restricting the funds they make available to the small

---

[11]See Paul F. McGouldrick and John E. Peterson, "Monetary Restraint and Borrowing and Capital Spending by Large State and Local Governments in 1966," *Federal Reserve Bulletin,* July 1968, pp. 552–581. Also see John E. Peterson, "Response of State and Local Governments to Varying Credit Conditions," *Federal Reserve Bulletin,* March 1971, pp. 209–232.

businesses that have no easy alternative to bank borrowing. This set of arguments is hard to assess empirically, as are similar arguments that restrictive monetary policies impose a greater burden on lower-income groups than on others. However, the point is well taken that the fear (realistic or not) that a restrictive monetary policy imposes a particularly harsh burden on specific sectors of the economy can foster a reluctance to aggressively employ monetary restraint, particularly if the highly interest-responsive sectors are deemed socially worthy and politically powerful (as are the housing industry and state and local governments).

Financial Market Stability and Monetary Control

A concern with erratic movements in prices and yields on government securities, with a disorderly market, is most evident when the Treasury is engaged in marketing a new security issue. The appearance on the market of a large, new issue tends to depress government security prices abruptly and hence would raise interest yields in step. To prevent the security issue from failing to be fully subscribed at face value, and to avoid the abrupt increase in interest yields on government securities that would otherwise occur, the Fed can maintain an "even keel" policy. That is, to support bond prices, it can serve as a buyer of last resort, when the Treasury markets its new issue. Because the Treasury frequently appears in the securities market to finance current deficits and to refinance outstanding debt, an even keel policy must often be followed.

Other factors besides Treasury debt issues can cause swings in interest rates. The Fed judges any abrupt changes in interest rates to be undesirable, because, in addition to threatening the success of the Treasury's financing operations, they increase uncertainty and can cause inefficient, temporary shifts of resources from one use to another. Hence, the Fed attempts to stabilize interest rates on a short-term basis, without regard for the source of instability.

To accomplish this, the Fed must abdicate control of the supply of money, as was indicated before. Therefore, under such a policy, the money supply responds elastically to changes in money demand. However, as we also know, not all changes in money demand are random or seasonal. Some are the result of changes in the level of economic activity of the sort that must be offset if the country's macroeconomic goals are to be achieved. Unfortunately, except in the case of stable seasonal variations in money demand, there is no way the Fed can distinguish changes in money demand that, because of their random nature, should be accommodated by a change in the money supply, from changes that reflect unwanted alterations in economic activity and therefore should be met with an offsetting adjustment in the money supply and interest rates. There is some latitude for the Fed to accommodate daily or weekly shocks to the market for money while it still gives prime consideration over a longer time horizon (such as a quarter) to achieving changes in monetary aggregates and interest rates which are judged necessary for aggregate stabilization purposes. However, the Fed must be on guard against the widely recognized possibility that successive "special situations" might require a money supply response that cumulatively forces the money stock and interest rates away from the paths needed for aggregate stabilization purposes. The existence of random disturbances in the market for money, to which the Fed must respond, clearly complicates its control task.

No doubt, we could extend our list of the limitations that monetary policy makers must face in employing monetary policy for stabilization purposes. Our brief list, though, should leave no doubt that using discretionary monetary policy in a manner that contributes to domestic stability is a difficult task. Even so, the majority of economists believe that discretionary monetary policy can make a substantial contribution to the achievement of aggregate goals.[12]

Summary

We know that money is important and that by altering the money supply, the central bank can change the level of aggregate demand. This chapter has provided an aggregate money supply model that illustrates the roles of the most important factors that influence the money supply. Since the Fed can exert control over some of those factors, notably the reserve ratio and the volume of reserves, it can control the money supply. Given the Fed's ability to control the money supply, there remain enough difficulties in the application of monetary policy to arouse concern over the usefulness of discretionary monetary policy as a stabilization tool. Among those difficulties, this chapter has reviewed: (1) problems that arise because of lengthy lags between the emergence of need for policy and the impact of policy implementation and (2) restrictions on the freedom of the monetary authority to pursue its domestic stabilization goals due to international financial considerations and fear of the uneven impact of monetary restraint. There is little wonder that the past performance of discretionary monetary policy has fallen short of the theoretical ideal.

More importantly, all economists recognize that our understanding of the influence of monetary policy on the economy is incomplete. Most fundamentally, too little is known about the precise power and timing of monetary influences on aggregate demand, and differences in judgment on such basic issues cause profound disagreements on the appropriate application of monetary policy. Clearly, there is a need for continued research in the money arena. But since money supply changes have a powerful effect on economic

---

[12]For a readable insider's view of the monetary management process, see Sherman J. Maisel, *Managing the Dollar* (New York: W.W. Norton & Company, 1973).

activity, the application of monetary policy cannot wait for a complete resolution of all the existing uncertainties on money's role. In the meantime, most economists believe that, based on what is known, discretionary monetary policy can be used to pursue important national objectives. Increasingly, however, with diminishment of faith in the Fed's ability to combat cyclical fluctuations in economic activity, the emphasis has shifted to the pursuit of long-term goals.

Questions

1. Explain the logic of the process through which the commercial banking system can use an increase in reserves to generate a multiple increase in the stock of money.

2. Build a formal money supply model. What role does the market interest rate play in determining the size of the money stock? Use your model to explain how the Fed can alter the money supply.

3. What accounts for the lag in monetary policy? Does the length of time of that lag make a difference?

4. Considering the current state of economic affairs, what kind of monetary policy would you prescribe for the next six months?

5. Explain how the unique aspects of the residential construction market may have limited the use of monetary policy. Can you think of any other discriminatory effects of monetary policy?

Suggested Readings

Cagan, Phillip. *Determinants and Effects of Changes in the Stock of Money: 1875–1960.* New York: National Bureau of Economic Research, 1965.

deLeeuw, Frank, and Gramlich, Edward. "The Channels of Monetary Policy." *Federal Reserve Bulletin,* 40: June 1969, pp. 472–491.

Friedman, Milton. *A Program for Monetary Stability.* New York: Fordham University Press, 1959.

Friedman, Milton. "The Role of Monetary Policy." *The American Economic Review* 43 (1968): pp. 1–17.

Gambs, Carl. "Money—A Changing Concept in a Changing World." *Federal Reserve Bank of Kansas City Review,* January 1977, pp. 3–12.

Hafer, R. W. "The New Monetary Aggregates." *Federal Reserve Bank of St. Louis Review,* February 1980, pp. 25–32.

Jordan, Jerry. "Elements of Money Stock Determination." *Federal Reserve Bank of St. Louis Review,* October 1969, pp. 10–19.

Lang, Richard W. "The FOMC in 1979: Introducing Reserve Targeting." *Federal Reserve Bank of St. Louis Review,* March 1980, pp. 2–25.

Maisel, Sherman. *Managing the Dollar.* New York: W. W. Norton & Co., 1973.

McNeill, Charles R. "The Depository Institutions Deregulatory and Monetary Control Act of 1980." *Federal Reserve Bulletin* 66, June 1980, pp. 444–453.

Poole, William. "Current Issues in Monetary Control," *Federal Reserve Bank of Richmond Review* 66, July/August 1980, pp. 20–27.

Ritter, Lawrence. "Income Velocity and Anti-Inflationary Monetary Policy." *The American Economic Review* 49 (1959): pp. 120–129.

Smith, Warren L. "The Instruments of General Monetary Control." *National Banking Review* 1 (1963): pp. 47–76.

Tatom, John A. "Money Stock Control Under Alternative Definitions of Money." *Federal Reserve Bank of St. Louis Review*, November 1979, pp. 3–9.

Teigen, Ronald. "The Demand for and Supply of Money." In *Readings in Money, National Income, and Stabilization Policy,* edited by W. L. Smith and R. L. Teigen, pp. 68–103. 3rd ed. Homewood, Ill.: Richard D. Irwin, 1974.

Chapter 14 Implementing Fiscal Policy

Until the Great Depression, the government sector of the economy was quite small. Total government receipts during the 1920s were less than 10 percent of GNP and federal government receipts were less than half of the total. The government budget philosophy was one of alleged "fiscal responsibility"; it was tacitly assumed that a government budget should be balanced annually.

It is fortunate that the government budget was small during that period. With equality between tax receipts and expenditures *required,* the decline in tax receipts experienced during a business contraction would require a reduction in government spending or an increase in tax rates, while the growth in tax receipts during expansions would call for increased government spending or reduced tax rates. This budget philosophy is clearly procyclical, tending to amplify the strength of an ongoing contraction or expansion.

With government budgets of the size we have had since the depression, attempting to maintain an annually balanced budget would have been highly destabilizing. In the post-World War II era, though, there has been widespread recognition of the need, at the federal level, of *compensatory finance* policies of the type rationalized in Keynes' *General Theory*. As we already know, Keynesian analysis calls for increased government spending or reduced tax collections when income is falling and for reduced government spending or increased taxes during excessive expansions, conscious actions that lead to budget imbalances. As large as the federal government's economic role is today, such compensatory finance policies can have a powerful effect on the level of general business activity.

Compensatory Budgets:
Two Forms of Fiscal Response to Income Cycles

A government that deliberately alters tax rates and planned outlays in an effort to stabilize the economy is practicing what is termed *discretionary* fiscal policy. In addition to discretionary adjustments in taxes and outlays, there are some *automatic* tax and outlay changes that act to dampen fluctuations in income, automatic in the sense that they occur in response to a change in the level of GNP without any deliberate (discretionary) action by government. Logically enough, these automatic changes in taxes and revenues are called *automatic stabilizers*, or *built-in stabilizers*.

The Major Automatic Stabilizers

The two main automatic stabilizers of the U.S. economy are the federal income tax and the government income transfer programs, particularly unemployment compensation and welfare payments. As GNP falls during a contraction, some taxpayers find their income dropping below the taxable level; others fall into lower tax brackets; and taxes (whatever the percentage rate) are levied against a smaller income base. Thus, federal tax revenues are reduced as GNP falls. This is, of course, the direction in which tax collections should move to counter a contraction in economic activity. Conversely, when GNP is rising, many taxpayers are shifted into progressively higher tax brackets; some who previously had no taxable income become taxable; and given percentage tax rates are levied against a larger income base. Once again, federal tax revenues move in the direction required for stabilization.

On the transfer side, the most important stabilizer is unemployment insurance. During a contraction of business activity, insured workers who become unemployed are eligible for unemployment compensation benefits. Such transfers help to maintain disposable income (thus, consumption spending) as GNP falls. During expansions of business activity employment increases, and unemployment compensation declines.[1] Other forms of transfer payments (including old age and survivors' insurance, public assistance,

---

[1]Unemployment compensation is a joint federal-state program. The program is state administered but must be run in a manner that meets federal approval. Also, the federal government holds the program's accumulated reserves in the Employment Insurance Trust Fund. These funds are available for six months in most states with an additional three months of benefits available nation-wide when the national unemployment rate remains above 4½ percent for more than three months. Moreover, in 1974 Congress exhibited a willingness to provide additional unemployment assistance during periods of *aggravated* unemployment. In that year Congress temporarily authorized thirteen weeks of "special unemployment assistance" available when, for three months, the national unemployment rate has been 6 percent or greater or to an area in which the unemployment rate has been 6.5 percent or greater.

and other "welfare" payments) also tend to vary countercyclically, government outlays rising when GNP falls and falling when GNP rises.[2]

The existence of automatic stabilizers makes cyclical fluctuations in GNP smaller than they otherwise would be. (In terms of the models we have built, the size of any multiplier is reduced by the existence of a budget structure that includes these types of tax and transfer programs.) While they act to reduce the size of cyclical fluctuations in GNP, built-in stabilizers clearly cannot prevent such cycles because the automatic changes in taxes and transfers are *induced;* they occur only if and when GNP has already changed.[3]

Automatic Stabilizers and the Budget Surplus (Deficit). Because federal tax receipts and outlays vary automatically in response to changes in business activity, the size of the federal budget surplus or deficit changes automatically with every change in GNP. With the rates for tax liabilities and for transfer payments given, the federal budget will show a larger surplus or smaller deficit (due to larger tax revenues and reduced transfer payments) for higher levels of business activity, and a smaller surplus or larger deficit (due to reduced tax revenues and increased transfer payments) for depressed levels of business activity.

Figure 14—1 illustrates the effect on the government budget of a change in the level of business activity, assuming that no discretionary changes in

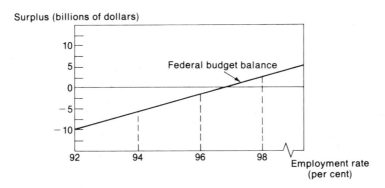

Figure 14—1 / Employment and the Budget Surplus (Deficit)

[2]While you are thinking about automatic stabilizers, you should recall that the monetary dampener also serves to stabilize the economy. For example, with output growing, the interest rate climbs, reducing investment spending and, consequently, reducing the strength of the business expansion. While our focus in this chapter is on fiscal policy, we should not forget the role of the monetary sector.

[3]While the automatic stabilizers work without discretionary government action, the tax and transfer programs that provide automatic stabilization are the result of earlier legislation. These tax and transfer programs were established with goals other than economic stability in mind, their contribution to the smoothing of business cycles being purely a by-product of their basic function.

taxes or transfers occur as GNP changes. For the hypothetical budget structure reflected in Figure 14—1, an unemployment rate of 8 percent, representing a depressed level of economic activity, would result in a $10 billion
deficit. With business activity at a very buoyant level, corresponding, say,
to 4 percent unemployment, the deficit would be some $2½ billion. If busi-
ness activity could expand so that only 2 percent of the labor force were
unemployed, the federal budget would show a surplus of some $2 billion.
Because of those government tax and outlay programs that act as built-in
stabilizers, net taxes (taxes minus transfers) and the actual *measured* surplus
or deficit varies with the prevailing level of income and employment.

More on Discretionary Fiscal Policy

Discretionary fiscal policy entails a change in the *structure* of the government budget. A discretionary change in tax schedules alters the volume of
tax revenues collected at any selected level of economic activity; a discretionary change in government transfer programs results in a changed level
of transfer payments at any level of business activity; and so on. Thus, a
discretionary fiscal policy action shifts the schedule in Figure 14—1 that
shows the federal budget balance associated with different levels of business
activity. For example, a discretionary increase in taxes (by, say, a reduction
in the exemption level or by an across-the-board increase in percentage tax
rates) would shift the budget balance schedule upward to reflect an increase
in the surplus (decrease in the deficit) that accompanies any level of economic activity.

In Figure 14—2 there are two schedules representing, with different sets
of government tax and outlay programs, the state of budget balance associated with different levels of business activity. If schedule A in Figure 14—
2 accurately reflects the relationship between employment and the budget
balance prior to a discretionary fiscal policy action, a budget shift in the
direction of schedule B could result from a discretionary increase in taxes,

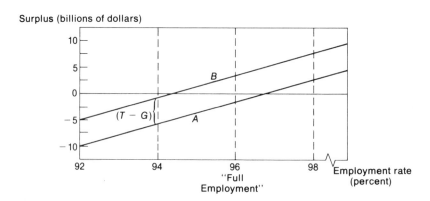

Figure 14—2 / Discretionary Fiscal Policy and the Budget Surplus

a discretionary reduction in transfer payments, or a discretionary reduction in government spending. Reversing the direction of the discretionary change in tax structure or outlays would shift the schedule representing the budget balance downward (as from schedule *B* toward schedule *A*).

During an extended contraction, the appropriate fiscal response of a movement toward budget deficit can result, obviously, from discretionary policy actions as well as from an automatic response in tax receipts and government outlays. Conversely, during an overly rapid, prolonged expansion, discretionary policy actions can produce the movement toward budget surplus that stabilization requires. Of the two budget postures (reflecting, again, a given set of government tax, transfer, and expenditure programs) represented in Figure 14—2, budget *A* is clearly more expansionary than budget *B* because the budget deficit is larger (surplus smaller) at every level of economic activity with budget *A*.

Measuring the Impact of Fiscal Policy: The Full Employment Surplus

Historically, the degree of stimulation (or restriction) of economic activity stemming from fiscal policy has been regarded as dependent on the size of the *observed* budget surplus or deficit. The budget has been popularly regarded as stimulative when in deficit (government outlays exceeding revenues), and restrictive when accruing a surplus. A glance back at Figure 14—2 should dispel the notion that observed surpluses or deficits are adequate measures of the impact of fiscal policy. Because the observed surplus or deficit is the result both of the structure of the budget and of the current level of economic activity, it is impossible to obtain a clear-cut judgment on the impact of fiscal policy from the currently measured surplus or deficit. A budget deficit may just reflect a depressed level of economic activity rather than a stimulative fiscal policy program. Hence, the very same budget structure might be judged restrictive, expansionary, or neutral, depending on the prevailing level of economic activity.

The *relative* impact of two alternative fiscal policy programs can be judged by comparing the surplus (or deficit) generated by those alternative programs at a given level of employment. While this comparison can be made at any arbitrarily selected level of employment, the comparison is conventionally made at an assumed level of employment of 96 percent of the measured labor force. In the 1960s, this level of employment was assumed to approximate full employment; consequently, the resulting measure of budget posture was labeled the *full employment surplus*. It is now more frequently referred to as the *high employment surplus* or deficit.

In Figure 14—2, budget *A* shows, at "full employment," a deficit (negative high employment surplus) of some $3 billion while budget *B* yields just under a $4 billion surplus. With the larger high employment deficit under budget program *A* reflecting either larger government outlays or smaller tax revenues at any level of employment, fiscal program A is more stimulative (or less restrictive) than program B is. This conclusion, of course, does not rest on the observed government budget balance. Indeed, the great advantage of the high employment surplus as a measure of fiscal influence on the economy lies in its ability to separate discretionary changes in the budget from induced (automatic) budget balance changes. The high employment surplus, while vastly superior to observed deficits and surpluses as a measure of fiscal posture, is still strictly limited; it only permits us to *compare* budgets, to identify more or less expansionary budget programs. To go further, to judge whether any particular budget program is compatible with noninflationary, full-employment equilibrium, we would need more information than is contained in a budget balance schedule. We also would need to know the strength of private demand for consumption goods, investment goods, and net exports.[4]

When private demand is excessively buoyant, a government budget that provides a high employment surplus would be optimal. With unduly anemic private demand, discretionary fiscal policy actions that provide a high employment deficit would be ideal. More specifically, if for simplicity we ignore the international sector of the economy, we know that commodity market equilibrium prevails only when planned injections into the income stream (investment and government spending) are equal to leakages (private saving plus net tax revenues) from that stream. That is, the equilibrium condition is $I + G = S + T$ or, rearranging, $I - S = T - G$.

If, with output at the full-employment level, planned saving exceeds planned investment (a private sector surplus), then equilibrium can prevail only if government spending exceeds net tax revenues (a government sector deficit at full employment). If full-employment planned saving falls short of planned investment (a private sector deficit), equilibrium would prevail only if net tax collections exceed government spending (a public sector surplus). For a budget structure that yields government budget balance at full employment to be compatible with full-employment equilibrium, the private sector must be planning to invest and save equally (private sector budget balance) at full employment.[5]

Redirecting attention to Figure 14—2, with the budget structure represented by schedule A, were the economy in equilibrium with 6 percent unemployment, the measured budget deficit $(T - G)$ would correspond to an equal excess of planned saving over planned investment. While the budget would be permitting a sizable measured deficit, it could not legitimately be called expansionary because it permits the 6 percent unemployment level of output to remain the equilibrium level. However, with a sizable increase

---

[4]For a more detailed discussion of the high employment surplus concept and its limitations, see Alan S. Blinder, *Fiscal Policy in Theory and Practice* (Morristown, N.J.: General Learning Press, 1973), pp. 6–12.

[5]James Tobin has clearly and elegantly explained the link between private demand and budget posture in "Deficit, Deficit, Who's Got the Deficit?", *National Economic Policy,* (New Haven, Conn.: Yale University Press, 1966).

in planned investment, the same budget would permit demand-pull inflation! The only budget consistent with full-employment equilibrium is one that fills the gap between full-employment output and aggregate demand. It goes without saying that the budget structure which fills that gap, providing full-employment equilibrium, is not independent of monetary policy because money supply changes also alter private demand.

Case In Point IX

Reading the Fiscal Policy Record

The figure below shows vividly the extent to which the actual budget surplus (or deficit) can differ from the high employment surplus (or deficit). Remember, the high employment surplus is the hypothetical measure of budget balance that would prevail if 96 percent of the labor force were employed. Thus, the actual budget surplus (deficit) can exceed the high employment surplus (deficit) only when unemployment is below the 4 percent full employment level. For a brief period in the mid-1950s, and for a more sustained period in the second half of the 1960s, the actual budget surplus exceeded the high employment surplus. For the rest of the time interval (1952–1979) covered by that chart, the actual budget surplus fell short of the high employment surplus as, with unemployment above the "full employment" level used in the high employment budget calculations, tax revenues were lower and government outlays higher than they would have been with 4 percent unemployment.

By abstracting from the impact of cyclical changes in tax revenues and government outlays, the chart of the high employment surplus allows a simple interpretation of changes in fiscal policy. According to the chart, there was a persistent and sizable increase in the high employment surplus during the 1950s. This reflects a sizable cutback in government's defense expenditures (following the end of the Korean War) without a corresponding discretionary reduction in taxes.

At the end of that decade, a further rise in the high employment surplus, to the +$20 billion range by the decade's end, signaled a further shift toward fiscal restraint. This corresponded to efforts by the Eisenhower administration to maintain balance (a zero surplus or deficit) in the *actual* budget. With the fiscal and monetary policies that were imposed in this period, economic expansion was weak in 1959–60, and the economy slid into recession in 1960–61.

In recognition of the restrictive effects of the Eisenhower budget, President Kennedy's Council of Economic Advisers called for discretionary tax reductions in the early 1960s. In 1964, taxes were cut, and those discretionary tax reductions along with increased government spending for a "War on Poverty," for "Great Society" programs, and for the Vietnam War

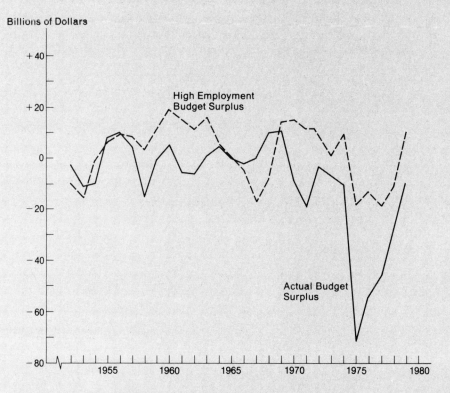

Figure 14—3 / The Actual and High Employment Surplus (Deficit), 1952–1979

Source: Council of Economic Advisers. *Economic Report of the President* (Washington, D.C.: U.S. Government Printing Office)

shoved the high employment budget strongly in the direction of deficit as the 1960s proceeded. The stimulus to the economy during that period lifted employment above the "full employment" level, as already indicated.

In the late 1960s, an accelerating inflation prompted a discretionary increase in taxes; a 10 percent surcharge on personal and corporate income taxes levied in mid-1968. This tax levy, combined with some cutbacks in government programs, shifted the budget in the direction of restraint at the end of the decade.

With rapid inflation in the late 1960s, and continuing into the 1970s, tax receipts were boosted as income earners were shifted into higher tax brackets. As a consequence, a sizable high employment surplus was maintained even though the surtax imposed in 1968 was allowed to expire in 1970. The economy suffered from a mild recession in 1970–71, but, because of inflation concerns, no major fiscal stimulus actions were taken. In 1975, however, with the economy plunging into its deepest contraction since the Great Depression, a combination of a one-time $8 billion tax rebate and reductions in taxes imposed both on personal and corporate incomes shifted the high employment budget sharply in the direction of fiscal stimulus.

In the last half of the 1970s, with the economy recovering but still plagued by persistent inflation, the high employment surplus was permitted to shift back in the direction of restraint. This shift was the result, largely, of inflation shifting taxpayers into higher percentage tax brackets.

The Budgetary Process

Because the record shows that budget adjustments are made in the hope of contributing to economic stability, our next task is to determine how budget adjustments are made. An understanding of this process will illuminate some of the specific difficulties attendant to the successful application of anti-cyclical *fiscal* policies.

Early each year, usually in January, the president sends his budget recommendations for the following fiscal year to Congress. The fiscal year runs from October 1 through September 30 of the following year. His budget proposal is the result of a full ten to twelve months of preparatory work involving the interaction of his office with the U.S. Office of Management and Budget and with affected government departments and agencies. The Council of Economic Advisers and the Treasury assist in the budget formulation process, advising on the feasibility of particular programs and on the *overall* budget impact of those programs.

Upon receipt of the president's budget recommendations, various subcommittees of the House of Representatives Appropriations Committee go to work separately reviewing, debating, and revising components of the original budget bill. The resulting recommendations are reported to the full Appropriations Committee which, in turn, reports its own actions to the entire House of Representatives. After the House passes its version of the budget, it must still be sent to the Senate for consideration. In the Senate it follows a sequence similar to that in the House, with subcommittees, full committees, then the entire Senate considering the budget. If the Senate's version of the budget differs from that of the House, the bill is resubmitted to committee. When both houses of Congress approve a common budget bill, that bill is sent to the president who can approve (sign the bill into law), veto, or allow the bill to become law without his approval. It is easy to see why adoption of a budget proposal might take some time, and how the resulting budget may be substantially altered from the president's proposed budget, both in the mix of public expenditures and in overall size.

Once a budget bill has become law, appropriation warrants are forwarded to the affected departments and agencies, which must revise their operating budgets to comply with approved appropriations. As the budgeted liabilities of the many government agencies accrue, the Treasury issues checks to cover them. Expenditure supervision is extensive; agency expenditures are reported regularly to the Office of Management and Budget with additional monitoring by the Treasury and the General Accounting Office (GAO).

Practical Limitations on Fiscal Policy: Problems of Timing and Budget Size

Our brief summary of the budgetary process indicates that a discretionary fiscal policy proposal must navigate a difficult, circuitous, and typically time-consuming course. By its very nature, this budgetary process is an impediment to the effective use of fiscal policy for stabilizing the economy. In addition, the constituency-oriented concerns of Congress have been a serious impediment to the effective application of fiscal policy.

Fiscal policy is national in scope, the important fiscal policy variables being the overall level of tax rates and the level of planned government outlays. For stabilization purposes, changes in *specific* tax, transfer, or expenditure programs are normally important only to the extent that they affect overall tax and outlay levels. In stark contrast, a U.S. senator or a member of the House of Representatives has as a primary concern specific tax changes and specific expenditure programs. His or her foremost fiscal concern is with the impact on his or her constituency of specific budget proposals; for example, with the level of government spending in the region on dams, highways, and military installations, and with the fairness to the constituency of proposed tax and transfer programs. The overall level of taxes and outlays is of distinctly secondary concern to the national legislator. Because a major budget package consists of many individual programs that have different impacts on different regions and groups, the time-consuming bargaining and compromise process in which Congress involves itself is inevitable. In that process, it is easy to lose focus on the stabilization objectives of the overall budget. As a consequence, Congress can provide, and often has provided, budgets that must be characterized as woefully inappropriate for stabilization needs.

The 1974 Reform of the Budget Review Process. In 1974, legislation was adopted to alter the congressional budget review process. That legislation requires Congress to initiate its role in the budget-making process by setting an overall expenditure goal and by specifying target levels for expenditures on each major functional category in the budget. The initial budget resolution that provides those totals must be completed by May 15 each year, and must also include a target for federal revenues with a recommendation for any discretionary changes in tax schedules deemed necessary.

With the guidelines provided by the first budget resolution, individual congressional committees proceed as before in considering individual budget proposals and presenting them to appropriations committees. When the appropriations committees have completed their deliberations, the full Congress must review the overall budget results and make any adjustments required for consistency with stabilization objectives.

Timing Problems Remain. By diverting congressional attention from the piecemeal consideration of individual budget bills to the size of the overall budget, the formal budget review process was devised produce fiscal programs that are more appropriate for stabilization purposes. At this point in time, it is not obvious that this goal has been achieved. Moreover, even if budget bills that provide the degree of fiscal stimulus or restraint that is judged appropriate for stabilization purposes are ultimately provided, the time required for their passage can still be so long that fiscal policy's usefulness as a countercyclical weapon is seriously compromised. In assessing the timing limitations on fiscal policy, we can use the same breakdown of the overall policy lag time that we used with monetary policy. The overall lag is just the sum of the three component lags, recognition, administrative, and operational, with the first two comprising the inside lag and the last the outside lag.

There is little reason to think that the recognition lag has to be much different for fiscal policy than it is for monetary policy because the same data series on economic activity are available to both fiscal and monetary authorities. As we have seen, the same claim cannot be made for the administrative lag. In practice, the administrative lag has been long enough to convince many analysts that fiscal policy cannot be effectively employed to combat short-run fluctuations in economic activity. However, there are techniques of instituting discretionary fiscal actions that can shorten that lag. As a first step, it has long been argued that institutional reforms are needed to separate as much as possible the formulation of national income policy (overall tax and outlay levels) from the establishment of specific tax programs and from the detailed allocation of budgeted expenditures to particular programs. The 1974 reform of the budget review process reflects formal, legislative recognition of the need for that separation. With recognition of that need, it is possible to design fiscal actions that affect the level of economic activity while minimizing the involvement of Congress in debates over questions of tax equity and resource allocation. The 10 percent surcharge on income taxes adopted during the Johnson administration reflects an effort to take advantage of that separation. While a surcharge on taxes raises the entire structure of tax rates, it leaves the progressive nature of the tax structure, the distribution of tax liabilities across the population, and the allocation of government outlays essentially unchanged. Even so, Congress imposed the 10 percent surcharge in July 1968, a year and a half after President Johnson requested it as an anti-inflation weapon early in 1967.

In recognition of the difficulty Congress has in quickly providing the fiscal policy actions appropriate for combating short-run income fluctuations, there have been proposals to transfer that responsibility to an automatic rule or to another part of government. One set of proposals suggests that the budget should be changed by formula. For example, Congress might establish a rule that all income taxes would automatically be raised by 10 percent when the unemployment rate falls below 5 percent, and fall by 10 percent when unemployment rises above 6 percent. Congress could make the formulas as simple or complex as desired, with taxes and outlays chang-ing automatically when unemployment, prices, production levels, and so on move past predetermined limits. Again, automatic (induced) changes in the budget can only reduce the size of unwanted fluctuations in economic ac-tivity, not prevent them. Moreover, constructing a rule that would provide the correct fiscal adjustment for the array of disturbances that can affect an industrialized economy is a task of awesome complexity (shades of the rules-versus-discretion arguments in Chapter 13). As an alternative, Con-gress could grant the president authority to change tax rates and expenditure levels within prescribed limits to help stabilize the economy, and a number of presidents have called for that authority during their terms in office. Perhaps the major difficulty with this proposal is political. Congress has jealously guarded its power to control taxes and expenditures. So far, it has refused to delegate any of that power to another branch of government; so the administrative lag remains a major stumbling block in the successful application of discretionary fiscal policy.

The final lag in applying stabilization policy, the outside or operational lag, can be far less troublesome with fiscal policy than with monetary policy. A personal income tax change can alter disposable income with little delay; a change in witholding rates will be reflected in the next paycheck. Of course, as our analysis of consumption behavior demonstrated, the size of the consumption response to an income tax change depends crucially on whether the public perceives that tax change as temporary or permanent. A 10 percent tax surcharge or tax rebate that is explicitly temporary may have a limited impact on aggregate demand even though disposable income can be quickly altered by such a tax change.

In contrast, fiscal legislation that calls for an altered level of expenditures on public works projects directly changes aggregate demand but with a longer lag. An increase in public works projects requires a planning period, the issuance of contracts, and so on. Moreover, a cutback in public works expenditures is inefficient (should projects be left unfinished?), and often not politically feasible. To partly relieve the extended outside lag, it has been suggested that the government maintain an inventory of carefully pre-planned projects. The funding for such "off-the-shelf" projects could be increased or decreased as required for stabilizing the economy.

Changes in the corporate tax rate or in the size of the investment tax credit also suffer from significant lags because they function by prompting revisions in investment commitments. However, government expenditure on labor could be changed quite quickly.

Just how quickly or slowly do changes in taxes and government spending affect the economy? It should come as no surprise that the precise timing of the impact of tax and expenditure changes cannot be assessed with cer-tainty. Modern research with empirical models of the aggregate economy suggests that both tax and expenditure changes have some effect on equi-librium output within the first quarter after the policy action, and that within one year either policy action strongly affects economy activity. The most comprehensive econometric models of the economy (the Brookings Model, the Wharton Model, the Federal Reserve-Penn-SSRC Model, and the BEA Model), discussed in detail in Chapter 17, exhibit general agreement on the strength and timing of fiscal policy actions. For example, the consensus from these models is that a $1 billion increase in government spending can be expected to raise GNP by $1 to 1½ billion within the quarter in which government spending rises, and by some $2½ to over 3 billion after two years.[6]

The Potential for Politically Motivated Fiscal Actions that Are Ultimately Destabilizing. At least brief consideration should be given to an additional problem that involves an inducement for fiscal actions to be destabilizing. This stems from the fact that, with changes in aggregate demand, *quantity* adjustments in employment and output occur more quickly than do *price* adjustments (changes in the inflation rate). Consider an economy with an inflation rate of 7 percent and an unemployment rate of 7 percent several months prior to national elections. It would be natural for the party in power under such circumstances to recognize that a stimulative fiscal policy, say, an income tax reduction, is apt to appeal to voters. Not only would voters view the tax cut as a direct income stimulus, but within a few months that fiscal stimulus could lower unemployment and raise production. Because there appears to be a longer lag in the inflation rate response (the short-run Phillips curve having a shallow slope), it may be after the election that the inflation cost of fiscal stimulus impinges on the economy, calling for restrictive stabilization actions. A pattern of actions like that described would clearly accentuate fluctuations in the economy.

A Brief Overview

What overall assessment have we obtained on the usefulness of fiscal policy as an anticyclical tool? Some analysts think our political institutions require an administrative lag that is too long to permit the use of fiscal policy for offsetting any fluctuations in economic activity. In contrast, there are some ardent supporters of active fiscal policy use who argue that the lags involved in applying discretionary fiscal policy are often quite short and, with relatively minor institutional changes, could become inconsequential. Because empirical evidence suggests that budget changes do have a strong effect on output within a few months, they argue that fiscal policy certainly can be relied on whenever the economy deviates significantly from its trend path of expansion. Notably, the periods of fiscal stimulus provided in the early 1960s and in the mid-1970s are generally viewed favorably in terms of their

---

[6]See Blinder, *Fiscal Policy in Theory and Practice*, p. 19; Gary Fromm and Lawrence R. Klein, "A Comparison of Eleven Econometric Models of the United States," *American Economic Review, Papers and Proceedings*, May 1973, pp. 389–393; and Albert A. Hirsch, "Policy Multipliers in the BEA Quarterly Econometric Model," *Survey of Current Business*, June 1977, pp. 60–72.

stabilizing effect on the economy. The 1968 tax increase was also clearly needed, although it should have come earlier. At the same time, fiscal actions can certainly contribute to instability. The persistent drift toward added fiscal stimulus during the period 1965–1967 contributed to the over-heating of the economy. At this point, it appears that the majority of economists agree that frequent budget adjustments, aimed at "fine tuning" the economy's expansion path, are not justified on the basis of our experience with fiscal policy, while any persistent tendency for the economy to deviate from its full-employment expansion path justifies consideration of fiscal remedies.

A More Detailed Review
of the Vietnam War and its Aftermath

The primary source of fiscal stimulus in 1965 had nothing to do with, indeed was at odds with, stabilization policy. In the 1965–1968 period, government expenditures were increased rapidly, both because of the war build-up in Vietnam and because of a sizable expansion in social program ("Great Society") outlays. In the face of quickening inflation in 1966, Congress temporarily suspended the 7 percent tax credit on investment, a modest action that was more than offset by increases in government spending. However, because monetary policy was quite restrictive, a general slowdown in economic expansion and a marked decline in construction developed toward the end of 1966. Fearful of stifling the prolonged economic expansion that had been underway since the beginning of the decade, Congress quickly restored the investment tax credit and the Federal Reserve eased monetary policy. With that policy reversal, the spectre of inflation reappeared.

Growing inflationary pressures finally prompted President Johnson to ask Congress for an income tax surcharge in January 1967. After an extended debate centering on the relative merits of an expenditure cut versus a tax increase, the Congress, in June of 1968, provided a 10 percent surtax coupled with a planned expenditure cut of some $6 billion (holding outlays to $180.1 billion for the fiscal year). However, the apparently strong shift toward fiscal restraint (the high employment budget shifted toward surplus by more than $27 billion from the first half of 1968 to the second half of 1969) failed to have the expected depressing effect on the economy. Unemployment remained below 4 percent, and the inflation rate actually accelerated through the fourth quarter of 1969. With the tax surcharge extended for a second year, the investment tax credit once again repealed, and a strong shift toward monetary stringency beginning in the first half of 1969, a substantial slowdown in economic activity began to surface by the end of the year. However, with well-entrenched inflationary expectations, the *deliberately engineered* slowdown in economic activity that began at the end of 1969 did not immediately slow inflation to an acceptable rate. Even so, it did lead to the elimination of generalized excess demand as the source of inflation pressure. The degree of slack introduced into the economy was reflected in an increase in the unemployment rate from the 3.5 percent average of 1969 to over 6 percent by the end of 1970.

While a tax relief and reform bill passed in December 1969, coupled with the June 1969 expiration of the surtax and an increase in government outlays, shifted the high-employment budget toward a less restrictive posture, the high employment budget still showed a sizable surplus of nearly $10 billion for all of 1970. With a 6 percent unemployment rate judged to be intolerably high, actions taken in 1971 included introduction of more liberal capital depreciation guidelines for tax purposes, reenactment of an investment tax credit, a personal income tax cut, and a sizable increase in government outlays. It was hoped that this tightwire-walking attempt to simultaneously lower unemployment and inflation could be pulled off with the help of wage-price controls. Gratifyingly, through 1972 employment and output rose briskly while the inflation rate declined. Unfortunately, though, the honeymoon was short-lived. The confrontation of swelling demands, fueled by a world-wide inflationary boom, with large-scale crop failures and critically short supplies of basic materials and energy sources, put strong upward pressure on prices during 1973 and 1974. In addition, the depreciation of the dollar in foreign exchange markets raised the prices of imported goods and transferred demand to domestic production. While both fiscal and monetary authorities might have better anticipated some of the special events that renewed inflationary pressures in 1973 and accentuated them in 1974, it is hard to imagine which stabilization policies might have achieved a markedly lower rate of inflation without massively increasing unemployment. In fact, restraint on aggregate demand in 1974, achieved primarily through a marked reduction in the rate of monetary expansion, raised unemployment to over 7 percent of the labor force at the close of 1974, while "double digit" inflation continued. Of course, theoretical arguments and empirical observations suggest that, with a lag, the slack that restrictive stabilization policies introduced during 1974 would slow inflation, and in the early months of 1975 the public received the good news that inflation was moderating. The accompanying bad news was the reason! During the last quarter of 1974 and the first few months of 1975, the economy was experiencing its sharpest and most persistent contraction since the depression. So abrupt was the contraction that it prompted a dramatically rapid reversal of stabilization strategy by the Ford administration. After calling for restrictive policies (including a 5 percent income tax surcharge) to combat inflation in October 1974, the Ford administration reversed its stance and requested a modest package of tax relief in January 1975. Just over two months later, Congress passed a $23 billion tax cut package that included a rebate on individual income taxes paid on 1974 income, a reduction in individual tax obligations in 1975, and an increase in the investment tax credit to a 10 percent rate for two years.

Some of the personal income tax provisions of the 1975 tax reduction program were extended, with modifications, through 1976, 1977, and 1978.

Notably, there were continuing increases in the "standard deduction" used in calculating personal income tax liabilities, and a tax credit based on the number of tax exemptions was maintained. Fiscal and monetary policy in this time interval was supportive of a strong expansion in demand, and, in 1976, real GNP rose by more than 6 percent with employment expanding by over 3 percent. Employment and output continued expanding through 1977, but with the labor force growing briskly, unemployment rates remained above desired levels. Serving as an offset to the shift toward fiscal restraint that inflationary increases in incomes provide, the Tax Reduction and Simplification Act of 1977, passed at the end of May, provided for the maintenance through 1978 of some earlier tax cuts (cited above) and authorized government outlays for creation of jobs through state and local government.

In 1978, inflation accelerated and unemployment fell faster than the Carter administration had anticipated. As a consequence, fiscal and monetary policy were allowed to shift in the direction of restraint. On the fiscal front, the effect of inflation on nominal incomes and, hence, tax brackets, combined with a slower than anticipated growth in federal outlays were the dominant factors shifting the high employment budget in the direction of restraint. With inflation persisting at an accelerated rate in 1979, the high employment budget was permitted to shift toward a larger surplus and, as the year progressed, monetary restraint pushed interest rates upward briskly.

World oil prices roughly doubled in 1979. With energy cost increases the single dominant force and with support from rapid increases in housing costs and food prices, the Consumer Price Index leaped upward by 13.3 percent in 1979. That intolerable inflation trajectory called forth a restrictive monetary stance (which drove interest rates to record levels in 1980), accompanied by a further shift upward in the high employment budget. The result was a sharp contraction in economic activity in 1980, setting the stage for a broad array of tax reduction proposals by Carter, Reagan, and congressional committees as the 1980 elections approached.

To briefly summarize the lesson in fiscal philosophy that can be drawn from our postwar experience, there have been major changes in accepted budget policy in just a few decades. We have moved from the view that government budgets should always be balanced, to broad acceptance in the 1960s and 1970s of the active use of discretionary fiscal policy as a basic tool of stabilization policy. At the beginning of the 1980s, however, there exists a growing contingent that believes that the pendulum has swung too far; that a highly activist fiscal policy is as likely to be destabilizing as stabilizing. It is noteworthy, however, as an indicator of the current commitment to modern fiscal theory, that, since the early 1960s, both liberal and conservative administrations have relied on the high-employment budget concept to justify budgets that have yielded very large measured imbalances; and both parties continue to advocate fiscal actions in the face of fluctuations in economic activity. What is most evident is that much remains to be learned about the optimal role of fiscal policy. More detailed information on the actual impact of particular fiscal policy actions is needed. It is also essential that policy makers improve their ability to forecast the strength of private demand and, indeed, the level of future government spending. And even with a much improved understanding of the influence of fiscal actions, there remains a need for institutional reforms that would permit a quicker fiscal response to economic developments.

Some Contemporary Fiscal Policy Proposals

With stabilization policy failing to elicit an acceptable performance from the U.S. economy for many years, the search for effective fiscal actions has produced an assortment of proposals that range from imaginative innovations in the structure of tax levies to the return to budget philosophies of an earlier age.

Tax Incentives to Slow Inflation

Prominent among the innovative proposals for dealing with stagflation are *tax-based income policies* (abbreviated TIP), which would use tax incentives to obtain labor compliance with a guideline for permissable rates of wage increase. One form of TIP policy would lower the tax obligations (through tax credits) of workers who accept wage increases below the guideline rate. In another form of TIP program, employers would be subject to tax penalties if they granted wage increases exceeding the guideline rate. In either case, the supply side of the economy is viewed as maintaining upward pressure on prices. Opposition to these policies stems partially from reluctance to blame the labor sector for persistent inflation and also from the recognition of potential problems in the application of either form of TIP policy. Critics contend that, with tax relief for minimizing wage increases, disposable income and, hence, aggregate demand may be left at excessive (inflationary) levels. With tax penalties for granting wage increases above the guideline rate, it has been suggested that production would be inhibited, prompting the price increases that the TIP program was intended to prevent. This could happen if the wage restrictions resulted in strikes. In addition, in expanding industries that might need to accelerate wage offer increases to attract sufficient labor, the tax penalties might reduce the incentive for expansion, resulting in restricted supplies (and higher prices) in those industries over time.

The Kemp-Roth View

Representing a broader view of the role of tax incentives (or disincentives), some critics of traditional fiscal policy argue that effective tax rates in the United States have climbed so high that they discourage individual production efforts and business capital formation. As a result, the growth of labor productivity is lagging, contributing (again from the supply side of the economy) to continued inflation. According to this view, if the government's budget were decisively reduced (say, 30 percent over a three-year period), so that fewer resources were diverted to government use, the reduced tax disincentives to generating income would prompt a vigorous expansion of economic activity. This view is reflected in the Kemp-Roth bill, which has languished in Congress for an extended period.

As an added bonus of the cutback in government resource usage, supporters of this view occasionally argue that, in spite of lowered tax rates, total tax revenues would actually expand as a consequence of the vigorous induced expansion in production and, hence, income. This argument is the basis of the Laffer Curve, to which you may have seen references. As illustrated in Figure 14—4, the Laffer Curve thesis asserts that there is some tax rate *(t*)* that maximizes total tax revenues and that further increases in tax rates, by depressing production, result in lowered tax revenues. In the Laffer view of the economy, tax rates are above *t** so that tax rate reductions, rather than increases, would be needed to eliminate a budget deficit. While economists are generally much concerned with the production disincentives stemming from taxation, and while many would prefer that government absorb a smaller fraction of the economy's productive resources (holding *t* at a lower rate), relatively few have adopted the thesis, reflected in the Kemp-Roth bill and the Laffer Curve, that tax rates are above the level *(t*)* that would maximize tax revenues.

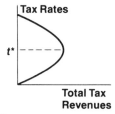

Figure 14—4 / The Laffer Curve

The Balanced Budget Cure

There have always been advocates of government budget balance, but, with rapid inflation persisting, the support for budget balance has become more widespread and insistent in recent years. Reflecting a view of the requirements for macroeconomic equilibrium that has been reviewed in this chapter, former Council of Economic Advisors Chairman Arthur Okun argued in 1980 that adoption of any proposal for balancing the fiscal 1981 federal budget would be merely a symbolic act rather than a cure for inflation. To illustrate that claim, he offered the following argument: "Suppose that federal expenditures for fiscal 1981 were reduced by $20 billion with no accompanying tax reduction or any other measure. That expenditure cut would amount to four-fifths of one percent of GNP. By the end of 1981, such a reduction might be expected to cut the total of private and public expenditures for goods and services—the dollar value of our GNP—by roughly 1.5 percent (using a "multiplier" of 2). That 1.5 percent cutback in total national spending would be divided into two components: a reduction in the price level and a reduction in output. While any estimate of the shares of these two components is uncertain, the statistical evidence indicates clearly that the reduction in output would be the larger component. On my own best guess, the reduction in the inflation rate at the end of 1981 would be 0.3 of 1 percent (with a 1.2 percent reduction in output)—although I could envision the possibility of a reduction as large as 0.6 of 1 percent.

All the evidence of U.S. price-wage behavior indicates that the payoff to this hypothetical program would be a mere fraction of a point on the inflation rate. The evidence from other nations confirms that balanced budgets are neither a necessary nor a sufficient cure for inflation. The two major industrial countries with the least inflation in recent years, namely Germany and Japan, had total government deficits in 1979 of 3 percent and 5 percent of GNP, respectively, or the equivalent of $75 billion and $125 billion for an economy of our size. Moreover, both had much larger total government deficits than ours consistently in 1976, 1977, and 1978.

As my numerical estimates make clear, whether or not the federal budget is balanced for fiscal 1981 is an issue of limited economic importance. But it is of utmost importance to recognize a placebo for what it is. Public officials must not fool themselves or the American public into believing that a balanced budget for 1981 is the cure for inflation."[7]

Supporters of budget balancing might respond that even the symbolism of balancing the budget could have a favorable effect on inflationary expectations. However, more important, they would argue, are the long-term effects of budget imbalances. These include: (1) a boost in interest rates, accompanied by a squeeze in private capital formation as government borrowing competes for funds with private business borrowing; and (2) pressure on the Fed to boost the money supply (fueling inflation) in an effort to prevent unpopular increases in interest rates. Okun himself would give these potential long-term consequences of budget imbalances careful consideration but would emphasize that budget balance is no "silver bullet solution" for persistent inflation.

Further Refinements in Fiscal Theory: Government Finance with Unbalanced Budgets

Recognition that stabilization policy might require a budget that is chronically out of balance forces us to be more deeply concerned with nontax methods of budget finance. Actually, this subject was broached in Chapter 8 when we tried to carefully distinguish *pure* monetary and fiscal policies from *combined* monetary-fiscal policies. To refresh your memory by example, in that chapter a pure fiscal policy was defined as a government budget change that leaves an *exogenously* determined money supply unaltered; its impact in the aggregate model stemmed from a shift in the *IS* schedule. Now that our analysis has shown that the money supply is positively related to the interest rate, with the Fed able to exogenously control the volume of reserves made available to the financial system, we have to

---

[7]Arthur Okun, "The Balanced Budget Is a Placebo," *Challenge,* May/June 1980, p. 3.

think of a pure fiscal policy as one that leaves the volume of reserves the Fed chooses to provide (thus, the position of our *LM* schedule) unchanged. As before, the impact of a pure fiscal policy stems from a shift in the *IS* schedule. In contrast, a fiscal policy action can be financed in a way that alters the volume of reserves, such a combined fiscal-monetary policy involving a simultaneous shift in both the *IS* and *LM* schedules in the aggregate model.

At this point, we can profit by briefly reviewing and, in one new way, amplifying our earlier discussion of the ramifications of alternative techniques of financing unbalanced budgets. The amplification involves recognizing that an unbalanced budget produces a change in society's wealth by altering the volume of government debt it holds. With government purchases in excess of tax revenues, the public will acquire additional government bonds or money (interest-bearing or noninterest-bearing government debt) in the amount of the deficit. Conversely, with the government running a surplus, the public will lose ownership of government debt, bonds or money, in the amount of the surplus. If consumption demand responds positively to changes in society's wealth, the direct impact on aggregate demand of fiscal policy actions will be strengthened by the wealth effect that an unbalanced budget provides. For example, a fiscal policy action that directly increases aggregate demand (an increase in government spending, a reduction in tax collections, or both) can, through an enlarged deficit that increases society's wealth, provide additional stimulation by raising the consumption component of aggregate demand.

Deficit Finance

Turning attention now to specific techniques of financing budget imbalances, consider, first, the consequences of financing an enlarged deficit by selling bonds to the public. When an increase in the budget deficit is financed by bond sales to the public, the public acquires government bonds in exchange for money. However, when the Treasury spends the money proceeds of its bond sales, it exactly restores the public's money holdings, leaving financial system reserves and the total money stock unchanged, but leaving the public's wealth increased by the amount of the bond issue. While the wealth increase may reinforce any direct increase in aggregate demand (rightward shift in the *IS* curve) stemming from the fiscal policy action, the *LM* schedule is unaffected by the deficit.[8] Fiscal actions that enlarge the deficit, as long as they are financed through bond sales to the public, still qualify as "pure" fiscal policies.

Our arguments are altered if the Treasury finances an increase in the

---

[8]If the demand for money depends on the volume of wealth, any increase in wealth would shift the money demand schedule and, consequently, the *LM* schedule. For an analysis of the impact of fiscal policy with money demand assumed to be a positive function of wealth, see William Silber, "Fiscal Policy in *IS-LM* Analysis: A Correction," *Journal of Money, Credit, and Banking,* 2 (1970): 461–472.

deficit through bond sales to the central bank. In this case, the Treasury swaps bonds with the Fed for deposits (at the Fed) that it can spend by check. When the Treasury spends its new deposits to cover the deficit increase, it merely transfers ownership of those deposits to the public by check. The recipients of the checks the Treasury draws on its account at the Fed, holders of new government debt, deposit those checks in their checking accounts, providing additional reserves (in the amount of the deficit) to the financial system. Those new reserves can support a multiple expansion of the money supply. The increase in reserves, a debt of a government unit (the central bank), reflects the increase in wealth the deficit bestows on the public. More important is the increase in money supply that results from this technique of deficit finance. A fiscal policy action that generates a deficit becomes a combination fiscal-monetary policy if the deficit is financed through bond sales to the central bank. The rightward shift of the *IS* curve is accompanied by a rightward shift in the *LM* curve.[9]

Financing a deficit via bond sales to the central bank is equivalent to financing the deficit through the printing of new money (currency). In either case, society's wealth and the volume of reserve money available to the financial system are increased by the amount of the deficit. Consequently, such bond sales are said to *monetize* the new government debt. As we already know, with a money supply increase combined with an expansionary fiscal policy, the interest rate rise that normally accompanies expansion is offset, permitting a stronger expansion than a pure fiscal policy of the same size would provide.

Surplus Finance

Just as fiscal actions can generate deficits, they can also generate surpluses. How the economy reacts depends in part on what the government does with its surplus—whether it is used to retire publicly held government bond debt or to retire bonds held by the central bank, or is just held idle.

With the tax bill, which the public pays to the government by check, exceeding government spending, the public's money holdings are reduced by the amount of the budget surplus. However, if the government uses that surplus to retire (buy back) government bonds held by the public, the same volume of money balances is returned to the public. Banking system reserves (and the *LM* curve) are left unchanged while the public's wealth is reduced by the amount of the surplus; that is, by the amount its bond holdings have declined with this pure fiscal policy. Thus, a restrictive fiscal policy that generates an increased surplus is a pure fiscal policy if the surplus is used to retire publicly owned government bonds.

---

[9]As an example of just such a combination fiscal-monetary policy, when the Treasury offers large volumes of new bonds for sale in order to refinance maturing bond debt and cover any current deficit, the Fed pursues an "even-keel" policy of maintaining interest rates (bond prices). To maintain bond prices in the face of an increased supply of bonds, the Fed must willingly purchase bonds at the support price.

On the other hand, if the surplus money proceeds that the fiscal program provides are used to retire bonds held by the central bank, the money supply will decline by a multiple of the surplus. In this case, the Treasury, through a check drawn on an account it keeps in the banking system, exchanges its surplus tax proceeds with the central bank for existing bonds. With that exchange, the financial system loses reserves in the amount of the surplus, inducing a multiple contraction of the money supply. The loss of reserves reflects society's loss of wealth, but more important is the money supply shrinkage. With a reduction in reserves accompanying a restrictive fiscal policy (both *IS* and *LM* shifted leftward), the resulting contraction would be stronger than one produced by a pure fiscal policy. These arguments continue to apply if the Treasury simply holds its surplus tax proceeds idle in its demand deposit account with the Fed. When the Treasury transfers deposits from its banking system account to its Fed account, the financial system loses an equal volume of reserves, causing a contraction of the money supply. It makes little difference to the Treasury whether the budget surplus is actually used to retire bonds held by the Fed, or is simply deposited in its account with the Fed. Each year the Fed returns its "profits" (which are substantial) to the Treasury, including interest revenues earned by the Fed on its government bond holdings.

In practice, virtually all stabilization policies are mixed monetary-fiscal policies. Still, those policy actions are separable into pure fiscal actions controlled by Congress (shifting only the *IS* curve), and monetary policy actions (shifting the *LM* curve) that are controlled by the Fed because the Fed can decide *independently* whether it wishes to be a net purchaser or seller of government bonds during any time period. Of course, the Fed may often act in a way that reinforces fiscal policy. An expansionary fiscal policy, as we know, tends to increase interest rates. If the Fed wishes to hold down interest rates as an aid to economic expansion, it must increase the money supply. In fact, as long as the Fed follows a policy of "leaning against the wind" (i.e., permitting the money stock to grow in an ostensibly "tight" money market in which the interest rate is rising, and reducing the money stock in a slack market in which the interest rate is falling), its actions will reinforce fiscal policy.

Deficit Finance and the Burden of the National Debt

With cumulative budget deficits that have exceeded cumulative surpluses, and the difference financed largely through public bond sales, the United States has seen its national debt grow from just over $1 billion at the beginning of the century to around $850 billion at the end of 1979. While a large share of the existing government debt is the result of war financing, the budgetary effects of government investments and recession (particularly in recent years) have contributed substantially to the total. Should the use of fiscal policy for stabilization purposes necessitate chronic budget deficits in the future, the public debt will continue to mount.

For decades, "fiscally responsible" politicians and conservative editorialists have warned of the dire consequences of the "bankrupting" growth in national debt. If they are correct in suggesting that an increasing national debt imposes heavy burdens on society, policy makers should carefully weigh those burdens before deciding to employ fiscal policies that raise the debt.

As a background to examining the burdens that debt finance can actually impose on society, we need to deal with a pair of ancillary issues that frequently intrude in discussions of the debt burden. First, we must disabuse ourselves of the notion that the government is just like a business firm. Too often, it seems, political commentators argue by analogy that the federal government, like a business firm, cannot indefinitely spend more than it collects in (tax) revenues without becoming bankrupt. Decidedly unlike a business firm, the federal government has virtually unlimited debt repayment power. Should it choose to fully retire the existing debt, though there is no reason why it should, it could do so through taxation or through the creation of new money. The government cannot go bankrupt. Furthermore, even the claim that business firms must have revenues that cover their full costs is patently absurd. Business firms can and often do borrow (run a deficit) as a normal practice. In fact, the growth in business debt in the United States since World War II has outrun the growth of the national debt.

The second ancillary issue arises because, historically, the debate among economists and other antagonists over the burden of debt-financed government spending has had a broad focus. In addition to analyzing the implications of bond as opposed to tax finance of a specific level of government spending, that debate has dealt with the productiveness of government resource usage. So that we can focus attention on the burdens that may result solely from the choice of bond issue as a means of financing government outlays, we first need to deal with the matter of the productiveness of government resource usage.

With the spending power gained through either tax levies or bond sales, the government can procure real resources (land, labor, and capital) for *public* use. With the economy operating at full employment, those resources have to be shifted from private use. Whether the resource transfer from private to public use imposes a burden on society depends on the benefits society reaps from that transfer. If the benefits from government use of resources are greater than those that flowed from their private use, it is wrong to talk about that resource usage imposing a burden on society. If that is not the case, if government resource use is less productive than private use, a burden is imposed on society; aggregate economic welfare will be reduced. Again, this burden stems from an inefficient allocation of resources (more resources allocated to public use and less to private use than optimum allocation would call for) and is not dependent on the technique used for financing the government spending; it exists whether that spending is bond or tax financed.

On the other hand, if government spending (however it is financed) puts real resources to work that would otherwise be idle, the question of a burden from inefficient resource usage is moot. If production is raised by government resource usage (some real resources that would otherwise lie idle being used to provide goods and services), society's welfare is unequivocally enhanced by the government's spending, though some other method of mobilizing those resources might be preferred.[10]

Comparable arguments apply to concerns over the impact that current government resource usage has on the well-being of future generations, our children and grandchildren. Once again there is a burden from wasteful resource usage by government. If the government squanders real resources, some of which would have been used to enhance the economy's productive capacity, future generations inherit a reduced capacity to provide wanted goods and services. In fact, if the government's resource usage simply enhances current consumption at the expense of investment, the same conclusion holds. On the other hand, if the government productively invests the resources it commands, for example, for school and highway construction, medical research, and parks, it is possible for future generations to enjoy a standard of living higher than would be attained without the resource transfer from private to public use. We must remind ourselves, though, that the burdens (or benefits) which flow to future generations as a direct result of current government resource usage are not the direct and unavoidable consequence of the technique chosen for financing government spending. Whether the government uses taxes or bonds to finance the acquisition of productive resources, if it uses those resources less (more) productively than the private economy would have, future generations will be burdened (benefited).

Burdens from the Choice of Bond (Debt) Finance

We can now focus attention narrowly on assessing the burdens that may arise directly from the choice to finance some government outlays by bond sales rather than through tax levies. Of course, to the continuing dismay of fiscal conservatives, it is because debt issue was frequently relied on to finance government outlays that, by the end of 1979, the national debt had risen to the $850 billion level cited earlier. In their strident pleas for balancing the government budget, lay critics of deficit finance have often buttressed their offensive with emotion-packed statements of "fact." With a population of some 220 million, it could be claimed in 1979 that ". . . each man, woman, and child in the United States (even newborn babies) is saddled with more than $3800 in debt, whether he knows it or not." The in-

---

[10]At times stabilization actions employing government budget adjustments may be constrained (as they should be) by concern over their influence on resource allocation. See Richard Musgrave, *The Theory of Public Finance* (New York: McGraw-Hill, 1959), pp. 517–520; and Julius Margolis, "Public Works and Economic Stability," *Journal of Political Economy* 57 (1949): 293–303.

tended imagery is clear. Because we as taxpayers bear ultimate responsibility for servicing the national debt, we and our children (and their children) owe for the national debt, and our obligations grow with each successive budget deficit.

Fortunately, in spite of the visions of imminent economic ruin that they can evoke, the harshest critics of debt finance have clearly overstated their case for the burden of debt finance, leaving their arguments open to easy attack. It is true that, as taxpayers, we citizens of the United States are responsible for the national debt. In addition, with recurrent deficits, future generations will owe an enlarged debt. However, the national debt, current and future, must be owed to someone, and, to the extent that it is an *internally* held debt, that someone is the U.S. citizenry. United States citizens may face higher tax obligations because of a national debt, but in the aggregate those higher tax payments would be just matched by higher interest payments to U.S. citizens as long as the debt is domestically owned. For an internally held public debt, the tax obligation burden has often been dismissed by economists with the quip, "we owe it to ourselves." With no externally held debt, future generations of U.S. citizens both own (in the form of bonds) and owe (as taxpayers) the debt inherited from earlier generations. The mere creation of paper securities (bonds that are assets to the owners and equivalent liabilities to the issuer) can neither enrich nor impoverish a nation. Thus, it is far from obvious that increasing the national debt (the national *credit* held by bond-owning U.S. citizens) will alter the nation's accumulation of real wealth or its production of real goods and services.

Actual Burdens from Debt Finance

While the propositions in the preceding paragraph effectively disenfranchise the simplistic layman's notion of the manner in which debt-financing government spending may impose a burden on future generations, it would be a mistake to conclude that there are no such burdens. There are, and economists have long been concerned with them. To begin with, in response to the quip that "we owe it [the public debt] to ourselves," it is obvious that not all individuals or families hold interest-bearing government debt in proportion to the debt-servicing tax liabilities they face. Hence, even if on aggregation the taxes destined for paying interest on the inherited national debt are matched by interest receipts, there can be a distributional burden from servicing the debt. While the evidence is not clear-cut, it is generally thought that bond holdings are concentrated in higher income groups so that the debt service tends to be regressive, redistributing income from lower to higher income groups (from taxpayers in general to bondholders). If servicing the debt increases income inequality, conflicting with the social objective of reducing inequality in income distribution, a legitimate debt burden exists. However, it is usually agreed that quantitatively this burden is of relatively minor consequence in the United States.

As an additional burden, as earlier noted, an increase in tax rates to service a growing debt may reduce national output through its "disincentive" effects. The higher the income tax rate, the smaller is the reward obtained by foregoing leisure and working more hours or working more intensively. If the federal debt grows at a faster rate than the GNP does, or if the interest yield government must offer on new security issues rises enough, an increase in tax rates to meet the interest charges on the debt could be required. However, the national debt has grown less rapidly than the GNP since World War II (permitting a decline in the ratio of debt to GNP from 130 percent of GNP in 1945 to about 35 percent of GNP in 1979); and, in spite of an increase in interest rates to record levels in recent years, annual interest payments have barely edged above the 1½ to 2 percent of GNP range where they have resided for nearly three decades.

A third potential source of a burden that deficits can impose on future generations causes more concern among U.S. economists than the income redistribution and work disincentives that deficits may entail. To illustrate that source of burden, suppose the economy is operating at a noninflationary, full-employment equilibrium with a balanced budget. Of course, for equilibrium the appropriate monetary policy stance (the correct size money stock) must prevail. Now, let government spending rise. The added expenditure would be inflationary, but aggregate demand may be kept at the equilibrium level by an appropriate income tax increase accompanied by no monetary policy action. In that case, the greater use of resources by government would be at the expense of private consumption for the most part.

Alternatively, if the additional government spending is bond financed, inflation can be avoided only by employing a restrictive monetary policy, which raises the interest rate to reduce aggregate demand. The higher interest rate simply frees the resources, primarily from private investment, that are required for government usage. With a reduction in investment spending on new plants and equipment, future generations will inherit a smaller capital stock. A burden of reduced productive capacity is transferred to future generations as a consequence of the choice to bond, rather than tax, finance a prescribed level of government spending. The role of deficit finance in generating a "capital shortage" is clearly a matter of current concern.

There is general agreement among economists that the three potential burdens of (internal) debt finance that we have confronted are legitimate concerns. With somewhat less unanimity that list could be extended,[11] but with no further documentation, the qualitative implications of the debt bur-

---

[11]A fourth argument in support of the claim that deficits transfer a burden onto future generations is championed by James Buchanan. According to this argument, whatever level of expenditures the government chooses, if it finances those expenditures through debt issue, the bonds the government issues are *voluntarily* purchased by individual citizens and firms. The purchasers willingly surrender present command over real resources or privately issued securities because the return they expect to receive on their "investment" exceeds their subjective estimate of the yield foregone. Because all transactions are voluntary, it can be argued that no current burden is involved in the debt-financed transfer of productive resources from

den discussion are clear. There is some burden to debt finance, and the burden may be transferred to future generations.

External Debt

So far we have restricted our discussion to consideration of a domestically owned national debt; but, because a significant and growing proportion of the U.S. debt is foreign held (around 15 percent in 1979), the burden of an external debt deserves brief exploration. At first blush, it might seem that an external debt entails a far heavier burden than an internal debt. Rather than providing transfer payments that shift command over an unchanged volume of productive resources among a country's citizenry, the tax levies for servicing an external debt transmit control over real resources to foreign debt holders. The output of real goods and services available for domestic use would be larger if the debt were forgiven. However, this argument ignores the international transfer of real resources that occurred when the foreign-held debt was issued. In exchange for U.S. government securities, foreign citizens gave up command (in the form of pounds, marks, yen, and so on) over foreign-owned real resources. The U.S. government used the acquired foreign currency purchasing power to acquire goods and services from abroad, or exchanged that purchasing power with U.S. households and firms that wanted to buy foreign goods and services. In contrast to the case with internal debt, the volume of real productive resources available for domestic use was enlarged by the debt sales abroad, while no net change in the ownership of real resources occurred. In subsequent periods tax levies are required to service the foreign debt, but the taxes are levied on an income that is larger because of the exchange of government securities for real resources. Integrating resource allocation issues into the external debt discussion, if the imported resources were productively invested, future generations could be better off, even after allowance is made for the foreign debt service. In fact, governments of countries around the world regularly issue external debt, expecting the resources acquired through that debt issue to lift domestic output by enough to repay the externally held debt and leave a residual for domestic enjoyment.[12] It is possible, of course, that the returns reaped from the use of resources acquired through foreign bond sales will not service the debt, leaving future generations worse off on balance. Once again, that is because the resource usage was *unprofitable,* not because the

---

private to government use. However, according to Buchanan, the deficit does impose a burden on future generations. Because the private securities that government bond holders could have purchased offer yields that are little different from the yields on government bonds, the purchasers of the government bond issue will not be materially better off in the future owing to the issuance of public debt. In contrast, the members of the future generation who are *coerced* into paying tax levies to finance the interest charges on the public debt are clearly worse off. In this sense, a burden is imposed on future taxpayers as a consequence of the choice to debt finance current government spending. See James M. Buchanan and Marilyn R. Flowers, *The Public Finances* (Homewood, Ill.: Richard D. Irwin, 1975), Chapter 29.

[12]Does it make sense for business firms to finance the acquisition of capital goods externally?

debt was externally financed. For our purposes there is no reason to make a major distinction between internal and external debt issue.

Multiple Goals and the Coordination of Monetary and Fiscal Policies

Because debt finance does involve some burdens, it is reasonable to ask whether it is rational for the government to employ unbalanced budgets for stabilization purposes. As we know, both fiscal and monetary policy can be used to influence the overall level of aggregate demand; so, in principle, it should be possible to maintain full-employment equilibrium with a balanced budget. Hence, the ultimate justification for maintaining discretionary control over the state of budget balance must be the need to pursue more than just one policy goal at a time. The choice of an appropriate combination of monetary and fiscal policies must rest on the influence that choice has on secondary goals, including the economy's growth, the division of resource use between government and the private sector of the economy, the provision of housing, the maintenance of balance of payments equilibrium, and so on.

Under ideal conditions, the stabilization authorities would be able to maintain full-employment equilibrium without relying on countercyclical changes in government spending. The volume of scarce productive resources that the government employs (by spending) would be determined on grounds of resource allocation. However crude the calculation of benefits must be in practice, resources would be allocated to government production only to the extent that the benefits provided to society by government's production exceed the benefits that would accrue from private use of those resources. Inefficient variations in government spending (leaving projects unfinished when cutbacks occur and rushing into possibly ill-conceived projects when spending is accelerated) would be avoided. Of course, as long as discretionary control over taxes (hence over the state of budget balance) is maintained, the stabilization authorities would still have a fiscal policy tool available, and the choice of a monetary-fiscal policy mix would have to be made.

As we know, whether government spending is used as a control tool or not, alternative combinations of monetary and fiscal policies have differing effects on the economy's growth path. With no change in the anticipated rate of inflation, an expansionary (restrictive) monetary policy lowers (raises) the interest rate, while expansionary (restrictive) fiscal policy raises (lowers) the interest rate. If full employment is maintained by combining an expansionary monetary policy with a restrictive fiscal policy, the interest rate will be reduced. As a consequence, more of full-employment output will be allocated to investment, which contributes to future productive capacity, and less to current consumption. In contrast, a shift to a more restrictive monetary stance combined with a more expansionary fiscal policy would raise the interest rate, shifting resources out of investment and into current consumption use. The choice that the stabilization authorities make with regard to the appropriate combination of monetary and fiscal policy must be influenced by their preferences for current, as opposed to future, consumption standards, and only by coincidence would the policy combination preferred on such grounds provide a balanced government budget.

Also, as indicated in Chapter 13, when designing a stabilization program consideration must be given to any restrictions that may impinge on monetary policy. Perhaps most importantly, it has been noted that monetary policy can have an uneven impact on various sectors of the economy. High interest rates have a particularly harsh effect on home construction, on state and local borrowing, and perhaps on small business. Concern over such side effects of countercyclical monetary policy has contributed to the growing degree of agreement in recent years that the monetary authorities should normally press for a relatively steady expansion of the money supply, avoiding excessive swings in the money stock's growth rate that would produce excessive variations in the interest rate. However, if any constraint keeps one control tool from being used for domestic stabilization purposes, some other control device must be relied on to assume its role. In general, a separate control instrument is required for every target that must be pursued. With so many targets, full employment, price stability, rapid growth, external equilibrium, the provision of housing for a growing population, and so on, it is no wonder that the government has felt compelled to use every control instrument it has available without imposing an equality constraint on government spending and tax collections. Fiscal policy has borne and, in the foreseeable future, will continue to bear a substantial responsibility for stabilization policy. Of course, as we have explained, fiscal policy has a number of limitations in the imperfect real world. In practice, the administrative lag has been a severe impediment to the active employment of budget adjustments for stabilization purposes. Moreover, variations in most lines of government spending involve an operational lag that can be quite extended unless a shelf of ready projects is maintained. As a consequence, both in principle and in practice, countercyclical variations in tax rates have received a great deal of critical attention in recent years. Of course, countercyclical tax changes that are clearly temporary have a weaker impact on spending than do "permanent" tax changes. However, there is ample empirical evidence that tax variations which are not explicitly temporary can have a prompt and substantial effect on aggregate demand. Many economists hope that, with continued refinements in our understanding of the macroeconomy and modest institutional reform of the budget-changing process, we will be able in the future to successfully apply fiscal and monetary policy in tandem in the pursuit of economic welfare. In the meantime, there is widespread agreement that, while fiscal policy can be used to combat persistent deviations of output from its full-employment expansion path, attempts to fine tune the economy's expansion with fiscal tools are likely to be unsuccessful and may, in fact, be destabilizing.

Summary

This chapter has attempted to formalize and refine our understanding of *fiscal policy,* discretionary changes in the structure of the budget undertaken in the interest of stabilizing the economy. Our discussion showed that, once the structure of the government budget is established, changes in output automatically induce changes in tax collections and government outlays that act to damp fluctuations in output. Because of the programs that provide such automatic revenue and outlay responses, the so-called *automatic stabilizers,* if we want to compare the relative impact of two alternative budget structures, we have to compare the surpluses or deficits they would generate at a common output level. While this *high employment surplus* comparison provides a handy guide to the direction of change in fiscal policy, in order to go further and determine what particular budget program is needed to povide full employment with stable prices, a more detailed understanding of the structure of the private economy is needed. Only with that information can policy makers design a budget policy that, given the growth rate of the money supply, matches aggregate demand with the full-employment capacity to produce.

A major complication in the active use of fiscal policy exists because of the potentially long lag between emergence of a need for fiscal stimulus or restraint and the effective application of the needed policy. While in recent years there has been a growing awareness in Congress itself of the need for streamlining the fiscal policy-making apparatus, the administrative lag remains a major impediment to the effective use of fiscal policy in countering income fluctuations. In addition, in the past, the nature of the concerns of members of Congress has often left overall budget policy a political orphan while attention was focused on the specific tax and outlay proposals that directly and intimately affect congressmen's constituents. With the budget reform of 1974, congressional bargaining is pushed to generate an overall budget that is more closely attuned to stabilization needs.

Because the active use of fiscal policy requires the budget to frequently be out of balance, if fiscal policy is to be employed, policy makers must be concerned with the implications of alternative government-financing techniques. We have seen that the impact on the economy of a particular budget policy is stronger if any imbalance in the budget is financed in a way that alters the money supply. Attention was also focused on some potential burdens stemming from deficit finance, although we concluded that, in practice, the benefits from being able to pursue a larger number of targets when government can alter its spending and tax revenues independently are likely to outweigh the burdens involved in relying on debt finance to the degree that the United States has in the past. While policy makers need to be mindful of the burdens deficit spending can impose, particularly through the influence debt finance can have on capital accumulation, we would be ill advised to limit the use of discretionary fiscal policy by requiring a balanced government budget.

It is notable that, since the publication of Keynes' *General Theory* in

1936, there has been a revolutionary change in our perception of the role of government in the economic process. The Keynesian notion that government should use its monetary and fiscal powers to influence the level of economic activity has become commonly accepted, perhaps too widely accepted. We still have a great deal to learn about the response of the aggregate economy to policy actions and about the limits on stabilization policy's ability to improve the economy's performance. Improvement of our models of the economy is an ongoing task in which a large number of economists are currently involved. Only with better models and institutional reforms to make stabilization tools more effective will the government be able to improve its performance in contributing to economic welfare. Even with the present state of knowledge, most economists believe that discretionary stabilization policy (both fiscal and monetary) has improved the performance of the U.S. economy. These feelings are well represented in a statement from Arthur Burns, former chairman of the Board of Governors of the Federal Reserve System. Burns argues that "Discretionary economic policy, while it has at times led to mistakes, has more often proved reasonably successful. The disappearance of business depressions, which in earlier times spelled mass unemployment for workers and mass bankruptcies for businessmen, is largely attributable to . . . stabilization policies. . . ."[13] Whether Burn's contention will appear reasonable or absurd by the time you read this text depends on the course that ongoing macroeconomic processes follow.

Questions

1. Popular wisdom apparently holds that all deficits are expansionary and all surpluses restrictive. Evaluate that belief.

2. Explain the sense in which the high-employment budget gives a better indication of changes in the role of fiscal policy than the actual budget does.

3. How does inflation affect the high-employment surplus or deficit? Why?

4. Describe the nature of the lag in fiscal policy and explain how that lag influences the effectiveness of fiscal policy. What other impediment to the effective use of fiscal policy stems from the fact that Congress has control power over the budget?

5. Why can we not rely solely on automatic stabilizers to control the economy? With those automatic stabilizers, what happens to the government budget over time, and what happens to equilibrium income as a result?

---

[13]Letter from Arthur Burns to Senator William Proxmire, Vice Chairman of the Joint Economic Committee, reprinted in *Federal Reserve Bank of St. Louis Review*, November 1973, pp. 15–22.

6. Watch the newspapers and listen to radio and TV news for a statement on the dangers of the national debt. Evaluate that statement, explaining carefully what is right or wrong with it. Are there legitimate burdens that stem from a national debt?

7. Use the full aggregate model to evaluate the effects of a stimulative fiscal policy consisting of an increase in government spending financed by bond sales to the central bank. What difference does it make how a deficit is financed?

8. Evaluate the effectiveness of a 10 percent surcharge on taxes. Be sure to address yourself to the importance of the perceived permanence of that tax.

9. Considering the current state of economic affairs, what fiscal policy would you prescribe for the next six months?

10. How would you characterize the overall stabilization program (fiscal and monetary) that has been effectuated in recent months?

Suggested Readings

Blinder, Alan S. *Fiscal Policy in Theory and Practice*. Morristown, N.J.: General Learning Press, 1973.

"Budget Policy, 1958–1963." *Economic Report of the President,* pp. 77–84. Washington, D.C.: U.S. Government Printing Office, 1962.

The Council of Economic Advisers. *Economic Report of the President*. Washington, D.C.: U.S. Government Printing Office, annually. Read sections on budget policy in the last issue.

"Federal Fiscal Policy, 1965–1972." *Federal Reserve Bulletin,* June 1973, pp. 383–402.

Heller, Walter. *New Dimensions of Political Economy*. New York: W.W. Norton, 1967.

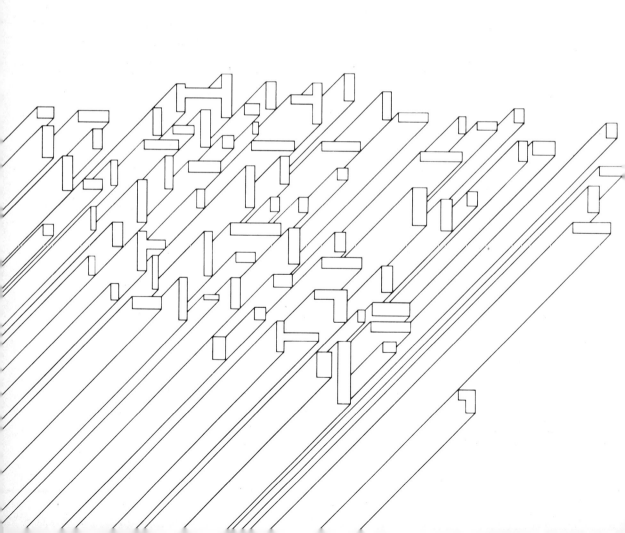

Part V

Extending and Refining the Macro Model

While the treatment of the topics covered in this concluding section of the text goes further than needed for a basic understanding of the domestic macro-economy, studying the three chapters in this section will add substantial breadth and some depth to your comprehension of macroeconomic concerns. Chapter 15 fully integrates international economic linkages into the analysis of our own economy's performance. This requires consideration both of trade (export and import) linkages and financial linkages. Alternative exchange rate systems are explained and the balance-of-payments receives brief attention.

Chapter 16 vastly lengthens the time interval to which our analysis is confined by considering the long-run growth of the economy's production capacity. Arguments over the desirability of growth are aired, and the conditions under which sustained growth can take place and the determinants of the economy's growth path are explored. Empirical evidence on the *sources of growth* in the United States is introduced. Chapter 17 maintains a focus on the dynamic properties of the macroeconomy by dealing with formal explanations of *business fluctuations* and by providing a descriptive introduction to methods of economic forecasting.

Chapter 15

International Economic Relations and Macroeconomic Equilibrium

Up to now we have dealt primarily with models of closed systems, paying scant attention to the foreign sector of the economy. However, when there is trade among nations, the domestic economies of those nations are linked together so that economic conditions in one country are affected by conditions in the rest of the world. Our understanding of how one country's level of economic activity is determined cannot be complete until these international linkages are considered.

The importance of U.S. participation in the world economic community has been highlighted in the past two decades by a highly publicized U.S. gold drain, by a switch in the early 1970s to a system of floating exchange rates, by an embargo on oil shipments to the U.S. from the OPEC countries in 1973, by persistent balance-of-payments deficits, and by a declining international exchange value of the dollar. Happily, analyses of headline-winning phenomena like those cited, and of the overall role of the foreign sector of the economy, can be accommodated readily in the *IS-LM* framework developed earlier. To begin that task, this chapter first analyzes the direct effects of international trade on the domestic level of economic activity by demonstrating the impact of the foreign sector on the commodity market component of the *IS-LM* model. Attention will then be turned to the international monetary system and to balance-of-payments concerns.

Foreign Trade and the Commodity Market

The introduction of foreign purchasers of U.S.-produced goods and services simply adds one more component, export sales, to U.S. aggregate demand. With this addition, domestic output is absorbed by consumption, investment, government, and *exports*. However, part of U.S. consumption, investment, and government purchases will be foreign-produced (imported) goods. To cite some common examples, consumption spending on French wines and Japanese radios, and investment expenditures on German machine tools do not contribute directly to demand for domestically produced output. Therefore, all spending on imports must be deducted from the total of final expenditures on consumption, investment, and government purchases in deriving a measure of aggregate demand for *domestic* production. Total demand for U.S. output then is

$$(C + I + G - M) + X \qquad\qquad [15\text{—}1]$$

where C is consumption, I investment, G government spending, X exports, and M imports. Rearranging the equation, aggregate demand is

$$C + I + G + (X - M) \qquad\qquad [15\text{—}1a]$$

where the role of foreign trade in determining aggregate demand is captured in the *net exports* or *trade balance term* $(X - M)$.

For commodity market equilibrium it is still necessary for planned spending to be equal to output,

$$Y = C + I + G + (X - M) \qquad\qquad [15\text{—}2]$$

or for leakages to equal injections,

$$S + T + M = I + G + X \qquad\qquad [15\text{—}2a]$$

Just as before, the appropriate behavioral relationships must be plugged into these equilibrium conditions to provide a solvable income determination model. To do that, the determinants of the volumes of exports and imports must be specified in usable (mathematical) form.

Exports (Sales) to and Imports (Purchases) from the Rest of the World

Foreign agents buy U.S.-produced goods and services when the items demanded cannot be bought from other sources at a lower delivered price. Foreign purchases of domestic output must depend then on international price differences as well as on tastes and income in the purchasing country. For purposes of incorporating a foreign sector into an *IS-LM* model, it will be assumed that the foreign/domestic price ratio does not vary with changes in U.S. output. Then, once the complete model with a foreign sector is constructed, that model will be used to analyze the impact of price disturbances. Also, it will be assumed initially that changes in U.S. output have a negligible effect on the income level in the rest of the world.[1] These simplifying assumptions allow us to treat our exports as *exogenously determined*.

Imports, on the other hand, must be treated as endogenously determined, even in the absence of a change in domestic and foreign price levels. With increases in income, consumption spending on both domestically and foreign-produced goods and services rises. In addition, with increased output, producing firms purchase larger volumes of inputs including foreign-produced inputs (transistors, shipping services, and so on). Thus, *imports are a positive function of aggregate income*. The marginal propensity to import has a value between zero and one, and for simplicity we can assume its value to be constant.

The *IS* Curve with Foreign Trade

With the addition of the export and import functions to the existing catalogue of behavioral relations we have employed in modeling the aggregate economy, our analysis of international trade will employ a commodity market equilibrium *(IS)* schedule based on the following functions:[2]

$$
\begin{array}{ll}
\text{Saving} & S = S(Y) \\
\text{Investment} & I = I(i) \\
\text{Exports} & X = \overline{X} \\
\text{Imports} & M = M(Y) \\
\text{Government} & \\
\quad\text{Spending} & G = \overline{G} \\
\text{Taxes} & T = \overline{T}
\end{array}
\qquad [15\text{—}3]
$$

For commodity market equilibrium, leakages must equal injections, or, in algebraic form,

$$
S(Y) + \overline{T} + M(Y) = I(i) + \overline{G} + \overline{X} \qquad [15\text{—}3a]
$$

In Figure 15—1, suppose we know one combination of an interest rate and an income level (i_0, Y_0) that provides commodity market equilibrium (that

---

[1]A change in the U.S. output (income) level will change U.S. import purchases. Unless offset by the domestic stabilization policies of our trading partners, an increase in their exports to the United States would stimulate their economies. Assuming this response is negligible is tantamount to assuming that our trading partners pursue their own domestic policy goals in a manner that offsets any undesired change in their foreign sector's net sales.

[2]Some of the behavioral functions are more simplistic than those worked with previously. For example, the responses of investment and taxes to changes in the income level are ignored. Using these simple functions makes the exposition of this section easier without requiring us to sacrifice any understanding of the role of the foreign sector.

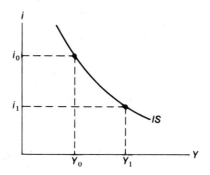

Figure 15—1 / The *IS* Curve for an Open Economy

is, we know one point on the *IS* curve). At the lower interest rate i_1, investment (thus total injections with $\overline{G}$ and $\overline{X}$ fixed) would be larger, requiring leakages to be enlarged if product market equilibrium is to be maintained. Leakages, saving and imports, are a positive function of income implying that some increase in income (say, to Y_1) is sufficient to restore the equality of leakages and injections. The *IS* curve again slopes downward from left to right just as before. However, the slope of the *IS* curve is greater for the open economy than for the closed economy. A fall in the interest rate stimulates investment leading, through the multiplier process, to a higher level of income. With the import leakage response added to the saving response of the closed system, a smaller increase in income will suffice to reestablish the equality of leakages and injections required for equilibrium.[3]

Shifts in the *IS* Curve. As was the case for closed systems, the *IS* curve is shifted rightward by any autonomous increase in spending on domestically produced output and leftward by any decrease. In addition to autonomous

---

[3]For commodity market equilibrium in the open economy,

$$Y = C + I + G + (X - M)$$

or, using simple linear forms of our behavioral functions,

$$Y = a + bY + \overline{I} + I(i) + \overline{G} + \overline{X} - \overline{M} - mY$$

Differentiating this equilibrium condition yields:

$$dY = b \cdot dY + \frac{\partial I}{\partial i} di - m \cdot dY$$

or

$$dY(1 - b + m) = \frac{\partial I}{\partial i} di$$

The slope of the *IS* curve is

$$\frac{di}{dY} = \frac{1 - b + m}{\dfrac{\partial I}{\partial i}}$$

This slope must be greater with the positive marginal propensity to import *(m)* present in the numerator.

changes in domestic consumption, investment, or government spending, changes in exports also generate such a shift; foreign purchases are no different from domestic purchases in their effect on output. An increase in exports shifts the *IS* curve rightward (increased aggregate demand must be matched by increased output for equilibrium to be maintained) and a decrease shifts it leftward. Likewise, a reduction in spending on imports, if that spending were redirected to purchases of domestic output, would shift the *IS* curve rightward while a redirection of spending away from domestic goods and into imports would shift the *IS* curve leftward.

The size of the shift in the *IS* curve generated by an autonomous spending change, measured at a constant interest rate, will be smaller for an open economy. That, again, is because any income adjustment results in a larger change in leakages when import purchases are sensitive to income changes than it does when they are not. The numerical value of the parallel shift in the *IS* curve is given by the product of the simple multiplier (assuming no interest rate change and, thus, no monetary dampener) and the autonomous change in spending.

Just as before, an increase in tax collections shifts the *IS* curve leftward and a tax reduction shifts the *IS* curve rightward. To anticipate an important concern that will be dealt with more fully later, you might pause to think about the impact in the commodity market of an increase in the domestic price level relative to the foreign price level. If such a price change affects exports or imports, the *IS* curve is shifted.

Equilibrium Income. The modified *IS* curve can be combined with the standard *LM* (money market equilibrium) schedule to determine *internal,* or *domestic,* equilibrium values of the interest rate, the level of income, employment, consumption, investment, and so on. The intersection of IS_0-LM_0 in Figure 15—2 depicts an economy with domestic equilibrium at the income and interest rate levels Y_0 and i_0, respectively.

An autonomous increase in net exports would shift the *IS* curve rightward to a position like IS_1, raising the domestic equilibrium values of income, the

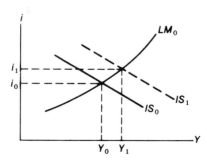

Figure 15—2 / The Domestic Impact of an Autonomous Change in Net Exports

interest rate, consumption, saving, and employment, while reducing investment in this model.[4] Conversely, an autonomous fall in net exports would shift the *IS* curve leftward, reducing the domestic income and interest rate levels and so on. What would be the direct effect on equilibrium of an increase in the U.S. price level relative to that of our trading partners? A generally accepted answer is easy to provide. A rise in U.S. prices relative to those in other countries would prompt a substitution of imported products for domestic purchases while, with U.S. goods and services more costly, U.S. exports would decline. With exports reduced and imports increased, aggregate demand is reduced (the *IS* curve shifted leftward), prompting a contraction in economic activity. What would be the effect of an increase in the level of income in other countries? Of a change in tastes with vacations in Europe, foreign cars, and imported clothes and wine becoming more fashionable in the United States? Of legislation that raises tariffs (tax levies) on imports while providing subsidies to exports? You must provide your own detailed answers to these questions, but any disturbance that raises exports or shifts expenditures from imported to domestic production raises aggregate demand (shifts the *IS* curve rightward), stimulating economic activity. Conversely, any disturbance that reduces exports or shifts spending from domestic to imported production reduces aggregate demand, fostering a contraction in the domestic economy.

Balance-of-Payments Concerns. With only minor modifications in the *IS-LM* apparatus, it has been possible to analyze the direct effects on the domestic economy of disturbances that impinge on a country's foreign trade balance. In addition, the modified *IS-LM* model can provide some important insights into the role of foreign trade in determining the state of a country's *balance-of-payments*. To initiate our discussion of the balance-of-payments, it must be noted that any domestic equilibrium position (*IS-LM* intersection) that could be located in Figure 15—2 *might* be consistent with *external*, or balance-of-payments, equilibrium. However, under a system of fixed international exchange rates, such as prevailed in one form or another for most of this century (until February 1973), such a result would be sheer coincidence. The probability is great that domestic equilibrium (an *IS-LM* intersection) will be accompanied by disequilibrium, i.e., a surplus or deficit, in the balance-of-payments. Indeed, as a case in point the United States experienced a chronic balance-of-payments deficit in the era between 1960 and the late 1970s.

With fixed exchange rates, the size of a balance-of-payments surplus or deficit is, of course, altered by autonomous changes in exports or imports, an issue to which we will return momentarily. In addition, the expansions and contractions in economic activity that stem from domestic sources produce systematic changes in the balance-of-payments. Consider, for example, an economic expansion fueled by an autonomous increase in domestic

---

[4]Recall that we have assumed away the response of investment to income in this model.

investment. As output (income) rises, imports are stimulated aggravating any existing balance-of-payments deficit or reducing a previous surplus. In addition, as output rises prices may also rise, making domestic output more expensive relative to foreign production. As prices rise, imports are encouraged and exports discouraged, so the balance-of-payments response to an income increase may be reinforced by any accompanying price increase. Similar arguments may be offered for economic expansions fueled by increased domestic consumption or government purchases. On the other hand, an economic contraction that stems from a fall in domestic consumption, investment, or government spending will enlarge a balance-of-payments surplus or reduce a deficit. Again that must be so because imports fall with income, providing a balance-of-payments response that may be reinforced by any decline in domestic (relative to foreign) prices during the contraction.

An autonomous increase in exports would shift the balance-of-payments toward surplus; but an increase in exports raises the equilibrium level of income, and, as income rises, imports rise. This induced import response must partially offset the effect on the balance-of-payments of the autonomous increase in exports, and the remaining gap may be partly closed if the domestic expansion prompts an increase in prices. Conversely, an autonomous decline in exports would lower income (and perhaps domestic prices relative to foreign prices), inducing in the balance-of-payments a partial offset of the initial contraction in export sales. In a similar vein, any autonomous change in imports will induce further changes in imports (as income changes) that partially offset the balance-of-payments impact of the autonomous change, a tendency reinforced by any price level change that accompanies the change in economic activity.

Quite obviously, because the balance-of-payments may be affected by changes in the level of income (the trade balance being inversely related to income, *ceteris paribus*), the use of stabilization policies to pursue domestic goals may result in balance-of-payments disequilibrium. If balance-of-payments equilibrium is itself a desirable end, our ability to pursue the domestic goals of full employment and price stability may be seriously constrained. For example, if a full-employment level of output results in an unacceptable balance-of-payments deficit, policy makers may have to accept a lower level of output and employment to maintain balance-of-payments equilibrium. There are alternatives, including direct intervention in foreign trade (employing tariffs, quotas, export subsidies, and exchange controls that limit the right to exchange domestic for foreign currency), which can and have been relied on in efforts to reconcile domestic and external goals. A balance-of-payments disequilibrium cannot persist indefinitely without a corrective adjustment; and, under some forms of international exchange systems, the requirements of balance-of-payments equilibrium can seriously hinder the pursuit of domestic goals.

Thus far, our accomplishments in formulating our model of the economy to permit foreign trade are fundamental. We have shown the direct effect of export sales and import purchases on aggregate demand and, hence, on equilibrium income. In addition, we have examined the interdependence of the domestic equilibrium level of income and the balance-of-payments, an interdependence that can be quite troublesome because efforts to achieve full employment may result in balance-of-payments disequilibrium. With these accomplishments our introduction to the macroeconomic role of international economic linkages is complete. However, a comprehensive view of the macroeconomic consequences of involvement in the world economic community requires further analysis. At the outset, it must be recognized that the state of the balance-of-payments is not determined only by the balance of trade. Capital flows between countries (from investment, loans, grants, and the like) are also determinants of the overall state of the balance-of-payments. Furthermore, it must be recognized that a balance-of-payments surplus or deficit has important feedback effects on the domestic economy that, as we shall see, can be manifest in shifts in the *LM* curve. To permit illumination of the balance-of-payments feedback, en route to a comprehensive assessment of the influences of our international economic involvement, familiarity with the international monetary system is imperative.

The International Monetary System

To permit efficient settlement of the net credits (credits minus debits) generated by international transactions, there is an elaborate international monetary system. The original foundation for the postwar system was established in 1946 with creation of the International Monetary Fund (IMF), an institution that now includes in its membership nearly all of the free world nations.

With the establishment of the IMF, the domestic currencies of the *member* countries had their par values defined in terms of gold. For years (in fact, from 1934 until August 1971), the official dollar price of gold was $35 an ounce. With the official British pound sterling price of gold at 14.58 pound sterling per ounce, the official dollar-pound exchange rate was $2.40 per pound. It should be clear from this example that defining national currency values in terms of gold also defines their values in relation to one another.

With clearly defined exchange ratios between different national currencies, individual transactions that take place across the borders are simple to accommodate financially. A tire maker in Akron, Ohio, wants to receive dollar payments for his sales in Texas. Likewise, he wants dollar payments for his sales abroad. In turn, a British exporter will want, ultimately, to have payment for his exports in the form of pounds sterling. In general, private transactions across borders can be, and ultimately are, settled in national currencies.

A U.S. firm that imports British sports cars may remit payment for those imports in dollars or pounds (or even in some third currency). If payment is made in dollars, the British exporter can sell those dollars to his bank at the prevailing exchange rate, receiving credit for deposits of pounds in exchange. To remit payment in pounds, the U.S. importer could, at the prevailing exchange rate, swap his dollar deposits for a bank draft denominated in pounds. How are the exchange rates determined, and what happens to foreign currency deposits sold to domestic banks (for example, any dollars sold to the British exporter's bank)?

A Two-Country Model of the Foreign Exchange Market

To answer the questions posed above, and to ensure an understanding of the functioning of the international monetary system, consider a simple, two-country example of a "foreign exchange" market. Let the two countries be the United States and England, and let us suppose that all debt payments between the countries are made in pounds. The foreign exchange market for the two-country example encompasses those institutions through which dollars and pounds are exchanged for each other. Included are private banks in the United States and Britain, foreign exchange dealers, and the central bank agencies of both countries.

In this simple two-country world, there is a variety of British products and marketable assets that Americans demand. That is, Americans are willing to exchange some of their dollar purchasing power for English linen and china, English shipping services, stock in English companies, English real estate, and so on. Because English suppliers want to be paid in pounds, let us place on American importers the burden of exchanging their dollars for the pounds they need. The demand for British goods, services, and capital assets then generates a demand for pounds (and a supply of dollars to pay for them) in the foreign exchange market. The higher the exchange value of pounds (the more dollars that must be given up to acquire a pound), the higher is the dollar price of British purchases to American buyers. With the dollar price of purchases increased, Americans will buy less from Britain, reducing the quantity of pounds demanded (dollars supplied) in the foreign exchange market.

Similarly, English demand for American goods, services, securities, and real estate creates a supply of pounds (in exchange for dollars) in the foreign exchange market because American suppliers want to be paid in dollars. The higher the value of pounds (the more dollars a British importer can get in exchange for a pound), the larger the quantity of pounds supplied in the foreign exchange market because each pound would buy a larger volume of American goods, services, or securities.[5] The foreign exchange market for

---

[5]To be more precise, a rise in the exchange rate will definitely increase the dollar volume of British purchases from America. Whether, with more dollars available per pound of expenditure, this results in an increased quantity of pounds supplied depends on the elasticity of British demand for U.S. purchases. The statement in the text implicitly assumes that this demand is elastic.

pounds might appear as depicted in Figure 15—3 with the market-clearing exchange rate $2.40 = £1. Changes in supply or demand would lead to changes in the market-clearing exchange rate. For example, an increase in American demand for British goods and thus for pounds, reflected in the rightward shift from demand schedule D to demand schedule D_1 in Figure 15—3, raises the market-clearing exchange rate to $2.80 = £1. What would be the impact of an increase in British demand for American goods?[6]

Flexible Exchange Rates. If demand and supply are left free to determine the foreign exchange rate, that rate will be forced to the market-clearing level. In that case if, at an exchange rate of $2.40 = £1, Americans are demanding more pounds for purchases from Britain than the British are supplying through their purchases from the United States (that is, there is an excess demand for pounds for foreign exchange), the exchange rate will rise. How far? To the level at which U.S. demand for pounds is reduced to equality with the enlarged supply of pounds, that is, to the market-clearing level. A movement in the exchange rate from $2.40 = £1 to $2.80 = £1, as in Figure 15—3, would reflect such an adjustment. An exchange rate change of this sort would be referred to as a *depreciation* of the dollar relative to the pound, or as an *appreciation* of the pound. The currency that was previously *undervalued* (the pound) has risen in foreign exchange value, and the currency that was previously *overvalued* (the dollar) has fallen in value.

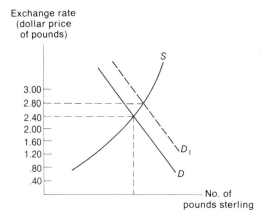

Figure 15—3 / A Foreign Exchange Market

---

[6]With international payments also made in dollars, there would also be a market for dollars in England. The price (exchange rate) determined by supply and demand in that market would have to match the price determined in the market for pounds. Why? To offer an analogy that may be familiar to you, if the price of eggs (or pounds) in two regions differs, *arbitragers* will enter the market, buying in the low-price market (increasing demand and pushing the price up there) while selling in the high-price market (increasing supply and forcing the price down in that market) until no price differential from which they can profit remains.

What would happen if suddenly the United States should decide to send more troops abroad, or if its citizens should find British cars more attractive because of a fall in their prices? Either of these disturbances would increase the demand for pounds in our two-country world and thereby raise the exchange rate. On the other hand, domestic (U.S.) inflation would make our goods and services more expensive relative to those in England. This would increase U.S. demand for British goods (thus U.S. demand for pounds) and would reduce British demand for U.S. goods (thus reducing the supply of pounds in the foreign exchange market). With increased demand for pounds and reduced supply, the exchange rate would be driven upward.

Fixed Exchange Rates. The flexible exchange rate system discussed above has direct current relevance. Yet, most of the post-World War II period has been characterized by *fixed* exchange rates, rates that were initially agreed to at the 1944 meeting at Bretton Woods, New Hampshire, in which the postwar international monetary apparatus was created. Under the original Bretton Woods agreement, exchange rates were fixed as countries were required to take the steps necessary to keep exchange rates from varying by more than 1 percent from specified par values.

The steps that are necessary for achieving such stabilization of exchange rates can be illustrated using our two-country example. Suppose, beginning with a $2.40 = £1 exchange rate, that Britain has responsibility for maintaining the value of the pound within 1 percent of par. With that responsibility, a tendency for the dollar price of pounds to rise above the legal limit must be met by Britain with the offer of pounds (for dollars). Conversely, downward pressure on the exchange rate would require the British government to absorb pounds by furnishing dollars. Figure 15—4 shows the foreign exchange market with Britain responsible for stabilizing the pound. As that figure shows, the Bank of England, as England's monetary agent, must

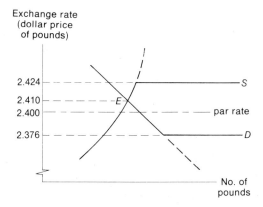

Figure 15—4 / The Stabilized Pound Market—No Intervention Required

stand ready to supply pounds (for dollars) perfectly elastically at the *upper band* price of $2.424 (= $2.40 × 1.01), and must be willing to buy pounds in whatever quantities offered (by selling dollars) at the *lower band* price of $2.376 (= $2.40 × .99).

With the market situation as depicted in Figure 15—4, no intervention by the Bank of England is required. The free market equilibrium price of $2.41 = £1 (point *E*) is well within the bands of allowable exchange rate variation. In this case, the supply of pounds resulting from U.S. sales to Britain is matched by U.S. demand for pounds to pay for purchases from Britain.

This situation can change quickly. Suppose U.S. demand for British goods, and thus for pounds, increases, shifting the demand schedule for pounds to D_1 in Figure 15—5. With floating (flexible) exchange rates, the exchange rate would rise to $2.45 = £1. However, under the postwar IMF system, Britain would have to limit the rise to the upper band value of $2.424. The number of pounds supplied to the foreign exchange market as a result of purchases from the United States is quantity *OA* in Figure 15—5, while the number of pounds demanded for financing U.S. purchases from Britain is *OB*. The difference *(AB)* is the number of pounds the Bank of England would have to supply in exchange for dollars offered in the foreign exchange market. In this case, the Bank of England's dollar holdings clearly would be growing.

As the obvious counterexample of exchange rate stabilization, suppose the demand for pounds had shifted leftward to position D_2 in Figure 15—6. In this case, Britain would be absorbing pounds in volume *CD* by providing dollars out of its accumulated stock of dollar *reserves*. That is, the supply of pounds from British purchases from the United States *(OC)* would exceed the U.S. demand for pounds *(OC)* for making payments to Britain. Out of its dollar reserves the Bank of England would have to exchange dollars for the excess pounds in order to prevent the exchange rate from falling below the permissible lower band value. Clearly, in order to provide this support

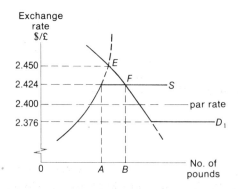

**Figure 15—5 / The Stabilized Market—
Bank of England Supplying Pounds**

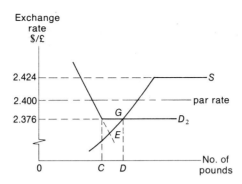

**Figure 15—6 / The Stabilized Market—
Bank of England Absorbing Pounds**

for the pound, the Bank of England would need substantial reserves either in the form of dollars or in assets that can be exchanged for dollars.

Typically, the reserves that a central bank possesses would have been accumulated during a period of balance-of-payments surplus (like that in Figure 15—5). Figure 15—6, on the other hand, shows Britain in a balance-of-payments deficit situation in which she is required to use accumulated reserves to absorb pounds in order to meet her IMF responsibility for maintaining the exchange rate

In our two-country example then, Britain would have met her responsibility to the IMF by buying or selling pounds (dollars) as required to keep the exchange rate stabilized within the allowable range around par. The United States would have met its obligation by readily buying gold from or selling gold to Britain at thirty-five dollars per ounce.

With the United States stabilizing the price of gold and Britain stabilizing the foreign exchange rate, there is a fixed relationship between both national currencies and gold. With these arrangements, when Britain has a balance-of-payments surplus (accumulating reserves), she can hold those reserves in a number of forms. They could be held in idle (noninterest-yielding) dollar deposit form; in the form of gold; or in the form of short-term, interest-bearing, U.S. securities. Gold or dollars serve equally well as reserves in this two-country system. Consequently, total (two-country) world reserves would be increased either by new gold being introduced into monetary usage, or by the United States running a balance-of-payments deficit settled by Britain's acceptance of the excess supply of dollars in reserves.

Extend this simple system to accommodate some 125 countries instead of 2, and we will have captured the essential features of the real world international monetary system as established at Bretton Woods. With the currencies of all member countries of the IMF defined in gold, par values between those currencies were established. In the post-Bretton Woods era, countries other than the United States kept their exchange rates within the allowable bands around par value with the dollar by exchanging their currencies for dollars. The United States, in turn, by exchanging gold for dollars at thirty-five dollars per ounce, maintained the required link between the dollar and gold and, consequently, between all other national currencies and gold. In this system the dollar, "as good as gold" in the early postwar period, served as a basic reserve asset.

Adjustments for Fundamental Disequilibrium. While the fixed exchange rate system worked well enough to allow an unprecedented postwar growth in world trade, it did permit periodic monetary crises to occur that threatened world-wide economic progress. The major crises stemmed from persistent balance-of-payments deficits in Britain and, more importantly, the United States.

Looking first at the British case, beginning with British purchases from the rest of the world in balance with purchases from Britain (so Britain was neither gaining nor losing reserves), assume that Britain experiences a domestic inflation at a rate exceeding that in the rest of the world. With fixed exchange rates, the relative price of British goods, services, and securities would be rising in world markets. Thus, world purchases from Britain (and demand for pounds) would fall and British purchases from the rest of the world (and the supply of pounds) would be increasing. The result, as in the situation depicted in Figure 15—6, is a balance-of-payments deficit requiring Britain to absorb pounds by exchanging its reserves (of other national currencies or gold) for those pounds.

A persistent deficit would gradually exhaust the deficit country's reserves if allowed to continue. However, the Bretton Woods agreement included provision for a country with such a chronic deficit (a country in *fundamental disequilibrium*) to alter its exchange rate to make its products more competitive in world markets. By redefining the gold value of the pound, making each pound worth less in terms of gold (an action called *devaluation*), Britain could *depreciate* the pound against other currencies (lower the exchange rate).[7] With that *official* devaluation, Britain would have to intervene in the foreign exchange market (selling or absorbing pounds) at the new set of allowable exchange rates. With dollars, marks, francs, pesos, and so on exchangeable for more pounds, purchases from Britain are made less dear in the rest of the world, while British purchases from the rest of the world are made more costly. With a suitable devaluation (and resulting depreciation of the pound against other currencies), a balance-of-payments deficit could be eliminated or reversed.[8]

---

[7]A depreciation of the pound against other currencies is an appreciation of those other currencies relative to the pound. The surplus countries could appreciate their currencies in relation to the pound by *revaluing* (raising their currency's value in terms of gold). However, this technique has been used rarely to combat balance-of-payments difficulties.

[8]Recognizing the increase in living costs suffered in the devaluation, the British could react to the increase in the pound price of imports by demanding higher incomes. Higher income payments, however, require higher product prices. By raising the domestic price level sufficiently, the effects of the devaluation (both on living costs and on the balance-of-payments) could be negated. For a full discussion of the impact of devaluation on the balance-of-payments, see Harry G. Johnson, "Toward a General Theory of Balance of Payments," in *International Trade and Economic Growth,* ed. H. G. Johnson (London: George Allen and Unwin, 1958).

The pound sterling was, in fact, a weak link in the international monetary system and, as a prelude to the tremors that reordered world monetary arrangements in the early 1970s, was subjected to devaluation in 1967. Devaluation of the pound was disruptive primarily because the pound has been held as a reserve currency by the Commonwealth countries. Of course, a depreciation of the pound reduced the purchasing power in world markets embodied in those reserves, and hence reinforced the reluctance of the world community to hold reserves in a form other than gold or a *strong* (generally balance-of-payments surplus) currency. When the confidence-shaking devaluation of the pound occurred, the dollar was anything but strong.

The Dollar. As suggested earlier, in the wake of the Bretton Woods agreement, the dollar was the "key currency" in terms of which international trade and finance were implemented. Both private and government reserves were held, to a large extent, in dollar form (in cash, bank deposits, and short-term U.S. securities). With world trade growing rapidly after World War II, a limited volume of international gold reserves made the world happy to hold, as reserves, the large outflow of *safe, stable* dollars that a chronic U.S. balance-of-payments deficit provided. In fact, there was an international "dollar shortage" during that period. Toward the end of the 1950s the demand for dollar reserves appears to have been satiated, and the surplus dollars the continuing U.S. deficit provided were, increasingly, sold back to the U.S. central bank for gold reserves.

As we progressed into the 1960s, U.S. gold reserves were being depleted at a substantial rate.[9] The 1967 devaluation of the pound ended the pretense that reserve currencies were "as good as gold." With world-wide confidence in reserve currencies shaken, there followed a period of intense pressure on the dollar (a *run* into gold). The intense upward pressure on the price of gold (downward pressure on the dollar) resulted in establishment of a two-tier price structure for gold. In the "free market" tier, jewelers and dentists, industrial users, Arab sheiks, and European speculators bid for gold in an unconstrained market.[10] In the official tier, international debts were still cleared with thirty-five dollar an ounce gold.

With the U.S. balance-of-payments deficit growing explosively in 1970 and 1971, another massive crisis arose with a 1971 run against the dollar in favor of the strong German mark and Japanese yen. On August 15, 1971, President Nixon was prompted to abandon gold convertibility, a cornerstone of the system created at Bretton Woods.

In December, an emergency meeting of the main IMF members at the Smithsonian Institution in Washington produced an interim realignment of

---

[9]From a high of $29 billion in 1949, the U.S. gold stock was halved by the mid-1960s; and, with the deficit not merely continuing but growing, that gold stock had shrunk to near $10 billion by August 1971 when gold convertibility was abolished.

[10]Since central bank intervention in the gold market ceased, free market gold prices have soared.

currency values. The dollar was devalued (the official price of gold was raised from thirty-five to thirty-eight dollars an ounce), and a number of other currencies were *revalued*. The overall impact was to depreciate the dollar relative to most European currencies by something under 10 percent while the German mark ended up with a relative appreciation of 14 percent and the Japanese yen appreciated 17 percent. In addition, the "bands" that demark the allowable outside limits on exchange rate variations were widened from 1 percent on either side of par to 2½ percent.

The Smithsonian agreement provided only temporary peace in the foreign exchange market. Under crisis conditions once again, the dollar was devalued to $42.22 per ounce of gold in February 1973, and shortly thereafter *official intervention in foreign exchange markets to maintain fixed exchange rates was ended*. Thus, early in 1973 the world was shuttled to a system of floating exchange rates. Since that time, central bank intervention in foreign exchange markets has resumed but on a scale that leaves us on an essentially floating exchange rate system. Rather than attempting to maintain fixed exchange rates, current central bank intervention aims: (1) at smoothing adjustments in the exchange rate by eliminating short-run jumps in those rates; and (2) to some extent, at limiting the size of exchange rate adjustments over longer time intervals. The fact that the U.S. and other countries have continued to experience balance-of-payments imbalances indicates that exchange rates have not been freed completely. Instead, we have what is labeled a "dirty" float of exchange rates, rather than a completely free or "clean" float. It is notable that, under this system, the United States has experienced sizable deficits in the latter half of the 1970s. That was so even though the dollar was being depreciated in foreign exchange markets (by some 18 percent from the beginning of 1976 to the beginning of 1980).

The Balance-of-Payments Account

On our path back to the central concern of this chapter, the role of international involvement in shaping domestic macroeconomic conditions, we can add precision to our understanding of the transactions we have reviewed by taking a brief formal look at the U.S. balance-of-payments account that summarizes those transactions. Formally, the balance-of-payments account is just a summary representation of all the international economic transactions of a country and its citizens during a prescribed time period, typically a year. The U.S. balance-of-payments account for 1979 appears in Table 15—1. In this account, credit items (those with positive signs) represent the export of something: a commodity, a service, a security, a bank deposit, or gold. In return, such transactions provide residents with claims on the foreign exchange balances of foreigners. Debit items (those with negative signs) reflect an import from the same array of items and, hence, create claims by foreign residents on domestic funds.

The balance-of-payments can be viewed as consisting of three basic component accounts: the *current account*, the *capital account*, and *balancing*

Table 15—1 / U.S. Balance-of-Payments, 1979 (billions of dollars)

I.	Current account		
	1. Merchandise trade balance	−29.5	
	2. Exports	182.1	
	3. Imports	211.5	
	4. Investment income (net)	32.3	
	5. Other services	2.5	
	6. Balance on goods and services (1+4+5)		5.4
	7. Unilateral transfers, private and government	−5.7	
	8. Balance on current account (6+7)		−0.3
II.	Capital account		
	9. U.S. direct investment abroad	−24.8	
	10. Foreign direct investment in the United States	7.7	
	11. U.S. net purchases (−) of foreign securities	−5.0	
	12. Foreign net purchases (+) of U.S. securities	7.6	
	13. Bank-reported claims on foreigners and other	5.0	
	14. Balance on capital account (9+10+11+12+13+14)		−9.4
	15. Statistical discrepancy		29.8
	16. Total to be offset (8+14+15)	20.1	
III.	Balancing items		
	17. Foreign official assets in the United States	−15.2	
	18. U.S. official reserve assets	−1.1	
	19. U.S. government assets other than official reserve assets	−3.8	
	20. Overall balance		0.0

Source: Laurence R. Jacobson, "U.S. International Transactions in 1979: Another Round of Oil Price Increases," *Federal Reserve Bulletin*, April 1980, pp. 283–289.

items. Basically, the current account shows the difference between our exports of commodities and services and our imports of them, though in some countries' accounts (as revealed in the U.S. account in the table below) transfer payments are included. U.S. commodity exports range from raw agricultural products to sophisticated electronic devices. Service exports include shipping, transportation on U.S. airlines, insurance, and the services of U.S. capital and technology abroad. Total revenues from exports also appear in the national income and product accounts as exports, and total U.S. expenditures on imported goods and services appear in those accounts as imports. The difference between exports and imports, designated net exports *(X − M)*, is the balance on goods and services in the overall balance-of-payments account (item 6 in Table 15—1).

The *capital account* measures the international purchase and sale of assets. Foreign lending and investment by U.S. citizens, businesses, or the government itself is tantamount to the *import* of securities or IOUs. My purchase of a Swiss bond, General Motor's acquisition of a truck plant in Spain, and the government's loan to the Philippines appear as debit items in the capital account because they all provide dollar claims against the U.S. The U.S. export of securities or IOUs, private or government (constituting foreign lending and investment in the United States), is a credit item. The balance on capital account (line 14) shows a deficit of $9.4 billion in 1979. That is the amount by which U.S. loans and investments abroad exceeded "nonofficial" foreign loans and investments in the United States, augmenting foreign claims on domestic funds, during 1979. Combining the *current account* and *capital account* balances, and adding a whopping 29.8 billion of errors and omissions[11] (line 15) provides the measure of payment credits of $20.1 billion that must be offset or "financed" by a flow of balancing or settlement items.

In 1979, the Federal Reserve acquired $1.1 billion of foreign currencies or their equivalent (foreign official reserve assets). Meanwhile, official foreign asset holdings in the United States were reduced by $15.2 billion as foreign central banks exchanged dollars for their own currencies in order to support the foreign exchange value of their currencies. The acquisition by our government of any other foreign assets besides official reserve assets also provides a flow of dollar claims into foreign banks as the entry in line 19 of Table 15—1 shows.

It should be noted that, like all balance sheets, Table 15—1 exhibits an overall balance as the −$20.1 billion of balancing item flows just covers the combined deficit on the current and capital accounts. This accounting balance says nothing, however, about the presence or absence of balance-of-payments equilibrium. It is an unsustainable surplus or deficit in the current and capital accounts combined that indicates a balance-of-payments disequilibrium. With those two component parts of the balance-of-payments account in mind, we can proceed to identify the fundamental determinants of the state of the balance-of-payments.

Maintaining Overall Balance-of-Payments Equilibrium

Early in this chapter, the determinants of the state of balance of the *current account* were discussed. Imports were treated as a positive function of the level of domestic income while exports were treated as exogenous. Thus, net exports (the balance on current account) were an inverse function of the level of income. By adding an explanation of the state of balance of the capital account, the conditions under which a country will find its stock of international reserves neither growing nor dwindling can be determined.

Loans and investments are attracted by higher interest returns. The higher are foreign interest yields relative to U.S. yields, the larger the fraction of any increment in U.S. wealth that will be loaned or invested abroad and the smaller the fraction of any increment in foreign wealth that will be loaned or invested in the United States. A rise in U.S. yield rates in relation to foreign rates would attract an inflow of capital into U.S. assets (or, on balance, would reduce the size of any net outflow). Thus, the *net* outflow of capital (the balance on capital account) is an inverse function of the U.S. interest rate. Algebraically,

---

[11]According to Laurence Jacobson, "The explanation for the widening gap in the statistics probably lies in unmeasured purchases of financial assets by foreign residents or unmeasured net reduction of foreign claims to U.S. residents. . . ." See Jacobson, "U.S. International Transactions in 1979: Another Round of Oil Price Increases," *Federal Reserve Bulletin,* April 1980, p. 289.

$$F = F(i) \qquad s.t. \; \frac{\Delta F}{\Delta i} < 0 \qquad\qquad [15\text{—}4]$$

where F is the net capital outflow and i is the U.S. interest rate.

Balance-of-Payments Equilibrium

As indicated earlier, for our purposes we can identify a period of balance-of-payments equilibrium if, for that period, any surplus (deficit) in the current account is offset by an equal deficit (surplus) in the capital account. With net exports a function of income and net capital outflows dependent on the interest rate, there is always some interest rate level that can be paired with a specified income level to yield an overall balance-of-payments equilibrium.

Suppose we know one income and interest rate combination that provides balance-of-payments equilibrium (i_0, Y_0 in Figure 15—7). An increase in the level of income (say to Y_1) would, by stimulating imports, reduce net exports and move the current account toward a larger deficit (or smaller surplus). Overall balance-of-payments equilibrium could be maintained only if an increase in the capital account surplus (or decrease in its deficit) could be obtained. With capital flowing toward attractive interest yields, there is some increase in the U.S. interest rate (say to i_1) that would generate the increase in capital inflows necessary to maintain overall balance-of-payments equilibrium. Schedule ff in Figure 15—7 plots all the combinations of i and Y that permit balance-of-payments equilibrium, its upward slope showing, again, that deterioration in the current account balance caused by a rise in the level of income requires a capital-inflow-stimulating rise in interest rates if overall equilibrium in the balance-of-payments account is to be maintained. The larger the response of import purchases to any change in the

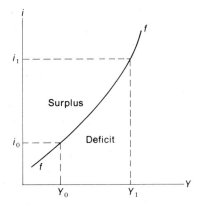

Figure 15—7 / Combinations of i and Y that Provide Balance-of-Payments Equilibrium

domestic income level, the larger the capital-flow-inducing interest rate increase required to maintain balance-of-payments equilibrium, that is, the steeper will be the *ff* schedule. In contrast, the stronger is the capital flow response to a change in the domestic interest rate, the larger the required import-generating change in the income level, the flatter the *ff* schedule must be. In fact, with a "perfect" world capital market (foreign assets perfect substitutes for domestic assets, no transactions costs of shifting between foreign and domestic assets, no government controls on international capital flows, and so on), the *ff* schedule would be horizontal. The smallest change in the domestic interest rate would prompt massive international capital flows (inflows for an interest rate increase and outflows for a decline in the domestic interest rate). Because imperfections (including transactions costs and government controls on capital flows) do exist in the international market for capital, a horizontal *ff* schedule is not realistic.

With all the interest rate-income combinations that provide balance-of-payments equilibrium represented by the *ff* schedule, every other *i*, *Y* combination must provide a balance-of-payments surplus or deficit. Any combination of *i* and *Y* that falls below the *ff* schedule yields a balance-of-payments deficit because the interest rate is too low to provide a capital inflow large enough to offset the accompanying deficit on current accounts. Conversely, any combination of *i* and *Y* above *ff* yields a balance-of-payments surplus.

By plotting the *ff* schedule in the same diagram with the *IS-LM* model, we can tell (for a given exchange rate and given domestic and foreign price levels) whether any *internal equilibrium* point (*IS-LM* intersection) will yield a balance-of-payments surplus or deficit. Figure 15—8(a) shows a domestic equilibrium that would be accompanied by a balance-of-payments surplus because the domestic equilibrium interest rate (i_0) is above the level needed for balance-of-payments equilibrium (i_1) at income level Y_0. In contrast, Figure 15—8(b) shows a domestic equilibrium that would be accompanied by a balance-of-payments deficit. In this case, the interest rate would have to be raised to level i_2 to produce balance-of-payments equilibrium at income level Y_0.

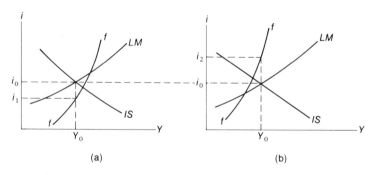

(a)   (b)

Figure 15—8 / Internal Equilibrium and External Disequilibrium

Systematic Shifts in the *ff* Schedule. A change in the domestic price level relative to the foreign price level will shift the *ff* schedule, as will any change in the foreign exchange rate. As previously argued, an increase in the domestic price level will stimulate U.S. purchases from abroad as foreign goods, services, and capital assets become relatively cheaper, while reducing foreign purchases from the United States because U.S. goods, services, and assets are made more costly by the price increase. A domestic inflation at a rate that exceeds that of our trading partners then shifts the *ff* schedule leftward, requiring a higher interest rate (to attract capital inflows) or a lower income level (to boost net exports) to maintain balance-of-payments equilibrium. Of course, the *IS* schedule is also shifted leftward as net exports decline.

A fall in foreign prices while the U.S. price level stays constant would have the same effects because U.S. purchases from abroad would be made less costly and foreign purchases from the U.S. would be made relatively more costly. On the other hand, a fall in the U.S. price level or a rise in the foreign price level would shift the *ff* schedule (and the *IS* schedule) to the right.

An increase in the foreign exchange rate, like a fall in the domestic price level or a rise in the foreign price level, shifts the *ff* curve downward. As an illustration, in our two-country world suppose that the dollar is depreciated from an exchange rate of $2.40 = £1 to $2.80 = £1. This depreciation raises the dollar price of U.S. purchases from Britain and lowers the pound price of British purchases from the United States. Domestic equilibrium positions (*IS-LM* intersections) that provided balance-of-payments equilibrium prior to the depreciation (that fell on the original *ff* curve) would provide surpluses afterward as U.S. purchases from Britain are reduced and British purchases from the U.S. increased. On the other hand, a reduction in the foreign exchange rate (an appreciation of the domestic currency) would shift the *ff* curve upward so that domestic equilibrium positions that previously yielded balance-of-payments equilibrium would produce deficits after the exchange rate alteration. Before continuing to the next section, you should be sure you can account for the impact on *both* balance-of-payments equilibrium and commodity market equilibrium of changes in the exchange rate and changes in the domestic price level relative to the foreign price level.

Automatic Responses to Balance-of-Payments Disequilibrium

Early in this chapter we indicated that a balance-of-payments disequilibrium produces important feedback effects on the domestic economy. With what we now know about the determinants of the balance-of-payments and the nature of alternative exchange rate systems, we can direct our attention to the automatic responses that balance-of-payments disequilibria produce.

Because the nature of the adjustments differs, we must look at the response to a balance-of-payments disequilibrium with both flexible and fixed exchange rates.

The Flexible Exchange Rate Case

With flexible exchange rates, the adjustment to a balance-of-payments disequilibrium requires little explanation. In fact, you already know that if the exchange rate is determined by a free market, neither surpluses nor deficits in the balance-of-payments can persist no matter what the domestic equilibrium position. Supply and demand would force a floating exchange rate to the level that equates the volume of foreign currency demanded for domestic purchases of foreign goods, services, and assets with the available supply.

Figure 15—9 illustrates the macroeconomic adjustment prompted by the appearance of a balance-of-payments surplus (due, say, to an exogenous increase in foreign investment). Interest rate-income combination i_0, Y_0 denotes the initial domestic equilibrium position; schedule f_0f_0 is the initial balance-of-payments equilibrium schedule; and, for reference, the full-employment output level is labeled Y_f. With the volume of foreign currency being provided by foreign purchases of domestic goods, services, and assets exceeding domestic demand for that currency, the domestic currency will appreciate (the foreign currency depreciate), making foreign purchases from our economy more costly and reducing the cost of domestic purchases from abroad. As a result, exports will fall and imports increase, shifting both the *ff* and *IS* schedules leftward. This adjustment must continue until both domestic and external equilibrium prevails, as at the intersection of IS_1, f_1f_1, LM_0. Because a flexible exchange rate provides balance-of-payments equilibrium at any domestic equilibrium position, domestic policy makers are free to use monetary and fiscal policy to pursue the domestic goals of price stability and full employment (the latter of which now appears to need some attention), unfettered by balance-of-payments concerns.

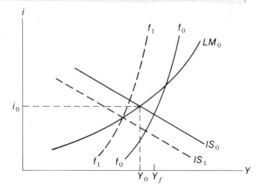

Figure 15—9 / Adjustment to a Balance-of-Payments Surplus with Flexible Exchange Rates

The Fixed Exchange Rate Case

For most of our history, exchange rates have not been free to vary continuously but have been fixed. With fixed exchange rates, persistent balance-of-payments surpluses and deficits can be generated, and those surpluses and deficits can affect the domestic economy in a manner that has not been explored yet.

With a balance-of-payments surplus, the domestic commercial banking system and the central bank will be experiencing an increase in reserves. With U.S. buyers offering fewer dollars in world markets than foreigners demand for financing their purchases from the U.S., financial institutions in the United States will be receiving for deposit a net inflow of funds (currency and checks) denominated in foreign currencies. When depository institutions turn these checks over to the central bank, they have their reserve accounts with the central bank credited in the appropriate dollar amount (given the current exchange rate) and the central bank can use the foreign checks to obtain currency, bank deposits, short-term securities, or gold from the issuing country.

Our main concern now is with the impact of the change in domestic monetary reserves. As long as the central bank permits a balance-of-payments surplus to increase reserves, those depository institutions will be expanding the domestic money supply, shifting our LM curve rightward. Thus, the economy represented in Figure 15—10 by schedules IS_0, LM_0, $f_0 f_0$ cannot be in full equilibrium at i_0, Y_0.

The balance-of-payments surplus generated with the economy at i_0, Y_0 would increase the domestic money supply, shifting the LM curve rightward. The resulting increase in aggregate demand would induce an increase in the level of income and an increase in the price level (preventing the LM schedule from shifting rightward as far as it would with prices constant). A rising domestic price level, by increasing the relative cost of U.S. products in the world market, would reduce net foreign purchases from the United States, shifting the IS curve downward.[12] At the same time, with foreign

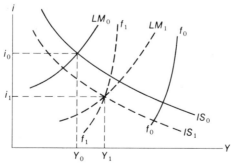

Figure 15—10 / Adjustment to a Balance-of-Payments Surplus with Fixed Exchange Rates

---

[12]In addition, any real balance effect on consumption would reinforce this downward shift.

purchases of U.S. goods, services, and assets depressed by increases in U.S. prices, the balance-of-payments (*ff*) schedule would be drifting leftward as prices rise. Eventually, full equilibrium would be reached at a point like i_1, Y_1 with income and prices above their original levels and the interest rate reduced. Clearly, the domestic money supply response to a balance-of-payments surplus will, if permitted, eliminate that surplus even with exchange rates fixed. Likewise, a balance-of-payments deficit could, through its impact on the *LM* curve, ultimately eliminate itself, but only after a fall in domestic income and prices and a rise in the interest rate.

Monetary and Fiscal Policy in an Open Economy

As we have shown for both flexible and fixed exchange rates, without government intervention there are automatic adjustments that will eliminate a balance-of-payments disequilibrium. However, those automatic adjustments result in changes in domestic output and employment levels, the price level, and the interest rate. In general, these changes cannot be expected to be consistent with domestic policy preferences. For example, few countries are apt to welcome a sizable increase in unemployment in order to combat a balance-of-payments deficit, or a domestic inflation to cure a surplus. Domestic policy makers will want to continue the pursuit of full employment and price stability in the face of a balance-of-payments surplus or deficit.

In both of the adjustment processes analyzed above, the economy ended up with commodity and money market equilibrium and with balance-of-payments equilibrium. However, in both cases there remained unemployed labor at the end of the adjustment process. If an excess supply of labor results in a fall in money wages, further adjustments would take place that ultimately provide full employment too. A fall in money wages would permit the price level to fall, shifting the *LM* and *ff* schedules rightward until equilibrium is achieved at full employment. If money wages did not fall, or fell so slowly that waiting for an automatic return to full employment would be unacceptable, policy makers would want to use monetary and fiscal policy to pursue full employment. In a similar vein, with money market, goods market, and balance-of-payments equilibrium at an output level above the full employment level, a price rise would permit reestablishment of full employment with stable prices. If the price rise is unwanted, monetary and fiscal actions may be taken to reduce aggregate demand. We need to assess the effectiveness of fiscal and monetary policy in an open economy.

Fiscal Policy with Fixed Exchange Rates

In Figure 15—11 the economy is represented with the money market, commodity market, and balance-of-payments in equilibrium at i_0, Y_0. The full-employment level of output is Y_f, so an expansionary fiscal policy (increase in government spending or cut in taxes) would appear to be in order. Fiscal

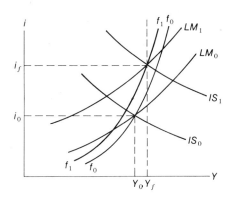

Figure 15—11 / Fiscal Stimulus with Fixed Exchange Rates

stimulus (a rightward shift of the *IS* curve) would raise the level of income and, because the trade balance is inversely related to income, push the balance-of-payments into a deficit. However, the expansion of income would raise the interest rate as money demand is increased, and the interest rate increase would attract capital inflows, pushing the balance-of-payments back toward equilibrium. Should the capital flow attracted by the higher interest rate not fully offset the trade balance deficit, leaving an overall balance-of-payments deficit, the central bank would have to provide the needed additional foreign currency, swapping that currency for domestic currency (otherwise the excess supply of domestic currency in the foreign exchange market would produce an unallowable change in exchange rates). As domestic currency is absorbed by the central bank, the domestic money supply falls (shifting the *LM* curve leftward), raising the interest rate until capital inflows are sufficient to restore balance-of-payments equilibrium.[13] The final equilibrium would occur at a position like that denoted by i_f, Y_f with external equilibrium and domestic equilibrium at full employment. The *ff* schedule is shown shifted to the left of its original position to allow for the effect on the balance-of-payments of any price increase that accompanies the economic expansion. With fixed exchange rates, fiscal policy remains effective.

Monetary Policy with Fixed Exchange Rates

Earlier we demonstrated that, with a balance-of-payments deficit and the central bank committed to maintaining a fixed exchange rate, the money

---

[13]As indicated earlier, the more mobile is international capital, the flatter is the *ff* schedule. If the capital inflows that the interest rate rise induces are greater than the trade imbalance induced by the expansion, providing a balance-of-payments surplus, the domestic money supply will grow and depress the interest rate until balance-of-payments equilibrium is restored. Fiscal policy in this case is reinforced by an induced monetary expansion.

supply automatically contracts until balance-of-payments equilibrium is restored. By implication, with money supply control subservient to the requirements of maintaining a fixed exchange rate, a second master—domestic stabilization—cannot be served. A corroborative demonstration of the indicated impotence of monetary policy when exchange rates are fixed is easily provided. With the economy at rest below the full-employment level (at i_0, Y_0 in Figure 15—12), let the central bank attempt to increase the level of income by increasing the money supply (shifting the LM curve rightward to position LM'). In Figure 15—12, the money supply increase is shown reducing the domestic interest rate to level i', but we have not yet taken account of the international reaction to a reduced domestic interest rate.

As soon as the domestic interest rate falls, a capital outflow will begin; dollars will be rapidly withdrawn from domestic assets for reinvestment in foreign assets that offer a more attractive interest yield. To buy those foreign assets, dollars (the domestic currency) must be exchanged for other currencies. Of course, as additional dollars appear on foreign exchange markets there will be a downward pressure on the dollar in those markets. However, under a system of fixed exchange rates, the central bank must support the value of the dollar, trading foreign currencies (or gold) for dollars at the allowable (fixed) exchange rate. As dollars are exchanged for other currencies, the domestic money supply shrinks, shifting the LM curve leftward and reducing aggregate demand. If capital were perfectly mobile internationally (a possibility we have briefly encountered before), the capital outflow and the resulting shrinkage of the domestic money supply would continue as long as the domestic interest rate remained below the interest rate prevailing in other countries. Thus, with other central banks maintaining unchanged interest rates in their countries, the U.S. capital outflow would return the LM curve to its original position when the central bank has bought, in the foreign exchange market, the money it attempted to pump into the domestic economy. With perfect capital markets only one interest rate can prevail world-wide, and the slightest change in rates would call forth a shift in funds that equalizes all rates.

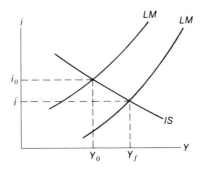

Figure 15—12 / Monetary Policy with Fixed Exchange Rates

For monetary policy to have any domestic impact in a fixed exchange rate world with *perfectly* mobile capital, it would have to alter interest rates world-wide. To do that, massive monetary policy actions that are not offset by foreign central banks would be required for *small* domestic effects. Of course, foreign assets are not perfect substitutes for domestic assets, and there are transactions costs involved in shifting from one set of assets to another. Hence, complete equalization of interest rates between countries is not required in reality. Individual central banks do have some power to influence their domestic economies,[14] but the limits that fixed exchange rates place on the central bank's ability to pursue an independent monetary policy have compelled countries to seek additional control tools, as we shall see below.

Monetary and Fiscal Policy with Flexible Exchange Rates

As we already know, with flexible exchange rates it is the exchange rate itself (rather than the domestic money supply) that adjusts to maintain balance-of-payments equilibrium. Hence, both monetary and fiscal policy can be used to pursue domestic goals with flexible exchange rates. (You should provide a graphical demonstration of this claim.) In effect, the flexible exchange rate serves as an additional policy instrument, maintaining balance-of-payments equilibrium so that our monetary and fiscal tools are free to serve other masters.

Additional Balance-of-Payments Control Instruments

Historical experience with a fixed exchange rate system has demonstrated clearly the reluctance of countries to sacrifice the pursuit of national ends for maintaining external equilibrium. Often, quite extraordinary measures have been taken to insulate domestic economies from the automatic adjustments that payment imbalances provoke. As we have already shown, with fixed exchange rates a balance-of-payments deficit prompts a contraction in the domestic money supply and, hence, in the level of economic activity. If the monetary authorities are unwilling to tolerate an economic contraction, they can "sterilize" the international flow of currency by returning to circulation every dollar that is absorbed by support actions in the foreign exchange market. Likewise, a payments surplus can be sterilized by removing from circulation every dollar that the surplus adds to the domestic money supply. Of course, with sterilization a balance-of-payments disequilibrium will persist; the use of monetary policy for domestic goals negates

---

[14]See William Branson, "The Minimum Covered Interest Differential Needed for International Arbitrage Activity," *Journal of Political Economy* 77 (1969): 1028–1035. According to Branson, the U.S. interest rate can enjoy a swing of .36 percent without enticing short-term capital movements between the United States and Canada or the United States and Britain.

its use in pursuing any other goal. Thus, a payments deficit that would ultimately exhaust a country's available reserve assets could persist, as could a payments surplus that adds continuously to the idle stock of reserve assets accumulated by the country experiencing that surplus. Certainly, sterilization efforts in a fixed exchange rate system can only postpone adjustments that can provide balance-of-payments equilibrium.

Altering "Fixed" Exchange Rates

Figure 15—13 depicts a country with a balance-of-payments surplus. If this country thinks its current domestic equilibrium position is optimal and wishes to avoid both the inflation that would allow the surplus to bring about its own end and the accumulation of idle foreign currency that sterilization of the surplus requires, it could lower its foreign exchange rate (appreciate its currency relative to other currencies) to eliminate the surplus. The appropriate *appreciation* of the domestic currency would shift the *ff* curve leftward to $f_1 f_1$ so that the original domestic equilibrium could be maintained.[15] Germany, persistently in surplus, appreciated the mark in 1961 and again in 1969.

To avoid domestic contraction, a country with a persistent deficit can depreciate its currency relative to other currencies, shifting its *ff* curve rightward. As we have mentioned earlier, England devalued the pound in 1967, producing a sizable depreciation of the pound relative to most other currencies,[16] and the United States undertook two devaluations in the early 1970s.

Exchange rate adjustments are simple and straightforward. Yet, from the Bretton Woods meeting until 1971 exchange rate adjustments were infrequently used, usually only under crisis conditions. While there are a number of reasons (not all rational) for reluctance to alter exchange rates, the most prominent concerns seem to have been the following:

1. A depreciation means an increase in the cost of purchases from abroad, thus, in the cost of living. For countries that depend heavily on imports, like Britain and the Netherlands, the impact is conspicuous (and politically costly). In real terms, a country that is experiencing a balance-of-payments deficit can be enjoying a greater flow of real goods and services than the domestic economy produces, a privilege that is hard to give up.
2. National pride is often cited as a reason for avoiding devaluation, as though some monumental loss of national face would be generated by a

---

[15]Maintaining equilibrium at i_0, Y_0 would also require some shift toward more expansionary fiscal policy because the currency appreciation will reduce net exports and, thus, domestic aggregate demand. It should be clear that with fiscal, monetary, and exchange rate policy, we could place the full equilibrium position (the *IS-LM-ff* intersection) at any point we wish in Figure 15—10.

[16]A number of Commonwealth countries devalued with England so that the pound was neither depreciated nor appreciated relative to their currencies.

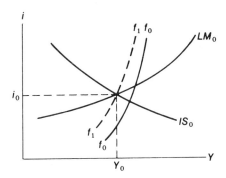

Figure 15—13 / Exchange Rate Adjustment to Combat a Surplus

realignment of currency values. In the past, our own political leaders seem to have been smitten by an irrational concern for "cheapening the dollar."

3. While the threat of exhausting its international reserves necessitates a balance-of-payments adjustment in deficit countries, no comparable incentive impinges upon a country with a surplus (which it can sterilize). With well-entrenched, politically powerful export- and import-competing industries that would see their sales reduced by appreciation of the undervalued domestic currency, we would not expect to see frequent currency revaluations.

Other Practical Adjustment Techniques

In lieu of exchange rate alterations, a host of other direct restrictions on international trade and capital flows can be deployed to combat a balance-of-payments disequilibrium. By shifting the external balance schedule such direct restrictions serve as an additional policy instrument. Commonly employed direct controls include tariffs and quotas to limit imports, subsidies to exports making it possible for domestic firms to sell their products abroad at more attractive prices, restrictions on foreign aid, and quotas or taxes on foreign capital flows. Exchange controls that limit the volume of foreign exchange made available to domestic firms and households have also been employed by some countries.

There are many familiar illustrations of the application of direct controls. A common ploy is to limit tourist spending abroad. The techniques range from exhortations to "see America first," to restrictive limits on the value of goods tourists may bring home duty-free, to the prescription of maximum daily travel allowances while abroad. Exports are subsidized in a number of European countries where a domestic *value added tax* is rebated on exports and levied on imports. Foreign aid transfers are frequently tied to expenditures on the donor country's products, and in the 1970s the United

States, which has shouldered a large share of the world's burden both for development aid and for world-wide defense, asked the other developed free world nations to assume a larger share of those burdens. In the capital flow arena (which has displayed a chronic deficit in the United States as a result of foreign investment), direct controls on U.S. foreign investment by banks and nonfinancial institutions were imposed in 1965. These controls reinforced the restraint provided by an 11½ percent *interest equalization tax* on all American purchases of foreign stocks and long-term bonds (these restrictions were lifted in 1973).

Needless to say, direct controls distort the trade and capital flows that would be observed in unfettered world markets in which each country would emphasize production of those items with which it enjoyed a relative cost advantage. Instead, with direct controls, the total volume of world trade is reduced, resulting in some decrease in the efficiency and material well-being of the world community. While *protectionist* direct controls are officially denounced by Western governments that ostensibly recognize the gains in production efficiency and world consumption offered by free trade, those governments all maintain some barriers (generally tariffs, quotas, and "voluntary" restrictions) on the free flow of goods, services, and capital.

Coordinated Mixes of Monetary and Fiscal Policy

For completeness, we need to extend our discussion of the techniques that countries with foreign exchange rates that are not market determined have for overcoming conflicts between domestic goals and balance-of-payments equilibrium. We must consider the use of alternative *combinations* of monetary and fiscal policies. For example, consider again an economy that suffers from a balance-of-payments deficit when operating at full-employment (domestic) equilibrium. Such an economy is represented in Figure 15—14 with Y_f the full-employment level of output and i_0 the equilibrium interest rate. Now, with domestic equilibrium at output level Y_f, balance-of-payments equilibrium would prevail if only the interest rate were i_1 instead of i_0. Logically, a reduction in the domestic money supply (shifting the *LM* curve to *LM'*) could be employed to lift the interest rate and attract capital inflows.[17] To maintain full employment an expansionary fiscal policy (shifting the *IS* curve to *IS'*) would have to accompany the *restrictive* monetary policy.

More generally, if the economy were suffering from both a depressed level of economic activity and a balance-of-payments deficit (as at Y_0, i_0 in

---

[17]As we have already indicated, with the passage of time a balance-of-payments deficit would automatically reduce the domestic money supply *(ceteris paribus)*, shifting the *LM* curve leftward until balance-of-payments equilibrium is restored. The central bank can reduce the money supply without waiting for the domestic currency outflow to produce a domestic money stock contraction.

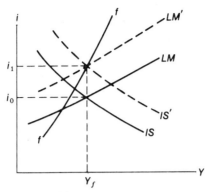

**Figure 15—14 / Combination Policies to
Maintain Internal and External Equilibrium**

Figure 15—15), it is still theoretically possible for an appropriate combination policy to achieve both full employment and balance-of-payments equilibrium. Once again, expansionary fiscal policy (shifting the *IS* curve to *IS'*) could be used to pursue the domestic goal of full employment while monetary policy is employed to achieve external balance (shifting *LM* to *LM'*).

Leaving graphical proofs to you, we need to acknowledge that it is also theoretically possible to employ mixed monetary-fiscal policies to deal with the combination of underemployment and a balance-of-payments surplus, with inflation (domestic demand greater than full-employment output) and a balance-of-payments surplus, inflation and a balance-of-payments deficit, and so on. In each case, with capital flows between countries sensitive to interest rate changes, monetary policy bears the responsibility for external balance (the subservience of monetary policy to the requirements of external balance is illustrated again), while fiscal policy must be used to achieve and maintain full employment. Unfortunately, the government generally must pursue more than two policy goals so that simple combination policies of the type we have illustrated may not be of much use. For example, the provision of a rapidly expanding stock of housing is usually accorded a high priority (at least in the United States). However, residential construction is depressed by the high interest rates a monetary-fiscal policy mix aimed at combating a balance-of-payments deficit requires. More generally, high interest rates depress all investment plans, slowing the growth of productive capacity in general. It is quite logical that governments typically look for additional instruments for reducing a deficit that limit reliance on high interest rates. Moreover, even when some simple mixed monetary and fiscal policy is appropriate, proper application of such a policy would require rather precise knowledge of the strength and timing of impact of both monetary and fiscal actions, knowledge that is not available now. It is no wonder that direct controls on international transactions have enjoyed such popularity.

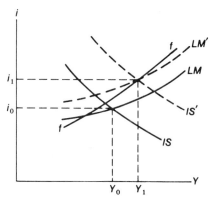

Figure 15—15 / A Cure for Unemployment and a Balance-of-Payments Deficit

Exchange Rates in the 1970s

What has happened to the value of the dollar in foreign exchange markets since the August 1971 breakdown of the Bretton Woods system? Figure 15—16 provides guidance in answering that question. In that figure, index measures of the exchange value relative to the dollar of the currencies of a sample of economically advanced countries are plotted. Note that the Canadian dollar, the British pound, and the Italian lira depreciated relative to the dollar in the 1970s. In contrast, the Swiss franc, the German mark and, until recent months, the Japanese yen appeared to be *strong* currencies during the 1970s, appreciating relative to the dollar. Figure 15—16 also shows a "trade-weighted" index of currencies representing the value relative to the dollar of a market basket of foreign currencies, with their values weighted by each country's share in U.S. trade. The rising schedule (the heavy black line) representing this index shows that the value of the dollar eroded relative to the *average* value of the currencies of trading partners of the U.S. during the 1970s.

Without attempting to provide a full explanation of the downward pressure on the exchange value of the dollar through the 1970s, it may be noted that such an explanation would include consideration of:

1. Relative rates of inflation in the United States and in the countries the U.S. trades with. A more rapid inflation rate would cause a country's exports to become more expensive and imports to become cheaper, leading to an increase in the supply of that country's currency in foreign exchange markets just as demand for the currency is being reduced. Thus, the exchange value of the currency of a country with more rapid inflation than that of its trading partners would fall.
2. Because of high investment abroad, generous military aid, and related sources of outflows of dollars during the 1950s and 1960s, the rest of the

world accumulated a vast stock of dollars that still resides in foreign hands. This "overhang" of dollars loses purchasing power as U.S. prices rise and the exchange value of dollars falls. As a consequence, holders of dollars have an incentive to exchange them for other, "stronger" currencies. Of course, the increased supply of dollars tends to further depress its exchange value.

3. Heavy dependence on foreign oil supplies in an era when OPEC actions have greatly raised the world price of oil contributed to sizable balance-of-payments deficits in the last half of the 1970s, exerting additional downward pressure on the dollar.

With high interest rates and an economic slowdown, a continuing depreciation of the dollar may be halted. This was clearly recognized in policy actions taken in late 1979 and early 1980 as interest rates in the United States were pushed to record levels and budgetary restrictions were pressed. Over the longer haul, however, maintenance of balance-of-payments equilibrium will require slower domestic inflation (proposals to slow wage increases and stimulate productivity are often made on this score), a speed-up in inflation in other countries, or a further depreciation of the dollar. For unclear reasons (national pride?), the public at large is more fearful of further depreciation of the dollar than are most economists. The majority of economists view the depreciation of a currency as simply a reflection of, for the most part, different inflation rates in the domestic economy and

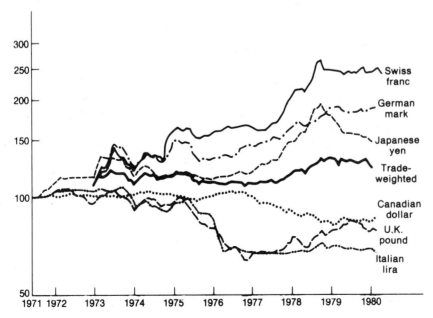

Figure 15—16 / Indexes of Effective Exchange Rates, 1971–1980:1

Source: International Monetary Fund

abroad. It is notable, however, that there is some professional concern over the possibility of a *vicious circle* of domestic inflation, currency depreciation, further domestic inflation, a further currency depreciation, etc.

The vicious circle begins with a disturbance that can cause domestic prices to increase. As an example, consider an expansionary monetary policy action that lowers interest rates. In view of the capital outflows that can be expected, this results in the anticipation of an exchange depreciation and, as those capital flows occur, the domestic currency's value will fall. With the currency depreciation, the domestic price of foreign goods is increased and export prices decline. As a result, consumers will increase their demand for domestic products and export demand will rise as well. With product demand increased, employment may rise. However, with prices increased through the currency depreciation, the rate of wage inflation rises as labor attempts to maintain its real wage. The increase in domestic demand reinforces the upward pressure on prices.

In turn, rising domestic prices reduce the competitive advantage previously enjoyed and, as this occurs, demand for domestic production contracts, the balance of trade shifts negatively, and the currency depreciates again. With monetary policy actions that strive to prevent contractions in employment and output (even when labor raises money wages to maintain a stable real wage in the face of a currency depreciation), a continuing cycle of domestic inflation, exchange depreciation, and further inflation may be possible. Detailed consideration of the restrictive conditions required for this process to occur are beyond the scope of this text,[18] but recognition of the possible existence of the "vicious circle" is clearly indicative of potential problems in a floating exchange rate system.

The Future of the International Monetary System

Quotas and tariffs, export subsidies, restrictions on capital flows, indeed all manner of direct control techniques for combating a balance-of-payments disequilibrium are stopgap measures that carry a heavy cost in that they disrupt efficient patterns of world resource utilization. As we have seen, they were quite naturally relied on, increasingly through the 1960s and into the 1970s, until the final breakdown of the Bretton Woods system in the spring of 1973.

As indicated earlier, the breakdown of the old order resulted in a system of managed floating exchange rates. While this system has allowed some fairly wide swings in exchange rates, it has survived the serious challenges generated by the massive balance-of-payments imbalances that have accompanied a world-wide protein shortage in early 1973 and the oil crisis that began in the fall of 1973, both developments that probably would have been far more disruptive of world financial order under a system of fixed exchange rates. Encouraged by that experience, the negotiating members of the IMF

---

[18]See Marion Bond, "Exchange Rates, Inflation, and the Vicious Circle," *Finance and Development,* March 1980, pp. 27–31.

appear unwilling at this time to adopt any formal world-wide exchange rate system that imposes limits on exchange rate adjustments. That is true in spite of the fact that, while freely floating exchange rates provide for automatic maintenance of balance-of-payments equilibrium, freeing domestic stabilization tools for the pursuit of domestic goals, it is often argued (especially by bankers and the world business community) that freely floating exchange rates are fraught with too much *uncertainty* and, hence, are disruptive of long-term sales and investment commitments. To focus on the essential concern, with floating exchange rates a U.S. firm cannot know the dollar value of the pound payments it will receive one, two, or five years from now on delivery of a shipment of wheat or a complex computer installation. In response to that charge, it can be argued that firms can guarantee the domestic currency values of their foreign contracts by selling those contracts in international currency markets known as *futures* markets (for example, a U.S. firm can exchange pounds to be received in the future for dollars). However, to the extent that flexible exchange rates do increase uncertainty, ensuring the domestic value of contracts will raise the transactions costs firms face, reducing the volume of international trade.

Until now, the use of futures markets, continuing *management* of exchange rates, and the choice by some countries to continue pegging their currencies to those of their major trading partners has permitted a continued expansion of world trade. However, the existing managed float system has yet to be tested in a period of serious recession that simultaneously affects the major trading nations.[19]

Summary

In this chapter, we have tried to provide a fairly comprehensive understanding of the macroeconomic ramifications of international trade and finance. Accommodating the role of exports and imports of goods and services was straightforward because net exports are a component of aggregate, commodity market demand. An increase in net exports shifted the *IS* curve rightward in the *IS-LM* model, stimulating the domestic economy, while a reduction in net exports shifted the *IS* schedule leftward, inducing a domestic contraction.

By extending our analysis to look at international financial flows, we were able to analyze a second, indirect way (or set of ways) in which the domestic level of economic activity may be affected by involvement in the world market place. In a fixed exchange rate world, when international transactions produce a surplus in the balance-of-payments (a net acquisition of reserve assets or foreign-issued claims exchangeable for those assets), the

[19]Monetarist views of the causes of inflation and balance-of-payments adjustments are cogently presented in Thomas Humphrey, "A Monetarist Model of World Inflation and the Balance of Payments," *Federal Reserve Bank of Richmond Economic Review*, November/December 1976, pp. 13–22.

net inflow of foreign currency deposits into the domestic financial system raises reserves. The reaction of depository institutions increases the domestic money supply, shifting the *LM* curve rightward and stimulating the domestic economy. On the other hand, a balance-of-payments deficit drains reserves, producing a reduction in the domestic money supply. The accompanying leftward shift in the *LM* curve results in a domestic contraction.

The automatic response to balance-of-payments disequilibrium in a fixed exchange rate world can, however, be postponed (the balance-of-payments disequilibrium perpetuated) if the central bank sterilizes the international deposit flows that accompany the disequilibrium. Central banks, in fact, have frequently short-circuited the automatic adjustment mechanism because the internal changes in income, prices, and interest rates that are necessary for automatic elimination of a balance-of-payments disequilibrium were typically inconsistent with domestic policy objectives. Still, concern for disequilibrium, at least in the deficit case where ultimate exhaustion of reserves is a threat, all too often resulted in the imposition of a host of controls on trade, tourism, and capital flows. In addition, there is little doubt that domestic policies in the postwar period were, on occasion, seriously constrained by balance-of-payments difficulties.

A glimpse at postwar experience suggests that the main shortcoming of the Bretton Woods system was the operational inflexibility of official exchange rates. Under that system, currency parities were changed only infrequently and always under crisis conditions, after the existence of fundamental disequilibrium was clearly confirmed. With the breakdown of the Bretton Woods system in 1973, we were shuttled to a system that provides, and certainly will continue to provide, more flexibility in exchange rates. That system, as well as serving to avoid crises of confidence in currencies, frees monetary policy for the pursuit of domestic goals. Exchange rate uncertainties and even the possibility of cycles of inflations and currency depreciation illustrate the fact that no system of payments is free of problems.

Questions

1. Draw the flow diagram appropriate for an open economy's commodity market and write out the equilibrium condition(s) for that market. Explain how commodity market equilibrium is affected by:
   a. an increase in foreign income,
   b. depreciation of the domestic currency,
   c. an increase in the domestic price level.

2. Explain the slope of the *ff* curve. Explain how that schedule is affected by:
   a. appreciation of the domestic currency,
   b. foreign inflation,
   c. import controls,
   d. export subsidies,
   e. exhortations to "see America first."

3. Explain how the exchange rate is determined under a system of floating exchange rates. Why did we rely on fixed rather than floating exchange rates until the early 1970s?

4. Suppose, to combat a balance-of-payments deficit, import restrictions are imposed. Analyze the impact on income, employment, the interest rate, and the balance-of-payments in a fixed exchange rate world.

5. Suppose a devaluation is utilized to reduce a balance-of-payments deficit. What fiscal policy should accompany that devaluation if no change in domestic income is desired?

6. We have assumed that the volume of export sales is independent of domestic income. Critically evaluate that assumption.

7. Suppose, under a system of fixed exchange rates, a country is considering two alternative policies to improve its balance-of-payments: (1) a formal devaluation; and (2) an income reduction through restrictive monetary and fiscal policy. Which policy would you recommend? Why?

8. Evaluate the effectiveness of using monetary policy to raise the level of domestic employment:
    a. with fixed exchange rates,
    b. with flexible exchange rates.

Suggested Readings

Branson, William H. "Monetarist and Keynesian Models of the Transmission of Inflation," *The American Economic Review* 65 (1975): 115–19.

Caves, R. E. "Flexible Exchange Rates." *The American Economic Review* 53 (1963): 120—129.

Friedman, Milton. "The Case for Flexible Exchange Rates." In *Essays in Positive Economics,* edited by Milton Friedman, pp. 157–203. Chicago: University of Chicago Press, 1953.

Mundell, Robert A. "The Appropriate Use of Monetary and Fiscal Policy for External and Internal Balance." *IMF Staff Papers* 9 (1962): 70–79.

Mundell, Robert A. "The Monetary Dynamics of International Adjustments Under Fixed and Flexible Exchange Rates." *Quarterly Journal of Economics* 74 (1960): 227–257.

Schmidt, Wilson E. *The U.S. Balance of Payments and the Sinking Dollar.* New York: New York University Press, 1979.

Stern, Robert, *et al., The Presentation of the U.S. Balance of Payments: A Symposium,* pp. 1–11. Princeton Essays in International Finance, No. 123. Princeton, N.J.: Department of Economics, Princeton University, August 1977.

Whitman, Marina v.N. "Global Monetarism and the Monetary Approach to the Balance of Payments." *Brookings Papers on Economic Activity,* 6, No. 3 (1975): 491–536.

Chapter 16   Economic Growth

Up to now, our analysis has involved a relatively short time perspective. We have attempted to account for gaps between potential output (full-employment output) and aggregate demand, and to show how government action might close those gaps. For the most part, *potential* output has been considered fixed because, by assumption, the time horizon with which we were concerned was too short to allow any change in the size or quality of the labor force, the state of technology, the stock of capital, or the quantity and quality of land and natural resources. We have recognized that even in the short-run, there is *net investment,* by definition a change in the capital stock. So, at least one of the assumptions employed in short-run analysis was somewhat suspect. It was necessary for us to argue that the assumption of a constant capital stock is *approximately* correct; in the short-run, net investment is small enough relative to the accumulated stock of capital that the stock can be treated as approximately constant.

As the time horizon with which we are concerned lengthens, it becomes increasingly unreasonable to assume that the quantity and quality of our factors of production stay constant. Our discussion of supply-oriented policies in Chapter 12 reflects recognition of the role of those factors. With increases in the size and quality of the labor force, with growth in the stock of capital, with technological innovation, and with the exploitation of new land areas (and other natural resources), an economy's capacity to produce grows. Indeed, production capacity in the United States has grown at a rate that has permitted transformation of a primitive, agricultural economy into a world production leader in considerably less than 200 years.

This chapter is directly concerned with the functioning of the economy when the time horizon with which we are concerned is vastly extended. Specifically, instead of focusing on cyclical movements in economic activity, this chapter is concerned with the long-run growth of production capacity. Matters of interest include the conditions under which economic growth takes place and identification of the determinants of an economy's equilibrium rate of growth.

Concern for the Rate of Economic Growth

There are a number of reasons for a country to be concerned about its rate of economic growth. With population growth, output must expand just to maintain per capita income (output). To satisfy the desire for higher levels of real per capita income, real output must grow faster than the population. Among those in the lower ranges of the income distribution, even in the affluent United States, there is no question about the desirability of per capita income growth. While, among the more affluent, it is easier to find individuals who castigate the pursuit of ever larger volumes of material goods and services, the vast majority of all income classes appear unwilling to sacrifice their color TVs, automobiles, vacation homes, beach vacations, and so on.

We also should point out that an expanding economy provides more opportunities for individuals to be productively employed, a distinct plus, particularly in the eyes of nonwhites and women whose unemployment rates always exceed the unemployment rate for white males by a wide margin. In addition, growth may provide the most politically practical way for a country to accommodate growing public service needs. With growth in productive capacity, increased volumes of resources can be devoted to public use, providing such public goods as schools, highways, and national defense without an absolute reduction in private resource use. Extending this line of argument, it is often contended that the conflict between rich and poor can be eased by growth because, with growth, the level of income channeled to low income groups can be raised without lowering the absolute level of income enjoyed by the relatively well-to-do. With income stagnant, the poor could be made richer only through a sacrifice of the current *absolute* living standards of the nonpoor, a requirement that is claimed to be more painful than the sacrifice of an improvement in the living standard that has not been experienced would be.

In the past, particularly during the 1950s and early 1960s (prior to "detente"), many analysts favored rapid growth because of our competitive relationship with the Soviet Union. Through growth, increasing productive capacity is made available for national defense items. Perhaps more significantly, brisk U.S. growth was called for to provide evidence to the ideologically uncommitted nations of the world that democratic capitalistic governments can provide rapidly rising standards of living. The less-developed countries have never seriously entertained the notion that higher levels of production of material goods are not essential to overall social well-being.

Of course, we must not ignore the fact that, in addition to generating benefits, growth does levy burdens (costs) on society. First and foremost, to raise future output levels, resources must be freed from current consumption use to provide the physical (plant and equipment) capital and human (skills and motivation) capital required for increased productive capacity. That is, *current* consumption must be sacrificed to provide the investment necessary for raising future output levels. A more prominent concern in recent years has centered on the possible trade-off between increases in GNP (as traditionally measured) and reductions in the *quality* of life. An extreme view of the results of growth has been offered by the British economist E. J. Mishan who blames growth for "the appalling traffic congestion in our towns, cities, and suburbs, . . . erosion of the countryside, the 'uglification' of coastal towns, . . . and a wide heritage of natural beauty being wantonly destroyed."[1] Some observers foresee even more dire consequences of continued growth. They argue that the world population is consuming the earth's exhaustible resources, including its clean air and water, at an unsustainable rate. The very survival of the human species, they claim, depends on a restoration of harmony between economic activity and the demands of the ecosystem, a restoration that can be accomplished only with a cessation of growth before the "spaceship earth" is made unlivable.

The vast majority of economists are far more sanguine in their view of the impact of continued growth, for growth does not have to be as destructive of the quality of life as its harshest critics contend. Rather than deny the beneficial, productive use of our resources, most economists call for actions which would promote the pattern of resource allocation, including use of resources to increase productive capacity, that would be automatically provided by a competitive market economy in which the *full social costs* of production are reflected in product prices. Where production processes have the potential for generating socially undesirable by-products, the emission of those by-products can be legally restricted. Alternatively, as economists would generally prefer, the emission of negative by-products can be discouraged through tax levies that reflect the costs those by-products impose on society. If the users of such *free* resources as our exhaustible supplies of clean air and water and our uncluttered open spaces must pay

---

[1]Edward J. Mishan, *Technology and Growth* (New York: Praeger, 1969), pp. 6–7.

user fees (tax levies) for fouling those resources, there is a compelling incentive to cut back on the production that generates those by-products, and there is encouragement for modification of production techniques to reduce or eliminate the effluents previously emitted.

Where production threatens to deplete exhaustible basic resources, market forces will dictate a modification of the production processes that employ those resources. As any particular resource becomes more scarce, its price will rise. The price increase will: (1) prompt efforts to find and develop additional sources of the scarce resource; (2) reduce the use of that resource by raising the cost of products manufactured using that resource; and (3) encourage the development of production processes that use the scarce resource more efficiently, or that use a substitute for that resource.[2] Much of the economic progress we have enjoyed can be traced to the discoveries and innovations prompted by scarcity.

We have by no means exhausted the list of potential benefits and costs associated with the growth process. Still, our list gives a clear indication of the variety of concerns of both supporters and opponents of the growth ethic. It should be clear that what any individual picks as an appropriate growth target is dictated by value judgments, and every individual places his own weights on the specific benefits and costs he associates with growth.

In contrast to the doomsday predictions of ecologists, most economists agree that society's well-being is best served by continued economic growth. Of course, it is generally recognized that not all output growth is desirable; not all output growth makes a positive net contribution to social welfare after allowing for the by-products of that growth. However, output growth that does make a net contribution to social welfare is welcomed. To adopt a no-growth policy, because output growth can produce undesirable side effects, smacks of a "throw out the baby with the bath water" attitude. Indeed, only with a growing productive capacity can we maintain our current consumption standards *and* provide the capital investment needed for cleaning our air, water, and countryside; for improving our transportation system; and so on. The remainder of the chapter examines the conditions under which sustained growth can take place and the factors that determine the growth path, first in the context of formal economic "growth models," then in terms of statistical attempts to measure the contributions of particular factors to U.S. growth.

Fixed-Proportion Growth Models

The intensity of national concern over the rate of growth fluctuates with the performance of the economy. After many years of sluggish growth in the 1950s, actions advocated by the Kennedy administration to spur growth

---

[2]Among its other effects, rapidly rising world oil prices (imposed by a cartel arrangement) have: (1) substantially increased oil exploration activities; (2) slowed the rate of growth of oil usage; and (3) made small cars more popular and stimulated interest in nuclear, solar, and other forms of energy.

commanded widespread attention and support. With output growing vigorously in the mid-1960s, growth was taken for granted and national concern turned to other issues. Since 1969, though, the rate of real output growth has slowed and inflation has accelerated. It is, once again, fashionable for society to worry about the rate of growth, although that concern is tempered by an awareness of the ecological implications of alternative growth patterns.

Economists themselves have always been highly concerned with economic growth. Consequently, there was only a short time lapse after the publication of the *General Theory* in 1936 before academic economists began to concern themselves with growth in a Keynesian world. In fact, a landmark in the evolution of modern theoretical explanations of growth appeared in 1939 with the publication of Roy Harrod's "An Essay in Dynamic Theory."[3]

The Harrod-Domar Model

While not identical, very similar attempts to extend the Keynesian model to analyze long-run economic growth were developed by Harrod and Evsey Domar. The basic model they developed is most often presented as the *Harrod-Domar model* in textbook reviews of the evolution of growth model analysis. While the Harrod-Domar model is quite simple, it provides some insights into the growth process that have directly affected growth planning in many countries.

The Harrod-Domar analysis focuses attention on the dual role that investment plays once we lengthen our time horizon sufficiently to let the capital stock grow significantly. On the one hand, investment expenditure, as Keynesian models emphasize, is a component of aggregate *demand*. On the other hand, net investment increases the stock of capital and, thus, increases the economy's potential *supply* of real goods and services over time. The Harrod-Domar analysis focuses on determining the (possibly restrictive) requirements for ensuring that aggregate supply and demand grow in step.

The formal Harrod-Domar model is constructed assuming a simple closed economy so aggregate *demand* is the sum of consumption *(C)* and autonomous investment $(\bar{I})$, as indicated in Equation (16—1).

$$\text{Demand} = Y_D = C + I \qquad [16-1]$$
$$= a + bY + \bar{I}.$$

Because aggregate spending (demand) is identical to aggregate income, the equilibrium level of aggregate demand is

$$Y_D = \frac{1}{1-b}(a + \bar{I}) \qquad [16-2]$$

[3]Roy Harrod, "An Essay in Dynamic Theory," *Economic Journal* 49 (1939): 14–33. See also Evsey Domar, "Expansion and Employment," *The American Economic Review* 37 (1947): 34–55.

or

$$Y_D = \frac{1}{s}(a + \bar{I})$$

where s is the marginal propensity to save. The change in aggregate demand that stems from a change in investment is just

$$\Delta Y_D = \frac{1}{s}\Delta \bar{I} \qquad\qquad [16\text{--}3]$$

the change in investment times the simple multiplier.

To know how aggregate *supply* changes over time, we must know the nature of the relationship between output and the volume of factor inputs employed. The first production relationship in the Harrod-Domar model assumes that aggregate potential supply is directly proportional to the volume of capital stock available. That is,

$$\text{Supply} = Y_S = \sigma K \qquad\qquad [16\text{--}4]$$

where K is the stock of capital and σ is the "output-capital" ratio.[4] With a constant output to capital ratio, the change in potential supply during any time period is

$$\Delta Y_S = \sigma \Delta K \qquad\qquad [16\text{--}5]$$

However, because by definition the change in capital stock during any period is net investment, Equation (16—5) can be rewritten to show the change in aggregate supply in any period as

$$\Delta Y_S = \sigma I \qquad\qquad [16\text{--}6]$$

The dual role of investment mentioned earlier is easily seen in Equation (16—3), showing the influence of investment on aggregate demand, and in Equation (16—6), showing the influence of investment on aggregate supply.

Starting with equality of aggregate supply and demand, if full employment of the capital stock is to be maintained over time, aggregate demand must grow in step with supply. If this equality ($\Delta Y_D = \Delta Y_S$) holds over time, from Equations (16—3) and (16—6)

$$\frac{1}{s}\Delta I = \sigma I \qquad\qquad [16\text{--}7]$$

or

$$\frac{\Delta I}{I} = s\sigma \qquad\qquad [16\text{--}7A]$$

---

[4]If $Y = \sigma K$, $\sigma = Y/K$, the output-capital ratio.

The term $\Delta I/I$ in Equation (16—7A) is the proportional rate at which investment itself *must grow* over time to maintain full utilization of the growing stock of capital. If, for example, the output to capital ratio is .5 and the marginal propensity to save is .1, the required rate of growth of investment for maintaining full use of the capital stock is .05 or 5 percent annually ($s\sigma = .1 \times .5 = .05$).

Should the marginal propensity to save increase to .2, the rate at which investment must grow to maintain full utilization of the capital stock becomes 10 percent. That is, the larger the fraction of any addition to output that is saved (the smaller the fraction consumed), the larger the required addition to investment if aggregate demand is to absorb the full volume of production that an enlarged capital stock can provide.

At what rate will aggregate output be growing with investment expanding at rate $s\sigma$? From Equation (16—6), output grows in absolute terms by

$$\Delta Y_S = \sigma I \qquad\qquad [16—8]$$

For the economy to be in equilibrium, saving must equal investment, and, in the long-run, saving is a constant fraction of income. In this case, the average and marginal propensities to save are identical so total saving is sY where s is both the average and marginal propensity to save. Substituting saving (sY) for investment in Equation (16—8) yields

$$\Delta Y = \sigma s Y \qquad\qquad [16—9]$$

so the rate of growth of output is

$$\frac{\Delta Y}{Y} = s\sigma \qquad\qquad [16—10]$$

Thus, output grows at the rate at which investment grows.

Growth rate $s\sigma$, the rate of growth of investment and output at which the expanding capital stock will remain fully utilized over time, is what Harrod called the *warranted* rate of growth (G_W). It is the rate of growth that will result in investors' expectations being *realized* or *warranted*, i.e., all investment exactly fully utilized. There are two important lessons for growth planning implied by Equation (16—10). First, that equation indicates that the rate of growth is positively related to the saving rate. Saving frees resources for investment, and it is investment that provides for a growing productive capacity. Secondly, Equation (16—10) indicates that the growth rate is directly related to the output-capital ratio (the productivity of capital). By raising the saving rate and investing in more productive capital, it appears a country can raise its warranted growth rate.

Labor Force Utilization

To know whether warranted growth rate $s\sigma$ permits maintenance of full employment of the labor force, we need to know the rate at which the labor force grows; and we need to know, from the aggregate production function, the relationship between labor utilization and output. The production relationship summarized in Equation (16—4) indicates only that aggregate supply is proportional to the stock of capital employed and tells us nothing about the labor requirement in the production process. We know though that labor inputs are required in the production process. Thus, for capital to serve as a strict constraint on output, as indicated in Equation (16—4), the aggregate production function must require labor and capital to be combined in *fixed proportions*, as shown in Figure 16—1. The heavy L-shaped lines in that illustration are production *isoquants*, showing the combinations of labor and capital that can provide particular levels of aggregate output. With the production function represented by Figure 16—1, one unit of output can be produced with two units of capital and four units of labor (point *A*). The addition of more units of labor has no impact on output as long as the stock of capital is held constant (point *B* in Figure 16—1). Similarly, increasing the quantity of capital with the quantity of labor held constant, for example, at the four-unit level, leaves output unchanged.

The proportionate capital-labor ratio that just permits one, two, or more units of output to be produced with no surplus labor or capital is 1 to 2, one unit of capital to two units of labor. The Harrod-Domar production function clearly assumes that the ratio of required capital to labor is *fixed* for all income levels. With this highly restrictive form of production function, the economy can grow at the warranted rate only if there is surplus labor or if the effective labor supply is growing as rapidly as investment and output are growing. To return to our earlier example in which the warranted rate of growth was 5 percent annually, if the economy begins with both capital and labor fully utilized, the labor force would have to grow at a 5 percent

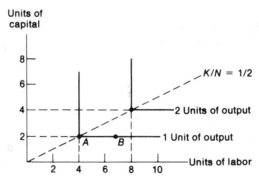

Figure 16—1 / A Fixed-Proportion Production Function

or greater annual rate to prevent labor scarcity from constraining output's growth to a slower rate. If, for example, the rate of growth of the labor force is only 3 percent annually, the rate of growth of investment and output would be constrained to be 3 percent or less annually. That conclusion holds, ultimately, even if the economy initially has unemployed labor available. Once labor is fully utilized, if the capital stock grows faster than the labor force, there will be redundant capital that, as our production function discussion has shown, has zero productivity; it simply is not used. The rate of population growth serves as a powerful constraint on the growth of output and the capital stock in the Harrod-Domar model.

Labor Force Growth. In the Harrod-Domar model, the labor force is assumed to grow at a biologically determined, constant, proportional rate, $\Delta N/N$. If the rate of growth of output is constrained by the rate of population growth, there is one way in which the growth rate can be raised. If it is possible to invest in new, *technologically improved* capital (rather than just in more units of an existing sort of capital), the average productivity of labor can be increased over time so that a smaller labor input can be combined with a given "size" of capital input to produce the same output as before. Hence, with "labor-saving" technological progress, the rate at which the economy's productive capacity grows can be raised. In its effect on productive capacity, a continous increase over time in the average productivity of labor is equivalent to having the labor force grow more rapidly with average productivity unchanged. Thus, the rate of growth of the "effective" labor force or of "augmented" labor is the sum of the rate of growth of man-hours of labor and of the rate of growth of average labor productivity. That is, "effective" labor supply's growth rate, which in the Harrod-Domar analysis is called the *natural* rate of growth, is:

$$G_N = \frac{\Delta N_e}{N_e} = \frac{\Delta N}{N} + \lambda \qquad\qquad [16\text{--}11]$$

where λ is the rate of growth of average labor productivity and $\Delta N/N$, as before, is the rate of growth of manpower.

The rate of growth of output is still strictly constrained, but with labor-saving technological progress, it is constrained to equality with the warranted rate of growth ($s\sigma$) or the natural rate of growth of *augmented* labor, whichever is smaller. Thus, the emphasis in the full Harrod-Domar model is on the important role of the rate of saving and investment as the determinant of the warranted rate of growth and on the roles of population growth and technological progress as determinants of the natural rate of growth. To accelerate growth, a country must save (invest) a larger fraction of its current output and/or must employ policies that increase the rate of technological progress. A full equilibrium rate of growth would be one that maintained full utilization of both the capital stock and the labor force over time. In full equilibrium, then,

$$\frac{\Delta Y}{Y} = s\sigma = \frac{\Delta N}{N} + \lambda \qquad [16\text{—}12]$$

or

$$G_W = G_N$$

In full equilibrium, the economy would expand along a production ray like K/N in Figure 16—1, with output and the stock of capital expanding at precisely the rate dictated by the expansion of the augmented labor force. While steady growth at the natural rate is possible, with no mechanism that coordinates the growth of the capital stock with the *natural* rate of growth (determination of s, σ, $\Delta N/N$, and λ are all independent), the probability that expansion will take place along the one *razor's edge* expansion path that maintains full utilization of labor and capital is extremely small.

Should the natural rate of growth be smaller than the warranted rate, excess capital stock will ultimately appear. Immediately the marginal product of new capital drops to zero, eliminating the incentive for investment. With investment and, thus, aggregate demand falling, excess capacity would be growing making it appear that firms had been investing at too rapid a rate when, in fact, more investment would be needed to stave off a major contraction. Conditions are little better if the natural rate exceeds the warranted rate. In that case, there would be increasing unemployment of labor over time. The equilibrium growth path represented by the Harrod-Domar model is clearly a difficult path for the economy to follow.

Happily, the real world appears less demanding in its requirements for permitting the full utilization of both labor and capital as the economy expands. Dissatisfied with the pessimistic predictions in the razor's edge model, growth theorists soon provided alternative accounts of the growth process. These alternative models of growth showed that the demanding conditions for full equilibrium in the Harrod-Domar model stemmed from the rigidity of the assumptions on which the model was built: a constant capital-output ratio, a constant saving ratio, and a constant rate of growth of the augmented labor force. By relaxing one or more of these restrictive assumptions, the razor-edge rigidity in the Harrod-Domar analysis can be eliminated.

Neoclassical Growth Models

In a seminal contribution to the new generation of growth models, in 1956 Robert Solow constructed a neoclassical growth model that: (1) generalized the Harrod-Domar analysis by employing a production function that permits substitution between capital and labor inputs; and (2) focused attention on the supply of factor inputs rather than on demand as the basic determinant of the long-run growth path.[5] In conjunction with the assumption of capital-labor substitution, Solow also assumed a competitive economy (with no wage or price rigidities), providing assurance that all factor inputs would be fully utilized and that the commodity market would clear (planned investment and saving equal) at the full capacity level of production. Because the fundamental assumptions employed in the Solow analysis are common to neoclassical theory, the resulting growth model is *neoclassical*. With full employment assured, the neoclassical growth model is concerned with the equilibrium growth rate and with the contributions that labor, capital, and technological progress make to growth.

The Generalized Production Function and Output Changes

As shown in Figure 16—2, when capital and labor are substitutes, production can take place with an unlimited number of different capital to labor ratios.[6] Each of the heavy lines in that figure is an isoquant that shows the various combinations of capital and labor that can be used to produce a particular volume of output. Two possible output expansion rays are shown in Figure 16—2, one for a capital-labor of 2 to 1, and one with $K/N = 1/2$.

Examination of either of the possible expansion paths plotted in Figure 16—2 shows that an equiproportional change in both factor inputs changes output by the same proportion; for example, doubling the quantity of labor and capital employed along the $K/N = 2/1$ ray doubles output. Thus, the production function that provides the isoquants in Figure 16—2 assumes constant returns to scale.[7] At the same time, it assumes diminishing returns to any one variable factor input. That is, adding more and more units of a variable factor input to a fixed quantity of other inputs is assumed to raise output at a diminishing rate, the *marginal product* of any factor input that is allowed to vary in quantity declining as additional units of the variable factor are employed.

The general algebraic form of the production function specified above is simply

$$Y = Y(K, N) \quad s.t. \quad \frac{\Delta Y}{\Delta K} > 0$$

$$\frac{\Delta Y}{\Delta N} > 0$$

[16—13]

---

[5]Robert M. Solow, "A Contribution to the Theory of Economic Growth," *Quarterly Journal of Economics* 70 (1956): 65–94. Also see idem, "Technical Change and the Aggregate Production Function," *Review of Economics and Statistics* 39 (1957): 312–320.

[6]The neoclassical production function that provides the isoquants (constant output schedules) in Figure 16—2 is the general form we assumed throughout our analysis of short-run income determination models.

[7]A production function that exhibits constant returns to scale is frequently described as *linearly homogeneous* or homogeneous of degree 1. For any function $Y = Y(K, N)$, if $Y(\eta K, \eta N) = \eta Y$, the function is linearly homogeneous.

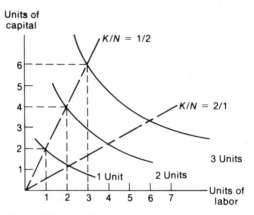

**Figure 16—2 / Neoclassical Production
Isoquants—Capital and Labor Substitutable**

Because changes in the size of either the labor force or the capital stock produce changes in output, it is definitionally true from Equation (16—13) that

$$\Delta Y = \left(\frac{\Delta Y}{\Delta K}\right) \cdot \Delta K + \left(\frac{\Delta Y}{\Delta N}\right) \cdot \Delta N \qquad [16\text{—}14]$$

Recognizing that $(\Delta Y/\Delta K)$ and $(\Delta Y/\Delta N)$ are just the marginal products *(MP)* of capital and labor respectively, the change in output is,

$$\Delta Y = MP_K \cdot \Delta K + MP_N \cdot \Delta N \qquad [16\text{—}15]$$

Because multiplying and dividing any expression by the same term has no impact on that expression's value, Equation (16—15) can be rewritten as

$$Y \cdot \left(\frac{\Delta Y}{Y}\right) = K \cdot MP_K \left(\frac{\Delta K}{K}\right) + N \cdot MP_N \left(\frac{\Delta N}{N}\right) \qquad [16\text{—}16]$$

or

$$\frac{\Delta Y}{Y} = \frac{K \cdot MP_K}{Y} \left(\frac{\Delta K}{K}\right) + \frac{N \cdot MP_N}{Y} \left(\frac{\Delta N}{N}\right) \qquad [16\text{—}17]$$

Equation (16—17) then defines the proportional rate of change of output in terms of the rates of change of the capital stock and the labor force. Because the neoclassical model assumes the economy is perfectly competitive, labor and capital are paid their respective marginal products. Thus, as indicated in Equation (16—17), labor's total income is $N \cdot MP_N$, capital's income is $K \cdot MP_K$, $(N \cdot MP_N)/Y$ is labor's *relative share* of total output, and

$(K \cdot MP_K)/Y$ is capital's relative share of total output. If, for economy of exposition, we label capital's fractional share of output α [that is, let $(K \cdot MP_K)/Y = \alpha$] then labor's relative share is $(1 - \alpha)$ and Equation (16—17) becomes

$$\frac{\Delta Y}{Y} = \alpha \left(\frac{\Delta K}{K}\right) + (1 - \alpha)\left(\frac{\Delta N}{N}\right) \qquad [16—18]$$

With the production function exhibiting constant returns to scale, if capital and labor should grow at the same proportional rate, output also grows at that rate. As we shall see, with equality of planned saving and investment maintained in the neoclassical model, there are forces that drive the growth rates of capital and output to equality with the rate of growth of the labor force which is, once again, biologically determined. In full equilibrium, then, there is only one possible output-capital ratio and one possible capital-labor ratio.

Equilibrium Growth in the Neoclassical Model

For equilibrium, planned saving must equal planned net investment. With long-run saving proportional to income $(S = sY)$ and net investment simply the change in capital stock (ΔK), equilibrium requires

$$\Delta K = sY \qquad [16—19]$$

Substituting this expression for ΔK in Equation (16—18) yields

$$\frac{\Delta Y}{Y} = \alpha s \frac{Y}{K} + (1 - \alpha)\frac{\Delta N}{N} \qquad [16—20]$$

Equation (16—20) shows that the rate of growth of output is directly proportional *(ceteris paribus)* to the output to capital ratio (Y/K). In Figure 16—3, the rate of growth of output $(\Delta Y/Y)$ is plotted as a function of the output-capital ratio for assumed, constant values of the relative income shares of capital and labor, the marginal propensity to save, and the labor force growth rate.

From Equation (16—19), the rate of growth of the capital stock is

$$\frac{\Delta K}{K} = s \frac{Y}{K} \qquad [16—21]$$

showing that, for a given marginal propensity to save, the rate of growth of the capital stock rises in direct proportion to the output-capital ratio. This relationship is also plotted in Figure 16—3.

From the diagram, it is easy to see that the economy will move toward one equilibrium growth path over time. If we started with the output-capital

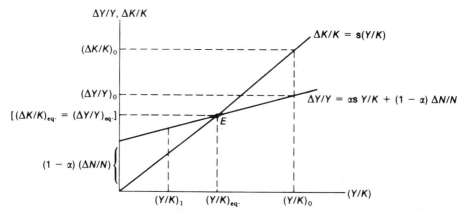

Figure 16—3 / The Equilibrium Growth Rate

ratio above its equilibrium value [say, value $(Y/K)_0$ in Figure 16—3], the rate of growth of the capital stock, $(\Delta K/K)_0$, would exceed the rate of growth of output, $(\Delta Y/Y)_0$, resulting in a decline in the output-capital ratio. With the output-capital ratio below the equilibrium value [as at $(Y/K)_1$ in Figure 16—3], output would be growing at a higher rate than capital, raising the output-capital ratio. Thus, there is convergence toward point E in Figure 16—3, which provides the ultimate equilibrium growth rate for output and capital, $(\Delta Y/Y)_{eq.} = (\Delta K/K)_{eq.}$ and establishes the equilibrium output-capital ratio, $(Y/K)_{eq.}$.

Because, in equilibrium, $\Delta K/K = \Delta Y/Y$, Equation (16—20) can be re-written as

$$\frac{\Delta Y}{Y} = \frac{\Delta K}{K} = \alpha s \frac{Y}{K} + (1 - \alpha) \frac{\Delta N}{N} \qquad [16\text{—}22]$$

Substituting the value for $\Delta K/K$ given by Equation (16—21) yields

$$s \frac{Y}{K} = \alpha s \frac{Y}{K} + (1 - \alpha) \frac{\Delta N}{N} \qquad [16\text{—}23]$$

Solving for $s(Y/K)$ yields

$$s \frac{Y}{K} = \frac{(1 - \alpha)}{(1 - \alpha)} \frac{\Delta N}{N}$$

$$= \frac{\Delta N}{N} \qquad [16\text{—}24]$$

Because $s(Y/K) = \Delta K/K$, in equilibrium

$$\left(\frac{\Delta Y}{Y}\right)_{eq.} = \left(\frac{\Delta K}{K}\right)_{eq.} = \left(\frac{\Delta N}{N}\right)_{eq.} = s \frac{Y}{K} \qquad [16\text{—}25]$$

Thus, output and the capital stock will ultimately be constrained to grow at the rate of growth of the labor force.[8]

The Propensity to Save and the Equilibrium Growth Rate

Equation (16—25) shows that, in contrast to the Harrod-Domar conclusion, when the labor force is not a constraint on growth, *the equilibrium rate of growth is independent of the value of the marginal propensity to save.* This conclusion, that the growth rate cannot be raised permanently by having an increased proportion of output devoted to investment instead of consumption, rests on the assumption of diminishing returns in the production process. An increase in the propensity to save does immediately raise the growth rate of the capital stock above its previous equilibrium level and, because the marginal product of capital is positive, this lifts output's growth rate above its previous equilibrium level. However, as long as capital grows more rapidly than labor, thereby raising the capital-labor ratio, the marginal product of capital will be falling. This reduces the rate at which output grows and, because investment is just the saving ratio times output, reduces the rate at which the capital stock grows. Ultimately, the growth rate of output and capital would fall to equality with the labor force growth rate, halting the rise in the capital-labor ratio. Thus, long-run equilibrium would finally be restored with output and the capital stock growing at the same rate as the labor force.

While an increase in the saving rate cannot permanently raise the equilibrium growth rate, it would raise the equilibrium capital-labor ratio. Because this change would provide labor with more units of capital to work with, raising the marginal product of labor, a labor force of any size would be able to produce a larger absolute level of output after the rise in the saving ratio. The economy would be placed on a permanently *higher level* equilibrium growth path by the increase in the marginal propensity to save. The impact of an altered saving rate is reflected in the growth paths plotted in Figure 16—4, with the higher *absolute level* growth path corresponding to the increased propensity to save.[9]

We should be sure to note that, by employing a more general and flexible production function, the neoclassical model has avoided the disturbing conclusions provided by the Harrod-Domar model. In Solow's words,

---

[8]So far, we have not allowed for technological progress in the neoclassical model. We will do so shortly.

[9]For convenience, the natural logarithm of output is measured on the vertical axis of Figure 16—4. With output growing at a constant percentage rate, the time path of the natural logarithm of output is a straight line as drawn. The slope of the growth paths plotted in Figure 16—4 is the equilibrium growth rate which is unaffected by changes in the saving rate.

As indicated, the level of the equilibrium growth path is altered by changes in the saving rate. Hence, the question arises of what saving rate and accompanying growth path for output are optimal. For consideration of that question, see Edmund Phelps, "The Golden Age of Accumulation: A Fable for Growthmen," *American Economic Review* 51 (1961): 638–643.

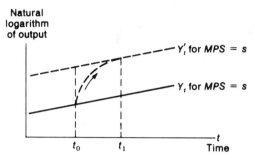

Figure 16—4 / Impact on the Growth Path of a Changed Saving Ratio

When production takes place under the usual neoclassical assumption of variable proportions and constant returns to scale, no simple opposition between natural and warranted rates of growth is possible. . . . The system can adjust to any given rate of growth of the labor force, and eventually approach a state of steady proportional expansion.[10]

Of course, to argue that capital and labor can be fully employed continuously, Solow's assumption that the economy is essentially competitive is required because, under competitive conditions, relative prices of capital and labor are free to adjust sufficiently to make employers willing to fully utilize the available volumes of both inputs. Even so, economic progress appears to be limited in nature. With output and labor destined to grow at the same rate in the long-run, output per capita stays constant, hardly a condition that portends a rising standard of living. With technological progress, the long-run outlook becomes more promising.

Technological Progress and Growth

Equation (16—18) showed the rate of growth of output as determined by the rates of growth of the capital stock and labor force with no provision for the role of technological progress. With a slight modification of that equation, technological progress can be introduced into the neoclassical model. Equation (16—26) below is the resulting expression for the rate of growth of output. In that equation r is the rate of technological progress, the annual rate of increase in output that would result from technological progress

$$\frac{\Delta Y}{Y} = r + \alpha \frac{\Delta K}{K} + (1 - \alpha) \frac{\Delta N}{N} \qquad [16\text{—}26]$$

even if the stock of capital and the number of man-hours of available labor are unchanged.[11]

---

[10]Solow, "A Contribution to the Theory of Economic Growth," p. 458.

[11]Throughout our analysis we have failed to provide an explanation of the generation of technological progress. On that issue, see Edwin Mansfield, *The Economics of Technological Change* (New York: W. W. Norton, 1968).

To deduce the implications for the growth process of the introduction of technological progress, we can repeat the manipulations performed with the neoclassical growth model that ignored technological change. Recalling from Equation (16—21) that $\Delta K/K = s\,(Y/K)$, Equation (16—26) can be rewritten to define the growth rate of output as a function of the output-capital ratio as shown in Equation (16—27)

$$\frac{\Delta Y}{Y} = r + \alpha s\,\frac{Y}{K} + (1 - \alpha)\,\frac{\Delta N}{N} \qquad [16\text{—}27]$$

In Figure 16—5, the relationships between the growth rate of output and the output-capital ratio are shown for zero $(r = 0)$ and positive $(r = \bar{r})$ rates of technological progress. The relationship between the output-capital ratio and the growth rate of the capital stock is also plotted in that figure. The presence of technological progress clearly raises the equilibrium growth rate of output and the capital stock while the equality between those growth rates is maintained. In addition, the equilibrium output to capital ratio is raised.

What is the new equilibrium growth rate of output and capital? Because we now know that output and capital grow at the same equilibrium rate $(\Delta Y/Y = \Delta K/K)$, we can rewrite Equation (16—26) as

$$\frac{\Delta Y}{Y} = \frac{\Delta K}{K} = r + \alpha\,\frac{\Delta K}{K} + (1 - \alpha)\,\frac{\Delta N}{N} \qquad [16\text{—}28]$$

Solving for the equilibrium growth rate yields

$$\frac{\Delta Y}{Y} = \frac{\Delta K}{K} = \frac{r}{1 - \alpha} + \frac{\Delta N}{N} \qquad [16\text{—}29]$$

showing that, with technological progress introduced, the equilibrium growth rate of capital and output becomes equal to the rate of growth of effective or augmented labor. Thus, output's growth rate is determined by

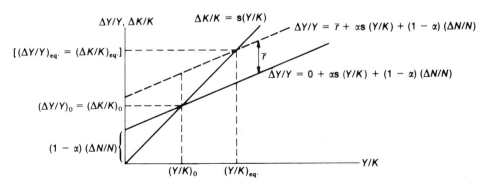

Figure 16—5 / Equilibrium Growth with Technological Progress

the rate of population growth, the rate of technological progress, and the size of labor's relative share of output.[12]

Because the rate of growth of output per worker is

$$\frac{\Delta Y}{Y} - \frac{\Delta N}{N} = \frac{r}{1 - \alpha} \qquad [16\text{—}30]$$

there can be no increase in output per worker according to this model unless there is technological progress (r positive).

---

[12] Because it exhibits constant returns to scale and diminishing marginal productivity to changes in the quantity of any *one* factor input employed, a particular, simple production relation, known as the Cobb-Douglas production function, has been widely used in the construction of growth models. Most commonly, this function takes the form

$$Y = AK^{\alpha}N^{1-\alpha} \tag{a}$$

where A and α are constants and Y, K, and N are output, capital, and labor. Differentiating this function with respect to time yields

$$\frac{dY}{dt} = K^{\alpha}N^{1-\alpha}\frac{dA}{dt} + \alpha AK^{\alpha-1}N^{1-\alpha}\frac{dK}{dt} + (1 - \alpha) AK^{\alpha}N^{1-\alpha}\frac{dN}{dt} \tag{b}$$

Dividing both sides of this expression by Y $(= AK^{\alpha}N^{1-\alpha})$ yields

$$\frac{1}{Y}\frac{dY}{dt} = \frac{1}{A}\frac{dA}{dt} + \alpha\frac{1}{K}\frac{dK}{dt} + (1 - \alpha)\frac{1}{N}\frac{dN}{dt} \tag{c}$$

the percentage rate of growth of output expressed as a function of the percentage rate of "disembodied" technical progress and the percentage rates of growth of the capital stock and the labor force. If output, the capital stock, and investment all grow at constant (long-run equilibrium) percentage rates y, k, and i over time, their values at any point in time are given by: $Y_t = Y_0e^{yt}$ $K = K_0e^{kt}$ $I = I_0e^{it}$

With investment identical to the rate of change of capital stock,

$$I = \frac{dK}{dt} = kK_0e^{kt} = I_0d^{it} \tag{d}$$

Because in equilibrium saving, which is $s \cdot Y_0e^{yt}$, must equal investment, our set of equalities can be expanded to

$$I = \frac{dK}{dt} = sY_0e^{yt} = kK_0e^{kt} = I_0e^{it} \tag{e}$$

For this set of equalities to hold continuously over time, the percentage growth rates of output, investment, and the capital stock must all be equal ($y = k = i$).

With the growth rate of output equal to that of the capital stock (call the rate G_Y), equation (c) can be rewritten as

$$G_Y = \alpha \cdot G_Y + \frac{1}{A}\frac{dA}{dt} + (1 - \alpha)\frac{1}{N}\frac{dN}{dt} \tag{f}$$

Solving for G_Y yields

$$G_Y = \frac{1}{1 - \alpha}\frac{1}{A}\frac{dA}{dt} + \frac{1}{N}\frac{dN}{dt} \tag{g}$$

which is comparable to Equation (16—29) in the text.

Once again, the equilibrium growth is independent of the saving rate. While an increase in the saving rate temporarily raises the growth rates of capital and output, diminishing returns will ultimately push their growth rates back to equality with the growth rate of augmented labor. During the transition, with capital growing more rapidly than the effective labor force, the marginal product of capital will be falling, lowering the rate of growth of output and thus of capital formation ($= s\,Y$). This adjustment will continue until output, capital, and augmented labor grow at the same rate, $\Delta N/N + r/(1 - \alpha)$.

Agreement of Theory and Empirical Evidence on the Determinants of Growth

The neoclassical model we have developed is representative of growth theory in the mid- to late 1950s. As we have seen, this neoclassical model contradicts the Harrod-Domar conclusion that the willingness of society to forego current consumption and save is a potent determinant of the *rate* of economic growth and, thus, of society's future well-being. While the saving-investment rate remained a crucial determinant of the *level* of the growth path, changes in the investment rate could not be counted on to accelerate the long-run growth rate. This suggests that policy prescriptions for permanently altering the rate of growth would have to be focused on programs that change the quality of the factors of production, for example, on technological innovation that raises the productivity of labor or capital, and on labor productivity enhancing education.

Paralleling theoretical developments, by the late 1950s there had been several attempts to empirically account for the U.S. growth experience. The typical empirical study provided a statistically fitted aggregate production function that related output growth to growth in manpower and the stock of capital, and to the rate of technological progress. Such regressions provide a means of identifying the important *sources* of growth and measuring their individual contributions to growth.

The results of those studies were consistent with the conclusions of the neoclassical growth model. *Capital deepening,* raising the capital-to-labor ratio by adding more units of identical capital to the existing stock of capital that labor has to work with, appeared to explain only a small part of the total growth of output per worker that the United States has experienced, while technological change reigned as the primary determinant of growth in output per worker. Taking a brief look at some of those empirical results, in two different papers Robert Solow offered evidence on the sources of U.S. growth. In 1957, he fitted a production function to U.S. data spanning the period 1909–1949.[13] His regression results suggested that technological progress was responsible for a full 87½ percent of the increase in output per worker during the period analyzed, while only a paltry 12½ percent of the increase could be attributed to capital deepening.

---

[13]Robert Solow, "Technical Change and the Aggregate Production Function," *Review of Economics and Statistics* 39 (1957): 312–320.

In a later study that updated the time period covered to span 1929–1961, Solow found that U.S. output grew at a 2½ percent annual rate just as a result of technological progress.[14] Persistent growth in the labor force also accounted for substantial increases in the total volume of output over that period, with an elasticity of output with respect to changes in the labor force of .89. However, the elasticity of output with respect to the capital stock was only .11, implying that a 1 percent increase in the rate of growth of capital would produce, even in the short run, only a .1 percent increase in the rate of growth of output.

Similar results were obtained by Richard Nelson. For the period 1929–1960, he found that only 18 percent of the increase in output per worker could be attributed to an increase in the quantity of capital per worker.[15] Thus, both theory and empirical evidence offered a gloomy outlook on the possibility of affecting the growth rate by employing policies that alter the investment rate. In fact, the empirical evidence cast doubt on the ability of changes in the investment rate to significantly alter the *level* of the growth path, so small were the apparent elasticities of output with respect to changes in the capital stock. Rather than depending on capital deepening, it appeared that policies to stimulate research and education would be required to foster the productivity increases necessary for maintaining a rising standard of living.

However, those pessimistic conclusions on the role of investment in altering the growth rate were probably wrong or, at best, were badly misleading. Both the theoretical and empirical results were generated using models that assumed technological progress was *disembodied;* that the rate of technological progress, which results in increased aggregate productive capacity, is *independent* of the rates at which the labor force and the capital stock are growing [look back at Equation (16—26) to see that this is the case in the neoclassical model]. Yet, much (probably most) of technological advance is *embodied* in new capital goods, so that investment in newly produced capital is necessary for that technological advance to take place. As a consequence, an increase in the rate of *gross* investment brings with it an increase in the rate at which the "efficiency" of the capital stock is raised.

The need to distinguish between embodied and disembodied technological progress was clearly recognized in the early 1960s. The proponents of the resulting theory stressed the role of investment in modernizing the capital stock as much as in deepening it. Official government recognition of this view was reflected in a 1961 statement by the Council of Economic Advisers:

---

[14]Robert Solow, "Technical Progress, Capital Formation, and Economic Growth," *The American Economic Review* 52 (1962): 76–86.

[15]Richard Nelson, "Aggregate Production Functions and Medium-Range Growth Projections," *The American Economic Review* 54 (1964): 575–606.

One of the reasons for the recent slowdown in the rate of growth of productivity and output is a corresponding slowdown in the rate at which the stock of capital has been renewed and modernized. . . . As has been confirmed by more recent research, the great importance of capital investment lies in its interactions with improved skills and technological progress. New ideas lie fallow without the modern equipment to give them life. From this point of view, the function of capital formation is as much in modernizing the equipment of the industrial worker as in simply adding to it.[16]

In 1962, Edmund Phelps published a paper analyzing the properties of a growth model that makes the distinction between embodied and disembodied technological progress.[17] His model recognizes that the latest, most efficient technology can only be exploited by putting new capital goods embodying that technology in place, either to replace old capital or as a net addition to the capital stock. Because new capital is more productive than old capital, it is necessary to distinguish between different *vintages* of capital goods. The later the vintage (the newer the capital good), the more advanced the technology and, hence, the greater the output per unit of labor a unit of capital can produce. In the aggregate then, the lower the average age of the capital stock the greater is the average productivity of labor.

The average age of the capital stock can be temporarily lowered by increasing the rate of saving and gross investment. In this way, the rate of growth of labor productivity and, thus, of output can be accelerated. However, as in the earlier neoclassical growth model, the rate of growth will ultimately return to its initial value.

Large investments today result in a large volume of old capital in the future that will tend to raise the average age of the capital stock. The average age of the capital stock will ultimately rise to its old equilibrium value and output will grow at the old rate. To obtain a permanent modernization of the capital stock would require the investment ratio to rise without limit, a clear impossibility. Thus, a once-and-for all increase in the investment ratio is limited in the long-run to increasing the capital-labor ratio with the average age of the enlarged capital stock unchanged. As in the old view model, the economy is shifted to a *higher level* growth path by the capital deepening a higher investment ratio provides, but grows at the old equilibrium growth rate.

It seems that our theoretical conclusions are little altered by allowing for embodied technological change. However, the empirical evidence that casts doubt on the effectiveness of investment ratio changes in altering the growth path is called into question because it was obtained by treating all technological progress as disembodied or organizational.

---

[16]U.S. Congress Joint Economic Committee, ''The American Economy in 1961: Problems and Policies,'' in Council of Economic Advisers, *Hearings on the Economic Report of the President* (Washington, D.C.: U.S. Government Printing Office, 1961), p. 338.

[17]Edmund Phelps, ''The New View of Investment: A Neoclassical Analysis,'' *Quarterly Journal of Economics* 76 (1962): 548–567.

The Empirical Evidence with Technological Change Embodied

It was expected that fitting a model which treats technical progress as embodied, so that investment is required for such progress, would reveal a far more important role for investment in controlling the economy's growth path. To test that hypothesis, Solow fitted an extreme form of the new view model that assumed *all* technological innovation was embodied. To account for embodied improvements in capital, Solow adjusted his capital stock figures to make recent additions to the capital stock more productive than older ones. This is accomplished by multiplying each vintage of capital by a productivity improvement factor $(1 + \lambda)^v$, where λ is the annual rate of technical advance and v is the vintage of the unit of capital. His model also adjusted each vintage of capital for depreciation by assuming that, from gross investment in year v of $I(v)$, the amount of capital "surviving" in year t is portion $B(t-v)$. Thus, his "equivalent stock of capital," adding up the survivors of each vintage and weighting by the appropriate productivity improvement factor was:

$$J(t) = \sum_{v=-\infty}^{t} (1 + \lambda)^v B(t - v) \, I \, (v) \qquad [16{-}31]$$

This measure of the effective capital stock was used in fitting an aggregate production function. The results for the 1929–1961 period indicate an elasticity of output with respect to capital stock of .51 as opposed to the .11 obtained assuming only disembodied technical change. Tangible investment in new capital goods appears to have retained some of its traditionally assumed importance. Still, because we do not have any measure of the fraction of technological advance that is embodied, we cannot know how to weight the two extreme-case results produced by Solow to find the true output-capital elasticity.[18]

Though a number of other studies by Denison, Kendrick, Jorgenson, and others have attempted to quantify the contribution to growth of changes in the quantities of factor inputs and of technological progress, the empirical results remain controversial. Yet, a policy for controlling the growth path cannot be intelligently formulated without measures of the response of output to changes in each of its determinants. As an example of the dilemma a policy maker faces, we know that technological advance is important to growth, but we need to know the extent to which technical advance is

---

[18]Some more recent studies assume various breakdowns of overall technical advance to try to identify the appropriate division. This effort has not been successful. One paper tests thirty-six model variations. The authors find both types of technical advance important and obtain output-capital elasticities intermediate to the extremes obtained by Solow. See Lester C. Thurow and L. D. Taylor, "The Interaction Between the Actual and Potential Rate of Growth," *Review of Economics and Statistics* 48 (1966): 351–360. For more recent results, see Robert M. Coen and Bert G. Hickman, "Investment and Growth in an Econometric Model of the United States," *The American Economic Review* 70 (1980): 214–219.

embodied in new capital formation. The greater the degree of embodiment the larger the growth payoff to a policy that stimulates investment, for example, an investment tax credit. On the other hand, if the elasticity of output to changes in the capital stock is small, policies to improve the labor force (such as subsidies to education and to research to improve education) and policies to encourage basic technical research might be more appropriate.

Case in Point X

Denison's Evaluation of Sources of Growth

In a sequence of studies beginning in the early 1960s, Edward Denison of the Brookings Institution has provided statistical analyses of the sources of growth in the U.S. economy. His estimates have been generated for a model that is largely consistent with the formal models described so far in this chapter. Notably, economic growth is viewed as stemming from increases in the quality or quantity of factor inputs, or from organizational improvements in production, and changes in income shares of different factors are viewed as reflecting changes in factor productivity. In contrast to our formal growth models and the empirical work based directly on these models, Denison disaggregates the factor variables (e.g., "labor") to permit changes in output growth rates to be associated with particular characteristic changes in the provision of services from those variables. His measures of *labor* are also broad enough to accommodate quality improvements that are specific to labor, and his measure of increases in output per unit of input permits assessment of the roles of specific informational and organizational improvements in production as well as measurement of the role of scale economies.

The table below summarizes Denison's measures over the period 1929–1976. Over that period it appears that real natural income grew by 2.98 percent annually with increases in effective (augmented) labor accounting for 1.36 percentage points of annual growth, and increases in capital accounting for .46 percentage points of annual growth, with the remaining 1.16 percent of annual output growth accounted for mainly by improvements in the state of technology (.73 percent), improvements in resource allocation (.26 percent), and economies of scale (.27 percent).

From the point of view of policy efforts to alter the growth path (the short-run growth rate and the long-run level) of income, the contributions to the growth rate of increased education (.41 percent), additions to the stock of capital (.46 percent), and advances in knowledge (.73 percent) are particularly notable. These measures suggest that the growth rate might be subject to some modification through policies that alter the rate of investment, educational attainment, and outlays on research and development; just over half of the annual output increase stemmed from these sources.

**Table 16—1 / Source of Growth of Total
Output, 1929–1976 (annual percentage growth rates)**

Real national income			2.98
Increase in "quantity" of inputs			1.82
Labor		1.36	
Employment level	1.09		
Impact of shorter hours	− .24		
Age/sex composition	− .08		
Education	.41		
Other	.18		
Capital		.46	
Inventories	.09		
Nonresidential structures and equipment	.18		
Dwellings	.17		
International assets	.02		
Increase in output per unit of input			1.16
Advances in knowledge		.73	
Improved resource allocation		.26	
Farm	.21		
Nonfarm	.05		
Legal and human environment		− .04	
Pollution abatement	− .02		
Worker safety and health	− .01		
Dishonesty and crime	− .01		
Economies of scale		.27	
Other		− .06	

Source: Edward Denison, *Accounting for Slower Economic Growth, the United States in the 1970s* (Washington, D.C.: The Brookings Institution, 1979), p. 104.

Still, it is hard to imagine generating a large percentage increase in the yearly growth rate (during the transition to a higher level expansion path) with politically acceptable policies to influence investment, education, and R&D outlays. It is also notable that Denison's estimating procedure recognizes Environmental Protection Agency (EPA) and Occupational Safety and Health Administration (OSHA) type regulations, though the "legal and human environment" factors were responsible for a very modest decline in output growth over the 1929–1976 period, according to his measures.

The Basis for Policy Choices. For the time being, our best indicators of the directions in which we might profitably focus our growth-determining efforts appear to be measures of the rates of return available to alternative uses of our resources. Because a factor input's contribution to output determines the reward it receives in a market economy, the rates of return to alternative investments can be compared, assuming that a higher rate of return is an indication of relative underinvestment. In fact, comparing the rate of return to investment in education and the rate on tangible, physical investment indicates that there is little difference in the rates of return to those two directions of investment allocation. For example, Gary Becker found a rate of return on investment for a four-year college education of around 9 percent and a rate on tangible investment in the same range.[19] Such evidence suggests that investment in both human and tangible capital is appropriate. Currently available measures of the rate of return to intangible investment in research and development are highly tentative.[20] However, the tentative estimates suggest that in many sectors of the economy the rate of return to additional research would exceed that on investment in physical capital.

Given current limitations on our quantitative understanding of the determinants of growth, it is difficult to formulate a specific growth policy. However, as our knowledge improves, we are likely to think more seriously about a comprehensive growth plan. In formulating such a plan, we must remain aware of the fact that *growth is not free*. The immediate and direct cost that must be borne to stimulate growth is the consumption that must be foregone in order to free resources for tangible or intangible investment. Never will our goal be the maximum possible growth rate or the highest level growth path. Instead, we will want the *optimum* growth path, the path that, accounting for both the costs and benefits of growth, maximizes society's total well-being over time. Until our knowledge of the determinants of growth improves, probably the best positive growth policy recommendation would be to avoid short-run recessions that stifle normal expansionary forces.

Still, fiscal and monetary policy actions that are taken for stabilization purposes influence the economy's growth path in important ways that should not be ignored. An increase in taxes raises *gross* saving (private saving plus government saving in the form of a budget surplus) out of full employment income, freeing resources from consumption. If those resources are invested, the economy's capital stock is enlarged and, generally, improved in overall quality. Of course, as we already know the attractiveness of private investment can be affected by tax changes too (recall the role of corporate taxes and the investment tax credit).

On the expenditures side of the government budget, the economy's productive capacity is enlarged by greater government spending on: (1) education, including worker retraining, (2) basic and applied research, (3) transportation systems, and so on. On the other hand, monetary policy has its important influence on growth through its effect on private investment. To assess the long-run role of money in the growth process, James Tobin introduced government-issued paper money into the neoclassical growth

---

[19]Gary Becker, "Underinvestment in College Education?" *The American Economic Review* 50 (1960): 346–354.

[20]For a brief summary of the difficulties involved in obtaining such measures, as well as some tentative estimates, see Edwin Mansfield, "Technological Change and Industrial Research," in *The Goal of Economic Growth,* ed. Edmund Phelps (New York: W. W. Norton, 1969), pp. 153–171.

model.[21] Paper money serves both as a medium of exchange and as a second asset in which the public can hold wealth (real capital from past investment being the other). By altering the yield on (cost of) holding wealth in money form, monetary policy has its long-run influence on investment. For example, an increase in the rate of monetary expansion that results in a continuing inflation lowers the yield on (raises the cost of holding) money balances. In Tobin's two-asset world, the increased inflation rate will induce a portfolio adjustment with wealth holders purchasing more physical assets, lowering the marginal product of capital until, at the margin, the yield on money and physical assets is equalized. With a higher capital-labor ratio, output per capita is increased; the equilibrium growth path is permanently raised. Money, then, is not neutral in the long-run according to Tobin.

Because policy makers have both fiscal and monetary policy tools available, it is possible for some control to be exerted over the economy's growth path even while the primary objective of maintaining a noninflationary full-employment equilibrium is pursued. If a shift toward a more restrictive fiscal posture, which would depress the economy, is accompanied by a shift toward a more expansionary monetary policy, equality of aggregate demand and supply can be maintained. At the same time, such a combination monetary-fiscal policy will result in more of current output going into investment at a lowered interest rate while less output is devoted to consumption and/or government use. A shift to such a combination policy would accelerate growth in the short-run and raise the level of the equilibrium growth path in the long-run. What would be the effect of a shift to a combination of restrictive monetary and expansionary fiscal policy?

Summary

Historically, the United States has enjoyed a rapid growth rate. In this century alone, real U.S. output has grown at a rate of over 3 percent annually, and per capita output has grown by some 1½ percent annually. In this chapter, we have taken a brief look at some of the models economists have built as they have tried to unravel the mysteries of the extraordinary growth in productive capacity that the *developed* countries, like the United States, have experienced in the last two or three centuries.

The first model we looked at, the Harrod-Domar model, attached a great deal of importance to the saving-investment rate. In that model, the warranted growth rate was directly proportional to the saving ratio so that the higher the saving ratio, the greater the proportional rate at which the economy could grow. Of course, equilibrium growth required maintenance of equality between planned saving and investment, an often difficult task. In addition, output expansion was strictly limited by the rate of growth of the

---

[21]James Tobin, "A Dynamic Aggregative Model," *Econometrica* 33 (1965): 671–684.

effective labor force because capital and labor had to be combined in fixed proportions to be productive. The Harrod-Domar model provided disturbing predictions; the economy in a Harrod-Domar world was subject to chronic unemployment if the natural rate of growth exceeded the warranted rate, and to a collapse of aggregate demand if the natural rate should fall short of the warranted rate.

The dire predictions on the likelihood of steady growth with full employment of labor and capital were the result of the restrictive assumptions employed in the Harrod-Domar analysis. By the mid-1950s, a new generation of growth models had emerged that employed the standard neoclassical assumptions of capital-labor substitutability and perfect competition. In these neoclassical growth models, the conflict between the natural and warranted rates of growth was eliminated. At the same time, because production with a neoclassical production function is characterized by diminishing marginal productivity, the possibility of changes in the investment ratio altering the equilibrium growth rate was eliminated. In the neoclassical model, a rise in the investment ratio would accelerate output growth only in the short-run (which could, of course, be a substantial length of calendar time). However, raising the investment ratio could, by permanently raising the capital-labor ratio, shift the economy to a *higher level* long-run growth path.

To enable output per worker to rise when the economy was on its long-run equilibrium growth path, technological progress had to be introduced into the neoclassical model. Theoretically, it made little difference in the implications we drew from the neoclassical model whether technological progress was treated as embodied or disembodied. In either case, while the rate of growth would be accelerated in the short-run by an increase in the investment ratio, only the level of the long-run, equilibrium growth path would be increased by such an investment ratio change. However, there is substantial quantitative difference in the role the investment ratio appears to play in the growth process when production function regression models are altered to treat technological progress, as embodied in new capital goods. Indeed, the traditional view of the close link between economic well-being and investment in tangible capital is far more strongly supported by models that permit investment to modernize the capital stock as well as enlarge it.

While the United States and other countries are facing problems of ecological damage and resource depletion that have prompted some critics to call for a policy of no growth, majority opinion among economists and the public seems committed to the continuation of growth. A rational (welfare-maximizing) growth policy would require expansion of the use of resources in growth-enhancing activities (tangible investment, research, education) until the marginal social benefit from the last resource unit so employed is just equal to the marginal social cost (*including* environmental damage) of its use. Few think that this condition is satisfied by a zero growth rate, though no technique is now available for objectively determining what growth rate would be socially optimal.

Questions

1. In what sense are Harrod-Domar models razor's edge models? To what can this property be attributed?

2. Of what importance are changes in the saving rate and the productivity of capital:
   a. in the Harrod-Domar model?
   b. in the neoclassical model?

3. In neoclassical growth models, the rate of growth of output is independent of the fraction of income that is saved and invested. Explain why this is so.

4. It is often alleged that the Soviet Union is now a major industrial power only because Soviet planners required a massive sacrifice of living standards in the interwar period. Evaluate that claim.

5. Write a brief essay discussing factors that might have contributed to a slowing of the U.S. growth rate in the 1970s.

Suggested Readings

Britto, Ronald. "Some Recent Developments in the Theory of Economic Growth: An Interpretation." *Journal of Economic Literature* 11 (1973): 1343–66.

Denison, Edward F. *The Sources of Economic Growth in the United States and the Alternatives Before Us*. New York: Committee for Economic Development, 1962.

Denison, Edward F. "How to Raise the High-Employment Growth Rate by One Percentage Point." *The American Economic Review* 52 (1962): 67–75.

Denison, Edward F. *Accounting for Slower Economic Growth: The United States in the 1970s*. Washington, D.C.: Brookings Institution, 1979.

Dernburg, Thomas F., and Dernburg, Judith D. *Macroeconomic Analysis*, Chapters 10–11. Reading, Mass.: Addison-Wesley, 1968.

Hahn, F. H., and Matthews, R. C. O. "The Theory of Economic Growth: A Survey." *Economic Journal* 74 (1964): 779–907.

Phelps, Edmund. "The Golden Age of Accumulation: A Fable for Growthmen." *The American Economic Review* 51 (1961): 638–643.

Schultz, T. W. "Investment in Human Capital." *The American Economic Review* 51 (1961): 1–17.

Solow, Robert W. *Growth Theory*. Oxford: Oxford University Press, 1970.

Swan, T. W. "Economic Growth and Capital Accumulation." *Economic Record* 32 (1956): 334–361.

Weintraub, Andrew; Schwartz, Eli; and Aranson, J. R., eds. *The Economic Growth Controversy*. White Plains, N.Y.: International Arts and Sciences Press, 1973.

Chapter 17

Business Cycles and Forecasting

While long-run growth in productive capacity has been a characteristic of the United States and other developed economies, the growth in economic activity has not been smooth. Indeed, economic history shows all industrial economies as having been plagued by sizable fluctuations: periods of recession following periods of expansion followed by recession in a seemingly endless cycle. This boom-bust sequence has been so common that virtually every U.S. citizen feels comfortable discussing the "business cycle." This chapter pays homage to the importance of business fluctuations by, first, reviewing a sample of formal business cycle models and, second, providing an introduction to forecasting, an activity that, increasingly, is performed by relying on econometric models of the economy. A detailed exploration of empirical forecasting models is beyond the scope of this text, but a description of the form of some prominent models is provided.

The Anatomy of Business Cycles

Cyclical movements can be observed in any number of economic variables. As macroeconomic examples, consumption, investment, unemployment, and output all exhibit cyclical fluctuations. However, because it is a comprehensive measure of the overall level of economic activity, movements in GNP may be the best single indicator of business cycle developments.

During the *expansion phase* of the business cycle, GNP grows more rapidly than its long-run trend growth rate, and more rapidly than the rate of growth of productive capacity, the proportion of productive capacity employed increasing. At some point, the GNP series reaches its *upper turning point* and the *contraction phase* of the cycle begins. In the contraction, GNP may grow more slowly than its trend rate, or may even fall in absolute value. During this phase, the proportion of productive capacity utilized falls. Finally, the GNP series reaches its *lower turning point* and expansion begins. In the idealized cycle in Figure 17—1, two upper turning points (U and U') and two lower turning points (L and L') are labeled.

The amount of time required for completion of one complete cycle, called the *period* of the cycle, can be measured from cycle *peak* to *peak* (U to U') or from *trough* to *trough* (L to L'). The magnitude of the cycle is measured by the maximum percentage deviation of the observed value of GNP from its trend value. In our idealized graph, the cycle's magnitude, usually called its *amplitude*, would be reflected in vertical distances, A, A', A'', and A''' in Figure 17—1.

Figure 17—2 shows a plot of actual U.S. GNP for 1900 through 1979 contrasted with trend growth in GNP. Clearly, neither the amplitude nor the duration of the observed GNP cycle is as regular in actuality as they are in our ideal cycle. In fact, the periodic expansions and contractions of economic activity have occurred with such irregularity, especially in recent years, that most modern economists feel more comfortable labeling swings

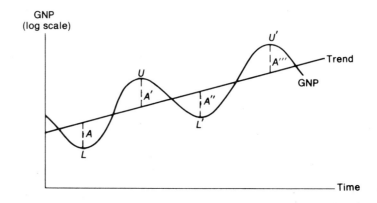

Figure 17—1 / Idealized Cycle of GNP Around Trend

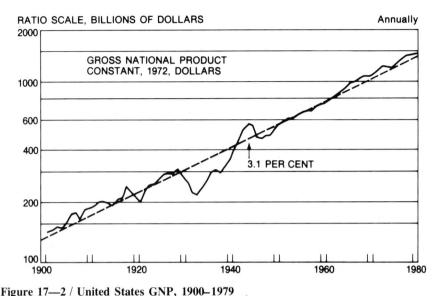

RATIO SCALE, BILLIONS OF DOLLARS   Annually

GROSS NATIONAL PRODUCT
CONSTANT, 1972, DOLLARS

3.1 PER CENT

Figure 17—2 / United States GNP, 1900–1979

Source: Board of Governors of the Federal Reserve System, *Historical Chart Book* (Washington, D.C.: Publications Services, Board of Governors of the Federal Reserve System, 1980).

in economic activity business ''fluctuations'' rather than ''cycles,'' the latter term carrying too strong a connotation of regularity. Also, as you may already know, not all sectors of the economy expand and contract in step with aggregate output. Construction, for example, often fluctuates in a distinctly *countercyclical* pattern and industrial production is often out of step with aggregate final sales. Because of the irregularities in actual business fluctuations, it is no easy matter to identify cycle turning points (peaks and troughs). Compounding that problem, the *rate of growth* of output can decline for a time, allowing output to lag further and further behind productive capacity, without any absolute decline in output. In such a *growth recession*, the economy suffers the undesired consequences of swelling unemployment of labor and capital, but no *peak* in output is identifiable. Clearly, our scheme for labeling cycle-turning points, hence expansion and contraction periods, is somewhat arbitrary.

In spite of the difficulties involved, with a frame of reference like ours the National Bureau of Economic Research (the NBER) has attempted to identify the approximate dates when peaks and troughs in aggregate economic activity have occurred.[1] The turning points identified by the NBER for the postwar period in the United States are shown in Table 17—1.

---

[1] For a detailed discussion of the identification of reference cycle-turning points, see Arthur F. Burns and Wesley C. Mitchell, *Measuring Business Cycles* (New York: National Bureau of Economic Research, 1946).

Table 17—1 / Reference Cycle-Turning Points

Trough	Peak	Months in: Contraction[a]	Expansion[b]
Oct. 1945	Nov. 1948	8	37
Oct. 1949	July 1953	11	45
Aug. 1954	July 1957	13	35
Apr. 1958	April 1960	9	24
Feb. 1961	Dec. 1969	10	106
Nov. 1970	Nov. 1973	11	36
Mar. 1975	Jan. 1980[c]	16	74

[a]From previous peak.
[b]From previous trough.
[c]Tentative.
Source: U.S. Department of Commerce, *Business Conditions Digest*, January 1980.

Explaining Business Fluctuations: Formal Cycle Theories

While the rhythm of the observed fluctuations in economic activity has not matched that of our idealized cycle, it has been regular enough to suggest that fluctuations might be the result of certain systematic and recurring causes.[2] Efforts to identify those causes (to explain business fluctuations) have a long, if not impressively successful, history. However, since World War II confidence in the ability of the government to stabilize the economy through the active use of monetary and fiscal policy increased until interest in identifying the fundamental sources of business fluctuations virtually evaporated. Faith in the effectiveness of stabilization policy appears to have peaked in the middle 1960s, but since then the belief has spread that the business cycle has not even been domesticated, much less eliminated. Current research, however, continues to accord formal cycle theories a relatively low priority, so that no new, elaborate formal cycle theories can be described in this chapter. Hence, the sample of cycle models that are reviewed in this section are those that have enjoyed prominence in the past. Those models can contribute to our understanding of some of the forces that fuel expansions and contractions. In particular, they account for momentum in expansions and contractions and indicate how cumulative movements in production may be reversed.

External and Internal Cycle Theories

There have been a great number of proposed explanations of business fluctuations. Those explanations can be grouped in a number of ways, but a basic distinction has long been made between two broad classes of models. The first class attributes cycles to forces *external* to the systematic interactions of the component parts of the economic system. Historically, these

---

[2]Since 1854 the average length of the reference cycles identified by the NBER has been close to four years, with the average expansion close to twice the duration of the average contraction. The shortest cycle lasted twenty-eight months.

external theories of the cycle have focused attention on wars, the chance discovery of gold mines, and major innovations (like the railroad, the automobile, and the computer) as prime movers in generating fluctuations in business activity. As an interesting alternative source of fluctuations, in a frequently cited external theory (not necessarily because of its validity), the noted nineteenth-century economists W. S. and H. S. Jevons attributed business cycles to changes in the level of sunspot activity. According to the sunspot theory, changes in sunspot activity affected the earth's climate which in turn affected crop yields. Fluctuations in agricultural output and prices resulted in fluctuations in the overall level of economic activity.

The second class of cycle theories, the internal theories, ascribe business fluctuations to endogenous forces, forces within the economy that automatically reverse cumulative expansions and contractions in economic activity. While there are numerous alternative *internal* explanations of the business cycle, the majority ascribe a major role to movements in investment. In order to acquire a basic understanding of what is involved in modern business cycle analysis, as our next task we will take a close look at one prominent, post-Keynesian example of an internal cycle model.

The Multiplier-Accelerator Interaction. Interaction between the income multiplier and the accelerator mechanism has played a central role in virtually all modern business cycle models. The simple accelerator relates the level of net investment to the rate of change of output. According to the simple accelerator, with output growing continuously net additions to the capital stock are required. For net investment to take place at a uniform *level* over time, the rate of growth of output must stay constant. As soon as the rate of output growth declines, even if it remains positive, investment falls.

The multiplier concept, relating changes in the level of income to changes in individual spending schedules, should be even more familiar because we have used it frequently in developing and manipulating income determination models. In the late 1930s, Alvin Hansen suggested that, under some not implausible conditions, the economy might generate cyclical fluctuations internally as a result of interactions between the multiplier and the accelerator. Paul Samuelson provided a formal demonstration of Hansen's suggestion in an elegantly simple model.[3]

Ignoring the government and foreign sectors of the economy, net income (output) in period t is

$$Y_t = C_t + I_t \qquad [17-1]$$

Assuming that households' consumption responds to income with a simple, one-period lag, consumption is

$$C_t = bY_{t-1} \qquad [17-2]$$

---

[3]Paul Samuelson, "Interaction Between the Multiplier Analysis and the Principle of Acceleration," *Review of Economics and Statistics* 21 (1939): 75–78.

Net investment, which takes place to provide the productive capacity necessary for satisfying aggregate consumption demand, consists of an autonomous component ($\bar{I}$) plus an *induced* component given by the simple accelerator. Net investment then is

$$I_t = \bar{I} + A(C_t - C_{t-1}) \qquad [17\text{—}3]$$

where A is the aggregate accelerator coefficient. Plugging into Equation (17—1) and solving for Y_t yields

$$Y_t = \bar{I} + b(1 + A)Y_{t-1} - AbY_{t-2} \qquad [17\text{—}4]$$

For this economic system to be in *static* equilibrium, income must be constant through time. That is, it must be the case that $Y_t = Y_{t-1} = Y_{t-2} = \ldots = Y_{t-n} = \ldots$. By imposing this equilibrium condition, Equation (17—4) can be solved for the *static* equilibrium level of income, yielding

$$Y_{\text{eq.}} = \frac{1}{1 - b} \cdot \bar{I} \qquad [17\text{—}5]$$

an expression that has a familiar form. However, if static equilibrium is disturbed in this model, the system *may not return to equilibrium* and, even if it does, the time path of adjustment back to equilibrium is of interest to us as it may exhibit a cyclical pattern.

To illustrate our investigation of the consequences of a shock to our simple system, we can introduce some ''reasonable'' numerical values into that system. To begin with, we will assume an MPC of .5, an accelerator coefficient of 2, and a value of autonomous investment of $20 billion. With these values, the equilibrium level of income is

$$Y_{\text{eq.}} = \frac{1}{1 - b} \cdot \bar{I} = \frac{1}{1 - .5} \cdot 20 \text{ billion} = \$40 \text{ billion} \qquad [17\text{—}5a]$$

Consumption would be $.5Y = \$20$ billion. Also, because, with no *change* in income, there is no *change* in consumption and thus no induced investment; total investment is just the $20 billion of autonomous investment.

Suppose there is a $10 billion rise in autonomous investment so $\bar{I}$ is lifted to a new level of $30 billion. The dynamic response of the simple economic system is traced in Table 17—2. In period 1 in that table, the system is in equilibrium with $Y_{\text{eq.}} = \$40$ billion and with both consumption and autonomous investment equal to $20 billion.

In period 2, autonomous investment has increased by $10 billion so that income in period 2 (Y_2) becomes $50 billion. In the next period, consumption responds to period 2's income rise, increasing to $25 billion, and the multiplier expansion process is underway.

In isolation, the multiplier would generate an increase in income to a new equilibrium value of

$$Y_{\text{eq.}} = \frac{1}{1 - b} \cdot \bar{I} = \frac{1}{1 - .5} \cdot 30 \text{ billion} = \$60 \text{ billion} \qquad [17\text{—}5b]$$

**Table 17—2 / Dynamic Adjustment
with Multiplier-Accelerator Interaction**[a]

Period	(1) $\bar{I}$	(2) $C = .5Y_{t-1}$	Induced $I =$ (3) $2(C_t - C_{t-1})$	(4) $Y = C + I$
1	20	20	0	40
2	30	20	0	50
3	.	25	10	65
4	.	33	16	79
5	.	40	14	84
6	.	42	4	76
7	.	38	−8	60
8	.	30	−16	44
9	.	22	−16	36
10	.	18	−8	40
11	.	20	8	58
12	.	29	18	77

[a]Figures rounded to nearest billion dollars.

However, the multiplier no longer operates in isolation. Through the accelerator, the rise in consumption in period 3 *induces* $10 billion of additional investment in that period, raising income in period 3 to $65 billion. By period 4, we should note, the *rate* of increase in income has begun to fall. Consequently, the rate of increase in consumption declines in period 5 producing a smaller volume of *induced* investment in period 5. With investment falling, the stage is set for a contraction and, in period 6, income begins to fall. With the accelerator inducing net *disinvestment* beginning in period 7, a major contraction is underway.

By period 9, income has fallen well below its original equilibrium level. However, in that period the rate of decline of income slows. As a consequence, consumption's fall is slowed in period 10 and, with it, the rate of net disinvestment slows. The recovery from contraction is underway, as indicated by period 10's increase in income back to $40 billion.

If we continued to trace the adjustment path of our simple economic system, we would find income following a time path like that shown in Figure 17—3. Income would fluctuate around the $60 billion income level that the simple multiplier gives as a static equilibrium income level with *no tendency* for convergence toward that value.[4] It should be clear that the

---

[4]A mathematician would not have to plod through the one-step-at-a-time "iterative" process we employed in the text in order to know how our model behaves. He would recognize Equation (14—4) as a "second-order difference equation" that can be solved analytically for an expression for income in any time period. For readable expositions of the method of solving difference equations, see Alpha Chiang, *Fundamental Methods of Mathematical Economics* (New York: McGraw-Hill, 1975), Chapters 16—17, and William Baumol, *Economic Dynamics* (New York: Macmillan, 1970), Chapters 9–11.

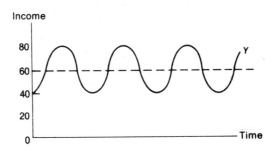

Figure 17—3 / A Cycle with Constant Amplitude

particular path of adjustment that our example economic system traced was dictated by the values we assumed for the MPC and the accelerator coefficient (given the form of the model). For alternative values of these parameters, a rich variety of adjustment paths are possible. Figure 17—4 shows the general patterns of adjustment that may occur.

Path (a) shows a monotonic[5] adjustment of income from the original income level (Y_0) toward the new equilibrium level (Y_1) which it approaches asymptotically. Path (b) is monotonic, but instead of income converging on a new equilibrium level, it grows exponentially. Path (c) shows income oscillating in a damped manner (the amplitude of the cycle diminishing over time) so that income converges on its static equilibrium value. Path (d) is the path traced by the economy in our example, the amplitude of the cycle remaining constant over time. And, finally, path (e) is an explosive cycle. Clearly for an economy characterized by an adjustment path like (b), (d),

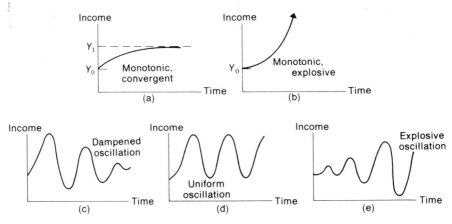

Figure 17—4 / Possible Adjustment Patterns in the Multiplier-Accelerator Model

[5]A function is monotonic if, for every point on the function, the slope (first derivative) of the function has the same sign. The function in part (a) of Figure 14—4 is rising (slope positive) throughout. Thus, that function shows income increasing monotonically.

or (e) we could not expect the static equilibrium value of income to be achievable once income is disturbed.

Figure 17—5 summarizes the combinations of values of the MPC and the accelerator coefficient that, in the Samuelson multiplier-accelerator, yield the various forms of adjustment path shown in Figure 17—4. Area I shows the combinations that permit income to adjust asymptotically from one equilibrium income to another as shown by path (a) in Figure 17—4. Area II shows the combinations that produce damped cycles. The combinations in area III produce explosive oscillations, while the combinations in area IV produce monotonic but explosive growth. The values of the MPC and the accelerator coefficient that provide the uniform cycles of our example (.5 and .2 respectively) fall on the boundary between areas II and III.

The Model's Shortcomings. The multiplier-accelerator model offers a highly simplified explanation of business fluctuations. However, it has enjoyed prominence in modern business cycle analysis because, as well as being one of the first of the post-Keynesian breed of dynamic models, it captures an interaction between the multiplier and the accelerator that is surely a basic ingredient of all *endogenously* generated cycles. Still, its extreme simplicity has compromised its validity as a complete cycle model. With values for the accelerator coefficient and the MPC in the range typically found in the United States, the multiplier-accelerator model would generate cyclically or monotonically explosive changes in income (areas III or IV of Figure 17—5). Because this kind of instability has not been observed in the United States, some modifications of the basic multiplier-accelerator model are necessary in the interest of realism. If, for example, the simple accelerator is replaced with an investment function that calls for extended lags in the

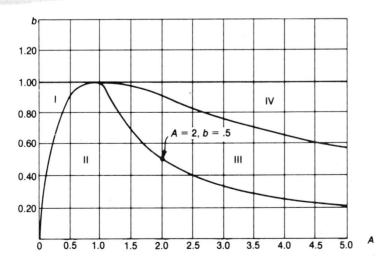

**Figure 17—5 / Regions Showing
Different Adjustment Paths of Aggregate Income**

response of investment to changes in the level of sales, the probability of explosive adjustments in income is moderated. Even if the simple accelerator is retained, with no lag in the response of investment to sales changes, there are logical reasons for expecting a ceiling on the upswing of income, which can halt a potentially explosive expansion and lead automatically to contraction, as well as a floor under the system's contractions that stops those contractions and leads to subsequent expansions.[6]

Ceilings and Floors. In the basic multiplier-accelerator model there is no limit on the rate of expansion until output has reached the full capacity level. However, at that point output is constrained by the ceiling of productive capacity and can grow only as fast as productive capacity grows, say, 4 to 5 percent annually in the United States. This rate of growth must be less than the rate at which output was growing before it reached the ceiling, or that contact would never have occurred. With the annual rate of growth of sales slowed (to the rate of growth of productive capacity), the volume of induced investment called for by the accelerator falls and a contraction would be initiated in our model. Thus, the production ceiling provides an upper turning point to the time path of output, even if the observed values of the propensity to save and the accelerator imply a dynamically unstable (explosive) adjustment path for the basic multiplier-accelerator model. The ceiling not only limits the expansion of output, but also provides for an automatic switch to the contraction phase of the cycle.

Shifting our focus to the contraction phase of the business cycle, we now need to determine what it is that provides a floor under output once contraction begins. According to the simple model, a fall in sales induces disinvestment in the next period, which lowers income inducing more disinvestment, and so on. However, it is unlikely that investment and income would ever fall to zero in actuality, no matter what the basic multiplier-accelerator model suggests when our best estimates of the accelerator coefficient (A) and the MPC are built into the model. As a contraction proceeds, income ultimately falls to the level at which all income is consumed. At that point, even if there were no gross investment, the minimum level of gross income would have been reached. While *negative* net investment could, in theory, be so large that net income (consumption plus net investment) was zero or negative, in reality disinvestment is likely to be limited to the amount of depreciation, a value that can be much smaller (in absolute terms) than the disinvestment called for by the simple accelerator. Algebraically, if gross investment should ever fall to the zero level, minimum or *floor* net income would be $Y_{min} = C_0 - D$, where C_0 is the break-even level of consumption spending and D is depreciation. Typically, though, gross investment could never fall to zero because that would require zero gross investment for every firm. There is, most analysts would argue, a minimum value of au-

---

[6]The reasons for expecting a *ceiling* on income expansions and a *floor* under contractions are described in John M. Hicks, *A Contribution to the Theory of the Trade Cycle* (Oxford: Oxford University Press), 1940.

tonomous investment that takes place independent of the level of income or its rate of change as business firms try to modernize their capital stock. In fact, to cite evidence that strengthens our belief in a floor under output, gross investment remained positive even in the depths of the Great Depression. With firms' net disinvestment plans limited to the amount of depreciation, and with substantial volumes of income-independent (autonomous) investment forthcoming, contractions are constrained by a positive floor of minimum net output given by $Y_{min} = 1/(1 - b) \cdot I_{min}$, where I_{min}, minimum net investment, is autonomous investment minus depreciation. Historical evidence suggests that in most contractions the volume of autonomous investment has been substantially larger than the volume of depreciation so that the floor on income has strictly limited the extent to which a contraction could proceed.

Once the floor value of output is reached, the contraction's progress is ended. With income no longer falling, the volume of induced investment called for by the simple accelerator (which was negative during the contraction) is increased (to zero) and we are returned to the expansion phase of the cycle.[7] It is easy to see, then, that even when the values of the MPC and the accelerator imply an explosive system, there are simple and sensible arguments which indicate that business fluctuations will be constrained to a pattern that accords with observed history. The basic multiplier-accelerator model just failed to explicitly incorporate the required floor of minimum output and ceiling of maximum productive capacity.

Monetary Theories of the Cycle

Multiplier-accelerator models pay no heed to the role of the financial sector of the economy in generating business fluctuations, but the business cycle literature abounds with monetary or financial theories of the cycle (most of which would fit in the more general category of *expectations theories* because they rely on endogenous changes in expectations to provide cycle-turning points). A prominent example of such theories was provided decades ago by R. G. Hawtrey, who attributed prime responsibility for business fluctuations to monetary instability.[8]

Hawtrey argued that, with the economy in recession, banks have reserve funds with which they can extend loans and that interest rates are low. With interest rates depressed, the interest cost of holding inventories is low so inventory investment is stimulated. The increase in planned inventory investment raises production and income, raising sales. In turn, the sales increase raises expected future sales, stimulating inventory investment

---

[7]To be more precise about the shift to expansion, with disinvestment limited to the amount of depreciation, considerable excess productive capacity can be left by the contraction. Several periods of stagnation, during which income does not grow, would be required in this case for the excess stock of capital to be depreciated away before investment rises to a positive level (the negative D term disappearing), carrying income with it and initiating the cumulative expansion.

[8]Ralph G. Hawtrey, *Trade and Credit* (London: Green and Co., 1928), Chapter 5.

which raises production and income, and so it goes in a cumulative expansion. The financial system, eager to extend loans to profitable businesses operating in what is expected to be an expanding economy, supports the cumulative expansion through credit extension out of its loanable reserves. However, loanable reserves must finally be depleted and interest rates rise. The boom is ended.

With the interest cost of holding stocks of inventories increased, planned investment in inventories is cut, reducing production and income. With income reduced, sales fall, eroding confidence in future sales and further reducing inventory investment. The cumulative contraction is underway. With business firms repaying existing (high interest) loans and not borrowing additional funds to finance new inventory purchases, the volume of credit extended by the banking system falls and its loanable reserves are replenished. Interest rates then fall and the stage is set for another boom.

According to Hawtrey, banks exhibit a lemming-like herd behavior that is inimical to economic stability. In the cumulative expansion, banks (collectively) extend more credit than would be required at a full-employment equilibrium output level as they share the business community's optimistic expectations about future business conditions. Analogously, after the peak in activity they allow a contraction in credit larger than that required to restore full-employment equilibrium so the cycle can continue.

Hawtrey's analysis correctly identifies inventory investment as the most volatile component of aggregate demand. Also, his concern with financial considerations broadens our perspective on the sources of economic fluctuations. His failure to provide for any accelerator mechanism and his emphasis on the response only of inventory investment to changes in credit conditions limit the usefulness of his model. Like all cycle models, Hawtrey's is a caricature of a reality that, because of its complexity, has not yet been adequately represented in a cycle model. Our selection of specific cycle theories to discuss could be vastly extended, but we would make little progress toward the objective of providing a general explanation of business fluctuations. As an alternative, before considering the role of government in business fluctuations, we can provide a summary description of the different sorts of cycle models that have enjoyed prominence.[9] To that end, we can usefully subdivide cycle models into monetary cycle theories, nonmonetary demand theories, and supply theories, though some explanations of the cycle may overlap these categories. In the monetary theories, fluctuations in the interest rate and in the availability of loanable funds are held responsible for fluctuations in investment and, hence, in overall activity. Hawtrey's explanation of the business cycle fits this category quite well.

In nonmonetary demand theories of the cycle, expansions and contractions are generally assumed to be prompted by an inconsistency between

---

[9]For a comprehensive treatment of cycle models, the interested reader may consult any standard text on business cycles, such as Louis A. Dow, *Business Fluctuations in a Dynamic Economy* (Columbus, O.: Charles E. Merrill, 1968).

consumer demand and the existing capital stock. Fluctuations in the investment component of aggregate demand account for turning points in the cycle. Many of the models that fit in this category employ some version of the accelerator principle, as do the multiplier-accelerator models we have reviewed.

In supply theories of business fluctuations, it is fluctuations in operating costs and profit margins that are thought to bear the responsibility for propagating business fluctuations. Typically, changes in profit margins are held responsible for cycle-turning points through their effects on expectations and thus on investment.[10]

The Modern Role of Government in the Cycle

The introduction of a government that has the tools to influence aggregate demand provides a new set of possible constraints on income fluctuations. Rather than waiting for endogenous forces (such as a production ceiling or the exhaustion of reserve funds in the financial system) to halt an expansion, the government may intervene, limiting the growth of aggregate demand in order to avoid the inflation that high levels of capacity utilization can foster. Conversely, rather than allowing a contraction to proceed until income reaches an endogenously determined floor level, the government could stimulate aggregate demand. A government that succeeded in using its fiscal and monetary policy tools to manage aggregate demand in this countercyclical manner would be pursuing a *countercyclical stabilization policy.*

In the latter stages of a buoyant expansion, whatever its ultimate cause, the government would need restrictive fiscal and/or monetary policies to prevent aggregate demand from outrunning productive capacity. Conversely, in a downswing (whatever its cause) the government would need to impose an expansionary monetary-fiscal program to stimulate aggregate demand. Appropriately administered, such a stabilization program would reduce the amplitude of the cycle. Figure 17—6 shows a time path of GNP

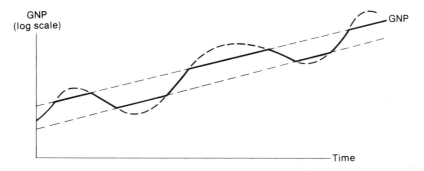

Figure 17—6 / Cyclical Fluctuations Constrained by Stabilization Policy

[10]The leading proponent of supply-side theories of the business cycle was Wesley C. Mitchell. See Mitchell, *Business Cycles and Their Causes* (Berkeley: University of California Press, 1941).

with stabilization policy imposing bands (a floor and a ceiling if you prefer) on the swings in output. Unfortunately, *appropriate* administration of stabilization policy is difficult to achieve. While there are a number of reasons for government's inability to adequately employ a stabilization policy, as discussed earlier, a large share of those limitations can be classified as *timing* problems. If, to avoid inflation, the government undertakes policy actions designed to constrain demand, but does so too late in the cycle, the policy actions will have their impact on demand after the peak of the cycle when income is already falling. Thus, that restrictive policy would reinforce and accelerate the contraction. On the other hand, a restrictive policy put in effect too early in the expansion phase of the cycle would stop a desirable expansion, limiting the growth of real output well before inflationary pressures are a serious threat. Similar timing difficulties plague efforts to limit contractions.

Clearly, poorly timed pursuit of a stabilization policy can be *destabilizing!* As Milton Friedman is fond of pointing out, the road to increased *instability* can be paved with good intentions. Almost everyone would agree that our quantitative knowledge of the size and timing of impact of monetary and fiscal policy actions is, at present, too limited to make stabilization policy a straightforward administrative task. Indeed, there is little doubt but that government's stabilization efforts have, at times, been misguided and, thus, destabilizing. Still, relatively few economists are convinced that the record is bad enough to warrant total rejection of the use of stabilization policies. We must be mindful, however, that, at least in the postwar period, government economic activity has been an integral contributor to the pattern of the observed business cycle. In fact, some economists hold the government directly, and essentially independently, responsible for the cyclical swings we see in economic activity.

The Destabilizing Effects of Government Policy in an Inherently Stable Economy

While it remains a minority opinion, the view that the government's own monetary and fiscal actions are the major cause of economic instability has attracted growing attention in recent years. According to this view, the economy is inherently more stable than endogenous cycle models, such as the basic multiplier-accelerator model developed in this chapter, suggest. Proponents of this view claim that history offers no evidence that ceilings and floors have played significant roles in producing turning points in economic activity. The thrust of these claims is that when a free market economy is *occasionally* pushed out of static equilibrium the economy automatically adjusts back to equilibrium, perhaps monotonically, but at worst with mild and quickly damped cycles. The appearance of continuing fluctuations must be attributed to new shocks to the system that start fresh cycles or strengthen ongoing but decaying cycles. While other sources are possible, in a modern economy in which the government plays an active economic role, emphasis is focused on the government's ability to produce fluctuations. An informal, modern external theory of the business cycle results with government providing the impetus for cycle-turning points.

Stop and Go Policy

Beginning with the economy in a mild recession and with no significant inflation, an activist government might be expected to use expansionary monetary and fiscal policies to raise employment and output. With no inflation expected, the expansionary policy may succeed in markedly reducing unemployment with only a moderate immediate increase in the inflation rate; along the *short-run* Phillips curve the employment-output trade-off may be quite favorable. However, with any significant rise in the inflation rate, expectations will gradually be revised, shifting the short-run Phillips curve upward. Hence, maintenance of a sharply reduced unemployment rate (one below the natural rate) would require an accelerating inflation rate.

Eventually, government policy makers have to turn their attention to reducing the inflation rate, sacrificing the goal of high employment. As explained in Chapter 11, with a reduction in aggregate demand the inflation rate will recede and, with a lag, so will inflation expectations, so that the short-run Phillips curve is shifted downward. However, it is unlikely that the stabilization authorities will allow the economy to remain in a recessionary situation very long. With unemployment growing, there is powerful political pressure for a solution to the unemployment problem. With any significant reduction of the inflation rate, the focus of stabilization policy is quickly shifted from combating inflation to raising employment. Because expectations adjust with a lag, even when stabilization policy has shifted to an expansive stance, the expected rate of inflation will still be falling, shifting the short-run Phillips curve downward. Hence, the apparent trade-off between unemployment and inflation is again quite favorable. However, with the shift to an expansionary policy, a reacceleration of inflation is unavoidable. The stop and go nature of stabilization policy, as government awkwardly pursues admirable goals, has produced a full cycle in economic activity and set the stage for its repetition.

As indicated earlier, there is general agreement that the government *can* act in a destabilizing way. However, few would be willing to attribute to the stabilization authorities a role as pernicious as the one just described. Moreover, the majority of economists continue to subscribe to the Keynesian notion that the economy is frequently disturbed by forces over which the stabilization authorities have little direct control. Changes in society's thriftiness as a result of spontaneous alterations in expectations; bursts of investment opportunity; swings in agricultural exports because of foreign droughts; shortfalls in domestic agricultural production because of late spring floods and early freezes; oil embargoes by the Organization of Petroleum Exporting Countries; and other shocks to the economy can generate cumulative swings in economic activity. If the economy is subjected to many small shocks that are randomly distributed over time, those shocks might be expected to cancel each other out eventually, but apparently they do not. We observe irregular fluctuations in the economy. Notably, some cyclical fluctuations can be observed in production levels in the Soviet Union, even though there are no cycles in the central planning mechanism that dictates production targets.[11]

Engineers have theories of wave-generating mechanisms that can explain the bunching of traffic along streets and highways, the simultaneous appearance of elevators (and buses) that were dispatched at random time intervals, and so on. Economic analysis has not yet provided comparable explanations of the wave-like fluctuations in economic activity because the economic system is much more complex than the physical systems that have already yielded to engineering analysis. However, research effort is currently being expended to enhance our understanding of the dynamic behavior of the economy, and to ascertain the requirements for devising government policies that will induce the economy to expand along a desired, stable growth path. Some of that research is making use of a sophisticated set of mathematical techniques designated *control theory,* which in the main evolved from engineering analysis of *control problems,* i.e., the problems of optimally controlling a chemical processing plant, a spaceship trajectory, a cargo ship's course, and so on.

Formally, control theory is concerned with the analysis of systems, including mechanical, electrical, industrial, physiological, biological, and economic systems, so as to determine the manner in which control instruments may affect the evolution of that system over time, and the values which those control variables would have to possess for the system to produce certain desired results. The economy is a system in which there are a number of *state variables* (indicating the state of the economy) in which we are interested: output, employment, the price level and its rate of change, and so on. There are also a number of *control instruments* available in that system, including money supply changes, government spending changes, tax rate changes, and exchange rate changes, that can be employed to modify movements of the state variables over time. It is hoped that the application of control theory will allow us to determine how available control instruments should be applied and what new control instruments (automatic or otherwise) might be employed in the pursuit of full employment, price stability, and any other policy goal. A great deal of challenging work remains to be done before control theory will make a useful contribution to the formulation of stabilization policy. Interestingly, initial attempts at the simple task of building automatic steering devices in ships were less than an overwhelming success. Those automatic devices steered an unstable course with the ships oscillating in an undamped cycle around their desired course. Steering the economy is much more difficult than steering a ship.

---

[11]For a model which shows that cycles can be generated from random shocks, see R. Frisch, "Propagation Problems and Impulse Problems in Dynamic Economics," in *Economic Essays in Honor of Gustav Cassel* (London: George Allen and Unwin, 1933).

System Stability and Static Macroeconomic Analysis

There remains an important implication of the dynamic analysis in this chapter which we have not yet considered. The static equilibrium level of income in the basic multiplier-accelerator model was given by the familiar expression $Y_{eq.} = [1/(1-b)] \cdot \bar{I}$ [see Equation (17—5)]. This expression shows that the static equilibrium value of income is independent of the value of the accelerator coefficient. As we have seen, however, for different combinations of the accelerator coefficient and the MPC our model traces different dynamic adjustment paths and, for many combinations, a static equilibrium can never be attained; that is, the system is explosive or exhibits cycles of constant amplitude. To illustrate this point, with an MPC of .5 and $\bar{I}$ = \$30 billion the static equilibrium value of income was \$60 billion. However, with an accelerator coefficient equal to 2, income did not converge with that value but fluctuated around it in a cycle of constant amplitude. In contrast, had the accelerator coefficient taken the value .8, income would have followed a damped cyclical path, ultimately converging on the income level indicated by Equation (17—5) while, with an accelerator value of 3, income would have traced an explosive cyclical path.

Of the three example values chosen for the accelerator coefficient, one value ($A = .8$) yields an adjustment path that allows income to converge on the static equilibrium value. In the other two cases, the system is *unstable*. These clear-cut results permit us to draw an important analytical rule. It is obvious that there are numerous alternative models which demonstrate different patterns of dynamic behavior while yielding the same static equilibrium results. For the conclusions drawn from a static analysis (with which most of this book has dealt) to be valid, the system must be dynamically stable. Thus, to provide a necessary condition for the conclusions we draw from analysis with static models to be valid, our models must be tested for the property of dynamic stability. The required tests involve the use of analytical techniques (differential equations, difference equations, computer simulation, and so on) that are outside the scope of this text, but the student should recognize that dynamic analysis is an indispensable adjunct to static analysis.

An Introduction to Economic Forecasting

In both the last chapter on economic growth and the current chapter on business fluctuations, we have been directly concerned with tracing movements in aggregate income and its components over time. A natural *applied* extension of that interest entails the forecasting of future national economic developments.

It is in its application to forecasting that macroeconomics has its broadest audience. As our analysis has indicated already, for the federal government to make intelligent decisions on corrective stabilization policy actions, it must know what path the economy is following; it must have forecasts of future economic developments. Such interest in forecasting is not limited to government policy makers. Because aggregate economic developments alter incomes, the behavior of consumers, and the behavior of firms, economic forecasts are essential inputs in the decisions firms must make. Long-term plans for investment in production facilities, for development of distribution networks, and for acquiring and disposing of subsidiaries depend heavily on business forecasts. So, too, do financing strategies, inventory purchase plans, and hiring plans. Finally, with economic forecasts rciving widespread news media coverage, households might be expected to alter their expectations of the future on the basis of those forecasts and modify their purchase and work choices accordingly.

Forecasting with Macroeconometric Models

Following Jan Tinbergen's pathbreaking 1939 effort to construct an econometric model of the U.S. economy, interest in the construction and application of macroeconometric models has mushroomed.[12] The U.S. central bank (the Federal Reserve System), in conjunction with a group of economists at the Massachusetts Institute of Technology and the University of Pennsylvania, has built and now operates an econometric model of the U.S. economy (the Federal Reserve-MIT-Penn model). The commerce department has its own model, too. Other models are maintained by the Wharton School of Finance and Commerce at the University of Pennsylvania, by the University of Michigan, by Princeton University, and by the Brookings Institution. Also, a number of large business firms have such models and many other firms purchase forecasts from the Wharton School model, from Chase Econometrics (a subsidiary of Chase Manhattan Bank), and from Data Resources Incorporated.

In principle, the task of constructing an econometric model of the economy is straightforward and familiar. Beginning with a theoretical model of the economy, the behavioral functions in that model are fitted to historical data. The number of behavioral functions so fitted differs depending on: (1) the model builder's interest, and (2) the degree of *disaggregation* required for obtaining *stable* regression equations (regression equations with stable parameters) that can be depended upon for prediction purposes. On the first score, a *small* model (for example, an econometric analog of a static macro model) can be employed if predictions of movements in broad aggregates such as output, employment, the general price level, and total consumption are the concern. On the other hand, to get detailed subsector predictions on the component parts of aggregate measures such as consumption (divided, say, into nondurables and services, autos and parts, and other durables) and investment (in plant and equipment, inventories, and housing) would require a separate explanatory equation for each component variable.

---

[12]Jan Tinbergen, *Statistical Testing of Business Cycle Theories,* vol. I (Geneva: League of Nations Economic Intelligence, 1939.)

Similarly, added equations may be necessary to obtain stable regressions. That need arises when the behavior patterns of the component parts of some important variable differ. For example, consumer purchases of services and nondurables are far more stable over the cycle than are durable purchases. Thus, to obtain regression equations that can accurately predict total consumption spending, the model builder may be required to disaggregate consumption, i.e., to divide total consumption spending into its component parts with a separate explanatory equation for each part.

Whatever the number of regression equations required, those regressions and any accompanying identities comprise a set of simultaneous equations that can be employed for prediction purposes. Based on known or anticipated changes in factors that are exogenous to the econometric model (including monetary and fiscal policy variables), that model can be directly applied to forecasting future economic developments. Moreover, an econometric model can be used to trace the time pattern of effects of alternative policy actions. (Computers do the hard work of iteratively solving the system of equations for each period's solution values of the endogenous variables in the model.) Because some of the behavioral relations in econometric models of the economy involve lagged responses, and because the values of exogenous variables change over time, those models can exhibit cycles, reflecting (the model builder would hope) the dynamic properties of the modeled economy. It is natural that interest in formal cycle models has waned because econometric models provide a representation of the dynamic properties of the economy with far more detailed attention to the economy's structure than formal cycle models contain. (The largest econometric models of the economy contain several hundred equations, while a few models contain less than ten equations.)

Even though the practice of macroeconometric modeling is relatively young, there has been considerable improvement in the forecasting capability of those models. While potential for substantial improvement remains, even now forecasts made with the more prominent existing macroeconometric models compare favorably with those made using more pragmatic techniques. Moreover, while much remains to be learned, work with those models has shed substantial light on the structure of the economy and on the effectiveness of monetary and fiscal policy weapons. Models in which both monetary and fiscal policies contribute importantly to the path of economic activity now dominate even though room for disagreement on the economy's structure and, hence, on the roles of monetary and fiscal policies remains. A brief description of a handful of the more prominent macroeconometric models is sufficient to illustrate the link between our model-building efforts and statistical model building. It will also serve to illustrate the variety of modeling approaches that are available.

The Brookings Institution Model. The oldest of the large models now being used is the Brookings Institution model. It has been revised many times and, in fact, is currently revised as needed. It can contain hundreds of equations (depending upon the version).

The Brookings model is basically a Keynesian model, having its foundation in the *IS-LM* framework developed in Chapter 8; that is, the *IS-LM* framework forms the bond between the financial sector and the real sector of the economy, with output and employment determined primarily from the demand side.

Consumption, the largest component of aggregate demand, responds only gradually to changes in income as a large portion of *current* income changes go into saving (consistent with the permanent income and life cycle consumption models). Consumption is also positively related to liquid assets, as it is in monetarist models, but aggregate demand is not primarily determined by monetary variables.

Investment, as would be expected in a Keynesian-style model, is a prominent and volatile determinant of aggregate demand. Business investment is positively related to expected production capacity needs and, through a complex cost-of-capital relationship, is inversely related to interest rates. Investment in residential structures is particularly sensitive to financial market conditions; it is influenced by both the long-term interest rate and the extent of credit rationing.

Changes in the level of government spending, which are determined exogenously by congressional action, also have a powerful effect in this model. The foreign sector has a much less prominent influence on aggregate demand; the net demand from abroad responds (1) positively to a growth in world trade, (2) negatively to a rise in the U.S. price level in relation to foreign prices, and (3) negatively to an expansion in domestic income, because that raises import purchases.

The remaining part of the model represents the financial sector. The model separates the demand for money into demands for demand deposits and for time deposits, and it relates the supply of money to free reserves. In the liquidity preference framework, the demand for and the supply of money determine short-term interest rate levels, and changes in the short-term interest rate influence other yields, notably the time deposit rate and long-term rates. The Fed, generally through open market operations, can influence the financial sector and hence the real sector of the economy. In turn, because the demand for money is positively related to GNP, changes in the real sector are transmitted to the financial sector in *IS-LM* fashion.

In summary, then, the Brookings model is closely associated with traditional *IS-LM* analysis. Output is significantly affected by fluctuations in current investment expenditures and by changes in the government budget. The investment variables are, in turn, influenced by changes in interest rates.

The Federal Reserve-MIT-Penn Model. Another basically Keynesian model, but with variations, is the Federal Reserve-MIT-Penn (FRMP) model. In this model, consumption is composed of the services provided by stocks of durable goods plus expenditures on nondurable goods and on services. (This model distinguishes between services yielded by durable goods and expenditures on durable goods.) The consumption variable is related to current and past income. The FRMP model, employing a consumption function drawn from the life cycle theory, also links household wealth to aggregate consumption. As a result of this linkage, monetary policy changes play a very important role in this model, as money supply changes alter yields on, and the capitalized value of, equity claims, which in turn alter consumption. This model also assesses a credit-rationing effect.

As for investment, the "neoclassical" theory of the firm is used as the basis for plant and equipment equations, but allowances are made for such factors as lags in the formation of expectations and technological changes. Interest rates and tax effects are considered in terms of the impact they have on investment returns. Equations are included in an attempt to separate builders and owners of housing from users so that housing starts may be predicted. Municipal government spending (and taxes) are endogenous in the model.

On the financial side, the behavior of financial markets is described, given GNP and some variables determined by Fed policy. Unborrowed bank reserves are exogenous and are related to deposits, reserve requirements, and free reserves. The Treasury bill rate is determined as the money market interest rate and is used to estimate various other short-term rates and the long-term interest rate; the latter, in turn, is used to estimate dividend yields on stocks (which are substitutes for bonds), which, as a capitalization rate, can be used to estimate the market value of stocks.

The FRMP model has several paths by which the monetary sector can affect the real sector of the economy. In general, the financial sector influences the real sector by affecting investment expenditures through interest rates. Thus the model is basically Keynesian.

The Wharton School Model. The Wharton School model is quite similar to the FRMP model with regard to the financial sector. Equations for money demand and money supply are estimated, and interest rates are determined. However, consumption changes in this model are a function of changes in liquid assets rather than in total wealth. The degree of credit availability is also a factor influencing consumption in the Wharton model.

Like the FRMP model, the Wharton model has several paths by which monetary policy (financial change) affects spending in the real sector. Again, this is basically a Keynesian model, because interest rates are the primary means of transmission from the financial sector to the real sector (by affecting investment spending). Both models differ from the straightforward Keynesian analysis, however, in that *wealth* effects are considered in consumption demand.

The St. Louis Federal Reserve Model. The three models discussed above are all basically Keynesian, varying only in degree of departure from basic

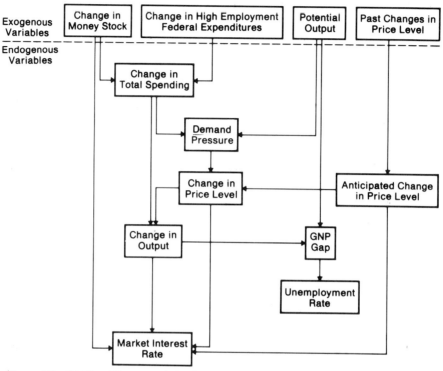

Figure 17—7 / Flow Diagram of the St. Louis Federal Reserve Model

Source: Leonall C. Andersen and Keith M. Carlson, "A Monetarist Model for Economic Stabilization," *Federal Reserve Bank of St. Louis Bank Review*, April 1970, p. 10.

Keynesian concepts. A completely different approach, representing monetarist reasoning, underlies the St. Louis Federal Reserve model. In this
approach, money supply plays the dominant role in the determination of
money GNP. A flow diagram of this model is shown in Figure 17—7.

This model assumes that there are multiple channels through which monetary factors influence GNP, but it does not spell out what those channels
are or test the importance of alternative channels. Fiscal variables, which
are treated as exogenous, are included as possible determinants of GNP,
but, in statistical tests with the model, they have no measured lasting influence on nominal income (if unaccompanied by changes in money).

The St. Louis model actually has no financial sector as such, but it corresponds to the models considered previously in that money can be assumed
to affect GNP. Total spending is a function of both monetary and fiscal
actions. Mony supply is viewed as an exogenous variable that is determined by Fed actions. Because of this, there is no feedback link from interest rates to money supply. Also, although the model determines an interest rate, that rate has no direct effect on spending, output, and prices.
This model has no formal theoretical basis, like the *IS-LM* framework which

consists of a specific set of structural equations. It is also a very *small* model, containing only eight equations and only three exogenous variables.[13]

Other Forecasting Techniques:
Naive Forecasts and Leading Indicators

As alternatives to econometric modeling, there are forecasting techniques that require little knowledge of the structure of the economy. The practice of *extrapolating observed patterns* of economic change and the use of *leading indicators* for predicting cycle-turning points are commonplace examples of alternative forecasting methods.

A forecaster who relied exclusively on the simple extrapolation of observed patterns could be replaced by a parrot calling, for example, for the ''same (absolute or percentage) change this period as last period.'' With no concern for identifying the causal forces that influence economic activity, that extrapolation technique assumes that the forces which produce each period's pattern of economic change will persist. This forecasting technique will fail to indicate every cyclical turning point in economic activity, and fail to make use of any available information on changes in the economic environment that might keep past patterns from being repeated. Extrapolative models also fail to add to our understanding of the macroeconomy. Hence, they have nothing to say about the effects of monetary and fiscal policy actions. Still, because cumulative swings in economic activity have a great deal of momentum, the most naive forecaster may have a respectable track record. In addition, with a reasonable understanding of which disturbances have an important influence on the economy and, hence, may alter the course of economic events, extrapolations may be adjusted in an *ad hoc* manner to provide an improved forecasting performance.

The practice of forecasting with leading indicators is more exotic, and comprehension of that forecasting method requires some background information. With the hope of uncovering information that would be useful in explaining and forecasting business fluctuations, several decades ago the National Bureau of Economic Research (NBER) began the task of examining more than 1,000 economic time series for cyclical patterns of movement over time. Some 400 of the series were found to vary cyclically, and a number of those were identified as *leading* indicators of the business cycle. That is, cyclical peaks and troughs in a number of those variables were found generally to precede in time (lead) the peaks and troughs in overall business activity so that forecasts on cycle turning points could be obtained by following the paths of those variables.

---

[13]See Leonall C. Andersen and Keith M. Carlson, ''A Monetarist Model for Economic Stabilization,'' *Federal Reserve Bank of St. Louis Review,* April 1970, p. 9 for a list of equations and variables. The main equation expresses changes in money income as a function of dollar changes in both money stock and high-employment federal expenditures (each on a current and a lagged basis); the monetary changes are found to exert a statistically significant influence on total spending while fiscal actions exert no lasting effect.

The series of leading indicators (along with series of coincident and lagging indicators) are continuously refined and updated by the NBER. At present, a list of some thirty-six time series is maintained and reported in the Department of Commerce's *Business Conditions Digest*. Out of that comprehensive collection, attention is most frequently focused on a short list of a dozen leading indicators including the average workweek of production workers, the weekly *new* claims on unemployment insurance, net business formation, new orders for durable goods, new building permits, stock prices, and so on. In the postwar period, declines in the leading indicators have preceded, without fail, outright declines in output or slowdowns in the rate of growth of output. Of course, predicting a change in the pattern of economic events says little about the magnitude of the ensuing expansion or slowdown. Moreover, forecasting cycle developments without a firm explanation of the reasons for those developments is frustrating. Still, leading indicators are relied on extensively as crude predictors of coming economic events.

Anticipations and Intentions Data

Forecasters and the news media also devote considerable attention to *anticipations and intentions* data. The Survey Research Center at the University of Michigan compiles monthly data on consumer sentiment (economic optimism or pessimism) and on consumer intentions to purchase (a house, a car, and so on). A number of private and public organizations compile data on planned investment outlays by business firms. The two most frequently cited investment intentions series are compiled by McGraw-Hill and jointly by the Office of Business Economics and the Securities and Exchange Commission. The McGraw-Hill survey is undertaken only once a year while the OBE-SEC series is available quarterly. Forecasters pay considerable attention to sizable shifts in consumer and business purchase plans as reported in the anticipations and intentions series because changes in planned spending are reflected in changes in aggregate demand for goods and services.

Summary

Developed economies have experienced recurrent waves of prosperity followed by recession in a pattern that, historically, has been regular enough to be labeled the business cycle or trade cycle. In this chapter, a formal model of the economy was constructed that was capable of endogenously generating just such a cyclical pattern of movement in production activity. Consistent with traditional business cycle analysis, the model we constructed (the well-known multiplier-accelerator model) focused on the investment component of aggregate demand as the prime source of instability. With investment determined by the accelerator principle, a small percentage increase in consumption demand was seen to generate a sizable response in the demand for investment goods, initiating a cumulative expansion in output. On the other hand, with consumption demand failing to grow at a sufficiently rapid rate, the accelerator was seen to induce a drop in investment, initiating a cumulative contraction. The accelerator acted as a strong source of instability.

In fact, with plausible values for the MPC and the accelerator, the basic multiplier-accelerator model suggested such an unstable system that we found it necessary to constrain fluctuations in income by the *ceiling* of full capacity and the *floor* of minimum output. Alternatively, modifications of the lag structure of the model were claimed capable of making the system more stable.

In working with the multiplier-accelerator, we discovered that alternative forms of a model that yield identical static *equilibrium* results can yield distinctly different dynamic adjustment paths, with some of those paths convergent and some not. From this we were forced to conclude that the inferences drawn from analysis with static models can be valid only if the model being employed is dynamically stable.

As the financial counterpart to the multiplier-accelerator analysis, we took a brief look at a monetary theory of the cycle. In that theory, excessive credit expansions and contractions fueled the business cycle with the depletion of loanable reserve funds and their replenishment providing cycle-turning points. While the role of the financial sector is no doubt exaggerated in such monetary demand theories of the cycle, cumulative monetary expansions and contractions may well reinforce cyclical movements in general business activity.

Our discussion in this chapter also recognized the potential of government, both for acting as a stabilizer and as a destabilizer. To cite recent experience, from 1961 until late 1969 the United States experienced an unbroken expansion. The active use of stabilization policy is widely credited for that favorable performance. Yet, in the latter half of that period, mistakes in the application of stabilization policy were made, and the results of those mistakes combined with more recent ones still plague us.

A major increase in government spending was necessitated, beginning in 1965, by the rapid escalation of the Vietnam War. The expansionary boom of 1966 can be directly tied to the war-induced increase in government spending that was not accompanied by an alteration of the federal tax structure. The ensuing inflation prompted the government to impose restrictive stabilization policies in 1968 and 1969. The recession of 1969–1970 was the direct result of those restrictive policies, not of any inherent cyclical forces endogenous to the economy. An easing of monetary and fiscal policy allowed income expansion to resume in 1971, clearly before inflationary forces were quelled, and restrictive monetary policy in 1974 contributed to a sharp contraction in economic activity that began in 1974. More expansionary policies led to a strong growth in employment and output in the mid-1970s, but an underestimate of the strength of economic expansion in 1977 and 1978 resulted in the maintenance of overly stimulative policies that permitted an abrupt acceleration of inflation in 1979 and 1980.

Quite apparently, the government's monetary and fiscal actions have been both a source of progress and of disruption. The government-managed expansion that began in 1961 and lasted until the end of the 1960s suggested that an endless boom-bust sequence is not inevitable, that judiciously applied stabilization policy can smooth the path of income growth. Still, our experience from the late 1960s to the present highlights the difficulties of properly applying stabilization policy, particularly when a well-entrenched cumulative expansion or contraction is underway.

Finally, this chapter provided a brief introduction to forecasting, a natural extension of dynamic macroeconomic analysis. Our discussion of forecasting was restricted to four popular approaches: (1) forecasting with econometric models, (2) forecasts using extrapolation procedures, (3) forecasting with leading indicators, and (4) forecasting with anticipations and intentions data. All of these techniques are employed extensively by those public and private organizations that must make decisions based on expected future economic conditions.

Questions

1. Provide a verbal explanation of the way in which interaction between the multiplier and the accelerator can result in economic cycles.

2. Under what conditions must floors and ceilings be introduced into the basic multiplier-accelerator model?

3. With a cycle model that calls for damped fluctuations in income when the best available estimates of the system's parameters are plugged into the model, how can continued fluctuations be explained?

4. Explain and criticize the argument that the government is responsible for causing the business cycle.

5. Is it important to check any model used for policy purposes for stability? Explain your answer.

6. Briefly discuss the "inevitability" of the cycle.

7. In an earlier chapter, we argued that spending on investment goods was inversely related to the interest cost of borrowing. If this is the case, what are the implications for multiplier-accelerator analysis?

8. Should you continue studying economics and attend graduate school, do you suppose any unsolved problems in designing stabilization policies will remain to challenge you by the time you finish your training?

Suggested Readings

Baumol, William J. *Economic Dynamics,* Chapters 1–3, 7–10. 3rd edition. London: Macmillan, 1970.

Carlson, Keith M. "Does the St. Louis Equation Now Believe in Fiscal Policy?" *Federal Reserve Bank of St. Louis Review,* February 1978, pp. 13–19.

Goodwin, Richard. M. "The Non-linear Accelerator and the Persistence of Business Cycles." *Econometrica* 19 (1951):1–17.

Gordon, Robert A. *Business Fluctuations.* 2nd edition. New York: Harper & Row, 1961.

Hicks, John R. *A Contribution to the Theory of the Trade Cycle.* Oxford: Oxford University Press, 1950.

Matthews, R. C. O. *The Trade Cycle.* Cambridge: Cambridge University Press, 1959.

Metzler, Floyd A. "The Nature and Stability of Inventory Cycles." *Review of Economic Statistics* 23 (1941):113–129.

Samuelson, Paul A. "Interactions Between the Multiplier Analysis and the Principle of Acceleration." *Review of Economic Statistics* 21 (1939):75–78.

Glossary

accelerated depreciation. A shortening of the guideline lives firms are allowed to use in calculating depreciation costs on capital assets.

accelerator theory. An explanation of investment that links net investment to output (or its rate of change) through the production function.

accommodating monetary policy. An expansion of the money supply to keep interest rates from rising and ''crowding out'' private spending when a stimulative fiscal policy is being applied.

adaptive expectations. Expectations that are altered or ''adapted'' to experienced events.

adjustable peg. An international monetary system under which exchange rates of different currencies are pegged but adjustable under some circumstances. The International Monetary Fund maintained such a system for almost two decades after World War II.

aggregate demand. The total value of all planned purchases of final goods and ser-

vices during a chosen period (usually a year). The sum of planned consumption, investment, government purchases, and net exports.

aggregate demand schedule. A schedule showing the inverse relationship between the general price level and aggregate demand.

aggregate supply. The total volume of real final goods and services provided by businesses to the product market each accounting period.

aggregate supply schedule. The schedule, derived from the labor market and the economy's production function, that shows the relationship between the general price level and the volume of real goods and services business firms supply to the product market, holding constant the state of technology and the quantity and quality of nonlabor factor inputs.

amplitude. The magnitude (peak to trough) of the business cycle.

annually balanced budget. The requirement

that government's outlays and tax revenues be kept equal every year.

anticipations and intentions data. Survey questionnaire data on the expectations and purchase plans of households and business firms, used to make economic forecasts.

appreciation. An increase in value. In foreign exchange, an increase in the exchange value of a currency.

arbitrage. The purchase of an item in one market for resale in a market where the price is higher. Arbitrage tends to equalize the prices of an item that prevail in different markets with allowances for transportation costs, risk, and so on.

assets. Items owned by a firm or individual that have value.

augmented labor. The effective volume of labor input in the production process adjusted for the influence of growth in labor productivity.

automatic stabilizers. Automatic changes in tax revenue, outlays, interest rates, etc. that reduce the magnitude of the multiplier and hence reduce the size of expansions and contractions.

autonomous consumption. That minimum level of consumption that is undertaken independent of the level of disposable income. In a linear consumption function, the autonomous component is the intercept.

autonomous investment. That investment undertaken without regard to the level of economic activity.

average product. Total output per unit of some variable factor input used to produce that product.

average propensity to consume. The fraction of income that is spent on consumption goods.

average propensity to save. The fraction of income that is saved.

balanced budget. A budget in which total revenues and total outlays are equal.

balanced budget multiplier. A predictor of the impact on equilibrium income of an equal change in government spending and tax revenues. In commodity market models the balanced budget multiplier has a value of one.

balance-of-payments. The difference between a country's payments to foreigners and its receipts from foreigners, reflecting all of the international economic transactions of a country and its citizens during a particular time period.

balance-of-payments disequilibrium. A balance-of-payments surplus or deficit that can not persist indefinitely.

balance of trade. The portion of a country's overall balance-of-payments consisting of exports and imports. A balance of trade surplus, often referred to as a "favorable" balance of trade, exists when exports exceed imports. There is a balance of trade deficit when the reverse is true.

balance sheet. A summary statement of a firm's financial condition showing what the firm owns (its assets), what it owes (its liabilities), and the residual net worth of the firm on a given date.

barter. The exchange of goods and services without the use of money.

base year. A reference year employed for purposes of making comparisons.

black market. An illegal market. With reference to wage-price controls a market in which a commodity or service is sold for more than the legal ceiling price.

Board of Governors of the Federal Reserve System. The seven-member board that supervises the Federal Reserve System. Members are appointed by the president for fourteen-year terms, with the term of one member expiring every two years.

bond. A financial instrument entitling the holder to payments of interest and principal, generally at prescribed future dates. Both corporations and governmental units (federal, state, and local) issue bonds.

business cycles. Periodic fluctuations in economic activity.

capital. A produced means of further production (machinery, equipment, inventories, and structures). Human resources can be considered *human capital*.

capital account. That part of the balance-of-payments consisting of the purchase and sale of assets. The U.S. typically invests more abroad than foreigners invest in the U.S., creating a deficit in the U.S. capital account.

capital consumption allowance. A measure of the physical capital "used up" during the accounting period, consisting mainly of normal depreciation although the accidental destruction of capital goods is also reflected.

capital deepening. With no change in technology, an increase in the quantity of capital employed with other resources.

capital gain (loss). A change in the value of an asset that has not been altered.

capital-output ratio. The amount of capital required per unit of output. This concept is applied in both a *total* and a *marginal* sense.

cartel. An organization of producers in the same industry that regulates prices and allocates markets to cartel members with the objective of generating monopoly profits.

checkable deposits. Deposits in banks and other depository institutions upon which drafts may be drawn for payments to third parties.

circular flow. The flow of factor services and real products between households, firms, government, and foreigners and the corresponding flow of payments.

classical economics. That body of economic thought developed by Adam Smith in the 18th century and prevailing until the 1930s, based on the assumptions that the economy was self-regulating and needed no government intervention to maintain noninflationary, full-employment equilibrium.

closed economy. An economy that is involved in no international transactions.

coefficient of determination (R^2). A measure of "goodness of fit" that is the proportion of the variation in a dependent variable explained by movements in the independent variable(s) in a regression equation.

coincident indicators. Measures of particular lines of economic activity that tend to move in step with general economic activity.

commercial bank. A federal- or state-chartered bank that deals directly with the public, holding deposits (primarily demand or checking account deposits) for individuals and firms and extending loans to individuals and firms. The checkable deposit liabilities of commercial banks serve as money.

comparative statistics. Analysis that compares the attributes of a system at rest before and after some specific shock has disturbed that system.

compensation of employees. Wages and salaries, tips, business Social Security contributions, and other sources of labor compensation.

compound interest. Interest accrued both on a principal sum and on the interest earned by that sum as of a prescribed date.

concentration ratio. A proxy for monopoly power that measures the degree to which an industry is dominated by a few firms. Typically the percentage of an industry's sales accounted for by the four largest firms.

consol. A bond with no maturity date that provides a set coupon interest payment each accounting period forever.

constant dollars. Dollars of unchanged purchasing power.

Consumer Price Index. A measure of the average price of those goods and services bought by the residents of urban areas.

consumption. Basically, household expenditures on those durable goods, nondurables, and services that render satisfaction directly. Alternatively, when a measure of the true "using up" of consumer goods is desired, expenditures on nondurables and services plus the use value of consumer durables.

consumption function. The relationship between income and consumption (*ceteris paribus*).

control theory. A set of mathematical techniques that are applicable to the task of optimally controlling the adjustment path of a number of types of systems, including economic systems.

coordinated policies. The simultaneous and coordinated application of two or more policy instrument in pursuit of two or more policy goals.

cost-push inflation. That inflation that stems from an upward shift of the aggregate supply schedule. Often, organized labor and concentrated businesses are blamed for using their market power in a manner that drives up production *costs*, hence prices.

crawling peg. A proposed foreign exchange system in which frequent and automatic *small* adjustments in the par value of a currency would occur as that currency's market value persistently presses against the "floor" or "ceiling" of allowable exchange rates.

credit "availability" or "rationing." The presence or absence of a nonprice restriction on the volume of loan funds business firms can acquire for investment purposes.

credit expansion multiplier. See money supply multiplier.

credit markets. The financial markets in which borrowers and lenders are brought together. A complex array of financial institutions provide these markets.

creeping inflation. A gradual (say, less than 3 percent annually) but persistent increase in the general price level.

cross-section data. Observations across a population collected at a point in time.

crowding-out effect. A reduction in private spending that results from and offsets the stimulative effects of an expansionary fiscal policy. According to this thesis, an increase in government spending can reduce private investment by a like amount through increases in the interest rate.

currency. Coins or paper money.

current dollars. Observed, nominal values that have been subjected to no adjustment for price changes.

deflation. A statistical adjustment of nominal values to express those values in terms of base year prices. Also, a decline in the general price level (the opposite of an inflation).

demand deposit. An obligation of a commercial bank to pay, *on demand,* an amount specified by the customer who owns the deposit. Such deposits constitute *checkbook* money.

demand-pull inflation. An inflation that results from a rightward shifting aggregate demand schedule which produces a generalized excess demand for real goods and services at current prices.

deposit expansion multiplier. A predictor of the impact of a change in the volume of reserves, or high-powered money, on the volume of demand deposits and money.

depreciation. The annual shrinkage in the stock of productive capital assets due to wear and obsolence.

depression. A highly depressed state of economic activity. In the Great Depression of the 1930s, as an example, the U.S. suffered an unemployment rate that reached 25 percent of the labor force.

devaluation. An official reduction in the par value of a currency.

diminishing returns. With technology held constant, as additional units of a variable factor input are combined with other factors production rises, but, ultimately, output will rise at a diminished rate (the *marginal* additions to output decline). At that point, diminishing returns have emerged. Diminishing returns to a factor and diminishing marginal productivity of that factor are two labels for the same phenomenon.

discount rate. The interest rate at which the Federal Reserve System lends reserves to depository institutions.

discouraged workers. Those potential workers who have stopped actively seeking work because they are convinced further job search will not uncover an obtainable job. Such individuals are not counted as unemployed because one must be actively seeking work to be a part of the labor force as currently defined.

discretionary fiscal policy. The deliberate alteration of tax rates and government outlays in an effort to stabilize the economy.

"disembodied" technical change. Changes in the state of technology (such as organizational improvements) that can raise the economy's productive capacity without investment being made in new capital goods.

disguised unemployment (underemployment). Unutilized or underutilized productive resources that are not counted as unemployed because of the *special* definitions used in calculating unemployment measures.

disintermediation. A withdrawal of funds from financial intermediaries for direct lending in the securities market when interest rates rise.

disinvestment. A reduction in the size of the capital stock that results when gross investment falls short of capital consumption.

disposable personal income. That income left after the payment of personal tax liabilities.

dissaving. Consumption in excess of income.

dividends. Payments by corporations to stockholders representing the reward for providing the firms with capital.

dynamics. An analysis in which the time path of economic adjustment is traced.

dynamic stability analysis. Analysis of a system's time path of adjustment to determine whether that system will migrate to a static equilibrium position after it is disturbed by some specific shock.

econometrics. A combination of economic theory and statistical analysis that provides a test and quantification of theory.

economic growth. An increase in a nation's real production over time. Generally measured by an increase in real Gross National Product or per capita real Gross National Product.

economic indicators. Time series of economic variables that are employed in analyzing and forecasting business cycles. Indicators can lead, lag, or be coincident with general economic activity.

elasticity. A measure of *responsiveness.* Price elasticity is the percentage change in quantity demanded (or supplied) per unit percentage change in price. Other elasticities are also frequently employed in economic analysis.

"embodied" technical change. Changes in the state of technology that are embodied in capital goods and, hence, require investment in technologically advanced capital goods if they are to add to the economy's production capacity.

employment. As measured in the U.S., the number of individuals who, during a given survey period: (1) worked any amount of time as a paid employee, (2) were self-employed, (3) worked fifteen hours or more in a family enterprise, or (4) did not work but had jobs from which they were temporarily absent due to illness, labor dispute, vacation, bad weather, and so on.

Employment Act of 1946. An act of Congress which declared that ". . . it is the continuing responsibility of the Federal Government. . . to promote maximum employment, production, and purchasing power." This act formally recognizes the federal government's responsibility for employing policies that stabilize the economy.

endogenous. Determined within the system.

equation of exchange. The identity $MV = PY$ that relates the stock of money and its velocity to the general price level and the level of real output. This identity is fundamental to classical analysis.

equilibrium. A rest position. A state of balance between opposing forces so that no adjustments are produced (for example, in quantity, price, income, and so on).

equilibrium in the commodity market. The rest position that prevails when the aggregate demand for and supply of real goods and services are equal.

equilibrium in the money market. The rest position that prevails when the supply of and demand for money (bonds) are equal.

escalator. A formula that automatically adjusts a money flow in response to changes in the price level.

excess reserves. The surplus of a depository institution's actual reserves over its required reserves.

exchange controls. Controls that limit the access of individuals and firms to foreign exchange markets.

excise tax. A tax levied on the production or sale of specific items such as liquor, gasoline, jewelry, and so on.

exogenous. Determined outside the system and hence not influenced by events within the system.

expected price level. The general price level that is expected to prevail in the future.

expenditure approach. A method of constructing measures of aggregate output (income) by summing the expenditures of different sectors (the household, business, government, and foreign sectors) of the economy.

exports. Sales of domestically produced goods and services to the rest of the world.

external balance (ff) schedule. A schedule showing all the interest rate-income combinations that provide balance-of-payments equilibrium.

factors of production. Those human and nonhuman resources that are used in the production process. These can be classified into four broad groups: land, labor, capital, and entrepreneurial talent.

Federal Open Market Committee. The chief policy making body in the Federal Reserve System, consisting of the seven-member Board of Governors of the Federal Reserve System and representatives of five district banks.

Federal Open Market Committee (FOMC) directives. Instructions on the target ranges for the federal funds rate and the rates of growth of monetary aggregates.

Federal Reserve System. The central banking system of the United States. Created by Congress in 1913, the system includes twelve district banks (with additional branch offices) administered by a presidentially appointed Board of Governors, the Federal Open Market Committee, and several thousand member banks.

final products. Consumer goods and newly produced capital goods that are bought not for resale but for *final* use.

financial intermediaries. Financial institutions, including banks, savings and loan associations, mutual savings banks, insurance companies, credit unions, and so on. These institutions channel savings to borrowers.

fiscal policy. Stabilization policy involving changes in government spending, taxes, or transfers.

finished goods producer price index. An index measure of the average price of commodities that are to be sold to final demanders, both consumers and producers.

fixed investment.   Investment in plant, equipment, and residential structures, exclusive of inventory investment.

fixed-proportion production.   A production process in which factor inputs (labor and capital for example) must be combined in strictly fixed proportions with no opportunity for substituting one factor input for another.

flexible money wages and prices.   Money wage rates and prices that change freely in response to changes in supply or demand schedules (as assumed in classical analysis).

flexible or floating exchange rates.   Foreign exchange rates that are determined in a free market by the interaction of supply and demand.

flow variable.   A variable that must be measured over a time period, such as income, output, consumption, investment, and saving.

foreign exchange.   Currency, checks, bills of exchange, and related instruments used for international payments.

foreign exchange rate.   The price of one nation's currency in terms of another.

frictional unemployment (search unemployment).   Temporary unemployment of those engaged in the process of job search. Job seekers and job slots cannot be matched frictionlessly and instantly because of imperfect information, imperfect labor mobility, and so on.

full employment.   In simple terms a situation in which a job is *available* for everyone who wants to work at the prevailing real wage. In terms of measured unemployment most economists would accept an unemployment rate in the 4½–5½ percent range as full employment.

full-employment surplus (deficit).   The federal budget surplus or deficit that would prevail if the economy were at *full* employment, arbitrarily defined as 4 percent unemployment.

full information.   Complete information, usually on the general price level.

general equilibrium.   Simultaneous equilibrium in all markets in the economy.

general price level.   The "average" price level economy-wide, which is probably best represented by the implicit GNP deflator, though no price index can adequately measure the economy-wide price level.

GNP gap.   The difference between actual GNP and the GNP that would be produced at full employment. Often used as a rough measure of the foregone production cost of a depressed level of economic activity.

gold standard.   An international monetary system in which each nation's currency is defined in terms of a fixed weight of gold with gold bullion used to clear international payments imbalances.

government purchases of goods and services.   Federal, state, and local government expenditures on products and factor services. This total appears in the national income and product accounts as a measure of production of final goods and services.

Gross National Product (GNP).   The total market value of all final goods and services produced by an economy in a year.

gross private domestic investment.   Total expenditures on newly produced capital goods (including additions to inventories) with no adjustment for depreciation of the existing stock of capital.

growth recession.   A slowdown in the economy's rate of growth during which unemployment of labor and capital swells but output continues to rise although more slowly than productive capacity.

high employment surplus.   See full-employment surplus.

high-powered money.   See reserve money.

horizontal integration.   The merging under single ownership of firms involved in the production of like goods or services.

human capital.   The mental and physical productive capabilities of the population. People invest in human capital through formal education, on-the-job training, and so on.

hyperinflation.   A very rapid, "runaway" inflation in which the nation's monetary system is threatened.

hypothesis.   A tentatively accepted relationship subject to refutation on the basis of observed reality.

implicit price deflator.   A *broad* measure of the general price level equal to the ratio of nominal GNP to real GNP.

import quota.   A legal restriction on the quantity of an item that may be imported during a given period.

imports.   Domestic purchases of goods and services produced abroad.

imputations.   Constructed values of economic activity employed where direct observation is impossible. Notable imputations are made for the rental value of owner-occupied houses and for farm produce consumed on the farm.

income approach.   A method of constructing measures of aggregate income (output) by summing the earned incomes of the factor inputs employed in the production process.

income tax.   A tax levied on income so that tax revenues rise with income. The personal income tax and the corporate income tax are the major examples in the U. S.

index numbers.   Numbers, typically expressed in percentage form, that reveal the value of a series relative to some base period.

indexing.   The attachment of inflation escalator clauses to all forms of contractual arrangements involving money transfers.

indifference curve.   A schedule showing all the alternative combinations of commodities, of risk and expected return on a portfolio, etc., that would leave an individual equally satisfied.

indirect business taxes.   Sales taxes, excise taxes, and similar levies that are not based on firms' profits. Such taxes entail costs to business firms for which no productive services are directly rendered.

induced spending (consumption or investment).   That spending that is induced by a change in income.

inflation.   A significant and sustained rise in the general price level.

inflation tax.   An inflation-induced wealth transfer from the holders of money balances to government.

injection.   Any addition to the spending stream that does not stem directly from the income accruing to the household sector. Business investment, government purchases, and exports represent injections.

innovation.   Adoption of a new, "improved" method of production, or of a new and different product.

inside lag.   The time that elapses between emergence of a need for a policy action and the time that policy action is undertaken.

interest.   The price of loanable funds, hence the opportunity cost of holding money. As a factor reward, the return earned by those who provide money capital.

intermediate products.   Items purchased for resale rather than for final use.

internal rate of return.   The percentage rate of return a firm can expect to earn on investment in a capital asset.

International Monetary Fund (IMF).   The international organization that has administered the international monetary system since the Bretton Woods conference in 1944.

inventory.   Stocks of raw materials, semi-finished goods, and finished goods that firms have on hand for further processing or for sale.

investment.   Expenditure on newly produced, physical capital goods. Expenditures on plant, equipment, residential structures, and inventory additions are included.

investment tax credit.   A credit against a business's profit tax liability based on the amount of investment the firm undertakes.

involuntary unemployment.   That unemployment (over and above normal "search" unemployment) that exists when a depressed level of aggregate demand for goods and services leaves the number of jobs business firms are willing to offer at the prevailing real wage short of the number of jobs workers would willingly accept.

IS **curve.**   A schedule showing all of the alternative combinations of an interest rate and an income level that provide commodity market equilibrium.

labor force.   The employed plus all those individuals, sixteen years of age or older, who are unemployed but actively seeking work.

labor force participation rate.   The proportion of a population that actively participates in the labor force, either working or seeking employment.

labor productivity.   The ratio of output to labor input.

labor services.   The productive services of people.

Laspeyres index.   An index obtained using base year weights.

leading indicators.   Measures of particular economic activities that tend to move ahead of movements in general economic activity.

leakages.   Withdrawals from the flow of spending on domestically produced output, encompassing saving, taxes, and imports.

lender of last resort.   An important duty of

the Federal Reserve System as it was originally envisioned, i.e., standing by to lend funds to member commercial banks when they were faced with extraordinarily large withdrawals during times of uncertainty.

liability. A claim against the assets of an individual or a firm by any other individual, firm, or institution.

linear regression equation. An equation that relates variations in a dependent variable to movements in one or more causal variables.

liquidity. An asset is more liquid the more easily it can be disposed of without appreciable transaction costs and without loss of market value. Money is the most liquid of all assets.

LM **curve.** A schedule showing all the combinations of the interest rate and the level of real income that provide equilibrium in the money (bond) market.

macroeconometric models. Econometric models of the macroeconomy that are useful for explaining and predicting macroeconomic events.

macroeconomics. That portion of economic analysis that focuses attention on the economy as a whole.

markets. Institutions that permit more efficient exchange of goods or services by providing readily accessible lines of communication between buyers and sellers.

marginal cost. The change in total costs of production stemming from a one unit change in output.

marginal efficiency of capital (MEC). The expected rate of return on a one-unit addition to the stock of capital, holding constant the state of technology, the quantity and quality of other factor inputs, the prices of factor inputs over the life of the asset, and the demand for products manufactured by that asset over its lifetime.

marginal efficiency of investment (MEI). The expected rate of return on a one-unit increase in the flow rate of aggregate investment, holding constant the stock of capital, the strength of demand for final goods, and the other determinants of the position of the marginal efficiency of *capital* schedule. The marginal efficiency of investment schedule slopes downward because of rising marginal costs in the capital goods producing industry.

marginal product. The extra output that is generated by a one unit increase in the quantity of one variable input employed.

marginal propensity to consume. The change in consumption that results from a one-unit change in income.

marginal propensity to save. The change in saving that results from a one-unit change in income.

marginal revenue. The change in revenue that results from a unit change in sales.

marginal tax rate. The change in tax collections per unit of change in income, typically expressed in percentage form.

measure of economic welfare (MEW). A measure of society's economic well-being that is broader than GNP though obtained by modifying GNP figures.

member banks. Those commercial banks that are members of the Federal Reserve System.

merger. The combining of two or more firms under one ownership.

microeconomics. That portion of economic analysis that focuses on the behavior of individual economic units (individual households, firms, and industries).

model. A theoretical explanation of some real world phenomenon involving hypothesized relationships, interrelationships among hypotheses, and the logical implications that can be drawn therefrom.

monetarist. A modern quantity theorist who contends that money supply changes are the dominant cause of macroeconomic adjustments, while fiscal policy does little more than alter the allocation of resources.

monetary dampener. A mechanism that tends to weaken expansions and contractions as changes in the level of income change money demand, the interest rate, and thus investment spending.

monetary effects of fiscal policy. The money supply changes that may result from fiscal actions, depending on the method the government uses to finance its spending.

monetary policy. Stabilization policy applied through changes in the money supply.

money. Any asset that is readily accepted as a medium of exchange. In addition to serving as a medium of exchange, money serves as a store of purchasing power and as a standard or measure of value. Money can be narrowly defined as publicly owned currency plus checkable deposits.

money capital. The funds used by business firms to buy physical capital.

money market. A convenient construct in which money can be considered to be supplied and demanded.

money market certificates. Short-term obligations of financial institutions that offer an interest yield which is tied to the Treasury bill rate.

money supply multiplier. A measure of the multiple change in the nominal money supply that results from a unit change in the volume of reserves.

money wage. The nominal wage without regard to its real purchasing power.

monopoly. A market structure in which one seller controls market supply and hence has some control over market price.

multiplier. A measure of the impact on equilibrium income of an autonomous change in spending or net tax collections.

multiplier-accelerator model. A model that combines the multiplier and accelerator to show that cyclical fluctuations can be generated internally.

national income. A measure of income *earned* by productive factor inputs that can be obtained using either the income or the expenditure approach.

national income and product accounts. A set of data on aggregate output (income) and its components which are crucial to macroeconomic analysis.

natural rate of unemployment. The measured rate of unemployment that would prevail when the economy is neither in a recession nor suffering from inflationary pressures. The unemployment remaining under these conditions can be considered to represent *search* unemployment.

near monies. Highly liquid assets such as savings deposits, short-term government bonds, and the like that can be readily converted into money and that perform some of the same functions as money (e.g., store of value).

neoclassical growth models. Growth models developed in the postwar period that focus attention on the supply of factor inputs rather than on demand as the basic determinant of an economy's long-run growth path.

net exports. Exports minus imports.

net interest. Interest payments from business firms to households and government.

net national product (NNP). The economy's *net* output for the year which is available for consumption, government use, and additions

to the existing capital stock. It is obtained by subtracting capital consumption from GNP.

net private domestic investment. That investment which increases the accumulated stock of capital goods; gross investment minus capital consumption.

net taxes. Taxes minus transfer payments.

net worth. The difference between assets and liabilities representing an individual or firm's owned "wealth."

nominal interest rate. The observed, market interest rate which differs from the real rate of interest when a non-zero inflation rate is anticipated.

nominal value. Current dollar value with no adjustment for price level changes.

nominal wage. The wage rate measured in current dollars.

normative economics. Economics analysis that is concerned with what "ought to be" rather than with what "is." It ultimately rests on value judgments.

NOW accounts. Negotiable Order for Withdrawal accounts consist of deposits that earn interest, but upon which drafts may be drawn (like checks) for payments to third parties.

open economy. An economy that is involved in international transactions.

open market operations. Purchases and sales of government securities undertaken by the Federal Reserve System to alter the volume of reserves and, hence, the money supply.

ordinary least-squares technique. A technique of fitting a linear regression equation that minimizes the sum of squared deviations of actual observed values of the dependent variable from the values predicted by the regression equation.

outside lag. In simple terms, the time interval between a policy action and the point in time when that action has a significant effect on the economy. It must be remembered that policy actions have influences on the economy that are actually distributed in time.

Paasche index. A price index obtained using latter (current period) weights.

partial correlation coefficient. A measure of the covariation of two variables with adjustment made for the influence of other variables. The stronger the tendency for two variables to move together, the closer is the value of the partial correlation coefficient to one.

par value of a currency. The "official" exchange rate between its currency and another country's currency that a country was required to maintain under the postwar IMF system.

past income. In the Duesenberry model, the highest level of income attained in the past.

period. In business cycle analysis, the amount of time required for completion of one cycle.

permanent income. That flow of expenditures that a household believes it can enjoy in the foreseeable future without a loss of capital value or wealth.

personal income. The total of income *received* by households without personal tax liabilities deducted.

Phillips curve. A schedule showing the trade-off between unemployment and inflation.

positive economics. Economic analysis concerned with what "is" rather than what "should be."

potential Gross National Product. The volume of Gross National Product that the economy could provide with *full* employment.

present value. The discounted, *present* worth of a stream of future receipts obtained using the interest cost of capital as the discount rate.

price index. A measure of price level change between two periods, typically expressed as a percentage.

prime rate. The interest rate charged by commercial banks on loans to their most credit-worthy business customers.

private sector. That portion of the economy incorporating households and business firms but excluding government.

producer price index. A measure of the average price of commodities at the time they are involved in their first important commercial transaction.

production function. The relationship between output and the volume of factor inputs used to produce that output.

product market. The market in which real goods and services are bought and sold.

profit. The residual income, after payment of wages, rent, and interest, which accrues to entrepreneurs.

profit-push inflation. An inflation that is alleged to stem from monopolistic firms using their market power to push up profits by raising prices.

progressive tax. A tax levy in which the percentage tax rate rises as the tax base grows.

proprietors' income. Income accruing to all unincorporated businesses, including single proprietorships and partnerships.

public debt. The outstanding bond debt of government.

pure interest rate. The theoretical interest rate that would be earned on a riskless security issue on which administrative costs are negligible.

quantity adjustments. Changes in real output and employment.

quantifiable. Measurable in numerical terms.

quantity theory of money. In classical analysis, the theory that money supply changes bring about equal proportional changes in prices with no change in real variables. The *modern* quantity theory assumes money supply changes produce changes in real output as well as prices in the short-run, but still provides a proportional relationship between money and prices with output at the full-employment level in the long run.

quota. See import quota.

rate of interest. The pure rate of interest or a weighted average of all observed market interest rates.

rational expectations. Expectations based on an understanding of the economy's responses to the shocks that impinge upon it.

razor's edge models. Simplistic growth models that yield pessimistic predictions on the probability of the economy expanding along a path that maintains full utilization of all factor inputs.

real Gross National Product. The economy's annual output of final goods and services valued in terms of base year prices.

real income. The purchasing power embodied in a flow of money income.

real interest rate. The observed, market interest rate less the expected inflation rate.

real wage. The purchasing power embodied in the money wage, and inversely proportional to the price level.

recession. A period of depressed economic activity in which unemployment rises. As a rule of thumb, when real GNP declines for two successive quarters, the economy is in a recession.

recovery. The expansion phase of the business cycle in which employment and output rise.

relative income. The value of a household's income relative to the average for its peer group.

rent. The return received for the use of real property (land in the broad classification of factor inputs).

rental income of persons. Rental income of those whose primary occupation is something other than the renting of real property. Included is the imputed rental value of owner-occupied homes.

replacement investment. That portion of total investment that is required to replace the capital that is worn out, made obsolete, or accidentally destroyed each year.

required reserve ratio. The fixed percentage of deposit liabilities that commercial banks must hold as reserves.

reservation wage. The minimum wage a job seeker is willing to accept.

reserve money (high-powered money). Reserves of depository institutions and currency, each dollar of which can support the existence of a multiple amount of publicly held money.

risk. The dispersion of possible outcomes (such as gains or losses) when a particular course of action is followed. When the possible outcomes are distributed *normally*, the standard deviation of the distribution can be used as a measure of risk.

sales tax. A fixed percentage tax levied on the retail prices of commodities and services.

saving. That part of disposable income that is not consumed.

Say's Law. "Supply creates its own demand." The argument, fundamental to classical analysis, that there could never be a generalized glut (excess supply) of goods and services of the type that Keynes claimed would send the economy reeling into recession. The proposition bears the name of French economist Jean Baptiste Say (1767–1832).

scientific method. A method of analyzing phenomena involving the construction and testing of models that attempt to explain those phenomena.

search unemployment. See frictional unemployment.

shoeleather costs of inflation. The money and time costs of society's efforts to economize on money balances to minimize the inflation tax on those balances.

shortage. An excess of demand over supply at the prevailing price.

special drawing rights (SDRs). "Paper gold" reserves in the form of bookkeeping entries in the accounts kept by the International Monetary Fund. SDRs were created in 1969 to supplement gold as a reserve asset as world trade continued to grow.

speculative demand for money. The demand for money as an asset in order to avoid the capital losses that are expected on bonds as interest rates rise.

statistical discrepancy. The difference, attributed to measurement errors, between the level of national income obtained using the "expenditure approach," and that obtained using the "income approach."

sterilization. The actions of a country's central bank when (using open market operations or other means) it offsets the money supply changes caused by a balance-of-payments surplus or deficit.

stock. The accumulated volume of an item that is measurable at an instant in time.

stop-and-go stabilization policy. A cyclical pattern of expansionary, then contractionary, then expansionary stabilization actions that result in inflationary booms followed by inflationary recessions.

structural unemployment. A *hard-core* residual of unemployment afflicting those whose lack of skills, location, and so on, keep the value of their potential contributions to production below the wage they must be paid to be employed.

supply shocks. Disturbances that impinge upon or stem from the supply side of the economy.

surtax. An additional tax levied on an existing tax base.

tariff. A tax on imports.

tax. A compulsory levy exacted by government for which no particular service is provided in turn to the taxpayer.

technological progress. Changes in the state of technology that permit more output to be produced with an unchanged *quantity* of factor inputs.

time deposits. Savings accounts and certificates of deposit owed to depositors by commercial banks but legally subject to withdrawal only if notice is given at a specified advance time.

time series. A set of data with observations generated over time.

total revenue. The product of sales price and number of units sold, representing the total sales receipts of a firm.

transactions demand. Demand for money to use as a medium of exchange, financing those transactions that occur between the points in time when income is received.

transfer payments. Payments for which no current productive services are rendered. Pension, unemployment compensation, welfare payments, veterans benefits, and interest on the national debt are prominent examples.

transitory. A temporary, random, chance, unexpected increment in consumption or income.

Treasury bills. Short-term (up to one year) obligations of the U.S. Treasury.

trend. The long-run pattern of a time series with the seasonal and cyclical influences on that series removed.

unemployment rate. The percentage of the civilian labor force that is not employed (see employment).

union. An organization of workers that, with the right to strike, has greater bargaining power with management over wages, working conditions, fringe benefits, and so on, than would individual, unorganized workers.

unplanned (unintended) inventory investment. A change in accumulated inventories that occurs because aggregate planned spending differs from the volume of output firms are producing for final sale. The commodity market is in disequilibrium when there is unplanned inventory investment.

upward bias. A tendency to overstatement, e.g., the tendency of Laspeyres price indexes to overstate the amount of inflation.

value added. The additions to the value of an item as it goes through each stage of the production process.

verification. The testing of hypotheses against observed reality to see whether actual observations tend to support or refute the hypotheses.

vertical integration. The merging under a single ownership of firms engaged in different stages of the processing of raw materials into finished products.

vintage. Dates of origin of capital goods. The later the vintage, presumably the more advanced the technology embodied in the capital goods involved.

wage-price controls. Legal restrictions on the wages firms can pay and the prices they can charge.

wage-push inflation. The inflation that is attributed to organized labor contracting for wage increases that exceed labor's increase in productivity.

wages. The income earned by labor in the production process.

wealth. An accumulated stock of valuable assets, financial or real.

yield. The return on an investment.

Index